"Dr. Feingold has written a truly excellent introduction to Fundamental Theology. Since the issues considered in Fundamental Theology are of such critical importance, having an introduction that is comprehensive, clearly written, and faithful to the tradition of the Church is of very great value. Dr. Feingold doesn't shy away from treating the difficult issues and does so with balance and sound judgement in a very user-friendly way. Highly recommended."

—Ralph Martin,
Director of Graduate Theology Programs in the New Evangelization
Sacred Heart Major Seminary

"Dr. Lawrence Feingold's *Faith Comes from What Is Heard* is a magnificent work. This Fundamental Theology textbook is rooted in the Catholic Church's rich theological tradition. Dr. Feingold covers the major areas of Fundamental Theology, with ample recourse to Sacred Scripture, to important documents from the Church's Magisterium, as well as to classic texts from St. Thomas Aquinas, St. Augustine, and numerous Church Fathers. Dr. Feingold's writing has that rare clarity and depth that make this book a true gem. I heartily recommend this book for courses on Fundamental Theology, or even as a complementary text for courses in Sacred Scripture or Apologetics. Not only would this be an ideal textbook for Catholic universities, colleges, and seminaries, but it would also be an excellent book for readers interested in understanding their Catholic faith at a deeper level. I will be using this text in my own courses, and I can't wait to reread through it with my students. More than that, I will be recommending this text to friends interested in learning more about the Catholic faith."

—Jeffrey L. Morrow,
Assistant Professor of Catholic Theology
Seton Hall University's Immaculate Conception Seminary School of Theology

"Dr. Feingold has assembled a wide collection of materials that will help the student of theology to discover many riches of the Catholic tradition. The book will especially help programs that aim to train the laity. A useful tool from a good scholar!"

—Fr. Romanus Cessario, O.P.,
Saint John's Seminary, Brighton, Massachusetts

"Teachers and students of Fundamental Theology will welcome Lawrence Feingold's *Faith Comes from What Is Heard* because of its detailed treatment of revelation and faith, tradition and Scripture. It is moreover magisterial in its treatment of the Church's Magisterium on all these topics, but most especially in its treatment of Scripture, its inspiration and truth, the historicity and apostolicity of the Gospels, and the issues surrounding typology. Scripture is here appreciated in its properly theological character. The volume will therefore also serve as an admirable introduction to theology as a whole, whose nature it treats by way of an extended commentary on the first question of the *Summa*. While the text nicely distinguishes apologetics and Fundamental Theology, its treatment both of the credibility of faith and the historicity of the Gospels will, in fact, strengthen the faith of all who read it. Because of its scope, Fundamental Theology is hard to organize satisfactorily, but teachers will recognize here a thoughtful and convincing, logical and theological, progression of topics."

—Fr. Guy Mansini,
Professor of Systematic Theology
Saint Meinrad Seminary & School of Theology

"Lawrence Feingold's *Faith Comes from What Is Heard* is a brilliant exposition of the foundations of theology. It is a trustworthy guide for all who seek a more profound knowledge of truth. It is a modern expression of the timeless theology of St. Thomas Aquinas that contains many golden nuggets from the greatest minds of the Church. If you desire to dig deeply into the Church's storehouse of treasures, here is your guide to that in-depth reasoning so essential to good theology."

—Kenneth J. Howell,
Author, Founder and Director of the Eucharist Project

FAITH COMES FROM WHAT IS HEARD

An Introduction to
Fundamental Theology

FAITH COMES FROM WHAT IS HEARD

An Introduction to Fundamental Theology

LAWRENCE FEINGOLD

EMMAUS
ACADEMIC

Steubenville, Ohio
www.EmmausAcademic.com

EMMAUS
ACADEMIC
Steubenville, Ohio
www.emmausacademic.com

A Division of The St. Paul Center for Biblical Theology
Editor-in-Chief: Scott Hahn
1468 Parkview Circle
Steubenville, Ohio 43952

Library of Congress Control Number: 2016937323
ISBN: 978-1-941447-54-3

Cover design and layout by Margaret Ryland

Cover art by Rembrandt Harmensz van Rijn, Christ Preaching ("La Petite Tombe")
(c. 1652) National Gallery of Art, Washington.

To Mary, Mother of the Church,
and to Marsha, my wife, who spent countless hours
editing and improving the text

*"So faith comes from what is heard,
and what is heard comes by the preaching of Christ.
But I ask, have they not heard? Indeed they have; for
'Their voice has gone out to all the earth,
and their words to the ends of the world.'"*
(Romans 10:17–18)

*"And these words which I command you this day shall be upon your heart;
and you shall teach them diligently to your children,
and shall talk of them when you sit in your house,
and when you walk by the way,
and when you lie down, and when you rise."*
(Deuteronomy 6:6–7)

"Always be prepared to make a defense to any one who calls you to account for the hope that is in you, yet do it with gentleness and reverence."
(1 Peter 3:15)

TABLE OF CONTENTS

PART 3 Transmission of Revelation through Tradition and the Magisterium

ABBREVIATIONS

Magisterial Sources:

AAS   *Acta Apostolicae Sedis*; available at http://www.vatican.va/
archive/aas/index_sp.htm.

DS   Denzinger, Heinrich. *Enchiridion Symbolorum. Compendium of Creeds, Definitions, and Declarations on Matters of Faith and Morals.* 43rd ed. Edited by Peter Hünermann; English edition edited by Robert Fastiggi and Anne Englund Nash. San Francisco: Ignatius Press, 2012.

SD   *The Scripture Documents: An Anthology of Official Catholic Teachings.* Edited by Dean P. Béchard, S.J. Collegeville, MN: Liturgical Press, 2002.

CCC   *Catechism of the Catholic Church.* 2nd ed. Washington, DC: United States Catholic Conference, 2000.

DV   Second Vatican Council, Dogmatic Constitution on Divine Revelation *Dei Verbum.*

LG   Second Vatican Council, Dogmatic Constitution on the Church *Lumen gentium.*

PBC   Pontifical Biblical Commission.

CDF   Congregation for the Doctrine of the Faith.

Patristic and Medieval Sources:

ANF   *The Ante-Nicene Fathers.* Peabody, MA: Hendrickson, 1994.

CCL   *Corpus Christianorum: Series Latina.* Turnhout: Brepols, 1953–.

CSEL   *Corpus Scriptorum Ecclesiasticorum Latinorum.* Vienna, Prague, and Leipzig: Tempsky, 1865–.

NPNF1   *Nicene and Post-Nicene Fathers,* 1st ser. Peabody, MA: Hendrickson Publishers, 1994.

NPNF2   *Nicene and Post-Nicene Fathers.* 2nd ser. Peabody, MA: Hendrickson Publishers, 1994.

PG   *Patrologiae cursus completus.* Series Graeca. Edited by J. P. Migne, Paris, 1856–1867.

PL   *Patrologiae cursus completus.* Series Latina. Edited by J. P. Migne, Paris, 1844–1865.

St. Thomas Aquinas:

ST   *Summa theologiae of St. Thomas Aquinas.* 2nd ed. Translated by Fathers of the English Dominican Province. London: Burns, Oates, & Washbourne, 1920–1932.

SCG   *Summa contra gentiles.* Translated by Anton Pegis, James Anderson, Vernon Bourke, and Charles O'Neil. 4 vols. Notre Dame, IN: University of Notre Dame Press, 1975.

bk.   book

ch.   chapter

q.   question

a.   article

Subsections of the articles in *ST* and other of Aquinas's works include the *corpus* (corp.), objections (obj.), replies to objections (ad), and the *sed contra* (sc), and Roman numerals refer to the major "parts" (groups of questions).

In Aquinas's works, "Marietti no." refers to the paragraph numbers used in the Latin editions produced by Casa Editrice Marietti in Turin, Italy.

Citations from the Second Vatican Council are taken from *The Sixteen Documents of Vatican II.* Boston: Pauline Books & Media, 1999.

INTRODUCTION

This book is the fruit of ten years of teaching Fundamental Theology, first in the Institute of Pastoral Theology of Ave Maria University and then at Kenrick-Glennon Seminary in St. Louis. It is designed to serve as a textbook for courses in Fundamental Theology in seminaries and in graduate and undergraduate programs in theology. It can also serve as a textbook for courses on Introduction to Theology and Introduction to Scripture. It aims, furthermore, also at all Catholics who want to understand their faith and its foundations more deeply.

The work is inspired by the conviction that theology ought to inform both the mind and heart, bringing them together to foster growth in faith, hope, and charity. This textbook also seeks to bring together dogmatic and biblical theology, the Thomistic tradition, the Fathers of the Church, and the contemporary Magisterium. The theologians that I draw on most heavily are St. Thomas Aquinas, Blessed John Henry Newman, Joseph Ratzinger, and St. John Paul II. The magisterial text that is most central to this book is the Second Vatican Council's Dogmatic Constitution on Divine Revelation, *Dei Verbum*.

The subject of this textbook is the Foundations of Catholic Theology, or Fundamental Theology, which is *theology's reflection on itself as a discipline, its method, and its foundation in God's Revelation transmitted to us through Scripture and Tradition.* The book is divided into six parts: (1) Revelation and faith as man's response to God's Word; (2)

the nature of Theology and theological method; (3) the transmission of Revelation through Tradition and the Magisterium; (4) the inspiration and truth of Scripture and principles of biblical interpretation; (5) the historical character of the Gospels; and (6) biblical typology. Since Scripture is the principal foundation and "soul" of theology,[1] half of the book deals with Scripture and its interpretation.

Part 1 studies God's Revelation, the nature of divine faith as the human response to God's Word (chapter 2), and the motives of credibility for faith (chapter 3). Since theology is "faith seeking understanding," to use the traditional formulation found in St. Anselm's *Proslogion*, it follows that faith provides the necessary disposition for doing theology. Faith is the human response, made possible by grace, to God's Revelation.

Part 2 is a reflection on the nature of theology understood as faith seeking understanding. This reflection is guided by the brilliant and brief introduction to theology by St. Thomas Aquinas in the first question of his *Summa theologiae*.

Parts 3–6 study the sources of theology, which are the means by which Revelation is transmitted to us, preserved over time, and safeguarded. These means are Tradition, the Magisterium, and Scripture. Part 3 treats the transmission of Revelation in the Church through her apostolic Tradition, under the guidance of her Magisterium. Part 4 treats the other channel through which God's Revelation is transmitted, which is Sacred Scripture, and discusses its inspiration and truth, following *Dei Verbum* §11. The fundamental principles of biblical interpretation are treated under the guidance of *Dei Verbum* §12.

Particular attention to the historicity of the Gospels (part 5) is appropriate for Fundamental Theology because Christ is the culmination and center of Revelation and His life and words are given to us directly in the Gospels. If the historical character of the Gospels is put in doubt, then the culmination and center of Revelation would become obscure, confused, and the subject of endless controversy. If, in the words of St. Jerome, ignorance of the Old Testament is ignorance of Christ, how much more true it is that doubt or ignorance about the

---

[1] *DV* §24.

historical character of the Gospels leads to ignorance of Christ and doubt about His divine claim!

The final section explores the classical doctrine of the four senses of Scripture and biblical typology, by which God uses sensible and historical events to prefigure Christ, the Church, and the Christian life.

Some of the material has appeared in an earlier form. Chapters 7 and 8 are modified versions of chapters 6–7 of Feingold, *The Mystery of Israel and the Church*, volume 3, *The Messianic Kingdom of Israel* (St. Louis: The Miriam Press, 2010), 89–124. Some of the material in chapters 2–3 also appeared previously in Feingold, *The Mystery of Israel and the Church*, volume 2, *Things New and Old* (St. Louis: The Miriam Press, 2010), 1–21.

PART 1

Revelation and Faith: God Speaks to Man and Our Response

CHAPTER ONE

Revelation and Salvation History

God Speaks to Man

The existence of sacred theology as a discipline distinct from philosophy is based on the fact that God speaks to man in history and man is capable of hearing, receiving, and discerning God's revealed Word. This fact of divine Revelation is the beginning and first foundation of sacred theology.[1] That God speaks to man is also the initial wonder of theology and the foundation of all the other wonders disclosed by God's Word. That the eternal God speaks to man, a little part of His creation,[2] is logically unexpected, but is secretly longed for as a sign that we are loved by the source of our being. And He speaks to us precisely to call us into intimate communion with Himself, which is the purpose or final cause of Revelation.

Dei Verbum §2 begins with this marvelous fact of God's self-communication and its purpose to bring us into intimacy with God:

> In His goodness and wisdom God chose to reveal Himself and to make known to us the hidden purpose of His will (see Eph. 1:9) by which through Christ, the Word made flesh,

---

[1] See René Latourelle, *Theology of Revelation* (Staten Island: Alba House, 1966), 13–14: "God's word to humanity is the first Christian reality: the first fact, the first mystery, the first category.... Revelation is the original mystery; it communicates every other mystery."

[2] See St. Augustine, *Confessions* 1.1.1, trans. Henry Chadwick (Oxford, UK: Oxford University Press, 1991), 3.

man might in the Holy Spirit have access to the Father and come to share in the divine nature (see Eph. 2:18; 2 Peter 1:4). Through this revelation, therefore, the invisible God (see Col. 1:15; 1 Tim. 1:17) out of the abundance of His love speaks to men as friends (see Ex. 33:11; John 15:14–15) and lives among them (see Bar. 3:38), so that He may invite and take them into fellowship with Himself.

The principal subject of Revelation is twofold: God Himself and His plan of salvation for mankind. God reveals Himself as the origin and goal of creation and of history. He reveals Himself first of all through seeking out man and calling him into communion. These two aspects of Revelation, therefore, are inextricably bound together. God reveals Himself through revealing His love for man and His plan of salvation (centered on the Incarnation and Passion of the Son of God) to merit the forgiveness of sins and make us, through grace, sons of God in the Son.

In the fullness of Revelation, God reveals Himself to be a communion of Persons—Father, Son, and Holy Spirit—and He invites us to enter into that communion both as sons in the Son and as brides of the Son, who is the eternal Bridegroom.

Two Movements of Revelation

Revelation thus has two directions or movements. God marvelously lowers Himself and, through that "condescension," no less marvelously elevates man to enter into communion with Himself. Revelation is an extended dialogue between two infinitely unequal partners who interact through descent and ascent: God descends to man so that man can ascend to Him. God pursues man so that man might seek God and be lifted up to enter into an infinitely gratuitous filial and spousal relationship with Him. All of Revelation reveals this dialogical structure. We see it in the work of creation, the covenants, the Incarnation, and the sacraments.

The *Catechism of the Catholic Church*, like *Dei Verbum* §2, begins with a summary view of God's Revelation in which we see these two dialogical movements of God's descent and man's ascent:

> God, infinitely perfect and blessed in himself, in a plan of sheer goodness freely created man to make him share in his own blessed life. For this reason, at every time and in every place, God draws close to man. He calls man to seek him, to know him, to love him with all his strength. He calls together all men, scattered and divided by sin, into the unity of his family, the Church. To accomplish this, when the fullness of time had come, God sent his Son as Redeemer and Savior. In his Son and through him, he invites men to become, in the Holy Spirit, his adopted children and thus heirs of his blessed life.[3]

St. Thomas Aquinas structures his *Summa theologiae* around this double movement.[4] He begins part I with God who creates the cosmos in such a way that rational creatures can be elevated to return to Him through moral action (part II), and through God's ultimate self-emptying in the Incarnation of Christ and the sacraments of the Church (part III). The classic formulation of this structure is *exitus/reditus*. Creation comes forth (*exitus*) from God so that it can return (*reditus*) to Him in knowledge and love.

Already in creation, God reveals Himself in a certain way through the things that are made. His providence shows Him bending over His creation in loving care so that it can return to Him by doing the actions for which it was made. Man in particular is made with a rest-

---

[3]   CCC §1.

[4]   The *Summa theologiae* was written between 1265 and 1274 and is the classical masterpiece of Catholic theology. This manual for "beginners" (as St. Thomas describes it in the prologue) explores the themes of God, man, Revelation, the world, virtue, vice, and all the main points of doctrine in a systematic and well-reasoned manner. Each question begins with several objections against St. Thomas' thesis, followed by an argument from authority in favor of his view (the *sed contra*). He then demonstrates his position in the body of the article (the *corpus*), followed by a response to each objection (ad 1; ad 2; etc.). The *Summa* will be our main guide through the foundational points of Catholic theology in this work. Translations from the *Summa* are generally my own, done on the basis of the translation of the Fathers of the English Dominican province.

less heart that seeks to return to its Maker. According to the classic words of St. Augustine: "You stir man to take pleasure in praising you, because you have made us for yourself, and our heart is restless until it rests in you."[5] God created man with a natural inclination and desire to know and love God and to enter into relation with Him. Both the capacity and the desire for ascent and elevation are built into man's nature.[6]

Thus man naturally seeks God,[7] and we see evidence for this in all the natural religions and forms of worship that mark all human cultures.[8] This means that, when God speaks to man, He speaks to one who is already made to seek Him and search for His Word, whether consciously or unconsciously, explicitly or implicitly.[9] Man's search for God, however, if left to man himself, is extremely arduous, and requires "every effort of intellect, a sound will, 'an upright heart,' as well as the witness of others who teach him to seek God."[10]

God, thankfully, does not leave man to himself, despite original sin, but condescends to man to call him into covenant, speaking to men as friends. That God should enter into covenant with man, an infinitely unequal partner, is utterly gratuitous and should amaze us. This condescension culminates in the Incarnation of the Son who

---

[5] St. Augustine, *Confessions* 1.1.1 (Chadwick, 3).

[6] For the theme of the natural desire for God, see Lawrence Feingold, *The Natural Desire to See God According to St. Thomas Aquinas and His Interpreters* (Ave Maria: Sapientia Press, 2010).

[7] See CCC §27: "The desire for God is written in the human heart, because man is created by God and for God; and God never ceases to draw man to himself. Only in God will he find the truth and happiness he never stops searching for: 'The dignity of man rests above all on the fact that he is called to communion with God. This invitation to converse with God is addressed to man as soon as he comes into being. For if man exists, it is because God has created him through love, and through love continues to hold him in existence. He cannot live fully according to truth unless he freely acknowledges that love and entrusts himself to his creator' (*Gaudium et spes* §19)."

[8] See CCC §28: "In many ways, throughout history down to the present day, men have given expression to their quest for God in their religious beliefs and behavior: in their prayers, sacrifices, rituals, meditations, and so forth. These forms of religious expression, despite the ambiguities they often bring with them, are so universal that one may well call man a *religious being*."

[9] See Vatican II, Pastoral Constitution on the Church in the Modern World *Gaudium et spes* §21: "Above all the Church knows that her message is in harmony with the most secret desires of the human heart when she champions the dignity of the human vocation."

[10] CCC §30.

empties Himself even to death on the Cross (see Phil 2:6–8).

Already in the Garden of Eden, man was immeasurably elevated above His natural state by the gift of intimacy with God, who walked with them "in the cool of the day," and by access to the tree of life in the center of the Garden, representing supernatural and eternal life. After these gifts were lost and man descended through the fall from grace, the drama of man's elevation is more dramatic. The Son of God descends into our history and condition to elevate us to share in His. The Fathers of the Church speak of this as the "economy" of salvation. Christ takes what is ours—human life, history, culture, obedience, weakness, and humiliation—in order to win for us a share in what is His: eternal life, intimate communion with the Father in the Holy Spirit, perfect love and knowledge, and the dignity of sons.

The Eucharist exemplifies the double movement of Revelation. God comes forth to man first in the liturgy of the Word, and then still more marvelously in the Real Presence and in Holy Communion. However, the descent of God unto the altar takes place so that there can be an elevation. The supreme elevation is to make man not only a participant in Christ's divine nature through Communion, but also a participant in His perfect worship of the Father, so that the Church offers God to God in the sacrifice of the Mass.

The Principal Content of the Gospel Is the Incarnation and Our Nuptial Union with the Incarnate Word

The culmination of God's Revelation is the Incarnation and our union with God through becoming sons in the Son in His Church, here on earth and in heaven. St. Thomas Aquinas makes this summary of Revelation when he comments on the meaning of the word "Gospel" in Romans 1:1 in his commentary on the epistle:

> *Gospel* means good news. For it announces the news of man's union with God, which is man's good: "it is good for me to cleave to God" (Ps 73:28). Indeed, a threefold union of man

with God is announced in the Gospel. The first is by the grace of union: "the Word was made flesh" (John 1:14). The second is by the grace of adoption, as implied in the Psalm: "I say: you are gods, sons of the Most High, all of you" (Ps 82:6). The third is by the glory of attainment: "this is eternal life, that they know you" (John 17:3).[11]

All of Revelation either treats of the Incarnation and our union with God in Christ and the Church, or else prepares for it in a marvelous way by promise, prophecy, worship, the commandments, and the formation of the People of God in whom He will become incarnate.

St. Thomas says that "the Son of God is deservedly said to be called the subject matter of the Holy Scriptures, which reveal the divine wisdom, as Deuteronomy declares (Deut 4:6). . . . For the Son is said to be the Word and wisdom, begotten: *Christ, the power of God and the wisdom of God* (1 Cor 1:24)."[12] All of Revelation is Christocentric.

As all Revelation centers on Christ, so too all Revelation centers on the preparation for our union with Him, which is represented as a nuptial mystery in which we are to be brides of Christ, the Bridegroom. Revelation is the story of a wedding to which all of mankind is called.

The betrothal is announced in the Old Testament. God promises through the prophet Hosea: "And I will betroth you to me for ever; I will betroth you to me in righteousness and in justice, in steadfast love, and in mercy. I will betroth you to me in faithfulness; and you shall know the Lord" (Hos 2:19–20). Ezekiel 16 recounts the story of God's courtship of Israel despite her infidelities. The Song of Songs is an allegory of the desire and love of the bride and groom. When the Word became flesh, John the Baptist announced that he was the

---

[11] St. Thomas Aquinas, *Commentary on the Letter of Saint Paul to the Romans*, Marietti nos. 23–24, trans. F. R. Larcher (Lander: The Aquinas Institute for the Study of Sacred Doctrine, 2012), 9. For an excellent reflection on Aquinas's understanding of the "Gospel" in his commentaries on St. Paul, see Matthew Levering, *Engaging the Doctrine of Revelation: Mediation of the Gospel through Church and Scripture* (Grand Rapids: Baker Academic, 2014), 121–138

[12] Ibid., 11n9.

friend of the Bridegroom, who was Jesus: "He who has the bride is the bridegroom; the friend of the bridegroom, who stands and hears him, rejoices greatly at the bridegroom's voice; therefore this joy of mine is now full" (John 3:29). When questioned why His disciples did not fast, Jesus answered: "Can the wedding guests mourn as long as the bridegroom is with them? The days will come, when the bridegroom is taken away from them, and then they will fast" (Matt 9:15). In His parables, He compared the Kingdom to a wedding feast for the king's son, to which a great multitude had been invited.[13] The final book of the Bible culminates with the angel's message: "Write this: Blessed are those who are invited to the marriage supper of the Lamb" (Rev 19:9). As usual, the analogy falls infinitely short—we are invited to the wedding of the Lamb not as guests, but as the Bride!

The Communication of Revelation: Mediation

How does God reveal Himself to man? There is a fundamental principle of reason that is of great importance in theology: everything is received according to the mode of the receiver. When applied to Revelation, this implies that God reveals Himself according to the mode of human nature so that we can receive Him in a human way. That Revelation be received in a human way implies several key elements: our natural mode of learning is first through sensible realities; it is socially and culturally mediated; and it is progressive and unfolding. God's Revelation therefore comes to man through sensible realities, is socially communicated, is embedded in historical events, and progressively unfolds in history.

Sensible Realities

It is a fundamental principle of the philosophy of man that all human knowledge naturally begins with sense knowledge. We come to know higher realities (such as universal metaphysical ideas) through sense experience and abstraction from sense experience. God makes

---

[13] Matt 22:1–14.

use of sensible realities by revealing Himself in history through historical events, through the human words and actions of the prophets, through the worship that God gave to Israel and the Church, and above all through the humanity of Christ, His Passion, and Resurrection. As we shall see in part 6, this foundation in sense knowledge is the key principle behind biblical typology, by which God reveals deeper mysteries through historical events such as the Exodus. The use of sensible realities in Revelation is also a crucial principle behind the sacraments and the liturgy.

Social Mediation of Revelation

The social dimension of Revelation implies that God speaks to man not in an individualistic way, but in and through a society—Israel and the Church. The Second Vatican Council expressed this truth in *Lumen gentium* §9:

> At all times and in every race God has given welcome to whosoever fears Him and does what is right. God, however, does not make men holy and save them *merely as individuals*, without bond or link between one another. Rather has *it pleased Him to bring men together as one people*, a people which acknowledges Him in truth and serves Him in holiness.

Since man is a social animal,[14] it makes sense that God would will to save him through a society. It is also fitting that God speak to man socially because of the principle of mediation. God speaks to a society—Israel and the Church—through certain members of that society who are established as mediators between God and mankind. The classic example is Moses, through whom God spoke to all of Israel at that time and in the centuries to come. The mediator of Revelation is referred to as a prophet. The prophet receives a communication from God not simply for his own edification, but to be communicated socially to others to build up the faith of the People of God.

---

[14] This is famously stated by Aristotle in his *Politics* 1.2.1253a.

Revelation and History

God reveals Himself in the web of human history and through historical events of which He is the protagonist. He revealed Himself to man already in the Garden of Eden, establishing a primordial covenant. After the Fall, He revealed a plan to destroy the serpent's head through a Woman and her offspring (Gen 3:15). To prepare for that event, He called Abraham out of his father's house to become the father of a new people chosen to be the People of God and gave him the promise that the people would be blessed and extremely numerous and that, in his seed, all nations would be blessed (Gen 12). He revealed Himself in the events of the Exodus, bringing the Chosen People out of bondage in Egypt with an "outstretched arm" and miraculous works and leading them to Mount Sinai, where he sealed the covenant with them and gave them the Torah to guide moral action and worship. His Revelation continued through the life of Israel, the teachings of the prophets, and especially the promise of the Messiah and the kingdom He was to establish. God's Revelation culminates in the historical event of the fulfillment of these promises in the birth, life, death, and Resurrection of Jesus Christ, followed by the expansion of the apostolic Church.

Pope St. John Paul II, in §§11–12 of his encyclical *Fides et ratio*, speaks about the inseparable connection between Revelation and history:

> God's Revelation is therefore immersed in time and history. Jesus Christ took flesh in the "fullness of time" (*Gal* 4:4); and two thousand years later, I feel bound to restate forcefully that "in Christianity time has a fundamental importance."[15] It is within time that the whole work of creation and salvation comes to light; and it emerges clearly above all that, with the Incarnation of the Son of God, our life is even now a foretaste of the fulfilment of time which is to come (cf. *Heb* 1:2).

---

[15] Here quoting his own Apostolic Letter on Preparation for the Jubilee of the Year 2000 *Tertio millennio adveniente* (1994), §10e; in *AAS* 87 (1995), 11.

The truth about himself and his life which God has entrusted to humanity is immersed therefore in time and history; and it was declared once and for all in the mystery of Jesus of Nazareth. . . . For the People of God, therefore, history becomes a path to be followed to the end, so that by the unceasing action of the Holy Spirit (cf. Jn 16:13) the contents of revealed truth may find their full expression. This is the teaching of the Constitution *Dei Verbum* [§8] when it states that "as the centuries succeed one another, the Church constantly progresses towards the fullness of divine truth, until the words of God reach their complete fulfilment in her."

History therefore becomes the arena where we see what God does for humanity. God comes to us in the things we know best and can verify most easily, the things of our everyday life, apart from which we cannot understand ourselves.

Revelation makes known to the eyes of faith that human history is the arena of salvation: salvation history.

This sacred history, in addition to being the Revelation of God and His plan of salvation, is also a protracted and unremitting battle between God's plan for redemption and those who oppose it, even unknowingly, throughout history. St. Augustine, in his great work, *The City of God*, expresses this battle in terms of two opposing "cities" or civilizations. He shows that the most fundamental structure of human history is the conflict between these two "cities," or types of civilization, found in every age. These two cities are determined by their acceptance or rejection of the first precept of the Law of God, which is the double commandment of love. St. Augustine perfectly expresses this radical alternative in terms of two opposing loves: "Two cities have been formed by two loves: the earthly by the love of self, even to the contempt of God; the heavenly by the love of God, even to the contempt of self. The former, in a word, glories in itself, the latter in the Lord."[16]

The City of God, insofar as it exists visibly in this world, culmi-

---

[16] *City of God* 14.28 (*NPNF1*, 2:282–283).

nates in the Catholic Church. Its origin, however, lies at the beginning of history. The Fathers of the Church see the City of God as beginning with Abel, who offered cult to God with a spirit of humility and reverence. It continues in the line of Seth and in the family of Noah, and then in Abraham and the formation of the Chosen People through his descendants. This People would be the privileged place for the City of God until the coming of its King and eternal Ruler, Christ our Lord, and the founding of the Church as His Mystical Body in which all nations are to be gathered.[17] Obviously, not all the members of the People of the Old and the New Covenant work to build up the City of God. Many are constructors of the worldly city, sowing weeds in the field of the Lord; on the Day of Judgment, they will be definitively separated from her. On the other hand, outside of the visible Church, there are many who are in fact invisibly in relationship with her.[18] Although ignorant of the Church through no fault of their own, they ardently desire to serve God as He wishes to be served, and thus are animated by the Spirit of God, who is the "soul" of the Church.

The Progressive Nature of Revelation

Revelation is the education of the human race, as taught by God Himself. Now, just as no sensible teacher teaches everything at once, but rather teaches progressively according to the growing capacity of the students, so also God wisely reveals Himself progressively to mankind, in stages, gradually preparing His pupils for more difficult lessons.

Revelation has three principal stages: the primitive Revelation to Adam and Eve and the first patriarchs (about which we know very little), the Revelation contained in the Old Testament given to Israel through the patriarchs and prophets, and finally the fullness of Revelation given in Jesus Christ.

---

[17] See *LG* §9.

[18] See *LG* §16 and Pius XII, Encyclical Letter on the Mystical Body of Christ *Mystici Corporis Christi* (1943), §103: "For even though by an unconscious desire and longing they have a certain relationship with the Mystical Body of the Redeemer, they still remain deprived of those many heavenly gifts and helps which can only be enjoyed in the Catholic Church."

Dei Verbum §§3–4 summarizes these stages of Revelation:

Planning to make known the way of heavenly salvation, He went further and from the start manifested Himself to our first parents. Then after their fall His promise of redemption aroused in them the hope of being saved (see Gen. 3:15) and from that time on He ceaselessly kept the human race in His care, to give eternal life to those who perseveringly do good in search of salvation (see Rom. 2:6–7). Then, at the time He had appointed He called Abraham in order to make of him a great nation (see Gen. 12:2). Through the patriarchs, and after them through Moses and the prophets, He taught this people to acknowledge Himself the one living and true God, provident father and just judge, and to wait for the Savior promised by Him, and in this manner prepared the way for the Gospel down through the centuries. Then, after speaking in many and varied ways through the prophets, "now at last in these days God has spoken to us in His Son" (Heb. 1:1–2).

A broad sketch of these stages of salvation history is given in an allegorical interpretation of the parable of the Good Samaritan.[19] Origen records this interpretation, and he states that it is not original with him, but was passed down by the "elders":

One of the elders wanted to interpret the parable as follows. The man who was going down is Adam. Jerusalem is paradise, and Jericho is the world. The robbers are hostile powers. The priest is the Law, the Levite is the prophets, and the Samaritan is Christ. The wounds are disobedience, the beast is the Lord's body, and the stable, which accepts all who wish to enter, is the Church. . . . The manager of the stable is the head of the Church, to whom its care has been entrusted. And the fact that the Samaritan promises he will return represents the Sav-

---

[19] This is an interpretation of the parable in the literal sense, as an allegory of salvation history. The parable also has a moral sense, explaining the duty of the Christian to help his neighbor, who is every man.

ior's second coming. All of this has been said reasonably and beautifully.[20]

The man coming down from Jerusalem before he is robbed signifies Adam in original justice. The robbery is the Fall, which brings on the second stage of salvation history, in which fallen man is without the preternatural gifts and without sacramental grace. During this period, the man remains wounded and without salvation. The third stage is marked by the Levite and the priest. As symbols of the Old Covenant, they have the power to awaken hope, but cannot save fallen Adam. The Samaritan's work of healing represents the sacramental economy of the Church, in which grace is not only signified by rituals, as in the Old Testament, but efficaciously given through the sacraments of the Church. The Samaritan, who represents Christ, brings the victim to an inn and departs, promising to return and to pay all charges in full. The inn is the Church, where we live the Christian life, and the return signifies the Second Coming that will inaugurate the final stage of consummated beatitude.

This progressive character of Revelation is beautifully stated in the first two verses of the Letter to the Hebrews: "In many and various ways God spoke of old to our fathers by the prophets; but in these last days he has spoken to us by a Son, whom he appointed the heir of all things, through whom also he created the world."[21] As we see in this text, the progressive character of Revelation is not indefinite, interminable, forever progressing and never arriving at fullness. Rath-

---

[20] Homily 34 on Luke 10:25–37, in *Origen: Homilies on Luke; Fragments on Luke*, trans. Joseph Lienhard, S.J., (Washington, DC: Catholic University of America Press, 1996), 138. The Christological interpretation of the parable of the Good Samaritan is extremely common in the Fathers. We find it first in St. Irenaeus, *Adversus haereses* 3.17.3 (*ANF* 1:641–42), in which he says that the Lord "Himself compassionated, and bound up his wounds, giving two royal denaria." We find it also in Clement of Alexandria, *Who Is the Rich Man That Shall Be Saved?* 29 (PG, 9:634). See Jean Cardinal Daniélou, S.J., "Le bon Samaritain," in *Mélanges bibliques rédigés en l'honneur de André Robert* (Paris, 1956), 457–465; D. Sanchis, "Samaritanus ille," *Recherches de Science Religieuse* 49 (1961): 414ff.; A. Orbe, *Parabolas evangélicas de S. Ireneo* (Madrid: BAC, 1972), 105–153; W. Monselewski, *Der Barmherzige Samaritaner: Eine auslegungsgeschichtliche Untersuchung zu Lukas 10: 25–37* (Tübingen: Mohr-Siebeck, 1967); and Bertrand de Margerie, S.J., *An Introduction to the History of Exegesis*, vol. 1, *The Greek Fathers* (Petersham: Saint Bede's, 1993), 70–75.

[21] Heb 1:1–2 is quoted in *DV* §4.

er, its fullness is achieved in Christ and His Paschal mystery, and it culminates in the sending of the Holy Spirit to the Apostles to guide them "into all the truth" (John 16:13).

The human sciences, in contrast, are always progressive, for we will never arrive at the absolute fullness of knowledge about physics, biology, ethics, or metaphysics. Thus, it is easy for modern man to think of Revelation also as intrinsically and necessarily always progressive. If all the sciences naturally progress with history as each age builds on its predecessors, why not Revelation?

Here we need a distinction. The science of theology progresses over time like other sciences. Revelation, however, progressed only until its culmination in Christ's Paschal mystery and the sending of the Holy Spirit, in which God achieved His purpose and revealed all that needed to be publicly revealed to mankind.

An important thesis of Modernism, condemned by Pope St. Pius X at the beginning of the twentieth century, is that Revelation continues through the ages. In 1907, the Holy Office condemned a list of Modernist propositions in the document, *Lamentabili sane*, or Syllabus Condemning the Errors of the Modernists. Proposition 21 condemns the statement that "Revelation, constituting the object of the Catholic faith, was not completed with the apostles."[22] This condemnation confirms the constant faith of the Church that public Revelation was completed with the death of St. John the Evangelist, the last of the Apostles, about the year 100.

The Modernist idea that Revelation continues to progress indefinitely rests on a naturalistic idea of Revelation. According to the most radical form of Modernism, Revelation is "nothing else than the consciousness man acquired of his relation to God"[23] through the development of his religious sense. Modernism denies the Catholic understanding of Revelation as something having its origin in God, not in man's natural faculties, which thus transcends the human mind. This false naturalistic conception of Revelation can be clearly seen in prop-

---

[22] Holy Office, Decree Condemning Certain Errors of the Modernists *Lamentabili sane* (1907), §21 (DS, 3421).

[23] Ibid., §20 (DS, 3420).

osition 22 of *Lamentabili*, which condemns the following statement: "The dogmas the Church presents as revealed are not truths fallen from heaven, but a certain interpretation of religious facts that the human mind has acquired by laborious effort."[24] If Revelation were actually acquired by laborious human effort in the development of man's religious sense, then it is reasonable to think that it would continue to progress or change as long as man continues to think about his relationship with God.

However, the Church continues to believe—and will always do so—that the truths of Revelation are indeed "*truths fallen from heaven.*" They have their origin in the eternal wisdom of God. Through divine Revelation and the virtue of divine faith by which we give our assent to revealed truth, we already have here on earth a certain participation in the divine wisdom, which is enjoyed in its fullness by the angels and saints in heaven.

Now, since Revelation is a divine and not a human work, it must be perfectly ordered, which means it must be directed to some definite goal. An infinite process of Revelation would have no goal or culmination, and thus would have no order, but would be random, which is not worthy of the divine wisdom. In fact, all of Revelation has a very concrete culmination: the Incarnation, life, death, and Resurrection of Christ our Lord. In the Incarnation and Passion, God has given nothing less than Himself, and given Himself to the end,[25] to the shedding of all His blood for man and giving us His Body and Blood in the Eucharist so that we may finally attain to the beatific vision. There is nothing greater to give in any possible world, even for the omnipotence of God! The great Dominican biblical scholar, Marie-Joseph Lagrange, eloquently explains:

> If religion has any meaning, it indicates relations with God. The aim of religion is to draw us closer to God, and the most perfect religion is that which draws us closest to Him. When the union is such that the mind cannot conceive anything

---

[24] DS, 3422.

[25] See John 3:16; 13:1; Gal 4:4–5; 1 John 1:1–4; and Phil 2:6–11.

more intimate, we have attained, I think, the final degree of perfection in so far as man is capable of attaining thereunto. Our religion proposes to our belief that God united Himself to the human race by the Incarnation, that having become incarnate He unites Himself to us in this life by the Holy Eucharist, and that, while further uniting Himself to us by grace, He offers us union with Him in glory by penetrating into the very vision of His inscrutable nature. The impossibility of any further "religious progress" stands out clearly from this simple summary of religious teaching.[26]

All Revelation before Christ was progressive because it was a preparation for the Incarnation of God. The prophets announced the future coming of the Messiah, and the mysteries of Christ were prefigured in the ancient Jewish ceremonies. However, once the Messiah has come, once the second Person of the Trinity has taken on flesh, once the Passion of our Lord has redeemed man and offered to God a perfect sacrifice of expiation, once the Holy Spirit was given on Pentecost and the Church was formed and began to spread on the apostolic foundation, Revelation is complete. No further public Revelation is to be expected.

And not only do we not expect such Revelation, but if someone claims to have received further public Revelation, he should not be believed. St. Paul says categorically in the Letter to the Galatians (1:8): "But though we, or an angel from heaven, preach a gospel to you besides that which we have preached to you, let him be anathema."

Once the fullness has come, we must not expect or crave anything further until we are admitted into the presence of God in heaven. All public Revelation culminates in Christ, "in whom are hidden all the treasures of wisdom and knowledge" (Col 2:3). To expect anything more is to derogate the dignity of Christ, the perfect Word of the Father, perfect God and perfect man. *Dei Verbum* §4 states: "The Christian economy, therefore, since it is the new and definitive covenant,

---

[26] Marie-Joseph Lagrange, *Historical Criticism and the Old Testament*, trans. Edward Myers (London: Catholic Truth Society, 1906), 25.

will never pass away; and no new public revelation is to be expected before the glorious manifestation of our Lord, Jesus Christ." This teaching was reaffirmed once more in the document *Dominus Iesus* §§5–6, in which it is stated to be *"contrary to the faith of the Church"* to affirm that the Revelation completed in Christ is somehow incomplete and capable of being complemented by other religious traditions.[27]

In *Fides et ratio*, John Paul II highlights the centrality of Christ in giving the fullness of meaning to God's entire plan of salvation history:

> In the Incarnation of the Son of God we see forged the enduring and definitive synthesis which the human mind of itself could not even have imagined: the Eternal enters time, the Whole lies hidden in the part, God takes on a human face. The truth communicated in Christ's Revelation is therefore no longer confined to a particular place or culture, but is offered to every man and woman who would welcome it as the word which is the absolutely valid source of meaning for human life. Now, in Christ, all have access to the Father, since by his Death and Resurrection Christ has bestowed the divine life which the first Adam had refused (cf. *Rom* 5:12–15). Through this Revelation, men and women are offered the ultimate truth about their own life and about the goal of history. As the Constitution *Gaudium et spes* [§22] puts it, "only in the mystery of the incarnate Word does the mystery of man take on light." Seen in any other terms, the mystery of personal existence remains an insoluble riddle. Where might the human being seek the answer to dramatic questions such as pain, the suffering of the innocent and death, if not in the

---

[27] CDF, Declaration on the Unicity and Salvific Universality of Jesus Christ and the Church *Dominus Iesus* (August 6, 2000), §6: "Therefore, the theory of the limited, incomplete, or imperfect character of the revelation of Jesus Christ, which would be complementary to that found in other religions, is contrary to the Church's faith. Such a position would claim to be based on the notion that the truth about God cannot be grasped and manifested in its globality and completeness by any historical religion, neither by Christianity nor by Jesus Christ."

light streaming from the mystery of Christ's Passion, Death and Resurrection?[28]

The Mystery of God and the Mystery of Man Progressively Revealed

As we have seen, God's Revelation has a double focus: the God who descends toward man and man who is mysteriously capable of being elevated to union with God. Thus, there is a double mystery at the heart of Revelation: the mystery of God who is love and the mystery of man who is *capax Dei*—capable of union with God despite the mystery of sin. Man's capacity for union with God is the mystery of grace, by which man is made a "sharer of the divine nature," according to the profound words of 2 Peter 1:4. The divine pedagogy at work in salvation history progressively develops each aspect—the mystery of God and the mystery of man's union with God.

God begins to unveil His mystery first by revealing to Israel His Providence, oneness, fullness of Being, and man's corresponding duty to love Him above all things. A key text is Deuteronomy 6:4–5: "Hear, O Israel: The Lord our God is one Lord; and you shall love the Lord your God with all your heart, and with all your soul, and with all your might." Another is Exodus 3:14: "God said to Moses, 'I AM WHO AM.' And he said, 'Say this to the people of Israel, "I AM has sent me to you."'" God, however, did not fully and explicitly reveal the mystery of His inner life to Israel. It is only in Christ that the mystery of the Trinity is explicitly revealed.[29]

In a similar way, in the books of Moses, God did not explicitly reveal man's supernatural end to see God face to face. It is alluded to in the prophets, but it is Christ who explicitly announces that the pure in heart shall *see God*. By revealing our supernatural end, as well as the Resurrection of the body, Christ fully reveals man and his exalted destiny.[30] As stated in *Gaudium et spes* §22:

---

[28] John Paul II, Encyclical Letter on Faith and Reason *Fides et ratio* (1998), §12.

[29] See Feingold, *Mystery of Israel and the Church*, vol. 2, *Things New and Old* (St. Louis: Miriam Press, 2010), 146–163.

[30] For the progressive revelation of the Last Things, see ibid., 43–54.

The truth is that only in the mystery of the incarnate Word does the mystery of man take on light. For Adam, the first man, was a figure of Him Who was to come, namely Christ the Lord. Christ, the final Adam, by the revelation of the mystery of the Father and His love, fully reveals man to man himself and makes his supreme calling clear.

The Communication of Revelation: Prophecy

When God reveals Himself to a prophet, He infuses knowledge directly into his mind, temporarily giving him a new and more potent intellectual light to perceive new truths that exceed his natural reason and to rightly judge whatever God wills him to affirm.[31]

The charism of prophecy involves two aspects. First, God may infuse new knowledge into the mind of the prophet concerning His plan of salvation. This involves either seeing a vision, hearing, or simply understanding a divine communication.[32] Secondly, He gives a light to rightly judge concerning an aspect of salvation history. This right judgment may concern new knowledge or simply confirm in a supernatural way what the prophet already knows from previous prophecy, Tradition, or experience, or it may give a new interpretation and insight to that previous knowledge.[33] Of these two aspects, St. Thomas Aquinas holds that the gift of right judgment through di-

---

[31] See Paul Synave and Pierre Benoit, *Prophecy and Inspiration: A Commentary on the Summa theologica II-II, questions 171–178*, trans. Avery R. Dulles, S.J., and Thomas L. Sheridan (New York: Desclee Co., 1961).

[32] St. Thomas holds that this may happen through the mediation of angels. See *ST* II-II, q. 172, a. 2. The Old Testament seems to indicate this, in that Revelation is often attributed to an "angel of the Lord" who conveys the Word of the Lord.

[33] For example, if the author of Genesis 1–11 made use of narrative traditions common to other cultures in the Ancient Near East, as in the account of creation, the fall, and the flood, we should think that the prophetic light enabled the prophet to rightly judge what elements of the received narrative to include and how they were to be modified and rightly understood. See the PBC's Decree of June 27, 1906, which reads: "Whether it may be granted without prejudice to the Mosaic authenticity that Moses in the production of his work made use of sources, whether written documents or oral traditions, and from these, in accordance with his special purposes and under the influence of divine inspiration, he selected some things, either verbatim or in substance, summarized or amplified, and inserted them into his work. Response: Affirmative" (DS, 3396; *SD*, 189).

vine illumination is most decisive and is always present in the prophet, whereas the seeing of visions and the like need not be present and would not be sufficient by itself to communicate Revelation.[34] It is not enough to see a vision or hear a message infused by God, as did King Nebuchadnezzar (cf. Dan 2) or Pharaoh (Gen 41); the prophet, like Daniel or Joseph, must also be able, through divine illumination, to understand it rightly and communicate it.

Revelation thus implies a supernatural illumination of the mind, which is not to be identified with a special sensibility on the part of the prophet.[35] Prophecy is not a natural gift, like perfect pitch or mathematical genius. It is entirely a gratuitous gift (charism) of God that occurs whenever God wishes, and only then, and to the extent that God wishes. The prophets did not always receive divine communications, but only intermittently.[36] The human mind is passive in this regard.[37] The prophets did not always completely understand what was revealed to them.[38] The extent to which they did so depended on the will of God and the illumination they were given.

---

[34] See *ST* II-II, q. 173, a. 2: "But it is the first of these two that holds the chief place in prophecy, since judgment is the complement of knowledge. Wherefore if certain things are divinely represented to any man by means of imaginary likenesses, as happened to Pharaoh (Gen 41:1–7) and to Nabuchodonosor (Dan 4:1–2), or even by bodily likenesses, as happened to Balthasar (Dan 5:5), such a man is not to be considered a prophet, unless his mind be enlightened for the purpose of judgment.... And yet a man will be a prophet, if his intellect be enlightened merely for the purpose of judging of things seen in imagination by others, as in the case of Joseph who interpreted Pharaoh's dream." See also q. 174, a. 2.

[35] See ibid., q. 172, a. 3.

[36] See ibid., q. 171, a. 2: "Now the prophetic light is not in the prophet's intellect by way of an abiding form, else a prophet would always be able to prophesy, which is clearly false.... It follows therefore that the prophetic light is in the prophet's soul by way of a passion or transitory impression.... Hence it is that even as the air is ever in need of a fresh enlightening, so too the prophet's mind is always in need of a fresh revelation; thus a disciple who has not yet acquired the principles of an art needs to have every detail explained to him."

[37] See ibid., q. 171, a. 2, ad 1: "For just as, in natural knowledge, the possible intellect is passive to the light of the active intellect, so too in prophetic knowledge the human intellect is passive to the enlightening of the Divine light."

[38] See ibid., q. 173, a. 4: "Nevertheless it must be observed that since the prophet's mind is a defective instrument ... even true prophets know not all that the Holy Spirit means by the things they see, or speak, or even do."

Jesus Christ is the supreme prophet because, unlike the other prophets, He proclaimed the full and definitive contents of Revelation both in words and through His entire life. He is the supreme Revealer because He Himself is the principal content of Revelation, and because He has a perfect knowledge of the plans He came to realize. Only in the human soul of Jesus Christ was Revelation received in a way that was continuous, entire, and absolute. This is because Jesus Christ, in His humanity, by an absolutely unique privilege, enjoyed the beatific vision from the moment of His conception. This has been the common teaching of the great theologians, and it was taught authoritatively by Pius XII in *Mystici Corporis Christi*.[39] Christ, who is the Revealer of the Father, taught what He knew by sight and vision, not by faith, conjecture, or arduous religious investigations. Christ is the "author of faith,"[40] but He Himself did not have faith because He already had the vision of God in its fullness.[41]

The humanity of Jesus Christ is also the supreme Mediator of Revelation, for He is able to reveal the Father not only through words communicated from another, but in His every action, for every act of Christ is an act of the Son of God on our behalf, in relation to the Father. Thus, every act of Christ, especially His Passion and Resurrection, reveals the love of God for mankind in a way that infinitely surpasses all words. Thus Jesus says to Philip, who asked Him to show them the Father:

> Have I been with you so long, and yet you do not know me, Philip? He who has seen me has seen the Father; how can you say, "Show us the Father"? Do you not believe that I am in the Father and the Father in me? The words that I say to you I do not speak on my own authority; but the Father who dwells in me does his works. (John 14:9–10)

---

[39] §§48 and 75.

[40] See Heb 12:2: "Looking at Jesus, the author and finisher of faith," Confraternity of Christian Doctrine translation (New York: Benziger Bros., 1958).

[41] See St. Thomas, *ST* III, q. 9, a. 2; q. 10. See also Lawrence Feingold, "Vision of God in Christ: 'Who Loved Me and Gave Himself for Me,'" in *Love and Friendship: Maritain and the Tradition*, ed. Montague Brown (Washington, DC: Catholic University of America Press, 2013), 218–232.

Revelation through the Holy Spirit

Although Christ is the central focus of Revelation, the Holy Spirit is the hidden agent of Revelation. Although God speaks through humble created realities such as human words and historical events, those human words and events are elevated by the power of the Holy Spirit so that they can produce a divine work and a divine fruitfulness. Thus, all Revelation and prophecy is through the power of the Holy Spirit, and we profess in the Nicene Creed that the Holy Spirit "has spoken through the prophets." As 2 Peter 1:21 states: "No prophecy ever came by the impulse of man, but men moved by the Holy Spirit spoke from God." The Holy Spirit is at work also in the transmission of Revelation through Scripture, for He inspires the sacred authors. The power of the Holy Spirit works not only in the mind of the prophet and sacred author, but must also be at work in the minds of those who receive Revelation through faith, as will be seen below. Thus St. Paul says: "No one can say 'Jesus is Lord' except by the Holy Spirit" (1 Cor 12:3). The Holy Spirit is also the protagonist of the Church's constant mission to transmit Revelation through evangelization and to understand more deeply the content of Revelation through the work of theologians.

Inexhaustible Nature of Revelation

Although Revelation culminates in the Paschal mystery and the sending of the Holy Spirit to the Apostles to open their minds to the fullness of what Christ had said and done, Revelation is still capable of being developed more and more over time. Thus, even though public Revelation is completed, mankind will never be able to *fully* receive and understand it in this world. The Word of God that comes to man, especially in Christ, is a superabundantly fruitful Word. It has a power to impregnate human minds, hearts, and cultures. Theology will never exhaust the mystery and will never complete its work before Christ returns.

It will be only in the vision of God that Revelation will be fully and completely understood, for then we shall see Him as He is, and no longer through deficient signs that point to Him as "in a mirror dimly" (1 Cor 13:12).

Study Questions

1. What is the final cause of God's Revelation?
2. Explain the two movements of condescension and elevation involved in divine Revelation.
3. Explain the Christocentrism of Revelation.
4. Explain the relevance to Revelation of the principle that "everything is received according to the mode of the receiver."
5. Why is God's Revelation essentially historical in nature?
6. Why is Revelation progressive? What are the fundamental stages of Revelation?
7. Is public Revelation still continuing? Contrast this with the Modernist understanding of Revelation.
8. Explain the social and ecclesial nature of Revelation. Why does God not speak with everyone individually?
9. How is the Holy Spirit the hidden agent of Revelation?

Suggestions for Further Reading

Dei Verbum §§1–4.

Pope St. John Paul II. Encyclical Letter on the Relationship between Faith and Reason Fides et ratio, §§1–15. September 14, 1998.

Congregation for the Doctrine of the Faith. Declaration on the Unicity and Salvific Universality of Jesus Christ and the Church Dominus Iesus. August 6, 2000.

Summa theologiae II-II, qq. 171–174.

Latourelle, Rene, S.J. Theology of Revelation. Staten Island: Alba House, 1966.

CHAPTER TWO

The Virtue of Divine Faith

When God speaks to man, how is His Word able to be received by man? Man, who hears the Word of God, needs a power of assenting to that Word, which power we call divine faith. Since sacred theology is a science built on the foundation of faith in God's Word, Fundamental Theology must examine the act and habit of divine faith itself, as that by which we receive the Word of God that comes to us in Revelation.[1]

Human Faith

In order to understand divine faith, something must first be said about the nature of faith in general. Faith in general, which includes human faith, is a *firm assent of the mind to things unseen*. It is an act of the intellect characterized by two elements: firm assent and an unseen object.

What does it mean for faith to be about things unseen? An object can be seen in two ways: by the senses and by the mind. Things are seen by the senses when they are empirically observed. However, something is also said to be seen when the mind grasps that it is necessarily true. In this second way the mind "sees" first principles of reason, such as the principles that nothing can be and not be in the same way at the same time, that every change has a cause, that the whole is

---

[1] On the subject of faith, see Feingold, *The Mystery of Israel and the Church*, vol. 2, chs. 1 and 2 (1–38).

greater than the part, and that good is to be sought and evil avoided, as well as the golden rule. These principles are self-evident and thus are "seen" by the mind. Furthermore, everything that is logically deduced or inferred from evident principles is also seen by the mind as a result of the reasoning process. The conclusions of mathematical, scientific, and philosophical demonstrations fall into this category. Something is unseen, therefore, if it is neither empirically observed, nor self-evident, nor deduced from evident principles through a sound process of reasoning.

When something is seen by the mind, whether through empirical observation, as a first principle, or as a conclusion from evident principles, the intellect naturally and spontaneously assents to the truth. In these cases, the intrinsic evidence of the object naturally causes the assent of the intellect. When the object is unseen, however, the intellect does not assent naturally and spontaneously. Nevertheless, experience shows that we can *freely choose* to assent to an unseen object, or not. This free assent of the intellect requires another cause in addition to the object. Since the will is man's executive faculty and all our free movements are moved by the will, it follows that assent to something unseen happens if and only if the will commands it. No explicit command or choice of the will is necessary for the intellect to give assent to something self-evident, as in the case of "two plus two equals four" or "the whole is greater than the part."[2] When the object is unseen, however, the assent needs to be chosen because the object by itself is insufficient to bring it forth. St. Thomas writes:

> Faith implies assent of the intellect to that which is believed. Now the intellect assents to a thing in two ways. First, through being moved to assent by its very object, which is known either by itself (as in the case of first principles, which are held by the habit of understanding), or through something else already known (as in the case of conclusions which are held by

---

[2] It is true that assent can be freely withheld even in cases of self-evident truth by a positive command of the will, as in a skeptic. However, it seems that people withhold assent in such cases only in philosophical discussions, and not in their practical life.

the habit of science). Secondly the intellect assents to something not through being sufficiently moved to this assent by its proper object, but through an act of choice, whereby it turns voluntarily to one side rather than to the other: and if this be accompanied by doubt or fear of the opposite side, there will be opinion, while, if there is certainty and no fear of the other side, there will be faith.[3]

Why would the will choose that the intellect assent to something unseen? The will never acts without a motive, for the free choice of the will results from some deliberation of reason. Therefore the intellect can be moved by the will to assent to an unseen object only if there is some motive for giving assent. If the motive for assent is uncertain, then the resulting act is called opinion. If the motive is so strong that the assent is firm, than the resulting act is called faith.

What would justify such firmness when one cannot see what one is affirming? Normally the firmness of the act of faith is motivated by the testimony of a *witness* who is judged to be sufficiently credible and who claims to see or have seen—whether through empirical evidence or through reasoning from evident principles—what, for the believer, remains unseen. The firm assent of faith is not arbitrary or without reason, but is motivated by the *authority* of a witness whom one has some reason to trust. Since there may be reasons both to trust and to doubt a given witness, the choice to believe on his word is a free choice motivated by a free prudential judgment assessing the credibility of the witness.

Faith therefore can be defined as assent not moved by the intrinsic evidence of truths, but rather by a firm impulse of the will based on a sufficiently credible witness. In the act of faith, the intellect assents to a given truth (or falsehood) because the will chooses to do so on account of *motives of credibility* judged to be weighty.

Every rational person chooses to make acts of human faith very frequently, and no one could live without doing so. All society and culture is based on trust in the witness of other people who have seen

---

3   *ST* II-II, q. 1, a. 4.

what we have not. For most of human history (until DNA testing), the identity of our own parents could be known only by human faith. All education begins with human faith in our parents and teachers. We learn primarily by human faith, trusting in the authority of teachers, books, the media, public opinion, and friends. The goal of education is to lead the student to see for himself through right reasoning whatever can be seen. However, every pupil must begin by putting his trust in the teacher until he comes to see for himself what he has been taught. Such faith is frequently a moral duty, for one *ought* to believe when the witness who vouches for a certain truth is known to be trustworthy. Withholding assent in such a case, without cogent reasons to the contrary, would be irrational and contrary to social communion and friendship.

Faith in general is an act midway between scientific demonstration and opinion. The essence of faith is that one does not directly see the intrinsic reason for the truth of a given proposition. In this sense, it is like opinion. However, faith differs from opinion in its certitude. In the act of faith, one sees clearly that the proposition merits firm assent on account of the authority of those who teach it, though not on account of its own intrinsic evidence. It is held as certain, and so mere opinion or deliberate doubt cannot coexist with faith, for they are mutually exclusive. A religious opinion is distinct from an act of religious faith, for the former is held to be uncertain or without sufficient foundation.

Supernatural Faith

What has been said about human faith also applies analogously to the Catholic faith. The Catholic faith concerns unseen objects such as God, heaven, grace, the Trinity, the Incarnation, etc. Why should we believe in these unseen objects? The only morally compelling reason to assent to something unseen is the trustworthiness of the witness. With regard to things that can only be seen by God Himself, such as His inner life and free plan of mercy for our salvation, there can be no other sufficient witness than God, if He chooses to reveal Himself. The act of divine faith is made possible when one grasps that God, who is the First Truth who can neither deceive nor be deceived, has indeed revealed Himself. This is the source of the firmness of divine faith and the grounds for the moral duty of believing.

But here a host of objections crop up. First of all, how does one know that God exists? And if He exists, how does one know that He has revealed Himself to men, and if so, where? Reason can begin to help us to answer these questions. Philosophical reason can determine that God exists. Historical reason can prudently judge that it is reasonable to believe that He has spoken to men through the Jewish prophets and the person of Jesus Christ and that this deposit of faith has been entrusted to the Catholic Church. This prior work of reason, often referred to as the "preambles of faith," constitutes the three principal parts of apologetics, which shows the reasonableness of belief in God, Christ, and the Church.

Once reason has shown the existence of the divine Witness, it is not hard to show that He is worthy of supreme trust. However, the difficulty is to determine *where God has spoken.* The Catholic faith tells us that He has spoken, above all, in the Incarnation of the Son of God two thousand years ago. But how do we know this? Here too, we must trust the witness of others who preceded Christ, who accompanied His Incarnation, and who came after Him. There are three classes of witnesses here, divided according to their chronological relationship—before, during, and after—to the Incarnation. These witnesses are: first the prophets who announced His coming, then the Apostles who witnessed His Incarnation (preaching, Passion, and Resurrection), and finally the Church, which preserves and passes on the deposit of faith.[4]

---

[4] See John Henry Newman, "Faith and Private Judgment," in *Discourses Addressed to Mixed Congregations* (Boston: Patrick Donahoe, 1853), 143–159, at 145–146: "Now in the first place what is faith? It is assenting to a doctrine as true, which we do not see, which we cannot prove, because God says it is true, who cannot lie. And further than this, since God says it is true, not with His own voice, but by the voice of His messengers, it is assenting to what man says, not simply viewed as a man, but to what he is commissioned to declare, as a messenger, prophet, or ambassador from God.... Faith has two peculiarities;—it is most certain, decided, positive, immoveable in its assent, and it gives this assent not because it sees with eye, or sees with the reason, but because it is told by one who comes from God."

Recognition of the trustworthiness of these witnesses is the work of reason. It would be irrational to believe if reason could not somehow recognize that God Himself has spoken in human history. Reason is indispensable in this task. However, it is not necessary to have extraordinary intelligence to do this. It is enough to sincerely seek religious truth and not be blinded by prejudice.

Note also that, because reason is necessary, the act of faith is not a blind leap, as Protestants say. We place our full trust in what God has said because reason first shows us that this is reasonable, and then grace gives us the certainty of that judgment.

Although indispensable, reason is not the only cause of the act of divine faith. Faith is a firm assent of the mind to unseen truth, commanded by the will, which is persuaded by reason. However, this persuasion of reason is insufficient in matters of divine faith on two grounds. First, it is insufficient on account of the transcendence and transcendent importance of the unseen objects of faith—the divine mysteries—which, in addition to being unseen, are often contrary to the order of things encountered in ordinary experience. Faith requires one to hold onto what is unseen in preference to the regularities of the empirical world that are subject to our dominion. Second, reason requires aid because the divine witness also remains unseen and needs to be recognized as speaking through very humble mediators. In coming to this recognition, reason therefore needs the help of the grace of God, which illumines the mind to see the motives for believing that the unseen witness is indeed ultimately God speaking through a mediator. The will also needs the aid of grace strengthening and purifying it to sincerely seek those motives and, once they are seen, to cleave to the Word of the unseen God. For this aid the only recourse is prayer. Denying the necessity of grace for the act of salvific faith is the error of semi-Pelagianism.[5]

---

[5] For the necessity of grace for the act of faith, see *ST* II-II, q. 6, a. 1: "The Pelagians held that this cause was nothing else than man's free-will: and consequently they said that the beginning of faith is from ourselves, inasmuch as it is in our power to be ready to assent to things which are of faith, but that the consummation of faith is from God, Who proposes to us the things we have to believe. But this is false, for, since man, by assenting to matters of faith, is raised above his nature, this must needs accrue to him from some supernatural principle moving him inwardly; and this

Joseph Ratzinger has written about the intrinsic difficulty of the act of faith, due to its unseen character, in his *Introduction to Christianity*:

> It [faith] signifies the deliberate view that what cannot be seen, what can in no wise move into the field of vision, is not unreal; that, on the contrary, what cannot be seen in fact represents true reality, the element that supports and makes possible all the rest of reality. And it signifies the view that this element that makes reality as a whole possible is also what grants man a truly human existence, what makes him possible as a human being existing in a human way. In other words, belief signifies the decision that at the very core of human existence there is a point that cannot be nourished and supported on the visible and tangible, that encounters and comes into contact with what cannot be seen and finds that it is a necessity for its own existence.
>
> Such an attitude is certainly to be attained only by what the language of the Bible calls "turning back," "con-version." Man's natural inclination draws him to the visible, to what he can take in his hand and hold as his own. He has to turn around inwardly in order to see how badly he is neglecting his own interests by letting himself be drawn along in this way by his natural inclination. He must turn around to recognize how blind he is if he trusts only what he sees with his eyes. Without this change of direction, without this resistance to the natural inclination, there can be no belief. Indeed belief is the conversion in which man discovers that he is following an illusion if he devotes himself only to the tangible. This is at the same time the fundamental reason why belief is not demonstrable: it is an about-turn; only he who turns about is receptive to it; and because our inclination does not cease to point us in another direction, it remains a turn that is new

is God. Therefore faith, as regards the assent which is the chief act of faith, is from God moving man inwardly by grace."

every day; only in a lifelong conversion can we become aware of what it means to say "I believe."

From this we can see that it is not just today, in the specific conditions of our modern situation, that belief or faith is problematical, indeed almost something that seems impossible, but that it has always meant a leap, a somewhat less obvious and less easily recognizable one perhaps, across an infinite gulf, a leap, namely, out of the tangible world that presses on man from every side. Belief has always had something of an adventurous break or leap about it, because in every age it represents the risky enterprise of accepting what plainly cannot be seen as the truly real and fundamental.[6]

The merit of the act of divine faith comes from the difficulty of entrusting ourselves to God's unseen truth and preferring His unseen Word to our sight of lesser things.

Hebrews 11:1

The fact that faith concerns things unseen is emphasized in a brief and enigmatic definition of faith given in Hebrews 11:1: "Faith is the substance of things to be hoped for, the evidence of things that are not seen." The first clause distinguishes divine faith from human faith. Divine faith concerns not just any unseen thing, but the ultimate object of human hope: the supernatural end of union with God promised by God Himself. "Substance" (*substantia*) is the literal translation of the Greek *hypostasis*[7] and indicates that faith gives us the foundation, already here in time, of the things we hope for.[8] The second clause

---

[6] Joseph Ratzinger, *Introduction to Christianity* (San Francisco: Ignatius Press, 1990), 50–52.

[7] The RSV translates *hypostasis* as "assurance." However, it seems that "substance" would be a more exact translation. See Pope Benedict XVI, Encyclical Letter on Christian Hope *Spe salvi*, §7.

[8] See St. Thomas's explanation of the definition of faith in Heb 11:1 in *ST* II-II, q. 4, a. 1: "The relation of the act of faith to its end which is the object of the will, is indicated by the words: 'Faith is the substance of things to be hoped for.' For we often use the term substance to refer to the first beginning of a thing, especially when the whole subsequent thing is virtually contained in the first beginning. For instance, we might say that the first self-evident principles are the substance

emphasizes the two aspects of faith mentioned above: firmness and an unseen object. Faith is the evidence, which here seems to mean *certainty*, of things not seen.

Divine faith is not only the foundation for things hoped for, but also the first step in their realization. Through faith, the believer enters into a certain preliminary union with God on the level of knowledge, sharing in God's knowledge of Himself and of His plan for mankind. It is a participation in the knowledge that will be possessed in full in the beatific vision. Faith also prepares for a union of wills, for one cannot love and desire what one does not know. Without faith, supernatural hope and charity are impossible. In this sense, faith is the foundation of the spiritual life.

Pope Benedict XVI has a very interesting commentary on Hebrews 11:1 in his *Spe salvi* §7. Commenting on the word here translated as "substance," he says:

> Faith is a *habitus*, that is, a stable disposition of the spirit, through which eternal life takes root in us and reason is led to consent to what it does not see. The concept of "substance" is therefore modified in the sense that through faith, in a tentative way, or as we might say "in embryo"—and thus according to the "substance"—there are already present in us the things that are hoped for: the whole, true life. And precisely because the thing itself is already present, this presence of what is to come also creates certainty: this "thing" which must come is not yet visible in the external world (it does not "appear"), but because of the fact that, as an initial and dynamic reality, we carry it within us, a certain perception of it has even now come into existence.

---

of science, because these principles are in us the first beginnings of science, the whole of which is itself contained in them virtually. In this way then faith is said to be the 'substance of things to be hoped for,' for the reason that in us the first beginning of things to be hoped for is brought about by the assent of faith, which contains virtually all things to be hoped for. Because we hope to be made happy through seeing the unveiled truth to which our faith cleaves. . . . Accordingly if anyone would reduce the foregoing words to the form of a definition, he may say that *faith is a habit of the mind whereby eternal life is begun in us, making the intellect assent to what is non-apparent*."

Because divine faith is the presence "in embryo" of what we hope for, this faith can only be the fruit of God's grace.

Divine faith can be understood in two ways: as an act and as a habitual readiness or capacity to make that act. In the latter sense, faith is a *habitus*, a "stable disposition of the spirit," and a supernatural virtue. Human faith, on the contrary, lacks stability and is not a virtue, for it is not always good to believe everyone who makes some claim. Divine faith, rather, is always virtuous, since it is always good to assent to God's Word. Furthermore, divine faith is a theological virtue because it attains to God Himself. Its object is God as the First Truth, as known through God's own Revelation of Himself. Because faith is a supernatural virtue, both the act and habit of faith must have their point of departure in God's grace.

Definition of Divine Faith

At this point we can give a definition of divine faith. There are four fundamental elements that enter into this definition: (1) what kind of thing it is; (2) its object; (3) its efficient cause; and (4) its motive. First, divine faith is a supernatural virtue. Second, the object of faith is God's Revelation of Himself. Third, the first efficient cause of the act of faith is the grace of God. Fourth, the motive of divine faith is the credibility of God and not the intrinsic evidence of the things believed. Divine faith is therefore a supernatural virtue by which we believe the truths God has revealed, moved by God's grace and motivated by God as Truth.[9] The First Vatican Council includes these four aspects in its classic definition of divine faith as a

> supernatural virtue whereby, inspired and assisted by the grace of God, we believe that what he has revealed is true, not because the intrinsic truth of things is recognized by the

---

[9] See *The Roman Catechism*, trans. Robert I. Bradley and Eugene Kevane (Boston: St. Paul, 1985), 20: "By this divine faith we give a firm and unhesitating assent to God revealing His mysterious truths." *The Roman Catechism* also defines faith as that "by which we give our unhesitating assent to whatever the authority of our Holy Mother the Church teaches us as revealed by Almighty God" (ibid., 15). Notice that the Church is brought in here as the vehicle of Revelation.

natural light of reason, but because of the authority of God himself who reveals them, who can neither err nor deceive.[10]

Through the virtue of divine faith, we are able to commit our mind and will to God's self-revelation precisely because we recognize the presence of His Word, the living Truth who "can neither err nor deceive." Any other motivation for believing would be neither supernatural nor worthy of God. For example, if one believed for social reasons, or because the content of Revelation seemed reasonable, this would not be supernatural faith, because that faith must be motivated principally by committing oneself to the witness of God, who is Truth.

Dei Verbum §5 further develops Vatican I's treatment of faith, adding a new aspect by speaking of faith as the "obedience by which man commits his whole self freely to God":[11]

"The obedience of faith" (Rom 16:26; see 1:5; 2 Cor 10:5–6) is to be given to God who reveals, an obedience by which man commits his whole self freely to God, offering "the full submission of intellect and will to God who reveals,"[12] and freely assenting to the truth revealed by Him. To make this act of faith, the grace of God and the interior help of the Holy Spirit must precede and assist, moving the heart and turning it to God, opening the eyes of the mind and giving "joy and ease to everyone in assenting to the truth and believing it."[13] To bring about an ever deeper understanding of revelation the same Holy Spirit constantly brings faith to completion by His gifts.

---

[10] First Vatican Council, Dogmatic Constitution on the Catholic Faith *Dei Filius* (1870), ch. 3 (DS, 3008.)

[11] Nevertheless, the teachings of Vatican I and Vatican II on faith are clearly equivalent, for we give our whole self freely to God in the act of faith (*DV* §5) precisely through the habitual submission of our intellect and will to God who reveals Himself (*Dei Filius*, ch. 3). This habitual submission of mind and will is realized through the supernatural virtue of faith, infused by God into our souls.

[12] See Vatican I, *Dei Filius*, ch. 3 (DS, 3008).

[13] Ibid. (DS, 3010).

Since Revelation consists in God *revealing Himself* to us, revealing to us His love, faith likewise consists in returning that love by *entrusting our whole self* to God. This is done through making intellectual assent to God's Word, committing our lives to that unseen Truth that we have embraced, and believing Him without reservation. Our assent, in turn, is moved by a free choice of the will, and the will is moved efficaciously by God's grace that "gives joy and ease" to our assent to the Truth. All mature virtues, in fact, give joy and ease to their exercise, and faith is no exception. It can be seen here that the greatest obstacles to the act of faith are the fear of entrusting ourselves to God and to the Church in which we receive His Word and the pride by which we wish to be autonomous, refusing to submit to any superior, even one who is Love and Truth.

Faith Is Light

Paradoxically, the act of faith involves both light and darkness. The definition of faith given in Hebrews 11:1 alludes to both aspects when it speaks of faith as "the *evidence* of things *unseen.*" Insofar as faith is of things unseen, it involves a darkness, for we cannot directly see what we believe to be true. The life of faith always involves walking in a darkness that is disconcerting to the natural man and his natural desire to see where he is going.

However, supernatural faith is essentially light, for it provides an irrefutable evidence—God's testimony—in favor of the most important truths that a human being can know in this life. Faith lights up the path of man by disclosing his transcendent Source and the goal of his life: the Triune God. Psalm 119:105 emphasizes this aspect of faith: "Thy word is a lamp to my feet and a light to my path." As God's Word is light, so is the virtue of faith that receives God's Word as truth. *The Catechism of the Catholic Church* §26 gives a definition of faith that makes use of the aspect of light: "Faith is man's response to God, who reveals himself and gives himself to man, at the same time bringing man a superabundant light as he searches for the ultimate meaning of his life." Faith is light because it provides "the definitive, superabundant answer to the questions that man asks himself about the meaning and purpose of his life."[14]

The modern secular world, however, tends increasingly to view Christian faith as principally sentiment rather than light. Faith has undergone a drastic category shift. From being understood as a virtue that perfects the intellect to know supernatural truths, it is seen rather as a pure option of the will to help one get through life. As such, it can be tolerated perhaps within the confines of the Church, but must be banished from any influence in the public square.

In response to this caricature of faith, Pope Francis stresses that faith is light:

> There is an urgent need, then, to see once again that faith is a light, for once the flame of faith dies out, all other lights begin to dim. The light of faith is unique, since it is capable of illuminating every aspect of human existence. A light this powerful cannot come from ourselves but from a more primordial source: in a word, it must come from God. Faith is born of an encounter with the living God who calls us and reveals his love, a love which precedes us and upon which we can lean for security and for building our lives. Transformed by this love, we gain fresh vision, new eyes to see; we realize that it contains a great promise of fulfilment, and that a vision of the future opens up before us. Faith, received from God as a supernatural gift, becomes a light for our way, guiding our journey through time.[15]

Faith Is Not Subject to Error

The light of divine faith, unlike human faith, is not subject to error, for faith is properly divine or supernatural only insofar as it is belief in what has actually been revealed by God. For this reason, divine faith

---

[14] CCC §68.

[15] Encyclical Letter on Faith *Lumen fidei* (2013), §4.

is strong enough to be described as "the *substance* of things hoped for." Divine faith has a certainty that comes from its divine source that enables it to be a sufficient foundation for man's journey to his supernatural end. *Lumen fidei* §10 speaks of this aspect of faith:

> Faith understands that something so apparently ephemeral and fleeting as a word, when spoken by the God who is fidelity, becomes absolutely certain and unshakable, guaranteeing the continuity of our journey through history. Faith accepts this word as a solid rock upon which we can build a straight highway on which we can travel. In the Bible, faith is expressed by the Hebrew word *'emûnāh*, derived from the verb *'amān*, whose root means "to uphold." The term *'emûnāh* can signify both God's fidelity and man's faith. The man of faith gains strength by putting himself in the hands of the God who is faithful.

Thus the proper response to God's word is appropriately expressed by the Hebrew term *Amen*.

However, it sometimes happens that a believer is mistaken in thinking that something has been revealed by God that has not in fact been revealed. When someone believes something false in matters of religion, the error should not be attributed to the virtue of divine faith, but rather to human faith in some heresy or false interpretation or insight that is mistaken for divine Revelation. Something has been believed out of ignorance or negligence that ought not to have been believed.

Belief in the teachings of religions other than Christianity and Judaism lacks an essential element of divine faith. Although members of those other religions may have an exemplary interior disposition of self-abandonment to God and His will (which may be salvific[16]),

---

[16] See *LG* §16: "Those also can attain to salvation who through no fault of their own do not know the Gospel of Christ or His Church, yet sincerely seek God and, moved by grace, strive by their deeds to do His will as it is known to them through the dictates of conscience. Nor does Divine Providence deny the helps necessary for salvation to those who, without blame on their part, have not yet arrived at an explicit knowledge of God and with His grace strive to live a good life.

they cannot firmly adhere to His revealed Word, to which they lack access. The doctrines of other religions should be understood as human beliefs arising from *man's search for God*, rather than a supernatural response to *God's seeking out man* and revealing Himself to him. The natural religions of the world contain many elements of religious truth pertaining to the natural order, but their foundation is mankind's religious insight rather than God's public Revelation attested to by sufficient motives of credibility. The Congregation of the Doctrine of the Faith's Declaration in 2000, *Dominus Iesus*, explains in §7 this distinction between divine *faith* in revealed truth and *belief* in the religious wisdom contained in other religions:

> For this reason, the distinction between *theological faith* and *belief* in the other religions must be *firmly held*. If faith is the acceptance in grace of revealed truth, which "makes it possible to penetrate the mystery in a way that allows us to understand it coherently," then belief, in the other religions, is that sum of experience and thought that constitutes the human treasury of wisdom and religious aspiration, which man in his search for truth has conceived and acted upon in his relationship to God and the Absolute. This distinction is not always borne in mind in current theological reflection. Thus, theological faith (the acceptance of the truth revealed by the One and Triune God) is often identified with belief in other religions, which is religious experience still in search of the absolute truth and still lacking assent to God who reveals himself.

In summary, divine faith is the freely chosen, firm, stable, joyful, and self-abandoning adherence of the mind, moved by divine grace, to the truths revealed by God about Himself and His plan of salvation, not on account of their own intrinsic evidence, but based on the veracity of God, who cannot err or deceive.

Whatever good or truth is found amongst them is looked upon by the Church as a preparation for the Gospel."

The Certainty of Faith and Grades of Certainty

Because faith is based on the recognition of God's Word, it has a certainty that is proper to itself, distinct from other kinds of certainty. Philosophers distinguish moral certainty, scientific (or physical) certainty, metaphysical certainty, and the certainty of faith.

"Moral certainty" is the kind of certainty we can have about moral realities, such as the moral character of witnesses, and about the morality of our actions in daily life. Human faith is based on the trustworthiness of a witness, whether of another person or of one's conscience. The firmness of human faith depends on our certainty about the moral character of the people whose witness we believe. Obviously, moral certainty can be subject to error. But it would be impossible to live without acting on the basis of moral certainties and without trusting the testimony of a great many people.

Scientific certainty is the certainty we have that nature will follow its natural laws. We have scientific certainty that things will fall according to the law of gravitation. It is not completely certain for two reasons. First, science can always be improved, and secondly, God can work miracles that do not obey the ordinary laws of nature in some regard, for God can work outside of those laws.

The third kind of certainty is metaphysical certainty. This is the certainty we have of first principles, both theoretical and practical/moral. Theoretical principles include the principle of non-contradiction, causality (every effect has a cause), finality (every agent acts for some end). Practical/moral principles include: that good is to be done and evil is to be avoided, the golden rule, the double commandment of love, and the primacy of the common good over the private good. These first principles are absolutely certain. Even God cannot suspend them or contradict them. Some people sometimes put some of them in doubt in an intellectual way, but in practice we cannot stop being aware of their truth.

Finally, there is the certainty of faith. This is the certainty that God's revealed Word is true because God is the Truth and cannot err or deceive. Because it rests on God who is the Truth, the certainty of faith has a unique power to serve as the foundation for human life.

This is the meaning of Jesus's parable about the house built on the rock in Matthew 7:24–27. Faith in Christ's words enables one to build one's life on the firmest of foundations.

In the process of coming to the certainty of faith we have to make use of metaphysical certainties and moral certainties with regard to the human mediators of Revelation. However, the certainty of faith is not simply the product of natural certainties or probabilities, but rests also on the power of God's grace. Precisely because faith involves a properly divine certainty, it is impossible without His supernatural aid.[17]

Private Judgment and the "Dogmatic Principle"

Martin Luther laid the seeds of a radically changed notion of faith by disconnecting it from the witness of the Church and her Magisterium.[18] The eventual result of this severance is the Protestant doctrine of *private judgment*. Nevertheless, the original Reformers did not intend to extend the freedom of private judgment to all believers. Thus Luther attacked (and rightly so, from the Catholic perspective) the more radical wing of his fellow Protestants as being heretical in their denial of the Real Presence and the necessity of infant Baptism.

"The right of examining what we ought to believe is the foundation of Protestantism," said Madame de Staël. However, "the first Protestants did not so understand it: they thought that they could fix the Pillars of Hercules of the human mind at the boundary of their own knowledge; but they were wrong in fancying that men would submit to their decisions as if they were infallible; they who rejected

---

[17] See *ST* II-II, q. 6, a. 1.

[18] This denial appeared publicly for the first time in 1519 in a dispute with Johann Eck, a Catholic theologian. Luther was forced to affirm that ecumenical councils could err and actually did err in the condemnation of John Huss (condemned by the Council of Constance in 1415). Eck rightly responded that if ecumenical councils were subject to error, then there could no longer be any certainty on any point of faith. The denial of the infallibility of ecumenical councils and popes undermines the faith of the Church. For, how does the believer know what truths God has revealed if there is no infallible authority to interpret Revelation?

all authority of this sort in the Catholic religion."[19] The principle of private judgment used by Luther, Zwingli, and Calvin was naturally taken up, contrary to their intention, as a principle applicable to all, and it inevitably led to the division of the churches and the multiplication of sects.[20] This fragmentation of beliefs and churches led to religious indifferentism and liberalism in the nineteenth century, which can be considered the inevitable offspring of the original Protestantism, even though it seems in many ways to be its opposite.

In consequence of the multiplication of Christian denominations, faith has increasingly become identified with mere religious sentiment or opinion. At first, such a view was characteristic of liberal Protestantism of the nineteenth century.[21] It has since come to be shared by many Catholics as well, aptly referred to as "cafeteria Catholics." This view of faith, which has steadily grown in influence throughout the last two centuries, was characterized by Blessed John Henry Newman as follows:

---

[19] Madame de Staël, *Germany*, part 4, ch. 2, ed. O. W. Wight (New York: Derby and Jackson, 1859), 2:298.

[20] See the nineteenth-century Spanish writer, Jaime Balmes, *Protestantism and Catholicity Compared in Their Effects on the Civilization of Europe* (Baltimore: J. Murphy, 1851), 26–27: "If there be any thing constant in Protestantism, it is undoubtedly the substitution of private judgment for public and lawful authority. This is always found in union with it, and is, properly speaking, its fundamental principle: it is the only point of contact among the various Protestant sects,—the basis of their mutual resemblance. It is very remarkable that this exists, for the most part, unintentionally, and sometimes against their express wishes. . . . If you examine the words and the acts of the first Reformers, you will find that they made use of this principle as a means of resisting the authority which controlled them, but that they never dreamed of establishing it permanently; that if they labored to upset lawful authority, it was for the purpose of usurping the command themselves; that is to say, that they followed in this respect, the example of revolutionaries of all kinds, of all ages, and of all countries. . . . Within the vast limits marked out by this name [Protestantism], there is room for every error and for every sect. You may deny with the Lutherans the liberty of man, or renew with the Arminians the errors of Pelagius. You may admit with some that real presence, which you are free to reject with the Calvinists and Zwinglians; you may join with the Socinians in denying the divinity of Jesus Christ; you may attach yourself to Episcopalians, to Puritans, or, if you please, to the extravagances of the Quakers; it is of no consequence, for you always remain a Protestant, for you protest against the authority of the Church; your field is so extensive, that you can hardly escape from it, however great may be your wanderings; it contains all the vast extent that we behold on coming forth from the gates of the Holy City."

[21] See Friedrich Schleiermacher, *On Religion: Speeches to Its Cultured Despisers*, trans. Richard Crouter (New York: Cambridge University Press, 1988).

That truth and falsehood in religion are but matter of opinion; that one doctrine is as good as another; that the Governor of the world does not intend that we should gain the truth; that there is no truth; that we are not more acceptable to God by believing this than by believing that; that no one is answerable for his opinions; that they are a matter of necessity or accident; that it is enough if we sincerely hold what we profess; that our merit lies in seeking, not in possessing; that it is a duty to follow what seems to us true, without a fear lest it should not be true; that it may be a gain to succeed, and can be no harm to fail; that we may take up and lay down opinions at pleasure; that belief belongs to the mere intellect, not to the heart also; that we may safely trust to ourselves in matters of Faith, and need no other guide,—this is the principle of philosophies and heresies, which is very weakness.[22]

Newman contrasts this view of faith as sentiment/opinion with what he refers to as the "dogmatic principle." By this, he means the conviction that God has revealed definite dogmas of faith to mankind, which it is our grace and glory to hold with a unique firmness as the rock on which we build our lives. In his great work *An Essay on the Development of Christian Doctrine*, which he wrote in the process of his conversion to Catholicism, he describes the "dogmatic principle" and its understanding of faith as follows:

That there is a truth then; that there is one truth; that religious error is in itself of an immoral nature; that its maintainers, unless involuntarily such, are guilty in maintaining it; that it is to be dreaded; that the search for truth is not the gratification of curiosity; that its attainment has nothing of the excitement of a discovery; that the mind is below truth, not above it, and is bound not to descant upon it, but to venerate it; that truth and falsehood are set before us for the trial

---

[22] *An Essay on the Development of Christian Doctrine*, 6th ed. (Notre Dame: University of Notre Dame Press, 1989), 357–358.

of our hearts; that our choice is an awful giving forth of lots on which salvation or rejection is inscribed; that "before all things it is necessary to hold the Catholic faith"; that "he that would be saved must thus think," and not otherwise; that, "if thou criest after knowledge, and liftest up thy voice for understanding, if thou seeketh her as silver, and searchest for her as for hid treasure, then shalt thou understand the fear of the Lord, and find the knowledge of God,"—this is the dogmatical principle, which has strength.[23]

The "dogmatic principle" has strength because it makes possible an unwavering and heroic assent to God's Word as it comes to us through the Church. It enables men to build their lives on the rock of truth without vacillation or doubt. It enabled the martyrs to shed their blood for Christ and His truth; the Middle Ages to build the cathedrals; the Scholastics, like St. Thomas Aquinas, to write their *summas*; Sts. Benedict, Francis, Dominic, and Ignatius to found their respective orders; and the great mystics like St. Teresa and St. John of the Cross to make their spiritual ascent of Mount Carmel.

The notion of private judgment, on the contrary, is weakness because it attacks the very possibility of making the total gift of one's mind to God. Divine faith is the supernatural submission of the intellect to God, the divine Teacher. This submission is actually a great liberation, freeing the mind from ignorance. But this submission will never be total if one retains the prerogative of private judgment.[24]

---

[23] Ibid., 357.

[24] Newman, while still an Anglican, wrote a powerful critique of the notion of private judgment of Scripture in his essay, "Private Judgment," in *Essays, Critical and Historical* (London: Basil Montagu Pickering, 1871), 2:336–374; see especially 351–352: "While, then, the conversions recorded in Scripture are brought about in a very marked way through a *teacher*, and *not* by means of private judgment, so again, if an appeal *is* made to private judgment, this is done in order to settle who the teacher is, and what are his notes or tokens, rather than to substantiate this or that religious opinion or practice. And if such instances bear upon our conduct at this day, as it is natural to think they do, then of course the practical question before us is, *who* is the teacher now, from whose mouth we are to seek the law, and *what are his notes?*" See also his "Faith and Private Judgment," in *Discourses Addressed to Mixed Congregations*.

Divine Faith Is Lost through Formal Heresy

Heresy is a particular kind of disbelief by which someone who believes in Christ obstinately rejects the authority of the Church to define doctrine and corrupts or denies some truths of faith. They "choose" and obstinately hold their tenets of faith according to their own reason and will, which they put above the authority of the Church. Interestingly, the word "heresy" comes from the Greek for election or choice.[25] Every heresy involves a kind of picking and choosing of the faith according to one's own personal (or group) criteria. This is the same spirit that leads to "cafeteria Catholicism."

It is important to distinguish "formal heresy" from "material heresy." Heresy, properly speaking, always implies a *culpable resistance* to the faith that involves *obstinacy* in rejecting truths revealed by God that one knows to be taught infallibly as such by the Church. This presupposes that one has been baptized and exposed to sufficient motives of credibility to recognize the authority of the Church in conscience, and thus cannot be considered invincibly ignorant. This obstinate rejection of dogmas of faith by such a person is formal heresy, and it is gravely sinful. St. Augustine characterizes formal heresy as follows: "In Christ's Church those are heretics who hold mischievous and erroneous opinions and when rebuked that they may think soundly and rightly, offer a stubborn resistance, and, refusing to mend their pernicious and deadly doctrines, persist in defending them."[26] Canon 751 of *The Code of Canon Law* defines heresy as "the obstinate denial or obstinate doubt after the reception of baptism of some truth which is to be believed by divine and Catholic faith."

It is possible, however, to be in error with regard to the tenets of the faith simply through ignorance, but without obstinacy or willfulness. In this case one is said to be a "material heretic," but not a "formal heretic." Of these St. Thomas, citing St. Augustine, says:

> As Augustine says . . . "By no means should we accuse of heresy those who, however false and perverse their opinion may

---

[25] See *ST* II-II, q. 11, a. 1.

[26] *De civitate Dei* 18.51 (PL, 41:613).

be, defend it without obstinate fervor, and seek the truth with careful anxiety, ready to mend their opinion, when they have found the truth," because, to wit, they do not make a choice in contradiction to the doctrine of the Church. Accordingly, certain doctors seem to have differed . . . even in matters of faith, which were not as yet defined by the Church; although if anyone were obstinately to deny them after they had been defined by the authority of the universal Church, he would be deemed a heretic. This authority resides chiefly in the Sovereign Pontiff.[27]

Many great Catholic theologians, including the Doctors of the Church, have held mistaken views on matters of faith that were later defined by the Church. St. Thomas, for example, erred with regard to the Immaculate Conception, which was not yet infallibly taught in his day. Such mistakes should be regarded as material rather than formal heresy.

The members of Christian denominations that profess heretical views, such as the various families of Protestantism (as well as Nestorians, Monophysites, etc.), should not simply be regarded as formal heretics, for very often they follow a heresy in good faith. This occurs when they have never been properly exposed to the motives of credibility of the Catholic Church and, following their conscience, they do not obstinately resist the impulses of interior grace leading them towards Catholic unity. Such persons are material rather than formal heretics.

Nevertheless, it is reasonable to think that the founders of heretical sects were heretics in the formal sense because, while still within the bosom of the Church, they obstinately opposed the voice of her authentic Magisterium. Nevertheless, God alone knows the interior state of the heart.

The sin of formal heresy has a very special gravity because it goes against the common good of a Christian society in a very weighty matter. The patrimony of faith in a generally Christian society is certainly

---

[27] *ST* II-II, q. 11, a. 2, ad 3.

one of the most significant components (indeed, the most significant) of the true common good of that society. If this patrimony is lost by heresy or apostasy, the common good is injured more grievously than by any other catastrophe.

What happens to the virtue of faith when a person who once had faith obstinately denies an article of faith proposed by the Church or anything infallibly taught by her? St. Thomas teaches that a formal heretic entirely loses the virtue of faith by obstinately denying one sole article of faith, whatever it may be.[28] This is because, when a heretic denies one article of faith, the other truths of faith that he continues to affirm are no longer held by supernatural faith, but simply by human faith or religious opinion. In other words, by rejecting some truth of faith that has been infallibly taught and sufficiently promulgated by the Church, the heretic rejects not only that particular truth, but also the very reason why he ought to believe all the articles of faith. For, faith obliges him to submit his fallible reason to the divine wisdom of Christ's Church. By rejecting this rule of faith in one article, the heretic has elevated his own judgment over the Church and no longer holds any article simply on the basis of the authority of God and the Church, but rather on the basis of his own will. He has substituted religious opinion for divine faith, and while it may be correct or incorrect in its content, it lacks divine merit, for it is not moved by a humble and loving submission of the intellect to God who speaks through the Church.

In the act of supernatural faith, man transcends the limits of his own nature and makes a divine act through the grace of God. The formal heretic, on the contrary, refuses to conform himself to the grace of God and the authority of the Church, preferring to maintain his private judgment. For example, if a man believes every Catholic dogma with the exception of one, such as the Real Presence, or certain moral teachings such as the illicitness of contraception or homo-

---

[28] St. Thomas explains this succinctly in *ST* II-II, q. 5, a. 3: "The formal object of divine faith is the divine truth manifested in Sacred Scripture and in the doctrine of the Church. Therefore, any person who does not adhere in all things to the doctrine of the Church, as to a certain and infallible rule ... does not have the virtue of faith, but rather holds [the remaining] truths of faith in a way different from that of faith."

sexual acts, can it be said that such a person has divine faith? He still has divine faith if his error in matters of faith is really through inculpable ignorance, but if he knows that the Church teaches these truths and he still denies them because they seem unreasonable or absurd to him, then he prefers his own opinion to the oracle of God. In this case, he believes what he does on the basis of human, rather than divine, faith.

Dispositions for Faith

Scripture frequently praises those who are ready to believe God, such as the centurion in Matthew 8:10, Nathanael, who believed because Jesus said that he saw him under the fig tree (John 1:50), and the Canaanite woman who answered that "even the dogs eat the crumbs that fall from their masters' table" (Matt 15:27–28). Similarly, those are severely blamed who obstinately refuse to believe despite having received signs that serve as motives of credibility, as in the archetypical case of Pharaoh. For this reason Jesus castigates Chorazin and Bethsaida in Matthew 11:21: "Woe to you, Chorazin! woe to you, Bethsaida! for if the mighty works done in you had been done in Tyre and Sidon, they would have repented long ago in sackcloth and ashes."

It is clear from this that there is a praiseworthy disposition to believe possessed by some and not by others. Or even the same person could have this disposition at some points in his life and not at others. Newman, in a brilliant sermon on this topic from 1856,[29] describes the fact of this disposition for faith as follows:

> that with good dispositions faith *is* easy, and that without good dispositions, faith is *not* easy; and that those who were praised for their faith, were such as had already the good dispositions, and that those who were blamed for their unbelief, were such as were wanting in this respect, and would have be

---

[29] "Dispositions for Faith," in *Sermons Preached on Various Occasions* (London: Burns and Lambert, 1858), 79–99.

lieved, or believed sooner, had they possessed the necessary dispositions for believing, or a greater share of them.[30]

This disposition for faith is something virtuous,[31] and its lack is something for which we are rightly blamed. It is for this reason that the act of faith, when sufficient motives of credibility are presented, can serve as a test of the heart and of the goodness of the will, and be a matter of salvation.

At the same time Scripture attributes this good disposition to the aid of grace.[32] Thus we can say that there is a cooperation of God's grace that first excites this disposition in us, and then man's habitual cooperation with this grace to foster and develop it over time. In those who do not have divine faith, we can assume that God's grace has touched them in different ways to excite this disposition for faith but that it has not yet been sufficiently cooperated with, or that sufficient motives of credibility have not yet been presented.

Newman sees the principal disposition for faith as arising from attention to conscience, which gives rise to three convictions. First, conscience speaks with an interior authority that judges one's own will, motives, and actions. Its voice is experienced by us as something that, although it is in us, nevertheless in some way transcends us because we experience its voice as a judgment on our actions. This leads to the conviction that it comes from God and is His witness in our heart.

Secondly, however, when conscience convicts us with regard to many of our actions, we perceive the need of divine forgiveness, as when St. Paul, in Romans 7:21–24, laments:

So I find it to be a law that when I want to do right, evil lies close at hand. For I delight in the law of God, in my inmost self, but I see in my members another law at war with the law

---

[30] Ibid., 83.

[31] I would say that it is a combination of virtues in which the virtue of penance plays a leading role.

[32] See Eph 2:8–9: "For by grace you have been saved through faith; and this is not your own doing, it is the gift of God—not because of works, lest any man should boast."

of my mind and making me captive to the law of sin which dwells in my members. Wretched man that I am! Who will deliver me from this body of death?

Attentiveness to conscience leads the upright man to ardently desire some means of forgiveness for his sin. Thus it leads to hope for a revelation of God's mercy with respect to those who repent. This is the disposition ready to respond when a voice cries: "The time is fulfilled, and the kingdom of God is at hand; repent, and believe in the gospel" (Mark 1:15).

Third, we also experience the uncertainty of some of the judgments of conscience and the difficulty of discerning conscience from self-interest. This, for Newman, leads to the disposition of hoping for a Revelation from God to clarify man's path in following conscience and holiness. The man with the right disposition for faith is "on the lookout" for a Revelation from God. He hopes and longs for it, and this gives him the "eyes to see" it when God's Revelation is presented to him. Newman writes:

So that the gift of conscience raises a desire for what it does not itself fully supply. It inspires in them the idea of authoritative guidance, of a divine law; and the desire of possessing it in its fullness, not in mere fragmentary portions or indirect suggestions. It creates in them a thirst, an impatience, for the knowledge of that Unseen Lord, and Governor, and Judge, who as yet speaks to them only secretly, who whispers in their hearts, who tells them something, but not nearly so much as they wish and as they need. Thus you see, my Brethren, a religious man, who has not the blessing of the infallible teaching of revelation, is led to *look out* for it, for the very reason that he *is* religious. He has something, but not all; and if he did not desire more, it would be a proof that he had not used, that he had not profited by, what he had.[33]

---

[33] Newman, "Dispositions for Faith," 87–88.

Jesus spoke about the disposition for faith most directly in the parable of the sower,[34] which is presented as a parable of fundamental importance (see Mark 4:13). The four kinds of soil represent four different dispositions of the heart for receiving the seed of the sower, which represents the word of Christ. Jesus is warning the disciples that not all—but only one group among four—have the proper dispositions for receiving the Word in faith and persevering in it.

Study Questions

1. What is the difference between supernatural faith, human faith, and religious opinion?
2. Give a definition of divine faith, including four elements: kind or genus, object, efficient cause, and motive.
3. What is the motive for the act of divine faith? Explain.
4. What is a good disposition for receiving the virtue of faith? In what sense is the act of religious faith, or its refusal, a test of the heart?
5. What does Cardinal Newman mean by the dogmatic principle in religion? How does he characterize the opposing attitude of religious liberalism?
6. What is the difference between formal and material heresy?
7. Can a heretic have divine faith in the articles of faith in which he believes?

Suggestions for Further Reading

Summa theologiae II-II, qq. 1–16.

Pope Benedict XVI. Encyclical Letter on Christian Hope *Spe salvi*. November 30, 2007.

Dubay, Thomas, S.M. *Faith and Certitude*. San Francisco: Ignatius Press, 1985.

Dulles, Avery, S.J. *The Assurance of Things Hoped For: A Theology of Christian Faith*. New York: Oxford University Press, 1994.

---

[34] Matt 13:3–23; Mark 4:3–20.

Pope Francis. Encyclical Letter on Faith *Lumen fidei*. June 29, 2013.

Newman, John Henry Cardinal. "Dispositions for Faith." In *Sermons Preached on Various Occasions*, 79–99. London: Burns and Lambert, 1858.

——. *An Essay in Aid of a Grammar of Assent*. New York: Catholic Publication Society, 1870.

——. "Faith and Private Judgment." In *Discourses Addressed to Mixed Congregations*, 143–159. Boston: Patrick Donahoe, 1853.

——. "Private Judgment." In *Essays, Critical and Historical*. Vol. 2, 336–374. London: Basil Montagu Pickering, 1871.

CHAPTER THREE

Motives of Credibility for Faith

Motives of Credibility

As we have seen in the previous chapter, the great difficulty in making the act of divine faith lies in recognizing where God has truly spoken in human history, for He speaks through mediators chosen and sent by Him. God cannot speak to man directly without created and sensible mediation (apart from the beatific vision), but must condescend to our nature and speak to us through sensible and empirical means. Furthermore, God does not speak directly to everyone in an individualistic fashion; rather, He speaks to mankind socially through certain freely chosen intermediaries who are entrusted with a divine mission of being the instruments of God's Revelation. These intermediaries are the Old Testament patriarchs and prophets, the Apostles and Evangelists, and above all the humanity of Jesus Christ. The Magisterium of the Church also has the mediating role of safeguarding and authoritatively transmitting that Revelation. Since God speaks to all through intermediaries, it must be possible for mankind to be able to recognize these intermediaries and become certain of their divine commission. Otherwise it would be extremely imprudent to believe, for one would run the risk of being deceived by any charlatan (or even an honestly mistaken person) about God's Revelation concerning the most important matters of human life. If God is to effectively reveal Himself, He must make it clear who are His true spokesmen and give them some kind of trustworthy sign or badge of their divine credentials. These signs can be called *motives of credibility*.[1]

Motives of credibility are supernatural signs that manifest the miraculous action of God. Their purpose is to show that an alleged revelation from God is truly His Word, not that of a false prophet. These motives allow us to make the transition from human faith in the word of a prophet to divine faith in God who speaks through the prophet. Proportionate motives of credibility show that the act of faith is reasonable and morally compelling. With sufficient motives of credibility, it would be unreasonable not to believe; without such motives, it would be unreasonable to believe. Belief in an alleged revelation that is not supported by sufficient reasons to think that God is its source would put one in danger of attributing mere human words and claims to God.

To show the divine origin of the Revelation received by Israel and the Church, the Catholic Tradition speaks of three principal objective miraculous signs: the miracles worked by the prophets, Christ, and the Apostles; the prophecies about the Messiah and the Church; and the very existence of the Catholic Church, which can be seen to be something more than a merely human society by its universal spread, continuity, and holiness.[2] The life of the Catholic Church is a motive of credibility through her four marks: one, holy, catholic, and apostolic. The *Catechism of the Catholic Church* §156, quoting Vatican I, speaks of these three objective motives of credibility:

> Thus the miracles of Christ and the saints, prophecies, the Church's growth and holiness, and her fruitfulness and stability "are the most certain signs of divine Revelation, adapted to the intelligence of all"; they are "motives of credibility" (*motiva credibilitatis*), which show that the assent of faith is "by no means a blind impulse of the mind."

---

[1]   This section is a modification of material first published in Lawrence Feingold, *The Mystery of Israel and the Church*, vol. 2, *Things New and Old* (St. Louis: Miriam Press, 2010), 4–11.

[2]   See First Vatican Council, Dogmatic Constitution on the Catholic Faith *Dei Filius* (1870), ch. 3 (DS, 3009 and 3013).

I think that a fourth motive of credibility should also be included, which is the holiness of the revealed doctrine, especially of the person of Jesus Christ, and the correspondence of this Revelation with the "reasons of the heart." This last motive is less objective in nature, and thus more difficult to evaluate, but no less important than the others in practice, precisely because of its subjective aspect.

The Witness of Miracles

Let us begin with miracles, for the other motives of credibility are particular kinds of miracles and can be reduced to this one. Prophecy is a miracle of knowledge that points to the divine omniscience. The four marks of the Church over the last two millennia likewise are miracles in the order of human affairs pointing to the divine providence. The holiness of the Church, especially of her head, the person of Christ, is the greatest miracle of all, manifesting to the world the divine holiness and wisdom.

When God revealed Himself to Moses, He attracted his attention by an evident miracle: a burning bush that was not consumed. When God then asked him to be His messenger to Pharaoh and the elders of Israel, Moses in turn asked for a miraculous sign by which his divine commission would be recognized:

> Then Moses answered, "But behold, they will not believe me or listen to my voice, for they will say, 'The Lord did not appear to you.'" The Lord said to him, "What is that in your hand?" He said, "A rod." And he said, "Cast it on the ground." So he cast it on the ground, and it became a serpent; and Moses fled from it. But the Lord said to Moses, "Put out your hand, and take it by the tail"—so he put out his hand and caught it, and it became a rod in his hand—"that they may believe that the Lord, the God of their fathers, the God of Abraham, the God of Isaac, and the God of Jacob, has appeared to you."[3]

---

[3] Exod 4:1–5.

This witness of miracles was continually manifested by Moses and then by Joshua in the succession of the ten plagues, the miraculous crossing of the Red Sea, the column of fire and cloud that led the people, the manna by which they were fed in the wilderness, the water brought out from the rock by the rod of Moses, the divine fire on Mt. Sinai, the tablets of the Law written by the finger of God, the miraculous crossing of the Jordan River, the falling of the walls of Jericho, etc. Every step of the way of the Chosen People was marked by this witness of a power that could only come from God. Moses repeatedly reminded the Chosen People of these motives of credibility—the prodigious miracles by which God took them out of Egypt with a "mighty hand" and an "outstretched arm."[4]

When, centuries later, the Chosen People had fallen largely into the worship of Baal, Elijah also made use of a miracle to defend the true God. He challenged the prophets of Baal to demonstrate the truth of their religion by having fire descend from heaven to consume a sacrificial offering. Of course, they were unable to do this. Elijah then prepared an altar for sacrifice and doused it with water, and fire came down from heaven at his invocation to show that the worship of the God of Israel is the true religion:

> And at the time of the offering of the oblation, Elijah the prophet came near and said, "O Lord, God of Abraham, Isaac, and Israel, let it be known this day that thou art God in Israel, and that I am thy servant, and that I have done all these things at thy word. Answer me, O Lord, answer me, that this people may know that thou, O Lord, art God, and that thou hast turned their hearts back." Then the fire of the Lord fell, and consumed the burnt offering, and the wood, and the stones, and the dust, and licked up the water that was in the trench. And when all the people saw it, they fell on their faces; and they said, "The Lord, he is God; the Lord, he is God."[5]

---

[4] See Deut 4:34; 7:8. In Deut 29:1–5, before telling the Israelites of the punishments that would come upon them for infidelity, Moses calls to mind all the prodigies they witnessed.

[5] 1 Kings 18:36–39.

The same witness of miracles was constantly given by Christ as proof that He was who He claimed to be. When messengers came from John the Baptist in prison, asking Jesus if He was the one that Israel was awaiting, Jesus replied solely by referring to the witness of His miracles (Matt 11:4–5): "Go and tell John what you hear and see: the blind receive their sight and the lame walk, lepers are cleansed and the deaf hear, and the dead are raised up, and the poor have good news preached to them." Or again, He said to the people in Jerusalem on the feast of Chanukah (John 10:25, 37–38):

> The works that I do in my Father's name, they bear witness to me.... If I am not doing the works of my Father, then do not believe me; but if I do them, even though you do not believe me, believe the works, that you may know and understand that the Father is in me and I am in the Father.

All of His great teachings were preceded by miracles to show the truth of what He said. The multiplication of the loaves and fishes preceded His teaching on the Bread of Life in the synagogue in Capernaum. The raising of Lazarus shortly preceded His Paschal mystery, which was then confirmed by the miracle of the Resurrection, witnessed by the Apostles and more than five hundred of the disciples, as St. Paul tells us.[6] The birth of the Church was confirmed by the miracle of Pentecost and the cures worked by the Apostles.

With regard to the witness of miracles, there is a perfect harmony between the Old and the New Testaments, and indeed between these and the entire life of the Church, in which miracles continue to manifest the glory of God.

The Witness of Prophecy

Prophecy as a miraculous witness is taken here in the restricted sense in which it refers to a foretelling of future free events in the name of

---

6   See 1 Cor 15:6.

God, which then occur as foretold.[7] Such prophecy is a special kind of miracle involving God's unique knowledge of future free events. Since only God can know such events, the fact that they are foretold by human beings indicates that such knowledge comes from God. This provides a motive of credibility for thinking that the other words spoken by the prophet are also from God. Moses speaks of this motive of credibility in Deuteronomy 18:21–22:

> And if you say in your heart, "How may we know the word which the Lord has not spoken?"—when a prophet speaks in the name of the Lord, if the word does not come to pass or come true, that is a word which the Lord has not spoken; the prophet has spoken it presumptuously, you need not be afraid of him.

Often, one prophecy whose fulfillment is close at hand serves to provide the motive of credibility for other prophecies whose fulfillment is more distant. The prophecies of Jeremiah and Isaiah about the Babylonian exile and the return after seventy years[8] served as the motive of credibility to recognize the inspired nature of their entire prophetic witness, including their prophecies about the Messiah.

Messianic Prophecies

The messianic prophecies are a unique kind of motive of credibility for various reasons:[9] they are very numerous; they come in a great variety; and their object, who is the Redeemer of the world, has a universal importance. Stretching from Abraham (ca. 2000 BC) to the book of Wisdom (first century BC?), some fifty prophetic texts[10] allude

---

[7] Prophecy in general can also mean proclamation of the revealed Word of God, a power which is given to all the faithful.

[8] For the seventy years of exile, see Jer 25:11–12; 29:10. For the name of the Persion king, Cyrus, who would enable the Israelites to return and rebuild the Temple, see Isaiah 44:26–28.

[9] See Feingold, *The Mystery of Israel and the Church*, vol. 1, *Figure and Fulfillment* (St. Louis: Miriam Press, 2010), 15–72.

[10] Messianic prophecies recognized in the Catholic Tradition include the following: Gen 3:15;

to a great diversity of aspects of the Messiah's life and work.

Because of these characteristics, these motives "validate," as it were, Christ's claim to be that Redeemer. St. Justin Martyr lays great emphasis on the value of prophecy in establishing the reasonability of faith in Christ:

> We could produce many other prophecies, but we refrain from doing so, since we think that those above-mentioned are sufficient to convince those who have ears to hear and understand, and we assume that these persons are also capable of perceiving that we do not make bare statements, such as the fables of the supposed sons of Jupiter, without being able to prove them. *Why should we believe a crucified Man that He was the First-begotten of an Unbegotten God, and that He will pass judgment on the entire human race, unless we had found testimonies concerning Him foretold before He came* and was made Man, and unless we had seen events happen just as foretold, namely, the devastation of the Jewish land, and men of every race believing through the teaching of His Apostles, and turning away from old customs which they had practiced in error.[11]

Blaise Pascal, the French philosopher, stresses the cumulative value of the prophecies:

> If a single man had written a book foretelling the time and manner of Jesus' coming and Jesus had come in conformity with these prophecies, this would carry infinite weight. But

---

12:3; 18:18; 22:18; 26:4; 28:14; 49:10; Num 24:17–19; Deut 18:15–19; 2 Sam 7:12–16; 1 Chron 22:10; Job 19:25; Ps 2:7–8; 16:15; 22:6–8; 22:14–18; 31; 40:6–8; 72; 89; 110; 118; 132; Wis 2:12–20; Isa 7:14; 9:1–7; 11:1–12; 12:1–6; 25:6–8; 42:1–7; 49:1–12; 50:5–7; 52:13–53:12; 55:1–5; 60; 61; 62; Jer 23:5–6; 31:31–34; Ezra 36:25–27; Dan 2:31–45; 7:13–14; 9:24–27; Hos 2:19–23; Mic 5:2; Zech 2:10–11; 9:9–10; 11:12–13; 12:10; Mal 1:11; 3;1–4; and Bar 3:37.

[11] St. Justin, *First Apology*, ch. 53, in *The First Apology, The Second Apology, Dialogue with Trypho, Exhortation to the Greeks, Discourse to the Greeks, The Monarchy or The Rule of God*, trans. T. B. Falls, The Fathers of the Church, vol. 6 (Washington, DC: The Catholic University of America Press, 1948), 90 (my italics).

there is much more here. There is a succession of men over a period of four thousand years, coming consistently and invariably one after the other, to foretell the same coming; there is an entire people proclaiming it, existing for four thousand years to testify in a body to the certainty they feel about it, from which they cannot be deflected by whatever threats and persecutions they may suffer. This is of a quite different order of importance.[12]

Not only do the messianic prophecies stem from a succession of many different prophets, they also speak of disparate and seemingly irreconcilable aspects of the Messiah and His mission, for example to suffer and be slain but yet to rule forever over an eternal kingdom that will include all nations. The fact that such apparently contrasting prophecies come together perfectly in Jesus Christ gives to the prophecies a supernatural weight.[13] As Pascal observes, "It takes boldness to foretell the same thing in so many ways."[14]

The Witness of the People of God

Many people object that they themselves did not personally witness the miracles recorded in the Bible. However, we do see those miracles today *indirectly* through their effect in forming the People of God in the Old and New Testament: the synagogue and the Church. The miracles of the Exodus and Mt. Sinai formed the very existence of the Jewish people and, in a sense, have continued to conserve their

---

[12] *Pensées*, sec. 1, ser. 24, no. 332, trans. A. J. Krailsheimer (New York: Penguin Classics, 1966), 129.

[13] See Charles Journet, "The Mysterious Destinies of Israel," in *The Bridge: A Yearbook of Judaeo-Christian Studies*, ed. John Oesterreicher (New York: Pantheon Books, 1956), 2:c51: "Saying that the contents of the prophecies surpassed the prophets' knowledge of them is the same as saying that the realization of the prophecies was itself a revelation, indeed the greatest of all. Jesus alone could explain the past and give Israel's history its full significance; He alone could put at one what had seemed disparate. He did so when he brought together in his own person the scattered traits of the promised Messiah, and when he announced that the messianic kingdom of glory and power and majesty would begin as a kingdom crucified."

[14] *Pensées*, sec. 1, ser. 24, no. 336 (Krailsheimer, 130).

existence until today in the most trying of circumstances, in which it seems that God is silent. Jews see the continued existence of the Jewish people and faith through so many centuries and in the midst of so many calamities, including that of a two-thousand-year exile from their homeland, as a great sign of credibility for the truth of the Mosaic Revelation on Mt. Sinai that formed that faith. A contemporary Jewish theologian, Michael Wyschogrod, states: "Above all, it seems to be an indestructible people. While all the peoples of the ancient world have long disappeared, the Jewish people continues to live and has lived for two thousand years without a homeland, dispersed over most of the globe."[15] If those events of the Exodus did not truly occur, how can we explain the continuity of the faith of the Jewish people and their continued vitality through so many centuries until today? They have maintained the same faith for well over three millennia!

In the same way, the miracles of Christ, His Resurrection, the miracle of Pentecost, and the miracles worked by the Apostles formed the Church and gave her a force of expansion in the most adverse circumstances of tremendous persecution for the first three centuries of her life. Pinchas Lapide, a Jewish theologian, makes this point in a forceful and surprising way. He sees both the historical events of Exodus and the Resurrection of Christ as necessary to explain the ensuing historical reality of Israel and the Church. Although he does not believe in the divinity of Christ, he thinks that the Resurrection of Jesus truly occurred as the only way to explain the rise of the early Church:

> Thus, according to my opinion, the resurrection belongs to the category of the truly real and effective occurrences, for without a fact of history there is no act of true faith. A fact which indeed is withheld from objective science, photography . . . but not from the believing scrutiny of history. . . . Without the Sinai experience—no Judaism; without the Easter experience—no Christianity. Both were Jewish faith

---

[15] *The Body of Faith: Judaism as Corporeal Election* (New York: The Seabury Press, 1983), 10.

experiences whose radiating power, in a different way, was meant for the world of nations. For inscrutable reasons the resurrection faith of Golgotha was necessary in order to carry the message of Sinai into the world.[16]

Furthermore, the continued existence of Israel, and the two-thousand-year expansion of the Church built on the rock of Peter are the visible fulfillment of most audacious prophecies.[17] These prophecies are fulfilled in a reality that is before our eyes today. No one can say that the realization of these prophecies perhaps did not really occur, as perhaps one could in the case of prophecies that were fulfilled long ago but whose evidence no longer remains, as in the division of the vestments of Christ (Ps 22:18). We ourselves are witnesses of their realization. For this reason, the unity, miraculous expansion, holiness, and continuity of the Catholic Church in time and space are great signs of its being truly founded by the Messiah, and thus by God.

The Church can be considered the most impressive fulfillment of the prophecies. Who could have imagined, in the centuries before Christ, that the pagan nations would come to believe in one God, the God of Israel, and become incorporated into one *spiritual kingdom*— the new Israel—and share the faith of Israel in the Jewish Messiah? Who could imagine that this spiritual kingdom, to be augmented continually by the incorporation of the Gentiles, would last until the end of time and be universal in scope? This is a prophecy of enormous magnitude.

---

[16] Pinchas Lapide, *The Resurrection of Jesus: a Jewish Perspective* (Minneapolis: Augsburg, 1983), 92. He makes the same argument in his work with Jürgen Moltmann, *Jewish Monotheism and Christian Trinitarian Doctrine: A Dialogue*, trans. Leonard Swidler (Philadelphia: Fortress Press, 1981), 60: "If they [the Apostles], through such a concrete historical event as the crucifixion, were so totally in despair and crushed, as all the four evangelists report to us, then no less concrete a historical event was needed in order to bring them out of the deep valley of their despair and within a short time to transform them into a community of salvation rejoicing to the high heavens."

[17] With regard to Israel, see Gen 12:2; 22:17; with regard to the Church, see Matt 16:18 and Dan 7:14 and 2:44.

The Four Marks of the Church as Motives of Credibility

In the New Covenant, the Church is a motive of credibility insofar as she appears with four marks that show a supernatural origin. We profess these four marks in the Creed when we say that the Church is one, holy, catholic, and apostolic. The universal spread and continuity of the Catholic Church—which professes the same holy faith and exhibits the same sacramental form of government based on apostolic succession through twenty centuries, with great numbers of persons living that holy life—is a kind of miracle visible to all generations, including our own.[18]

Division of human societies is natural and does not suggest a supernatural cause. That a human institution retain its core unity—in faith, sacraments, and government—over twenty centuries of tremendous growth and volatile development, is something startling and miraculous. That it be so one in government as to retain the unbroken succession from its original founders, the eleven Apostles, is still more surprising. That a society expand vigorously in its beginnings is natural, but that it do so especially in the midst of the most tremendous persecutions is miraculous. That a society be multinational is somewhat unusual, but that it continue to expand through the centuries so that it is progressively spread over the whole world, present in almost every human culture today, points to the work of God. This is the note of catholicity.

Although harder to document, the note of holiness is perhaps the most important motive of credibility in practice. Despite the sins of the members of the Church, who recede from her life through their sin, the holiness of the Church remains visible in her martyrs, in her worship, and in the lives of her saints, both those canonized and many more unrecognized in the midst of ordinary life. The First Vatican Council stresses this aspect of the Church. After speaking of the necessity of faith for salvation, it goes on to speak of the Church as a perpetual motive of credibility:

---

[18] On the four marks of the Church as motives of credibility, see Feingold, *The Mystery of Israel and the Church*, vol. 3, *The Messianic Kingdom of Israel* (St. Louis: Miriam Press, 2010), 53–107.

To enable us to fulfill the obligation to embrace the true faith and persistently to persevere in it, God has instituted the Church through his only begotten Son and has endowed her with manifest marks of his institution so that she may be recognized by all men as the guardian and teacher of the revealed word.

In fact, it is to the Catholic Church alone that belong all those signs that are so numerous and so wonderfully arranged by God to make evident the credibility of the Christian faith. In fact, the Church herself by reason of her astonishing propagation, her outstanding holiness and her inexhaustible fertility in every kind of goodness, by her Catholic unity and her unconquerable stability, is a kind of great and perpetual motive of credibility and an incontrovertible evidence of her own divine mission.[19]

This motive of credibility, however, requires serious knowledge of history[20] and the ability to distinguish the holiness of the Church from the sins and scandals of Catholics who, in their sin, act contrary to the Church's own teaching and thus fail to live in and manifest her supernatural life. Jesus's parable of the wheat and the weeds illustrates the difficulty of this motive of credibility. In the parable, when one looked at the wheat field, one saw weeds planted by an enemy in addition to the wheat, and the master insisted that the weeds not be uprooted lest the wheat be harmed. Similarly, in the Church, one sees fruits of holiness that point to her divine source, as well as sin that points away from that source and serves to make her appear like the rest of the world.

Does the existence of sin in the Church make this motive of credibility useless? No, but it means that the Church as a motive of credibility should be sought not in what makes her like the rest of human

---

[19] *Dei Filius*, ch. 3, no. 12 (DS, 3012–3013).

[20] See the famous line of Blessed John Henry Newman: "To be deep in history is to cease to be a Protestant," in *Essay on the Development of Christian Doctrine*, 6th ed. (Notre Dame: University of Notre Dame Press, 1989), 8.

institutions, but rather in that which makes her stand out as marked by a reflected transcendence that comes from and dimly reveals her source. This is first of all the lives of the saints and martyrs, as well as the cultural patrimony that the Church has given rise to: Christian art, architecture, and music; the medieval universities; the rise of modern science; and the recognition of the dignity of man.[21] Modern man is still attracted by beauty, and the beauty generated by the faith—in culture and in the lives of the saints—is capable of revealing the Church as a motive of credibility. Joseph Ratzinger has expressed this eloquently in an address of 2002 at a meeting of the ecclesial movement, Communion and Liberation:

> The encounter with the beautiful can become the wound of the arrow that strikes the heart and in this way opens our eyes, so that later, from this experience, we take the criteria for judgment and can correctly evaluate the arguments. For me an unforgettable experience was the Bach concert that Leonard Bernstein conducted in Munich after the sudden death of Karl Richter. I was sitting next to the Lutheran Bishop Hanselmann. When the last note of one of the great Thomas-Kantor-Cantatas triumphantly faded away, we looked at each other spontaneously and right then we said: "Anyone who has heard this knows that the faith is true."
>
> The music had such an extraordinary force of reality that we realized, no longer by deduction but by the impact on our hearts, that it could not have originated from nothingness but could only have come to be through the power of the Truth that became real in the composer's inspiration. Isn't the same thing evident when we allow ourselves to be moved by the icon of the Trinity of Rublev? . . .
>
> To admire the icons and the great masterpieces of Christian art in general leads us on an inner way, a way of overcom-

---

[21] For works on the Church as motive of credibility, see Thomas E. Woods, *How the Catholic Church Built Western Civilization* (Washington, DC: Regnery, 2005). A different kind of apologetics of the Church is given by Luigi Giussani, *Why the Church?* trans. Vivianne Hewitt (Montreal: Mc-Gill-Queen's University Press, 2001).

ing ourselves; thus in this purification of vision that is a purification of the heart, it reveals the beautiful to us or at least a ray of it. In this way we are brought into contact with the power of the truth. I have often affirmed my conviction that the true apology of Christian faith, the most convincing demonstration of its truth against every denial, are the saints and the beauty that the faith has generated. Today, for faith to grow, we must lead ourselves and the persons we meet to encounter the saints and to enter into contact with the Beautiful.[22]

The Sanctity of God's Revelation as a Motive of Credibility

We have seen that the Church is a motive of credibility above all insofar as she is endowed with a holiness that points to her source. This means that the Person of Jesus, embodying the divine Wisdom, is the principal motive of credibility. Thus, we can say that there is a fourth motive of credibility that consists in the supernatural sanctity, nobility, and wisdom of God's Revelation, especially in the very Person of Jesus. If God makes Himself known to mankind, this Revelation should be a supernatural wisdom above the wisdom of the world, but not in conflict with the voice of conscience, which likewise comes from God. On the contrary, Revelation ought to be in perfect harmony with the secret dictates of conscience and the aspirations of the human heart.

This motive of credibility is frequent in the Old Testament. In Deuteronomy 4:5–8, Moses says to the people:

Behold, I have taught you statutes and ordinances, as the Lord my God commanded me, that you should do them in the land which you are entering to take possession of it. Keep them and do them; for that will be your *wisdom and your un-*

---

[22] Message to the Communion and Liberation Meeting at Rimini (August 24–30, 2002), "The Feeling of Things, the Contemplation of Beauty," at http://www.vatican.va/roman_curia/congregations/cfaith/documents/rc_con_cfaith_doc_20020824_ratzinger-cl-rimini_en.html.

derstanding in the sight of the peoples, who, when they hear all these statutes, will say, "Surely this great nation is a wise and understanding people." For what great nation is there that has a god so near to it as the Lord our God is to us, whenever we call upon him? And what great nation is there, that has statutes and ordinances so righteous as all this law which I set before you this day?[23]

The truth of God's Revelation in the Old Testament is witnessed to by the human conscience, which finds the moral law announced in the Ten Commandments and summarized in the double commandment of love[24] to be also that written upon the human heart.[25]

The supernatural wisdom of Revelation is also beautifully revealed in the theophany of the burning bush. We have seen that Moses asked for miracles to serve as motives of credibility for his mission. However, before asking for miracles, he first asked for the *name of God* to tell the elders of Israel, so that they might believe that God is speaking through him:

> Then Moses said to God, "If I come to the people of Israel and say to them, 'The God of your fathers has sent me to you,' and they ask me, 'What is his name?' what shall I say to them?" God said to Moses, "I AM WHO AM." And he said, "Say this to the people of Israel, 'I AM has sent me to you.'" God also said to Moses, "Say this to the people of Israel, 'The Lord, the God of your fathers, the God of Abraham, the God of Isaac, and the God of Jacob, has sent me to you: this is my name for ever, and thus I am to be remembered throughout all generations.'"[26]

---

[23] See also Ps 147:19–20.

[24] Deut 6:5 and Lev 19:18.

[25] See Rom 2:15 and CCC §§2070–71.

[26] Exod 3:13–15. For the divine name in Exod 3:14, I have used the Confraternity of Christian Doctrine translation (New York: Benziger Bros., 1958).

The Hebrew word that is translated in our modern bibles as "Lord" is the sacred Tetragrammaton, which is comprised of the four consonants YHWH (יהוה). This was translated first into Greek (in the Septuagint translation) in the third century BC as "He who is."[27] Because of the sacredness of this name, observant Jews of all times do not pronounce it so that the name is not profaned or made to sound like just another name of God used by the peoples of the world. Instead, the title "Adonai," which means "Lord,"[28] is said in place of the Tetragrammaton.

It is surely extraordinary that God revealed His name to Moses and the Jewish people around 1400 BC in such a way that it coincides with the culmination of metaphysical insight about the nature of God: that God's very essence is *TO BE*—BEING in all its fullness. God is *He who is*—*Being* by essence—whereas all other things *receive* being or *have* being in limited ways through participation from God.[29] God revealed Himself as the Lord of Being. He can give being to all other things because He is all perfection of being, and He has dominion over all finite and created being (being by participation) as its Lord and infinite Source.

In the same way, the clear Revelation of the oneness of God, as well as our resulting duty to love Him with all our heart, mind, and soul, is a marvelous sign of the supernatural wisdom of the Revelation to Israel. All devout Jews recite the text of Deuteronomy 6:4–5 morning and evening: "Hear, O Israel: The Lord our God is one Lord; and

---

[27] The verb "is" here could also be translated into the future, or simply indicate eternal being, for the verb form is imperfect (continuous). Pope Benedict XVI's Regensburg Lecture (September 12, 2006) has an interesting commentary on the translation of the divine name: "Today we know that the Greek translation of the Old Testament produced at Alexandria—the Septuagint—is more than a simple (and in that sense really less than satisfactory) translation of the Hebrew text: it is an independent textual witness and a distinct and important step in the history of revelation, one which brought about this encounter [between Biblical faith and Greek thought] in a way that was decisive for the birth and spread of Christianity." For the text of the Regensburg Lecture, see James V. Schall, *The Regensburg Lecture* (South Bend: St. Augustine's Press, 2007).

[28] *Adonai* was translated into Greek as *Kyrios* and into Latin as *Dominus*.

[29] St. Thomas Aquinas comments on this in *SCG* I, ch. 22 (no. 10): "Moses was taught this sublime truth by the Lord. . . . God showed that his proper name is HE WHO IS. All names are given to signify the nature or essence of something. Therefore it follows that the divine Being Itself is His very essence or nature."

you shall love the Lord your God with all your heart, and with all your soul, and with all your might."

Human philosophy can understand that God is one, and it seems that Plato and Aristotle came to this insight. Nevertheless, that this should have been so clearly proclaimed almost a thousand years earlier in the midst of a world utterly dominated by polytheism and in a people without any philosophical culture is surely miraculous and a sign of a divine Revelation. This argument does not work with regard to Islam, for this teaching in the Quran is derivative from the Bible and came at least eighteen centuries after it was revealed to Moses.

Like the ethos of the Old Testament, the moral and religious teaching of Jesus (as in the Sermon on the Mount) comes to us with the same divine claim to absolute authority and the same nobility that touches the depths of the human conscience.

A corollary to this motive of credibility is that no supposedly revealed doctrine that is manifestly contrary to the dictates of conscience and natural reason can possibly be God's true Revelation. A religion that proclaims the use of violence in the establishment of religion or the licitness of polygamy is, by that very fact, shown not to be from God.[30]

Pope Benedict XVI was very brave to speak about this in his well-known Regensburg lecture, when he cited the Byzantine emperor Manuel II Paleologus (1391), who said: "Show me just what Mohammed brought that was new, and there you will find things only evil and inhuman, such as his command to spread by the sword the faith he preached." Benedict goes on to comment:

> The emperor, after having expressed himself so forcefully, goes on to explain in detail the reasons why spreading the faith through violence is something unreasonable. Violence is incompatible with the nature of God and the nature of the soul. "God," he says, "is not pleased by blood—and not acting

---

[30] It is one thing for polygamy to be tolerated for a time in a certain society, as was the case in the early history of Israel, and quite another thing for it to be formally approved as licit and good, as is the case in Mormonism and Islam.

reasonably (σὺν λόγῳ) is contrary to God's nature. Faith is born of the soul, not the body. Whoever would lead someone to faith needs the ability to speak well and to reason properly, without violence and threats. . . . To convince a reasonable soul, one does not need a strong arm, or weapons of any kind, or any other means of threatening a person with death."[31]

Holiness of the Revelation in the Person of Jesus Christ and His Cross

The holiness of Revelation is evident above all in the Person of Jesus Christ, the One who reveals the face of the Father in His life, deeds, and words, as communicated to us above all through the four Gospels. The prologue of the Letter to the Hebrews (1:1–3) bears witness to the revelatory power of the very Person of the Son of God. God's holiness was communicated in the "many and various ways God spoke of old to our fathers by the prophets; but in these last days he has spoken to us by a Son, whom he appointed the heir of all things, through whom also he created the world. He reflects the glory of God and bears the very stamp of his nature."

This unique holiness is present throughout, but shines in a culminating way in Christ's Passion. For this reason, the Gospel of John frequently speaks of the Cross as Christ's glorification, for it alone reveals the full extent of His love. In John 8:28, Jesus says: "When you have lifted up the Son of man, then you will know that I am he." Still more emphatically, in John 12:31–32, He says: "Now is the judgment of this world, now shall the ruler of this world be cast out; and I, when I am lifted up from the earth, will draw all men to myself." Christ's crucifixion draws all men to Himself by revealing the holiness of a love "to the end."[32]

The holiness revealed in the Cross of Christ is a sign that requires a heart that is well-disposed to recognize the overpassing love of God

---

[31] Benedict XVI, Regensburg Lecture.

[32] See John 13:1: "When Jesus knew that his hour had come to depart out of this world to the Father, having loved his own who were in the world, he loved them to the end."

who wills to die for the salvation of His creatures. St. Paul speaks of the ambivalent nature of the Cross as a sign of the truth of the Christian faith in 1 Corinthians 1:18–25:

> For the word of the cross is folly to those who are perishing, but to us who are being saved it is the power of God. . . . For Jews demand signs and Greeks seek wisdom, but we preach Christ crucified, a stumbling block to Jews and folly to Gentiles, but to those who are called, both Jews and Greeks, Christ the power of God and the wisdom of God. For the foolishness of God is wiser than men, and the weakness of God is stronger than men.

Although more difficult to verify objectively than the other motives of credibility, this reason for belief based on the sanctity of God's Revelation and of the Person and Cross of Jesus Christ in whom Revelation culminates is most important in practice.

A good summary of the harmony of these four motives of credibility—miracles, prophecy, the witness of the Church, and the supernatural wisdom and holiness of the doctrine revealed and of the Person of the Revealer—was given in the middle of the nineteenth century by Blessed Pius IX:

> But, how many, how wonderful, how splendid are the proofs at hand by which human reason ought to be entirely and most clearly convinced that the religion of Christ is divine, and that "every principle of our dogmas has received its root from above." . . . For, in truth, this faith is the teacher of life, the guide to salvation, expelling all faults, and in fruitfulness giving birth to and nurturing the virtues, confirmed by the birth, life, death, Resurrection, wisdom, miracles, and prophecies of its divine author and consummator, Christ Jesus; everywhere resplendent with the light of a supernatural teaching . . . preeminent in the highest degree through the predictions of so many prophets, the splendor of so many miracles,

the constancy of so many martyrs, the glory of so many saints, revealing the salutary laws of Christ and acquiring greater strength every day from these most cruel persecutions, [this faith] has pervaded the whole earth, land and sea, from the rising to the setting of the sun, under the one standard of the Cross, and also, having overcome the deceits of idols and torn away the mist of errors and triumphed over enemies of every kind, it has illuminated with the light of divine knowledge all peoples, races, nations. . . .[33]

The Reasons of the Heart for Faith: Love Disposes to Faith

Pascal observed that the most effective arguments for convincing people of the existence of God and the truths of religion are reasons of the *heart*, rather than rigorous logical arguments.[34] These arguments of the heart give us a sharpened insight into our most fundamental convictions, which are based on the experience of love and contrition. Although we often say that love is blind, as in the case of infatuation, experience shows that true love greatly enhances our ability to see the truth, goodness, and beauty (and thus profound dignity and value) of the beloved. This insight of love can lead a person to draw a conclusion through a kind of abbreviated, intuitive reasoning. For example, people's understanding of sexual morality is greatly sharpened when it concerns their own children, as opposed to a merely abstract consideration.

In this way, love for other persons and contrition for having wounded them can better dispose us to grasp the arguments for God's existence and to recognize His Revelation, in which He makes known His infinite love for those whom we love. And to the extent that desire

---

[33] Pope Pius IX, Encyclical Letter on Faith and Religion *Qui pluribus* (1846), §8 (DS, 2779).

[34] "The heart has its reasons of which reason knows nothing: we know this in countless ways. . . . It is the heart which perceives God and not the reason. That is what faith is: God perceived by the heart, not by the reason" (Krailsheimer, 154). By "reason," here, Pascal seems to understand reason used (in a Cartesian way) without the aid of the heart.

and love for God is already in our heart, that desire or love enables us to better recognize the actions of God by a certain connaturality born of desire for Him or friendship with Him.

Blessed John Henry Newman speaks eloquently about the importance of reasons of the heart:

> The best argument, better than all the books in the world, better than all that astronomy, and geology, and physiology, and all other sciences, can supply,—an argument intelligible to those who cannot read as well as to those who can,—an argument which is "within us,"—an argument intellectually conclusive, and practically persuasive, whether for proving the Being of a God, or for laying the ground for Christianity,—is that which *arises out of a careful attention to the teachings of our heart, and a comparison between the claims of conscience and the announcements of the Gospel.*[35]

This mutual interaction between love and faith can be described as a *vital circle* (or vital spiral). Reasons of the heart presuppose a genuine love for human persons that disposes us to recognize the existence of the divine love at the origin of the human person. And this incipient love for God, whose existence is thus grasped in an intuitive way by reason as the Source of love, disposes one to recognize the actions of God in salvation history, thus engendering faith in His Revelation. And faith in the Revelation of His deeds of love provides new motives for loving God back.

These arguments of the heart can be formulated in various ways. For example, we can grasp the notion that, if God does not exist or does not concern Himself with our salvation, then the hunger of man's heart that seeks to love Absolute Goodness will have no object worthy of its love, no object in which man's aspirations can come finally to rest. No one has expressed this better than St. Augustine, at the beginning of his *Confessions*: "You stir man to take pleasure in praising you, because you have made us for yourself, and our heart is

---

[35] Newman, "Dispositions for Faith," 98–99 (my italics).

restless until it rests in you."[36] Who has not tasted, in some way, this bitter discontent as he strayed from God?

Furthermore, it is well known that the experience of genuine human love, whether of parents, spouse, children, or intimate friends, is an excellent preparation for better understanding the existence of God and His love for man because it shows us that our loved ones need and *deserve* more love than we are able to give them. We sense dimly that our finality is to love and be loved in a divine way, more than any finite person could offer. If God does not exist, this finality of the human person would be forever in vain.

We also grasp that men deserve this greater or divine love because we sense dimly the truth of the biblical phrase that man is made in the image and likeness of God. Disinterested love discovers this likeness in our neighbor to which self-love is blind. We naturally recognize that man has a dignity, a worthiness of being loved that transcends the material universe and can only come from God. Therefore God exists and has an absolute dignity in which the human person shares or participates in a limited way because of God's paternal love for man.

Finally, if God does not exist, then there is no loving providence at the very basis of our existence as the ultimate reason for our coming into the world. We would be nothing more than products of blind chance and freak accidents of an intrinsically meaningless world, as Sartre, Nietzsche, Jacques Monod, and others would have it. But love tells us that this cannot be so, that the human person cannot fail to be the product of divine love, in which he is destined to share if he does not fail to correspond to the divine vocation.

Let me confess here that this was the argument that convinced me of the truth of God's existence at age twenty-nine. On a certain day, after several years of marriage, I realized that I was not able to love my wife with the unconditional love that she deserved. The thought that God must exist if human life is not to be completely absurd and in vain then came to me with vivid force. And I realized that the ability to love is God's gift, which must be implored through prayer.

---

[36] St. Augustine, *Confessions* 1.1.1 (Chadwick, 3).

Who can explain the impressions that are made on our minds under the impulse of God's grace, which sharpens its power to see?

There is no doubt that the arguments of the heart are effective to persuade, but are they also true proofs with a foundation in reason and its grasp of reality? Pascal himself did not speak of them in that way, but perhaps he underestimated their philosophical basis.[37] I would argue that Pascal makes an excessive division, for rhetorical purposes, between the reasons of the *heart* and of the *reason*, excessively limiting the latter to mere *reasoning* (the third operation of the mind). Nevertheless, what Pascal refers to as the "heart" includes what St. Thomas refers to as the habit of first principles, by which we see first principles as evidently true. This is the work of intellect taken in the broad Thomistic and classical sense, which includes all three operations of the mind, and not just the third. The heart also includes the affective movements of the will, which dispose the mind to be attentive to see the presence of value and goodness. These affective movements, in turn, are open to being strengthened by the impulses of grace and the gifts of the Holy Spirit.[38] In sum, the "reasons of the heart" are not irrational! On the contrary, they are supremely rational, even though they are not formulated as syllogisms.

The reasons of the heart, as outlined here, are based on fundamental principles of reason, even if they are not enunciated in the form of a strict syllogism and thus skip many steps. They presuppose the principle of reason that all things have a natural finality that they tend to realize. This finality corresponds with a natural desire in the thing, and natural desire cannot be in vain. If a given nature tends naturally and consistently towards a certain end, then that end must not be naturally or intrinsically impossible. For, if it were impossible, then the creature would be absurd in that it has a natural inclination to something that is naturally impossible. This would be inexplica-

---

[37] See Peter Kreeft, *Christianity for Modern Pagans: Pascal's Pensées Edited, Outlined, and Explained* (San Francisco: Ignatius Press, 1993), 229–230.

[38] St. Thomas understands the gifts of the Holy Spirit of understanding and wisdom as heightened abilities to understand divine things through the influence of supernatural charity, by which one has a certain connaturality with the things of God.

ble, for it would be simultaneously ordered and not ordered to some end. Now, the rational creature, who is capable of conceiving absolute good, tends towards the possession of an absolute good. Therefore, such an end must be possible to attain and also, therefore, must exist. And an absolute good can be nothing other than a loving God who is possessed by being known and loved.

The arguments of the heart are efficacious not only for leading to belief in God's existence, but especially for recognizing the fullness of Revelation in Jesus Christ. For, the Gospel is essentially the proclamation that we have been loved by God *to the death*. In the words of John 3:16, "God so loved the world that he gave his only Son, that whoever believes in him should not perish but have eternal life." Or as St. Paul says in Romans 8:32–39:

> He who did not spare his own Son but gave him up for us all, will he not also give us all things with him? Who shall bring any charge against God's elect? It is God who justifies; who is to condemn? Is it Christ Jesus, who died, yes, who was raised from the dead, who is at the right hand of God, who indeed intercedes for us? Who shall separate us from the love of Christ? Shall tribulation, or distress, or persecution, or famine, or nakedness, or peril, or sword? . . . For I am sure that neither death, nor life, nor angels, nor principalities, nor things present, nor things to come, nor powers, nor height, nor depth, nor anything else in all creation, will be able to separate us from the love of God in Christ Jesus our Lord.

In other words, the Gospel confirms our noblest intuitions about human dignity and promises to fulfill our wildest aspirations for unlimited love, goodness, truth, beauty, and communion.

St. Thomas Aquinas on the Motives of Credibility

St. Thomas treats the motives of credibility in an interesting (and politically incorrect) article in the *Summa contra gentiles* on the reasonability of the Catholic faith in comparison with Islam. He begins by stating that, since God has willed to reveal Himself, it is fitting for the divine Wisdom to manifest that Revelation through works that only God can do, such as different kinds of miracles:

> For these "secrets of divine Wisdom" (Job 11:6), the divine Wisdom itself, which knows all things to the full, has deigned to reveal to men. . . . In order to confirm those truths that exceed natural knowledge, it gives visible manifestation to works that surpass the ability of all nature. Thus, there are the wonderful cures of illnesses, there is the raising of the dead . . . and what is more wonderful, there is the inspiration given to human minds, so that simple and untutored persons, filled with the gift of the Holy Spirit, come to possess instantaneously the highest wisdom and the readiest eloquence.

Secondly, St. Thomas observes that mass conversions to Christianity, especially in the early Church, were largely motivated by these miracles, as witnessed to in the Acts of the Apostles. He also cites Hebrews 2:4, which mentions the miracles that confirmed the Gospel: "God also bore witness by signs and wonders and various miracles and by gifts of the Holy Spirit distributed according to his own will."

Such mass conversions, however, were more remarkable for four reasons. First, they took place in the midst of a terrible persecution lasting 250 years. Second, the Christian faith teaches supernatural mysteries exceeding the power of reason, such as the Trinity, the Incarnation and Passion, and grace. The human mind naturally resists what transcends its own powers. Third, Christianity teaches a high moral code, especially regarding marriage and the transmission of life. Fourth, Christian hope promises a supernatural beatitude—seeing God face to face with the eyes of the mind and rejoicing eternally in His glory—rather than sensual pleasures.

> When these arguments were examined, through the efficacy of the above-mentioned proof, and not the violent assault of

arms or the promise of pleasure, and (what is most wonderful of all) in the midst of the tyranny of the persecutors, an innumerable throng of people, both simple and most learned, flocked to the Christian faith. In this faith there are truths preached that surpass every human intellect; the pleasures of the flesh are curbed; it is taught that the things of the world should be spurned. Now, for the minds of mortal men to assent to these things is the greatest of miracles, just as it is a manifest work of divine inspiration that, spurning visible things, men should seek only what is invisible.[39]

The spread of the Catholic faith, given these adverse conditions, and its resulting universality, continuity, and holiness, built on the apostolic foundation, make the Catholic Church the most important miracle of all after the Resurrection of Christ. Before the expansion of the Church in the time of the Apostles, God worked many miracles to further its spread. Today these miraculous works are less necessary, at least where the Church is well established, because there all can see the Church that continues through the centuries as a perpetual miracle. This means that the past miracles in some sense continue to be visible in the Catholic Church in that her very presence today as one, holy, catholic, and apostolic is only explicable as a result of innumerable miracles throughout her history. Hence, St. Thomas says: "This wonderful conversion of the world to the Christian faith is the clearest witness of the signs given in the past; so that it is not necessary that they should be further repeated, since they appear most clearly in their effect."[40]

To show the force of the Church with her four marks as a motive of credibility, St. Thomas makes an argument in the form of a dilemma (forcing a choice between two difficult options): either the Church spread through many miracles or she spread without miracles. We believe that the former option is true. However, even if the second

---

[39] *SCG* I, ch. 6 (no. 1; Pegis et al, 1:71–72).

[40] Ibid. (no. 3; Pegis, 1:72).

option were true, it would be no less miraculous. Whichever way one resolves the dilemma, the spread of the Church involves miracles and is thus a motive of credibility. St. Thomas says:

> For it would be truly more wonderful than all signs if the world had been led by simple and humble men to believe such lofty truths, to accomplish such difficult actions, and to have such high hopes. Yet it is also a fact that, even in our own time, God does not cease to work miracles through His saints for the confirmation of the faith.[41]

Miracles are not as necessary in the mature age of the Church as they were in her infancy, but God still acts wonderfully in every generation in order to confirm and strengthen His followers, especially when the Church spreads to new regions. The apparition of Our Lady of Guadalupe in Mexico City in 1531 and the resulting conversion of some ten million Native Americans is the most remarkable example. This divine action continues in the miracles required for the canonization of saints, or in the miracles of places like Lourdes and Fatima.

But what signs can be alleged by the followers of Jehovah's Witnesses, Mormons, Buddhists, or Muslims? With regard to Muhammad, St. Thomas says:

> He did not bring forth any signs produced in a supernatural way, which alone fittingly gives witness to divine inspiration; for a visible action that can be only divine reveals an invisibly inspired teacher of truth. On the contrary, Muhammad said that he was sent in the power of his arms—which are signs not lacking even to robbers and tyrants. . . . Nor do divine pronouncements on the part of preceding prophets offer him any witness. . . . It is thus clear that those who place any faith in his words believe foolishly.[42]

---

[41] Ibid. (Pegis, 1:72–73).

[42] Ibid. (no. 4; Pegis, 1:73–74).

This does not mean that Muslims or members of other religions do not believe *sincerely,* for of course they do. At issue here are objective motives for belief. St. Thomas is arguing that Islam does not have the same motives of credibility as the Catholic faith, for it lacks the argument from miracles and prophecy, as well as the four marks of the Church. Nor is the spread of Islam a motive of credibility, for it took place not under persecution but through the aid of the sword. Often Muslims put forth the beauty of the Quran as a motive of credibility. This is insufficient, however, for the beauty of religious texts is not in itself miraculous and is not a sufficient sign of divine Revelation. Man is a religious animal and gifted with a connatural religious and poetic sense.

The motives of credibility are useful not only to distinguish Christianity from other religions, but also to orient and illuminate the comparison between the Protestant denominations and the Catholic Church. Christ presented powerful motives of credibility before instituting the Church and substantially changing the religious worship of Israel; but the Protestant revolutionaries did not present any such motives of credibility for the changes in Church authority and worship they introduced. The meek and gentle St. Francis de Sales, who converted some seventy-two thousand Calvinists back to the Catholic faith, rebuked them for believing their ministers (Luther, Zwingli, Calvin) who opposed the Church and changed doctrine without being supported by prophecies or miracles:

> Your ministers have not been prophesied as preachers of the word of God, nor the time of their coming, nor a single one of their actions. They have made a revolution in the Church much greater and bolder than Our Lord made in the synagogue; for they have taken all away, only putting back certain shadows: but testimonies to this effect have they none. . . . Whence will they show me that the Church was ever to receive another form, or a like reformation to the one which our Lord made?[43]

---

[43] St. Francis de Sales, *The Catholic Controversy,* part 1, ch. 24 (Rockford: TAN Books, 1989), 27.

Instead of these signs, Protestantism generally justifies its extraordinary mission from God by its success and by the interior witness of the Holy Spirit inspiring the Reformers. However, the successful spread of Protestantism was not based on the continuity, unity, and universality of its organization and teaching. The result of the Protestant Reformation was rather the *multiplication* of churches and sects divided one from another in doctrine, numbering in the range of twenty thousand. Fragmentation and division are not miraculous signs, but rather the natural tendency of human institutions left to themselves (especially when governed by the principle of private interpretation of Scripture and dogma). These effects of Protestantism do not need to be explained by a divine cause!

What is miraculous is rather the internal unity of the Catholic Church in communion with the Roman Pontiff through twenty centuries, surviving great crises and historical vicissitudes and yet always preserving the same faith. Why did the Catholic Church not go the way of the Protestant denominations? What maintains its unity, catholicity, apostolicity, and holiness? It is clearly the rock of Peter, the papacy, on which Christ founded the Church (Matt 16:18). Catholics see this foundation—and the four marks that rest on it—as a sure sign of the divine origin of the Church.

Although the Protestant world lost the marks of unity, catholicity, and apostolicity (understood as apostolic succession), holiness in the Protestant world still remains as a motive of credibility.[44] This holiness, however, as Protestants would agree, comes from the gifts they received from the Church (and share with the Catholic Church today): Scripture, Baptism, the Nicene Creed, and so forth. This holiness thus points to its source in the Catholic Church and should impel to Catholic unity.[45]

---

[44] Newman, during the last part of his Anglican period, made much of this argument for remaining Anglican; see *Apologia pro vita sua* (New York: D. Appleton, 1865), 190–191.

[45] See *LG* §8.

On the Possibility of Miracles

Since the Enlightenment, it has become not uncommon for people to reject the very possibility of miracles on the grounds that the laws of nature are supposedly inviolable. This position would strike at the very heart of Christianity's claim to credibility.[46]

In the eighteenth century, the empiricist philosopher David Hume gave a famous argument against miracles in his *Enquiry Concerning Human Understanding*:

> A miracle is a violation of the laws of nature; and as a firm and unalterable experience has established these laws, the proof against a miracle, from the very nature of the fact, is as entire as any argument from experience can possibly be imagined. . . . There must, therefore, be a uniform experience against every miraculous event, otherwise the event would not merit that appellation. And as a uniform experience amounts to a proof, there is here a direct and full *proof*, from the nature of the fact, against the existence of any miracle; nor can such a proof be destroyed, or the miracle rendered credible, but by an opposite proof, which is superior.[47]

Hume makes an *a priori* argument against any miracle. He claims that our experience of nature's regularity ought to outweigh the evidence of any miracle that could be proposed to our consideration. The apparent regularity of the laws of nature ought to make us voluntarily disbelieve any report of a miraculous event as unworthy of belief.

---

[46] See the PBC's *The Inspiration and Truth of Sacred Scripture: The Word that Comes from God and Speaks of God for the Salvation of the World*, (Collegeville: Liturgical Press, 2014), 135: "For a long time, by reason of a scientific approach, simply taken for granted, and because of certain philosophical concepts, doubts arose as to the historicity of these stories. According to modern science, everything that happens in this world happens on the basis of invariable rules: the so-called laws of nature. Everything is determined by these laws, and there is no space for extraordinary happenings. There is also a widespread philosophical concept according to which God, although Creator of the world, does not intervene in its functioning, which runs according to fixed rules. In other words, it is asserted that there cannot be extraordinary events caused by God; the narratives which speak of these events, therefore, cannot have any historical truth."

[47] *An Enquiry Concerning Human Understanding*, (Amherst: Prometheus Books, 1988), 104–105.

The reason Hume and others think that belief in a miracle would never be warranted seems to be due to various *a priori* notions, such as a conception of God as limited to establishing and sustaining the laws of nature. But what is the evidence for this? Since God is omnipotent, He can do all things, except that which contradicts itself. For example, God cannot make a square circle, because a square thing and a not-square thing cannot be the same thing at the same time and in the same way. But there is nothing contradictory about a miracle. A law of nature establishes the action of God in ordinary cases, and in miracles the divine action deviates from the norm in exceptional cases in accordance with the plan of divine wisdom for the sake of our salvation.

Hume does allow, at least in theory, for a possible exception. It would be reasonable to believe a miracle only if it would be still more miraculous if it were supposed to be false:

> When anyone tells me that he saw a dead man restored to life, I immediately consider with myself whether it be more probable, that this person should either deceive or be deceived, or that the fact, which he relates should really have happened. I weigh the one miracle against the other; and according to the superiority, which I discover, I pronounce my decision and always reject the greater miracle. If the falsehood of his testimony would be more miraculous than the event which he relates; then, and not till then, can he pretend to command my belief or opinion.[48]

This, in fact, is a reasonable position. One should accept the evidence for a miracle only when the evidence for it is greater than the evidence against it. The only problem is that Hume thinks that this never occurs, whereas orthodox Christians think it does occur. G. K. Chesterton has a magnificent statement on why it is reasonable to sometimes believe miracles:

---

[48] Ibid., 106.

But my belief that miracles have happened in human history is not a mystical belief at all; I believe in them upon human evidences as I do in the discovery of America. Upon this point there is a simple logical fact that only requires to be stated and cleared up. Somehow or other an extraordinary idea has arisen that the disbelievers in miracles consider them coldly and fairly, while believers in miracles accept them only in connection with some dogma. The fact is quite the other way. The believers in miracles accept them (rightly or wrongly) because they have evidence for them. The disbelievers in miracles deny them (rightly or wrongly) because they have a doctrine against them. The open, obvious, democratic thing is to believe an old apple-woman when she bears testimony to a miracle, just as you believe an old apple-woman when she bears testimony to a murder . . . If it comes to human testimony there is a choking cataract of human testimony in favour of the supernatural. If you reject it, you can only mean one of two things . . . you either deny the main principle of democracy, or you affirm the main principle of materialism—the abstract impossibility of miracle. You have a perfect right to do so; but in that case you are the dogmatist. It is we Christians who accept all actual evidence—it is you rationalists who refuse actual evidence, being constrained to do so by your creed. But I am not constrained by any creed in the matter, and looking impartially into certain miracles of mediaeval and modern times, I have come to the conclusion that they occurred.[49]

Another type of objection to the possibility of miracles comes from a philosophical notion of physical determinism. For example, the great French mathematician and physicist Pierre-Simon Laplace (1749–1827) rejected miracles because they would be incompatible with an absolute physical determinism that he asserted:

---

[49] *Orthodoxy* (London; New York: John Lane, 1908), 278–280.

We ought then to regard the present state of the universe as the effect of its previous state and as the cause of the one which is to follow. Given for one instant a mind which could comprehend all the forces by which nature is animated and the respective situation of the beings that compose it . . . it would embrace in the same formula the movements of the greatest bodies of the universe and those of the lightest atom; for it, nothing would be uncertain and the future, as the past, would be present to its eyes.[50]

Stephen Hawking, in *The Grand Design*, rejects miracles on apparently the same grounds of the absolute determinism of physical laws:

Given the state of the universe at one time, a complete set of laws fully determines both the future and the past. That would exclude the possibility of miracles or an active role for God.[51]

Again Hawking writes: "This book is rooted in the concept of scientific determinism which implies that . . . there are no miracles, or exceptions to the laws of nature."[52] "These laws should hold everywhere and at all times; otherwise they wouldn't be laws. There could be no exceptions or miracles. God or demons couldn't intervene in the running of the universe."[53]

Ironically, the "concept of scientific determinism" cannot be known from empirical science. Empirical science cannot ever experimentally test the hypothesis of physical determinism. If scientists

---

[50] *A Philosophical Essay on Probabilities*, trans. F. W. Truscott and E. L. Emory (New York: Dover, 1951), 4. This claim of absolute determinism has been disproven even in the field of physics by quantum mechanics. However, even if there were an absolute determinism in the mechanics of closed physical systems, it would not mean that God could not intervene through miracles, nor rule the free actions of beings endowed with a spiritual and rational nature.

[51] Stephen Hawking and Leonard Mlodinow, *The Grand Design* (New York: Bantam Books, 2010), 30.

[52] Ibid., 34.

[53] Ibid., 171.

hold it, they do so as a kind of *a priori* dogma that lacks the possibility of verification or falsification through the methods of empirical science. The question of whether the general laws of nature completely determine every event in the universe is outside of the bounds of empirical science. This is a question more properly addressed by philosophy and theology.

A closely related rejection of miracles holds that they are incompatible with the scientific view of the world and are tied with the intellectual infancy of mankind. Richard Dawkins gives a good example:

> The nineteenth century is the last time when it was possible for an educated person to admit to believing in miracles like the virgin birth without embarrassment. When pressed, many educated Christians are too loyal to deny the virgin birth and the resurrection. But it embarrasses them because their rational minds know that it is absurd, so they would much rather not be asked.[54]

Many Christian theologians of the past two centuries have also rejected the possibility of miracles. Probably the most famous of them is Rudolf Bultmann, who said: "It is impossible to use electric light and the wireless and to avail ourselves of modern medical and surgical discoveries, and at the same time to believe in the New Testament world of spirits and miracles."[55] Why is this impossible? Bultmann, like the others mentioned above, holds it impossible because he believes in absolute determinism, a closed network of natural causes that admits no intervention by God:

> The historical method includes the presupposition that history is a unity in the sense of a closed continuum of effects in which individual events are connected by the succession

---

[54] Richard Dawkins, *The God Delusion* (New York: Houghton Mifflin, 2006), 187.

[55] Rudolf Bultmann, *New Testament and Mythology and Other Basic Writings*, ed. and trans. by Schubert Ogden (Philadelphia: Fortress Press, 1984), 4.

of cause and effect. [This continuum] cannot be rent by the interference of supernatural, transcendent powers.[56]

This tenet seems to be held as a kind of unproven dogma that belongs not to modern science *per se*, for no scientific principle is given to refute miracles, but only to a certain kind of worldview—known as Deism—that has become common among some intellectuals since the Enlightenment. This worldview holds that God must stay out of His creation. He is forbidden to trespass on the world that He has left subject to our dominion. It is not difficult to see that a motive for this view can be a disordered desire for complete autonomy, first evidenced in the original sin.

I think that, in practice, the last objection is the most important. Whether a person is willing to accept miracles depends in large part on the disposition of the heart. If he desires freedom understood as autonomy as the principal value, he will not be disposed to favor the idea of God intervening in history and the world. But if he is yearning for something beyond this world—a divine love—then it will seem not too unreasonable that God would want to intervene and show His hand and voice in the world.

Given the existence of God, the possibility of miracles is not hard to see. It can be shown that God has dominion over all created beings. God as the First Cause can cause directly anything that any secondary cause can bring to pass. All creatures are obedient to God if He wishes to move them directly and not just through the mediation of other created causes. St. Thomas and scholastic theologians refer to this power of creatures to directly obey God as obediential potency.[57]

Study Questions

1. What are motives of credibility? Explain the three motives of credibility given in *CCC* §156.

---

[56] Bultmann, *Existence and Faith*, ed. Schubert Ogden (New York: Meridian Books, 1960), 291–292.

[57] For the notion of obediential potency, see Feingold, *The Natural Desire to See God according to St. Thomas Aquinas and His Interpreters* (Ave Maria: Sapientia Press, 2010), 105–114.

2. Explain how the holiness of God's Revelation, culminating in the Person of Jesus Christ, is a motive of credibility.
3. What are "reasons of the heart" for belief in God and in Christianity? Are such arguments "rational"? Explain.
4. How can one respond to someone who denies the possibility of miracles?

Suggestions for Further Reading

Summa contra gentiles, bk. I, ch. 6.

Lewis, C. S. *Miracles*. San Francisco: HarperCollins Publishers, 2001. Originally published 1947.

Garrigou-Lagrange, Réginald. *The Principles of Catholic Apologetics.* Translated by T. J. Walsh. Eugene: Wipf & Stock, 2009. Originally published 1926.

Feingold, Lawrence. *The Mystery of Israel and the Church*, vol. 1, *Figure and Fulfillment*, 15–72. St. Louis: The Miriam Press, 2010 (on the messianic prophecies as motive of credibility).

———. Ibid., vol. 3, *The Messianic Kingdom of Israel*, 53–107. St. Louis: Miriam Press, 2010 (on the four marks of the Church as motives of credibility).

PART 2

Theology: Faith Seeking Understanding

CHAPTER FOUR

Should Theology Exist? Two Orders of Knowledge about God

Fundamental Theology is theology's self-reflection on its own nature and foundations. This second part, chapters 4–6, explores the nature and methods of theology by following the classic text on the subject, which is the first question of St. Thomas Aquinas's *Summa theologiae*.

Sacred Theology

What is theology? The word itself means the science or study of God, and in this broad sense, it can indicate two disciplines. It can either be the philosophical study of God as He can be known by *reason alone*, or it can be the study of God as known through *Revelation*, with faith and reason working together in harmony. The second of the two is a higher and greater form of theology, for God's Revelation allows our knowledge of Him to penetrate to His intimate life and to His gratuitous acts in salvation history. In this second sense, theology can also be defined as "faith seeking understanding." The two senses of theology are often distinguished by referring to the philosophical study as *natural theology* and that based on Revelation as *sacred theology*.[1] Normally, the word "theology," unless the context indicates otherwise, is

---

[1] In the first question of the *Summa*, Aquinas refers to Catholic theology based on Revelation as *sacra doctrina*, which can be translated as sacred doctrine, sacred science, sacred theology, or simply Catholic theology.

taken in this second and higher sense, and it is in this sense that it is used in this book. Theology is a science that necessarily presupposes faith in God's Revelation as its proper foundation and illuminates the content of faith using reason and the analogy that exists between revealed and natural truths.

Should Theology Exist? Rationalist and Agnostic Objections

The first question that St. Thomas poses in his *Summa of Theology* is whether there should exist a discipline such as sacred theology, and why. Aristotle and Aquinas speak about four fundamental questions that one must ask in every inquiry.[2] First, does something exist? Second, if it does exist, what is it? That is, what is its nature or essence? The last two questions follow: (third) what are its properties and attributes and (fourth) *why* does it have those properties and attributes? But it would be pointless to investigate the essence and properties of something that perhaps does not even exist. Thus, with regard to theology, we should first ascertain that it exists before we investigate its nature, properties, and methods of demonstration.

To show that a field of study exists, it would be sufficient to show that its object exists, and that we have some access to that object. In the case of theology, the object is God who reveals Himself and our access to Him is through reason enlightened by faith in His Revelation. Thus, sacred theology exists as a distinct science of God based on His Revelation. St. Thomas, however, is not content to answer in this abbreviated way, and he poses the deeper question as to why there is any need for "sacred doctrine" distinct from philosophy or the natural sciences. This question implies a still deeper question: why should God reveal Himself to mankind, making possible a sacred doctrine

---

[2] Aristotle, *Posterior Analytics* 2.2.89b36–90a4. See Aquinas's *Commentary on Aristotle's Posterior Analytics*, bk. 2, lec. 1, trans. Richard Berquist (Notre Dame: Dumb Ox Books, 2007), 231: "There are four things which we seek to know: *that it is so* [properties and attributes], *why it is so* [why those attributes?], *whether it is* [exists], and *what it is* [essence or nature]. Everything that is askable or knowable can be reduced to these four." In Latin the four questions are, respectively: *quia, propter quid, si est,* and *quid est.*

about God based on His Revelation? Why is it fitting that there be a body of knowledge of God that extends beyond what reason alone can know, based on Revelation and faith? Would not philosophy and empirical science be enough for man, as contemporary society affirms?

Aquinas begins every article with objections to the thesis he is considering. This first article begins with two very modern objections. One objection states that the empirical sciences and philosophy treat of all reality, including the first principles of things. Thus it would seem that there cannot exist any field of study above the empirical and philosophical sciences, or if it did, it would be superfluous.[3]

The philosophical position that underlies this kind of objection is known as "rationalism," which holds that no science higher than the empirical sciences and philosophy is necessary because they sufficiently attain to all of reality. Using this reasoning, adherents of the "New Atheism" vigorously and derisively deny the existence of theology.[4] Stephen Hawking's idea that physics could come up with

---

[3] *ST* I, q. 1, a. 1, obj. 2: "Furthermore, every science must be about being, for nothing can be known except what is true, and truth is convertible with being. But the philosophical sciences treat of all being, including even God. Thus a certain part of philosophy is referred to as theology, or the divine science, as is clear from the Philosopher in book 6 of the *Metaphysics*. Therefore it seems superfluous to have any other discipline than the philosophical sciences." St. Thomas does not distinguish here between the empirical and the philosophical sciences, as we would today. By "philosophical sciences" he presumably intends to include all human sciences that rely on reason unaided by Revelation.

[4] Some of the most important figures of the so-called "New Atheism" are Richard Dawkins, professor of zoology at Oxford; the late Christopher Hitchens, an Anglo-American journalist; Sam Harris, doctor of neuroscience and CEO of Project Reason, a nonprofit foundation for spreading scientific knowledge and secular values; Daniel Dennet, professor of philosophy at Tufts University; and Victor Stenger, professor of physics at the University of Hawaii. They have gained attention with a series of best-selling books: *The God Delusion* by Richard Dawkins (New York: Houghton Mifflin, 2006); *God Is Not Great: How Religion Poisons Everything* by Christopher Hitchens (New York: Twelve, 2007); *Breaking the Spell: Religion as a Natural Phenomenon* by Daniel Dennett (New York, Viking, 2006); *The End of Faith: Religion, Terror, and the Future of Reason* by Sam Harris (New York, W. W. Norton, 2004); and *God: The Failed Hypothesis: How Science Shows That God Does Not Exist* by Victor Stenger (Amherst: Prometheus Books, 2008). For good critiques of the New Atheism, see Alvin Plantinga, *Where the Conflict Really Lies: Science, Religion, and Naturalism* (Oxford: Oxford University Press, 2011); Peter Hitchens, *The Rage Against God: How Atheism Led Me to Faith* (Grand Rapids: Zondervan, 2010); David Bentley Hart, *Atheist Delusions: The Christian Revolution and Its Fashionable Enemies* (New Haven: Yale University Press, 2009), and "Believe It or Not," *First Things* (May 2010); Edward Feser, *The Last Superstition* (South Bend: St. Augustine's Press, 2008); and Michael Augros, *Who Designed the Designer?* (San Francisco: Ignatius Press, 2015).

a "theory of everything" is a good example of a rationalist rejection of theology as a field of study that transcends the empirical sciences.[5]

All forms of complete materialism would share this rejection of the existence of sacred theology. If all that exists is material, then the empirical sciences will, in principle, be sufficient to explain all of reality. Since Marxism is a radical form of materialism, it too vehemently—and often violently—rejects the possibility of sacred theology.

The weakness of the rationalist objection to theology is that it presupposes a quite inflated view of the power of unaided human reason. It is very unreasonable to think that unaided reason could ever arrive at a "theory of everything" because, in philosophical terms, this would mean a sufficient theory of the first causes of things. Although philosophy can speak about God as First Cause and demonstrate His existence and attributes, it does not adequately treat of Him because He always remains more unknown to human reason than known. Reason can recognize that it alone can never perfectly know the nature of the First Cause, since by definition, it must be uncaused, unlike all other causes, and thus it transcends the whole order of which it is the first uncaused cause. Thus there is room for a higher doctrine about God that exceeds the limits of natural reason if, indeed, God deigns to reveal Himself.

Rationalists, however, are not the only ones who reject the possibility of theology. It is possible to reject theology from a philosophical position that has too little confidence about the power of unaided human reason. St. Thomas therefore poses a second objection against the existence of sacred theology, quoting Sirach 3:23: "Seek not the

---

[5] See Stephen Hawking and Leonard Mlodinow, *The Grand Design* (New York: Bantam Books, 2010), 30: "Given the state of the universe at one time, a complete set of laws fully determines both the future and the past. That would exclude the possibility of miracles or an active role for God." However, eight years earlier, in a paper of July 20, 2002 ("Gödel and the End of Physics"), Hawking recognized that Gödel's theorem excludes the possibility of a theory of everything. He writes: "Some people will be very disappointed if there is not an ultimate theory that can be formulated as a finite number of principles. I used to belong to that camp, but I have changed my mind. I'm now glad that our search for understanding will never come to an end, and that we will always have the challenge of new discovery. Without it, we would stagnate. Godel's theorem ensured there would always be a job for mathematicians" (at http://www.hawking.org.uk/godel-and-the-end-of-physics.html).

things that are too high for you." This objection says that, even if there are realities above the bounds of our reason, we do not need a doctrine or science about such things, for the natural order should be sufficient for the aspirations of man. It seems that "man should not seek to know what is above reason,"[6] for what is above reason will be above human knowledge, language, action, and interest. How can there be a study of that which exceeds the limits of reason?

The philosophical position that lies behind this kind of objection is known as "agnosticism."[7] An agnostic position maintains that one should not seek a science higher than the empirical sciences and philosophy because, even though there may be many realities that transcend the limitations of such sciences, such realities simply cannot be known by man, for there are intrinsic limits to human speculative reason that cannot be overcome. For many, this would be the case for all "religious truths" or truths about God. In other words, an agnostic would deny that there can be any true knowledge by way of faith in God's historical Revelation. This kind of position was formulated most famously by Immanuel Kant in his *Critique of Pure Reason* (1781) and his *Religion within the Boundaries of Mere Reason* (1793).[8]

Another form of agnosticism is given by logical positivists, such as Ludwig Wittgenstein, in his preface to his *Tractatus Logico-Philosophicus*: "What can be said at all can be said clearly; and whereof

---

[6] *ST* I, q. 1, a. 1, obj. 1: "It seems that it is not necessary for there to be any other science besides the philosophical sciences. For man should not seek those things that are above reason, according to Sirach 3 [23]: 'Seek not things that are too high for you.' But what is accessible to reason is sufficiently treated in the philosophical sciences. Therefore it seems superfluous to have any other discipline than the philosophical sciences."

[7] "Agnosticism" comes from the Greek word that means "to not know." It does not refer to a temporary state of ignorance that could be overcome by new knowledge, but rather is the conviction that such ignorance is insuperable, that no one can have knowledge of that which transcends reason.

[8] See, for example, Immanuel Kant, *Religion within the Boundaries of Mere Reason and Other Writings*, part 3, ch. 5, trans. Allen Wood and George Di Giovanni (Cambridge, UK: Cambridge University Press, 1998; originally published 1793), 114: "Thus, 'not they who say Lord! Lord! But they who do the will of God,' those, therefore, who seek to become well-pleasing to him, not through loud praises of him (or of his envoy, as a being of divine origin) according to revealed concepts which not every human being can have, but through a good life conduct, regarding which everyone knows his will—these will be the ones who offer to him the true veneration that he desires."

one cannot speak thereof one must be silent. The book will, there-fore, draw a limit to thinking, or rather—not to thinking, but to the expression of thoughts."[9] The book ends by saying: "There is indeed the inexpressible. This *shows* itself, it is the mystical. . . . Whereof one cannot speak, thereof one must be silent."[10] According to logical pos-itivism,[11] sacred theology, and even metaphysics,[12] are matters about which "one must be silent." For Wittgenstein, one could perhaps think some kind of "mystical" (theological or metaphysical) thoughts and have some kind of religious faith, but not formulate such thoughts in a coherent doctrine.

The agnostic position can also be formulated in a more practical form. Instead of directly rejecting the possibility of knowing truths beyond the limits of reason, many simply have no interest in such knowledge. This lack of interest in the supernatural that dominates much of the contemporary world can be referred to as a kind of practi-cal "naturalism." Such a position is presented as virtuous, for it seems at once humble and pragmatic.

Why Is It Fitting That God Reveal Himself to Man?

St. Thomas gives two reasons for the necessity of a divinely revealed teaching about God. First, only such teaching can reveal the super-natural mysteries that surpass the limits of reason, especially the

---

[9] Ludwig Wittgenstein, *Tractatus Logico-Philosophicus*, in *Major Works: Selected Philosophical Writings* (New York: Harper Perennial, 2009), 3.

[10] Ibid., propositions 6.522 and 7 (Harper Perennial, 81–82).

[11] For a classical statement of logical positivism, see Alfred Jules Ayer, *Language, Truth, and Logic* (London: Victor Gollancz Ltd, 1936). Positivism is the philosophical position that only knowl-edge that can be empirically verified is warranted or meaningful. Of course, that statement is a philosophical statement and cannot be empirically verified!

[12] It should be noted that Wittgenstein's agnosticism applies not only to theology, but also to all metaphysics. See *Tractatus Logico-Philosophicus*, proposition 6.53: "The right method of philoso-phy would be this. To say nothing except what can be said, i.e., the propositions of natural science, i.e., something that has nothing to do with philosophy, and then always, when someone else wished to say something metaphysical, to demonstrate to him that he had given no meaning to certain signs in his propositions."

fact that God has ordered mankind to an end that exceeds human comprehension. Second, such teaching is necessary to give us secure knowledge of the truths of natural theology and of the natural moral law, truths that reason could know, but which, in practice, are known principally by faith:

> It was necessary for human salvation that there be some doctrine based on divine revelation distinct from the philosophical sciences that are studied by human reason. First, because man is ordered to God as to an end that transcends reason's grasp, according to Isaiah [64:4]: "Eye has not seen, O God, besides you, what you have prepared for those who love you." But men must know their end in advance, so as to order their intentions and actions to this end. Therefore it was necessary for the salvation of men that some things that exceed the power of human reason be made known to them by divine revelation.
>
> Even with regard to those things that human reason can investigate, it was necessary for mankind to be instructed by divine revelation. This is because the truth about God that can be grasped by reason would come to mankind only through a few, after a long time, and with many errors mixed in. But man's entire salvation, which lies in God, depends on the knowledge of this truth. Therefore, so that salvation may come to men in a more fitting and certain way, it was necessary that they be instructed in divine things by divine revelation. It was thus necessary that there should be a sacred doctrine based on revelation in addition to the philosophical sciences that are studied by reason.[13]

We need a revealed doctrine principally because God has willed to elevate us to a supernatural end, an intimate, face-to-face union with Him in heaven known as the beatific vision. We could never know this true end of man if God did not reveal it to us. And if our

---

[13] *ST* I, q. 1, a. 1.

end is supernatural and mysterious, so must be the means to get there. If God did not reveal to us these supernatural means, we could never direct our lives to attain our final end.

Dei Verbum §2 stresses that God's Revelation centers on man's supernatural end, which is participation in the Trinitarian life of God:

> In His goodness and wisdom God chose to reveal Himself and to make known to us the hidden purpose of His will (see Eph. 1:9) by which through Christ, the Word made flesh, man might in the Holy Spirit have access to the Father and come to share in the divine nature (see Eph. 2:18; 2 Peter 1:4). Through this revelation, therefore, the invisible God (see Col. 1:15, 1 Tim. 1:17) out of the abundance of His love speaks to men as friends (see Ex. 33:11; John 15:14–15) and lives among them (see Bar. 3:38), so that He may invite and take them into fellowship with Himself.

Thus man's elevation to share in the life of the Blessed Trinity through an intimate filial friendship is the principal reason for divine Revelation.[14]

It is also very fitting, however, that God reveals truths that natural reason could discover, such as the existence, goodness, omnipotence, and oneness of God[15] and the natural moral law. Natural theology (the truths about God that belong to the natural order) is the culmination of philosophy and its most difficult part. If God did not reveal such truths, as St. Thomas says, they would "come to mankind only through a few, after a long time, and with many errors mixed in." But the truths about God, including those accessible to reason, need to be known by man from the beginning of his moral life (that is, from the age of reason), so as to be the guiding principles of his action. God thus mercifully reveals to humanity both natural and supernatural

---

[14] See also CCC §52: "God, who 'dwells in unapproachable light' [1 Tim 6:16], wants to communicate his own divine life to the men he freely created, in order to adopt them as his sons in his only-begotten Son. By revealing himself God wishes to make them capable of responding to him, and of knowing him, and of loving him far beyond their own natural capacity."

[15] See, for example, Deut 6:4: "Hear, O Israel: the Lord our God is one Lord."

truths about Himself, about man and the moral law, and about the path of salvation. Therefore, sacred theology does not limit itself solely to supernatural mysteries that can only be known if God reveals them, such as the Trinity, the Incarnation, the Church, and the beatific vision, but also examines what St. Thomas calls the "preambles of faith"—those truths about God which reason can discover without the aid of Revelation and which help dispose a person to recognize Revelation.[16]

The position of St. Thomas on the fittingness of Revelation in the first article of the *Summa* was solemnly confirmed by the Magisterium of the Church in Vatican I:

> It is to be ascribed to this divine revelation that such truths among things divine that of themselves are not beyond human reason can, even in the present condition of mankind, be known by everyone with facility, with firm certainty, and with no admixture of error. It is, however, not for this reason that revelation is to be called absolutely necessary, but because God in His infinite goodness has ordained man to a supernatural end, viz., to share in the good things of God that utterly exceed the intelligence of the human mind, for "no eye has seen, nor ear heard, nor the heart of man conceived, what God has prepared for those who love Him" [1 Cor 2:9].[17]

Vatican II, in *Dei Verbum* §6, also reaffirmed this doctrine:

> Through divine revelation, God chose to show forth and communicate Himself and the eternal decisions of His will regarding the salvation of men. That is to say, He chose to share with them those divine treasures which totally transcend the understanding of the human mind.

---

16 For the notion of "preambles of faith," see Pope St. John Paul II, Encyclical Letter on Faith and Reason *Fides et ratio* §67.

17 First Vatican Council, Dogmatic Constitution on the Catholic Faith *Dei Filius* (1870), ch. 2 (DS, 3005).

As a sacred synod has affirmed,[18] God, the beginning and end of all things, can be known with certainty from created reality by the light of human reason (see Rom. 1:20); but teaches that it is through His revelation that those religious truths which are by their nature accessible to human reason can be known by all men with ease, with solid certitude and with no trace of error, even in this present state of the human race.[19]

The last step of St. Thomas's argument in this first article reasons that, since knowledge of God's Revelation is necessary for human life, it is also fitting that there be a discipline that systematically treats this knowledge, which is called sacred theology.

Reply to the Rationalist and Agnostic Objections

At this point it is easy to answer the objections posed at the beginning. If there are two sources of knowledge about God—reason and divine Revelation—it is fitting that there be two disciplines that study God: one through the light of reason alone and the other through the light of Revelation and reason. St. Thomas lays down the principle that "sciences are differentiated according to the different ways in

---

[18] Ibid.

[19] See also Pope Pius XII, Encyclical Letter Concerning Some False Opinions Threatening to Undermine the Foundations of Catholic Doctrine *Humani generis* (1950), §§2–3: "For though, absolutely speaking, human reason by its own natural force and light can arrive at a true and certain knowledge of the one personal God, Who by His providence watches over and governs the world, and also of the natural law, which the Creator has written in our hearts, still there are not a few obstacles to prevent reason from making efficient and fruitful use of its natural ability. The truths that have to do with God and the relations between God and men completely surpass the sensible order and demand self-surrender and self-abnegation in order to be put into practice and to influence practical life. Now, the human intellect, in gaining the knowledge of such truths is hampered both by the activity of the senses and the imagination, and by evil passions arising from original sin. Hence men easily persuade themselves in such matters that what they do not wish to believe is false or at least doubtful.

"It is for this reason that divine revelation must be considered morally necessary so that those religious and moral truths which are not of their nature beyond the reach of reason in the present condition of the human race may be known by all men readily with a firm certainty and with freedom from all error."

which things are known."[20] Sacred theology is not superfluous, even though it studies the same First Cause that is the object of natural theology, because sacred theology studies Him through a higher source of knowledge, which is God's own Revelation of Himself. Therefore, sacred theology "differs in kind from that theology which is a part of philosophy."[21] The rationalist objection would only be valid if it could be proven that God cannot or has not revealed Himself, or that reason can perfectly know the first causes of all things.

The other objection examined by St. Thomas concedes that reason has limits, but charges sacred theology with presumption in seeking to pass beyond them. St. Thomas answers by conceding that it would certainly be presumptuous and absurd for reason to seek to go beyond its own limits if God had not revealed Himself. If reason were all that we had, then we would have to be content with that. But since He has in fact deigned to reveal Himself, it would be an attitude of false humility for reason to close itself off from that higher knowledge and restrict itself to what it can achieve with its own unaided powers. The *truly humble attitude of reason is to open itself to faith* and seek to understand as much as possible what has been received through Revelation. It is both more reasonable and more humble to listen to God speak about Himself and try to understand what He has said than to dismiss it for being above our unaided powers. True humility is the ability to receive a gift graciously. St. Thomas writes:

> Although those things that are above man's knowledge ought not to be sought through reason, they are to be received by faith if God reveals them. Thus the sacred text [Sirach 3:23] continues: "You have been shown many things above the

---

[20] *ST* I, q. 1, a. 1, ad 2.

[21] Ibid.: "Sciences are differentiated according to different ways in which things are known. For the astronomer and the physicist can demonstrate the same conclusion, as, for example, that the earth is round. However, the astronomer demonstrates this by means of mathematics (abstracting from matter), whereas the physicist demonstrates it using a material means. Thus there is no reason why the same things, which are treated by philosophy insofar as they are knowable by the light of natural reason, cannot also be treated by another science insofar as they are known by divine revelation. Therefore that theology which pertains to sacred doctrine differs in kind from that theology which is a part of philosophy."

understanding of men." And sacred science consists in these things.[22]

Natural and Supernatural Knowledge of God

As we have seen, the distinction between sacred theology and natural theology depends on the distinction between two kinds of knowledge about God. The highest field of philosophy can investigate God, but only as He can be known by reason as the First Cause of the universe. This field of philosophy is called metaphysics or natural theology. It is very important to distinguish *natural theology*, which does not presuppose either faith or Revelation, from *sacred theology*, which is the science of God based on faith in His Revelation to man. Sacred theology investigates God as He is in Himself insofar as He has revealed Himself to man. Sacred theology is not accessible without faith, for it is based on God's Revelation that came to mankind first through Israel and culminated in the Incarnation and Paschal mystery of Christ, as revealed in the New Testament and the apostolic Tradition. Natural theology, since it is based on reason, was accessible to ancient philosophers without access to Revelation, such as Plato and Aristotle, and to all men in a rudimentary way. St. Paul affirms reason's access to God through creation in Romans 1:18–23:

> For the wrath of God is revealed from heaven against all ungodliness and wickedness of those men who in wickedness hold back the truth of God, seeing that what may be known about God is manifest to them. For God has manifested it to them. For *since the creation of the world his invisible attributes are clearly seen—his everlasting power also and divinity—being understood through the things that are made.* And so they are without excuse, seeing that, although they knew God, they did not glorify Him as God or give thanks, but became vain in their reasoning.

---

[22] Ibid., ad 1.

Notice that St. Paul affirms not only the ability of natural reason to know God's existence "through the things that are made," but also His "invisible attributes" and His "everlasting power." This is a consequence of the fact, affirmed, for example, in Psalm 19:1, that "the heavens are telling the glory of God; and the firmament proclaims his handiwork."

The First Vatican Council infallibly defined the capacity of natural reason to know God's existence with certainty through creation, as well as the distinction of natural and sacred theology:

> The same Holy Mother Church holds and teaches that God, the beginning and end of all things, can be known with certainty from the things that were created through the natural light of human reason, for "ever since the creation of the world his invisible nature . . . has been clearly perceived in the things that have been made" [Rom 1:20]; but it pleased His wisdom and goodness to reveal Himself and the eternal decrees of His will to the human race in another and supernatural way, as the Apostle says: "In many and various ways God spoke of old to our fathers by the prophets; but in these last days he has spoken to us by a Son" [Heb 1:1–2].[23]

Natural theology, for Plato and Aristotle, is the highest part of the most noble philosophical science, for it is the culmination of metaphysics. Metaphysics, which is the science of being as such (being *qua* being), investigates the properties and first causes of being. However, it cannot have God directly as its object precisely because it only employs natural reason and God always remains naturally unseen by the mind because He infinitely transcends all His creatures. He can thus only be known as the transcendent First Cause and Final End of being. God is known as the *hidden First Principle*, but not as the "protagonist" of the science of metaphysics.

Because of its elevation and difficulty, Plato and Aristotle assigned metaphysics the last place in the pedagogical order of the sci-

---

[23] *Dei Filius*, ch. 2 (DS, 3004).

ences. Since the mind attains to what is unseen on the basis of what is seen, and since God is understood only as the First Cause of creatures, we must study the creature before we can ascend to the First Principle. In fact, it was the opinion of Plato, Aristotle, and St. Thomas Aquinas that metaphysics is a science for the mature man.[24]

In the natural order of knowledge, God is the *last* subject to be studied. Philosophical reason can grasp, in a rigorous way, that He is the cause of being and its final end only at the end of the long road of philosophy.[25] And in this way, as St. Thomas points out, God is known by few, very imperfectly, at the end of a lifetime, and often with the admixture of great errors. In the supernatural order of Revelation, on the contrary, God is the *first* known, for the first thing that God reveals is Himself, as when He spoke to Moses in the burning bush. He makes Himself known as a personal God, the God of Abraham, Isaac, and Jacob, as He who is. God Himself is the "protagonist" of sacred theology.

It follows that there are two orders of knowledge about God, one natural and the other revealed. Philosophical knowledge of God only attains to Him as First Cause. Sacred theology, on the other hand, enables men to have access to God as He is in Himself, in His personal reality, inner Trinitarian life, and free actions in history. Blaise Pascal gave a famous description of the distinction of the two orders of knowledge about God in his "Memorial," a short text which he wore constantly on his heart: "Fire. 'God of Abraham, God of Isaac, God of Jacob,' not of philosophers and scholars."[26]

These two orders of knowledge about God follow two opposing itineraries. Philosophy starts with the world and with man in order to end up with a consideration of God as First Cause insofar as He can

---

[24] See Plato, *Republic* 7.539–540; Aristotle, *Nicomachean Ethics* 6.8.1142a15–20; St. Thomas, *Commentary on Aristotle's Nicomachean Ethics*, bk. 6, lec. 12 (Marietti nos. 1210–1211), trans. C. J. Litzinger (Notre Dame: Dumb Ox Books, 1993), 384.

[25] Nevertheless, natural reason can rather easily grasp the existence of God as First Cause in a *spontaneous and non-rigorous fashion*, which would be in line with what St. Paul says in Romans 1:20–21 about men being without excuse for not knowing of the existence of God and His attributes.

[26] *Pensées*, trans. A. J. Krailsheimer (New York: Penguin Classics, 1966), 285.

be known through creation. Sacred theology, on the contrary, begins with God's Revelation of Himself as Trinity, and then, in the light of the Triune God and His Revelation, proceeds to investigate His creation (and man in particular, who is ordered to return back to the Father in filial friendship with Him through Christ in the Holy Spirit). A good example of the use of this theological order is the structure of St. Thomas's *Summa*, which begins by studying God in Himself, then proceeds to look at creation, and concludes with the return of the rational creature to his Trinitarian source through grace and the moral life, the Incarnation, and the Church and her sacraments.

The distinction of the two orders of knowledge about God has been solemnly taught by the Church in the First Vatican Council:

> The perpetual common belief of the Catholic Church has held and holds also this: there is a *twofold order of knowledge*, distinct not only in its principle but also in its object; in its *principle*, because in the one we know by natural reason, in the other by divine faith; in its *object*, because apart from what natural reason can attain, there are proposed to our belief mysteries that are hidden in God that can never be known unless they are revealed by God.[27]

The *Catechism of the Catholic Church* §50 echoes Vatican I in teaching the existence of a twofold order of knowledge about God:

> By natural reason man can know God with certainty, on the basis of his works. But there is another order of knowledge, which man cannot possibly arrive at by his own powers: the order of divine Revelation. Through an utterly free decision, God has revealed himself and given himself to man. This he does by revealing the mystery, his plan of loving goodness, formed from all eternity in Christ, for the benefit of all men. God has fully revealed this plan by sending us his beloved Son, our Lord Jesus Christ, and the Holy Spirit.

---

[27] *Dei Filius*, ch. 4 (DS, 3015; my italics).

The same fundamental teaching is taken up by St. John Paul II in *Fides et ratio* §9. After citing Vatican I, he explains:

> Based upon God's testimony and enjoying the supernatural assistance of grace, faith is of an order other than philosophical knowledge, which depends upon sense perception and experience and which advances by the light of the intellect alone. Philosophy and the sciences function within the order of natural reason; while faith, enlightened and guided by the Spirit, recognizes in the message of salvation the "fullness of grace and truth" (cf. John 1:14) which God has willed to reveal in history and definitively through his Son, Jesus Christ.

Natural truths are those that can be attained through the natural light of reason. Supernatural truths are those that elude the grasp of reason alone, and can only be known through Revelation and the supernatural gift of faith. These truths are called mysteries. A mystery, in the strict sense of the word, is a truth that cannot be known if God does not reveal it, and which, even after it has been revealed, cannot be properly and fully comprehended by the human mind except through the beatific vision.[28]

St. Paul explains the sense of "mystery" in 1 Corinthians 2:7–11:

> But we impart a secret and hidden wisdom of God, which God decreed before the ages for our glorification. None of the rulers of this age understood this. . . . But, as it is written, "What no eye has seen, nor ear heard, nor the heart of man conceived, what God has prepared for those who love him," God has revealed to us through the Spirit. For the Spirit searches everything, even the depths of God. For what person knows a man's thoughts except the spirit of the man which is in him? So also no one comprehends the thoughts of God except the Spirit of God.

---

[28] For a classic exposition of the notion of mystery in Catholic theology, see Matthias Joseph Scheeben, *The Mysteries of Christianity*, trans. Cyril Vollert, S.J. (St. Louis: B. Herder, 1946).

This fundamental text of St. Paul contains a number of points. First, the mysteries of faith absolutely exceed the understanding of unaided reason, intuition, or natural inclination and, for this reason, are said to be "hidden." Second, God has graciously revealed these mysteries through the Spirit. Third, the mysteries center on man's supernatural end—"what God has prepared for those who love him." Fourth, even after being revealed, the mysteries are comprehended only by God. Fifth, the gifts of the Spirit enable the spiritual man to attain a certain penetration into the mysteries, for "we have the mind of Christ" (1 Cor 2:16). Sixth, the unspiritual man, although he can know revealed propositions, cannot enter into their meaning, "for they are spiritually discerned" (1 Cor 2:14).

In its discussion of supernatural truths, the First Vatican Council cites this text of St. Paul to explain the limits of our understanding of supernatural mysteries:

> Nevertheless, if reason illumined by faith inquires in an earnest, pious, and sober manner, it attains by God's grace a certain understanding of the mysteries, which is most fruitful, both from the analogy with the objects of its natural knowledge and from the connection of these mysteries with one another and with man's ultimate end. But it never becomes capable of understanding them in the way it does truths that constitute its proper object. For divine mysteries by their very nature so exceed the created intellect that, even when they have been communicated in revelation and received by faith, they remain covered by the veil of faith itself and shrouded, as it were, in darkness as long as in this mortal life "we are away from the Lord; for we walk by faith, not by sight" [2 Cor 5:6f].[29]

God reveals the mysteries so that they can be understood in some manner, both through the activity of sacred theology and the gifts of the Spirit. However, the mysteries, except in the light of glory, can

---

[29] *Dei Filius*, ch. 4 (DS, 3016).

never be understood in the same way as the mind can grasp natural truths accessible to unaided reason.

Examples of mysteries include the Blessed Trinity, the Incarnation, Redemption, sanctifying grace, the election of Israel and the Catholic Church, original justice and original sin, the seven sacraments, heaven, the resurrection of the body, the eternity of hell, the divine maternity of Mary, and the vision of God as man's final end. Reason alone would never arrive at these truths, and even after they are revealed, reason cannot fully grasp them because they transcend the natural analogies by which we can understand them in part.

Of course, as stated above, the Revelation of God is not limited to supernatural mysteries, for He can also reveal truths of the natural order that are accessible to reason. These truths include God's existence,[30] His unity,[31] His omnipotence[32] and perfect goodness,[33] His omniscience,[34] His freedom and providence,[35] His justice and mercy,[36] the spiritual nature and immortality of the soul,[37] man's free will,[38]

---

[30] See Exod 3:14: "God said to Moses, 'I AM WHO AM.'"

[31] See Deut 6:4: "Hear, O Israel: The Lord our God is one Lord."

[32] See Wis 11:17: "Thy all-powerful hand, which created the world out of formless matter."

[33] See Exod 33:19: "I will make all my goodness pass before you, and will proclaim before you my name 'The Lord'; and I will be gracious to whom I will be gracious, and will show mercy on whom I will show mercy."

[34] See Ps 139:1–16. See also Wis 15:18–19: "For great is the wisdom of the Lord; he is mighty in power and sees everything; his eyes are on those who fear him, and he knows every deed of man."

[35] See Matt 6:25–33.

[36] See Exod 34:6–7: "The Lord, a God merciful and gracious, slow to anger, and abounding in steadfast love and faithfulness, keeping steadfast love for thousands, forgiving iniquity and transgression and sin"; Wis 15:1: "But thou, our God, art kind and true, patient, and ruling all things in mercy"; and Eph 2:4–5: "But God, who is rich in mercy, out of the great love with which he loved us, even when we were dead through our trespasses, made us alive together with Christ."

[37] See Wis 3:4: "For though in the sight of men they were punished, their hope is full of immortality." See also Matt 22:31–32: "And as for the resurrection of the dead, have you not read what was said to you by God, 'I am the God of Abraham, and the God of Isaac, and the God of Jacob'? He is not God of the dead, but of the living."

[38] See Gen 4:6–8: "The Lord said to Cain . . . 'sin is crouching at the door; its desire is for you, but you must master it.'" See also Wis 15:14–17: "It was he who created man in the beginning, and he left him in the power of his own inclination. If you will, you can keep the commandments, and to act faithfully is a matter of your own choice. He has placed before you fire and water: stretch out your hand for whichever you wish. Before a man are life and death, and whichever he chooses will be given to him."

human dignity,[39] the Ten Commandments[40] and other precepts of the natural moral law,[41] and God's judgment of man's works[42] followed by reward and punishment in the hereafter.[43]

Study Questions

1. What are the two reasons why divine Revelation is necessary, according to St. Thomas (*ST* I, q. 1, a. 1)? Explain.
2. What is the difference between natural theology and Catholic theology (sacred theology)? Explain.
3. Why does sacred theology begin with God, whereas philosophy studies God last?
4. What are the major objections against the existence of sacred theology? How should one respond to those objections?
5. What is a mystery of faith? Can they be understood in some way?
6. Make a list of the principal supernatural mysteries and the natural truths about God knowable by reason.

Suggestions for Further Reading

Summa theologiae I, q. 1, a. 1.

Pope St. John Paul II. Encyclical Letter on the Relationship between Faith and Reason *Fides et ratio* §§1–35. September 14, 1998.

---

[39] See Gen 1:26.

[40] See Exod 20:1–17 and Deut 5:6–21.

[41] See, for example, Lev 19.

[42] See 1 Sam 2:10: "The Lord will judge the ends of the earth"; Ps 96:10: "He will judge the peoples with equity"; Matt 25; Acts 17:31; and 2 Tim 4:1.

[43] See Dan 12:3–4: "And many of those who sleep in the dust of the earth shall awake, some to everlasting life, and some to shame and everlasting contempt. And those who are wise shall shine like the brightness of the firmament; and those who turn many to righteousness, like the stars for ever and ever."

CHAPTER FIVE

The Science of Theology

The Scientific Character of Theology

After establishing that there should exist a sacred doctrine based on God's Revelation, the next question St. Thomas poses (*ST* I, q. 1, a. 2) is whether this sacred doctrine should be considered to be a science in the proper sense of the term. Can there be a *science* of the things believed through faith? For many people today, theology does not attain to the status of a science because science is generally equated with only the empirical sciences, such as physics, chemistry, biology, geology, etc. Observation and measurement are the tools of empirical science, and hypotheses are tested through empirical experimentation in order to verify their truth. It is obvious that theology is not an empirical science.

Aristotle, however, understood science in a broader way, as an *intellectual virtue*, an acquired *habit of mind* of rightly thinking about a particular subject, by which one gains a systematic body of knowledge of an object[1] through knowledge of its fundamental caus-

---

[1] For example: the object of physics is moving bodies; the object of biology is living bodies; the object of chemistry is the composition and properties of bodies; etc. For a Thomistic understanding of the notion of "object" see Lawrence Dewan, O.P., "'Objectum': Notes on the Invention of a Word," in *Wisdom, Law, and Virtue: Essays in Thomistic Ethics* (New York: Fordham University Press, 2007), 414. See also Reinhard Hütter, "What Is Faith? The Theocentric, Unitive, and Eschatologically Inchoative Character of Divine Faith," *Nova et Vetera* (English) 11, no. 2 (2013): 326–332.

es.[2] Scientific knowledge is generated by coming to understand the *causes* of the objects that we encounter by the deduction of conclusions from self-evident first principles[3] grasped by common sense[4] and induction from experience. In this sense, the philosophical disciplines are sciences with as much right to the term as the empirical sciences. Metaphysics, the philosophy of man, and ethics are sciences in which conclusions are deduced from evident first principles and phenomena of experience are understood through grasping their underlying causes.

Can sacred theology, the science of God as grasped by faith and reason, be considered a science in the Aristotelian sense of the word? If it is a science, it must have some self-evident principles and some experience from which it infers conclusions. At first glance, it seems that theology cannot have evident first principles if it is *faith seeking understanding*. After all, does not faith preclude evident principles, since it is belief in what is unseen? How can there be a *science of faith*? St. Thomas poses this very objection in the second article of the *Summa*:

> It seems that sacred theology is not a science. For every science is based on self-evident principles. But sacred theology is based on the articles of faith, which are not self-evident. In-

---

[2] For Aristotle's understanding of scientific knowledge, see his *Posterior Analytics* 1.2. Science as an intellectual virtue is an interior perfection of mind that enables one to know and contemplate a particular aspect of reality with a certain perfection.

[3] See, for example, *Nichomachean Ethics* 6.6.1140b31–34, trans. W. D. Ross, in *The Basic Works of Aristotle* (New York: Modern Library, 2001), 1027: "Scientific knowledge is judgment about things that are universal and necessary, and the conclusions of demonstration, and all scientific knowledge, follow from first principles (for scientific knowledge involves apprehension of a rational ground)." See also *Metaphysics* 1.2.

[4] "Common sense" here means the intuitive knowledge that is *common* to mankind, which is the knowledge of first principles. These include both the speculative first principles, such as that something cannot be and not be at the same time in the same way (the "principle of non-contradiction"), that every change has a cause, and that the whole is greater than the sum of its parts, and the moral first principles, such as that good is to be done and evil avoided, "do unto others as you would have them do unto you" (the "golden rule"), that what is good for all is more important than what is good for only one (the common good is greater than the private good), and that God is to be loved above all.

114

deed, not everyone holds them, "for not all men have faith," as stated in 2 Thessalonians [3:2]. Therefore, sacred theology is not a science.[5]

The objection is a good one. Theology does not appear to possess self-evident principles. Indeed, if Catholic theology were based on self-evident principles, there would be no unbelievers in the world, since all would see its truth. And if theology is not based on self-evident principles, it cannot be a science in the Aristotelian sense.

St. Thomas gives his solution to the question using an Aristotelian distinction between two types of sciences: principal and subordinate (subaltern). A principal science is one that stands on its own by building on its own self-evident principles. Euclidean geometry, for example, builds on its own axioms and definitions. A subordinate science, on the other hand, takes its principles from a higher science, which it does not question, and develops its own set of conclusions from these "borrowed" principles. Practical sciences and arts are generally of this type, for they take their principles from a theoretical science and apply them for practical ends. Medicine and engineering are the classic examples. Medicine accepts without question the principles from biology and chemistry and applies them to the practical concerns of curing illnesses. Engineering and architecture receive their principles from mathematics and physics and apply them to the problem of erecting structures capable of withstanding gravity, wind, and other forces. Sciences such as medicine and engineering are considered by Aristotle to be subordinate sciences. Other examples include acoustics, optics, perspective, and music (at least to the extent that the notes of a musical scale are based on mathematical ratios).

How can this distinction be helpful in considering the scientific status of theology? Should it be classified as a principal or a subordinate science? At first sight, one might think that St. Thomas would classify theology as a principal science on account of its great dignity as the science of God who reveals Himself. Indeed, as we shall see below, he holds it to be the queen of all the sciences. However, pre-

---

[5] *ST* I, q. 1, a. 2, obj. 1.

cisely because it is based on divine Revelation, it is to be classified as a subordinate science that borrows its principles from a higher science. However, this higher science from which it borrows is no mere human science. Since theology is the science built on God's self-revelation, it borrows its principles from God's "science" about Himself, which is more properly called *omniscience*. Theology is a science subordinated to God's omniscience, which He shares with mankind through Revelation. On the basis of the principles borrowed from God's Revelation accepted in faith, theology can rationally reflect on God and the ordering of all things to Him. St. Thomas writes:

> I respond that sacred theology is a science. But it must be recognized that there are two kinds of sciences. One kind is based on principles that are evident to the light of natural reason, such as arithmetic, geometry, and others of that sort. Another kind is based on principles evident in the light of a higher science, as the art of perspective is based on principles known by geometry, and music is based on principles known by arithmetic.[6] And in this way sacred theology is based on principles known by the light of a higher science, which is the science of God and the blessed. Therefore as music believes principles transmitted to it by mathematicians, so sacred theology believes principles revealed to it by God.[7]

In reply to the objection posed at the beginning, St. Thomas writes: "The principles of any science are either self-evident or derive from the knowledge of a superior science. And the principles of sacred theology are of the latter kind, as has been said."[8] It is not necessary that the principles of every science be self-evident. It is sufficient that they be received from a higher science in which they are evident or proven.

---

[6] St. Thomas says this because musical scales and harmonies are based on numerical ratios such as 2:1 (the octave); 3:2 (the fifth); and 4:3 (the fourth).

[7] *ST* I, q. 1, a. 2.

[8] Ibid., ad 1.

For the blessed in heaven, and obviously for God, the articles of faith are principles that are most evidently seen. In this way St. Thomas reconciles two apparently opposing aspects of theology. On the one hand, it has an imperfect mode of being a science because it is based on authority and does not "see" the intrinsic evidence of its own principles on which it is built. However, it has a most sublime dignity because it is a science subordinated to the science that God has of Himself and of His creation. Thus, sacred theology is the most certain of all the sciences, even though it treats of the most sublime questions, for it participates in the certainty of God's own omniscience.

This solution to the question of the scientific character of theology enables it to maintain a great humility, for the theologian must recognize that he never adequately penetrates into the principles that form the basis of his science. They always remain *borrowed principles*. Indeed, the entire science of theology is the result of gratuitous gifts given by God to man: His self-revelation and the elevation of man to a supernatural end.

However, precisely because of the incapacity of theology to have dominion over its principles, those principles have a divine nobility, for they are "borrowed" from God Himself! Theology's unique greatness and humility go hand in hand. It is humble in that it has no dominion over its own foundation. It is great because its foundation is divine.

Despite the borrowed nature of its principles, theology is similar to other sciences in that, from its borrowed principles, it builds a systematic body of knowledge by defining terms, making distinctions, demonstrating conclusions, clarifying through analogy, and defending its conclusions against those who attack them.

Theology as the Science of God

Theology, like every other science, is defined by the object it studies. The Greek word "theo-logy" literally means the science of God, the science that has God directly as its object. In *ST* I, q. 1, a. 7, St. Thomas discusses the proper subject studied by theology:

I answer that God is the subject of this science. The relation between a science and its subject is the same as that between a faculty or habit and its object. Properly speaking, that by reason of which everything is referred to a faculty or habit is said to be its object. For example, since both a man and a stone are referred to sight insofar as they are colored, color is the proper object of sight. Now everything is treated in sacred theology with reference to God, either because it is God Himself or because it is ordered to God as its source and end. It follows that God is truly the subject of this science. This is also manifest from the principles of this science, which are the articles of faith that are about God. Now, the subject of the first principles of a science and of the entire science are the same, because the whole science is contained virtually in its principles. Some people, however, looking at what is treated in this science rather than that by reason of which it is treated, have described the subject of this science in a different way: as "realities and signs," or "the work of reparation," or "the whole Christ, head and members." All of these things are indeed treated in this science, but in their ordering to God.

Theology studies not only God, but also all created things insofar as they are related to God as Creator, Legislator, and Final End. Hence, theology also studies creation, by which creatures proceed from God and thus have Him as their final end; ethics, by which rational creatures live according to God; and salvation history, by which God intervenes in history to lead human beings to Himself. The many themes studied in theology all relate to its main subject and unifying principle, which is God Himself.[9]

Since sacred theology is the science of God based on His own Revelation of Himself, it is only accessible through the virtue of faith. Thus theology can also be defined as the science which seeks a deeper understanding of what is known through faith, or *faith seeking under-*

---

[9] See *ST* I, q. 1, a. 7, ad 2: "Whatever other conclusions are reached in this sacred science are comprehended under God, not as parts or species or accidents but as in some way ordered to Him."

standing (*fides quaerens intellectum*). Here theology is defined by its special source of knowledge, which is the light of faith illuminating reason. In other words, theology is the science of God (and of creatures in their relation to God) as known through the light of faith and reason.

St. Augustine beautifully explains the relation between reason and faith in theology: "Directing my course according to this rule of faith, insofar as I could, and insofar as You made it possible for me, I sought You, and desired to see with my understanding that which I believed, and I have argued and labored much."[10] St. Anselm is well known for continuing this Augustinian understanding of theology and expresses it in a prayer at the beginning of his *Proslogion*: "I yearn to understand some measure of Your truth, which my heart believes and loves. For I do not seek to understand in order to believe, but I believe in order to understand [*credo ut intellegam*]. For I believe even this: that unless I believe, I shall not understand."[11]

Theology can also be understood as the science of Revelation.[12] However, since Revelation is the self-manifestation of God, it is better to hold God, insofar as He can be known through faith and reason, to be the object of theology. The unity of theology can be seen better when it is defined as the science of God and of all other things in their relation to God. The unity of theology is less evident if it is defined as the science of Revelation. What gives unity to God's Revelation? Surely that unity comes from its source, which is God Himself.[13]

A quite different definition of theology is given by Bernard Lonergan, who defines it as that which "mediates between a cultural matrix and the significance and role of a religion in that matrix."[14] This allows

---

[10] St. Augustine, *De Trinitate* 15.28.51, trans. Stephen McKenna, in *The Trinity* (Washington, DC: The Catholic University of America Press, 1963), 523.

[11] St. Anselm, *Proslogion* 1, in *Complete Philosophical and Theological Treatises of Anselm of Canterbury*, trans. Jasper Hopkins and Herbert Richardson (Minneapolis: Arthur J. Banning Press, 2000), 93.

[12] See, for example, Aidan Nichols, *The Shape of Catholic Theology* (Collegeville: Liturgical Press, 1991), 32ff.

[13] See the following section on the unity of theology.

[14] *Method in Theology* (New York: Herder and Herder, 1972), xi.

for an extremely pluralist understanding of theology. Theology here is defined not by its object (God who reveals Himself), nor by its source or formal light (Revelation),[15] but through its social function of mediation. There is no doubt that this mediation is a very important purpose of theology. However, various problems result if theology is defined in this way. First, theology would lose its primary focus on God who reveals Himself—its formal object[16]—and would seem to focus on man's self-understanding in relation to his culture and religion. Secondly, it would lose its essential unity that comes from its formal object, for there could be many distinct kinds of mediations between a cultural matrix and religion. Third, the distinction between natural and supernatural theology would be blurred, for both could be understood as mediations between culture and religion. According to this kind of definition, Plato's philosophy or Kant's *Religion within the Boundaries of Mere Reason* would qualify as a theology in much the same way as Catholic theology. Similarly, faith would no longer be a prerequisite for doing theology, understood in this Lonerganian sense. In the Augustinian and Thomistic understanding, on the contrary, supernatural faith is a *sine qua non* for doing sacred theology; faith is its portal, for it alone provides access to God's Revelation. *Fides quaerens intellectum* begins with faith.[17]

The Unity of Theology

After determining that theology is indeed a scientific study of God who reveals Himself, the next question is whether it is one science or many. Is theology, like philosophy, a genus that comprises a collection of distinct theological sciences, or on the contrary, is it just

---

[15] The formal light of a science is the source or cause of all the knowledge of that science, that by which everything that is known in that science is grasped. The formal light of philosophy is the natural light of reason and our natural grasp of first principles. The formal light of theology is Revelation.

[16] See the following section for an explanation of this term.

[17] See the profound treatment of this point in Romano Guardini, "Holy Scripture and the Science of Faith," trans. Scott G. Hefelfinger, *Letter & Spirit* 6 (2010): 414–432, originally published as "Heilige Schrift und Glaubenswissenschaft," *Die Schildgenossen* 8 (1928): 24–57.

one science that has an all-embracing scope? St. Thomas continues to flesh out the notion of theology as a science by posing this question here (*ST* I, q. 1, a. 3). Philosophy, for example, in the view of Aristotle, is not a single science, but rather a collection of related sciences including metaphysics, logic, philosophy of nature, philosophy of man, ethics (general ethics and social ethics), philosophy of art, etc.[18] These philosophical sciences are distinct because they have different objects, although they all have in common a method of investigation by which they look for the most fundamental causes of their respective objects and, thus, are different species of the genus of philosophy. In the same way, empirical science does not comprise one science, but is divided into distinct sciences: physics, chemistry, biology, etc. There is one common genus, "empirical science," that comes from sharing an empirical methodology, but each particular empirical science is distinct by reason of its object. Is theology likewise a collection of distinct sciences treating distinct objects—such as God, man, morality, salvation history, Sacred Scripture, the Incarnation, the Church and her history and law, the sacraments, and the liturgy—unified by a common theological method?

Indeed, the fact that theology studies God, human nature, morality, creation, salvation history, and canon law, would seem to indicate that it cannot be one science, just as no one human science studies all of those objects. In the human sciences, God is studied by metaphysics (whose object is being as such), which is a science distinct from the philosophy of man, which is distinct from ethics, which is distinct from cosmology, which is distinct from history, which is distinct from jurisprudence.[19] Thus, theology seems to be a collection of several dis-

---

[18] See Jacques Maritain, *Introduction to Philosophy*, trans. E. I. Watkin (New York: Sheed & Ward, 1947), 271. For the relationship between the philosophical and the empirical sciences, see ibid., 111–123. Empirical sciences look for the empirical and mathematically generalizable causes of their object of study, whereas philosophical sciences look for the first and deepest causes of their object of study.

[19] St. Thomas gives two objections. Obj. 1 states that "It seems that sacred theology is not one science. For according to the Philosopher in book 1 of the *Posterior Analytics* [1.28], that science is one whose subject matter is one in genus. But the Creator and the creature, which are both treated in sacred theology, are not contained in one genus. Therefore sacred theology is not one science." Obj. 2 states that "Furthermore, sacred theology treats of angels, corporeal creatures,

tinct theological sciences, unified only by their common reference to God's Revelation.

St. Thomas, on the contrary, argues that it is properly one science, whose unity comes from having one *formal object*, which is God:

> I respond that sacred theology is one science. The unity of a faculty or habit should be considered according to its object, not considered in a material way, but according to the formal aspect of the object. For example, a man, an ass, and a stone all share in one formal aspect of being colored, which is the object of sight. Therefore, since sacred Scripture considers things insofar as they are divinely revealed, as has been said above, whatever has been divinely revealed shares in one formal aspect of the object of this science. And thus they are contained in sacred theology as in one science.

Formal and Material Objects

A brief digression may be helpful here to explain the difference between the formal and material objects of a science, faculty, or virtue. Every science has a certain unity and particular identity by which it is distinguished from other sciences. This unity comes from the focus on one general or universal object, in the light of which everything else is considered. This limitation of the focus of a particular science is called its *formal object*. Every science has its own formal object, which is that determined aspect of reality in reference to which everything else is understood within the science. For example, the formal object of ethics is morality, or the moral quality of human actions. The formal object of mathematics is quantity, or the *quantitative* aspect of reality. The formal object of physics is the motion of bodies.

In the course of its investigation, a science will touch on many diverse aspects of reality and a great number of individual things that it considers through its one formal object. This diversity and multiplic-

---

and human morality. But these pertain to different philosophical sciences. Therefore, sacred theology is not one science."

ity of individual things that it considers is referred to as the science's *material object*, which is broader than the formal object. This distinction between the formal and material object can be clearly seen in our sense faculties. The formal object of sight is color, but the material object of sight includes all sensible things that can be known through color. Likewise, the formal object of hearing is sound, whereas its material object includes all physical reality that produces sound. Among the sciences, biology provides a simple example of this distinction. The formal object of biology is living organisms. However, the material object of biology is broader, for it also includes everything that relates to living organisms, such as their environment, nourishment, and chemical components.

This distinction between the formal and material objects of a science also applies to Catholic theology. The formal object of theology is God insofar as He is known through Revelation and reason, but theology also considers all of creation insofar as it is created by God, governed through His providence, and called to return to Him in the sanctification of men and society. Thus, the material object of theology actually includes all of reality, which no other science can claim. Nevertheless, theology has a proper unity and identity that comes from the *limitation of its formal object to one reality*: God. Everything else that is considered in theology is considered in its relation to God and His Revelation.

In this way, St. Thomas answers the objection that we posed above. Although theology treats many different realities that are also studied by different human sciences, nevertheless, all those realities are treated in theology under the one formal aspect of their relation to God, who is the proper subject of sacred theology. Thus, in his response to the first objection, St. Thomas writes: "Sacred theology does not treat equally of God and of creatures, but principally of God, and of creatures only insofar as they are ordered to God as their source and end."

In reply to the second objection, which argues that there should be a multiplicity of theological sciences similar to the multiplicity of human sciences, St. Thomas makes an interesting argument by analogy. He lays down the general principle that the higher and more noble a faculty or science, the greater is its breadth and extension: "Nothing prevents inferior faculties and habits from being diversified by those matters that fall together under a superior faculty or habit, because the superior faculty or habit views the object under a more universal formal aspect."[20] Our higher faculties thus have a more universal formal object than our lower ones. Our external senses, for example, are diversified according to different kinds of sensible formal objects: color, sound, smell, taste, and texture. Each external sense perceives only its own proper sensible object. Our internal senses, such as imagination and memory, on the other hand, are higher and attain to the formal objects of all the external senses. Our one faculty of memory retains things seen, heard, felt, smelled, and tasted, and our imagination likewise represents them all. Our spiritual faculties of intellect and will are higher still, and attain to all the objects of our external and internal senses, as well as to realities that are immaterial and not sensible at all, such as justice, virtue, and God. Intellect and will are our most noble faculties because they are open to every being.

Applying this to the sciences, we see that the empirical sciences are necessarily particular in studying one type of reality alone and leaving out other aspects of being, since each science studies a particular class of sensible beings. Physics is limited to investigating the motion of inanimate bodies and cannot attain to souls and morality, etc. Mathematics has a broader scope but is limited to quantity and quantitative relations and thus can only describe the numerical values and relations of things. The philosophical sciences have a greater breadth, for they are not limited by empirical observation received by the five senses. They study different aspects of being and their primary cause insofar as they can be deduced from experience and first principles. However, since the different aspects of being studied by the philosophical sciences are formally distinct, the philosophical sciences are distinct from one another. For example, logic studies reasoning, ethics studies the moral act, philosophy of nature studies the change and movement of bodies, philosophical anthropology studies human

---

[20] *ST* I, q. 1, a. 3, ad 2.

nature, and metaphysics studies being as such—thus all of these are distinct sciences that study distinct formal objects.

Sacred theology, however, can have a greater breadth than any of the philosophical sciences, for its formal object is God, to whom all created things are ordered. St. Thomas writes:

> As the object of the interior unifying sense [*sensus communis*] extends to all that is sensible, including both the visible and the audible, the unifying sense is one faculty that extends to all the different objects of the five exterior senses. Similarly, sacred theology can consider under one aspect those realities that are treated in different philosophical sciences, and still remain one. In this way sacred theology bears the stamp, in a certain way, of the divine science, which is one and simple, although extending to all things.[21]

By ascending higher than any human science, theology maintains its unity without sacrificing sharpness of vision. Because it reaches up to the lofty perspective of God's own Revelation, taking in all things in their relation to God, it can study realities as diverse as God and man, angels and salvation history, and the moral law and man's final end without losing its unity and divine focus.

This thesis has very important pedagogical consequences for the study of theology. Since theology is one science, despite the diversity of matters treated, theologians should seek a global vision, rather than overspecialize in one area, for theological wisdom comes from knowing the whole and seeing everything in relation to the Triune God, in whose inner life man has been granted a glorious participation. The more global theological formation is, the more it is properly theological: seeing all things from the most elevated point of view possible—God's own perspective as He has revealed it to us. Not least of the merits of St. Thomas's *Summa* is the way it manifests the unity of theology, organically ordering the manifold theological questions

---

[21] Ibid.

like a Gothic cathedral[22] or a living organism. Another classic work showing the unity of theology is Matthias Scheeben's *The Mysteries of Christianity*.[23]

Many theologians have lamented that contemporary theology has lost its unity. Avery Cardinal Dulles, at the end of his life, wrote:

> Over the past fifty years we have all heard the repeated complaint, amounting sometimes to a lamentation, that theology has lost its unity. Like Humpty Dumpty it has suffered a great fall, and all the pope's theologians have not succeeded in putting it together again. Theology is splintered into subdisciplines that insist on their own autonomy without regard for one another. Biblical studies go in one direction, historical scholarship goes in another, ethics in a third, and spirituality in a fourth.
>
> In addition to this fragmentation of disciplines, there is a growing breach between past and present. The classic statements of the faith are studied historically, in relation to the circumstances in which they arose. If their contemporary relevance is not denied, they are reinterpreted for today in ways that preserve little if anything of their original content.[24]

The danger of the splintering and separation of the theological disciplines is especially acute in the historical-critical study of Sacred Scripture, which is often treated in practice as if it were an autonomous science distinct from systematic theology and moral theology. Benedict XVI has spoken strongly against this tendency to separate exegesis from systematic theology. In *Verbum Domini*, he writes:

---

[22] See Erwin Panofsky, *Gothic Architecture and Scholasticism: An Inquiry into the Analogy of the Arts, Philosophy, and Religion in the Middle Ages* (New York: New American Library, 1976).

[23] Matthias Joseph Scheeben, *The Mysteries of Christianity*, trans. Cyril Vollert, S.J. (St. Louis: B. Herder, 1946).

[24] Avery Cardinal Dulles, S.J., "Wisdom as the Source of Unity for Theology," in *Wisdom and Holiness, Science and Scholarship: Essays in Honor of Matthew L. Lamb*, ed. Michael Dauphinais and Matthew Levering (Naples: Sapientia Press, 2007), 59f, quoted in Reinhard Hütter, *Dust Bound for Heaven: Explorations in the Theology of Thomas Aquinas* (Grand Rapids: William B. Eerdmans Publishing, 2012), 314.

> Unfortunately, a sterile separation sometimes creates a barrier between exegesis and theology, and this "occurs even at the highest academic levels." . . . In a word, "where exegesis is not theology, Scripture cannot be the soul of theology, and conversely, where theology is not essentially the interpretation of the Church's Scripture, such a theology no longer has a foundation."[25]

The splintering of theological disciplines into separate sciences would deaden the splintered parts, for every branch of theology intrinsically needs the complementary insights of the other branches, analogously to a living body whose various organs form a living whole.

The glue that holds the different branches of theology together as one science is divine faith. If a part of theology, such as biblical exegesis or moral theology, were practiced in such a way that its methods and conclusions were considered to be neutral with regard to faith commitments, relying exclusively on the methodology of various human sciences, then those disciplines would splinter off and no longer be part of one theological science held together by faith in God's Revelation.[26]

Is Sacred Theology a Practical or a Theoretical Science?

Given that theology is one science and not a collection of sciences, we may ask whether it is a theoretical or a practical science. St. Thomas addresses this in *ST* I, q. 1, a. 4. This question does not come up in the same way for philosophy, since it is a collection of philosophical sciences that contains both kinds. For example, metaphysics and philosophy of nature are theoretical, whereas ethics and logic are practical.

---

[25] Pope Benedict XVI, Apostolic Exhortation On the Word of God in the Life and Mission of the Church *Verbum Domini* §35 (2010). That biblical exegesis is a part of sacred theology was also reaffirmed in the document of the PBC, *The Interpretation of the Bible in the Church* (1993).

[26] See Hütter, *Dust Bound for Heaven*, 313: "Renewal will have to come about by way of recovering theology's inner unity. And the latter requires nothing less than allowing theology's soul—supernatural, divine faith—to inform again the whole body of theology."

A theoretical (or speculative) science is one that is principally ordered to knowledge of truth for its own sake, purely for the love of that
truth, whereas a practical science is one that is ordered to operation,
for love of another end that can be attained from that knowledge. If
this operation involves the making or production of things, then the
science is called an *art*; if it is directed to acting well, it is called *ethics*.
Theoretical and practical sciences differ therefore in their end or purpose: to know the truth simply for love of that truth or to know the
truth for the love of an action or operation. Examples of theoretical
sciences are metaphysics, pure mathematics, and theoretical physics.
Examples of practical sciences are engineering, the fine arts, medicine, psychotherapy, ethics, political science, economics, and spiritual direction. Theoretical sciences are higher than practical sciences
and have a certain priority, for they provide practical sciences with
their principles and ends. One must first know the truth about reality
and about one's nature and end before one can effectively determine
one's operation, for operation follows on being (*operatio sequitur esse*).

Where does theology fall? It has characteristics of both types. On
the one hand, theology is eminently practical because it is ordered
to action and teaches the pathway to heaven.[27] Indeed, Revelation is
largely concerned with the moral law. On the other hand, theology is
a theoretical science, for it provides knowledge of the highest truths
(the Trinity, the Incarnation, etc.) for love of those truths. Furthermore, its object is God, and God is not something that we produce
through our operations as an artifact or moral act, but a Person whom
we know and love. Therefore, although theology is both theoretical
and practical, it is principally theoretical. St. Thomas writes:

> On the contrary, every practical science is concerned with
> things that can be made by man, as ethics is concerned with
> human acts, and architecture with buildings. But sacred the-
> ology is principally about God, whose work man is, and not

---

[27] See *ST* I, q. 1, a. 4, obj. 1: "It seems that sacred theology is a practical science. For the end of practical science is operation, according to the Philosopher in book 2 of the *Metaphysics*. But sacred
theology is ordered to operation, according to James [1:22]: 'Be doers of the word, and not just
listeners.'"

vice versa. Therefore it is not a practical science, but rather a theoretical one.

I answer that sacred theology, while extending to things that pertain to different philosophical sciences, remains one, as was said above, on account of a common formal aspect that it considers in these different things, namely, that they are knowable by the divine light. Therefore, although philosophical sciences are divided into some that are theoretical and others that are practical, sacred theology includes both within itself, just as God both knows Himself and the things that He makes through one and the same science. However, it is more theoretical than practical, because it is more principally concerned with divine things than with human acts. The latter are treated insofar as through them man is ordered to a perfect knowledge of God in which eternal beatitude consists.[28]

Theology is unique in being simultaneously *theoretical and practical*. Indeed, it is both *more theoretical than any other science*, for it studies the First Truth in the light of His self-revelation, *and more practical than any other* because it lays out the way to man's supernatural final end. Study of the Triune God, the Incarnation, and salvation history is principally theoretical, for these truths are contemplated and loved now, as in eternity, simply because they are true, good, and beautiful, the summit and source of all truth and beauty. Nevertheless, every theological truth has immense practical implications, for the Trinity is the exemplar for the spiritual life. Prominent among the truths revealed by God is the truth concerning how one ought to live rightly and order human actions so as to merit heaven and glorify God, giving Him fitting worship. This is the practical aspect of theology that is studied in moral, spiritual, sacramental, and liturgical theology. Indeed, moral theology is the most practical of all sciences, for it is the most useful in teaching man how to arrive at his final end.

---

[28] *ST* I, q. 1, a. 4.

Because theology is both theoretical and practical, the theologian must be exemplary not only in clarity of thought, but also in the purity of his moral life. St. Thomas explains this in his commentary on the Letter to the Hebrews:

> Perfection is twofold: one is perfection according to the intellect, when someone has that judgment of intellect to discern and judge rightly about those things which are proposed to him; the other is perfection according to the affection that charity makes, which is when someone adheres totally to God.... For the doctrine of Sacred Scripture has this, that in it are not things only to be pondered, as in geometry, but also to be approved through the affection. Hence Matt 5:19: "But he that shall do and teach," etc. Therefore, in other sciences it suffices that a man be perfect according to his understanding, but in these it is required that he be perfect according to understanding and affection.[29]

Is Theology the Most Noble of the Sciences?

St. Thomas continues his introduction to theology (*ST* I, q. 1, a. 5) by asking whether it is the most noble of the sciences. This question is important also on account of its social consequences, for the noblest science ought to be promoted by society. Of course, Aquinas's answer is affirmative, and it follows from the preceding article (4), in which we have seen that theology is both the most practical and most theoretical of sciences. In the thirteenth century the supreme nobility of theology would have been a shared conviction governing the life of the university, but in the last three centuries this thesis has become less and less evident, and perhaps even laughable to many.

The first objection proposed by St. Thomas is based on the principle that the dignity of a science depends on its degree of certainty. But sacred theology is a science based on faith in God's Revelation, and

---

[29] *Commentary on the Epistle to the Hebrews*, ch. 5, lec. 2 (Marietti no. 273), trans. Chrysostom Baer (South Bend: St. Augustine's Press, 2006), 120.

the articles of faith can be, and are, doubted by all unbelievers. Thus it would seem that a science based on faith is not the most certain, but the most dubious.[30] This kind of objection took on great force beginning in the Enlightenment. A methodology of universal doubt, such as that used by Descartes and his followers, contributed to the growth of the persuasive power of this objection, giving rise to diverse rationalistic systems. Forms of rationalism, if they acknowledge theology's right to exist at all, deny its nobility and place it below the empirical sciences and philosophy precisely because theology is based on faith and not on self-evident principles known by reason.

The most extreme form of rationalism denies the validity of any knowledge based on faith, rejecting the existence of supernatural mysteries, the infallible authority of the Magisterium, and the inspiration of the Bible. A more moderate type of rationalism may profess allegiance to some revealed religion, but maintain the supremacy of human reason with respect to faith, and of philosophy and natural science with respect to sacred theology. This generally involves the claim that faith and Revelation teach the same moral truths as philosophy, but in a way that is symbolic and better suited to the masses, dressing truths up in mythical images or "picture-thinking."[31] Faith would be a type of knowledge that is suited to the uncultured and to a more primitive state of mankind. It is acknowledged as contributing ethical insights that were not yet philosophically or scientifically formulated. However, mankind that has come of age no longer has need of faith, which should be replaced by philosophy or science.

---

[30] *ST* I, q. 1, a. 5, obj. 1: "It seems that sacred theology is not more noble than other sciences. For certainty pertains to the dignity of a science. But other sciences, whose principles cannot be doubted, seem to be more certain than sacred theology, whose principles, such as the articles of faith, can be doubted. Therefore other sciences seem to be more noble than this."

[31] Georg Hegel, *Phenomenology of Spirit*, no. 788, trans. A. V. Miller (Oxford, UK: Oxford University Press, 1977), 479. Bultmann gives a good description of this position in *New Testament and Mythology and Other Basic Writings*, ed. and trans. by Schubert Ogden (Philadelphia: Fortress Press, 1984), 22: "Theology would be the predecessor of philosophy—something that can certainly be understood as a matter of intellectual history—which, having been surpassed by philosophy, is now only its unnecessary and tiresome competitor."

This moderate rationalist position was defended by the Muslim philosopher Averroes (1126–1198) in the twelfth century. An opposite reaction, fideism,[32] resulted in the Muslim world, rejecting the use of philosophy in the service of the faith, and philosophy never recovered its prestige there. Rationalist positions were defended later in the West by Spinoza (1632–1677), Kant (1724–1804),[33] and Hegel (1770–1831), who all held the supremacy of philosophy over religion (whether Judaism or Christianity).[34] The French philosopher Auguste Comte (1798–1857) held a somewhat more extreme rationalist position, putting theology at the most primitive historical stage of mankind's knowledge. The second, intermediate stage would be metaphysics (philosophy). However, the mature age of mankind recognizes the supremacy of the empirical sciences, which ought to replace both metaphysics and theology.

Such rationalist positions are only possible given the premise that God has not revealed Himself to mankind with a Revelation that transcends the power of reason. Rationalism presupposes *naturalism*, which is the *a priori* exclusion of the supernatural dimension.

In order to resolve this question about the place of theology among the sciences, one must clarify in what way one science should be regarded as higher than another. Since theology is both a theo-

---

[32] Fideism is the position that discounts the exercise of reason in religious matters, seeking to proceed by faith alone. It can be manifested in various forms, such as opposition to the use of metaphysics in theology or lack of interest in the naturally known truths that serve as preambles of faith.

[33] See Immanuel Kant, *Religion within the Boundaries of Mere Reason and Other Writings*, trans. Allen Wood and George Di Giovanni (Cambridge, UK: Cambridge University Press, 1998; originally published 1793).

[34] Hegel saw both religion and philosophy as stages in the development of the self-consciousness of absolute Spirit. However, he conceived religion as a way of communicating through pictorial language and metaphor, rather than through concepts and reasoning. Religion thus ought to progressively cede its place to philosophy as the more complete expression of self-consciousness; see, for example, *Phenomenology of Spirit*, no. 788: "The Spirit of the revealed religion has not yet surmounted its consciousness as such, or what is the same, its actual self-consciousness is not the object of its consciousness; Spirit itself as a whole, and the self-differentiated moments within it, fall within the sphere of picture-thinking and in the form of objectivity. The *content* of this picture-thinking is absolute Spirit; and all that now remains to be done is to supersede this mere form, or rather, since this belongs to *consciousness as such*, its truth must already have yielded itself in the shape of consciousness" (Miller, 479).

retical and a practical science, we must examine its nobility in both regards. Here (*ST* I, q. 1, a. 5), St. Thomas observes that the measure of nobility for a theoretical science depends on two factors: the dignity of its subject matter and its degree of certitude.[35] For example, mathematics excels in its degree of certitude but falls short in the dignity of its subject matter, which is only quantity. Biology is less noble in its certitude, but more noble in its subject matter. Theology, however, has God Himself as its object, and everything else insofar as it relates to Him. Thus it has the highest possible subject matter, including mysteries completely unknowable to other sciences, such as the inner life of the Triune God. With regard to its certitude, theology is based on the omniscience of God expressed in His Revelation, whereas other sciences have only the light of human reason, which can err. If Revelation is truly the Word of God, who can neither deceive nor be deceived, then the science based on Revelation will be the most certain of all sciences, at least in its revealed principles. Theology is therefore the most noble of theoretical sciences both as regards the nobility of its subject matter and the certainty of its principal teachings.[36]

Practical sciences are more noble to the degree that they aim at a higher end. The highest practical science would be the one that leads to the attainment of the ultimate end. This is the case of theology,

---

[35] *ST* I, q. 1, a. 5: "I answer that this science, which is theoretical in one respect and practical in another, transcends all others, whether theoretical or practical. One theoretical science is said to be nobler than another, on account both of its certainty and of the dignity of its subject matter. In both regards this science surpasses other theoretical sciences. With regard to its certainty because other sciences draw their certainty from the natural light of human reason which can err, whereas this science has its certainty from the light of the divine science, which cannot be deceived. According to the dignity of its subject matter, because this science is principally about things that transcend reason on account of their loftiness, whereas other sciences only treat what is accessible to reason. With regard to practical sciences, one is nobler than another if it attains to a higher end, as political science is higher than military science, for the good of the army is ordered to the good of civil society. Now the end of this doctrine, insofar as it is practical, is eternal beatitude, which is the final end to which all the other ends of the practical sciences are ultimately ordered. Therefore it is manifest that in all respects this science is nobler than others."

[36] As will be seen in the discussion of infallibility below, this maximum certainty is by no means contained in all the conclusions of theology, but only in those directly revealed by God or necessarily connected to that Revelation and guaranteed as such by the Church's infallible teaching office.

which shows us the way to eternal life—our supernatural final end. Other practical sciences, such as medicine and engineering, aim directly at intermediate and natural ends (health, material goods, etc.), not at the final supernatural end.

In his response to the first objection in article 5,[37] St. Thomas concedes that theology is not the most indubitable science, but this does not prevent it from being the most certain. Theology is not indubitable because the articles of faith are not directly seen by the human mind except through the beatific vision. Here St. Thomas brings in a helpful distinction made by Aristotle in book II of the *Metaphysics*. The articles of faith are not seen directly by the mind not because they are not manifest *in themselves*, but because they are not manifest *to us*, on account of the weakness of the human mind, which is likened to the eyes of a bat:

> Nothing prohibits something from being more certain according to nature, while being less certain with regard to us, on account of the weakness of our intellect, which is to the most manifest things of nature as the eye of a bat is to the light of the sun, as is said in book II of the *Metaphysics*.[38] Thus the doubt which some hold about the articles of faith is not on account of the uncertainty of the truths themselves, but on account of the weakness of the human intellect. And yet the least knowledge that can be had of the highest things is more desirable than the most certain knowledge that can be had of the least of things, as is said in book XI of *On Animals*.[39]

St. Thomas is admitting here that the mode of knowing of theology based on faith is inferior to the mode of human theoretical sciences that are not based on faith. For it is a higher mode of knowing to see a truth directly in itself than it is to hold a truth on the witness of

---

[37] Ibid., ad 1.

[38] Aristotle, *Metaphysics* 2.1.993b8–11 (Ross, *Basic Works of Aristotle*, 712).

[39] The reference is to Aristotle, *Parts of Animals* 1.5.644b25–645a1 (Ross, *Basic Works of Aristotle*, 656).

another. However, this inferiority of the mode of theology is super-abundantly compensated for in two ways. First, knowledge through faith enables theology to have access to God's own knowledge of Himself. And even a little access to God's own knowledge of Himself is immensely more satisfying than the most perfect knowledge of some limited aspects of creatures. For, in knowing any creature, the mind cannot help but desire to know adequately its first causes, which requires the knowledge of God and His purpose in creating, which are known through faith. Secondly, the imperfect mode of knowing through faith enables theology to surpass all human sciences even with regard to certainty. Though the truth of an article of faith is not seen in itself so as to render it psychologically indubitable, its truth is rendered most certain to the eyes of faith through the testimony of God as manifested through the Church's definitive teaching office and through the power of the supernatural virtue of faith, which is a gift from God.

In his response to the second objection in this article, St. Thomas addresses the relation of sacred theology to the human sciences whose aid it employs. The objection is that, if theology makes use of the human sciences—such as metaphysics, logic, history, and philology—in its work, it must depend on those human sciences, for the recipient depends on the supplier. Thus, theology is not the highest science.[40]

St. Thomas responds by pointing out that one science can use another in two ways: as a subordinate science uses a superior, or the reverse. In the former case, a subordinate science uses the conclusions of another as its own principles. In the latter case, a higher science uses the conclusions of another not to supply its own principles, but as an instrument for the sake of a greater manifestation of its own principles. This second way is the relation of theology to the human sciences. St. Thomas writes:

---

[40] *ST* I, q. 1, a. 5, obj. 2: "It belongs to an inferior science to receive from a superior one, as the musician receives from the mathematician. But sacred theology receives something from the philosophical disciplines.... Therefore, sacred theology is inferior to the other sciences."

This science can receive something from the philosophical disciplines, not because it stands in need of it by some necessity, but for the sake of a greater elucidation of what is passed on in this science. For it does not receive its principles from other sciences, but immediately from God by revelation. And thus it does not receive from other sciences as from superiors, but uses them as inferiors and handmaidens, as architectural sciences use others that supply their materials, and as political science uses military science.[41]

Why does theology need to use the human sciences at all? Some would like to strip theology of all use of philosophy, as if philosophy were water diluting and denaturing the wine of theology. As noted above, this anti-philosophical position is called fideism. St. Thomas explains that theology needs the aid of philosophy and the other human sciences not to receive principles from them, but because theology must always make use of *analogy* to understand what God has revealed:

That it uses them is not on account of its own defect or insufficiency, but on account of the defect of our intellect, which is more easily led to those things that transcend reason, that are treated in this science, through things known by natural reason, from which the other sciences proceed.[42]

Because Revelation transmits supernatural truths that exceed human experience, theology must labor to render them more intelligible through the analogy of natural things that are accessible to human experience, and which are treated in the human sciences. This use of analogy is constantly evident in Revelation itself. Christ and the prophets make frequent use of parables and metaphors for this purpose of elucidating supernatural truths by means of natural ones. Theology, therefore, must make use of philosophy to provide the best presentation of

---

[41] Ibid., ad 2.
[42] Ibid.

these natural truths. It especially uses metaphysics, but also the other philosophical sciences, such as logic, ethics, and the philosophy of man, as well as other human sciences such as history, rhetoric, philology, and, to a lesser degree, the empirical sciences. However, this does not mean that theology is subordinated to the human sciences, for theology makes use of them as an architect makes use of bricklayers and carpenters. Theology uses philosophy or history as a handmaid or servant.

However, in order for philosophy and the human sciences to be an adequate instrument to aid theology, the philosophy or science must be true and valid in its own order. A false or deficient philosophy would be a source of error and heresy. What is received from the philosophers must always be critically judged, case by case, according to its compatibility with faith, under the guidance of the Church's Magisterium. Only a true and adequate philosophy can serve theology as its handmaid.

The certitude of theology's conclusions does not come from philosophy, but rather from Revelation itself. We are certain that God is triune, for example, because the Church has defined that this is a truth revealed by God, not on account of any analogy that theology may receive from philosophy. Certitude in theology comes from faith in God's Revelation that comes to us through the Church. Nevertheless, theology needs the aid of philosophy in order to understand this Revelation, penetrate it more fully by means of analogy, and properly communicate what is believed.

Is Theology Wisdom?

One might think that, since we have shown that theology is a science, it could not also be wisdom, for science and wisdom appear to be different intellectual virtues. Indeed, many who are excellent in the sciences do not seem to be wise, and vice versa. St. Thomas, however, holds that, precisely because sacred theology is the noblest science, it is also supernatural wisdom.

Wisdom is generally understood to be the highest kind of knowledge by which one can rightly judge and order all things. Aristotle shows that this knowledge must be of the first and ultimate causes of all being, for only in the light of God (who is both the First Cause and Final End) can one rightly judge and order all things.[43] Wisdom seeks the ground and foundation of all that we encounter in human experience. On the natural level, this highest science—natural wisdom—is called metaphysics. Metaphysics is the science that studies being as being and the properties and first causes of all beings. Metaphysics alone of the human sciences can show the existence and attributes of God. Nevertheless, metaphysics is limited to what reason alone can know of God as the First Cause and Final End of all things. Natural theology is a part of metaphysics.

Sacred theology is a *supernatural* or *revealed* wisdom that penetrates more profoundly into the First Cause and Final End. It is a much higher wisdom than metaphysics, for it knows mysteries concerning God and His salvific will for mankind that reason alone could never grasp. Thus, sacred theology knows far more about God than the greatest minds, such as Plato or Aristotle, could know through metaphysics. In the light of divine Revelation, it can also judge and order all things more profoundly. As St. Thomas wrote in his commentary on the Apostles' Creed: "Before the coming of Christ, none of the philosophers was able, however great his effort, to know as much about God or about the means necessary for obtaining eternal life as any old woman knows by faith since Christ came down upon earth."[44] Our knowledge of the catechism gives us a wisdom immeasurably greater than that of Aristotle, and which he doubtless would have valued more than all his philosophy if he had but known that gift of God. Aristotle knew that the end of man must lie in a contemplation of God, but he could not know that it is a supernatural contemplation face to face for all eternity, which we attain by knowing God, loving Him, and serving Him on this earth through His grace.

---

[43] Aristotle, *Metaphysics* 1.1–2.

[44] *The Aquinas Catechism: A Simple Explanation of the Catholic Faith by the Church's Greatest Theologian* (Manchester: Sophia Institute Press, 2000), 6.

At the beginning of his earliest major work, his commentary on the *Sentences*, St. Thomas distinguishes the supernatural wisdom that is sacred theology from the natural wisdom that is the philosophical science of metaphysics. This clear distinction between these two orders of knowledge is one of his most important contributions, and it is interesting to see it present right from the beginning of his teaching. He writes:

> Theology is wisdom insofar as it considers the highest causes. . . . It is said to be wisdom more so than metaphysics, for it considers the highest causes according to the mode of the causes themselves, since it is accepted immediately from God through revelation. Metaphysics, on the other hand, considers the highest causes from viewpoints taken from the realm of creatures. Hence, this doctrine [theology] is said to be more divine than metaphysics, for it is divine in respect to the subject and the approach, whereas metaphysics is divine only in respect to the subject.[45]

Metaphysics or natural theology can be said to be divine because it studies God as First Cause, but sacred theology can be said to be a science doubly divine, for it studies God through God's own Revelation.

St. Thomas returns to this theme in the next article (6), in which he asks whether sacred theology qualifies as wisdom. In support of the identification of wisdom and theology, he cites Deuteronomy 4:6, in which God says of His Revelation in the Torah: "That will be your wisdom and your understanding in the sight of the peoples." Aquinas then explains that all wisdom enables the wise man to order and judge things, but there are also grades of wisdom, according to the height and universality of the principles by which one judges and orders. Both metaphysics and sacred theology judge all things in the light of God. However, metaphysics knows God only as First Cause and Final

---

[45] St. Thomas, *Scriptum super Sententiis* bk. 1, prologue, a. 3, solution 1 (my translation from the Latin text at http://www.corpusthomisticum.org/snp0001.html).

End, whereas sacred theology knows God in a far higher way through Revelation. Thus it can judge and order all things according to God in a far more perfect way than metaphysics. St. Thomas writes:

> This doctrine is most especially wisdom among all forms of human wisdom, and not just in any one order, but absolutely. Since it belongs to the wise man to order and judge, and since judgment of a lower matter is taken from a higher cause, he who considers the highest cause in any order is said to be wise in that order. Thus, in the order of building, the one who determines the form of the house is said to be wise and an architect with respect to inferior artisans who trim the wood and prepare the stones. Thus, in 1 Corinthians [3:10] it is said: "As a wise architect I have laid the foundations." Again, in the whole order of human life, the prudent person is said to be wise insofar as he orders human acts to their due end. Thus, in Proverbs [10:23] it is said that "wisdom is prudence for a man." Therefore, he who considers absolutely the highest cause of the entire universe, which is God, is said to be supremely wise. Thus, wisdom is said to be knowledge of divine things, as is clear from St. Augustine's *De Trinitate* [12.14]. Now, sacred theology most properly considers God insofar as He is the highest cause, because it considers Him not only insofar as He can be known through creatures . . . but also with regard to what He alone knows about Himself and has communicated to others through revelation. Thus, sacred theology is especially called wisdom.[46]

St. Thomas has some good objections to the identification of theology with wisdom. The first objection protests that "no doctrine that borrows its principles from another is worthy of the name of wisdom, for it belongs to the wise man to order and not to be ordered [Aristotle, *Metaphysics* 1.2]. But this doctrine borrows its principles from another, as is clear from what has been said. Therefore this doctrine is not

---

[46] *ST* I, q. 1, a. 6.

wisdom."[47] In other words, it seems that the science of faith is not wisdom because it does not *see* what it holds, but goes by the authority of another. This would be a valid objection for a merely human science. No subordinate or practical human science, such as engineering or medicine, has the dignity of wisdom, for such sciences are governed by the higher sciences from which they receive their principles. However, theology receives its principles directly from God, the author of every order. As St. Thomas replies, "Sacred doctrine derives its principles not from any human knowledge, but from the divine knowledge, through which, as through the highest wisdom, all our knowledge is set in order."[48]

Another objection denies that theology is wisdom because it is acquired by laborious study.[49] Scripture, however, speaks of a wisdom from above not acquired by study, but infused directly by God.[50] Indeed, we see that many canonized saints had great wisdom without having ever formally studied sacred theology.

This objection is answered by distinguishing three levels of wisdom: metaphysics, sacred theology, and the highest gift of the Holy Spirit, referred to as wisdom in Isaiah 11:2. Metaphysics and sacred theology are levels of wisdom acquired by study. The gift of the Holy Spirit, on the other hand, is an ability to judge all things in the light of God that works not through learning, but through the force of the person's inclination of love for God. Supernatural charity establishes friendship with God. Since the friend is like another self, all true friendship gives one a connatural knowledge of the interior dispositions of the friend and enables one to see the world through the eyes of the friend. Supernatural charity, therefore, confers on the one who loves God an ability to see the world, as it were, through the eyes of the Beloved. Charity thus gives us a connaturality with God, through

---

[47] Ibid., obj. 1.

[48] Ibid., ad 1.

[49] Ibid., obj. 3: "Furthermore, this doctrine is acquired by study. But wisdom is received by infusion, for it is numbered among the seven gifts of the Holy Spirit, as is clear from Isaiah 11. Therefore this doctrine is not wisdom."

[50] See James 1:5 and 3:17.

which the gift of wisdom can more deeply grasp the Divine plan.[51] The greater our charity and union with God, the better we are able to judge according to the mind of God.

The science of theology is not enough to attain the heights of supernatural wisdom. The gift of wisdom is the highest of the gifts of the Holy Spirit and gives a quasi-experiential knowledge of divine things through the perfection of charity.[52] Theologians are called to elevate their knowledge through the gift of wisdom. The greatness of St. Thomas Aquinas and the other Doctors of the Church is that they *combined to an eminent degree all three types of wisdom*: metaphysics, theology, and the gift of the Holy Spirit.[53]

---

[51] See *ST* II-II, q. 45, a. 2: "Wisdom denotes a certain rectitude of judgment according to the divine ideas. This rectitude of judgment can occur in two ways. One is according to the perfect use of reason, and the other is according to a certain connaturality with the matter that is to be judged. In matters of chastity, for example, one who has learned moral theology will judge properly through the investigation of reason, whereas one who has the habit of chastity will judge properly by virtue of a certain connaturality. In like manner, with regard to divine realities, a right judgment coming from the investigation of reason pertains to wisdom understood as an intellectual virtue. But to have a right judgment about them from a certain connaturality belongs to wisdom insofar as it is a gift of the Holy Spirit, as Dionysius says in the second chapter of the *Divine Names* (lect. 4), that 'Hierotheus is perfect in divine things, for he is taught not merely by learning, but by experiencing divine things.' This sympathy or connaturality for divine things is the result of charity, which unites us to God, according to 1 Corinthians 6:17: 'He who is joined to the Lord, is one spirit.' Consequently wisdom which is a gift, has its cause in the will, through charity, but it has its essence in the intellect, whose act is to judge rightly."

[52] See *ST* I, q. 1, a. 6, ad 3: "Since judgment pertains to wisdom, wisdom can be taken in two ways according to two modes of judgment. One can judge another in one way by mode of inclination, as he who has the habit of virtue rightly judges about virtuous actions insofar as he is inclined to them. Thus it is said in the tenth book of the *Ethics* that the virtuous person is the measure and rule of human acts. Another way is by mode of knowledge, as when someone who is instructed in moral science can judge of virtuous acts, even if he does not have virtue. The first way of judging divine things pertains to the wisdom that is counted as a gift of the Holy Spirit, according to 1 Corinthians [2:15]: 'The spiritual man judges all things.' And Dionysius says, in chapter 2 of the *Divine Names*, 'Hierotheus is taught not merely by learning, but by experiencing divine things.' The second mode of judging pertains to this doctrine, insofar as it is obtained by study, even though its principles are received by revelation."

[53] See Pope St John Paul II, Encyclical Letter on Faith and Reason *Fides et ratio* §44: "Another of the great insights of Saint Thomas was his perception of the role of the Holy Spirit in the process by which knowledge matures into wisdom. From the first pages of his *Summa Theologiae*, Aquinas was keen to show the primacy of the wisdom which is the gift of the Holy Spirit and which opens the way to a knowledge of divine realities. His theology allows us to understand what is distinctive of wisdom in its close link with faith and knowledge of the divine. This wisdom comes to know by way of connaturality; it presupposes faith and eventually formulates its right judgment

In the beginning of his earlier great systematic work, the *Summa contra gentiles*, St. Thomas praises sacred theology, or supernatural wisdom, as follows:

> Among all human pursuits, the pursuit of wisdom is the most perfect, noble, useful, and full of joy. It is most perfect because, insofar as a man gives himself to the pursuit of wisdom, to that extent does he even now have some share in true beatitude. And so the wise man has said: "Blessed is the man that shall continue in wisdom" (Sir 14:22).[54] It is most noble because, through this pursuit, man especially approaches to a likeness to God, Who "made all things in wisdom" (Ps 103:24). And since likeness is the cause of love, the pursuit of wisdom especially joins man to God in friendship. That is why it is said of wisdom that "she is an infinite treasure to men, by which they that use her become the friends of God" (Wis 7:14). It is most useful because through wisdom we arrive at the kingdom of immortality. For "the desire of wisdom brings one to the everlasting kingdom" (Wis 6:21). It is most full of joy because "her conversation has no bitterness, nor her company any tediousness, but joy and gladness" (Wis 7:16).[55]

This praise of wisdom belongs to all three levels of wisdom, which ought to grow together.

Theology and Prayer

In order to illuminate divine things, the theologian must first taste them through intimate contemplation. St. Thomas states this in his

---

on the basis of the truth of faith itself. . . . Yet the priority accorded this wisdom does not lead the Angelic Doctor to overlook the presence of two other complementary forms of wisdom—*philosophical wisdom*, which is based upon the capacity of the intellect, for all its natural limitations, to explore reality, and *theological wisdom*, which is based upon Revelation and which explores the contents of faith, entering the very mystery of God."

[54] Douay-Rheims version.

[55] *SCG*, bk. 1, ch. 2 (no. 1; Pegis, 1:61–62). I have slightly modified the translation.

Commentary on Psalm 33:9 (Vulgate), "O taste and see that the Lord is good":

⌈In material things we see first, and then we taste. But in spiritual things we taste first so that we can see, because no one knows who does not taste. And thus he says first taste, and then see.[56]⌋

Obviously, Thomas was writing from the depths of personal experience. Similarly, we see his life of prayer in the following text from his commentary on Dionysius's *Divine Names*:

⌈We should understand divine things according to this union of grace. It is not as if we draw divine things down to the level of the things of our experience, but rather that we are drawn out of ourselves and placed in God, so that by this union we are totally deified.[57]⌋

St. Thomas's early biographers give a marvelous description of St. Thomas's life of prayer. Bernard of Guy writes:

In Thomas the habit of prayer was extraordinarily developed; he seemed to be able to raise his mind to God as if the body's burden did not exist for him. He had a particular devotion to the Sacrament of the Altar; and no doubt the special profundity of his writings on this subject was due to the same grace which enabled him to say Mass so devoutly. This he did every day, unless prevented by sickness; after which he

---

[56] St. Thomas, *In psalmos Davidis expositio*, commentary on Ps 33 (Marietti no. 9): "In corporalibus namque prius videtur, et postea gustatur; sed in rebus spiritualibus prius gustatur, postea autem videtur; quia nullus cognoscit qui non gustat; et ideo dicit prius, gustate, et postea, videte"(http://www.corpusthomisticum.org/cps31.html). Ps 33:9 in the Vulgate corresponds to Ps 34:8 in the *RSV*; for the Latin of the Vulgate, see *Bibliorum Sacrorum: Nova Vulgata* (Vatican City: Libreria Editrice Vaticana, 1986).

[57] St. Thomas, *In librum beati Dionysii De Divinis nominibus expositio* ch. 7, lec. 1, ed. Ceslas Pera, O.P. (Turin: Marietti, 1950).

would hear, and usually also serve, another Mass said by his socius or some other priest. . . . While saying Mass he was utterly absorbed by the mystery, and his face ran with tears. At night, when our nature demands repose, he would rise, after a short sleep, and pray, lying prostrate on the ground; it was in those nights of prayer that he learned what he would write or dictate in the daytime. . . . He never set himself to study or argue a point, or lecture or write or dictate without first having recourse inwardly—but with tears—to prayer for the understanding and the words required by the subject. When perplexed by a difficulty he would kneel and pray and then, on returning to his writing or dictation, he was accustomed to find that his thought had become so clear that it seemed to show him inwardly, as in a book, the words he needed. All this is confirmed by his own statement to brother Reginald that prayer and the help of God had been of greater service to him in the search for truth than his natural intelligence and habit of study.[58]

In his continual recourse to prayer in the doing of theology, St. Thomas is a magnificent model for the theologian. The CDF's Instruction on the Ecclesial Vocation of the Theologian, *Donum veritatis* §8, stresses that "the theologian is called to deepen his own life of faith and continuously unite his scientific research with prayer. In this way he will become more open to the 'supernatural sense of faith' upon which he depends." Theology depends on prayer because it depends on living faith to grasp and penetrate its object, which is divine Revelation. Romano Guardini beautifully expresses this dependence of theology on living faith:

When Thomas Aquinas states that he carried out his *Summa theologiae* on his knees, it is not a pious remark but rather a methodological principle valid for every genuine theolo-

---

[58] Bernard Guy, *Historia ecclesiastica*, ch. 15, in Kenelm Foster, *The Life of Saint Thomas Aquinas: Biographical Documents* (Baltimore: Helicon Press, 1959), 36–37.

gy. It indicates not only that a theologian must be pious and ask for God's assistance; all of this would only have personal consequences. Even more so, it means that the living act of faith and its concrete activity, in prayer and Christian deeds, are together the methodological foundation of theological thought—just as the perception of a work of art is the basis for every possible aesthetic science. It is not at all accidental that the truly great theologians were saints—men of prayer.[59]

Study Questions

1. Is Catholic theology a science? Explain. If theology is a science, does it have self-evident principles on which it is based?
2. Is theology subordinated to any other science?
3. What is the subject of sacred theology? Explain.
4. Is sacred theology one science, or a collection of distinct theological sciences? Explain your answer. What accounts for the unity of theology?
5. Is sacred theology a practical or a theoretical science? Why?
6. Is theology the most noble of the sciences? Why?
7. What is rationalism, and how does it conceive the relationship between theology and the empirical and philosophical sciences? What is fideism?
8. Since theology makes use of human sciences such as philosophy and history, does this make it subordinate to them? Explain.
9. Is sacred theology wisdom? Explain the three levels of wisdom.
10. What is the relationship between sacred theology and metaphysics?
11. Is there a relationship between theology and prayer?

---

[59] Guardini, "Holy Scripture," 422.

Suggestions for Further Reading

Summa theologiae I, q. 1, aa. 2–7.

Pope St. John Paul II. Encyclical Letter on the Relationship between Faith and Reason *Fides et ratio* §§36–48. September 14, 1998.

Dulles, Avery Cardinal, S.J. "Wisdom as the Source of Unity for Theology." In *Wisdom and Holiness, Science and Scholarship: Essays in Honor of Matthew L. Lamb*, 59–71. Edited by Michael Dauphinais and Matthew Levering. Naples: Sapientia Press, 2007.

CHAPTER SIX

Theological Method

If theology is indeed a science, it must have its own methods of demonstration by which the science develops and grows in its penetration of the faith. As Aristotle observed, every field of inquiry should use a method proper to it and it is the mark of a fool to try to use the method of one field to understand a different field.[1] Thus, empirical methods are not appropriate for studying God and His Revelation, for God cannot be observed or be subject to experiment, but must be sought as the hidden first cause of all things. Philosophical rather than empirical methods are needed to demonstrate God's existence and attributes. And a method combining faith and philosophical reason is necessary to penetrate into God's Revelation. For, theology is a science based on faith in God's Revelation, but it must also use reason in order to think about what God has revealed. Theology, therefore, must have a method proper to it, different both from the empirical sciences and from philosophy.

Many people, Christians and non-Christians, might think that theology does not use rigorous or demonstrative arguments because it is based on the authority of Revelation and not on philosophical

---

[1] See Aristotle, *Nichomachean Ethics* 1.3.1094b12–29, trans. W. D. Ross, in *The Basic Works of Aristotle* (New York: Modern Library, 2001).

reasoning. This attitude is often referred to as "fideism." St. Thomas provides this as one of the possible (mistaken) objections:

> It seems this doctrine does not involve argumentation. For Ambrose says in book 1 of *De Fide*, "Put aside arguments when you are seeking faith." But in this doctrine faith is principally sought, for which reason it is said in John [20:31]: "These things are written that you may believe." Therefore sacred doctrine does not involve argumentation.[2]

⌈But if sacred theology had no place for reasoned argumentation, then it would not be a science, for all sciences develop by some kind of reasoning. In fact, theology not only makes use of arguments, but does so in multiple ways. There is a richness of means by which theology grows as a science. But what kind of reasoning does sacred theology employ?⌋

Arguments Based on Authority: Positive Theology

A question can be resolved in two ways: by appealing either to authority or to reason. An argument from authority does not indicate *why* something is true, but simply vouches for the truth of a statement because of the authority of the one who affirms it without setting forth the reasons for its truth. ⌈An example of an argument from authority is to maintain that something is true because Aristotle, Aquinas, Einstein, the Pope, or the Bible says so. ⌊In human sciences, arguments from authority are the weakest and never have more than probable value. However, they are very useful for orienting those who are learning and cannot yet fully see the arguments. ⌋

As mentioned above, there are four questions that one can pose about a given object. First, does something exist? Second, if it does exist, what is it—what is its nature? And then two other questions follow: (3) what are its properties and attributes and (4) why does it have

---

[2] *ST* I, q. 1, a. 8, obj. 1.

those properties and attributes? Sacred theology, like other sciences, poses all of these four questions. However, these different questions require different methods.

With regard to the things that God has revealed, the first and third of these questions can be answered by the authority of a witness. For example, we can assert the existence of the Trinity, grace, heaven, or the sacraments because Jesus testifies to them. Similarly, we can use arguments from authority for questions of fact, such as the attributes and properties of things (question 3). Thus we assert that Jesus is true God and true man on the basis of His testimony and that of the prophets and Apostles. The second and fourth questions penetrate further and cannot be answered simply by a witness, but require grasping the essence and the cause of a phenomenon.

So, does sacred theology use arguments from authority or from reason? There are problems with both alternatives. It would seem that if it used only arguments from reason, then it would be no different from natural theology, which is a part of philosophy. However, if it used arguments from authority, then this would be contrary to its dignity as *wisdom*, for arguments of authority are the weakest and fail to illuminate the mind as to the *why* of things and their *natures*.[4]

As is so often the case, the answer here is both/and. Sacred theology uses both. Clearly, theology must use arguments of authority, for we know the existence of supernatural things only from faith in the authority of God's Revelation. As our senses grasp the data in the empirical sciences, so the supernatural data used by sacred theology is grasped only from the authority of God, for, as St. Paul says in 1 Corinthians 2:9, "'what no eye has seen, nor ear heard, nor the heart of man conceived, what God has prepared for those who love him,' God has revealed to us through the Spirit." St. Thomas explains:

---

[3] See Aristotle, *Posterior Analytics* 2.2.89b36–90a4, in *Basic Works*.

[4] See *ST* I, q. 1, a. 8, obj. 2: "Furthermore, if it involves argumentation, it argues either from authority or from reason. If it argues from authority, this does not seem to accord with its dignity. For the argument from authority is the weakest, according to Boethius. But if it argues from reason, this does not seem to accord with its ends, for as Gregory says in a homily [*In Evang.* 2.26 (PL, 76:1197)], 'Faith does not have merit where human reason offers its own experience.' Therefore sacred theology does not involve argumentation."

It is especially proper for sacred theology to argue from authority, because the principles of this doctrine are received from revelation. Thus it is necessary to believe on the authority of those to whom revelation has been made. Nor is this contrary to the dignity of this doctrine, for although the value of an argument from authority based on human reason is the weakest, that based on divine revelation is the most efficacious.[5]

Furthermore, arguments from authority in theology are not limited to ascertaining that something is, or that something is true of something, but frequently also reveal some of the *what* and the *why* of the matter. For, God does not limit Himself to revealing bare facts, but reveals also the meaning and finality of the divine things that He communicates. Nevertheless, the minds of the faithful must always seek to penetrate more deeply into those meanings and purposes through theological reasoning.

Arguments from authority have an entirely different force in sacred theology than they have in the empirical and philosophical sciences, for theology is a science based on faith in God's Revelation, and God can neither deceive nor be deceived. As we have seen, theology is a subordinate science, taking its principles from God's knowledge of Himself communicated to man through Revelation. Therefore, in terms of certainty, the *strongest* possible argument in sacred theology is one from authority when the authority invoked is ultimately that of God Himself.[6] As will be seen in the following chapters, God's Revelation does not reach us without mediation, but is passed on through Scripture and Tradition (together, the "deposit of faith"). The true interpretation of those sources of Revelation is then discerned by the Magisterium of the Church, especially when it speaks with the charism of infallibility received from God. This interpretation of the Magisterium, in turn, then becomes part of Tradition passed on in the Church from generation to generation. Therefore, an argument

---

[5] Ibid., ad 2.

[6] See ibid.

from authority in theology must involve an examination of Scripture, Tradition, and the Magisterium.

Consequently, one type of theological argument is to manifest the authority that stands behind a particular affirmation. This can be done by showing that some particular truth is contained in Scripture or Tradition or has been taught by the Magisterium of the Church. This type of theological investigation into the sources of theological doctrine is called *positive theology*.

Such investigations involve an exegetical or historical approach. For example, if a particular truth has been infallibly defined by the Church, the Catholic theologian can show that this truth was already contained in Scripture and Tradition. Or if a truth has not yet been infallibly defined, the theologian can aid the Magisterium in arriving at the certainty that a given truth is actually contained in the deposit of faith. Positive theology, therefore, is an indispensable part of theology, requiring erudition in the interpretation of Scripture, in the history of the transmission of the apostolic Tradition in the life of the Church (especially in the Fathers), and in the development of magisterial teaching.

Pope Pius XII gives a good description of the noble task of positive theology in *Humani generis* §21:

It is also true that theologians must always return to the sources of divine revelation: for it belongs to them to point out how the doctrine of the living Teaching Authority is to be found either explicitly or implicitly in the Scriptures and in Tradition. Besides, each source of divinely revealed doctrine contains so many rich treasures of truth that they can really never be exhausted. Hence it is that theology through the study of its sacred sources remains ever fresh; on the other hand, speculation which neglects a deeper search into the deposit of faith proves sterile, as we know from experience.

Positive theology enriches the other branches of theology, for the sources of Revelation contain a rich and inexhaustible theological reflection that must always be the soul of all the branches of theology.

Furthermore, like all sacred theology, positive theology must be done in communion with the living Magisterium of the Church. The theologian cannot exercise "private judgment" with regard to the interpretation of either Scripture or Tradition. Rather, he must seek to read the sources of Revelation through the eyes of the Church and her living Magisterium, which clarifies and illuminates those sources. *Humani generis* §21 further states:

> For, together with the sources of positive theology God has given to His Church a living Teaching Authority to elucidate and explain what is contained in the deposit of faith only obscurely and implicitly. This deposit of faith our Divine Redeemer has given for authentic interpretation not to each of the faithful, not even to theologians, but only to the Teaching Authority of the Church. But if the Church does exercise this function of teaching, as she often has through the centuries, either in the ordinary or in the extraordinary way, it is clear how false is a procedure which would attempt to explain what is clear by means of what is obscure. Indeed, the very opposite procedure must be used. Hence Our Predecessor of immortal memory, Pius IX, teaching that the most noble office of theology is to show how a doctrine defined by the Church is contained in the sources of revelation, added these words, and with very good reason: "in that sense in which it has been defined by the Church."[7]

Systematic Theology and Theological Reasoning

Sacred theology, however, is not limited to arguments from authority. Its objective is not simply to establish a conclusion by way of the authority of God's Revelation, but also to penetrate that Revelation in a systematic and orderly way, insofar as this is possible. This func-

---

[7] Here citing Pius IX, Letter to the Episcopal Assembly at Fulda *Inter gravissimas* (October 28, 1870).

tion of theology is referred to as systematic theology.[8] For example, if God reveals that He gives grace to mankind, theology poses the questions as to what grace is, what are its causes and purposes, and whether there are different kinds of grace and how they differ. Theology thus inquires into the meaning, causes, essences, distinctions, interrelations, consequences, and implications of what God reveals. It *teaches the believer how to think through theological problems* so that he can see for himself the reasons for each conclusion and how they rest on revealed truths and valid universal principles, as well as how they are related to each other and to what we know by reason. Only in this way can theology be a science and gain some understanding, however limited, of the content of the faith. St. Thomas states his pedagogical objective in *Quodlibet* 4 (q. 9, a. 3):

> Disputed questions can be ordered to two ends. One kind of disputation is ordered to removing doubt about *whether* something is true, and in a theological disputation of this kind one must principally rely on authorities that are received by those with whom one is disputing. . . . Another kind of disputed question is that of masters in the schools, who seek not simply to remove error but to instruct their listeners and lead them to *understand* the truth under consideration. For this it is necessary that the argument be based on *arguments that uncover the root of the truth*, and make one see *how and why* the thesis is true. Otherwise, if the master decides the question simply by citing authorities, the listener may satisfy himself *that* the thesis is true, but he will acquire no science or understanding and will walk away with an empty mind.[9]

Theological disputations thus can have one of two purposes: to ascertain through an argument from authority that a given thesis is true (positive theology), or to show how and why a given thesis is true and how it relates to other truths (systematic theology). It is doubt-

---

[8] It is also sometimes referred to as "scholastic" theology (referring to the kind of theology taught in the higher schools or universities).

[9] My translation here is of the Latin text found at http://www.corpusthomisticum.org/q04.html.

less extremely useful to show that a given thesis is true because it is taught by Scripture, Tradition, or the Magisterium. As we have seen, this is "positive theology." If only this type of demonstration is used, however, the reader learns that a thesis is true, but does not come to understand it more deeply, nor to see its relation with other truths. This is not satisfying because the human mind has a natural desire to understand a given truth by seeing it in its cause or root, in its relations with other truths (both natural and supernatural), and in its purpose or finality. In other words, if possible, the theologian should offer arguments to show *why* a thesis is true—so that the student in turn becomes equipped to demonstrate it to others.

But here we have to reply to the objection posed above. If arguments of reason are used, will not the merit of faith be lost? Or will not theology be reduced to philosophy, and thus the greater certainty of its claims be lost? On the contrary, faith, which comes from grace, does not destroy reason or exist in opposition to it, but rather perfects the intellect as grace perfects nature. Thus faith can collaborate with reason and employ reason in its service.[10] This can happen in three different kinds of theological argumentation. With regard to revealed truths that belong to the natural order, such as God's existence and attributes, reason is employed to give a philosophical demonstration. With regard to mysteries, reason cannot demonstrate them, but it can demonstrate other truths from them, as corollaries. This is called theological deduction. Reason, finally, can also give analogies from the natural order or from Revelation in support of a mystery, which analogies are called arguments from fittingness.

Philosophical Demonstrations Used in Theology

We have seen that St. Thomas distinguishes two types of truth that are revealed by God: mysteries that are above the reach of reason

---

[10] St. Thomas states this crucial principle in *ST* I, q. 1, a. 8, ad 2: "Nevertheless, sacred theology indeed makes use of human reason, although not to prove the faith, because this would take away the merit of faith. Instead, it is used to manifest other things that are passed on in this doctrine. Since grace does not take away nature, but perfects it, it is necessary that natural reason serve the faith, as the natural inclination of the will yields to charity."

and truths about God and man that natural reason can discover. Philosophical arguments can *never be used to prove or demonstrate mysteries*, but they can and should be used to demonstrate truths that also belong to the natural order. Examples of revealed truths that can also be demonstrated by philosophical arguments include the existence of God, His attributes, the creation of the world out of nothing, the freedom of God in creating all things for His glory, the absolute dependence on God of every created thing, the goodness of the material world and of man, the spiritual nature and immortality of the soul, the substantial union of our body and soul, the freedom of the will, the dignity of the human person, the nature of love and the virtues, the existence of natural law, and even the existence of truth itself.

Even though the highest certainty of such truths of the natural order comes from Revelation, it is useful to give a philosophical proof for at least two reasons. First, because a philosophical demonstration shows the reasons and causes as to *why* something is the way it is. This is much more satisfying to the mind, which naturally desires to know not only *the fact* that something is a certain way, but *why* it is so. Thus, it helps believers to grasp the harmony of faith and reason.[11] Secondly, this type of philosophical demonstration is capable of teaching those who do not share the Catholic faith, for reason has a universal appeal. Thus, philosophical demonstrations help those whose belief in God is shaky or non-existent.

It is interesting to note that Revelation itself affirms the power of reason to come to a natural knowledge of God. The book of Wisdom treats of the natural evidence of God's existence in 13:1–9:

> For all men who were ignorant of God were foolish by nature; and they were unable from the good things that are seen to know him who exists, nor did they recognize the craftsman

---

[11] See Francisco Suarez, *Opera omnia*, vol. 1, *prooemium* (Paris: Vivès, 1856), xxiii: "Scholastic theologians . . . use natural theology as a servant, to confirm supernatural truths and from the harmony of both kinds of theology to enable the mind of the faithful to rest more easily in those truths."

while paying heed to his works; but they supposed that either fire or wind or swift air, or the circle of the stars, or turbulent water, or the luminaries of heaven were the gods that rule the world. If through delight in the beauty of these things men assumed them to be gods, let them know how much better than these is their Lord, for the author of beauty created them. And if men were amazed at their power and working, let them perceive from them how much more powerful is he who formed them. For *from the greatness and beauty of created things comes a corresponding perception of their Creator*. . . . Yet again, not even they are to be excused; for if they had the power to know so much that they could investigate the world, how did they fail to find sooner the Lord of these things?

In the *Summa* and elsewhere, St. Thomas makes very frequent use of this kind of philosophical argument to demonstrate revealed truths that belong to the natural order. Such arguments can be taken from any sound philosophy. Obviously a false philosophy cannot be used in the service of faith, and any philosophical argument that is contrary to a revealed truth is shown to be false by that very fact. Revelation and the Magisterium of the Church thus provide a great safeguard to Christian philosophy by preserving it from errors contrary to revealed truth, which thus enables it to more perfectly perform its task of illuminating the natural order. Pius XII, in *Humani generis* §29, writes:

It is well known how highly the Church regards human reason, for it falls to reason to demonstrate with certainty the existence of God, personal and one; to prove beyond doubt from divine signs the very foundations of the Christian faith; to express properly the law which the Creator has imprinted in the hearts of men; and finally to attain to some notion, indeed a very fruitful notion, of mysteries. But reason can perform these functions safely and well only when properly trained, that is, when imbued with that sound philosophy which has long been, as it were, a patrimony handed down by earlier Christian ages, and which moreover possesses an authority of an even higher order, since the Teaching Authority of the Church, in the light of divine revelation itself, has weighed its fundamental tenets, which have been elaborated and defined little by little by men of great genius. For this philosophy, acknowledged and accepted by the Church, safeguards the genuine validity of human knowledge, the unshakable metaphysical principles of sufficient reason, causality, and finality, and finally the mind's ability to attain certain and unchangeable truth.

Since philosophical arguments are not always free from error, they must always be used in theology with an awareness of their limitations and with a sense of intellectual humility. Obviously, they must never be confused with revealed truths, as St. Thomas explains:

> Sacred theology also uses philosophical authorities where they were able to know the truth through natural reason. Thus Paul, in Acts 17 [28], quotes Aratus where he says, "As even some of your poets have said, 'For we are indeed his offspring.'" But sacred theology uses these authorities as extrinsic and merely probable arguments. On the contrary, it uses the authorities of canonical Scripture as proper sources that establish conclusions with certainty. It also uses the authority of other doctors of the Church as proper sources of theological argumentation, but only furnishing probable arguments. For our faith rests on the revelation made to the apostles and prophets who wrote the books of canonical Scripture, and not on any revelation made to any other doctors.[12]

In this text St. Thomas establishes a hierarchy of sources that can be used in theology. In the first place is the authority of canonical

---

[12] *ST* I, q. 1, a. 8, ad 2.

Scripture. To it we must add the authority of the Magisterium of the Church. Then there are the writings of the Fathers and Doctors of the Church. However, insofar as they are speaking as private theologians, their authority merely establishes probability in their favor.[13] Finally, there are the arguments of good philosophers. Again, their authority merely establishes probability, and only in the philosophical sphere (truths accessible to reason regarding God and man), and their arguments must always be critically examined by both reason and faith.

Theological Deduction

Philosophical arguments are clearly useful with regard to revealed truths that are also accessible to human reason. But does reasoning have any role to play regarding supernatural mysteries not accessible to reason? Such mysteries include man's elevation to a supernatural end, the beatific vision, the Trinity, the Incarnation, the Redemption, sanctifying grace, the theological virtues, the sacraments, the Church, and the inspiration of Scripture. A fideist attitude would deny the utility of reason here, but the Catholic Tradition, on the contrary, holds that reason can help to understand such mysteries more deeply both through theological deduction and arguments from fittingness.

Reason can use revealed truths as the basis from which it *deduces* other truths as corollaries. This is called *theological deduction*. St. Thomas points out that theological reasoning begins with the articles of faith, and then proceeds to deduce conclusions from them:

> As other sciences do not argue to prove their principles, but argue from their principles to demonstrate other truths in these sciences, so *this doctrine does not argue in order to prove its principles, which are the articles of faith, but from them it goes on to prove something else;* as the Apostle from the resurrec-

---

[13] Where there is a consensus of the Fathers of the Church on a given point of doctrine as to be definitively held, it can be inferred that they are speaking not merely as private theologians, but as witnesses of apostolic Tradition.

tion of Christ argues in proof of the general resurrection (1 Cor 15).[14]

The reasoning in this particular case mentioned by St. Thomas (1 Cor 15) proceeds from two premises: that Christ truly rose from the dead and that Christ was constituted head of His Body, the Church, and is in intimate solidarity with His Body. Therefore, it can be inferred that the Resurrection of the Head of the Body indicates the destiny of the members of the Body, as long as they persevere in the Body to the end. Since Christ was resurrected, His Mystical Body and Bride will also be resurrected.[15]

For another example of theological deduction, we may begin with the truth of faith that Christ is true God and true man. On this basis the early ecumenical councils worked out Trinitarian and Christological doctrine. From Christ's true divinity, it can be deduced that He is omnipotent, omniscient, supremely merciful, supremely just, and consubstantial with the Father. Likewise, insofar as He is truly man, it can be deduced (against heresies like Monophysitism, which diminish Christ's humanity) that He has a rational soul with a human intellect like ours, as well as a free human will (distinct from the divine will)[16] and human passions, although all this without sin.

Some things that can be inferred by theological deduction may also be contained explicitly elsewhere in Revelation, whether in Scripture or in Tradition. But even in such cases, theological deduction is still useful because it enables these truths to be known in their relationship to other over-arching revealed truths. This is the case, for example, with Christ's free human will. It is known directly from many texts of Scripture, such as Christ's prayer in Gethsemane, and it can also be known by theological deduction from the broader truth of

---

[14] *ST* I, q. 1, a. 8.

[15] This example of the general resurrection is not only a theological deduction that follows from Christ's Resurrection, as St. Paul shows in 1 Cor 15, but also a revealed truth in its own right.

[16] See, for example, the Letter of St. Agatho to the Emperor (AD 680–681) against the Monothelite (one will) heresy: "For how is it possible not to acknowledge in him two wills, to wit, a human and a divine, when in him, even after the inseparable union, there are two natures according to the definitions of the synods" (trans. Henry R. Percival in *NPNF2*, 14:333).

Christ's humanity. Likewise, the general resurrection, which St. Paul shows can be inferred from Christ's Resurrection, is nevertheless a revealed truth in its own right.

Even when the conclusion is itself a revealed truth, as in the case of the general resurrection, theological deduction is still very useful in showing the connection and harmony between the mysteries and giving some insight into their hierarchy and necessity. When the theological conclusion is not directly revealed in itself, it is said to be "virtually" or implicitly contained in Revelation. Theological deduction then makes explicit what otherwise would only be implicit. This type of reasoning is very important both in combating heresies and in explaining the faith.[17]

Arguments from Fittingness

Theological deduction is not the only use of reason to deepen our understanding of the mysteries of faith. Reason can also provide *arguments from fittingness* to show that a given revealed truth is extremely fitting. An argument from fittingness is a method of argumentation used *not to prove* the truth of revealed supernatural mysteries, since they cannot be proved, but rather, *by means of analogy, to show why such a mystery makes sense and is worthy of God*. In formulating such an argument, one seeks to look at a question from God's perspective, considering how a particular revealed doctrine fits in or harmonizes with what we can grasp of God's nature and global purpose in salvation history. Such arguments presuppose the conviction that the wisest, most beautiful and harmonious plan or state of affairs is most likely to be true. God, as the divine artist, would choose the most beautiful plan of salvation. It is interesting to observe that scientists frequently use the same criterion in judging the truth of scientific hypotheses. The simplest and most elegant hypothesis is preferred— held to be more probable—even before decisive empirical observation is capable of confirming it.

---

[17] See the classic work on this topic by Francisco Marín-Sola, *La evolución homogénea del dogma católico* (Madrid: Biblioteca de Autores Cristianos, 1952).

There remains, of course, the problem of discernment. What appears to be wiser and more beautiful at first sight may turn out to be less wise and beautiful when one contemplates it more deeply, and vice versa. For example, the Cross of Christ may seem absurd at first sight, but it shows itself to be the wisdom and beauty of the divine Love. It follows that arguments from fittingness are not equally appreciated by every mind and require prayer, contemplation, and an upright disposition. Precisely for this reason, arguments from fittingness are not strict demonstrations, but means of progressively gaining insight and conviction.

Arguments from fittingness are directed primarily to those who already believe because of the authority of God's Revelation. When used by and for believers, they presuppose faith, but seek to penetrate to a certain extent why it is fitting that things should be as God has chosen. For example, reason alone cannot prove that God can become incarnate, or that He has actually done so. However, once we believe this on the authority of Christ and the Church, then we can ask why it is *fitting* that God has become incarnate. Reason can address why it is fitting that Christ established a Church, why He instituted seven sacraments, and why He suffered death on the Cross. Reason can address the fittingness of why God created the world, why He elevated men to the supernatural end of the beatific vision, why He gives them sanctifying grace, and why He instituted the Old Covenant and the Mosaic Law. We can even ask why it is fitting that God should be a Trinity.

Although these arguments are directed primarily to those who already believe, they can also be very helpful to those who are inquiring into the faith and are looking for its harmony with the eyes of reason alone. In such cases, however, it must be made clear that the argument from fittingness is not put forward as a cause of our holding it or as the source for our certainty. Catholics believe mysteries with firm faith not because we have great arguments from fittingness for them, but because they have been revealed by God and declared as such by the Church. St. Thomas speaks of arguments from fittingness in the *Summa contra gentiles*:

We only believe things which are above human reason because God has revealed them. Nevertheless, there are certain persuasive arguments that should be brought forth in order to make divine truth known. This should be done for the training and consolation of the faithful, and not with any idea of refuting those who are adversaries. For the very inadequacy of the arguments would rather strengthen them in their error, since they would imagine that our acceptance of the truth of faith was based on such weak arguments.[18]

Nevertheless, this type of theological argumentation is exceedingly fruitful and is perhaps the principal way in which faith seeks understanding. The arguments from fittingness have their foundation in *analogy*. They take a philosophical principle that is valid in the natural order and extend it analogically to the supernatural order. A good example of this is the explanation of the Trinitarian processions developed by St. Augustine and St. Thomas. They seek to explain the procession of the Second and Third Persons of the Trinity by an analogy with the operations of intellect and will, the highest operations in spiritual creatures. In men, the immanent operation of knowledge is fruitful in that it produces an interior word—the concept. Now it is reasonable to think that the eternal operation of knowing in God would be no less fruitful, and thus it should produce an interior word in God, a perfect Word or Image of the Father. However, everything that can be said to be in God *is* God, for God is absolutely simple. The Word of God thus *is* God and says everything that He is. And likewise it is reasonable to think that the eternal operation of love that is in God would also be fruitful, producing an eternal *Gift of self* which would ultimately also be God, for God is love. This procession of love in God is the procession of the Holy Spirit.[19]

---

[18] *SCG*, bk. 1, ch. 9.

[19] This argument from fittingness, often referred to as the "psychological analogy," was made first by St. Augustine in his classic, *De Trinitate*. St. Thomas refined it in *ST* I, q. 27, aa. 1–5. See also St. Thomas's *Commentary on John*, ch. 1, lec. 1, trans. Fabian Larcher and James Weisheipl (Washington, DC: Catholic University of America Press, 2010), 1:12–16.

Another argument from fittingness for the Trinity is taken from the notion of loving communion. A general principle of theology is that, since God is the source of all good and all perfection, He must possess everything that we know to be good, but without limitation. In our experience, we grasp that interpersonal communion, consisting in mutual self-giving, is a great good. A personal being is one capable of knowing and loving, and one who thus finds his perfection in knowing and self-giving love. If a person does not give himself to another person in love, his life is frustrated, as experienced by Adam in the Garden before the creation of Eve. John Paul II expressed this beautifully in *Redemptor hominis* §10: "Man cannot live without love. He remains a being that is incomprehensible for himself, his life is senseless, if love is not revealed to him, if he does not encounter love, if he does not experience it and make it his own, if he does not participate intimately in it."

God, who is pure act, must be infinite love realized in its highest form. The highest form of love is love of benevolence—willing the good for another in such a way that we give ourselves somehow to the other. Such a love implies a plurality of persons. Now, if God were a solitary being without interpersonal communion in His own nature, two unfitting consequences would follow. First of all, God would be deprived of a supreme perfection, the possibility of self-giving love, in His own inner divine life. Secondly, He would be dependent on creatures to realize this activity of love. Both possibilities seem incompatible with the perfection of God's nature.

John Paul II perfectly captured the fittingness of the doctrine of the Trinity: "It has been said, in a beautiful and profound way, that our God in his deepest mystery is not a solitude, but a family, since he has in himself fatherhood, sonship and the essence of the family, which is love."[20] Joseph Ratzinger has also made an interesting reflection on this topic:

---

[20] Homily of January 28, 1979 at Puebla, at http://w2.vatican.va/content/john-paul-ii/en/homilies/1979/documents/hf_jp-ii_hom_19790128_messico-puebla-seminario.html.

Although to us, the nondivine, it (God) is one and single, the one and only divine as opposed to all that is not divine; nevertheless in itself it is truly fullness and plurality, so that creaturely unity and plurality are both in the same degree a likeness and a share of the divine. Not only unity is divine; plurality, too, is something primordial and has its inner ground in God himself. . . . This has a further important consequence. To him who believes in God as tri-une, the highest unity is not the unity of inflexible monotony. The model of unity or oneness toward which one should strive is consequently not the indivisibility of the atom, the smallest unity, which cannot be divided up any further; the authentic acme of unity is the unity created by love. The multi-unity that grows in love is a more radical, truer unity than the unity of the "atom."[21]

These arguments from fittingness for the Trinity are extremely profound, but they are not sufficient of themselves to convince a non-believer that God is a Trinity of Persons. We know that God is a Trinity from the Revelation made by Christ. However, once we know that by faith, it is beautiful to seek to penetrate and understand, as far as possible, the mysteries that we believe and adore. This is faith seeking understanding. They can also serve the unbeliever to see that the mystery is not simply absurd, but worthy of contemplation.

Another beautiful example of an argument of fittingness is given by St. Thomas to explain why Christ instituted seven sacraments. As certain elements are necessary for man's natural life, so analogous elements are necessary for man's supernatural life. St. Thomas divides these necessary elements into two groups: those necessary for the life of each individual and those necessary for man as a social creature. What is necessary for each individual is birth, nourishment, maturity, healing in times of illness, and preparation for death. What is necessary for man's social life is marriage and government. So likewise in the supernatural life, these elements are necessary: spiritual rebirth through Baptism, spiritual nourishment in the Eucharist, spiritual

---

[21] *Introduction to Christianity* (San Francisco: Ignatius Press, 1990), 178–179.

maturity through Confirmation, spiritual healing through Penance, spiritual preparation for death through the sacrament of Anointing of the Sick, the elevation of matrimony to a sacrament, and spiritual government through the sacrament of Holy Orders.[22]

Such reasoning would be insufficient to demonstrate that Christ instituted seven sacraments. However, once the seven sacraments are known through Tradition, theology reflects on why Christ instituted precisely these seven sacraments by establishing an analogy between the natural and the supernatural life.

The First Vatican Council also explains this type of theological reasoning:

> If reason illumined by faith inquires in an earnest, pious and sober manner, it attains by God's grace a certain understanding of the mysteries, which is most fruitful, both from the *analogy* with the objects of its natural knowledge, and from the *connection* of these mysteries with one another and *with our ultimate end*. But it never becomes capable of understanding them in the way it does the truths which constitute its proper object. For divine mysteries by their very nature so excel the created intellect that, even when they have been communicated in Revelation and received by faith, they re-

---

[22] See *ST* III, q. 65, a. 1, and Aquinas's short treatise, "On the Articles of Faith and the Sacraments of the Church," in *The Aquinas Catechism* (Manchester: Sophia Institute Press, 2000), 254–256. See also the Council of Florence in its decree for the Armenians in 1439: "There are seven sacraments of the New Law. . . . The first five of these are ordained to the interior spiritual perfection of the person; the last two are ordained to the government and the increase of the whole Church. For by baptism we are spiritually reborn and by confirmation we grow in grace and are strengthened in the faith; being reborn and strengthened, we are nourished with the divine food of the Eucharist. If by sin we become sick in soul, we are healed spiritually by penance; we are also healed in spirit, and in body in so far as it is good for the soul, by extreme unction. Through Orders the Church is governed and receives spiritual growth; through matrimony she receives bodily growth" (DS, 1311). Paul VI took up this idea in his Apostolic Constitution on the Sacrament of Confirmation, *Divinae Consortium Naturae* (1971): "The sharing in the divine nature which is granted to men through the grace of Christ has a certain likeness to the origin, development, and nourishing of natural life. The faithful are born anew by Baptism, strengthened by the sacrament of Confirmation, and finally are sustained by the food of eternal life in the Eucharist"; see *Rite of Confirmation* (Washington, DC: United States Conference of Catholic Bishops, 2006), 11.

main covered by the veil of faith itself and shrouded as it were in darkness as long as in this mortal life "we are away from the Lord; for we walk by faith, not by sight" [2 Cor. 5:6].[23]

This text specifies that arguments from fittingness can shed light on a mystery of faith through the use of analogy in two ways. For one, a mystery can be compared to a natural reality known by human experience. An example of this is the analogy between the sacraments and the essential elements of human life, as seen above. In the second way, an analogy can be established between two mysteries. Thus St. Paul argues for the general resurrection of the faithful on the basis of Christ's Resurrection (1 Cor 15). An important subset of this second use of analogy occurs when another mystery of the faith is related to the mystery of man's supernatural end. Thus, the Incarnation and the Eucharist can be shown to be extremely fitting in relation to man's supernatural end of union with the Blessed Trinity.

Analogical Use of Philosophical Concepts in Theology

In making analogies between truths of the natural order and revealed truths, theological reason takes philosophical concepts and elevates them to speak analogically about supernatural mysteries. The First Council of Nicaea, for example, famously employed the philosophical term *consubstantial* (*homousios*), using the Greek notion of "substance" (*ousia*) to clarify the sense in which Christ's divinity is to be understood and to exclude the Arian heresy. Similarly, the word "person" (*hypostasis*) was used to speak about the Father, Son, and Holy Spirit.

We must always use analogy when we apply names to God, for we know God through creatures, and yet He infinitely surpasses all of them. St. Thomas explains that nothing can be properly predicated in a univocal sense of God and creatures. This is because we know God through His work of creation, but His creatures fall short of revealing the fullness of His power and being, for they are infinitely less than

---

[23] Dogmatic Constitution on the Faith *Dei Filius* (1870), ch. 4 (DS, 3016).

their Maker. This means that creatures truly reveal something about God to us, but they fall infinitely short in making Him known.

For example, creatures have power to do things according to their nature, and this tells us something about the power of God. However, the power of creatures is limited and finite, whereas that of God is infinite. Creatures have power, but God *is* power. Similarly, rational creatures can have wisdom that is limited and finite, but God is infinite wisdom. Neither power nor wisdom is predicated univocally of God and creatures. The same can be said for other names of God, such as Father. He is not Father as human fathers are, who must exist before their sons.

In a brilliant article on "whether what is said of God and of creatures is univocally predicated of them," St. Thomas explains:

> It is impossible to predicate a term univocally of God and creatures. This is because every effect unequal to the power of the agent cause receives a likeness of the agent not according to the same species, but in a deficient way, so that what is divided and manifold in the effect is simple and the same in the causes. As the sun, according to its one power, produces manifold and varied forms in these lower regions, similarly all the perfections of things which are divided and manifold in creatures exist in God united and simple. Thus when some name that pertains to perfection is said of a creature, it signifies that perfection distinct according to its nature from other perfections. . . . But when this name is said of God, we do not intend to signify anything distinct from His essence, or power, or being. . . . Thus nothing is said univocally of God and creatures.
>
> Nor are names applied to God and creatures in a purely equivocal way, as some have said. Because if that were so, nothing could be known or demonstrated about God at all from creatures, for the reasoning would always fall into the fallacy of equivocation. Such a view is both against the Philosopher, who proved many things about God, and also against

what the Apostle says: "His invisible nature . . . has been clearly perceived through the things that have been made" (Romans 1:20). Therefore it must be said that these names are said of God and creatures by analogy, that is, according to proportion.[24]

Architectonic Goal of Systematic Theology

Systematic or Scholastic theology uses all four of these types of theological reasoning—positive theology, philosophical arguments to demonstrate revealed truths accessible to reason, theological deduction, and arguments from fittingness for the mysteries of faith—and orders these arguments in an architectonic way, like a cathedral. The greatest master of systematic theology is St. Thomas, the "Common Doctor" of the Church, and the greatest work of systematic theology is his *Summa theologiae*. In the prologue, he states that he has attempted to present theology "according to the order of the subject matter," and not according to the purposes of controversy, so as to facilitate the students' grasp of theology as an organic, hierarchically structured, and balanced whole. In systematic theology, the order of presentation greatly helps to show the overarching unity of theology and the hierarchy and interpenetration of its various parts.

The structure of the *Summa* mirrors the structure and purpose of the world, which is an *exitus-reditus*: proceeding out from God so as to return back to God. The *Summa*, of course, especially focuses on man in this regard, who comes from God and returns to Him in beatitude through the moral life, through grace, and through Christ, His Church, and the sacraments. In part I of the *Summa*, after an introductory question on the nature of theology, St. Thomas begins with God, focusing on His existence, attributes, operations of intellect and will, and distinction of Persons. He then studies creation, focusing on the angels and especially on man. Part II studies the moral life by which man orders his actions so as to attain his final end of union with God. To make this possible, however, the Word became flesh and in-

---

[24] *ST* I, q. 13, a. 5.

stituted the Church and the sacraments, which are studied in part III. Peter Kreeft gives a good summary of the structure of the *Summa*:

> The structural outline of the *Summa Theologica* is a mirror of the structural outline of reality. It begins in God, Who is "in the beginning." It then proceeds to the act of creation and a consideration of creatures, centering on man, who alone is created in the image of God. Then it moves to man's return to God through his life of moral and religious choice, and culminates in the way or means to that end: Christ and His Church. Thus the overall scheme of the *Summa*, like that of the universe, is an *exitus-redditus*, an exit from and a return to God, Who is both Alpha and Omega. God is the ontological heart that pumps the blood of being through the arteries of creation into the body of the universe, which wears a human face, and receives it back through the veins of man's life of love and will. The structure of the *Summa*, and of the universe, is dynamic. It is not like information in a library, but like blood in a body.[25]

Within each of the three parts of the *Summa*, St. Thomas's method is also to proceed in a logical order that mirrors the operation of the mind and the structure of reality. As a good Aristotelian, he holds that, in any subject of inquiry, the mind asks certain fundamental questions, which should progress from the most general to the specific. The most basic question is whether something exists in reality, or, in the case of a mystery of faith, why it is fitting that it exist. After the existence of something has been ascertained, the mind wonders what it is and thus seeks a proper definition that manifests the inner nature of the thing. Finally, one proceeds to study its causes, purpose, subdivisions or kinds, properties, and actions. Action is studied last, following the common-sense notion that *operation follows on being* (*operatio sequitur esse*).

---

[25] Peter Kreeft, *A Summa of the Summa* (San Francisco: Ignatius Press, 1990), 15.

Branches of Systematic Theology

Although theology is one science because of the unity of its object— God in the light of His own Revelation—systematic theology must structure its investigation according to certain divisions that are developed in "treatises," or branches of theology. The subdivisions of the *Summa* correspond to the various treatises of systematic theology as practiced in the thirteenth century by the Church's greatest theologian.

The most central theological treatise is part I, on the Triune God (*De Deo uno et trino*). St. Thomas treats God in the unity of His nature in *ST* I, qq. 2–26, and with regard to the distinction of Persons in the Trinity in qq. 27–43. There follows a treatise on creation centering on the angels and men (qq. 44–119).

By far the largest part of the *Summa* is part II, which concerns Moral Theology, and is further divided into two parts: general and particular. General or Fundamental Moral Theology gives the general principles of Moral Theology and is studied in the *Prima secundae* (first part of the second part, abbreviated as "I-II"). Particular moral theology is studied in the *Secunda secundae* (second part of the second part, "II-II"), which examines the individual virtues, grouping them around the three theological and the four cardinal virtues (qq. 1–170), followed by the charisms and states of life (qq. 171–189).

The third part ("III") begins with Christology (qq. 1–59), which looks first at the ontological constitution of Christ, and then at the various mysteries of His life. Mariology is treated within the context of the mysteries of the life of Christ, as is Soteriology, which studies the Redemption worked by Christ's Passion and Resurrection.

After treating Christ, St. Thomas passes on to Sacramental Theology, in which he studies first the sacraments in general and then treats them one by one. The *Summa* was meant to conclude then with a treatise on Eschatology, which is the study of the Last Things: death, judgment (particular and final), heaven, and hell. St. Thomas never completed the project because of a powerful mystical experience on December 6, 1273, when writing on the Sacrament of Penance, which was followed by a rapid physical decline, and soon by death. The *Sup-*

plement contains corresponding articles from St. Thomas's earlier Commentary on the *Sentences* of Peter Lombard so as to provide a completed systematic treatment of the whole of theology.

Other parts of theology became distinct treatises after the time of St. Thomas. The general rule is that a branch of theology becomes further developed to the degree that it is opposed by heresy or the currents of civil society or is the subject of theological controversy. Ecclesiology became a distinct part of systematic theology after the Reformation in the sixteenth century as a response to controversies on the nature of the Church. Controversies between the Jesuit and Dominican schools over grace (the *de auxiliis* controversy) and the spiritual life led to further development of the theological treatise on grace (*ST* I-II, qq. 109–114). The sixteenth-century mystics, such as St. Teresa of Avila, St. John of the Cross, and St. Ignatius of Loyola, led to the development of "spiritual theology" as a distinct treatise. Through the influence of the Liturgical Movement in the nineteenth century, Liturgical Theology likewise developed as a distinct discipline. At the same time, the development of the Church's social doctrine in the late nineteenth century led to the development of Social Ethics as a distinct branch of theology. The theological study of marriage and the family has been fostered by the need to defend the Church's teaching in the face of the sexual revolution and the increasing breakdown of the family in Western society. John Paul II's development of the "Theology of the Body" is a response to this crisis.

Fundamental Theology

Another branch of theology developed above all in the last two centuries has been Fundamental Theology. One of the tasks of theology is to reflect in a systematic way on its nature, foundations, sources, and method. Fundamental Theology is that branch of theology that engages in the systematic reflection on the foundations of the Catholic faith: Revelation, faith, the transmission of Revelation through Scripture and Tradition, the nature of apostolic Tradition, the inspiration and inerrancy of Scripture, principles of biblical interpretation, the task of the Magisterium and her infallibility, the role of reason within theology, and the harmony of faith and reason.

St. Thomas studies the foundations of theology briefly in the first question of the *Summa*. A parallel treatment is given in the first nine chapters of the first book of the *Summa contra gentiles*. Fundamental Theology is reasonably studied first among the various branches of theology, for it investigates theology's own identity, object, scientific status, dignity, and methods. This must logically precede even the investigation of the Triune God.

Fundamental Theology differs from positive theology, which also studies the sources of Revelation, because Fundamental Theology studies the sources of Revelation in a systematic and global way. Positive theology studies those sources one by one, generally following an historical order.

John Paul II speaks of some of the tasks of Fundamental Theology in *Fides et ratio* §67:

> With its specific character as a discipline charged with giving an account of faith (cf. *1 Pet* 3:15), the concern of *fundamental theology* will be to justify and expound the relationship between faith and philosophical thought. Recalling the teaching of Saint Paul (cf. *Rom* 1:19–20), the First Vatican Council pointed to the existence of truths which are naturally, and thus philosophically, knowable; and an acceptance of God's Revelation necessarily presupposes knowledge of these truths. In studying Revelation and its credibility, as well as the corresponding act of faith, fundamental theology should show how, in the light of the knowledge conferred by faith, there emerge certain truths which reason, from its own independent enquiry, already perceives. Revelation endows these truths with their fullest meaning, directing them towards the richness of the revealed mystery in which they find their ultimate purpose. Consider, for example, the natural knowledge of God, the possibility of distinguishing divine Revelation from other phenomena or the recognition of its credibility,

the capacity of human language to speak in a true and meaningful way even of things which transcend all human experience. From all these truths, the mind is led to acknowledge the existence of a truly propaedeutic path to faith, one which can lead to the acceptance of Revelation without in any way compromising the principles and autonomy of the mind itself.

Similarly, fundamental theology should demonstrate the profound compatibility that exists between faith and its need to find expression by way of human reason fully free to give its assent. Faith will thus be able "to show fully the path to reason in a sincere search for the truth. Although faith, a gift of God, is not based on reason, it can certainly not dispense with it. At the same time, it becomes apparent that reason needs to be reinforced by faith, in order to discover horizons it cannot reach on its own."[26]

Apologetics

Apologetics uses the resources of theology—both systematic and positive—and the human sciences in order to defend the Catholic Church's claims that her doctrine corresponds to God's Revelation. The term "apologetics" comes from the Greek word *apologia*, meaning to defend or to justify. The English word "apology" comes from the same Greek word, but actually has an opposite meaning. To make an apology, in modern English, implies that you were wrong and that you admit this and seek to make amends. In the original Greek, however, *apologia* signifies a speech in defense of someone or some position[27] and in no way implies that one was in the wrong, but rather,

---

[26] Here he quotes from his Letter to Participants in the International Congress of Fundamental Theology on the 125th Anniversary of "Dei Filius" (September 30, 1995), §4, in which, as the note in *Fides et ratio* relates, he also states: "The search for the conditions in which man on his own initiative asks the first basic questions about the meaning of life, the purpose he wishes to give it and what awaits him after death constitutes the necessary preamble to fundamental theology, so that today too, faith can fully show the way to reason in a sincere search for the truth" (*L'Osservatore Romano*, October 3, 1995, 8).

[27] This comes from a Greek verb, *apologeomai*: to defend oneself; to speak in defense of someone.

in the right. "Apologetics" conserves this original sense and signifies a justification and defense of Catholicism as being the true religion. A term similar to apologetics was already used by the Fathers of the Church in the second century, during the Roman persecution. For example, Justin Martyr made two famous discourses called "apologies" before the pagan emperor Marcus Aurelius (who was also a Stoic philosopher). Obviously, the word "apology" here is not used in the modern sense, but in the sense of defending the Catholic faith as the true religion.

The Catholic faith can be rejected—and thus needs defending—in three progressively more radical ways: with regard to the Catholic Church, with regard to the divinity of Christ, and with regard to the existence of God and His attributes. Western society since the Renaissance has been progressively denying these three great pillars of faith. The Protestant rebellion attacked faith in the Catholic Church and her sacraments while maintaining belief in the divinity of Christ and the existence of God. The Enlightenment of the eighteenth century began to call into question the divinity of Christ without denying the existence of God. The nineteenth and twentieth centuries have witnessed the rejection not only of the Church and of Christ, but also of belief in God, the soul, and the public and personal duty of religion. Apologetics, as the defense of the Catholic faith, thus has three principal parts: the defense of the existence of God and His attributes and of the immortality of the soul and man's duties towards God; the defense of the divinity of Jesus Christ; and the defense of the Catholic Church as the supernatural society founded by Jesus Christ as the ark of salvation for mankind.

The theological dialogue of apologetics must begin with some shared foundation. St. Thomas explains that Catholic theology,

> since it has no science above itself, can dispute with one who denies its principles *only if the opponent admits at least some of the truths obtained through divine Revelation.* Thus we can argue with heretics from texts in Holy Scripture, and against those who deny one article of faith, we can argue from an-

other. If our opponent believes nothing of divine Revelation, there is no longer any means of proving the articles of faith by reasoning, but only of answering his objections—if he has any—against faith. Since faith rests upon infallible truth, and since the contrary of a truth can never be demonstrated, it is clear that the arguments brought against faith cannot be demonstrations, but are difficulties that can be answered.[28]

Apologetics has no choice but to *limit itself to the arms of its adversary.* Catholics can use arguments from sources of belief shared with Protestants (Scripture and some aspects of Tradition) to show that Protestants ought to accept other Catholic doctrines, insofar as they are implied in what they already accept. With Jews we are limited to the Old Testament, where the messianic prophecies and figures can be used to show how belief in Christ as the Messiah is in profound accord with their own history and faith. With Muslims, we are limited to the truths of faith that are found in the Koran, or which they accept through natural reason or tradition.

With atheists, dialogue principally takes the form of answering their objections against divine Revelation and using philosophy to demonstrate the "preambles of faith," those fundamental truths that can be known by reason without the help of faith and form the basis for belief in Revelation. These truths include an understanding of God, man, and our duties towards God. Knowledge of these truths makes one open to seeking God's Revelation and disposes one to recognize the true religion. Apologetics also has recourse to the science of history to show that God has truly revealed Himself to man. Here the historical credibility of Scripture and of the four marks of the Church (one, holy, catholic, and apostolic) are defended.

Apologetics, therefore, can take the form of positive theology, scriptural exegesis, historical verification, systematic theology, or philosophical demonstration, according to the needs and presuppositions of those to whom it is addressed.

---

[28] *ST* I, q. 1, a. 8 (my emphasis).

One of the first examples of apologetics is Justin Martyr's *Dialogue with Trypho* (a Jewish rabbi). Other examples include Aquinas's *Summa contra gentiles*, written circa 1264 to facilitate dialogue and debate with Muslim philosophers,[29] *The Catholic Controversy*, a work of St. Francis de Sales against the Calvinists written in 1594,[30] and John Henry Newman's *Essay on the Development of Christian Doctrine* of 1845. While writing this work, Newman converted to the Catholic faith because he saw that the Catholic faith was implied in what he already accepted of Tradition as an Anglican.

Apologetics is similar to Fundamental Theology in that both investigate the sources of Revelation in a systematic way. They differ in that apologetics is oriented toward disputation with particular interlocutors, defense of the faith against particular heresies, and the vanquishing of particular objections, whereas Fundamental Theology examines the foundations of the Catholic faith in a systematic, serene, and theoretical way.[31]

---

[29] The work was apparently undertaken at the request of a fellow Dominican, St. Raymund of Pennafort, who was working in the missions with the Moors. A work written in 1313 by Peter Marsilio, O.P., states: "Furthermore, strongly desiring the conversion of unbelievers, Raymond asked an outstanding Doctor of Sacred Scripture, a Master in Theology, Brother Thomas of Aquino of the same Order, who among all the clerics of the world was considered in philosophy to be, next to Brother Albert, the greatest, to compose a work against the errors of unbelievers, by which both the cloud of darkness might be dispelled and the teaching of the true Sun might be made manifest to those who refuse to believe. The renowned Master accomplished what the humility of so great a Father asked, and composed a work called the *Summa contra gentiles*, held to be without equal in its field" (quoted in Anton C. Pegis's introduction to *SCG*, Book One: *God*). See J. P. Torrell, *St. Thomas Aquinas: The Person and His Work*, trans. Robert Royal (Washington, DC: Catholic University of America Press, 2005), 101.

[30] *The Catholic Controversy: St. Francis de Sales' Defense of the Faith*, trans. Henry B. Mackey (Rockford: TAN Books, 1992).

[31] See Henri Bouillard, S.J., "Human Experience as the Starting Point of Fundamental Theology," in *The Church and the World: Fundamental Theology* (New York: Paulist Press, 1965), 79–80: "The treatise on the grounds of theology demonstrates how Scripture, Tradition, and the magisterium witness to divine revelation, and, on this score, they are the sources and criteria of theology. This discipline is invested with a dogmatic character from the fact that it receives in faith what these witnesses have to say about their own function and their authority. It posits what the Christian message itself considers to be the *dogmatic* foundations of the *science* of faith. The role of apologetics is quite different. Its task is to give an exposition, in a form legitimate in the eyes of the unbeliever, of what the believer considers to be the *rational* foundations of the *decision* to believe. To sum up, on the one hand the intention is to establish in faith the science of faith; on the other, we wish to lay foundations in reason for the act of faith."

The Ecclesial Character of Theology

Theology is an ecclesial science in two fundamental ways: in its principles and in its mission. Theology is ecclesial because its first principles are those of the faith of the Church, from which all its knowledge is derived. This theological knowledge is, in turn, meant to aid the Church in fulfilling the mission given her by Christ. Thus it is only from the Church and for the Church that theology can realize its full stature. John Paul II gives a good summary of these two complementary aspects of the ecclesial dimension of theology in *Veritatis splendor* §109:

> It is fundamental for defining the very identity of theology, and consequently for theology to carry out its proper mission, to recognize its *profound and vital connection with the Church, her mystery, her life and her mission:* "Theology is an ecclesial science because it grows in the Church and works on the Church. . . . It is a service to the Church and therefore ought to feel itself actively involved in the mission of the Church, particularly in its prophetic mission."[32] By its very nature and procedures, authentic theology can flourish and develop only through a committed and responsible participation in and "belonging" to the Church as a "community of faith." In turn, the fruits of theological research and deeper insight become a source of enrichment for the Church and her life of faith.

Since sacred or Catholic theology has as its first principles the content of Revelation, it can only exist integrally and in fullness within the Catholic Church, which received, maintains, and nurtures that deposit of Revelation. These first principles are derived from Scripture and Tradition (which includes the liturgy as an important element[33])

---

[32] Here quoting his own Address to the Professors and Students of the Pontifical Gregorian University, Dec. 15, 1979, §6.

[33] The liturgy uniquely reveals the Catholic understanding of the Triune God, the Church, salvation history, and the relationship between Scripture and Tradition.

and are authentically interpreted and defined by the Magisterium of the Church. Thus theology maintains its foundational principles in their integrity only within the Church and loses them through dissent and heresy.

Obviously, this does not mean that theology cannot be done outside the Catholic Church. To the extent that elements of Revelation are conserved outside the visible boundaries of the Catholic Church, there can be fertile reflection on God in the light of His authentic Revelation. This is true of Judaism and of Christian churches and ecclesial communities not in full communion with the successor of Peter. *Lumen gentium* §8 speaks of the "many elements of sanctification and truth" that are found outside the visible structure of the Catholic Church, which include the Old and New Testaments, oral Tradition, and the liturgy and sacraments. These elements make sacred theology possible and, by their very nature, lead to the fullness of Catholic truth: "These elements, as gifts belonging to the Church of Christ, are forces impelling toward catholic unity."

The more a theologian is steeped in Scripture and Tradition as it developed first in Israel and then in the Church throughout the centuries, the more his theology will be able to flourish for being rooted in fertile soil.[34] A great example of this is St. Thomas Aquinas. His work is a synthesis of the whole theological tradition preceding him. As Leo XIII says: "Aquinas, as Cajetan observes, because 'he most venerated the ancient Doctors of the Church, in a certain way seems to have inherited the intellect of all.'"[35]

Furthermore, a theologian must always seek to "think with the mind of the Church" (*sentire cum ecclesia*)[36] as manifested in her authentic Magisterium. This applies not only to the infallible Magisteri-

---

[34] See Germain Grisez, "The Inspiration and Inerrancy of Scripture," *Letter & Spirit* 6 (2010): 184: "He [God] speaks to us not only as individuals, but also, and especially, together, and together we must listen to and appropriate his message and be formed into the communities of faith we are called to be. Only the hearing of the whole Church is fully sound."

[35] Leo XIII, Encyclical Letter on the Eternal Father *Aeterni Patris* (1879), §17.

[36] This is the title of a list of rules for thinking with the Church in St. Ignatius of Loyola, *The Spiritual Exercises*, nos. 352–370, found in *The Spiritual Exercises of St. Ignatius: Based on Studies in the Language of the Autograph*, trans. Louis Puhl (New York: Vintage Books, 2000), 124–127.

um, but also to the ordinary Magisterium of the Church, interpreted through the hermeneutic of continuity,[37] by which earlier teachings are read in the light of later ones, and vice versa.

Theology is an ecclesial science not only due to its sources, but also on account of its *mission*. That mission involves building up the faith of the Church, which includes helping the Magisterium to define and teach the Catholic faith, aiding in evangelization, guiding the contemplation of her members, assisting in building a Christian culture, and defending the Church's faith from errors and attacks, whether from without or from within.

The Congregation for the Doctrine of the Faith has defended this notion of the mission of theology to build up the faith of the Church, stating that "the service of doctrine, implying as it does the believer's search for an understanding of the faith, i.e., theology, is therefore something indispensable for the Church."[38] Similarly, St. John Paul II, in *Veritatis splendor* §109, says that "the Church must constantly reawaken or 'rekindle' her own life of faith (see 2 Tim 1:6), particularly through an ever deeper reflection, under the guidance of the Holy Spirit, upon the content of faith itself." Throughout her journey through human history, the Church is called to imitate Mary, who pondered the mysteries of her Son "in her heart" (Luke 2:19, 51).

The ecclesial mission of theology has both a positive and a negative aspect: it is positive in reflecting on and expounding the faith, and negative in defending it from error. St. Thomas explains:

It belongs to one and the same science, however, both to pursue one of two contraries and to oppose the other. Medicine, for example, seeks to effect health and to eliminate illness. Hence, just as it belongs to the wise man to meditate especially on the truth belonging to the first principle and to teach

---

[37] See Benedict XVI, Address to the Roman Curia, December 22, 2005, at http://www.vatican.va/holy_father/benedict_xvi/speeches/2005/december/documents/hf_ben_xvi_spe_20051222_roman-curia_en.html, discussed below in ch. 9 (*The Magisterium of the Church and the Charism of Infallibility: Three Grades of Assent*), Hermeneutic of Continuity.

[38] CDF, Instruction on the Ecclesial Vocation of the Theologian *Donum veritatis* (1990), §1.

it to others, so it *belongs to him to refute the opposing falsehood*.

Appropriately, therefore, is the twofold office of the wise man shown from the mouth of Wisdom in our opening words (Proverbs 8:7): to meditate and speak forth of the divine truth, which is truth in person (Wisdom touches on this in the words "my mouth shall meditate truth"), and to refute the opposing error (which Wisdom touches on in the words "and my lips shall hate impiety"). By *impiety* is here meant falsehood against the divine truth.[39]

It is impossible to defend the faith against heresy or attack without doing theology.

Perhaps it is not superfluous to point out that the ecclesial nature of theology also applies to biblical exegesis. In the last two centuries, exegetes have not infrequently treated the Bible as if it were a document of ancient literature like any other, capable of being examined "impartially" without respect to faith commitments or ecclesial Tradition. This cannot be the case, for Scripture is "the very soul of theology" (*DV* §24). If theology only reaches its fullness within the Church, which it helps to defend and build up, then that part of theology that focuses on the interpretation of Scripture must likewise, and *a fortiori*, be an ecclesial science.

Benedict XVI stresses this point in *Verbum Domini*:

> The intrinsic link between the word and faith makes clear that authentic biblical hermeneutics can only be had within the faith of the Church, which has its paradigm in Mary's *fiat*. Saint Bonaventure states that without faith there is no key to throw open the sacred text: "This is the knowledge of Jesus Christ, from whom, as from a fountain, flow forth the certainty and the understanding of all sacred Scripture. Therefore it is impossible for anyone to attain to knowledge of that truth unless he first have infused faith in Christ, which is the lamp,

---

[39] *SCG*, bk. I, ch. 1, nos. 3–4 (Pegis, 1:60–61).

the gate and the foundation of all Scripture."[40] And Saint Thomas Aquinas, citing Saint Augustine, insists that "the letter, even that of the Gospel, would kill, were there not the inward grace of healing faith."[41]

Here we can point to a fundamental criterion of biblical hermeneutics: *the primary setting for scriptural interpretation is the life of the Church.* This is not to uphold the ecclesial context as an extrinsic rule to which exegetes must submit, but rather is something demanded by the very nature of the Scriptures and the way they gradually came into being.[42]

Pope Benedict then quotes the 1993 document of the Pontifical Biblical Commission, *The Interpretation of the Bible in the Church*:

Faith traditions formed the living context for the literary activity of the authors of sacred Scripture. Their insertion into this context also involved a sharing in both the liturgical and external life of the communities, in their intellectual world, in their culture and in the ups and downs of their shared history. In like manner, the interpretation of sacred Scripture requires full participation on the part of exegetes in the life and faith of the believing community of their own time.[43]

As Scripture was forged in the faith of Israel and the apostolic Church, so the interpretation of Scripture must always be made in the light of the apostolic faith that continues to live and organically develop in the Church.

---

[40] St. Bonaventure, *Breviloquium, Prol.*, in *Opera omnia*, vol. V (Quaracchi, IT: Patres Editores, College of Saint Bonaventure, 1891), 201–202.

[41] *ST* I-II, q. 106, a. 2.

[42] Benedict XVI, Apostolic Exhortation *Verbum Domini* (2010), §29 (italics original).

[43] PBC, *The Interpretation of the Bible in the Church* (1993), III.A.3 (*Enchiridion Vaticanum* 13, no. 3035).

Academic Freedom and the Theologian

The work of the theologian has a proper freedom of inquiry dictated by the demands of the truth. However, the academic freedom of the Catholic theologian must be understood in accordance with the sources of theology: Scripture, Tradition, and Magisterium. These do not limit the freedom of the theologian, but constitute the foundation of his science. They are internal to it, and not external. The CDF treats this profoundly in *Donum veritatis* §12:

> Freedom of research, which the academic community rightly holds most precious, means an openness to accepting the truth that emerges at the end of an investigation in which no element has intruded that is foreign to the methodology corresponding to the object under study.
>
> In theology this freedom of inquiry is the hallmark of a rational discipline whose object is given by Revelation, handed on and interpreted in the Church under the authority of the Magisterium, and received by faith. These givens have the force of principles. To eliminate them would mean to cease doing theology.

The Harmony of Faith and Reason

Since theology seeks to know God through faith and reason, it is essential that these two sources be kept in intimate harmony. Faith and reason, when rightly used, cannot conflict because they come from the same God, who is both the Creator and Revealer. Human faith in a false religion or cult, however, can be opposed to reason, for such faith does not come from God. Thus the conflict between faith and reason is felt much more acutely in religions other than Catholicism, as in Islam, Mormonism, the Jehovah's Witnesses, etc. The Catholic Church, on the other hand, has always been the great defender of human reason, and of the arts and sciences in general. Ironically, the Church's defense of reason has become increasingly energetic in the past 150 years, as Western culture, progressively distancing itself from Christian faith, has been gradually sinking into skepticism with regard to the power of reason to know theoretical or moral truth. Faith and reason, far from being adversaries, mutually support each other.

The First Vatican Council confirms the harmony of faith and reason:

> However, though faith is above reason, there can never be a real discrepancy between faith and reason, since the same God who reveals mysteries and infuses faith has bestowed the light of reason on the human mind, and God cannot deny himself, nor can truth ever contradict truth. The deceptive appearance of such a contradiction is mainly due to the fact that either the dogmas of faith have not been understood and expounded according to the mind of the Church or fanciful conjectures are taken for verdicts of reason. . . .
>
> Not only can there be no conflict between faith and reason, they also support each other since right reason demonstrates the foundations of faith and, illumined by its light, pursues the science of divine things, while faith frees and protects reason from errors and provides it with manifold insights. It is therefore far removed from the truth to say that the Church opposes the study of human arts and sciences; on the contrary, she supports and promotes them in many ways. She does not ignore or despise the benefits that human life derives from them. Indeed, she acknowledges that, just as they have come forth from God, the Lord of knowledge, so too, if rightly pursued, they lead to God with the help of his grace. Nor does the Church in any way forbid that these sciences, each in its own domain, should make use of their own principles and of the method proper to them. While, however, acknowledging this just freedom, she seriously warns lest they fall into error by going contrary to the divine doctrine or, stepping beyond their own limits, enter into the sphere of faith and create confusion.[44]

---

[44] *Dei Filius*, ch. 4 (DS, 3017 and 3019).

In *Fides et ratio,* John Paul II treats beautifully of the relationship between these two forms of knowledge. It opens with an affirmation of their complementary, harmonious, and equally necessary character:

> Faith and reason are like two wings on which the human spirit rises to the contemplation of truth; and God has placed in the human heart a desire to know the truth—in a word, to know himself—so that, by knowing and loving God, men and women may also come to the fullness of truth about themselves.

John Paul II also confirms the harmony of faith and reason in *Veritatis splendor* §109, quoting the CDF's *Donum veritatis:*

> "By its nature, faith appeals to reason because it reveals to man the truth of his destiny and the way to attain it. Revealed truth, to be sure, surpasses our telling. All our concepts fall short of its ultimately unfathomable grandeur (see Eph 3:19). Nonetheless, revealed truth beckons reason—God's gift fashioned for the assimilation of truth—to enter into its light and thereby come to understand in a certain measure what it has believed. Theological science responds to the invitation of truth as it seeks to understand the faith. It thereby aids the People of God in fulfilling the Apostle's command (see 1 Pt 3:15) to give an accounting for their hope to those who ask it."[45]

Pope Benedict XVI, in his famous Regensburg lecture, also discusses the importance of this synthesis of the Israelite principle of faith with the Greek patrimony of philosophy. He speaks of the danger of rejecting this Catholic understanding of the harmony between faith and reason, whether in the Islamic world, the Protestant world, or the modern secular world. He aroused the ire of the Islamic world by citing the comments of a Greek Byzantine emperor: "Show me

---

[45] *Donum veritatis* §6.

just what Mohammed brought that was new, and there you will find things only evil and inhuman, such as his command to spread by the sword the faith he preached."[46] Benedict comments on this as follows:

> The decisive statement in this argument against violent conversion is this: not to act in accordance with reason is contrary to God's nature.... For the emperor, as a Byzantine shaped by Greek philosophy, this statement is self-evident. But for Muslim teaching, God is absolutely transcendent. His will is not bound up with any of our categories, even that of rationality.[47]

Such an attitude makes it impossible to offer to God what St. Paul (Rom 12:1) calls our "reasonable service" or worship.[48] Benedict goes on to quote this text from Romans: "Consequently, Christian worship is, again to quote Paul—'λογικη λατρεία,' worship in harmony with the eternal Word and with our reason."[49] The Catholic conviction that every society is to offer to God through the Church whatever is valid in its philosophy and culture only makes sense with the belief that God is the *Logos*, the Word that is the source of all rationality, whose seeds have been scattered among all the sons of men.

After securing the attention of the world with this introduction concerning Islam, Benedict then focuses on the Catholic understanding of the harmony of faith and reason, especially with regard to its roots in classical Greek philosophy. Like St. Clement of Alexandria, he sees the conjunction of biblical faith and Greek philosophy as a providential event that was clearly part of God's plan for the entire life of the Church. Benedict points out an interesting symbol of the providential nature of this harmony in a curious event narrated in the

---

[46] In the footnote of the official text, Benedict explains: "In quoting the text of the Emperor Manuel II, I intended solely to draw out the essential relationship between faith and reason. On this point I am in agreement with Manuel II, but without endorsing his polemic."

[47] Benedict XVI, the Regensburg Lecture (Sept. 12, 2006), in James V. Schall, *The Regensburg Lecture* (South Bend: St. Augustine's Press, 2007), 134.

[48] Douay-Rheims translation. The Neo-Vulgate has *"rationabile obsequium,"* in *Bibliorum Sacrorum: Nova Vulgata* (Vatican City: Libreria Editrice Vaticana, 1986). The RSV translates this difficult phrase rather inadequately as "spiritual worship."

[49] Benedict XVI, Regensburg Lecture, 138.

Acts of the Apostles (16:9–10) during St. Paul's second missionary voyage, in which the Holy Spirit bars him from speaking the Word of God in Asia Minor (Turkey): "And a vision appeared to Paul in the night: a man of Macedonia was standing beseeching him and saying, 'Come over to Macedonia and help us.' And when he had seen the vision, immediately we sought to go on into Macedonia, concluding that God had called us to preach the gospel to them." As a result, St. Paul brought the Gospel to Greece for the first time, which Benedict interprets as "a 'distillation' of the intrinsic necessity of a rapprochement between biblical faith and Greek inquiry."[50] He comments:

> This inner rapprochement between biblical faith and Greek philosophical inquiry was an event of decisive importance not only from the standpoint of the history of religions, but also from that of world history—it is an event which concerns us even today. Given this convergence, it is not surprising that Christianity, despite its origins and some significant developments in the East, finally took on its historically decisive character in Europe. We can also express this the other way around: this convergence, with the subsequent addition of the Roman heritage, created Europe and remains the foundation of what can rightly be called Europe.
>
> The thesis that the critically purified Greek heritage forms an integral part of Christian faith has been countered by the call for a dehellenization of Christianity—a call which has more and more dominated theological discussions since the beginning of the modern age.[51]

Benedict critiques this attempt to de-hellenize Christianity because it would paradoxically take away the catholic (universal) character of the Church, which is universal by its openness to reason as such wherever it is found functioning rightly. The supernatural faith of the Church is the true answer to the philosopher's quest for the full

---

[50] Ibid., 135.
[51] Ibid., 138–139.

meaning of life. Thus the Church, which preserves and announces the supernatural Revelation of God, is called to be the Bride of the Logos, the Word who orders all things.

Study Questions

1. Why are arguments from authority especially important in theology? Why does theology need to use other arguments that are not from authority, but from reason?
2. What are the different types of argumentation used by Catholic theology?
3. What is an argument from fittingness? Give some examples.
4. How does Fundamental Theology differ from apologetics? What are the functions and methods of apologetics?
5. In what sense is Catholic theology an *ecclesial* science? Does Catholic theology presuppose the Catholic faith? Why?
6. How should we understand the proper autonomy of the work of the Catholic theologian? Does a requirement to adhere to magisterial teaching interfere with the proper autonomy of a Catholic theologian?
7. Can faith and reason ever contradict one another? Explain.
8. What would be the consequences for the Catholic faith of disparaging the role of reason in theology?
9. Why does Benedict XVI, in the Regensburg lecture, critique attempts to "de-hellenize" Christianity?

Suggestions for Further Reading

Summa theologiae I, q. 1, a. 8.
Congregation for the Doctrine of the Faith. Instruction on the Ecclesial Vocation of the Theologian *Donum veritatis*. May 24, 1990.
International Theological Commission. "Theology Today: Perspectives, Principles and Criteria." *Origins* 41, no. 40 (March 15, 2012): 641–661.

Ratzinger, Joseph Cardinal. *The Nature and Mission of Theology*. San Francisco: Ignatius Press, 1995.

Pope Benedict XVI. "Faith, Reason and the University: Memories and Reflections." Regensburg Lecture, September 12, 2006.

Schall, James V., S.J. *The Regensburg Lecture*. South Bend: St. Augustine's Press, 2007.

PART 3

Transmission of Revelation through Tradition and the Magisterium

CHAPTER SEVEN

Apostolic Tradition and the "Oral Torah"

Sacred Tradition

God reveals Himself so as to draw all men into His covenant and bring them into intimate communion with Himself. Yet, as we have seen, He reveals Himself historically and ecclesially through mediators. So that each person can encounter the salvific Word of God, it must be faithfully passed on to all believers until the end of time. How does God guarantee this transmission of Revelation in His Church? He has willed that this transmission of the Word take two complementary forms: oral and written. Revelation passed on through oral means and through the whole life of the People of God is called divine Tradition,[1] while Sacred Scripture is the inspired communication of God's Word in writing. Scripture and Tradition are the two channels by which the one deposit of God's Revelation is passed down through the ages.

In the Old Testament, Tradition was passed on orally through Moses, the other prophets, and the sages or scribes. This oral transmission preceded and ran parallel with the written transmission. In the New Testament, Tradition is the revealed doctrine on faith and morals given by Christ to the custody of the Church, which the Apostles trans-

---

[1] See *DV* §8: "The Church, in her teaching, life and worship, perpetuates and hands on to all generations all that she herself is, all that she believes."

mitted *orally* in their preaching, liturgy, and life, and which is continuously transmitted from generation to generation in the entire life of the Church through the action of the Holy Spirit. This also preceded and then accompanied the written transmission through the New Testament.

The word "tradition" comes from the Latin word *tradere*, which means to "pass on." Tradition is a sacred heritage passed on from generation to generation through the work of the Holy Spirit. It is life in Christ, with the faithful as living stones built together in the household of God upon Christ as their foundation.

The existence of Tradition can be seen in the missionary mandate given by Christ to the Apostles before His Ascension. In Mark 16:15, Jesus commands the Apostles: "Go into all the world and preach the gospel to the whole creation." He did not tell them to *write* the Gospel, but to preach it, which means to transmit orally the teaching they received. Likewise, in the missionary mandate in Matthew 28:18–20, Jesus gave the commission to His Apostles to "*make disciples* of all nations, baptizing them in the name of the Father and of the Son and of the Holy Spirit, *teaching* them to observe all that I have commanded you; and lo, I am with you always, to the close of the age." By teaching the nations all that Jesus taught them, the Apostles transmitted the salvific Tradition to the Church, especially to their successors, the bishops, who passed it on to their successors, and so on to the present day. This transmission will continue until the end of the world because of Jesus's promise that He will remain with them until the end of time. Thus, the Tradition that is imparted by the Apostles and their successors is a *living Tradition*, bringing each new generation of disciples into vital contact with Christ and His Gospel.

In Acts 1:8, Jesus's last reported words to the Apostles enjoin the same mission: "You shall receive power when the Holy Spirit has come upon you; and you shall be my witnesses in Jerusalem and in all Judea and Samaria and to the end of the earth." The witness of the Apostles and their successors in their preaching, liturgy, and governance of the Church is the principal way in which the apostolic Tradition is transmitted to all generations and places, imparting vital contact with

Jesus Christ, source of grace and truth. This witness is made possible, as Jesus makes clear, through the full outpouring of the power of the Holy Spirit on Pentecost. It follows that the Holy Spirit must be the main protagonist in the passing on of Tradition.

Acts 1:8 also shows us the itinerary of the passing on of Tradition in very condensed form: it began in Jerusalem in Judea and was brought to Samaria by Philip (Acts 8) and to Ethiopia through the eunuch; there was a community already in Damascus in Syria at the time of Paul's conversion; and it spread gradually to the rest of the world through the aid of the synagogues and God-fearing Gentiles in the diaspora. We might think of Tradition as a fountain of life-giving waters that comes from a high place—Jerusalem—and, under the governance of bishops and priests, progressively forms streams and rivers that water the valleys of the earth.

This image is used by prophets who speak of the transmission of the apostolic Tradition in various messianic prophecies. In Isaiah 2:2–4, the prophet pictures Tradition as going out from Zion:

> It shall come to pass in the latter days that the mountain of the house of the Lord shall be established as the highest of the mountains, and shall be raised above the hills; and all the nations shall flow to it, and many peoples shall come, and say: "Come, let us go up to the mountain of the Lord, to the house of the God of Jacob; that he may teach us his ways and that we may walk in his paths." For out of Zion shall go forth the law, and the word of the Lord from Jerusalem.

Another magnificent prophetic image of apostolic Tradition is given in Ezekiel 47 through the image of a spring of water coming out from the east gate of the Temple, giving life to the desert of Judah and making the waters of the Dead Sea fresh and full of life. The angel says to Ezekiel:

> This water flows toward the eastern region and goes down into the Arabah; and when it enters the stagnant waters of the

sea, the water will become fresh. And wherever the river goes every living creature which swarms will live, and there will be very many fish; for this water goes there, that the waters of the sea may become fresh; so everything will live where the river goes. (Ezek 47:8–9)

This is a beautiful type of the power of God's Revelation—the Gospel—to create supernatural life as it flows through history into the cultures of the world to transform them.

Tradition is the transmission of the very life of Christ through the Holy Spirit. Those who receive this life are incorporated into Christ. Thus the transmission of living Tradition "gathers" the new Israel to the one pastor of the flock—Jesus the Messiah. This is prophesied in Ezekiel 34:23, in which God promises to "set up over them one shepherd, my servant David, and he shall feed them."[2] Indeed, He feeds us with his own life in the Eucharist.

It should never be forgotten that the first recipients of the apostolic Tradition were the Israelites. Only by gathering a faithful remnant[3] of the lost sheep of Israel could the apostolic message then go out to the nations to incorporate them as well into the new Israel of the messianic age, which is the fulfillment of the prophecies of the messianic Kingdom. "For out of Zion shall go forth the law, and the word of the Lord from Jerusalem" (Isa 2:3). The Church, in its founding at Pentecost, was entirely Jewish. Jesus Himself says that He was sent to gather the lost sheep of Israel. He calls the Twelve Apostles to be the foundation of the new Israel, according to the biblical prophecies about the messianic age.

Benedict XVI speaks profoundly about this in his Wednesday Audiences on the Apostles. In an audience of 2006 he states:

It must be said that the message of Jesus is completely misunderstood if it is separated from the context of the faith and hope of the Chosen People: like John the Baptist, his direct

---

[2] See also Ezek 36:24.

[3] See Rom 9:27 and 11:5.

Precursor, *Jesus above all addresses Israel in order to "gather" it together in the eschatological time that arrived with him.*[4]

In the audience of the following week, he adds:

To whom would the Apostles be sent? In the Gospel Jesus seemed to limit his mission to Israel alone: "I was sent only to the lost sheep of the house of Israel." In a similar way he seemed to restrict the mission entrusted to the Twelve (Matt 10:5ff.).... A certain rationally inspired modern criticism saw these words as showing a lack of universal awareness by the Nazarene. Actually, they should be understood in the light of his special relationship with Israel, the community of the Covenant, in continuity with the history of salvation. According to the Messianic expectation, the divine promises directly addressed to Israel would reach fulfillment when God himself had gathered his people through his Chosen One as a shepherd gathers his flock: "I will save my flock, they shall no longer be a prey.... I will set up over them one shepherd, my servant David, and he shall feed them..." (Ezek 34:22–24).

Jesus is the eschatological shepherd who gathers the lost sheep of the house of Israel and goes in search of them because he knows and loves them. Through this "gathering together," the Kingdom of God is proclaimed to all peoples: "I will set my glory among the nations; and all the nations shall see my judgment..." (Ezek 39:21). And Jesus followed precisely this prophetic indication. His first step was to "gather together" the people of Israel, so that all the people called to gather in communion with the Lord might see and believe.

Thus the Twelve, taken on to share in the same mission as Jesus, cooperate with the Pastor of the last times, also seeking out the lost sheep of the house of Israel, that is, addressing the people of the promise whose reunion is the sign of salva-

---

[4] Benedict XVI, Audience of March 15, 2006, at http://w2.vatican.va/content/benedict-xvi/en/audiences/2006/documents/hf_ben-xvi_aud_20060315.html; my italics.

tion for all peoples, the beginning of the universalization of the Covenant. Far from belying the universal openness of the Nazarene's Messianic action, the initial restriction to Israel of his mission and of the Twelve thus becomes an even more effective prophetic sign.[5]

Christ laid the foundation for the "gathering" of Israel through His Incarnation, preaching, and Paschal mystery. The Apostles were inserted into His mission and were "sent" (the meaning of the word "apostle") through the power of the Spirit to continue to gather Israel through the transmission of the apostolic Tradition and through the administration of the sacraments of the New Law. They appointed successors to continue this mission until the end of time.

As they gathered the new Israel, they also gathered Gentiles into the Church through the power of the Spirit. St. Paul beautifully describes the place of the Gentiles in the inheritance of messianic Israel:

> So then you are no longer strangers and sojourners, but you are fellow citizens with the saints and members of the household of God, built upon the foundation of the apostles and prophets, Christ Jesus himself being the cornerstone, in whom the whole structure is joined together and grows into a holy temple in the Lord; in whom you also are built into it for a dwelling place of God in the Spirit.[6]

In the Acts of the Apostles and the letters of St. Paul, we see the prophetic image of the Word of the Lord that goes out from Zion to all nations progressively realized through the preaching of the Apostles. St. Paul solemnly gives witness of Tradition in 1 Corinthians 15:3–4: "I delivered to you as of first importance what I also received, that Christ died for our sins in accordance with the scriptures, that he was buried, that he was raised on the third day."

---

[5] Benedict XVI, Audience of March 22, 2006, at http://w2.vatican.va/content/benedict-xvi/en/audiences/2006/documents/hf_ben-xvi_aud_20060322.html.

[6] Eph 2:19–22.

Furthermore, St. Paul says that his oral preaching is the Word of God. In 1 Thessalonians 2:13, he writes: "And we also thank God constantly for this, that when you received the word of God which you heard from us, you accepted it not as the word of men, but as what it really is, the word of God, which is at work in you believers." And in 2 Thessalonians 2:15, he puts his oral preaching on the same level as his canonical letters: "So then, brethren, stand firm and hold to the *traditions* which you were taught by us, either by word of mouth or by letter." Earlier in the same chapter (2 Thess 2:5), speaking of the signs of the Second Coming of Christ, the Apostle says: "Do you not remember that when I was still with you I told you this?"

In 2 Timothy, St. Paul says his oral teaching is a sacred deposit that Timothy is to guard faithfully and pass on to others: "Hence I remind you to rekindle the gift of God that is within you through the laying on of my hands. . . . Follow the pattern of the sound words which you have heard from me; . . . guard the truth that has been entrusted to you by the Holy Spirit who dwells within us."[7] And again: "What you have heard from me before many witnesses entrust to faithful men who will be able to teach others also."[8] St. Paul implies that the effective transmission of the apostolic Tradition is not simply a matter of teaching, but involves a sacramental charism given by the Spirit through Holy Orders. This transmission was not to end with Paul and the other Apostles, but was sacramentally entrusted by Paul to Timothy and Titus (through the laying on of hands), who in turn were to sacramentally entrust the transmission of the sacred deposit to their successors.

Another fundamental text that speaks of Tradition is Romans 10:14–17:

> But how are men to call upon him in whom they have not believed? And how are they to believe in him of whom they have never heard? And how are they to hear without a preacher? And how can men preach unless they are sent? As it is written,

---

[7] 2 Tim 1:6, 13–14.

[8] 2 Tim 2:2.

"How beautiful are the feet of those who preach good news!"
But they have not all obeyed the gospel; for Isaiah says, "Lord,
who has believed what he has heard from us?" So faith comes
from what is heard, and what is heard comes by the preaching
of Christ.

The Gospel is transmitted to all nations and generations through
preaching, which is the oral transmission of the apostolic Tradition.

1 Peter 1:12 speaks of the preaching of the Gospel by the Apostles
as the work of the Holy Spirit, which the prophets glimpsed from afar:
"It was revealed to them that they were serving not themselves but you,
in the things which have now been announced to you by those who
preached the good news to you through the Holy Spirit sent from heaven,
things into which angels long to look."

One of the most tragic innovations of Protestantism was its denial
of Tradition as a source of Revelation (together with the denial of the
infallibility of the Magisterium), leaving Scripture as the only certain
norm of faith and morals. This position is summarized in the phrase
sola Scriptura. The existence of Tradition was solemnly defined as a
dogma of faith in the Council of Trent, against the position of Luther:

The holy, ecumenical and general Council of Trent . . . clearly perceives that these truths and instruction [of the Gospel]
are contained in the written books and in the *unwritten traditions*, which, received by the Apostles from the mouth of
Christ Himself, or from the Apostles themselves, the Holy
Spirit dictating, have come down to us, transmitted as it were
from hand to hand. Following, then, the examples of the orthodox Fathers, it receives and venerates with piety and reverence all the books both of the Old and New Testaments, since
one God is the author of both; *also the traditions, whether they
relate to faith or to morals, as having been dictated either orally
by Christ or by the Holy Spirit, and preserved in the Catholic
Church in unbroken succession.*[9]

---

[9]   Council of Trent, Session 4 (1546), in DS, 1501 (my italics).

The Function of Tradition

Many Protestant theologians admit the necessity of Tradition as a channel of Revelation only in the beginning of the Church, before the formation of the New Testament. Sacred Tradition, however, is necessary for the Church *in all times* for many reasons.

First, oral Tradition is chronologically prior to Sacred Scripture, both in Israel and the Church. Revelation is first manifested through the oral tradition of the patriarchs and prophets in Israel. God revealed Himself to our first parents, to Noah, to Abraham, Isaac, Jacob, and Joseph, but this Revelation was only written down many centuries later in Genesis. Even the great prophets first taught orally; their prophecies were put together and written down only later. Similarly, in the New Testament, the decisive Revelation is the Person of Jesus and His words and actions, especially the Paschal mystery. This was transmitted orally by the Apostles for the first generation of the Church's life. In both covenants, oral Tradition was present from the beginning and was written down in inspired form only at a later date. This shows that the living and spoken word is the first means chosen by God to reveal Himself.

Second, Scripture without Tradition is a dead letter, having no key for interpretation. Through the life-giving action of the Holy Spirit, Tradition conserves the true sense of Revelation and of Holy Scripture. Without Tradition, it would be impossible to defend the faith against heretics who cite Scripture against its true meaning. The Fathers and Doctors easily detected the presence of heresy because it clashed with their sense of the living Tradition. The fragmentation of the Protestant world into thousands of branches is a demonstration of what would happen to the Church if she were stripped of her authoritative Tradition.

The need for an authoritative Tradition for the interpretation of Scripture can be seen in Christ's parables. The disciples could not understand them, so Jesus Himself had to interpret them. Similarly, He interpreted the Old Testament texts that referred to His Paschal mystery on Easter Sunday and "opened their minds to understand the scriptures" (Luke 24:45). Tradition involves the living transmission of that understanding—given by the Lord to His Apostles—to all generations.

Third, Tradition is more ample than Holy Scripture and contains truths that are not *explicitly* contained in the Bible. St. John concludes his Gospel (21:25) with this affirmation: "But there are also many other things which Jesus did; were every one of them to be written, I suppose that the world itself could not contain the books that would be written." Evidently, St. John knew much more of the doctrine of Christ than he wrote in the Fourth Gospel, and therefore it is certain that he taught many truths orally that were never written down in the Bible. And on account of the reverence in which the Apostles were held, these truths were faithfully guarded and transmitted by the successors of the Apostles, the first bishops.

For example, St. Irenaeus, eminent Father of the Church and bishop of Lyons at the end of the second century and beginning of the third, tells how, in his early youth, he had heard many things— and remembered them with great clarity—from the holy martyr St. Polycarp, his master, who died in 169 after having been a bishop for perhaps some sixty or seventy years. St. Polycarp, in his turn, as a very young man had been a disciple of St. John the Evangelist at the end of the first century, as well as a disciple of St. Ignatius of Antioch, who was a direct disciple of St. Peter and St. John. Irenaeus writes:

> I have a clearer recollection of events at that time than of recent happenings—what we learn in childhood develops along with the mind and becomes a part of it—so that I can describe the place where blessed Polycarp sat and talked, his goings out and comings in, the character of his life, his personal appearance, his addresses to crowded congregations. I remember how he spoke of his intercourse with John and with the others who had seen the Lord, how he repeated their words from memory, and how the things that he had heard them say about the Lord, His miracles and His teaching, things that he had heard direct from the eye-witnesses of the Word of Life, were proclaimed by Polycarp in complete

harmony with Scripture. To these things I listened eagerly at that time, by the mercy of God shown to me, not committing them to writing but learning them by heart. By God's grace, I constantly and conscientiously ruminate on them.[10]

For St. Irenaeus, his memory of the oral Tradition stemming from the Apostles was, together with Scripture, his most precious possession and the subject of constant meditation.

The fact that the apostolic Tradition is more ample than the explicit contents of Sacred Scripture has important practical consequences. Not all revealed truths are found explicitly in the Bible, and therefore the Church can define dogmas of faith on the basis of her Tradition and what is only implicit in Scripture. For example, the Assumption of Our Lady is not narrated explicitly in Scripture, but was defined as dogma on the basis of the living Tradition. Similarly, the fittingness of the discipline of clerical celibacy (or more precisely, perfect continence for bishops, priests, and deacons) was understood by the Fathers to be an apostolic Tradition, even though it is not directly contained in Scripture.[11]

Another example is the canon of Scripture. No text of Scripture teaches which are the true books of the Bible. The canon of Scripture is known by the Church only through Tradition, confirmed by the Magisterium.[12] From the second to the fourth centuries, some local churches had certain doubts about which books were included in the canon of inspired Scripture. These doubts were gradually dissipated until, by the end of the fourth century, the true canon of Scripture was defined in councils in North Africa[13] and approved by the Roman

---

[10] In Eusebius, *Historia ecclesiastica* 5.20.6 (*NPNF2*, 1:227), in which Eusebius quotes a letter from St. Irenaeus to a Gnostic heretic named Florinus.

[11] See Stefan Heid, *Celibacy in the Early Church* (San Francisco: Ignatius Press, 2000); Christian Cochini, S.J., *Apostolic Origins of Priestly Celibacy* (San Francisco: Ignatius Press, 1990); and Alfons Maria Cardinal Stickler, *The Case for Clerical Celibacy* (San Francisco: Ignatius Press, 1995).

[12] See Mark P. Shea, *By What Authority? An Evangelical Discovers Catholic Tradition* (Huntington: Our Sunday Visitor, 1996), 78–171.

[13] See the PBC, *The Inspiration and Truth of Sacred Scripture: The Word that Comes from God and Speaks of God for the Salvation of the World*, §60 (Collegeville: Liturgical Press, 2014), 65.

Pontiff. This same canon was later infallibly defined in the Council of Trent. This means that Protestants, while rejecting the authority of Tradition, have nevertheless received their Bible from the Catholic Tradition (although a few books were left out).[14]

However, even when a truth of faith is contained directly in Scripture, Tradition is always necessary as a witness of the correct interpretation. Thus truths can be defined solely on the basis of Tradition (although with the aid of what is implicit in Scripture), but never on the basis of Scripture alone without Tradition. The two form an organic unity and together are "like a mirror in which the pilgrim Church on earth looks at God, from whom she has received everything, until she is brought finally to see Him as He is, face to face" (*DV* §7).

Tradition and Traditions

It is important to recognize that not everything taught by the Fathers of the Church is part of Tradition in the proper sense of the word. Any individual Father could make mistakes in particular matters. However, when the Fathers speak with a common and definitive voice concerning matters of faith and morals, we should recognize the presence of Tradition.[15] Numerical unanimity is not necessary and would be impossible to find or verify. The key criterion is moral unanimity, which means a general *consensus* on matters of faith and morals to be held by all the faithful.

Tradition with a capital "T" refers to the deposit of Revelation that has been entrusted to the Church. It is the apostolic Tradition. However, there are also venerable ecclesiastical traditions that do not necessarily form part of the deposit of Revelation, even though they have great importance in the life of the Church. These ecclesiastical traditions are not a matter of doctrine. They do not directly transmit

---

[14] Protestants rejected Tobit, Judith, Wisdom, Sirach, Baruch, 1 and 2 Maccabees, and parts of Esther and Daniel, despite the fact that these books had been accepted and used by the Church from the early centuries. The Council of Trent formally defined the Catholic canon of Scripture, in which these books are included.

[15] See the Council of Trent, Session 4 (April 8, 1546): "No one may dare to interpret the Scripture in a way contrary to the unanimous consensus of the Fathers" (DS, 1507).

a truth, but determine a particular way of acting or worshiping. They are disciplinary, and therefore they can change to a certain degree. Examples are the practice of fasting from meat on Fridays during Lent, praying facing towards the east, women's head coverings in church, and the like. The apostolic Tradition, on the other hand, cannot change, although it is gradually made more explicit over time.

Ecclesiastical traditions generally have a doctrinal root that certainly belongs to the apostolic Tradition.[16] Fasting and other penitential practices, for example, are based on the doctrinal truth that we must do penance of some sort for our sins and in remembrance of the Passion of Christ. The precise manner in which penance is done, however, is something that can and ought to vary according to different social and individual circumstances. Liturgical traditions, likewise, are based on the doctrinal truths concerning the essential elements of the sacraments and salvation history. Liturgical traditions develop organically in the life of the Church as worship interacts with culture. The doctrinal root, however, does not change. Although subject to reform and modification, ecclesiastical traditions merit great respect because of the Holy Spirit who works through them. It is a sign of a lack of ecclesial spirit to denigrate the venerable traditions of the Church, whether liturgical or ascetical.

Witnesses of Tradition

Given the importance of Tradition as a source of Revelation, it is necessary to determine how authentic Tradition is recognized. Theology speaks of five witnesses of Tradition: the Magisterium of the Church, which is the organ of Tradition; the Creeds recited in the liturgy and

---

[16] See Yves Congar, *The Meaning of Tradition*, trans. A. N. Woodrow (San Francisco: Ignatius Press, 2004), 44: "There exist . . . numerous traditions that are ecclesiastical by origin, having been laid down by the Church during her historical existence: institutions, rites, customs, discipline. Sometimes these are the historical form, or modification, perhaps, of a reality that is apostolic or even divine in origin. For example, the obligation of hearing Mass on Sunday or of the annual Easter Communion is an ecclesiastical modification of a divine or apostolic reality. The papacy, in the form fixed by centuries of history, is a historical form of a divine institution (that of Peter as supreme pastor and head of the apostolic college), itself already modified by an apostolic initiative (the fact that Peter had his 'see' at Rome)."

other professions of faith; the writings of the Fathers of the Church; the liturgy of the Church, for the rule of public prayer in the Church is also the rule of faith; and finally, the consensus of the great theologians of holy life and orthodox doctrine, such as St. Thomas Aquinas, St. Bonaventure, St. Bernard, etc. ⟩

When they exhibit a consensus, the Fathers of the Church have a special role in witnessing to the apostolic Tradition from the fact that they stand closer to it and because God has given them a special wisdom in accordance with their unique mission of standing at the head of the Church's theological Tradition.[17]

Vatican II on Tradition, Scripture, and the Magisterium

Dei Verbum §§7–10 discusses the transmission of Revelation in Tradition and Scripture and its preservation through the Church's Magisterium. Although Tradition and Scripture differ in the way they hand on Revelation, these two complementary channels flow from one original source—the words of Christ and the prophets—and work together in intimate union, forming one "sacred deposit" of faith.[18] Tradition came first, for the Apostles preached orally before the books of the New Testament were written down, just as Moses and the prophets preached before some of their words were written down in inspired form.

Tradition enabled the Apostles and their successors, through all ages of the Church, to "preserve this word of God faithfully, explain it, and make it more widely known" (*DV* §9). It will continue to perform this necessary function until the end of time. Tradition is always necessary in the Church, for Scripture does not make clear its own proper interpretation, nor does it explicitly contain all that God revealed. Even after the establishment of the New Testament and its canon, we

---

[17] See Pius XII, Encyclical Letter on Promoting Biblical Studies *Divino afflante Spiritu* (1943), §§28–29, and Congregation for Catholic Education, Instruction on the Study of the Fathers of the Church in the Formation of Priests (1989), in *Origins* 19, no. 34 (Jan. 25, 1990).

[18] See *DV* §10.

still need Tradition to ensure a true understanding of the message of Christ's Gospel.

Dei Verbum §9 magnificently describes the complementarity and unity of Scripture and Tradition in the transmission of Revelation:

> Hence there exists a close connection and communication between Sacred Tradition and Sacred Scripture. For both of them, flowing from the same divine wellspring, in a certain way merge into a unity and tend toward the same end. For Sacred Scripture is the Word of God inasmuch as it is consigned to writing under the inspiration of the divine Spirit, while Sacred Tradition takes the Word of God entrusted by Christ the Lord and the Holy Spirit to the Apostles, and hands it on to their successors in its full purity, so that led by the light of the Spirit of truth, they may, in proclaiming it, preserve this word of God faithfully, explain it, and make it more widely known. Consequently it is not from Sacred Scripture alone that the Church draws her certainty about everything which has been revealed. Therefore both Sacred Tradition and Sacred Scripture are to be accepted and venerated with the same sense of loyalty and reverence.

John Paul II, in an address of February 27, 2000, confirms this, saying:

> The Dogmatic Constitution *Dei Verbum* put the Word of God at the heart of the Church's life with renewed awareness. This centrality stems from a more vivid perception of the unity of Sacred Scripture and Sacred Tradition. The Word of God, which is kept alive by the faith of the holy people of believers under the guidance of the Magisterium, also asks each of us to accept our own responsibility for preserving intact the process of transmission.

In *Dei Verbum* §8, the content of Tradition is said to include the entire life of the Church:

Now what was handed on by the Apostles includes everything which contributes toward the holiness of life and increase in faith of the People of God; and so the Church, in her teaching, life, and worship, perpetuates and hands on to all generations *all that she herself is, all that she believes.*[19]

Development of Tradition

Dei Verbum §8 also treats the very important subject of the development of Tradition in the Church, which grows through a gradual increase in the understanding of God's Revelation:

This Tradition which comes from the Apostles develops in the Church with the help of the Holy Spirit. For there is a growth in the understanding of the realities and the words which have been handed down. This happens through the contemplation and study made by believers, who treasure these things in their hearts (see Luke 2:19, 51), through a penetrating understanding of the spiritual realities which they experience, and through the preaching of those who have received through episcopal succession the sure gift of truth. For as the centuries succeed one another, the Church constantly moves forward toward the fullness of divine truth until the words of God reach their complete fulfillment in her.

The continual enrichment of Tradition in the life of the Church is a very important doctrine with great practical consequences. In every period, the Church—through the continual action of the Holy Spirit in the contemplation of the faithful—is able to grasp certain revealed truths more profoundly and explicitly. Tradition grows, thus,

---

[19] Italics mine.

by the long process through which what was formerly implicit in Tradition and Scripture becomes more and more explicit. *Dei Verbum* §8 gives three causes of this growth: the continual contemplation of Revelation by the faithful on the model of Mary, who treasured it in her heart, the spiritual experience of the faithful, and the charism of preaching by those with the fullness of the sacrament of Holy Orders. The increased understanding of Revelation by which Tradition grows should not be thought of as a purely academic or intellectual process, as is the case in other sciences, for both the object of knowledge and the means of increased understanding are supernatural. Although theologians aid in this process of the development of Tradition, it is principally brought about by reception of the gifts of the Holy Spirit of knowledge, understanding, and wisdom, which grow in the faithful (whether theologians or not) as they progress in grace and charity. It is preserved and transmitted also through a supernatural means: the charism of preaching of the bishops that comes from the grace communicated through Holy Orders.

It follows from this truth about the development of Tradition that we cannot view any major period in the life of the Church as barren or unfruitful, as if Christ and His Spirit had failed to be present at that time. Every period of the Church's life and each region of the universal Church has something unique to contribute to the development of Tradition and to a deeper understanding of the deposit of faith and its inculturation.

A very common Protestant attitude is to think that the Church from the time of Constantine, more or less, had basically gone astray, until the advent of Martin Luther. Such an idea implies too little faith in the power of the Holy Spirit to maintain the faith of the Church through the centuries in accordance with the promise of our Redeemer to be present always with His Church, even to the end of time, and to send His Spirit to lead her into all truth. It is impossible that the divine fidelity would allow the key truths of the apostolic preaching to be lost or corrupted and cease to vivify the Church, even for a generation, although the Church is always in need of new evangelization and faithful reform.

Sometimes certain Catholics fall into a similar error, denigrating large epochs in the history of the Church, such as the Middle Ages, Scholasticism, the period from Trent to Vatican II, or the period since Vatican II. Such views betray a certain arrogance and party spirit and are incompatible with the development of Tradition in the life of the Church as affirmed in this text from *Dei Verbum* §8.

In order to help Protestants and others to rediscover the beauty of Tradition, *Dei Verbum* §8 mentions some great examples of the witness of Tradition from Patristic times:

> The words of the holy Fathers witness to the presence of this living Tradition, whose wealth is poured into the practice and life of the believing and praying Church. Through the same Tradition, the Church's full canon of the sacred books is known, and the sacred writings themselves are more profoundly understood and unceasingly made active in her; and thus God, who spoke of old, uninterruptedly converses with the bride of His beloved Son; and the Holy Spirit, through whom the living voice of the Gospel resounds in the Church, and through her, in the world, leads unto all truth those who believe and makes the word of Christ dwell abundantly in them (see Col 3:16).

Through their proximity to the apostolic Tradition, the Fathers received the life-giving Tradition near its source, made it known, and enriched it with their own contemplation and preaching. The canon of Scripture is known through Tradition, and the profound meaning of Scripture is likewise progressively made known and made fruitful in the life of the Church through the dynamic action of Tradition. Scripture and Tradition together enable the Church to enter into unceasing dialogue with the Lord.

Tradition in Israel: The Oral Torah

The notion of "Tradition," of course, is not an invention of the Church or of Jesus, but was present in Israel from the beginning of her existence. God's Revelation was given to Israel not only in the written form of Scripture, but also in oral form to be passed from generation to generation. Like the Church, Israel knew the canon of her sacred books from oral Tradition.

The notion of oral Tradition in Judaism is expressed in the words of the Mishnah: "Moses received Torah at Sinai and handed it on to Joshua, Joshua to elders, and elders to prophets. And prophets handed it on to the men of the great assembly."[20] The "Great Assembly" refers to the sages of the time of Ezra and Nehemiah, who were the link between the last prophets after the Exile (Haggai, Zechariah, and Malachi) and the rabbis of the following generations.

The Old Testament itself shows us that Israel's knowledge of revealed truth was in constant development. This can be seen in the gradual growth of knowledge about the Messiah and His Kingdom, as well as of the Last Things: the Resurrection, heaven and hell, the necessity of prayers for the faithful departed, and so forth. The Resurrection, for example, is mentioned in the book of 2 Maccabees 7, when the mother and her seven martyred sons proclaim their belief that God will gloriously raise their mutilated bodies.

Despite the infidelity of individual men and women, Revelation in Israel was maintained, passed on, and developed according to God's plan. This was accomplished by the mutual witness of the written and the oral Torah, for the written Torah is explained and understood by the light of the oral Tradition.

Although at work since the calling of Abraham and the Revelation on Sinai, the oral Torah took on a new prominence in the life of Israel after the destruction of the Temple in AD 70,[21] and especially after the exile of the Jews from Israel in AD 135 with the Second Jewish War. Since all sacrifice had to be offered in the one Temple, the de-

---

[20] Mishnah-tractate *Avot* 1:1, in Jacob Neusner, *The Mishnah: A New Translation* (New Haven: Yale University Press, 1988), 672.

[21] The Jews mourn that destruction in an annual fast, *Tisha B'Av* (ninth day of the Jewish month of Av).

struction of the Temple of Jerusalem meant the end of the sacrificial system. With the loss of the offering of sacrifice, the Old Testament priesthood lost its principal function and thus its reason for existing. As a result, Jewish life came to center on the synagogue rather than on the Temple and was led by the rabbis who interpreted the Mosaic Law rather than by the priests and Levites. In this context of upheaval and tragedy, it gradually became imperative to write down the oral Torah to preserve it for future generations. The Mishnah and Talmud were written at this time.

Interestingly, the formative period of the Church corresponded chronologically with the formative period of rabbinical Judaism, for the oral Torah was written down by the sages of Israel during the first through the seventh centuries.

Rabbinical Judaism as it has existed for the past fifteen hundred years cannot be understood without understanding the role of the "oral Torah" in shaping Jewish life and the Jewish world-view. What is the oral Torah? Rabbi Jacob Neusner gives a good explanation:

> Judaism has always maintained that God revealed a dual Torah to Moses at Sinai: One Torah was to be transmitted to the people of Israel through the medium of writing; the other was to be handed down orally, memorized by successive sages. These words of God were specifically formulated to be memorized.... The written Torah and the oral Torah together constitute a single whole Torah—the full and exhaustive statement of God's will for Israel and humanity....
>
> The writing down of the oral Torah began with the Mishnah, a philosophical law code, at ca. 200 C.E. It concluded with the closure of the Talmud of Babylonia, a sustained exposition of both the Mishnah and Scripture, at ca. 600 C.E.... Sayings in these documents derive from sages who flourished from somewhat before the first century C.E. to the conclusion of the Talmud of Babylonia, hence over a period of more than six hundred years.[22]

---

[22] Jacob Neusner, *The Oral Torah: The Sacred Books of Judaism: An Introduction* (San Francisco: Harper & Row, 1986), vii.

He continues:

> Authoritative writings that say a single harmonious truth constitute not a library, but a canon. The canon of Judaism, made up of the authoritative books, so constitutes not merely a collection of writings but a coherent and harmonious statement, that is, torah, or instruction. . . .
>
> At stake in this book is the integrity of Judaism. Why? The Judaic religion stands or falls on the claim of the unity and cogency of the one whole Torah, oral and written, of Sinai. If I make my point stick, then I provide the key to living and believing as an informed Jew. If I do not, then I contribute merely a useful source of information about some books. So much more matters, in the pages that follow, than mere questions of detail. Specifically, details flow together into a single, whole, and cogent proposition.[23]

The unity of the written and oral Torah is crucial for understanding the nature of the Church, for she also is founded on the Word of God known through Scripture and Tradition, transmitted in written and oral form. This twofold mode of transmission has been God's plan from the beginning.

Revelation came to Israel through this twofold channel. It continues to come to Israel and the Church in this twofold channel today and will continue in this way until the end of time. The two channels—oral and written—of the one Revelation of God form a unitary whole and enable the Church to remain in the whole truth.

It follows that the study of the history of the early centuries of the Church is not merely an investigation of details of history. Rather it is an investigation into the early sources of the Tradition that was transmitted from Christ to the Apostles, and from them to their successors, down to our day. In this chain of witnesses, the early Fathers have a special place.

---

[23] Ibid., ix.

The same was true in the formation of rabbinical Judaism. The Jewish Sages—rabbis from the first to the seventh centuries AD—formulated in writing the substance of the oral Torah. This written corpus is referred to as the Mishnah and the Talmud. Together with the written Scriptures, the Mishnah and Talmud form the basis of Jewish life.

As Neusner states, *"The Judaic religion stands or falls on the claim of the unity and cogency of the one whole Torah, oral and written, of Sinai."* In the same way, Christianity depends on the claim of the unity and cogency of the one whole Torah, oral and written, begun on Sinai and consummated in the teaching and Paschal mystery of Jesus the Messiah and transmitted to His Apostles and their successors, orally passed on from generation to generation in the life of the Church. This is why it is crucial to study the Fathers of the Church (as privileged transmitters of Tradition) together with the Scriptures.

Apostolic Tradition and the Oral Torah

What is the connection between the oral Torah and the apostolic Tradition of the Church? First of all, the apostolic Tradition includes the oral Torah, insofar as the oral Torah was an integral part of God's continuing Revelation to Israel. This Revelation culminated with the Incarnation, teaching, death, and Resurrection of the Messiah. The apostolic Tradition is thus the complete deposit of which the oral Torah was only a part in development. The deposit of faith that Jesus passed on to His Church through the Apostles included all the Revelation made to Israel, understood as leading up to and preparing for the mystery of the Messiah and the messianic Kingdom (Christ and the Church). That Revelation was illuminated and transfigured by the light of the fullness of Christ and the New Covenant sealed in His Blood.

Thus, after the Revelation of Christ, much of the oral Torah of Israel as put down later in the Talmud is not directly pertinent to the Church because it deals primarily with the ceremonial law and judicial precepts of the Mosaic Law, which are no longer binding in the

Church, for the Church has a new ceremonial law centering on the seven sacraments of the New Covenant.[24] Jewish Tradition, however, continues to be able to further illuminate the mystery of Christ,[25] as well as the themes of marriage and the family,[26] prayer, worship, and others.

Benedict XVI on Tradition

Benedict XVI has given a beautiful catechesis on the apostolic Tradition in his Wednesday Audience of April 26 and May 3, 2006, as an introduction to the series of catecheses on the Apostles and Fathers of the Church. He emphasizes that Tradition is the transmission of the Church's life to all succeeding generations. It is not simply the passing on of formulas committed to memory by the Apostles. Rather, it is the transmission of the "goods of salvation" and of the spirit of *life in Christ*, made possible by the communication of the Holy Spirit. Tradition cannot be understood apart from the Holy Spirit, who spoke through the prophets, and through whom all Revelation is communicated and kept alive in the Church. He writes:

> The Church's apostolic Tradition consists in this transmission of the goods of salvation which, through the power of the Spirit, makes the Christian community the permanent actualization of the original communion. It is called "original" because it was born of the witness of the Apostles and of the community of the disciples at the time of the origins. It was passed on under the guidance of the Holy Spirit in the New Testament writings and in the sacramental life, in the

---

[24] The medieval theologians, such as St. Thomas, distinguished three kinds of precepts in the Mosaic Law (whether written or oral): the moral law, the ceremonial law, and judicial precepts. Christ fulfilled the entire Law, but only the precepts of the moral law continue as such in the Church. See Lawrence Feingold, *The Mystery of Israel and the Church*, vol. 1, *Figure and Fulfillment* (St. Louis: Miriam Press, 2010), 133–139, and *ST* I-II, q. 99, a. 4.

[25] See Raphael Patai, *The Messiah Texts* (Detroit: Wayne State University Press, 1979).

[26] See, for example, Joseph Atkinson, *Biblical and Theological Foundations of the Family: The Domestic Church* (Washington, DC: Catholic University of America Press, 2014).

life of the faith, and the Church continuously refers to it—to this Tradition, which is the whole, ever up-to-date reality of Jesus' gift—as her foundation and her law, through the uninterrupted succession of the apostolic ministry.

. . . Tradition is the communion of the faithful around their legitimate Pastors down through history, a communion that the Holy Spirit nurtures, assuring the connection between the experience of the apostolic faith, lived in the original community of the disciples, and the actual experience of Christ in His Church.

In other words, Tradition is the practical continuity of the Church, the holy Temple of God the Father, built on the foundation of the Apostles and held together by the cornerstone, Christ, through the life-giving action of the Spirit: "So then you are no longer strangers and sojourners, but you are fellow citizens with the saints and members of the household of God, built upon the foundation of the apostles and prophets, Christ Jesus himself being the cornerstone, in whom the whole structure is joined together and grows into a holy temple in the Lord; in whom you also are built into it for a dwelling place of God in the Spirit" (Eph 2:19–22).

Thanks to Tradition, guaranteed by the ministry of the Apostles and by their successors, the water of life that flowed from Christ's side and His saving blood reach the women and men of all times. Thus, Tradition is the permanent presence of the Savior who comes to meet us, to redeem us and to sanctify us in the Spirit, through the ministry of His Church, to the glory of the Father.

Concluding and summing up, we can therefore say that Tradition is not the transmission of things or words, a collection of dead things. Tradition is the living river that links us to the origins, the living river in which the origins are ever present, the great river that leads us to the gates of eternity. And since this is so, in this living river the words of the

Lord . . . are ceaselessly brought about: "I am with you always, to the close of the age" (Matt 28:20).[27]

Apostolic Tradition is something essential to the Church of Christ: the true Church of Christ is that in which apostolic Tradition is continually transmitted and revered as the life-giving river by which each generation receives the deposit of faith in its fullness.

Study Questions

1. What is the twofold purpose of sacred Tradition in the life of the Church?
2. What is the difference between Tradition and venerable ecclesiastical traditions?
3. Compare the role of Tradition in the life of Israel and the Church.
4. What are the principal witnesses of Tradition?
5. Explain why *Dei Verbum* §10 says that "sacred tradition, Sacred Scripture and the teaching authority of the Church, in accord with God's most wise design, are so linked and joined together that one cannot stand without the others."
6. How should we understand the *development of Tradition* in the life of the Church? If public Revelation came to a close with the death of the Apostles, how can Tradition continue to develop? (Make reference to *Dei Verbum* §8).

Suggestions for Further Reading

Dei Verbum §§7–10.
Congar, Yves. *The Meaning of Tradition.* Translated by A. N. Woodrow. San Francisco: Ignatius Press, 2004.
Pope Benedict XVI. *Jesus, the Apostles, and the Early Church,* 7–38

---

[27] Benedict XVI, General Audience, April 26, 2006; in *Jesus, the Apostles, and the Early Church* (San Francisco: Ignatius Press, 2007), 25–28.

(General Audiences from March 15 to May 10, 2006). San Francisco: Ignatius Press, 2007.

Newman, John Henry Cardinal. *An Essay on the Development of Christian Doctrine*. 6th edition. Notre Dame: University of Notre Dame Press, 1989.

Ratzinger, Joseph Cardinal. "The Question of the Concept of Tradition." In *God's Word: Scripture—Tradition—Office*, 41–89. Edited by Peter Hünermann and Tomas Söding. Translated by Henry Taylor. San Francisco: Ignatius Press, 2008.

———. *Principles of Catholic Theology: Building Stones for a Fundamental Theology*, 85–152. Translated by Sr. Mary Frances McCarthy, S.N.D. San Francisco: Ignatius Press, 1987.

Shea, Mark P. *By What Authority? An Evangelical Discovers Catholic Tradition*. Huntington: Our Sunday Visitor, 1996.

CHAPTER EIGHT

Apostolic Succession: Hierarchical Nature of the Transmission of Revelation

The apostolicity of the Church refers to the sacramental succession of bishops from the Apostles, as well as the continual passing on of the apostolic doctrine. The apostolic succession makes possible and sacramentally guarantees the preservation and transmission of the apostolic Tradition through the assistance of the Holy Spirit.

Christ Built His Church on the Apostles

Part of the scandal of the Catholic Church to Protestants and unbelievers in general is the mystery that the "Kingdom of God" is built on the foundation of sometimes very imperfect human beings: the Apostles and their successors. People often think that a spiritual kingdom ought to be completely spiritual, without any visible *institutional* structures like the episcopal college, based on apostolic succession, or the papacy, based on succession from Peter. This scandal was at the heart of the Protestant revolt. How could God build His kingdom using mere men?

Throughout salvation history, it is clear that God is pleased to use the weak things of this world to confound the proud. He used the Apostles to show us that all the glory is His, and He continues to use men like them to govern His Church according to the same model that He established during His public ministry. The power of the Holy

Spirit works through human persons endowed with the sacramental gift of Holy Orders in its fullness. Pope Benedict XVI expresses this beautifully in his catechesis on the Apostles: "The Church is wholly of the Spirit but has a structure, the apostolic succession, which is responsible for guaranteeing that the Church endures in the truth given by Christ, from whom the capacity to love also comes."[1]

The fact that Christ built His Church on the Apostles is a beautiful example of the principle of mediation and of the sacramental principle. God wills to make use of mediators in His governance and salvation of mankind. He made use of Moses in giving the Law to Israel, and He made use of Aaron and his descendants to be High Priests. Above all, God makes use of the humanity of Christ as the Mediator between God and man, and He likewise makes use of Peter and the other Apostles as mediators with respect to the Mediator. The Apostles sacramentally represent Christ and share in His mediation. Christ said to the Apostles on Easter Sunday: "As the Father has sent me, even so I send you" (John 20:21). And in His priestly prayer after the Last Supper He prayed: "As thou didst send me into the world, so I have sent them into the world" (John 17:18).

In His government of the world, God could conceivably direct everything Himself immediately without giving any share of direction or kingship to any creature. We might think that such a way of governing would be more appropriate for the majesty of God and the manifestation of His glory. This would be the Protestant tendency, which seeks, at least in theory, to minimize human mediation.

However, this is not the way that God has ordered His creation. His glory is shown not by reserving all execution of power to Himself, but by giving a participation of His kingship to creatures in a hierarchical way. He has given to mankind in general a kingship over the material creation, as seen in the first chapters of Genesis. He set man in the Garden to tend and cultivate it, and He gave man the order to dominate the earth. In the words of Psalm 8:4–7:

---

[1] Benedict XVI, General Audience of April 5, 2006, in *Jesus, the Apostles, and the Early Church* (San Francisco: Ignatius Press, 2007), 22.

What is man that thou art mindful of him, and the son of man that thou dost care for him? Yet thou hast made him little less than God, and dost crown him with glory and honor. Thou hast given him dominion over the works of thy hands; thou hast put all things under his feet, all sheep and oxen, and also the beasts of the field.

The creation of angels is also hierarchical. It can be seen in Scripture that there is a hierarchy of angelic beings, and it is reasonable to think that the higher ones illuminate the lower ones. Pseudo-Dionysius profoundly developed this principle of mediation among the angelic hierarchies:

The first intelligences [angels] perfect, illuminate, and purify those of inferior status in such a fashion that the latter, having been lifted up through them to the universal and transcendent source, thereby acquire their due share of the purification, illumination, and perfection of the One who is the source of all perfection. The divine source of all order has established the all-embracing principle that beings of the second rank receive enlightenment from the Godhead through the beings of the first rank.[2]

Similarly, within human society, a share of God's authority and kingship is given to parents within the family and to governors over nations and societies. Without hierarchy and headship of some type, every human society would dissolve into anarchy. The same is true of intermediate societies formed by association. Every business requires a leader and every athletic team needs a captain.

Even the human body is hierarchical in that the head must lead the other members, all of which complement one another, even though some are more noble than others. Now, if this is true in the human body and in human societies, it is no less fitting that there be

---

[2] Pseudo-Dionysius, *The Celestial Hierarchy* 8.2, in *Pseudo-Dionysius: The Complete Works*, trans. Colm Luibheid (New York: Paulist Press, 1987), 168.

hierarchy in the supernatural order in the Church.

The worship of Israel was hierarchically ordered in the three grades of high priest, priest, and Levite, which prefigure the division of Holy Orders in the Church into bishops, priests, and deacons. The Levites, like deacons in the Catholic Church, aided the priests, who were under the supreme authority of the High Priest.

A revolt against the priestly hierarchy established by God in the Law of Moses was led by Korah, Dathan, and Abiram, who, although they were not priests, claimed equality in priestly power with Aaron and his descendants, saying that the entire community had been consecrated by the Lord, not just Aaron and his children. God defended the Aaronic priesthood by having the ground open, swallowing up Korah, Dathan, Abiram, and their followers.[3]

The Hierarchical Principle

The hierarchical principle is the idea that God's creation involves distinct levels of being and activity that mutually enrich each other in a complementary way. Each level receives a distinct share in God's kingship to be used for the common good. No creature is self-sufficient, but each is called to serve the others according to his particular state.

St. Paul develops this idea in his doctrine of the Body of Christ, which is composed of many members. Among these members there is also the head. The head is Christ, but He rules His Church through visible mediators, who share in a particular sacramental way in His kingship, through the Sacrament of Holy Orders. After His Ascension, Christ is the invisible head of the Church, but His Body must also have a visible headship, which is constituted first by Peter and his successors, but also by the successors of the other Apostles (the bishops) and priests and deacons. Through the power of Orders, those who receive it are enabled to act *in persona Christi*, in the very person of Christ. They do this when they consecrate the Eucharist, absolve

---

[3] Num 16:31–35.

sins in the Sacrament of Penance, or ordain men to the priesthood. The recipients of Holy Orders, especially in the highest grade of the episcopate, also participate in God's kingship through receiving the power of jurisdiction in the Church, the power to teach and govern the People of God.

The Apostles and their successors are mediators in two dimensions.[4] They mediate vertically, acting as God's vicar and oracle in their infallible teaching, and offer up the supplications of the Church in the liturgy to the Father. However, they also mediate horizontally through time. Each generation of the successors of the Apostles passes on to the following generation what they have received from their predecessors, which they ultimately received from Christ. This horizontal transmitting of the apostolic office from generation to generation is called apostolic succession. The true Church of Christ is the one that contains, and in fact is built on, this succession. Without this succession, what Jesus accomplished in forming the Apostles would have been lost after their death. Pope Leo XIII explains:

> It was consequently provided by God that the Magisterium instituted by Jesus Christ should not end with the life of the Apostles, but that it should be perpetuated. We see it in truth propagated, and, as it were, delivered from hand to hand. For the Apostles consecrated bishops and each one appointed those who were to succeed them immediately "in the ministry of the word." Nay more: they likewise required their successors to choose fitting men, to endow them with like authority, and to confide to them the office and mission of teaching. "Thou, therefore, my son, be strong in the grace which is in Christ Jesus: and the things which you have heard of me by many witnesses, the same command to faithful men, who shall be fit to teach others also" (2 Tim 2:1–2). Wherefore, as Christ was sent by God and the Apostles by Christ, so

---

4 See Charles Cardinal Journet, *Theology of the Church* (San Francisco: Ignatius Press, 2004), 155–156.

the Bishops and those who succeeded them were sent by the Apostles.[5]

The apostolic succession is parallel to that earlier succession by which the descendants of Aaron transmitted the high priesthood from generation to generation.

Apostolic Succession

Apostolicity is one of the four marks of the Church. As such, it is part of the essence of the Church and is a clear visible sign of the true Church. It is of the essence of the Church to be *apostolic*, built on the Apostles and their successors, just as biblical Israel was built on Moses, Aaron, and their successors.

Why must this be so? It is because the very essence of the Church is to be a continuation of Christ's humanity by which He can reach every human being on the planet throughout history. Christ's physical body has ascended into heaven, so He cannot touch us directly in that visible humanity that He assumed in the moment of the Annunciation.[6] Thus He instituted a plan of salvation in which His humanity continues in time and space through the sacraments. His direct contact with the members of His Church happens above all in the Eucharist and Penance, but it also happens in a no less important way through Holy Orders, the fullness of which is the episcopacy. The recipients of the fullness of this sacrament are the successors of the Apostles. Through these "other Christs" the sacraments are celebrated and the faithful continue to be taught and governed by Christ Himself.

---

[5] Leo XIII, Encyclical Letter on the Unity of the Church *Satis cognitum* (1896), §8.

[6] See John 16:7: "Nevertheless I tell you the truth: it is to your advantage that I go away, for if I do not go away, the Counselor will not come to you; but if I go, I will send him to you." See also John 20:17: "Jesus said to her, 'Do not hold me, for I have not yet ascended to the Father; but go to my brethren and say to them, I am ascending to my Father and your Father, to my God and your God.'"

He chose Apostles during His public ministry to be the sacramental continuation of His humanity and His heralds. Even Protestants recognize this, although they limit it to the apostolic age. However, the need for a sacramental ministry of headship was not limited to the time of Christ's public ministry and the first decades of the Church. Christ always needs visible and authorized apostles to continue His mission in a visible and sacramental way. The Church is to be structured on the apostolic succession until the end of time because the Church that Christ formed before His Ascension was to last for all time, and therefore He made it apostolic, entirely centered on the authoritative witness of the Twelve that He chose to be the pillars and foundation of the Church.

In Ephesians 2:19–20, St. Paul says: "You are ... members of the household of God, built upon the foundation of the Apostles and prophets, Christ Jesus Himself being the cornerstone." In Revelation 21:10–14, John is shown a vision of the New Jerusalem descending from heaven, the "Bride of the Lamb," which is the Church. The walls of this holy City are built on twelve foundations, on which are written "the twelve names of the twelve Apostles of the Lamb." The very structure and architecture of the Church is based on the apostolic office, which must always remain vital and continuous in the Church.

In his Letter to the Corinthians (96), Pope Clement I (St. Peter's third successor, ordained to the priesthood by him) stressed the doctrine of apostolic succession as coming from Christ and perpetuating the apostolic office in the Church in a permanent way:

So then Christ is from God, and the apostles are from Christ. Both, therefore, came of the will of God in good order. . . . So, preaching both in the country and in the towns, they [the apostles] appointed their first fruits, when they had tested them by the Spirit, to be bishops and deacons for the future believers. And this was no new thing they did. . . . Our apostles likewise knew, through our Lord Jesus Christ, that there would be strife over the bishop's office. For this reason, therefore, having received complete foreknowledge, they appointed the officials mentioned earlier and afterwards they gave the offices a permanent character; that is, if they should die, other approved men should succeed to their ministry.[7]

Around eighty years later, St. Irenaeus wrote:

True knowledge is the doctrine of the apostles, and the ancient constitution of the Church throughout all the world, and the distinctive manifestation of the body of Christ according to the *successions of the bishops*, by which they have handed down that Church which exists in every place, and has come even to us.[8]

Apostolic succession, in consequence, is a clear sign or mark of the true Church and has something of a miraculous nature in its constancy and continuation over time. It is a sacramental principle, for it renders visible and marks out what is by nature invisible: communion with Christ in faith over time and space. The Church founded by Christ is visibly apostolic, and it will be so until the end of time. If a Christian denomination cannot demonstrate apostolic succession, including Petrine succession, it cannot be the true Church.

The Relation of the Apostles to Peter

The Apostles were called and constituted by Christ before His Ascension to be the foundation of the Church. They were all given a unique and unrepeatable charism at Pentecost to fulfill this call. This charism consisted in being absolutely authoritative and infallible witnesses of Christ's humanity, His death and Resurrection, His teaching, His interpretation of the Old Testament Scriptures, His sacraments, and the lineaments of His Church. Each Apostle had a total authority in this regard.

---

[7] Clement I, *Letter to the Corinthians* 42 and 44, in *The Apostolic Fathers: Greek Texts and English Translations*, trans. and ed. Michael W. Holmes, 3rd ed. (Grand Rapids: Baker Academic, 2007), 101–103.

[8] Irenaeus, *Adversus haereses* 4.33.8 (*ANF*, 1:508; my italics).

Nevertheless, the apostolic witness was instituted to found *one* Church. Thus the other Apostles were constituted under Peter. They too were part of the flock that Christ entrusted to Peter when He said three times, "Feed my sheep" (John 21:15–17). *All* of Christ's sheep were entrusted to Peter, even the other Apostles.

All of the Apostles were endowed with infallibility in matters of faith and morals, but nevertheless, nothing was given to them collectively that was not given to Peter as their head.[9] The apostolic authority was infallible, but was under the headship of Peter and could never be separated from him or put in conflict with him.[10] Both the apostolic college and the Petrine primacy are from Christ, to work in the harmony of collegiality and headship.[11]

When the Apostles are listed in the Gospels, Peter is always put in the first place. For example, Matthew (10:2) says: "First, Simon, who is called Peter."[12] Peter speaks on behalf of the Twelve (Luke 12:41); together with James and John, he is witness to the Transfiguration and the agony of Jesus in Gethsemane; and he is cited as the first witness

---

[9] See Leo XIII, *Satis cognitum*, §14: "It is necessary, therefore, to bear this in mind, viz., that nothing was conferred on the apostles apart from Peter, but that several things were conferred upon Peter apart from the Apostles. St. John Chrysostom in explaining the words of Christ asks: 'Why, passing over the others, does He speak to Peter about these things?' And he replies unhesitatingly and at once, 'Because he was pre-eminent among the Apostles, the mouthpiece of the Disciples, and the head of the college' (Hom. lxxxviii. *in Joan.*, n. I). He alone was designated as the foundation of the Church. To him He gave the power of binding and *loosing*; to him alone was given the power of *feeding*. On the other hand, whatever authority and office the Apostles received, they received in conjunction with Peter. 'If the divine benignity willed anything to be in common between him and the other princes, whatever He did not deny to the others He gave only through him. So that whereas Peter alone received many things, He conferred nothing on any of the rest without Peter participating in it' (S. Leo M. sermo iv., cap. 2)."

[10] Journet explains this well in *Theology of the Church*, 129: "They [the Apostles] have presided at her birth, as it were, and have left their mark on her forever. Such privileges were found in an equal degree in each of the apostles. As they were granted, however, for the sake of founding the one Church, governed by one visible head, these privileges tended by their own force to move the apostles—in that which concerns the government of the universal Church—toward a dependence on the supreme transapostolic power confided to Peter by the Savior. Hence, the apostles themselves were ranked among the sheep of Christ, having Peter as their visible pastor. And when Peter died, they remained, with respect to the government of the Church, submitted to the supreme regular power of governing the Church, which Peter transmitted to his successors."

[11] See Joseph Ratzinger, "Primacy, Episcopacy, and *Successio Apostolica*," in *God's Word: Scripture—Tradition—Office*, trans. Henry Taylor (San Francisco: Ignatius Press, 2008), 13–39.

[12] See also Mark 3:16; Luke 6:14; and Acts 1:13.

to the Resurrection (Luke 24:34; 1 Cor 15:5). In the Book of Acts, it is Peter who appoints Matthias (Acts 1:15–26) and who speaks to the crowds after Pentecost (Acts 2); it is Peter who performs the first healing in Church history (Acts 3:1–16); he addresses the Sanhedrin (Acts 4:5–22); he has authority to discipline (Acts 5:1–12); he endorses the spread of the Gospel to Samaria and to the Gentiles (Acts 10, 11:1–18); and he sums up the teaching of the Council of Jerusalem (Acts 15:6–11).[13]

Another key text concerning the primacy of Peter is Luke 22:31–32. During the Last Supper, Jesus foretells Peter's imminent betrayal and conversion: "Simon, Simon, behold, Satan demanded to have you, that he might sift you like wheat, but I have prayed for you that your faith may not fail; and when you have turned again, strengthen your brethren." Now, when Christ prays for something, it cannot fail to be answered. Christ did not pray that Peter not fall into sin, but that his faith not fail and that he be able to strengthen his brethren in the faith, who are the other Apostles and disciples.

Leo XIII says: "He willed then that he whom He had designated as the foundation of the Church should be the defense of its faith."[14] And St. Ambrose said in the fourth century: "Could not Christ who confided to him the Kingdom by His own authority have strengthened the faith of one whom He designated a rock to show the foundation of the Church?"[15]

The Church has always understood this prayer—that Peter's faith not fail—to extend to all Peter's successors. For Christ's concern was not with the apostolic Church alone, but with the Church of all ages. What good would it have done if Peter's faith had not failed but that of his successors had: Linus, Cletus, Clement, Evaristus . . . up to the present pope?

---

[13] See *Ignatius Catholic Study Bible: The New Testament* (San Francisco: Ignatius Press, 2010), 211. The Acts of the Apostles does not mention St. Peter again after the Council of Jerusalem, perhaps because, given his importance and after repeated threats on his life, St. Luke could not safely reveal that he was residing in Rome.

[14] *Satis cognitum* §12.

[15] St. Ambrose of Milan, *De fide* 4.5.56, in *Corpus Scriptorum Ecclesiasticorum Latinorum*, vol. 78 (Vienna, AT: Hoelder-Pichler-Tempsky, 1962), 176.

The Petrine office is essentially that of conserving the faith, confirming the brethren in the faith and in the bond of charity, and of feeding *all* the sheep of Christ, maintaining in the bond of unity all the bishops scattered through the world. Joseph Ratzinger, as Cardinal Prefect of the Congregation for the Doctrine of the Faith, writes in *The Primacy of the Successor of Peter in the Mystery of the Church*:

> From the beginning and with increasing clarity, the Church has understood that, just as there is a succession of the Apostles in the ministry of Bishops, so too the ministry of unity entrusted to Peter belongs to the permanent structure of Christ's Church, and that this succession is established in the see of his martyrdom.[16]

Since Peter and his successors perform the ministry of unity in the Church, it is said that "Where Peter is, there you have the Church. Where the Church is, there you find not death but life eternal."[17]

The Primacy of Peter Serves the Word of God

Protestants often think of the Catholic claim of the primacy of Peter as an arrogant attempt to put a human authority above the Word of God, which would thus be a radical corruption of the teaching of Christ. However, Catholics understand the primacy to be entirely at the service of the Gospel. The task of the apostolic witness of the universal episcopacy and the Petrine witness of the bishop of Rome is to maintain the deposit of faith intact through all centuries so that all the faithful may have the freedom won for us by Christ.

This is beautifully explained in the CDF's above-mentioned document:

---

[16] CDF, *The Primacy of the Successor of Peter in the Mystery of the Church* (1998), §3 in *Origins* 28, no. 30 (January 28, 1999): 561.

[17] St. Ambrose of Milan, *Enarrationes in Psalmos* 40.30, in *Commentary of Saint Ambrose on Twelve Psalms*, trans. Íde M. Ní Riain, (Dublin, IE: Halcyon Press, 2000), 197. The original Latin is: "Ubi Petrus, ibi ergo Ecclesia, ubi Ecclesia, ibi nulla mors, sed vita aeterna."

The Roman Pontiff—like all the faithful—is subject to the Word of God, to the Catholic faith, and is the guarantor of the Church's obedience; in this sense he is *servus servorum Dei*. He does not make arbitrary decisions, but is spokesman for the will of the Lord, who speaks to man in the Scriptures lived and interpreted by Tradition; in other words, the *episkope* of the primacy has limits set by divine law and by the Church's divine, inviolable constitution found in Revelation. The Successor of Peter is the rock which guarantees a rigorous fidelity to the Word of God against arbitrariness and conformism: hence the martyrological nature of his primacy.[18]

Patristic Witness to Apostolic Succession and the Primacy of Peter

The early Fathers of the Church were very aware of the reality of apostolic succession and its importance. Perhaps the first significant witness outside the New Testament is given by Pope St. Clement, the third successor to St. Peter, in his letter to the Corinthians, usually dated circa 96. This work was so highly esteemed in the early Church that it was read in the liturgical assembly in some places as if it were a part of the canon of Scripture. The letter is addressing a schism in the Church in Corinth, where the bishops (*episkopoi*) and presbyters were being challenged by some claiming a more charismatic authority, based not on the Sacrament of Orders and apostolic succession, but on charismatic gifts and a higher knowledge (*gnosis*). Perhaps the schism was the work of incipient Gnosticism, the first major heresy to trouble the Church.

It is highly significant that Pope Clement and the Church of Rome intervened to settle the conflict with a mixture of authority and theological persuasion, focusing on examples from the Old Testament. He clearly saw the welfare of all the churches to be his responsibility, especially in an issue so central to the divine constitution of the Church:

---

[18] CDF, *Primacy of the Successor of Peter*, §7 (*Origins* 28.30, 562).

the hierarchical principle of ecclesiastical authority, given through the Sacrament of Orders. The Apostle John was still alive when this letter was written, but it is not John who writes to the Corinthians, but Peter's successor Clement.

St. Ignatius of Antioch stresses apostolic succession over and over again in his letters written on his journey to martyrdom in the Coliseum. In the beginning of his letter to the Romans, he seems to allude to a primacy of the see of Rome, although it is obscure and disputed. He addresses the church in Rome with a very formal and elaborate praise, as "the church ... which also *presides* in the place of the district of the Romans, worthy of God, worthy of honor, worthy of blessing, worthy of praise, worthy of success, worthy of sanctification, and *presiding over love*, observing the law of Christ."[19]

The expression, "presiding over love" (*agape*), could also be rendered, "presiding over the communion [of the Church]," in that the communion and unity of the Church is the proper fruit and expression of charity. The grammatical structure favors this interpretation, for one presides properly over a community, which here would be the universal church itself,[20] formed by the love of Christ, poured forth in our hearts through the Holy Spirit.[21] Furthermore, in other places, St. Ignatius uses the term "*agape*" to designate the communion of the

---

[19] St. Ignatius, *Letter to the Romans*, Salutation (Holmes, *The Apostolic Fathers*, 225; my italics). See the comments on this text by Benedict XVI in his General Audience of March 14, 2007: "Ignatius was the first person in Christian literature to attribute to the Church the adjective 'catholic' or 'universal': 'Wherever Jesus Christ is,' he said, 'there is the Catholic Church' (*Smyrnaeans*, 8.2). And precisely in the service of unity to the Catholic Church, the Christian community of Rome exercised a sort of primacy of love: 'The Church which presides in the place of the region of the Romans, and which is worthy of God, worthy of honour, worthy of the highest happiness ... and which presides over love, is named from Christ, and from the Father' (*Romans*, Prologue). As can be seen, Ignatius is truly the 'Doctor of Unity': unity of God and unity of Christ (despite the various heresies gaining ground which separated the human and the divine in Christ), unity of the Church, unity of the faithful in 'faith and love, to which nothing is to be preferred' (*Smyrnaeans*, 6.1)"; see Benedict XVI, *Church Fathers from Clement of Rome to Augustine: General Audiences March 7, 2007–February 27, 2008* (San Francisco: Ignatius Press, 2008), 15–16.

[20] See G. Bareille, "Ignace d'Antioche (saint)," in *Dictionnaire de théologie catholique*, vol. 7/1 (Paris: Librairie Letouzey et Ané, 1927), 709.

[21] See Rom 5.5. *Agape* also has a clear Eucharistic meaning in the letters of St. Ignatius, for the unity of charity is sacramentally communicated to the Church through the Eucharist.

church in various cities.[22] In his *Letter to the Romans* 4, he mentions that he does not give them orders "like Peter and Paul," thus alluding to the pre-eminent apostolic authority of the see of Rome.

Another great witness to the apostolic nature of the Church is St. Irenaeus, who died circa 202. He stressed the apostolic succession and the unity of the faith and the Tradition throughout the universal (Catholic) Church in his battle against the Gnostic heretics of his day, who claimed to have a secret apostolic authority that completely lacked any visible connection with the Apostles.

The Gnostics were divided into many sects, each one professing different esoteric doctrines that they claimed were passed down secretly to them from Christ and the Apostles. To counter this absurd claim, St. Irenaeus stressed the public teaching of the Church through the bishops who have succeeded the Apostles. The true faith is that which comes from the Apostles, has been taught always and everywhere in the Catholic Church,[23] and is taught now by the successors of the Apostles in communion with the successor of Peter.

The Gnostic heresiarchs, on the contrary, could not show that their doctrine came from Christ, nor that it had spread in an uninterrupted, unified form. They lacked the marks of unity, Catholicity, and apostolic origin. St. Irenaeus reproaches them: "For there were no Valentinians before Valentinus, or Marcionites before Marcion."[24] We can say the same in modern times: there were no Lutherans or Calvinists before Luther and Calvin.

---

[22] See St. Ignatius's *Letter to the Trallians* 13.1, *Letter to the Romans* 9.3, *Letter to the Philadelphians* 11.2, and *Letter to the Smyrnaeans* 12.1. Michael Holmes (*Apostolic Fathers*, 223, 235, 247, and 259, respectively) translates "agape" in these texts as "love," but it could also be translated here as "communion." See Francis Glimm, Joseph Marique and Gerald Walsh, eds., *The Apostolic Fathers* (New York: Cima Publishing, 1947), 107n2, 117n13, and 123n14.

[23] See Vincent of Lerins, who gives the classical expression of this doctrine in his *Commonitory*, ch. 2: "In the Catholic Church itself, all possible care must be taken, that we hold that faith which has been believed everywhere, always, and by all. For that is truly and in the strictest sense 'Catholic' which, as the name itself and the reason of the thing declare, comprehends all universally. This rule we shall observe if we follow universality, antiquity, consent" (*NPNF2*, 11:132; PL, 50:639).

[24] St. Irenaeus, *Adversus haereses* 3.4.3, trans. Cyril Richardson, in *Early Christian Fathers* (New York: Macmillan, 1970), 375.

To ascertain the true faith and avoid the heresies of the Gnostics, one should remain with the apostolic Tradition preserved in the Church through the apostolic succession. The true faith can be found in all doctrine taught by the successors of the Apostles in common. However, St. Irenaeus singles out the Church in Rome as being pre-eminent in the preservation of the faith, with which every other Church must agree:

> It is within the power of all, therefore, in every Church, who may wish to see the truth, to contemplate clearly the tradition of the apostles manifested throughout the whole world; and we are in a position to reckon up those who were by the apostles instituted bishops in the Churches, and [to demonstrate] the succession of these men to our own times. . . .
>
> Since, however, it would be very tedious, in such a volume as this, to reckon up the successions of all the Churches, we do put to confusion all those who, in whatever manner . . . assemble in unauthorized meetings, by indicating that tradition derived from the apostles, of the very great, the very ancient, and universally known Church founded and organized at *Rome* by the two most glorious apostles, Peter and Paul; as also [by pointing out] the faith preached to men, which comes down to our time by means of the successions of the bishops. For it is a *matter of necessity that every Church should agree with this Church, on account of its pre-eminent authority.*[25]

St. Irenaeus goes on to list the succession of twelve bishops of Rome up until his time:

> The blessed apostles, then, having founded and built up the Church, committed into the hands of Linus the office of the episcopate. Of this Linus, Paul makes mention in the Epistles to Timothy. To him succeeded Anacletus; and after him, in the third place from the apostles, Clement was allotted

---

[25] Ibid., 3.3.1–2 (*ANF*, 1:415).

the bishopric. This man, as he had seen the blessed apostles, and had been conversant with them, might be said to have the preaching of the apostles still echoing [in his ears], and their traditions before his eyes. Nor was he alone [in this], for there were many still remaining who had received instructions from the apostles. In the time of this Clement, no small dissension having occurred among the brethren at Corinth, the Church in Rome dispatched a most powerful letter to the Corinthians, exhorting them to peace, renewing their faith, and declaring the tradition which it had lately received from the apostles. . . . To this Clement there succeeded Evaristus. Alexander followed Evaristus; then, sixth from the apostles, Sixtus was appointed; after him, Telephorus, who was gloriously martyred; then Hyginus; after him, Pius; then after him, Anicetus. Sorer having succeeded Anicetus, Eleutherius does now, in the twelfth place from the apostles, hold the inheritance of the episcopate. *In this order, and by this succession, the ecclesiastical tradition from the apostles, and the preaching of the truth, have come down to us.* And this is most abundant proof that there is one and the same vivifying faith, which has been preserved in the Church from the apostles until now, and handed down in truth.[26]

About the same time as St. Irenaeus, Tertullian refuted the heretical sects of his time by saying:

Let them produce the original records of their churches; let them unfold the roll of their bishops, running down in due succession from the beginning in such a manner that that first bishop of theirs shall be able to show for his ordainer and predecessor one of the apostles or of apostolic men who were in communion with the apostles. For this is the manner in which the apostolic churches transmit their registers: as the church of Smyrna, which records that Polycarp was placed

---

[26] Ibid., 3.3.3 (*ANF*, 1:416; my italics).

therein by John; as also the church of Rome, which makes Clement to have been ordained in like manner by Peter.[27]

St. Cyprian, who died a martyr in 258, wrote a tract *On the Unity of the Church* in 251, in which he simply supports the primacy of the successor of Peter from the Gospels:

> But if anyone considers those things carefully, he will need no long discourse or arguments. The proof is simple and convincing, being summed up in a matter of fact. The Lord says to Peter: "I say to thee, that thou art Peter, and upon this rock I will build my Church." And he says to him again after the resurrection: "Feed my sheep" (John 21:17). It is on him that He builds the Church, and to him that He entrusts the sheep to feed. And although He assigns a like power to all the Apostles, yet He founded a single Chair, thus establishing by His own authority the source and hallmark of the [Church's] oneness. No doubt the others were all that Peter was, but a primacy is given to Peter, and it is made clear that there is but one Church and one Chair. So too, even if they are all shepherds, we are shown but one flock which is to be fed by all the Apostles in common accord. If a man does not hold fast to this oneness of Peter, does he imagine that he still holds the faith? If he deserts the Chair of Peter upon whom the Church was built, has he still confidence that he is in the Church? The authority of the bishops forms a unity, of which each holds his part in its totality.[28]

---

[27] Tertullian, *On Prescription against Heretics*, ch. 32 (*ANF*, 3:258).

[28] St. Cyprian, *On the Unity of the Church* 4, trans. Maurice Bévenot, in *De Lapsis and De Ecclesiae Catholicae Unitate* (Oxford, UK: Clarendon Press, 1971), 61–63. This important text exists in two versions. The other version, called the *textus receptus*, reads as follows: "it is on one man that He builds the Church and although He assigns a like power to all the Apostles after His resurrection, saying: 'As the Father hath sent me, I also send you' (John 20:21–23). Yet, in order that the oneness might be unmistakable, He established by His own authority a source for that oneness having its origin in one man alone. No doubt the other Apostles were all that Peter was, endowed with equal dignity and power, but the start comes from him alone, in order to show that the Church of Christ is unique" (ibid., 63).

St. Cyprian also refers to the Roman Church as "the Chair of Peter and ... the principal Church whence sacerdotal unity has sprung."[29] St. Cyprian goes on to formulate a very important principle: if someone separates himself from the apostolic Church in communion with Peter, then he cannot inherit the promises of the Church:

> Whoever breaks with the Church and enters on an adulterous union, cuts himself off from the promises made to the Church; and he who turns his back on the Church of Christ will not come to the rewards of Christ: he is an alien, a worldling, an enemy. *You cannot have God for your Father if you no longer have the Church for your mother.* If there was any escape for one who was outside the ark of Noah, there will be as much for one who is found to be outside the Church.[30]

Towards the end of the fourth century, St. Jerome wrote to Pope Damasus as follows: "My words are spoken to the successor of the Fisherman, to the disciple of the Cross. .... I communicate with none save your Blessedness, that is with the chair of Peter. For this I know is the rock on which the Church is built."[31]

In the same way, St. Augustine writes that in the Church of Rome "the primacy of the Apostolic chair always flourished."[32] He also says: "You are not to be looked upon as holding the true Catholic faith if you do not teach that the faith of Rome is to be held."[33] In the Pelagian controversy, Pelagius was condemned in a North African synod, which was sent to Rome for confirmation. When the confirmation arrived, St. Augustine said: "You see, there have already been two coun-

---

[29] St. Cyprian, *Epistle 59 to Cornelius* 14, in *Letters*, trans. Rose Donna (Washington, DC: Catholic Univeristy of America Press, 1964), 186.

[30] St. Cyprian, *Unity of the Church* 6 (Bévenot, 67).

[31] St. Jerome, *Letter 15 to Pope Damasus* 2 (trans. W. H. Fremantle in *NPNF2*, 6:18). See also *Letter 16 to Pope Damasus* 2 (*NPNF2*, 6:20): "He who clings to the chair of Peter is accepted by me."

[32] St. Augustine, Letter 43.7, in *St. Augustine: Letters*, vol. 1, trans. Wilfrid Parsons (New York: Fathers of the Church, Inc., 1951), 187. The Latin reads: "In qua semper apostolicæ cathedræ viguit principatus."

[33] St. Augustine, Sermon 120.13, cited in Leo XIII, *Satis cognitum* §13.

cils about this matter, and their decisions sent to the Apostolic See; from there rescripts have been sent back here. The case is finished; if only the error were finished too, sometime!"[34] This text has been popularized and reduced as follows: "*Roma locuta est, causa finita est*" ("Rome has spoken; the case is closed").

In the mid-fifth century, the greatest protector of the faith of the Church concerning the great Christological and Trinitarian controversies was Pope St. Leo the Great. With regard to the primacy, he says:

> Yet out of the whole world Peter alone has been chosen to be put in charge of the universal convocation of peoples as well as of every apostle and all the Fathers of the Church. Although there are many priests and many shepherds among the people of God, it is Peter who properly rules each one of those whom Christ also rules principally.[35]

A century and a half later, St. Gregory the Great writes to Emperor Maurice Augustus:

> It is clear, therefore, to all who know the gospel, that the Lord's voice committed the care of the whole Church to the apostle Saint Peter, the prince of all the apostles. Because it was to him that it was said: "Peter, do you love me? Feed my sheep." . . . Behold, he accepts the keys of the kingdom of Heaven; to him the power of binding and of loosing is attributed; to him the care of the whole Church.[36]

---

[34] St. Augustine, Sermon 131.10, in *The works of Saint Augustine: a Translation for the 21st Century: Part 3*, vol. 4, *(94A-147A) on the New Testament*, trans. and notes Edmund Hill, (Brooklyn: New City Press, 1992), 322.

[35] Pope St. Leo the Great, Sermon 4.2, in *St. Leo the Great: Sermons*, trans. Jane Freeland and Agnes Conway, The Fathers of the Church 93 (Washington, DC: Catholic University of America Press, 1996), 26.

[36] St. Gregory the Great, Letter 37 of book 5 to Maurice Augustus (June, 595), in *The Letters of Gregory the Great*, trans. John Martyn, vol. 2 (Toronto: Pontifical Institute of Mediaeval Studies, 2004), 352.

Nor should it be thought that the primacy of Peter and his successors was recognized only by the Western Latin Church. The Eastern
Church had repeatedly recognized the primacy of Peter in the most
important matters.[37] The See of Peter was the final court of appeal
in questions of faith and ecclesiastical government. Warren Carroll
writes:

> Papal primacy as a general proposition had been recognized
> in the Eastern Church *from the beginning of the Christian
> era*, with the letter of Pope Clement I to the Greek church in
> Corinth in AD 95. . . . Because of slow communication and
> transportation, Papal primacy was not exercised nearly as of-
> ten in the East as in the West in specific acts, such as confirm-
> ing or deposing bishops. But it had been not only acknowl-
> edged but trumpeted, made the basis of appeal after appeal
> for help, by the iconodule[38] bishops and monks throughout
> the iconoclastic controversy.[39]

Study Questions

1. Why does God use the principle of hierarchy and mediation in
   His work of creation?
2. Explain the harmony between hierarchy in the natural order and
   the supernatural and sacramental hierarchy of the Church.
3. How do Clement of Rome and St. Irenaeus explain the notion of
   apostolic succession?
4. Explain the harmony between apostolic succession and Petrine
   succession.
5. How does the Petrine primacy serve the Word of God?

---

[37] The first example is given by Clement I, in *Letter to the Corinthians*. Another example is the Council of Chalcedon (451).

[38] That is, those who defended the use of images of Christ and the saints against the iconoclasts.

[39] Warren Carroll, *The Building of Christendom* (Front Royal: Christendom College Press, 1987),
352.

Suggestions for Further Reading

Lumen gentium §§18–29.

Pope Leo XIII. Encyclical Letter on the Unity of the Church *Satis cognitum*. June 29, 1896.

Congregation for the Doctrine of the Faith, *The Primacy of the Successor of Peter in the Mystery of the Church*, in *L'Osservatore Romano*, November 18, 1998.

De la Soujeole, Benoît-Dominique, O.P. *Introduction to the Mystery of the Church*, 590–624. Translated by Michael J. Miller. Washington, DC: Catholic University of America Press, 2014.

Ratzinger, Joseph Cardinal. "Primacy, Episcopacy, and *Successio Apostolica*." In *God's Word: Scripture—Tradition—Office*, 13–39. Edited by Peter Hünermann and Tomas Söding and translated by Henry Taylor. San Francisco: Ignatius Press, 2008.

CHAPTER NINE

The Magisterium of the Church, the Charism of Infallibility, and Three Grades of Assent

We have seen that Revelation comes to us through two channels: Scripture and Tradition. The Magisterium, or Teaching Office, of the Church is not a third channel of Revelation, but rather an authoritative witness to the Revelation received by the Church through Scripture and Tradition so that it may be preserved in her in its integrity, rightly interpreted, until the end of time.[1] *Dei Verbum* §10 gives a description of the role of the Magisterium with regard to the preservation of Revelation:

> But the task of authentically interpreting the word of God, whether written or handed on, has been entrusted exclusively to the living teaching office of the Church, whose authority is exercised in the name of Jesus Christ. This teaching office is not above the word of God, but serves it, teaching only what has been handed on, listening to it devoutly, guarding it scrupulously and explaining it faithfully in accord with a divine commission and with the help of the Holy Spirit; it draws from this one deposit of faith everything which it presents for belief as divinely revealed.

---

[1] See Avery Cardinal Dulles, S.J., *Magisterium: Teacher and Guardian of the Faith* (Naples: Sapientia Press, 2007), 6–7.

The Magisterium pertains to the prophetic mission of the Church, and it stands in service of God's living revealed Word. The prophetic task of the Magisterium is distinct from (although intimately related to) the kingly office of governance that involves discipline and canon law. The object of the Magisterium is the clarification and manifestation of the truth contained in the deposit of faith or truths connected to the deposit and the mission of the Church. The proper response of the faithful to the teaching of the Magisterium is *assent* to those truths. This is distinct from the response that should be given to one's legitimate pastors in matters of discipline, which is *obedience*. In this chapter we are not concerned directly with discipline, but with the Church's prophetic mission of teaching and the assent of the faithful. Or to put it another way, the prophetic charism of infallibility concerns the content of *Tradition* (with a capital "T") and not disciplinary or liturgical *traditions*, which are intrinsically mutable and pertain rather to the Church's task of governance and sanctification.

The Fittingness and Necessity of an Infallible Teaching Office

The Church needs an infallible Magisterium as the rock and foundation on which she is built. This claim is clearly scriptural, for Christ Himself indicated that He wished to build His Church on an unshakeable apostolic authority. After Peter confessed Jesus as the Messiah and the Son of God, Christ promised him the primacy over the Church: "You are Peter, and on this rock I will build my Church, and the powers of death shall not prevail against it. I will give you the keys of the kingdom of heaven, and whatever you bind on earth shall be bound in heaven, and whatever you loose on earth shall be loosed in heaven" (Matt 16:18–19). The power to loose and bind with authority refers to all three of the *munera*, or offices, of Christ: prophetic, priestly, and kingly. Here we are concerned with the prophetic aspect of teaching with an authority that binds the conscience of the faithful.

Another key text that establishes the teaching authority of all the Apostles is Matthew 28:19–20: "Go therefore and make disciples of all nations, baptizing them in the name of the Father, and of the Son, and of the Holy Spirit, teaching them to observe all that I have commanded you; and behold, I am with you always, even unto the end of the world." The Gospel of Mark gives another form of this missionary mandate in 16:15–16: "Go into all the world and preach the gospel to the whole creation. He who believes and is baptized will be saved; but he who does not believe will be condemned." Pope Pius XI commented on these two texts: "These two commands of Christ, which must be fulfilled, the one, namely, to teach, and the other to believe, cannot even be understood unless the Church proposes a complete and easily understood teaching and is immune when it thus teaches from all danger of erring."[2]

Another argument for the necessity of an infallible teaching office is the lack of unity in Protestantism. Luther's denial of the authority of the Church led to the tremendous multiplication of Protestant sects that often profess radically different creeds and customs. The number of distinct Protestant churches that have existed has been estimated to be around 30,000, with the most diverse range of beliefs, from positions similar to those of the original Protestants to a liberal Protestantism that denies practically everything supernatural. If God has willed that Revelation be preserved in human history, an infallible teaching authority is necessary to protect the faith and the Church against the tendency of human organizations to splinter, and of opinions to change and divide.

Finally, reason alone can grasp the necessity of an infallible religious authority, if one presupposes that God wishes to reveal Himself and to establish a supernatural religion. In fact, the papacy and the dogma of papal infallibility—which is a scandal to many—is actually a clear sign of the presence of a religion different from other human sects and schools. The scandal comes from rejecting or not understanding the notion of a *supernatural* religion, a religion revealed and founded by God Himself. For, if God revealed His will to man in time and in history, He must provide some way of preserving what

---

[2] Pius XI, Encyclical Letter on Religious Unity *Mortalium animos* (1928), §8, in *The Papal Encyclicals*, vol. 3, *1903–1939*, ed. Claudia Carlen (Raleigh: The Pierian Press, 1990), 316.

He has revealed for the men of all times and places. This cannot be ensured without an infallible authority that continues in the contingent circumstances of history and can determine all religious questions that may arise. Blessed John Henry Newman states this point eloquently:

> The most obvious answer, then, to the question, why we yield to the authority of the Church in the questions and developments of faith, is, that some authority there must be if there is a revelation given, and other authority there is none but she. A revelation is not given if there be no authority to decide what it is that is given. . . . The absolute need of a spiritual supremacy is at present the strongest of arguments in favour of the fact of its supply.[3]

Furthermore, the principle of the infallibility of the Church is the precondition for all other acts of faith.[4] The infallibility of the Church is a necessary foundation for the act of supernatural faith as a firm and irrevocable assent to the Word of God that we have received in and from the Church. If the Church did not claim infallibility in the contents and interpretation of Revelation, how could the faithful make such an irrevocable assent, one that would be more than a fluctuating opinion based on one's own private judgment of the meaning of Scripture or Tradition?

Non-Catholics often see belief in the infallibility of the Church as an abdication of reason. There is nothing more reasonable, however, than submitting one's fallible and very limited reason to a divine teacher of truth. Thus, the fundamental question of religion is really this: has God revealed Himself to man, and presuming that He has, to whom has He entrusted this Revelation? The Catholic Church alone

---

[3] John Henry Newman, *An Essay on the Development of Christian Doctrine*, 6th ed. (Notre Dame: University of Notre Dame Press, 1989), 88–89.

[4] Newman, *An Essay in Aid of a Grammar of Assent* (New York: Catholic Publication Society, 1870), 146: "That the Church is the infallible oracle of truth is the fundamental dogma of the Catholic religion; and 'I believe what the Church proposes to be believed' is an act of real assent, including all particular assents."

claims that she is that living divine oracle to whom God authoritatively entrusted His Revelation, and who, due to the assistance of the Holy Spirit, possesses a unique privilege of infallibility in teaching in order to safeguard the deposit given for all generations.

Some people may object that the principle of authority is appropriate for mankind only before it comes of age, when it is in a youthful and immature stage of its development. According to this idea, the Church today ought to drop her claims to exercise an infallible authority. Theologians like Karl Rahner[5] and, more radically, Hans Küng[6] thought that the practical exercise of infallibility (while still existing in theory, at least according to Rahner) should be relegated the realm of past history. The Church today, because of a laudable theological pluralism, ought to seek to persuade by means other than that of authority, the use of which she should practically renounce.

In reality, a more advanced society needs the principle of authority more than ever because it is particularly susceptible to the danger of intellectual pride. The Protestant principle of private judgment is especially destructive in contemporary society because the technological advances of modern progress naturally lead man to think that he is completely autonomous, fully capable of solving all of his problems by himself, including those of a moral and religious nature. Therefore, if God has truly given a Revelation, an infallible authority is more than ever necessary to conserve it in our times.[7]

The Purpose of the Infallibility of the Church

The function of the infallibility of the Church is to preserve the deposit of Revelation as an inheritance for all generations. It is essentially

---

[5] See Karl Rahner, "On the Concept of Infallibility in Catholic Theology," in *Theological Investigations*, vol. 14, trans. David Bourke (New York: Seabury Press, 1976), 71–72: "In the foreseeable future there will be no further really new definitions. The situation lying before us in the future makes it impossible for the Church's teaching authority to produce any further infallible definitions in the manner in which it was conceived to do so formerly."

[6] See Hans Küng, *Infallible? An Inquiry*, trans. Edward Quinn (Garden City: Doubleday, 1971).

[7] Newman makes this point in *Essay on the Development of Christian Doctrine*, 89–90.

conservative. The Church makes use of her power of infallibility only when it is necessary to defend the faith against heresy and religious error, which are contrary to the deposit received from Christ and the Apostles. Cardinal Newman expresses this conservative principle very well:

> St. Paul says in one place that his Apostolical power is given him to edification, and not to destruction. There can be no better account of the Infallibility of the Church. It is a supply for a need, and it does not go beyond that need. Its object is, and its effect also, not to enfeeble the freedom or vigor of human thought in religious speculation, but to resist and control its extravagance. What have been its great works? All of them in the distinct province of theology—to put down Arianism, Eutychianism, Pelagianism, Manichaeism, Lutheranism, Jansenism.[8]

Newman explains that the charism of infallibility, like everything in the life of the Church, has developed in its mode of exercise, but has been consistent in its purpose, which is to make possible and safeguard dogmas of faith, and to be the means by which the Church is built on the rock of the authority and wisdom of God.

> The principle indeed of Dogmatism develops into Councils in the course of time; but it was active, nay sovereign from the first, in every part of Christendom. A conviction that truth was one; that it was a gift from without, a sacred trust, an inestimable blessing; that it was to be reverenced, guarded, defended, transmitted; that its absence was a grievous want, and its loss an unutterable calamity;—all this is quite consistent with perplexity or mistake as to what was truth in particular cases. . . . Councils and Popes are the guardians and instruments of the dogmatic principle: they are not that principle

---

[8] Newman, *Apologia pro Vita Sua* (London: J. M. Dent, 1993), 284.

themselves; they presuppose the principle; they are sum-
moned into action at the call of the principle.[9]

Infallibility refers to immunity from error in the teaching of the
Magisterium through the assistance of the Holy Spirit. It is a gift of
God to the Church, which St. Paul calls the "pillar and bulwark of
the truth" (1 Tim 3:15). The infallibility of the Magisterium is the
means elected by God to maintain the entire Church in the fullness
of revealed truth. It is a supernatural participation in the infallibility
of God,[10] who is the Truth in person.

How to Recognize When the Church Teaches
with Infallible Authority

Infallible teaching is a prerogative of the Roman Pontiff when he
speaks with his full authority, and also of the bishops in union with
the pope, either in an ecumenical council or dispersed in their dio-
ceses.[11] Without the pope, there can be no exercise of the infallible
Magisterium. That is to say, there are two modalities of infallibility:
the pope alone and the pope together with the bishops. The bishops
without the pope are *not* infallible. *Lumen gentium* §22 states: "But the
college or body of bishops has no authority unless it is understood together with the Roman Pontiff, the successor of Peter as its head. The
pope's power of primacy over all, both pastors and faithful, remains

---

[9] *Essay on the Development of Christian Doctrine,* 360.

[10] See the CDF, Declaration in Defense of the Catholic Doctrine on the Church against Certain
Errors of the Present Day *Mysterium ecclesiae* (1973), §2: "God, who is absolutely infallible, thus
deigned to bestow upon His new people, which is the Church, a certain shared infallibility,
which is restricted to matters of faith and morals."

[11] See *LG* §25: "Although the individual bishops do not enjoy the prerogative of infallibility, they
nevertheless proclaim Christ's doctrine infallibly whenever, even though dispersed through the
world, but still maintaining the bond of communion among themselves and with the successor
of Peter, and authentically teaching matters of faith and morals, they are in agreement on one
position as definitively to be held. This is even more clearly verified when, gathered together in
an ecumenical council, they are teachers and judges of faith and morals for the universal Church,
whose definitions must be adhered to with the submission of faith."

whole and intact."[12] An ecumenical council has no more doctrinal authority than the pope alone, and the authority of a council depends on its confirmation and promulgation by the pope.[13]

Popes have generally preferred, however, to use their infallible authority in the most collegial manner possible, making pronouncements together with the bishops of the world in ecumenical councils or promulgating infallible teaching in a papal document only after consultation with the bishops of the world.[14]

The Infallibility of the Roman Pontiff

The infallibility of the Roman Pontiff was solemnly defined by the First Vatican Council:

---

[12] See also Leo XIII, Encyclical On the Unity of the Church *Satis cognitum* (1896), §53: "Nothing has been conferred on the Apostles independently of Peter, whereas many things have been conferred on Peter independently of the Apostles. . . . On the contrary, everything that the Apostles have received with regard to the exercise of their functions and authority, they have received jointly with Peter. Thus it can be clearly seen that the bishops would lose the right and the power of governance if they were to separate themselves from Peter or his successors."

[13] The heresy of "conciliarism" considers a council to be above the Roman Pontiff. See Leo XIII, *Satis cognitum*, §58.

[14] For example, the definition of Mary's Assumption by Pius XII in 1950 was preceded by a consultation with the bishops of the world; see his Apostolic Constitution *Munificentissimus Deus*, §§11–12: "And, since we were dealing with a matter of such great moment and of such importance, we considered it opportune to ask all our venerable brethren in the episcopate directly and authoritatively that each of them should make known to us his mind in a formal statement. Hence, on May 1, 1946, we gave them our letter 'Deiparae Virginis Mariae,' a letter in which these words are contained: 'Do you, venerable brethren, in your outstanding wisdom and prudence, judge that the bodily Assumption of the Blessed Virgin can be proposed and defined as a dogma of faith? Do you, with your clergy and people, desire it?' But those whom 'the Holy Spirit has placed as bishops to rule the Church of God' gave an almost unanimous affirmative response to both these questions." Of the 1,181 bishops questioned, only six hesitated on whether the doctrine was revealed by God, and a few others thought that the definition was not opportune, whereas 1,169 bishops requested the definition. Similarly, Pope St. John Paul II consulted with the bishops of the world before making a definitive and infallible pronouncement on the grave moral evil of abortion in *Evangelium vitae* (1995); see §62: "Therefore, by the authority which Christ conferred upon Peter and his Successors, *in communion with the Bishops—who on various occasions have condemned abortion and who in the aforementioned consultation, albeit dispersed throughout the world, have shown unanimous agreement concerning this doctrine*—I declare that direct abortion, that is, abortion willed as an end or as a means, always constitutes a grave moral disorder" (my italics).

Faithfully keeping to the tradition received from the beginning of the Christian faith, ... [We] teach and define that it is
a dogma revealed by God:

That the Roman Pontiff, when he speaks *ex cathedra*, that
is, when, acting in the office of shepherd and teacher of all
Christians, he defines, by virtue of his supreme apostolic authority, a doctrine concerning faith or morals to be held by
the universal Church, possesses through the divine assistance promised to him in blessed Peter the infallibility with
which the divine Redeemer willed his Church to be endowed
in defining the doctrine concerning faith or morals; and that
such definitions of the Roman Pontiff are therefore irreformable of themselves, not because of the consent of the Church.[15]

According to this definition, the pope is said to speak *ex cathedra* ("from the chair" of St. Peter) when three conditions are fulfilled.
First, he must speak not as a private doctor but as universal Pastor
of all Christians and successor of the Apostles. Second, he must be
teaching on matters of faith and morals. Third, he must define or make
clear that something is to be held or believed *definitively* or *firmly* by
the universal Church. When these conditions are fulfilled, the pope's
decrees are "irreformable of themselves, not because of the consent of
the Church," or of the body of the faithful, or of a majority of them.[16]
When these conditions are not fulfilled, especially with regard to the
intention to teach something to be held definitively, the Magisterium
is authentic but not infallible. This means that it is not intrinsically
irreformable, or immune from modification.

The teaching of Vatican I regarding the criteria for infallible pronouncements was repeated in *Lumen gentium* §25:

This infallibility with which the Divine Redeemer willed His
Church to be endowed in defining doctrine of faith and mor-

---

[15] First Vatican Council, Dogmatic Constitution on the Church of Christ *Pastor aeternus*, ch. 4 (DS,
3073–3074).

[16] Ibid. (DS, 3074).

als, extends as far as the deposit of Revelation extends, which must be religiously guarded and faithfully expounded. And this is the infallibility which the Roman Pontiff, the head of the college of bishops, enjoys in virtue of his office, when, as the supreme shepherd and teacher of all the faithful, who confirms his brethren in their faith, by a definitive act he proclaims a doctrine of faith or morals. And therefore his definitions, of themselves, and not from the consent of the Church, are justly styled irreformable, since they are pronounced with the assistance of the Holy Spirit, promised to him in blessed Peter, and therefore they need no approval of others, nor do they allow an appeal to any other judgment. For then the Roman Pontiff is not pronouncing judgment as a private person, but as the supreme teacher of the universal Church, in whom the charism of infallibility of the Church itself is individually present, he is expounding or defending a doctrine of Catholic faith. The infallibility promised to the Church resides also in the body of Bishops, when that body exercises the supreme magisterium with the successor of Peter.[17]

The same criteria apply to an ecumenical council. The decrees of a council are infallible only when there is a manifest intention to define something to be believed definitively by the universal Church in matters of faith and morals. In the Second Vatican Council, it is generally held that there was no intention to infallibly define any new dogma.[18] The Council of Trent, on the contrary, infallibly defined a great

---

[17] *The Sixteen Documents of Vatican II* (Boston: Pauline Books & Media, 1999), 152–153. The widely used *Vatican Council II: The Conciliar and Post-Conciliar Documents*, ed. Austin Flannery (Boston: Daughters of St. Paul, 1988), gives an inadequate translation to the words "definitive act," rendering them instead as "absolute decision" (380). One may well ask, what is an "absolute decision"? The Latin text is very clear: "*definitivo actu proclamat.*" This doctrine is summarized in CCC §891: "The Roman Pontiff, head of the college of bishops, enjoys this infallibility in virtue of his office, when, as supreme pastor and teacher of all the faithful—who confirms his brethren in the faith—he proclaims by a definitive act a doctrine pertaining to faith or morals."

[18] Paul VI spoke of the theological qualification of the teachings of the Second Vatican Council in a General Audience of January 12, 1966: "There are those who ask what authority and what theological qualification the Council intended to give to its teachings, knowing that it avoided

number of teachings on crucial disputed points of doctrine, such as the canon of Scripture, justification, original sin, and the seven sacraments.

It must be borne in mind that there is no set formula of words that the pope or ecumenical council must use in making an infallible definition. No teaching declares itself to be infallible. It is enough that the Pope or council manifest the intention to speak as the successor of the Apostles, that they teach a truth concerning faith and morals with the manifest intention of definitively resolving an issue, to be firmly believed or held by all the faithful. Phrases that manifest this intention include (but are not limited to) the following: "we define,"[19] "must be firmly believed,"[20] "must be firmly held,"[21] "definitively held,"[22] and the condemnation, *"anathema sit."*

The Infallibility of the Ordinary and Universal Magisterium

The infallibility of the Magisterium is not restricted to the formal definitions of the popes and ecumenical councils. Doctrines are also taught in an infallible way without formal definitions in the exercise of the *ordinary and universal Magisterium.* This Magisterium is realized by the Roman Pontiff in union with the bishops dispersed throughout

---

issuing solemn dogmatic definitions engaging the infallibility of the ecclesiastical Magisterium. And the answer is known by all who remember the conciliar declaration of March 6, 1964, repeated on November 16, 1964. Given the Council's pastoral character, it avoided pronouncing, in an extraordinary manner, dogmas endowed with the note of infallibility. However, it gave its teachings the authority of the supreme ordinary Magisterium, which, being the ordinary Magisterium and thus manifestly authentic, must be docilely and sincerely accepted by all the faithful according to the mind of the Council with regard to the nature and ends of each of the documents"; see *Insegnamenti di Paolo VI* (Vatican City: Tipografia Poliglotta Vaticana, 1965–1979), 4:700.

[19] Pius IX, Apostolic Constitution on the Immaculate Conception *Ineffabilis Deus* (1854); see DS, 2803.

[20] DS, 2803; CDF, Declaration on the Unicity and Salvific Universality of Jesus Christ and the Church *Dominus Iesus* (2000), §§ 5, 10, 11, 13, 14, 16, and 20.

[21] *Dominus Iesus* §7.

[22] John Paul II, Apostolic Letter on Reserving Priestly Ordination to Men Alone *Ordinatio sacerdotalis* (1994), §4.

the Catholic world when they agree in teaching doctrines *definitively* as pertaining to the deposit of faith, but in their ordinary (as opposed to extraordinary or solemn) magisterial teaching, and without a single definitive act.[23] In other words, the pope together with the college of bishops can teach infallibly in two ways: (a) gathered together solemnly in an ecumenical council or (b) spread out through the world and over time, but united in teaching a truth of faith and morals definitively.

John Paul II has said that the universal ordinary Magisterium is the "usual expression of the Church's infallibility."[24] For example, in the first centuries, before the ecumenical councils, all of the infallible teachings of the Church were of this kind. As a rule, the ordinary and universal Magisterium suffices to protect the faith of the Church until it is attacked in a particularly grave way by some heresy, at which time it is expedient that the doctrine be explicitly and solemnly defined to remove any doubt. For example, the Council of Nicaea was called to protect the faith of the Church in the divinity of Christ against the heresy of Arius by the solemn definition of the dogma that the Son is consubstantial with the Father.

The consensus between the pope and the bishops on the definitive teaching of doctrine is infallible even if, at a later date, this consensus may be lost by a defection of a portion of the episcopate due to doctrinal dissent or the influence of heresy.[25] To counter such a

---

[23] See *LG* §25: "They [the bishops] nevertheless proclaim Christ's doctrine infallibly whenever, even though dispersed through the world, but still maintaining the bond of communion among themselves and with the successor of Peter, and authentically teaching matters of faith and morals, they are in agreement on one position as definitively to be held." See also Pius IX, Letter to the Archbishop of Munich-Freising *Tuas libenter*, December 21, 1863: "For even if it were a matter of that submission which must be manifested by an act of divine faith, nevertheless, this would not have to be limited to those matters that have been defined by explicit decrees of ecumenical councils or by the Roman pontiffs and by this Apostolic See, but would also have to be extended to those matters transmitted as divinely revealed by the ordinary Magisterium of the whole Church dispersed throughout the world" (DS, 2879).

[24] John Paul II, Address to Bishops from New York of Oct. 15, 1988, §4; in *Origins* 18, no. 21 (Nov. 3, 1988): 348. See the discussion of this text in John F. Kippley, *Sex and the Marriage Covenant: A Basis for Morality*, 2nd ed. (San Francisco: Ignatius Press, 2005), 144–145.

[25] See Tarcisio Bertone, Secretary of the Congregation of the Doctrine of the Faith, "Theological Observations by Archbishop Bertone" in *L'Osservatore Romano* (English), January 29, 1997, 6–7.

dissent, the pope may choose to infallibly confirm the teaching of the ordinary and universal Magisterium in an encyclical or apostolic letter.[26] This was done, for example, by John Paul II in *Evangelium vitae*[27] and *Ordinatio sacerdotalis*, as will be seen below.

See also Lawrence Welch, *The Presence of Christ in the Church* (Ave Maria: Sapientia Press, 2012). For an opposing viewpoint, see Francis A. Sullivan, "Recent Theological Observations on Magisterial Documents and Public Dissent," *Theological Studies* 58, (Sept. 1997): 509–515.

[26] See the CDF, Doctrinal Commentary on the Concluding Formula of the *Professio fidei* (1998), §9: "The Magisterium of the Church, however, teaches a doctrine to be *believed as divinely revealed* (first paragraph) or to be *held definitively* (second paragraph) with an act which is either *defining* or *non-defining*. In the case of a *defining* act, a truth is solemnly defined by an *ex cathedra* pronouncement by the Roman Pontiff or by the action of an ecumenical council. In the case of a *non-defining* act, a doctrine is taught *infallibly* by the ordinary and universal Magisterium of the Bishops dispersed throughout the world who are in communion with the Successor of Peter. *Such a doctrine can be confirmed or reaffirmed by the Roman Pontiff, even without recourse to a solemn definition*, by declaring explicitly that it belongs to the teaching of the ordinary and universal Magisterium as a truth that is divinely revealed (first paragraph) or as a truth of Catholic doctrine (second paragraph). Consequently, when there has not been a judgment on a doctrine in the solemn form of a definition, but this doctrine, belonging to the inheritance of the *depositum fidei*, is taught by the ordinary and universal Magisterium, which necessarily includes the pope, such a doctrine is to be understood as having been set forth infallibly. The declaration of *confirmation* or *reaffirmation* by the Roman Pontiff in this case is not a new dogmatic definition, but a formal attestation of a truth already possessed and infallibly transmitted by the Church"; see *Origins* 28, no. 8 (July 16, 1998): 118. See also Welch, *Presence of Christ*, 30–32.

[27] See *Evangelium vitae* §§57, 62, and 65. §62 declares the grave immorality of abortion: "Given such unanimity in the doctrinal and disciplinary tradition of the Church, Paul VI was able to declare that this tradition is unchanged and unchangeable. Therefore, by the authority which Christ conferred upon Peter and his Successors, in communion with the Bishops—who on various occasions have condemned abortion and who in the aforementioned consultation, albeit dispersed throughout the world, have shown unanimous agreement concerning this doctrine—*I declare that direct abortion, that is, abortion willed as an end or as a means, always constitutes a grave moral disorder*, since it is the deliberate killing of an innocent human being. This doctrine is based upon the natural law and upon the written Word of God, is transmitted by the Church's Tradition and taught by the ordinary and universal Magisterium (cf. *LG* §25)." §65 confirms the grave immorality of euthanasia: "Taking into account these distinctions, in harmony with the Magisterium of my Predecessors and in communion with the Bishops of the Catholic Church, *I confirm that euthanasia is a grave violation of the law of God*, since it is the deliberate and morally unacceptable killing of a human person. This doctrine is based upon the natural law and upon the written Word of God, is transmitted by the Church's Tradition and taught by the ordinary and universal Magisterium (cf. *LG* §25)."

Ordinary Magisterium

Even when magisterial teaching is not intended to be definitive, and thus infallible, the authentic ordinary Magisterium of the pope or the episcopal college still demands the internal assent of the faithful, referred to as "religious submission of mind and will." This is explained in *Lumen gentium* §25:

> This religious submission of mind and will must be shown in a special way to the authentic magisterium of the Roman Pontiff, even when he is not speaking *ex cathedra*; that is, it must be shown in such a way that his supreme magisterium is acknowledged with reverence, and the judgments made by him are sincerely adhered to, according to his manifest mind and will. His mind and will in the matter may be known either from the character of the documents, from his frequent repetition of the same doctrine, or from his manner of speaking.[28]

This religious submission of mind and will to the non-definitive ordinary Magisterium has great ecclesial importance, for the vast majority of magisterial teaching is of this kind. Pius XII explains in *Humani generis* §20:

> Nor must it be thought that what is expounded in Encyclical Letters does not of itself demand consent, since in writing such Letters the Popes do not exercise the supreme power of their Teaching Authority. For these matters are taught with the ordinary teaching authority, of which it is true to say: "*He who heareth you, heareth me*"; and generally what is expound-

---

[28] See CCC §892: "Divine assistance is also given to the successors of the apostles, teaching in communion with the successor of Peter, and, in a particular way, to the bishop of Rome, pastor of the whole Church, when, without arriving at an infallible definition and without pronouncing in a 'definitive manner,' they propose in the exercise of the ordinary Magisterium a teaching that leads to better understanding of Revelation in matters of faith and morals. To this ordinary teaching the faithful 'are to adhere to it with religious assent' which, though distinct from the assent of faith, is nonetheless an extension of it."

ed and inculcated in Encyclical Letters already for other reasons appertains to Catholic doctrine.[29]

Furthermore, a pope may also choose to use an encyclical to pass judgment on a question previously under dispute. After such an intervention, the issue "cannot be any longer considered a question open to discussion among theologians."[30] An example of this type of act is the declaration of the illicitness of contraception made in *Casti connubii*[31] and *Humanae vitae*.[32] After these encyclicals, the question of the illicitness of contraception was clearly no longer "open to discussion among theologians."[33] Another example of a papal document definitively settling a disputed question is the papal bull "On the Nullity of Anglican Orders," *Apostolicae curae*, issued by Leo XIII in 1896.[34] If

---

[29] DS, 3885. For the importance of the authority of the ordinary (non-infallible) Magisterium and the unfortunate tendency to regard only infallible Magisterium as requiring assent, see Ratzinger, *The Nature and Mission of Theology* (San Francisco: Ignatius Press, 1995), 111–113.

[30] Pius XII, Encyclical Letter Concerning Some False Opinions Threatening to Undermine the Foundations of Catholic Doctrine *Humani generis* (1950), §20: "But if the Supreme Pontiffs in their official documents purposely pass judgment on a matter up to that time under dispute, it is obvious that that matter, according to the mind and will of the Pontiffs, cannot be any longer considered a question open to discussion among theologians."

[31] See Pius XI, Encyclical on Christian Marriage *Casti connubii* (1930), §56: "Since, therefore, openly departing from the uninterrupted Christian tradition, some recently have judged it possible solemnly to declare another doctrine regarding this question, the Catholic Church, to whom God has entrusted the defense of the integrity and purity of morals, . . . raises her voice in token of her divine ambassadorship and through Our mouth proclaims anew: any use whatsoever of matrimony exercised in such a way that the act is deliberately frustrated in its natural power to generate life is an offense against the law of God and of nature, and those who indulge in such are branded with the guilt of a grave sin."

[32] See *Humanae vitae* §§11–12: "The Church, nevertheless, in urging men to the observance of the precepts of the natural law, which it interprets by its constant doctrine, teaches that each and every marital act must of necessity retain its intrinsic relationship to the procreation of human life. . . . This particular doctrine, often expounded by the magisterium of the Church, is based on the inseparable connection, established by God, which man on his own initiative may not break, between the unitive significance and the procreative significance which are both inherent to the marriage act."

[33] Contraception was not under dispute by Catholic theologians before *Casti connubii*, but by Anglicans in the Lambeth Conference of 1930, which was the first time a major Christian body dissented from the traditional teaching on contraception.

[34] See §36: "Wherefore, strictly adhering, in this matter, to the decrees of the pontiffs, our predecessors, and confirming them most fully, and, as it were, renewing them by our authority, of our

the pope expressly passes judgment on a previously disputed point, it is not unreasonable to conclude that this teaching is considered definitive and that the act of passing judgment was a definitive act. For this reason, theologians are no longer free to defend the opposite point of view.

The documents of the congregations of the Roman Curia, and especially the Congregation for the Doctrine of the Faith, approved by the Pope, form part of the ordinary Papal Magisterium.[35]

Three Grades of Assent

Since some magisterial teachings are definitive and infallible and others are not, it is clear that there must be different grades of interior assent on the part of the faithful to these different kinds of magisterial teaching. Recent magisterial documents speak of three distinct grades of assent that correspond to three different types of magisterial teaching, of which the first two are infallible and the third is not. These grades of assent are succinctly described in the "Profession of Faith" that is currently pronounced by Catholic priests, theologians, and others called to assume offices in the name of the Church.[36] This Profession consists of the Nicene-Constantinopolitan Creed and concludes with three propositions intended to manifest the threefold adhesion of the believer to three grades of magisterial teaching:

> With firm faith, I also believe everything contained in the word of God, whether written or handed down in Tradition, which the Church, either by a solemn judgment or by the ordinary and universal Magisterium, sets forth to be believed as divinely revealed.

---

own initiative and certain knowledge, we pronounce and declare that ordinations carried out according to the Anglican rite have been, and are, absolutely null and utterly void."

[35] See Second Vatican Council, Decree Concerning the Pastoral Office of Bishops in the Church *Christus Dominus* (1965), §9: "In exercising supreme, full, and immediate power in the universal Church, the Roman pontiff makes use of the departments of the Roman Curia which, therefore, perform their duties in his name and with his authority for the good of the churches and in the service of the sacred pastors."

[36] CDF, *Professio fidei* (DS, 5070).

I also accept and hold each and every thing definitively proposed by the Church regarding teaching on faith and morals.

Moreover, I adhere with religious submission of will and intellect to the teachings that either the Roman Pontiff or the College of Bishops enunciate when they exercise their authentic Magisterium, even if they do not intend to proclaim these teachings by a definitive act.

These three grades of assent outlined in the three concluding propositions of the *Professio fidei* are the subject of John Paul II's *Ad tuendam Fidem*,[37] accompanied by a very interesting "Doctrinal Commentary on the Concluding Formula of the *Professio fidei*," signed by the Prefect of the Congregation for the Doctrine of the Faith, then Cardinal Ratzinger, which explains and gives examples of the three grades of assent.

The first grade of assent is to truths revealed by God and taught definitively as such by the Church, either in a solemn definition or in her ordinary and universal Magisterium. These truths are called dogmas of faith and their obstinate rejection is called heresy. Since these truths are proposed by the Church as God's Word, transmitted through apostolic Tradition and Sacred Scripture, the response of the faithful is to firmly believe these truths with the virtue of divine faith, by which we give assent to divine Revelation.[38] To obstinately withhold assent to these truths, by heresy or deliberate doubt, is a grave sin against the virtue of faith. Examples of these teachings include the

---

[37] The Apostolic Letter (issued *motu proprio*) *Ad tuendam Fidem* (1998) has the purpose of inserting certain norms into the *Code of Canon Law* concerning the second proposition of the Profession. The *Code of Canon Law* promulgated in 1983 already contained penalties for the public and obstinate denial of magisterial teachings of the first and third type, but lacked a special canon for a denial of an infallible teaching of the second type. Therefore, the Pope published this document to make up for this lack and assign a canonical penalty for those public figures of the Church who deny infallible propositions requiring the second grade of assent ("ecclesiastical" faith). Although this may seem to be a purely legal affair, it is very important in the life of the Church, due to the attitude prevalent among certain dissenting theologians that they are free to deny any teaching of the Church that is not explicitly a defined dogma of faith.

[38] In Latin, dogmas requiring the first grade of assent are referred to as *credenda*: doctrines *to be believed*.

articles of the Creed, the seven sacraments, the Ten Commandments, the necessity of grace, and the canon of Scripture.[39] The Doctrinal Commentary gives the following examples:

> the articles of faith of the Creed, the various Christological dogmas and Marian dogmas; the doctrine of the institution of the sacraments by Christ and their efficacy with regard to grace; the doctrine of the real and substantial presence of Christ in the Eucharist and the sacrificial nature of the Eucharistic celebration; the foundation of the Church by the will of Christ; the doctrine on the primacy and infallibility of the Roman Pontiff; the doctrine on the existence of original sin; the doctrine on the immortality of the spiritual soul and on the immediate recompense after death; the absence of error in the inspired sacred texts; the doctrine on the grave immorality of direct and voluntary killing of an innocent human being [abortion].[40]

The second grade of assent is to truths concerning faith and morals taught definitively by the Magisterium of the Church, either in a solemn judgment or through the ordinary and universal Magisterium, but which are not proposed as directly contained in God's Revelation. Rather they are put forth by the Church as intrinsically connected to Revelation and the Church's mission of salvation and/or necessary for defending or expounding the faith.[41] This group of infallible teachings includes truths of the natural order (such as natural law), theological deductions from revealed truths, as well as historical truths connected with the mission of the Church.[42]

---

[39] Council of Trent, Session 4 (April 8, 1546); see DS, 1501–1505.

[40] CDF, *Professio fidei*, §11 (*Origins* 28, no. 8: 118).

[41] With regard to the second grade of assent, *Professio fidei* §6 explains that "the object taught by this formula includes *all those teachings belonging to the dogmatic or moral area, which are necessary for faithfully keeping and expounding the deposit of faith, even if they have not been proposed by the Magisterium of the Church as formally revealed*" (*Origins* 28, no. 8: 117; italics original).

[42] See ibid. §7: "The truths belonging to this second paragraph can be of various natures, thus giving different qualities to their relationship with Revelation. There are truths which are necessar-

An example of an historical question that pertains to the Church's mission of salvation is the identification of saints. It is not directly revealed by God that particular members of the faithful departed are in fact in heaven and that their lives are such as to be proposed to the faithful as exemplary witnesses of Christian life and heroic charity. Nevertheless, it belongs to the Church's mission to be able to put forth certain deceased Christians as exemplary intercessors and models for the faithful. Thus, the Church has the power to infallibly declare the heroic sanctity of particular Christians after their death. The canonization of saints is an infallible act of the Church, but not a dogma of faith because it is not directly revealed by God. The canonization of saints requires the second grade of assent from the faithful. Such truths are to be firmly held.

Another example of an historical question that is intrinsically connected with the mission of the Church is the validity of sacraments in particular circumstances. For example, did the Anglicans lose the Sacrament of Holy Orders during the period from 1552 to 1662, when the Edwardine Ordinal was in use, in which the words of ordination (sacramental form) were significantly altered, losing all reference to the priesthood and to the offering of the sacrifice of the Eucharist? The practice of the Catholic Church since the second half of the sixteenth century was to regard Anglican Orders as null and void because of invalid sacramental form. Pope Leo XIII definitively confirmed this practice in the Bull *Apostolicae curae* of 1896. The invalidity of Anglican Orders is obviously not a dogma of faith, for that fact is not directly revealed by God. However, the historical question has been definitively settled by the Church with an infallible teaching requiring the second grade of assent.

The Doctrinal Commentary gives some examples of teachings requiring the second grade of assent that are connected either historically or logically with the deposit of Revelation:

---

ily connected with Revelation by virtue of an *historical relationship*; while other truths evince a *logical connection* that expresses a stage in the maturation of understanding of Revelation which the Church is called to undertake" (*Origins* 28, no. 8: 117).

With regard to those truths connected to Revelation by historical necessity and which are to be held definitively, but are not able to be declared as divinely revealed, the following examples can be given: the legitimacy of the election of the Supreme Pontiff or of the celebration of an ecumenical council, the canonizations of saints (*dogmatic facts*), the declaration of Pope Leo XIII in the Apostolic Letter *Apostolicae curae* on the invalidity of Anglican ordinations.[43]

The CDF's document considers various examples of *truths* connected with Revelation by a logical necessity. One example is the immorality of euthanasia, taught in the encyclical *Evangelium vitae*:

Confirming that euthanasia is "a grave violation of the law of God," the Pope declares that "this doctrine is based upon the natural law and upon the written Word of God, is transmitted by the Church's Tradition and taught by the ordinary and universal Magisterium." It could seem that there is only a logical element in the doctrine on euthanasia, since Scripture does not seem to be aware of the concept. In this case, however, the interrelationship between the orders of faith and reason becomes apparent: Scripture, in fact, clearly excludes every form of the kind of self-determination of human existence that is presupposed in the theory and practice of euthanasia.[44]

Since these teachings on faith and morals requiring the second grade of assent are definitively proposed by the Church, they are infallible, according to the teaching of *Lumen gentium* §25. However, since these doctrines are not directly revealed by God, the act of assent of the faithful to these teachings receives a different name than the first grade of assent. Instead of having to "firmly believe" such teachings (for firm faith is reserved for God's own Word), the faithful

---

[43] Ibid. §11, (*Origins* 28, no. 8: 118–119).

[44] Ibid.

must "firmly accept and hold" them with an irrevocable assent, on the authority of the Church when she speaks in a definitive manner.[45] This grade of assent is also referred to as "ecclesiastical faith," for it presupposes faith in the Church's power to infallibly determine matters of faith and morals through the assistance of the Holy Spirit, even if they have not been expressly revealed by God. A denial of this type of teaching is a grave sin against the faith, even though it does not technically merit the name of heresy or its canonical penalty. It is referred to in various ways, such as "error in Catholic doctrine," or "proximate to heresy."

The second grade does not differ from the first grade with regard to the firm and irrevocable character of the assent. The only difference is with regard to the motive of assent. In the case of truths directly revealed by God, the assent is motivated directly by God's truthfulness. In the case of teachings requiring the second grade of assent, the assent is motivated by faith in the Church's trustworthiness, due to God's promise of assistance to keep her in the truth. The Doctrinal Commentary explains:

> The fact that these doctrines may not be proposed as formally revealed, insofar as they add to the data of faith *elements that are not revealed or which are not yet expressly recognized as such*, in no way diminishes their definitive character, which is required at least by their intrinsic connection with revealed truth. Moreover, it cannot be excluded that at a certain point in dogmatic development, the understanding of the realities and the words of the deposit of faith can progress in the life of the Church, and the Magisterium may proclaim some of these doctrines as also dogmas of divine and catholic faith.
>
> With regard to the *nature* of the assent owed to the truths set forth by the Church as divinely revealed (those of the first paragraph) or to be held definitively (those of the second paragraph), it is important to emphasize that there is no difference with respect to the full and irrevocable character of

---

[45] In Latin, the doctrines requiring the second grade of assent are referred to as *tenenda*: to be *held*.

the assent which is owed to these teachings. The difference concerns the supernatural virtue of faith: in the case of truths of the first paragraph, the assent is based directly on faith in the authority of the Word of God (doctrines *de fide credenda*); in the case of the truths of the second paragraph, the assent is based on faith in the Holy Spirit's assistance to the Magisterium and on the Catholic doctrine of the infallibility of the Magisterium (doctrines *de fide tenenda*).[46]

The third grade of assent, referred to as "religious submission of will and intellect," is extremely broad. It is the response of the faithful to the entire ordinary Magisterium of the pope or college of bishops (as in an ecumenical council) concerning faith and morals proposed as true or sure, although not in a definitive way. This religious submission of mind and will is based on faith that the Holy Spirit assists the Church's Magisterium even when it is not intending to speak definitively. This grade of assent is explained in the CDF's important *Donum veritatis*:

> Divine assistance is also given to the successors of the apostles teaching in communion with the successor of Peter, and in a particular way, to the Roman Pontiff as Pastor of the whole Church, when exercising their ordinary Magisterium, even should this not issue in an infallible definition or in a "definitive" pronouncement but in the proposal of some teaching which leads to a better understanding of Revelation in matters of faith and morals and to moral directives derived from such teaching.[47]

---

[46] Ibid. §§7–8 (*Origins* 28, no. 8: 117–118, italics original; DS, 5071).

[47] CDF, Instruction on the Ecclesial Vocation of the Theologian *Donum veritatis* (1990), §17. See also CDF, Declaration in Defence of the Catholic Doctrine on the Church against Certain Errors of the Present Day *Mysterium ecclesiae* (1973), §3: "In carrying out their task, the pastors of the Church enjoy the assistance of the Holy Spirit; this assistance reaches its highest point when they teach the People of God in such a manner that, through the promises of Christ made to Peter and the other Apostles, the doctrine they propose is necessarily immune from error."

The explanation of the faith contained in the documents of the Second Vatican Council (unless it is repeating something already definitively taught) requires this third grade of assent. Other examples include the teachings of encyclicals, apostolic exhortations, and papal discourses, such as the Wednesday audiences in which St. John Paul II taught on the Theology of the Body.[48]

Below these three grades of assent, there is a fourth grade that concerns disciplinary measures, prudential judgments, and conjectural matters. As mentioned above, the proper response of the faithful in such matters is not properly assent but obedience. This is described by *Donum veritatis* as follows:

> Finally, in order to serve the People of God as well as possible, in particular, by warning them of dangerous opinions which could lead to error, the Magisterium can intervene in questions under discussion which involve, in addition to solid principles, certain contingent and conjectural elements. It often only becomes possible with the passage of time to distinguish between what is necessary and what is contingent.[49]

An example of such a teaching would be when the Magisterium declares that a particular thesis cannot be safely taught.[50]

---

[48] John Paul II, *Man and Woman He Created Them: A Theology of the Body*, trans. with introduction by Michael Waldstein (Boston: Pauline Books & Media, 2006).

[49] §24. See also Benedict XVI, Christmas Discourse to the Roman Curia, Dec. 22, 2005: "In this process of innovation in continuity we must learn to undertand more practically than before that the Church's decisions on contingent matters—for example, certain practical forms of liberalism or a free interpretation of the Bible—should necessarily be contingent themselves, precisely because they refer to a specific reality that is changeable in itself. It was necessary to learn to recognize that in these decisions it is only the principles that express the permanent aspect, since they remain as an undercurrent, motivating decisions from within"; see, in *Origins* 35, no. 32 (January 26, 2006): 538.

[50] See, for example, DS, 3645, which states that it cannot be safely taught that it is not certain that Christ had the vision of God in His human soul during His earthly life.

Ordinatio sacerdotalis and the Claims for the Ordination of "Women Priests"

A good example of a teaching requiring the second grade of assent is that given in Pope John Paul II's *Ordinatio sacerdotalis*, which definitively and infallibly confirmed the constant Tradition of the Church according to which she acknowledges that she has not received the authority from Jesus Christ to ordain women priests:

> Although the teaching that priestly ordination is to be reserved to men alone has been preserved by the constant and universal Tradition of the Church and firmly taught by the Magisterium in its more recent documents, at the present time in some places it is nonetheless considered still open to debate, or the Church's judgment that women are not to be admitted to ordination is considered to have a merely disciplinary force. Wherefore, in order that all doubt may be removed regarding a matter of great importance, a matter which pertains to the Church's divine constitution itself, in virtue of my ministry of confirming the brethren (cf. Luke 22:32) I declare that the Church has no authority whatsoever to confer priestly ordination on women and that this judgment is to be *definitively* held by all the Church's faithful.[51]

In this paragraph, the Pope has expressed himself very precisely so as to make clear that this pronouncement is definitive and therefore *infallible*, and thus can never be changed by any future pope or council. All of the requirements given in *Lumen gentium* §25 (summarized in *CCC* §891) are clearly realized. First, the Pope confirms that he is acting as supreme pastor when he speaks "in virtue of my ministry of confirming the brethren." Second, he explicitly intends to make a definitive act ("this judgment is to be *definitively* held by all the Church's faithful"). Finally, he is teaching on a question pertaining to faith and morals, for he says that it is "a matter which pertains to the Church's divine constitution itself."

---

[51] §4 (DS, 4983; my italics).

Here the Pope states that the prohibition of women priests is necessarily connected to revealed truth, and hence included in the deposit of faith. The CDF's Doctrinal Commentary affirmed that the Church can teach a doctrine infallibly without solemnly proclaiming it to be a revealed dogma, because it is *necessarily connected* with revealed doctrine. The teaching of *Ordinatio sacerdotalis* falls (at least) into this second category, for the Pope does not explicitly say that this doctrine has been directly revealed by God.

This matter was further clarified by the Magisterium in two documents of the CDF. In a response to a question regarding *Ordinatio sacerdotalis*, the Congregation declared that the doctrine that the Church has no power to confer priestly ordination to women should be considered as "belonging to the *deposit of faith*." Evidently, if a teaching is definitively declared to belong to the deposit of faith, it has been infallibly taught and can never be changed. They go on to affirm:

> This teaching requires definitive assent, since, founded on the written Word of God, and from the beginning constantly preserved and applied in the Tradition of the Church, it has been set forth *infallibly* by the ordinary and universal Magisterium (cf. Second Vatican Council, Dogmatic Constitution on the Church *Lumen gentium* §§25, 2). Thus, in the present circumstances, the Roman Pontiff, exercising his proper office of confirming the brethren (cf. Luke 22:32), has handed on this same teaching by a formal declaration, explicitly stating what is to be held always, everywhere, and by all, as belonging to the deposit of the faith.[52]

The CDF returned again to this subject in 1998 in the Doctrinal Commentary on *Ad tuendam Fidem* to speak of the great importance of the definitive and infallible doctrines that require the second grade of assent:

---

[52] CDF, Response of October 28, 1995 (DS, 5041; my italics).

A similar process can be observed in the more recent teaching regarding the doctrine that priestly ordination is reserved only to men. The Supreme Pontiff, while not wishing to proceed to a dogmatic definition, intended to reaffirm that this doctrine is to be held *definitively*, since, founded on the written Word of God, constantly preserved and applied in the Tradition of the Church, it has been set forth *infallibly* by the ordinary and universal Magisterium. . . . This does not foreclose the possibility that, in the future, the consciousness of the Church might progress to the point where this teaching could be defined as a doctrine to be believed as divinely revealed [that is, a dogma of faith].[53]

Theological Censures

It was frequent in the past for magisterial documents to take the form of a list of condemned propositions. For example, Pope Leo X condemned forty-one propositions of Martin Luther in the papal bull of 1520, *Exsurge Domine*,[54] and in the same way the Holy See condemned propositions of Baius and Jansenius. Pope Pius IX condemned the errors of nineteenth-century naturalism and liberalism in the *Syllabus of Errors*,[55] and St. Pius X condemned the errors of Modernism in the Decree *Lamentabili*.

It is important to determine what degree of assent these condemnations require. This is determined by the "theological censures" that are attached to the condemned propositions. If it is merely said that a proposition "cannot be safely taught," then this is a disciplinary matter that requires obedience, but could change over time. For it could

---

[53] *Professio fidei* §11 (*Origins* 28, no. 8: 118).

[54] DS, 1451–1492.

[55] The Syllabus of Errors of 1864 (DS, 2901–2980) is a collection of positions previously condemned by Pius IX in encyclicals or addresses. Since the Syllabus is not signed or specifically approved by the Pope (it is from the Secretary of State) and does not indicate the definitive nature of the condemnations, these positions as presented in the Syllabus should *not* be held to be infallible, but rather serve to invite one to read the original document and grasp the exact meaning of the condemnations from their original context.

happen that what cannot be safely taught today could be safely taught in the future if significant clarifications are made.

If the propositions are condemned as heretical (or rejected with the formula *"anathema sit"*), then the opposite truth is to be considered a dogma of faith and is clearly an infallible teaching. If, on the other hand, the proposition is condemned in a *definitive* way as erroneous or false, then the opposing truth is not a dogma, but it is nevertheless *infallible* and must be *firmly held* by the faithful with the second degree of assent (ecclesiastical faith). However, the condemnation must not be taken more broadly than the precise formulation that is condemned, and it must always be understood in its own specific context.

Infallibility and the Development of Doctrine

We have seen above that doctrine develops in the life of the Church in an organic way, as the Church comes to articulate the deposit of faith in a clearer and more explicit way over the centuries. How does this affect the pronouncements of the Magisterium? The teachings of the ordinary non-definitive Magisterium can be substantially modified over time, precisely because they are not definitive and thus are reformable. One should not expect this to be the case, however, due to the divine assistance given also to the non-definitive Magisterium.

With regard to definitive and infallible Magisterium, the substance of the definitive teaching, properly interpreted according to the genuine intention of its authors, is guaranteed not to be false. Without changing the substance, however, the mode of expression can be perfected in a double sense. First, it can be made clearer in itself by introducing distinctions, qualifications, and more clearly defined terms. Second, it can be formulated in a new way so as to be more understandable in a new cultural context, but without changing its original meaning.

Pope St. John XXIII refers to this type of reformulation in his famous address at the opening of the Second Vatican Council, in which he set forth his expectation for the teaching of the Council. He wanted the teaching of the Church in its entirety, as proclaimed by the Council of Trent and Vatican I, to be contemplated anew, without any reduction, so that it could be formulated in a way that the modern world could hear and understand:

> The entirety of Catholic doctrine, with nothing left out, is to be the object of a renewed study by all, serene and peaceful, in that accurate manner of thought and expression that especially shines forth in the acts of the Council of Trent and the First Vatican Council. It is necessary . . . that this doctrine be made known more widely and with greater depth, and that the hearts of the faithful be more fully permeated and formed by it. This certain and immutable doctrine, faithfully assented to, needs to be investigated and proclaimed as our time demands. *One thing is the deposit of faith, that is, the truths contained in this venerable doctrine; another thing is the way in which they are proclaimed, while always preserving the same sense and judgment.* This method is to be given great importance and it is to be worked out, if need be, with patience. The mode of presentation should be most suited to a Magisterium that is predominantly pastoral in character.[56]

---

[56] John XXIII, Discourse of Oct. 11, 1962 at the solemn inauguration of the Council (my translation). The Latin text of this paragraph reads: "Verumtamen in praesenti oportet ut universa doctrina christiana, nulla parte inde detracta, his temporibus nostris ab omnibus accipiatur novo studio, mentibus serenis atque pacatis, tradita accurata illa ratione verba concipiendi et in formam redigendi, quae ex actis Concilii Tridentini et Vaticani Primi praesertim elucet; oportet ut . . . eadem doctrina amplius et altius cognoscatur eaque plenius animi imbuantur atque formentur; oportet ut haec doctrina certa et immutabilis, cui fidele obsequium est praestandum, ea ratione pervestigetur et exponatur, quam tempora postulant nostra. Est enim aliud ipsum depositum Fidei, seu veritates, quae veneranda doctrina nostra continentur, aliud modus, quo eaedem enuntiantur, eodem tamen sensu eademque sententia. Huic quippe modo plurimum tribuendum erit et patienter, si opus fuerit, in eo elaborandum; scilicet eae inducendae erunt rationes res exponendi, quae cum magisterio, cuius indoles praesertim pastoralis est, magis congruant"; found in *AAS* 54 (1962): 791–792. Both the English translations given in *Council Daybook: Vatican II, Session 1, 1962, and Sessions 2, 1963*, ed. Floyd Anderson (Washington, DC: National Catholic Welfare Conference, 1963), 27, and that found in *The Teachings of the Second Vatican Council: Complete Texts of the Constitutions, Decrees, and Declarations* (Westminster: The Newman Press, 1966), 7–8, depart significantly from the official Latin. On this translation problem, see Romano Amerio, *Iota Unum: A Study of Changes in the Catholic Church in the XXth Century*,

As John XXIII makes clear in this famous discourse, the development of doctrine does not imply doctrinal relativism! The words and style in which a doctrine is stated by the contemporary Magisterium should be chosen to make it as clear and profound as possible for the modern world, but without changing the meaning of the earlier dogmatic formulations. This famous speech is in complete harmony with the First Vatican Council's condemnation of doctrinal relativism in *Dei Filius*:

> For the doctrine of faith that God has revealed has not been proposed like a philosophical system to be perfected by human ingenuity; rather, it has been committed to the spouse of Christ as a divine trust to be faithfully kept and infallibly declared. Hence also that meaning of the sacred dogmas is perpetually to be retained which our Holy Mother Church has once declared, and there must never be a deviation from that meaning on the specious ground and title of a more profound understanding. "Therefore, let there be growth and abundant progress in understanding, knowledge, and wisdom, in each and all, in individuals and in the whole Church, at all times and in the progress of ages, but only within the proper limits, i.e., within the same dogma, the same meaning, the same judgment."[57]

The CDF's *Mysterium ecclesiae* reiterated the teaching of Vatican I:

> As for the *meaning* of dogmatic formulas, this remains ever true and constant in the Church, even when it is expressed with greater clarity or more developed. The faithful therefore must shun the opinion, first, that dogmatic formulas (or some category of them) cannot signify truth in a determinate way,

---

trans. John Parsons (Kansas City: Angelus Press, 1996), 77–80.

[57] Vatican I, Dogmatic Constitution on the Catholic Faith *Dei Filius* (1870), ch. 4 (DS, 3020). The quotation is of Vincent of Lérins, *Commonitorium primum* 23.3 (PL, 50:668A).

but can only offer changeable approximations to it, which to a certain extent distort or alter it; secondly, that these formulas signify the truth only in an indeterminate way, this truth being like a goal that is constantly being sought by means of such approximations. Those who hold such an opinion do not avoid dogmatic relativism and they corrupt the concept of the Church's infallibility relative to the truth to be taught or held in a determinate way.[58]

Mysterium ecclesiae §5 also speaks of the way in which dogmatic formulations can be perfected over time: "Moreover, it sometimes happens that some dogmatic truth is first expressed incompletely (but not falsely), and at a later date, when considered in a broader context of faith or human knowledge, it receives a fuller and more perfect expression." In this process, the earlier formulation is not contradicted or rendered false, but is clarified and protected against misunderstanding. A newer formulation never derogates the earlier formulation, rightly understood, but clarifies it.

Hermeneutic of Continuity

Since the development of doctrine builds on the dogmatic formulations of the past without ever substantially changing their meaning, it follows that a key criterion for the interpretation of magisterial documents is to interpret them in harmony with earlier Church teaching. We can call this, following Benedict XVI, the "*hermeneutic of continuity*." The opposing method would be the "hermeneutic of discontinuity and rupture." Benedict XVI applied these terms to the interpretation of the Second Vatican Council in his Christmas discourse to the Roman Curia of December 22, 2005.

Many theologians have interpreted Vatican II, especially in the years shortly after the Council, as if it stood in some kind of radical

---

[58] CDF, Declaration in Defense of the Catholic Doctrine on the Church against Certain Errors of the Present Day *Mysterium ecclesiae* (June 24, 1973), §5.

discontinuity with previous Church teaching.[59] Many put forth this idea by speaking of the "spirit of the Council" rather than referring to its actual texts. The media facilitated such an approach. Benedict responded to this as follows:

> The question arises: Why has the implementation of the Council, in large parts of the Church, thus far been so difficult? Well, it all depends on the correct interpretation of the Council or—as we would say today—on its proper hermeneutics, the correct key to its interpretation and application. The problems in its implementation arose from the fact that two contrary hermeneutics came face to face and quarreled with each other. One caused confusion, the other, silently but more and more visibly, bore and is bearing fruit.
>
> On the one hand, there is an interpretation that I would call "a hermeneutic of discontinuity and rupture"; it has frequently availed itself of the sympathies of the mass media, and also one trend of modern theology. On the other, there is the "hermeneutic of reform," of renewal in the continuity of the one subject-Church which the Lord has given to us. She is a subject that increases in time and develops, yet always remaining the same, the one subject of the journeying People of God.
>
> The hermeneutic of discontinuity risks ending in a split between the pre-conciliar Church and the post-conciliar Church. It asserts that the texts of the Council as such do not yet express the true spirit of the Council. It claims that they are the result of compromises in which, to reach unanimity, it was found necessary to keep and reconfirm many old things that are now pointless. However, the true spirit of the Council is not to be found in these compromises but instead in the impulses toward the new that are contained in the texts. . . . In a word: it would be necessary not to follow the

---

[59] See Agostino Marchetto, *The Second Vatican Ecumenical Council: A Counterpoint for the History of the Council*, trans. Kenneth D. Whitehead (Chicago: University of Scranton Press, 2010).

texts of the Council but its spirit. In this way, obviously, a vast margin was left open for the question on how this spirit should subsequently be defined and room was consequently made for every whim.

The nature of a Council as such is therefore basically misunderstood.[60]

Clearly Benedict XVI thought that a right criterion for interpreting Vatican II is of crucial importance for the contemporary Church. He returned to this theme in one of his last public discourses, an address to the parish priests and clergy of Rome on February 14, 2013, in which he contrasted the real Second Vatican Council with the Council as represented by the media. The real Council was working with the Holy Spirit in continuity with the Church of all time, whereas the media depicted it as a battle between liberals and conservatives for power in the Church:

> There was the council of the Fathers, the real council, but there was also the council of the media. It was almost a council apart, and the world perceived the council through the latter, through the media. . . . And while the council of the Fathers was conducted within the faith, . . . the council of the journalists naturally, was not conducted within the faith, but within the categories of today's media. . . . It was a political hermeneutic.
>
> For the media, the council was a political struggle, a power struggle between different trends in the Church. It was obvious that the media would take the side of those who seemed to them more closely allied with their world. . . . We know that this council of the media was accessible to everyone. Therefore, this was the dominant one, the more effective one, and it created so many disasters, so many problems, so much suffering: seminaries closed, convents closed, banal liturgy . . . and the real council had difficulty establishing itself and taking

---

[60] Benedict XVI, Christmas Discourse, 2005 (*Origins* 35.32, 536).

shape; the virtual council was stronger than the real council. But the real force of the council was present and, slowly but surely, established itself more and more and became the true force which is also the true reform, the true renewal of the Church. It seems to me that, 50 years after the council, we see that this virtual council is broken, is lost and there now appears the true council, with all its spiritual force.[61]

Doctrinal Dissent

As mentioned above, it should be borne in mind that the three grades of assent concern only teachings, not disciplinary decrees. Assent, properly speaking, is given to teachings formulated as propositions. Disciplinary decrees demand the response of obedience, which is distinct from assent. One might think that a disciplinary decree of an ecclesiastical authority is imprudent or unwise, while still giving obedience.

A theologian may think privately that a truth taught by the ordinary Magisterium is imperfectly expressed or could be explained in a better way. Nevertheless, one must still assent with mind and will to the teaching that is proposed, even though one recognizes that it could be modified in some way in the future so as to be more perfectly expressed, or even though one does not fully understand it or see how to answer objections against it. Thinking that the formulation or argumentation is imperfect is not the same as dissent. Dissent consists in deliberately withholding assent and thinking that the magisterial teaching (and not just discipline) is incorrect and needs to be substantially changed.

The theme of doctrinal dissent and the difficulties that theologians may experience with magisterial teachings is treated in the CDF's *Donum veritatis*. With regard to a theologian who has difficulty in accepting a non-definitive magisterial teaching, it states:

---

[61] Benedict XVI, Address of Feb. 14, 2013; in *Origins* 42, no. 38 (February 28, 2013): 607–608.

Such a disagreement could not be justified if it were based solely upon the fact that the validity of the given teaching is not evident or upon the opinion that the opposite position would be the more probable. Nor, furthermore, would the judgment of the subjective conscience of the theologian justify it because conscience does not constitute an autonomous and exclusive authority for deciding the truth of a doctrine.

In any case there should never be a diminishment of that fundamental openness loyally to accept the teaching of the Magisterium as is fitting for every believer by reason of the obedience of faith. The theologian will strive then to understand this teaching in its contents, arguments, and purposes. This will mean an intense and patient reflection on his part and a readiness, if need be, to revise his own opinions and examine the objections which his colleagues might offer him.

If, despite a loyal effort on the theologian's part, the difficulties persist, the theologian has the duty to make known to the magisterial authorities the problems raised by the teaching in itself, in the arguments proposed to justify it, or even in the manner in which it is presented. He should do this in an evangelical spirit and with a profound desire to resolve the difficulties. His objections could then contribute to real progress and provide a stimulus to the Magisterium to propose the teaching of the Church in greater depth and with a clearer presentation of the arguments.

In cases like these, the theologian should avoid turning to the "mass media," but have recourse to the responsible authority, for it is not by seeking to exert the pressure of public opinion that one contributes to the clarification of doctrinal issues and renders service to the truth.[62]

Public and obstinate dissent against non-definitive teachings of the ordinary Magisterium is very harmful to the Church, causes grave

---

[62] §§28–30.

scandal, and thus would not be without grave sin, especially when it is done by those who are seen to speak in the name of the Church.

Study Questions

1. Why is it fitting for the Church to have the charism of infallibility, and thus an infallible Magisterium?
2. Who can exercise the charism of teaching infallibly in the Church?
3. What are the three conditions, stated in Vatican I's *Pastor aeternus* and Vatican II's *Lumen gentium* §25 by which we can recognize that a papal (or conciliar) teaching is teaching something infallibly?
4. Explain the three grades of assent to magisterial teachings as expressed in the Profession of Faith and as explained in the document, *Ad tuendam Fidem* (and the doctrinal commentary appended to it). What is the difference between the three grades? Give some examples for each grade.
5. What is the ordinary and universal Magisterium? What grade of assent must be given to it? Give some examples.
6. What grade of assent must be given to the teaching of John Paul II's Apostolic Letter *Ordinatio sacerdotalis*? Explain.
7. Explain the "hermeneutic of continuity."

Suggestions for Further Reading

Lumen gentium §§21–25.
Pope Benedict XVI, Christmas Discourse to the Roman Curia, Dec. 22, 2005. In *Origins* 35, no. 32 (January 26, 2006): 534–539.
———. Address of February 14, 2013. In *Origins* 42, no. 38 (February 28, 2013): 601–608.
Congregation for the Doctrine of the Faith. Doctrinal Commentary on the Concluding Formula of the *Professio fidei*. In *Origins* 28, no. 8 (July 16, 1998): 116–119.

————. Instruction on the Ecclesial Vocation of the Theologian *Donum veritatis*. May 24, 1990.

————. Declaration on the Unicity and Salvific Universality of Jesus Christ and the Church *Dominus Iesus*. Aug. 6, 2000.

Pope St. John Paul II, Apostolic Letter on Reserving Priestly Ordination to Men Alone *Ordinatio sacerdotalis*. May 22, 1994.

Dulles, Avery, S.J. *Magisterium: Teacher and Guardian of the Faith*. Naples: Sapientia Press of Ave Maria University, 2007.

Welch, Lawrence. *The Presence of Christ in the Church*. Ave Maria: Sapientia Press, 2012.

PART 4

The Inspiration and Truth of Scripture: Biblical Hermeneutics

CHAPTER TEN

Inspiration of Scripture

Inspiration of Scripture

We have seen that God has willed His Revelation to reach all people until the end of time. For this reason He has established two means for the one deposit of Revelation to be transmitted: oral and written. The oral transmission is called Tradition and the written inspired transmission is Sacred Scripture.

God, being sovereignly free in the salvation of man, did not have to give the People of God an inspired Scripture. He could have revealed Himself to Israel and the Church and left the transmission of that orally communicated Revelation to oral Tradition, passed down from generation to generation through the assistance of the Holy Spirit. That, however, was not His plan. God has willed that His Revelation be communicated in Israel and the Church not only through Tradition, but also in an inspired collection of canonical books written over the course of many centuries that transmit Revelation in fixed form as God's own Word.

Since Revelation is a supernatural work of God that transcends the order of reason and nature and informs us about the supernatural order centering on the Incarnation, attested to by supernatural miracles and prophecies, it is fitting that God transmit and preserve that Revelation also by supernatural means. It is in harmony with the whole revealed plan of God that He give a supernatural assistance in the writing down of that Revelation, such that God Himself vouches for the written work as His own, although written by human authors using their natural faculties.[1] Marie-Joseph Lagrange explains:

> This special providence of God, these revelations and miracles cannot be seen by all men, and God has been pleased that they should be recorded in a book, since men are wont to use writing as the ordinary means of recording history. But who is to undertake the performance of this duty, unless he be incited thereto by God and helped by Him? Just as miracles confirm revelation, so does inspiration preserve supernatural teaching, and is to us a token of God's paternal designs in the work of our salvation.[2]

Inspiration is the unique privilege of the Old and New Testaments. Belief in the inspiration of Scripture and its inerrancy antedates the Church, for it was also the faith of the Jewish people. Christ reminded the Jews who were opposing Him of their belief in the divine quality of Scripture when He said in John 5:39: "You search the scriptures, because you think that in them you have eternal life; and it is they that bear witness to me." The Jewish historian Josephus (AD 37– ca. 100) says:

> For we have not an innumerable multitude of books among us, disagreeing from and contradicting one another [as the Greeks have] but only twenty-two books, which contain the records of all the past times; *which are justly believed to be divine.* . . . And how firmly we have given credit to those books of our own nation is evident by what we do; for during so many ages as have already passed, no one has been so bold as

---

[1] See Marie-Joseph Lagrange, *Historical Criticism and the Old Testament*, trans. Edward Myers (London: Catholic Truth Society, 1906), 85: "There was no absolute necessity for inspiration— God is always free—but as it is a supernatural assistance to write, it well befits a supernatural order which includes revelation."

[2] Ibid., 87.

either to add anything to them or take anything from them, or to make any change in them; but it becomes natural to all Jews, immediately and from their very birth, to esteem those books to contain divine doctrines, and to persist in them, and, if occasion be, willingly to die for them.[3]

The New Testament also presents the authority of Scripture as absolute and indisputable.[4] St. Paul affirms the inspiration of the (Old Testament) Scriptures in 2 Timothy 3:16–17: "All scripture is inspired by God and profitable for teaching, for reproof, for correction, and for training in righteousness, that the man of God may be complete, equipped for every good work." Here St. Paul commends Sacred Scripture on account of its source, its end, and its effects. The originating principle of Scripture is God Himself, and its goal or purpose is the perfection of man. The effect of Scripture is that it enlightens men's ignorance, reproves their moral faults, and moves them to acts of virtue. The divine origin of prophecy and Scripture is confirmed by St. Peter in 2 Peter 1:21: "No prophecy ever came by the impulse of man, but men moved by the Holy Spirit spoke from God."

God Is the Principal Author of Scripture

Inspiration comes from the word "spirit" or "breath," a divine breath that moves man as wind moves a sail. When we say that someone's actions are inspired, we mean that the principle of those actions lies outside of that person, for he is aided to accomplish something that unaided reason could not have attained. The most common use of the word is the metaphorical sense in which great works of literature, art, and music, are said to be "inspired." Mozart and Leonardo da Vinci, St. Augustine and St. Thomas Aquinas, all produced works with manifest special natural gifts of God, such as great intellect and profound

---

[3] Flavius Josephus, *Against Apion* 1.8, in *Josephus: Complete Works*, trans. William Whiston (Grand Rapids: Kregel Publications, 1978), 609.

[4] See, among others, Acts 1:16 and John 20:36.

creative ability. These works also inspire those who contemplate them.

However, the word "inspiration" is not used in the same sense with regard to Scripture as with works of art, for the Bible is not merely a work that reveals a religious genius or that inspires elevated religious sentiments.[5] If this were so, then it would certainly be arrogant to claim that biblical inspiration is strictly limited to the Old and New Testaments and is not present in the Koran, the Talmud, the Book of Mormon, the Bhagavad-Gita, the revelations of Reverend Moon, and others. Nevertheless, the Catholic faith firmly professes that "inspiration," in the strict theological sense, is not present in any book other than those in the Old and New Testaments.[6] Indeed, no other book will ever again be inspired in this strict sense, for it is the exclusive property of the Bible.

In other words, inspiration is an analogical term, and not a univocal one. A univocal term is always used in the same sense, with the same definition. An analogical term is used in different, though related, senses. Inspiration is an analogical term because it admits both a strict theological sense and a broad figurative sense. Therefore, biblical inspiration is not to be confused with the inspiration of a gifted artist or writer.

Artistic inspiration, however, can serve to shed some light on scriptural inspiration by analogy. Artistic inspiration implies that the artist receives some kind of special insight and a gift of judging how best to communicate it in the composition of his work. Likewise, artistic inspiration suggests the idea that the artist's work in some way transcends the human cause by virtue of some kind of "illumination" received by the artist, experienced as a gift. Artistic inspiration does

---

[5] Alfred Loisy, the most radical of the Modernists, seems to equate biblical inspiration with natural artistic and religious inspiration, dissolving the distinction between the supernatural and the natural orders, saying "God is the author of the Bible just as he is the architect of St. Peter's in Rome and Notre Dame in Paris," in his *Simple Réflections sur le Décret du Saint-Office Lamentabili sane Exitu et sur l'Encyclique Pascendi Dominici gregis*, 2nd ed. (Ceffonds, 1908), 45, trans. James T. Burtchaell in *Catholic Theories of Biblical Inspiration Since 1810: A Review and Critique* (London: Cambridge University Press, 1969), 228.

[6] See the CDF, Declaration on the Unicity and Salvific Universality of Jesus Christ and the Church *Dominus Iesus* (2000), §8: "The Church's tradition, however, reserves the designation of *inspired texts* to the canonical books of the Old and New Testaments, since these are inspired by the Holy Spirit" (DS, 5085).

not eliminate the need for arduous effort on the part of the artist to work out and communicate what he has been graced to have "seen" or "heard" in a glimpse. All of these elements apply to scriptural inspiration, and in a supreme way.

The difference, however, is that in biblical inspiration this interior illumination and gift of right judgment in composition is on a different order—supernatural rather than natural—and it is so decisive that God is properly considered to be the *principal author* of Scripture, which is never the case for any other work, whether artistic, literary, or religious. Artistic inspiration enables the artist to make *his own* work. Scriptural inspiration enables the sacred author to make *God's* word! The great profession of Catholic faith on the Bible is that God is its *primary* and *principal* author, and therefore Scripture is rightly said to be the Word of God in an exclusive sense. It is God's Word because He inspired its composition in such a way that the human author, using his faculties under the influence of divine grace, *wrote what God wished him to write, only that and nothing more.* This can never be said of any other human work, no matter how "inspired" it may seem to us.

Doctrine of the Magisterium on Inspiration

The First Vatican Council, faced with denials of biblical inspiration on the part of rationalists, gave a solemn definition of the inspiration of the whole canon of the Old and New Testaments:

> These books of the Old and the New Testaments are to be received as sacred and canonical in their integrity, with all their parts, as they are enumerated in the decree of the said council [Trent] and are contained in the ancient Latin edition of the Vulgate. These the Church holds to be sacred and canonical, not because, having been carefully composed by mere human industry, they were afterward approved by her authority or merely because they contain revelation with no admixture of error but because, having been written by the inspiration of

the Holy Spirit, they have God for their author and have been delivered as such to the Church herself.[7]

The canon of the Bible is the collection of all the works that the Church recognizes as inspired by God. The Church recognizes this inspiration through her constant Tradition, manifested especially in the liturgy in which these works are read as the Word of God. Since they are inspired by God, they are rightly said to have God as their principal author.

The Catholic understanding of inspiration is distinguished here from two erroneous conceptions that overly minimize the action of God in the sacred writer. The first error conceives of inspiration as an action of the Church herself, consisting in her authoritative approval of certain works deemed to accurately represent the faith, though written solely by human means. This position must be rejected because it removes true authorship from God, who could not be the principal author of Scripture unless He directly molded its creation by the influence of grace upon the faculties of the sacred writers. The inspiration of Scripture is not the *effect* of the solemn approval of the Church, but rather the *cause* of the Church's veneration for the canonical Scriptures!

The second error is to conceive of inspiration as simply a negative protection from mistakes in the communication of Revelation. This error implies considerable faith in the inerrancy of Scripture, but it is still gravely insufficient. For, if inspiration solely meant freedom from error, then the Bible could not truly be called the Word of God, nor could God be its author in the full sense. If a professor corrects a student's paper by eliminating all errors, the professor is still not the true author of the paper, but only its censor or editor. However, the Catholic faith holds that God is not the editor or censor of Scripture, but its true Author. In contrast, God is *not* said to be the proper author of the infallible decrees of the Church's Magisterium, although we

---

[7] First Vatican Council, Dogmatic Constitution on the Catholic Faith *Dei Filius* (1870), ch. 2 (DS, 3006). For the Vulgate, see *Bibliorum Sacrorum: Nova Vulgata* (Vatican City: Libreria Editrice Vaticana, 1986).

believe that these communicate Revelation without error. Infallible magisterial teachings are not called the Word of God as Scripture is.[8] This implies that inspiration is something deeper and more substantial than mere protection from error. Inspiration is divine authorship, not censorship.

In summary, Vatican I declares that the books of the Bible are sacred and canonical not because of a subsequent approval of the Church, nor even because they contain infallible religious truth. Rather, Scripture is inspired because of its efficient cause, the Holy Spirit, who interiorly moved the sacred writers to write, so that God most properly is its principal author. The Fathers of the Church compare the Scriptures to a letter written by our heavenly Father, and transmitted by the sacred writers (who are also true authors) to the human race in its pilgrimage so far from its heavenly country.[9]

Divine authorship is what puts the Bible immeasurably above any other book or written work, including the writings of the saints and magisterial documents, and gives it a divine power to move the soul to piety, for "the word of God is living and active, sharper than any two-edged sword, piercing to the division of soul and spirit" (Heb 4:12). The inspiration of Scripture is an article of faith that cannot be demonstrated and must be believed on the authority of the Church and her constant Tradition.

The Action of God in the Sacred Writers

Inspiration implies three distinct effects in the human author: illuminating the mind, efficaciously moving the will, and assisting in the execution of the work. In 1893, Pope Leo XIII explained this threefold action of divine inspiration in his great encyclical on the Bible, *Providentissimus Deus*:

---

[8] For further discussion of these positions condemned by Vatican I, see Burtchaell, *Catholic Theories of Biblical Inspiration*, 44–58.

[9] See Leo XIII, Encyclical Letter on the Study of Holy Scripture *Providentissimus Deus* (1893), §1. See St. John Chrysostom, Homily 2 on Genesis, no. 4; in *Homilies on Genesis*, trans. Robert Hill (Washington, DC: Catholic University of America Press, 1986), 31; and St. Gregory the Great, *Letters* 4.31 (to Theodorus); in *NPNF2*, 12b:156.

For, by supernatural power, He so moved and impelled them to write—He was so present to them—that the things which He ordered, and those only, they, *first, rightly understood, then willed faithfully to write down, and finally expressed in apt words and with infallible truth.* Otherwise, it could not be said that He was the Author of the entire Scripture. Such has always been the persuasion of the Fathers. "Therefore," says St. Augustine, "since they wrote the things which He showed and uttered to them, it cannot be pretended that He is not the writer; for His members executed what their Head dictated." And St. Gregory the Great thus pronounces: "Most superfluous it is to inquire who wrote these things—we loyally believe the Holy Ghost to be the Author of the book. He wrote it Who dictated it for writing; He wrote it Who inspired its execution."[10]

To say that God inspired the Scriptures and is their author is to say that God interiorly moved the sacred authors to rightly grasp what He willed them to understand and to will to write it down, assisting them during the process of writing so that they wrote it down in fitting words and expressions. Pope Benedict XV also spoke of this threefold action of divine inspiration in *Spiritus Paraclitus*, where he says that St. Jerome speaks the mind of the Church concerning the effects of divine inspiration:

> For he holds that God, through His grace, illumines the writer's mind regarding the particular truth which, "in the person of God," he is to set before men; he holds, moreover, that God moves the writer's will—nay, even impels it—to write; finally, that God abides with him unceasingly, in unique fashion, until his task is accomplished.[11]

---

[10] *Providentissimus Deus* §20 (my italics).

[11] Encyclical Letter on St. Jerome *Spiritus Paraclitus* (1920), §9.

The illumination of the mind of the sacred author may include direct revelation of new truths not previously known by the sacred author (prophecy), or it may be limited to forming a correct judgment of truths that he learned through oral or written tradition, or a combination of these. For example, St. Luke states in the introduction to his Gospel (Luke 1:1–4) that he has done a careful historical investigation of primary sources prior to writing:

> Inasmuch as many have undertaken to compile a narrative of the things which have been accomplished among us, just as they were delivered to us by those who from the beginning were eyewitnesses and ministers of the word, it seemed good to me also, having followed all things closely for some time past, to write an orderly account for you, most excellent Theophilus, that you may know the truth concerning the things of which you have been informed.

The divine illumination that Luke received to write his Gospel in no way dispensed him from using the ordinary human means employed by other reputable historians. However, it enabled him to discern and record correctly and infallibly the truths he learned from the primary sources that he diligently consulted. Another example of the sacred writer making use of existing sources is noted in the second book of Maccabees, in which the writer says that his work consisted in making a summary of another larger work in five books written by Jason of Cyrene. This summary also cost him a lot of sweat: "For us who have undertaken the toil of abbreviating, it is no light matter but calls for sweat and loss of sleep" (2 Macc 2:26).

The necessity of divine illumination also applies to the book of Genesis. Some basic aspects of the primitive history of mankind could have been known to the sacred author from the tradition received from Adam and Eve and their descendants, up to Abraham.[12] However, the oral communication of this tradition over the course of millennia must necessarily have become adulterated in very many re-

---

[12] See Lagrange, *Historical Criticism and the Old Testament*, 210–211.

spects.[13] It is clear that divine illumination was necessary for Moses[14] to judge the truth of the material that he may have known from oral tradition so as to distinguish true elements from false accretions and rightly grasp truths such as the creation of man in the image of God and in a state of friendship with God, original sin and its legacy, and the promise of redemption.

It is not enough, however, for God to enlighten the intellect of the sacred writer. He must also move the author's will to desire to write that which divine illumination has enabled him to conceive. And after moving his will, God must assist the sacred writer in the composition of the text so that the truths may be expressed aptly and with infallible truth. Some theologians have supposed that God only inspired the ideas of the sacred writers and not the actual words they used.[15] This position should be rejected as insufficiently respecting the faith of the Church that God is the principal author of Scripture. Since God is the principal author, He must have not only inspired the ideas of the sacred authors, but also guided their mode of expression, since this is clearly the responsibility of an author. Thus, God inspired the sacred writers in the execution of their work so that they were able to express their inspired ideas with apt words, literary forms, and metaphors. In summary, God's inspiration of the sacred writer consisted in an influence of efficacious grace that *illuminated* his intellect and

---

[13] This adulteration can be seen, for example, in the many accounts of the Flood that are found in most of the primitive cultures of the world, such as those of the Sumerians and Babylonians. In some of these accounts, the cause of the Flood is not said to be sin, but overpopulation: human beings were making too much noise! See the old Babylonian text, *Atrahasis*, tablet 1, in Stephanie Dalley, *Myths from Mesopotamia: Creation, the Flood, Gilgamesh and Others* (Oxford, UK: Oxford University Press, 1989), 5 and 18: "The country became too wide, the people too numerous. The country was as noisy as a bellowing bull. The God grew restless at their racket, Ellil had to listen to their noise. He addressed the great gods, 'The noise of mankind has become too much, I am losing sleep over their racket.'" See also Alexander Heidel, *The Gilgamesh Epic and Old Testament Parallels* (Chicago: University of Chicago Press, 1946), 225–227.

[14] I assume here that Moses is the substantial author of Genesis, according to the PBC's Response on the Mosaic Authorship of the Pentateuch of June 27, 1906 (DS, 3394–3387). However, the need for a divine illumination enabling the sacred author to rightly judge what he has received from previous tradition would apply equally to any others who may have been involved in the redaction of Genesis.

[15] See Burtchaell, *Catholic Theories of Biblical Inspiration*, 88–120.

reasoning (including historical research), *moved* his will, and *guided* all his faculties involved in the composition of his work, especially his imagination, memory, and literary judgment.[16]

Biblical Inspiration and Instrumental Causality

Biblical inspiration can be seen as a special case of instrumental causality.[17] Philosophers speak of this type of causality when a cause produces its effect by means of an instrument. Almost all human production makes use of instruments and instrumental causality. The will and intellect make use of the human hand itself and all the other organs as instruments. To further enhance their capabilities, the hands, eyes, ears, voice, and other organs use tools such as hammers, chisels, pencils, lenses, and microphones as instruments.

The instrumental cause acts as a kind of servant of the principal cause. The effect is produced through the cooperation of the instrumental cause under the direction of the principal cause. A paintbrush in the hands of a painter, a chisel in the hands of a sculptor, a pen in the hands of a writer, a violin in the hands of a violinist, and an orchestra under the direction of a conductor are all examples of instrumental causes. The canvas is painted by the paintbrush under the

---

[16] See Lagrange, *Historical Criticism and the Old Testament*, 91: "From the Church's definitions we may conclude that God's help is antecedent and not consequent, that it is an impulse, and so necessarily a light bestowed upon him, for man is no mere machine, and his will does not determine anything without a corresponding light in the intellect. Now since this help is antecedent to the whole operation, it must extend to the whole work, and consequently even to the very words; but since the sacred writer used his ordinary faculties, it impressed nothing ready-made upon the mind—not even the thoughts."

[17] See Benedict XV, *Spiritus Paraclitus*, §8: "This partnership of God and man in the production of a work in common Jerome illustrates by the case of a workman who uses *instruments* for the production of his work; for he says that whatsoever the sacred authors say 'is the word of God, and not their own; and *what the Lord says by their mouths He says, as it were, by means of an instrument*' (*Tract. de Ps.*, 88)." This category of instrumental causality was developed and perfected by St. Thomas Aquinas. However, it is already found in the early Fathers, who frequently speak of inspiration in these terms. See Athenagoras, writing in the second century (AD 177): "The words of the prophets . . . under the motion of the divine Spirit, spoke forth what was being wrought in them, the Spirit working with them, as it were a piper who breathed into his pipe," quoted in *A Catholic Commentary on Holy Scripture*, ed. Bernard Orchard (New York: Thomas Nelson and Sons, 1953), 47.

direction of the hand, eye, mind, and will of the artist. In this way, the paintbrush produces an effect that it could never have achieved without this superior direction and impulse stemming from the artist's mind. The effect transcends the power of the instrumental cause taken alone and manifests the power of the principal cause that moved and directed it.[18] Therefore, the effect is most properly attributed to the principal cause, which is the artist, and only secondarily to the paintbrush, chisel, pen, violin, or orchestra.[19] In other words, instrumental causality is present when, through the impulse and direction of a superior cause, *an inferior cause is elevated above its own level, and made capable of producing an effect that transcends its proper capacity taken alone.* Instrumental causes are moved movers, which create effects only insofar as they are moved by a higher cause, as the paintbrush is moved by the artist's hand and mind.[20]

The human authors of Sacred Scripture can thus be seen as a kind of instrumental cause. They served as *living and free instruments* for the composition of the sacred books at the instigation of God, like paintbrushes or chisels moved by His hands. They were enabled to produce an effect that infinitely transcends the capacity of any human author acting by his own powers alone. For this reason the effect is properly attributed to God, the principal author, just as a painting by Raphael is attributed more properly to Raphael than to his paintbrush.

The difference is that paintbrushes are not intelligent or free, and the human authors of Scripture were intelligent and free in the use of all their capacities, like any other author. The fact of being inspired

---

[18] See *ST* III, q. 62, a. 1: "An efficient cause is twofold: principal and instrumental. The principal cause works by the power of its form, to which form the effect is likened; just as fire by its own heat makes something hot. In this way none but God can cause grace.... But the instrumental cause works not by the power of its form, but only by the motion whereby it is moved by the principal agent, so that the effect is not likened to the instrument but to the principal agent: for instance, the couch is not like the axe, but like the art which is in the craftsman's mind."

[19] See *ST* I-II, q. 16, a. 1: "An action is not properly attributed to the instrument, but to the principal agent." See also *In IV sent.* d. 47, q. 2, a. 1, sol. 3, ad 2 (at http://www.corpusthomisticum.org/snp4047.html).

[20] See St. Thomas, *De veritate*, q. 27, a. 4: "It is the nature of an instrument, as such, to move other things insofar as it itself is moved"; in *Opera omnia*, vol. 22/3 (Rome: Editori di san Tommaso, 1976), 805.

did not in any way diminish the use of their human faculties and human choice.[21] It simply guided, aided, and elevated those truly human faculties to make them apt instruments in the communication of God's Revelation. Like the paintbrush or pen, the human authors wrote only what the divine Author directed them to do, as He inspired their minds and wills with grace. Perhaps the sacred writers were not always aware of this supernatural direction, for inspiration is not something sentimental that can be directly "felt." God's impulse to move the will and intellect lies on a higher plane than feelings or sentiments. It is an entirely supernatural movement, invisible to human senses. Inspiration, therefore, is a mystery and an article of faith.

Inspiration Does Not Annul the Individual Style of the Sacred Writer

When an artist or craftsman makes a work, the choice of tools is not arbitrary. Even though the principal cause is the artist, the instruments are chosen for their aptness to the task at hand, and their particular contribution can generally be seen in the effect that is produced. The sculptor uses different types of chisels for different purposes, and the composer uses different musical instruments to produce different effects.

In a similar way, God has chosen authors with differing experience, knowledge, temperament, and literary ability to be His instruments in the composition of Holy Scripture. The different instruments were chosen for their aptitude in being moved by God to achieve the particular effect that He had planned from all eternity for that particular part of Scripture. This explains why the different books of Scripture

---

[21] See the vigorous expression of Franz Anton Staudenmaier, *Encyclopädie der theologischen Wissenschaften als System der gesammelten Theologie*, 2nd ed. (Mainz: Florian Kupferberg; Wien: Karl Gerold, 1840), 1:347: "The divine agency in inspiration cannot be understood as if men whom the Spirit inspires are turned into involuntary, controlled machines, as if they had slumped into a passive state, deprived of all individuality and initiative. Personal traits of mind and character remain; and any influence of God that does not activate our intellectual capacities and make common cause with them, is surely an impossibility" (trans. Burtchaell in *Catholic Theories of Biblical Inspiration*, 22).

show different literary styles and levels of literary culture.[22] The principal author is one and the same, but the instruments used were distinct from each other and appropriate for the effect that God intended.

The divine Author also is capable of using the sacred authors in collaborative efforts, making use of traditional sources, either oral or written, and the work of later editors or compilers.[23] In such a case, it is reasonable to think that inspiration would be active in all those who collaborate, according to the extent of their collaboration.[24] Pierre Benoit writes:

> The question is asked: Who enjoyed scriptural inspiration: the last editor of the biblical text, or also those who preceded him? Does not the answer become clear once it is realized that the text is the result of a long history directed throughout by the Holy Spirit. Why economize the divine charism by reserving it to the last worker? Why refuse it to all of those who worked before him in the domain of revelation? . . . Anyone who cooperated in a positive way to produce the text had to be inspired, whatever his role; not only those who wrote the text, down to the minor copyist who added a literary detail admitted into the canonical text, but also those who contributed to the formulation of the oral tradition, and even those

---

[22] See Pius XII, Encyclical on Promoting Biblical Studies *Divino afflante Spiritu* (1943), §33: "Catholic theologians, following the teaching of the Holy Fathers and especially of the Angelic and Common Doctor, have examined and explained the nature and effects of biblical inspiration more exactly and more fully than was wont to be done in previous ages. For having begun by expounding minutely the principle that the inspired writer, in composing the sacred book, is the living and reasonable instrument of the Holy Spirit, they rightly observe that, impelled by the divine motion, he so uses his faculties and powers, that from the book composed by him all may easily infer 'the special character of each one and, as it were, his personal traits.' Let the interpreter then, with all care and without neglecting any light derived from recent research, endeavor to determine the peculiar character and circumstances of the sacred writer, the age in which he lived, the sources written or oral to which he had recourse and the forms of expression he employed."

[23] See PBC, Response of June 27, 1906 (DS, 3395–3397).

[24] See Pierre Benoit, *Aspects of Biblical Inspiration*, trans. Jerome Murphy-O'Connor and Keverne Ashe (Chicago: Priory Press, 1965), 24–26, and Denis Farkasfalvy, *Inspiration & Interpretation: A Theological Introduction to Sacred Scripture* (Washington, DC: Catholic University of America Press, 2010), 211.

whose acts constituted the living lesson of which the text is the record.[25]

Since man is a social and historical animal, God makes use of his social, historical, and collaborative nature in the genesis of Scripture, guiding the long and often collaborative process through the charism of inspiration.

The Sacred Writers Are True Authors

Some of the Church Fathers speak of the relation between God and the human authors of Scripture as that between an author and his secretary, so that inspiration would be a kind of divine "dictation."[26] This, however, must not be interpreted in the sense of a purely mechanical dictation! The human authors had to employ ordinary human means in their work, such as historical research and literary composition, like any other true author. *Dei Verbum* §11 states:

> To compose the sacred books, God chose certain men who, all the while he employed them in this task, made full use of their powers and faculties so that, though He acted in them and by them, it was as true authors that they consigned to writing whatever He wanted written, and no more.

It is not contradictory to assert that the human authors are also true authors of the Word of God, for the sacred authors and God are not authors in exactly the same way. The human authors are indeed true authors, but in a subordinate and instrumental sense. This does not mean that one part of the Bible is by God and another part is by the human authors, as might be the case in a collaborative effort by different human authors. On the contrary, the Church believes that all of Scripture is by God, but that all is also by various human au-

---

[25] Benoit, *Aspects of Biblical Inspiration*, 24–25.

[26] See, for example, Pope St. Gregory the Great, *Praef. in Job* 2 (cited in Leo XIII, *Providentissimus Deus*, §20) and Benedict XV, *Spiritus Paraclitus*, §8.

thors. The letters of St. Paul, for example, are simultaneously by St. Paul and by God.

The distinction is that God is the primary and principal author, whereas the human author is a secondary author as God's instrument. There is no competition or possible division between the human author and the divine author, just as there is no competition between Raphael and his paintbrushes. It would be ridiculous to isolate a part of a painting and say that this is by the painter alone, whereas another part is by the paintbrush alone. The whole painting was produced both by the artist as principal cause and by the paintbrushes as instrumental causes. Likewise, the whole of Scripture is both by God and by the sacred writers. No part of Scripture can be attributed only to the one or the other.

Some theologians have sought to limit inspiration only to those parts of Scripture that are directly religious in intent, so that other parts would be entirely the work of the human writers and thus might contain historical or scientific errors.[27] This view is clearly contrary to faith and has been repeatedly condemned by the Magisterium of the Church,[28] which holds that the entire Bible is inspired in all its parts.[29] Every part of Sacred Scripture has God as its principal author.

The fact that the sacred writers are only instrumental authors does not in the least lessen their dignity. The more completely we are moved by the grace of God, the more holy our actions become. The difficulty lies in removing the impediments that block the action of the Holy Spirit in our souls. The human authors of Scripture received

---

[27] This erroneous view was first defended by Henry Holden, an English priest, in *Analysis of Divine Faith* (Paris: [unidentified], 1658), 61: "It is to be noted that the special and divine assistance which is given to the author of every such book as the Church receives for the Word of God doth only extend itself to those things which are doctrinal, or at least have some near or necessary relation to them. But in those things which are written by the bye, or have reference to something else not concerning religion, I conceive the author had only such a divine assistance as other holy and saintly authors have"; quoted in *The Cambridge History of the Bible*, vol. 3, *The West from the Reformation to the Present Day* (New York: Cambridge University Press, 1963), 221.

[28] See Leo XIII, *Providentissimus Deus*, §20, and Pius XII, Encyclical Letter Concerning Some False Opinions Threatening to Undermine the Foundations of Catholic Doctrine *Humani generis* (1950), §22.

[29] See Vatican I, *Dei Filius*, ch. 2 (DS, 3006).

an absolutely special grace or charism by which God removed all obstacles that could impede His action of divine inspiration in them.

Inspiration and the Analogy with the Incarnation

The Second Vatican Council, in *Dei Verbum* §13, makes a profound analogy between the Incarnation and the inspiration of Scripture:

> In Sacred Scripture, therefore, while the truth and holiness of God always remains intact, the marvelous "condescension" of eternal wisdom is clearly shown, "that we may learn the gentle kindness of God, which words cannot express, and how far He has gone in adapting His language with thoughtful concern for our weak human nature."[30] For the words of God, expressed in human language, have been made like human discourse, just as the Word of the eternal Father, when He took to Himself the flesh of human weakness, was in every way made like men.

The point of the analogy is that Scripture transmits a truly divine Word and message without ceasing to be a truly human word, composed by human faculties and making use of all the cultural riches of the societies in which they were composed.[31] This analogy will be crucial with regard to the principles of biblical interpretation, as will be seen below.

Pope Benedict XVI develops this analogy with the Incarnation in his 2010 Apostolic Exhortation *Verbum Domini* §18:

> Here it might be helpful to recall the analogy drawn by the Fathers of the Church between the word of God which became "flesh" and the word which became a "book." The Dog-

---

[30] St. John Chrysostom, *In Genesis* 3.8 [Homily 17.1] (PG, 53:134). The Latin "attemperatio" [in English, "suitable adjustment"] is the translational equivalent of the Greek "synkatabasis."

[31] See Scott Hahn, "For the Sake of Our Salvation: The Truth and Humility of God's Word," in *Letter & Spirit* 6 (2010): 21–46.

matic Constitution *Dei Verbum* takes up this ancient tradition which holds, as Saint Ambrose says,[32] that "the body of the Son is the Scripture which we have received," and declares that "the words of God, expressed in human language, are in every way like human speech, just as the word of the eternal Father, when he took on himself the weak flesh of human beings, became like them." When understood in this way, sacred Scripture presents itself to us, in the variety of its many forms and content, as a single reality. Indeed, "through all the words of sacred Scripture, God speaks only one single word, his one utterance, in whom he expresses himself completely (cf. *Heb* 1:1–3)."[33] Saint Augustine had already made the point clearly: "Remember that one alone is the discourse of God which unfolds in all sacred Scripture, and one alone is the word which resounds on the lips of all the holy writers."[34]

The Canon of Inspired Books

In order for God's Word to reach men in all times and places, it is not enough for Revelation to be committed to written form through the inspiration of the Holy Spirit in the sacred authors. It is also necessary for mankind to be able to recognize, with certainty, which are the sacred books inspired by God. We refer to the list of the inspired book by the term *canon*.[35]

---

[32] *Expositio Evangelii secundum Lucam* 6.33 (PL, 15:1677).

[33] CCC §102.

[34] *Enarrationes in Psalmos* 103.4.1 (PL, 37:1378).

[35] The word "canon" is used here in the sense of authoritative norm or normative list. The list of "canonized" saints was another normative and authoritative list. In a similar sense, the recognized legal decrees of the Church were called canons, from which we derive "canon law." See Joseph Lienhard, S.J., *The Bible, the Church, and Authority: The Canon of the Christian Bible in History and Theology* (Collegeville: Liturgical Press, 1995), 60. For a good overview of the questions surrounding the biblical canon, see Miguel Ángel Tábet, *Introducción General a la Biblia*, 3rd ed. (Madrid: Ediciones Palabra, 2009), 175–223; Raymond E. Brown and Raymond F. Collins, "Canonicity," in *The New Jerome Biblical Commentary*, eds. Raymond Brown, Joseph Fitzmyer, and Roland Murphy (Englewood Cliffs: Prentice-Hall, 1990), 1034–1054.

In accordance with His plan of saving men in the communion of the Church, it is fitting that God has entrusted the knowledge of which are the sacred books to Israel and the Church, rather than simply to isolated individuals through some kind of personal inspiration. For the Scriptures are the books of the Church. Together with the sacraments and the Tradition, they are her dowry from the Lord.[36]

Liturgical Nature of the Canon

The canon of Scripture is most intimately connected with the liturgy because it is precisely the list of the works solemnly read in the liturgy with the glorious title, *Word of the Lord*.[37] The liturgical reading of Scripture goes back to the Temple services and the synagogue services in ancient Israel.

We have a description of the liturgy in the middle of the second century by St. Justin Martyr in his *First Apology*, in which he gives a brief description of the liturgy of the Mass celebrated every Sunday with all the faithful:

> On the day which is called Sunday we have a common assembly of all who live in the cities or in the outlying districts, and the memoirs of the Apostles or the writings of the Prophets are read, as long as there is time. Then, when the reader has

---

[36] See Ecumenical Study Group of Protestant and Catholic Theologians in Germany, *Binding Testimony: Holy Scripture and Tradition*, "Canon—Holy Scripture—Tradition: Joint Statement," ed. Theodor Schneider and Wolfhart Pannenberg, trans. Martha Matesich (Frankfurt am Main: Peter Lang, 2014), 37: "Indisputably the Christian canon was formed in the context of proclamation, believing and professing, thus in particular within the framework of the worship of the congregation, so that it is possible to say that the lived life of the church was instrumental in forming the canon. For this reason there can be no question of a fundamental opposition between Scripture and the church. It is also undeniable that the evolution of the canon of Scripture was a prolonged, complex and differentiated developmental process."

[37] See Scott Hahn, "Canon, Cult and Covenant: The Promise of Liturgical Hermeneutics," in *Canon and Biblical Interpretation*, eds. Craig G. Bartholomew, et al. (Grand Rapids: Zondervan, 2006), 209: "There is increasing recognition that the motives for establishing the canon were largely cultic and that cultic use was an important factor in determining which Scriptures were to be included in the canon. Put simply, the canon was drawn up to establish which books would be read when the community gathered for worship, and the books included in the canon were those that were already being read in the church's liturgy."

finished, the president of the assembly verbally admonishes and invites all to imitate such examples of virtue. Then we all stand up together and offer up our prayers, and, as we said before, after we finish our prayers, bread and wine and water are presented. He who presides likewise offers up prayers and thanksgivings, to the best of his ability, and the people express their approval by saying 'Amen.' The Eucharistic elements are distributed and consumed by those present, and to those who are absent they are sent through the deacons.[38]

The "memoirs of the Apostles" seems to refer primarily to the Gospels (but perhaps also to other books of the New Testament), whereas the "writings of the prophets" probably refers to the Old Testament in general. It is not insignificant that one of our earliest references to the Gospels speaks of them in the context of solemn liturgical reading.[39]

Definition of the Canon at the Council of Trent

The canon of Scripture was solemnly defined at the Council of Trent:

Following, then, the example of the orthodox Fathers, it [the Council of Trent] receives and venerates with the same sense of loyalty and reverence all the books of the Old and New Testament—for the one God is the author of both—together with all the traditions concerning faith and practice, as coming from the mouth of Christ or being inspired by the Holy Spirit and preserved in continuous succession in the Catholic Church. The Council has thought it proper to insert in this decree a list of the sacred books, so that no doubt may remain as to which books are recognized by the council. They are the following:

---

[38] St. Justin Martyr, *First Apology* 67, trans. Thomas Falls in *The First Apology, The Second Apology, Dialogue with Trypho, Exhortation to the Greeks, Discourse to the Greeks, The Monarchy or The Rule of God* (Washington, DC: The Catholic University of America Press, 1948), 106–107.

[39] See Farkasfalvy, *Inspiration & Interpretation*, 74.

Old Testament: The five [books] of Moses, that is, Genesis, Exodus, Leviticus, Numbers, Deuteronomy, Joshua, Judges, Ruth, four books of Kings [= two books of Samuel and
two books of Kings], two of Chronicles, the first book of Ezra,
and the second of Ezra called Nehemiah, Tobit, Judith, Esther, Job, the Psalter of David containing 150 psalms, Proverbs, Ecclesiastes, the Song of Songs, Wisdom, Ecclesiasticus
[= Sirach], Isaiah, Jeremiah with Baruch, Ezekiel, Daniel, the
twelve minor Prophets, that is, Hosea, Joel, Amos, Obadiah,
Jonah, Micah, Nahum, Habakkuk, Zephaniah, Haggai, Zach-
ariah, Malachi; two books of the Maccabees, that is, the first
and the second.

New Testament: The four Gospels according to Matthew,
Mark, Luke, and John; the Acts of the Apostles, written by
Luke the evangelist, fourteen Epistles of the apostle Paul, that
is, to the Romans, two to the Corinthians, to the Galatians,
Ephesians, Philippians, Colossians, two to the Thessalonians,
two to Timothy, to Titus, to Philemon, and the Hebrews, two
[epistles] of the apostle Peter, three of the apostle John, one of
the apostle James, one of the apostle Jude, and the Revelation
of the apostle John.

If anyone does not accept all these books in their entirety, with all their parts, as they are being read in the Catholic
Church and are contained in the ancient Latin Vulgate editions, as sacred and canonical and knowingly and deliberately
rejects the aforesaid traditions, let him be anathema.[40]

It is interesting that the Council of Trent defines the biblical
canon on the basis of the Church's tradition of reading these books
publicly in the liturgy as the *Word of the Lord*. It is impossible that
Christ—who promised to be with His Church until the end of time
and promised the assistance of His Spirit to maintain her in the
truth—would have allowed books to be publicly read in the universal

---

40 Council of Trent, Session 4 (1546); see DS, 1501–1505.

Church for many centuries as God's Word if they were not actually inspired by God.

History of the Definition of the Canon

We have seen that the canon of Scripture is one of the principal things transmitted not in Scripture, but through Tradition. The canon was transmitted principally through the liturgical reading of the sacred books. Eventually lists of the sacred books were produced in the different churches. We only have fragmentary lists from the second century.

The first complete and correct list that has been preserved is from three North African councils celebrated in Carthage in 393, 397 and 419.[41] Pope Innocent I sent a list of the canonical books to Exsuperius, the bishop of Toulouse, in 405 and excluded some other Gnostic texts: "under the names of Matthias or of James the Less, or under the name of Peter and John, or under the name of Thomas, and if there are any others, you know that they ought not only to be repudiated but also condemned."[42] A list of the canon was given in the Council of Florence's Decree for the Jacobites.[43]

Early Patristic References to the Old and New Testament

Before the list of the canon from North Africa, we find the Fathers of the Church citing all the books of Scripture. St. Irenaeus, for example, writing towards the end of the second century, quotes the New Testament extensively. According to Bruce Metzger, he quotes "1,075 passages from almost all of the books of the New Testament: 626 from the Gospels, 54 from Acts, 280 from the Pauline Epistles (but not

---

[41] DS, 186. The canon is also given, with insubstantial differences, in the Decree of Damasus (DS, 179).

[42] Letter of February 20, AD 405 (DS, 213).

[43] DS, 1335.

from Philemon), 15 from the Catholic Epistles (but not 2 Pet, 3 John, or Jude), and 29 from the book of Revelation."[44]

Protestant Canon and Deuterocanonical Works

Many may find it very surprising that the canon of Scripture was infallibly defined so late in the history of the Church. This actually shows, however, that the canon was rather peacefully accepted in the Church until the time of the Reformation, and thus no solemn definition was judged necessary, despite various uncertainties and discrepancies among local churches regarding the exact nature and extent of the canon.

Most biblical books, as later defined by Trent, were accepted as canonical in all the churches from the second century onwards, but there were some books both of the Old and New Testaments whose canonicity was doubted in some local churches through the end of the fourth century and beyond. These books are often referred to as *deuterocanonical*, which literally means "another (or secondary) canon," whereas the books unanimously received are referred to as *protocanonical*. New Testament books that were not received or were held as doubtful in some churches include Hebrews, Revelation, 2 Peter, 2–3 John, James, and Jude. Those of the Old Testament are Wisdom, Sirach (also called Ecclesiasticus), 1–2 Maccabees, Tobit, Judith, Baruch, and parts of Daniel and Esther. The principal reason for doubt about these Old Testament deuterocanonical books was the fact that these works were not finally included in the canon recognized by rabbinical Judaism. In addition to canonical books that were doubted, there were also extra-canonical books that were read in some churches in the second and third centuries. Such books include the *First Letter of Clement* and the *Shepherd of Hermas*.

There was debate both about the extent of the canon and also on the *degree* of canonicity of the disputed or deuterocanonical books. St. Jerome, the champion of the Hebrew text, held that although the

---

[44] Bruce M. Metzger, *The Canon of the New Testament: Its Origin, Development, and Significance* (Oxford, UK: Clarendon, 1987), 154.

Old Testament deuterocanonical books were read in the liturgy, were useful for the edification of the faithful, and he himself quoted them rather extensively, they were not to be regarded as fully canonical such that they could be used as an ultimate authority for the defense of ecclesiastical dogma.[45] Through the influence of St. Jerome, doubts about the full canonicity of the deuterocanonical books of the Old Testament continued sporadically in some theologians up to the beginning of the sixteenth century (including the great Thomistic commentator, Cardinal Cajetan). St. Jerome, however, in his attachment to the more restrictive Jewish canon of the Old Testament, is a notable exception to the general consensus on this issue, exemplified by the position of St. Augustine,[46] in favor of the more inclusive canon later defined at Trent.

The canon became again a contentious issue at the dawn of the Reformation in 1519, when Martin Luther, in a public debate with Johannes Eck, expressed doubts about the canonicity of 2 Maccabees and appealed to the Old Testament canon accepted by rabbinical Judaism,[47] which lacked the deuterocanonical books. As a result, the Protestant canon differs from the Catholic canon by rejecting the canonicity of Wisdom, Sirach, 1–2 Maccabees, Tobit, Judith, Baruch, and parts of Daniel and Esther,[48] which Protestants refer to as the *"Apocrypha."*

---

[45] See St. Jerome's preface to the books of Solomon, translated by W. H. Fremantle in *NPNF2*, 6:492: "As, then, the Church reads Judith, Tobit, and the books of Maccabees, but does not admit them among the canonical Scriptures, so let it read these two volumes [Wisdom and Sirach] for the edification of the people, not to give authority to the doctrines of the Church." For a summary of Jerome's position, see Edmon Gallagher, "The Old Testament 'Apocrypha' in Jerome's Canonical Theory," *Journal of Early Christian Studies* 20.2 (Summer 2012): 213–233; A.E. Breen, *A General Introduction to Holy Scripture*, 2nd ed. (reprint: Fort Collins: Roman Catholic Books, 2000), 441–465.

[46] See St. Augustine's discussion of the canon in *On Christian Doctrine* 2.8, in *NPNF1*, 2:538–539.

[47] See Lienhard, *The Bible, the Church, and Authority*, 67.

[48] For the deuterocanonical works and their reception into the canon, see, among others, Martin Hengel, *The Septuagint as Christian Scripture: Its Prehistory and the Problem of Its Canon*, trans. Mark Biddle (Edinburgh: T&T Clark, 2002), 91–94; Albert Sundberg, "The 'Old Testament': A Christian Canon," *Catholic Biblical Quarterly* 30 (1968): 143–155; R. J. Foster, "The Formation and History of the Canon," in Orchard, *A Catholic Commentary on Holy Scripture*, 13–18; Tábet, *Introducción General a la Biblia*, 187–194.

There is debate about the nature of the Jewish canon at the time of Christ. Often scholars speak of a Palestinian canon, which lacked the deuterocanonical books, and an Alexandrian canon witnessed by the Septuagint translation, which would be larger, including the deutero-canonical books and forming the foundation for the Catholic canon. It seems better, though, to see the Jewish canon as still somewhat fluid in the first century AD. The five books of Moses would have been the first to be seen by all as canonical, followed by the prophetic books. The third class of Old Testament books, referred to as the "writings" or wisdom literature,[49] was less clearly defined with regard to the canon until the end of the first century AD. The general liturgical practice of the early Church was to use the broader canon of the "writings" as given in the Septuagint, including the deuterocanonical books.[50]

Study Questions

1. In what sense does the Catholic faith hold that God is the principal author of the Bible? Explain the Catholic notion of inspiration.
2. What does Vatican I say about the inspiration of Scripture?
3. What does Vatican II say about the inspiration of Scripture in *Dei Verbum* §11?
4. Explain instrumental causality and how it can be used to explain the action of God and the sacred writers in the composition of Scripture.
5. How did God act in the inspired sacred writers in the process of inspiration? Make reference to Leo XIII's *Providentissimus Deus*.

---

[49] The threefold division of the books of the Old Testament is perhaps reflected in Luke 24:44: "These are my words which I spoke to you, while I was still with you, that everything written about me in the law of Moses and the prophets and the psalms must be fulfilled." The category of "writings" may be indicated here by Luke through his mention of the Psalms. Other books included in this third category in the rabbinical tradition are Proverbs, Job, Song of Songs, Ruth, Lamentations, Ecclesiastes, Esther, Daniel, Ezra, Nehemiah, and Chronicles. The tripartite division of the Old Testament books seems to be alluded to also in the prologue to the book of Sirach by Ben Sira's grandson and translator, who speaks of "the reading of the law and the prophets and the other books of our fathers."

[50] See Albert Sundberg, "The 'Old Testament': A Christian Canon," *Catholic Biblical Quarterly* 30 (1968): 154–155.

6. Why do Catholics have more books in the canon of Scripture than Protestants?

Suggestions for Further Reading

Pope Leo XIII, Encyclical Letter on the Study of Holy Scripture *Providentissimus Deus*. November 18, 1893.

Pope Pius XII. Encyclical on Promoting Biblical Studies *Divino afflante Spiritu*. September 30, 1943.

Dei Verbum §11.

Alonso-Schökel, Luis. *The Inspired Word: Scripture in the Light of Language and Literature*. Translated by Francis Martin. New York: Herder, 1965.

Benoit, Pierre. *Aspects of Biblical Inspiration*. Translated by Jerome Murphy-O'Connor and Keverne Ashe. Chicago: Priory Press, 1965.

Farkasfalvy, Denis. *Inspiration & Interpretation: A Theological Introduction to Sacred Scripture*. Washington, DC: Catholic University of America Press, 2010.

Lienhard, Joseph, S.J. *The Bible, the Church, and Authority: The Canon of the Christian Bible in History and Theology*. Collegeville: Liturgical Press, 1995.

Synave, Paul, and Pierre Benoit. *Prophecy and Inspiration; A Commentary on the Summa Theologica II-II, questions 171–178*. Translated by Avery R. Dulles, S.J., and Thomas L. Sheridan. New York: Desclee, 1961.

CHAPTER ELEVEN

The Truth of Scripture

The truth of Scripture, often referred to negatively as inerrancy, is a consequence of biblical inspiration. It is part of the deposit of faith taught constantly and definitively by the Church throughout the centuries.[1] Nevertheless, it has come under increasing challenge since the Enlightenment, and so, beginning with Pope Leo XIII, the Magisterium has responded by repeatedly clarifying and affirming it.

The truth of Scripture is one of the principal topics defended in the seminal encyclical on Scripture by Leo XIII *Providentissimus Deus* (1893).[2] It was taken up again forcefully by Pope Benedict XV in *Spiritus Paraclitus* (1920), an encyclical commemorating the fifteenth centenary of the death of St. Jerome. Pope Pius XII also treats this subject in his encyclical on the Bible, *Divino afflante Spiritu* (1943). The Second Vatican Council reaffirms the preceding teaching on this

---

[1] See the CDF, Doctrinal Commentary on the Concluding Formula of the *Professio fidei* (1998), §11, which lists "the absence of error in the inspired sacred texts" as an example of a truth of faith that requires the first degree of assent proper to dogma" (*Origins* 28, no. 8 [July 16, 1998]: 118).

[2] See Pius XII, Encyclical Letter on Promoting Biblical Studies *Divino afflante Spiritu* (1943), §3: "The first and greatest care of Leo XIII was to set forth the teaching on the truth of the Sacred Books and to defend it from attack." See also Augustin Cardinal Bea, *The Word of God and Mankind*, trans. Dorothy White (Chicago: Franciscan Herald Press, 1967), 186: "The doctrine of inerrancy was put forward and expounded chiefly by Leo XIII in his encyclical, *Providentissimus Deus*, which is largely dedicated to establishing and defining this doctrinal point. The encyclical first expounds the doctrine of inspiration in order to affirm that of inerrancy."

subject in its Dogmatic Constitution on Divine Revelation, *Dei Verbum* §11.[3]

The first and most important consequence of God's divine authorship of the Bible as His Word is the *truth of the Bible*. God, who is the eternal Wisdom and Truth itself, reveals Himself in order to communicate the truth about Himself and His plan of salvation history, and He would not reveal falsehood.[4] His self-communication, however, follows a pattern of progressive unfolding, which we can refer to as the "divine pedagogy." The truth is not revealed in its fullness from the beginning, but in stages. God's Revelation respects the common principle that *everything is received according to the mode of the receiver*.[5] God therefore reveals Himself progressively, in such a way that the earlier Revelation prepares for the later and fuller Revelation, gradually enlarging the mode of the receiver, which is the People of God.

God also reveals Himself using the literary forms, modes of speech and general conceptions of the world (even when He corrects them) in use in the culture in which He speaks and in which the books of Sacred Scripture were written. So the truth will be presented not only in a literal historical way, but also through metaphor, symbolism, hyperbole, allegory, and poetry.

Therefore, since the Bible is truly the Word of God, it must be true and holy in its doctrine, as God is veracious and holy, and it must simultaneously be accommodated to its recipient and the culture in which it was composed. To deny the truth of the Bible or the sanctity of its doctrine (in its progressive unfolding) would be tantamount to denying its divine authorship, and therefore its inspiration. Nevertheless, because of the progressive nature of Revelation, the earlier

---

[3] For many excellent articles on this subject, see *Letter & Spirit* 6 (2010). This volume has the title, *For the Sake of Our Salvation: The Truth and Humility of God's Word*.

[4] See PBC, *The Inspiration and Truth of Sacred Scripture: The Word that Comes from God and Speaks of God for the Salvation of the World*, §144 (Collegeville: Liturgical Press, 2014), 162: "Since it originates in God, Scripture has divine qualities. Among these is the fundamental one of attesting the truth, understood, however, not as an aggregate of exact information on the various aspects of human knowledge but as a revelation of God himself and his salvific plan." The principal purpose of this document is to clarify the sense in which we hold that all of Scripture is *true*.

[5] See, for example, *ST* I, q. 12, a. 4, and q. 14, a. 1, ad 3; q. 14, a. 5; and q. 84, a. 1: "For the received is in the receiver according to the mode of the receiver."

parts of Scripture must be interpreted in the light of the whole and of the fullness of Revelation in Christ.[6] In the Old Testament, there are parts that are "incomplete and temporary" considered in themselves, but which still serve to "show us true divine pedagogy."[7]

This claim of the truth of Scripture is a scandal to many because of the fact that the instrumental authors of Scripture are men, and we all know that men are naturally liable to error. The human author of Scripture, however, insofar as He is working as an instrument of God, is capable of producing an effect that transcends his natural capacity. The effect reveals more the power of the principal agent than that of the instrumental cause. We have seen that the human authors of Scripture were so moved by God that they understood, rightly judged, and wrote what He wished them to communicate at that stage of salvation history. And God, who is Truth, would not wish to be the author of error, although He reveals Himself in a progressive way that takes into account the developing disposition of the People of God to receive an ever fuller truth, culminating in the Word Incarnate.

New Testament Witness to the Truth of Scripture

The clearest texts on the truth of Scripture are found in statements of Jesus in the Gospels.[8] For example, in John 10:34–36, in an inter-

---

[6] See *DV* §16: "God, the inspirer and author of both Testaments, wisely arranged that the New Testament be hidden in the Old and the Old be made manifest in the New. For, though Christ established the new covenant in His blood (see Luke 22:20; 1 Cor 11:25), still the books of the Old Testament with all their parts, caught up into the proclamation of the Gospel, acquire and show forth their full meaning in the New Testament (see Matt 5:17; Luke 24:27; Rom 16:25–26; 2 Cor 3:14–16) and in turn shed light on it and explain it."

[7] See *DV* §15: "Now the books of the Old Testament, in accordance with the state of mankind before the time of salvation established by Christ, reveal to all men the knowledge of God and of man and the ways in which God, just and merciful, deals with men. These books, though they also contain some things which are incomplete and temporary, nevertheless show us true divine pedagogy." For a reflection on the "dark passages" of Scripture, see Matthew J. Ramage, *Dark Passages of the Bible: Engaging Scripture with Benedict XVI & Thomas Aquinas* (Washington, DC: The Catholic University of America Press, 2013), and the PBC, *The Inspiration and Truth of Sacred Scripture*, §§124–149 (pp. 143–168).

[8] See Scott Hahn, "For the Sake of Our Salvation: The Truth and Humility of God's Word," *Letter & Spirit* 6 (2010): 22–26.

change with the crowd, Jesus cites Psalm 83:6, which is a difficult text, and then says that one cannot discount this text because "Scripture cannot be broken":

> Is it not written in your law, 'I said, you are gods'? If he called them gods to whom the word of God came (and scripture cannot be broken), do you say of him whom the Father consecrated and sent into the world, 'You are blaspheming,' because I said, 'I am the Son of God'?

In speaking with the Sadducees about the resurrection of the dead, Jesus rebukes them: "You are wrong, because you know neither the scriptures nor the power of God" (Matt 22:29). When He is seized at Gethsemane, He tells Peter to put down His sword: "But how then should the scriptures be fulfilled, that it must be so?" (Matt 26:54). He then says to the crowd: "But all this has taken place, that the scriptures of the prophets might be fulfilled" (Matt 26:56). In John 5:39, 47, He says: "You search the scriptures, because you think that in them you have eternal life; and it is they that bear witness to me.... But if you do not believe his [Moses's] writings, how will you believe my words?"

Benedict XV, in *Spiritus Paraclitus* §28, gives a good summary of Jesus's testimony on the truth of Scripture:

> We know what He felt about Holy Scripture: when He said, "It is written," and "the Scripture must be fulfilled," we have therein an argument which admits of no exception and which should put an end to all controversy.... When Christ preached to the people, whether on the Mount by the lakeside, or in the synagogue at Nazareth, or in His own city of Capharnaum, He took His points and His arguments from the Bible. From the same source came His weapons when disputing with the Scribes and Pharisees. Whether teaching or disputing, He quotes from all parts of Scripture and takes His example from it; He quotes it as an argument which must

be accepted. . . . How solemn His witness to the truth of the sacred Books: " . . . Not the smallest letter or the smallest part of a letter will pass from the law, until all things have taken place" (Matt 5:18); and again: "The Scripture cannot be broken" (John 10:35).[9]

St. John also refers to the truth of his witness in his Gospel. At its conclusion (21:24), he says: "This is the disciple who is bearing witness to these things, and who has written these things; and we know that his testimony is true."

St. Paul, in 2 Timothy 3:16, connects the inspiration of Scripture with its trustworthiness for teaching: "All scripture is inspired by God and profitable for teaching, for reproof, for correction, and for training in righteousness."

The Fathers and Doctors of the Church on the Truth of Scripture

Faith in the inerrancy of Scripture was the universal conviction of the Fathers of the Church and practically all theologians up to recent times. Towards the end of the first century, Pope Clement I wrote in his celebrated Letter to the Corinthians: "You have searched the holy Scriptures, which are true, which were given by the Holy Spirit; you know that nothing unrighteous or counterfeit is written in them."[10] Here he is referring to the Old Testament.

In the middle of the second century, St. Justin says to Trypho:

You are sadly mistaken if you . . . hope of embarrassing me into admitting that some passages of Scripture contradict others, for I would not be so bold as to assert, or even imagine,

---

[9] Benedict XV, Encyclical Letter on St. Jerome *Spiritus Paraclitus* (1920), §28–29 (*SD*, 91–92; section numbering taken from http://w2.vatican.va/content/benedict-xv/en/encyclicals/documents/hf_ben-xv_enc_15091920_spiritus-paraclitus.html).

[10] Clement I, *Letter to the Corinthians* 45.2–3, in *The Apostolic Fathers: Greek Texts and English Translations*, ed. Michael W. Holmes, 3rd ed. (Grand Rapids: Baker Academic, 2007), 105.

such a thing. If such a passage were quoted, and apparently contradicted another (since I am positive that no passage contradicts another), I would rather openly confess that I do not know the meaning of the passage, and I shall do my utmost to have my opinion shared by those who imagine that the Scriptures are sometimes contradictory.[11]

The Patristic age's faith in the inerrancy of Scripture is well expressed by St. Augustine in a letter to St. Jerome:

> For, I admit to your Charity that it is from those books alone of the Scriptures, which are now called canonical, that I have learned to pay them such honor and respect as to believe most firmly that not one of their authors has erred in writing anything at all. If I do find anything in those books which seems contrary to truth, I decide that either the text is corrupt, or the translator did not follow what was really said, or that I failed to understand it. But, when I read other authors, however eminent they may be in sanctity and learning, I do not necessarily believe a thing is true because they think so, but because they have been able to convince me, either on the authority of the canonical writers or by a probable reason which is not inconsistent with truth. And I think that you, my brother, feel the same way; moreover, I say, I do not believe that you want your books to be read as if they were those of Prophets or Apostles, about whose writings, free of all error, it is unlawful to doubt.[12]

---

[11] Justin Martyr, *Dialogue with Trypho* 65, trans. T. B. Falls, in *Justin Martyr: The First Apology, The Second Apology, Dialogue with Trypho, Exhortation to the Greeks, Discourse to the Greeks, The Monarchy or The Rule of God* (Washington, DC: The Catholic University of America Press, 1948), 251.

[12] St. Augustine, Epistle 82.1, trans. W. Parsons, in *Letters (1–82)* (Washington, DC: The Catholic University of America Press, 1951), 392. See also Epistle 22 to St. Jerome: "I think it is extremely dangerous to admit that anything in the Sacred Books should be a lie; that is, that the men who have composed and written the Scriptures for us should have lied in their books. It is quite another question whether a good man should ever lie, and still another whether a writer of the Holy Scriptures ought to lie—but no, that is not another question: it is no question at all. If we once admit in that supreme authority even one polite lie, there will be nothing left of those books,

The same position is expressed in his treatise against Faustus, a Manichean:

> As regards our writings, which are not a rule of faith or prac-
> tice, but only a help to edification, we may suppose that they
> contain some things falling short of the truth in obscure and
> recondite matters, and that these mistakes may or may not be
> corrected in subsequent treatises. . . . Such writings are read
> with the right of judgment, and without any obligation to be-
> lieve. In order to leave room for such profitable discussions of
> difficult questions, there is a distinct boundary line separat-
> ing all productions subsequent to apostolic times from the au-
> thoritative canonical books of the Old and New Testaments.
> The authority of these books has come down to us from the
> apostles through the successions of bishops and the exten-
> sion of the Church, and, from a position of lofty supremacy,
> claims the submission of every faithful and pious mind. If we
> are perplexed by an apparent contradiction in Scripture, it is
> not allowable to say, "The author of this book is mistaken"; but
> either the manuscript is faulty, or the translation is wrong, or
> you have not understood. In the innumerable books that have
> been written latterly we may sometimes find the same truth
> as in Scripture, but there is not the same authority. Scripture
> has a sacredness peculiar to itself. In other books, the read-
> er may form his own opinion, and perhaps, from not under-
> standing the writer, may differ from him, and may pronounce
> in favor of what pleases him, or against what he dislikes. In
> such cases, a man is at liberty to withhold his belief, unless
> there is some clear demonstration or some canonical author-
> ity to show that the doctrine or statement either must or may
> be true. But in consequence of the distinctive peculiarity of
> the sacred writings, we are bound to receive as true whatev-

---

because, whenever anyone finds something difficult to practice or hard to believe, he will follow
this most dangerous precedent and explain it as the idea or practice of a lying author" (ibid.,
95–96).This passage concerns St. Jerome's interpretation of Gal 2:11–15.

er the canon shows to have been said by even one prophet, or apostle, or evangelist. Otherwise, not a single page will be left for the guidance of human fallibility, if contempt for the wholesome authority of the canonical books either puts an end to that authority altogether, or involves it in hopeless confusion.[13]

Later in the same work he writes:

As to Enoch and Elias and Moses, our belief is determined . . . by the declarations of Scripture, resting as they do on foundations of the strongest and surest evidence. . . . To give you in a word, without argument, the true reason of our faith, as regards Elias having been caught up to heaven from the earth, though only a man, and as regards Christ being truly born of a virgin, and truly dying on the cross, our belief in both cases is grounded on the declaration of Holy Scripture, which it is piety to believe, and impiety to disbelieve. . . . The reason of our believing Him to have been born of the Virgin Mary, is not that He could not otherwise have appeared among men in a true body, but because it is so written in the Scripture, which we must believe in order to be Christians, or to be saved. We believe, then, that Christ was born of the Virgin Mary, because it is so written in the Gospel; we believe that He died on the cross, because it is so written in the Gospel; we believe that both His birth and death were real, because the Gospel is no fiction.[14]

With regard to the charge of contradictions in the Gospels where parallel accounts do not exactly coincide, St. Augustine lays down the principle that differences in the narration of the same event may simply reflect the fact that one has given a more summary account;

---

[13] St. Augustine, *Reply to Faustus the Manichæan* 11.5 (Richard Stothert in *NPNF*1, 4:180).

[14] Ibid., 26.3, 6, 7 (*NPNF*1, 4:321–323).

an omission is not a contradiction. In his treatise against Faustus, he writes:

> But Faustus finds contradictions in the Gospels. Say, rather, that Faustus reads the Gospels in a wrong spirit. . . . If you were animated with piety instead of being misled by party spirit, you might easily, by examining these passages, discover a wonderful and most instructive harmony among the writers. Who, in reading two narratives of the same event, would think of charging one or both of the authors with error or falsehood, because one omits what the other mentions, or one tells concisely, but with substantial agreement, what the other relates in detail, so as to indicate not only what was done, but also how it was done? This is what Faustus does in his attempt to impeach the truth of the Gospels; as if Luke's omitting some saying of Christ recorded in Matthew implied a denial on the part of Luke of Matthew's statement. There is no real difficulty in the case.[15]

St. Jerome is just as emphatic as St. Augustine on the truth of Scripture. Benedict XV, in *Spiritus Paraclitus* §14, summarizes St. Jerome's views:

> For Jerome, a true prophet was to be distinguished from a false by this very note of truth:[16] "The Lord's words are true; for Him to say it, means that it is."[17] Again, "Scripture cannot lie";[18] it is wrong to say Scripture lies, nay,[19] it is impious even to admit the very notion of error where the Bible is concerned.[20] "The Apostles," he says, "are one thing; other writers"—that

---

[15] Ibid., 33.7, (*NPNF*1, 4:343–344).

[16] St. Jerome, *Commentary on Micah* 2:11 and 3:5–8 (CCL 76:451 and 459–460).

[17] Ibid., 4:1 (CCL 76:470).

[18] St. Jerome, *Commentary on Jeremiah* 6:27 (CSEL 59:407).

[19] St. Jerome, *Commentary on Nahum* 1:9 (CCL 76A:534).

[20] St. Jerome, *Letters* 57 (to Pammachius), no. 7 (CSEL 54:513).

is, profane writers—"are another"; "the former always tell the truth; the latter—as being mere men—sometimes err,"[21] and though many things are said in the Bible which seem incredible, yet they are true;[22] in this "word of truth" you cannot find things or statements which are contradictory, "there is nothing discordant nor conflicting";[23] consequently, "when Scripture seems to be in conflict with itself both passages are true despite their diversity."[24]

St. Thomas speaks for the Latin Middle Ages: "It must be held that whatever is found in Sacred Scripture is true. Anyone who holds anything contrary to this is a heretic."[25] However, it is the sense intended by the human and divine author, and not the exact words divorced from the author's intention, that we must hold to be true.[26] He also says:

It is unlawful to hold that any false assertion is contained either in the Gospel or in any canonical text of Scripture, or that its writers have told untruths, because faith would be deprived of its certitude which is based on the authority of Holy Scripture. That the words of certain people are reported in different ways in the Gospel and other sacred writings does not constitute a lie. Hence Augustine says (*On the Harmony*

---

[21] Ibid. 82 (to Theophilus), no. 7 (*CSEL* 55:114).

[22] Ibid. 72 (to Vitalis), no. 2 (*CSEL* 55:9).

[23] Ibid. 18A (to Damasus), no. 7 (*CSEL*, 54:83); cf. ibid. 46 (Paula and Eustochius to Marcella), no. 6 (*NPNF2*, 6:62).

[24] Ibid. 36 (to Damasus), no. 11 (*CSEL*, 54:277).

[25] St. Thomas, *Quodlibet* 12, q. 16, ad 1: "Hoc tamen tenendum est, quod quidquid in sacra Scriptura continetur, verum est; alias qui contra hoc sentiret, esset haereticus"; in *Opera Omnia*, vol. 25/2 (Rome: Commissio Leonina, 1996), 421. This question is numbered as q. 17, rather than 16, at http://www.corpusthomisticum.org/q12.html.

[26] See St. Thomas, *Super Evangelium S. Matthaei* 27:9, lec. 1 (Marietti no. 2321): "It is the duty of a good interpreter not to consider the [mere] words, but their meaning"; this is a direct translation from the Mareitti edition of 1951 (p. 358), which reads, "officium est enim boni interpretis non considerare verba, sed sensum." Joseph Ratzinger points to the importance of this principle of Aquinas and Augustine in "Biblical Interpretation in Conflict," in *God's Word: Scripture—Tradition—Office*, trans. Henry Taylor (San Francisco: Ignatius Press, 2008), 122.

of the Gospels 2): "He that has the prudence to understand that in order to know the truth it is necessary to get at the sense will conclude that he must not be the least troubled, no matter by what words that sense is expressed." Hence it is evident, as he adds (ibid.), that "we must not judge that someone is lying if several persons fail to describe in the same way and in the same words a thing which they remember to have seen or heard."[27]

At the beginning of the seventeenth century, St. Francis de Sales says:

Holy Scripture is in such sort the rule of the Christian faith that we are obliged by every kind of obligation to believe most exactly all that it contains, and not to believe anything which may be ever so little contrary to it: for if our Lord himself has sent the Jews to it to strengthen their faith (cf. John 5:39), it must be a most safe standard. The Sadducees erred because they did not understand the Scriptures; they would have done better to attend to them, as to a light shining in a dark place, according to the advice of St. Peter (cf. 2 Pet 1:19[28]), who having himself heard the voice of the Father in the Transfiguration of the Son, bases himself more firmly on the testimony of the Prophets than on this experience.[29]

---

[27] *ST* II-II, q. 110, a. 3, ad 1.

[28] 2 Pet 1:18–21: "For he received from God the Father honour and glory, when there came such a voice to him from the excellent glory, This is my beloved Son, in whom I am well pleased. And this voice which came from heaven we heard, when we were with him in the holy mount. We have also a more sure word of prophecy; whereunto ye do well that ye take heed, as unto a light that shineth in a dark place, until the day dawn, and the day star arise in your hearts; knowing this first, that no prophecy of the Scripture is of any private interpretation, because no prophecy ever came by the impulse of man, but men moved by the Holy Spirit spoke from God."

[29] *The Catholic Controversy: St. Francis de Sales' Defense of the Faith*, (Rockford: TAN Books, 1989), 88. The text continues (89–90): "The Holy Scripture is called the Book of the Old and of the New *Testament*. When a notary has drawn a contract or other deed, when a testament is confirmed by the death of the testator, there must not be added, withdrawn, or altered, one single word under penalty of falsification. Are not the Holy Scriptures the true testament of the eternal God, drawn by the notaries deputed for this purpose, duly sealed and signed with his blood, confirmed by

From Leo XIII to Pius XII on Inerrancy

Leo XIII

The constant conviction of the Church on the truth of Scripture was strongly reaffirmed by Leo XIII in his great encyclical on the Bible, *Providentissimus Deus*:

> It follows that those who maintain that an error is possible in any genuine passage of the sacred writings, either pervert the Catholic notion of inspiration, or make God the author of such error. And so emphatically were all the Fathers and Doctors agreed that the divine writings, as left by the hagiographers, are free from all error, that they labored earnestly, with no less skill than reverence, to reconcile with each other those numerous passages which seem at variance, . . . for they were unanimous in laying it down, that those writings, in their entirety and in all their parts were equally from the afflatus of Almighty God, and that God, speaking by the sacred writers, could not set down anything but what was true.[30]

The inerrancy of the Bible, therefore, is a fundamental principle of interpretation.[31] We must not accept any interpretation that would imply the presence of falsehood or contradiction in the inspired text. What is at stake is the trustworthiness of the Bible as a secure foundation for theology and the spiritual life.[32]

There are different grades of those who deny the absolute inerrancy of Scripture. The most radical proponents view the Bible as a

---

death? Being such, how can we alter even the smallest point without impiety? . . . Our Lord puts a value on the iotas, yea, the mere little points and accents of his holy words. How jealous then is He of their integrity, and what punishment shall they not deserve who violate this integrity!"

[30] Leo XIII, Encyclical Letter on the Study of Holy Scripture *Providentissimus Deus* (1893), §21.

[31] See Benedict XVI, Apostolic Exhortation *Verbum Domini* (2010), §19: "Theological reflection has always considered inspiration and truth as two key concepts for an ecclesial hermeneutic of the sacred Scriptures. Nonetheless, one must acknowledge the need today for a fuller and more adequate study of these realities, in order better to respond to the need to interpret the sacred texts in accordance with their nature."

[32] See Leo XIII, *Providentissimus Deus* §17.

merely human creation, containing errors like any other work. This view adheres to a naturalist understanding of the world that cannot admit that the sacred writers had supernatural aid in writing their work, and according to which the supernatural events narrated would necessarily lack historical truth and must be considered as myths and legends. Others take a much more moderate view, upholding the existence of the supernatural and the inerrancy of Scripture in matters directly concerning faith and morals, but denying it in purely historical matters.

This more moderate position (restricted inerrancy) has been formulated in various ways. Some hold that errors could be present in historical matters, since this was a mere clothing or shell of the religious truths contained therein, which would be the only inspired or inerrant part. In other words, inerrancy would be limited to matters of faith and morals and would not apply to history, except insofar as it is directly connected to our salvation.

In effect, this more moderate position would be tantamount to limiting the *inspiration* of the Bible to matters that directly concern faith and morals. Thus the Bible would effectively not be inspired in its entirety, but only in parts directly concerning faith and morals. Leo XIII rejects this position in *Providentissimus Deus* §20:

> It is true, no doubt, that copyists have made mistakes in the text of the Bible; this question, when it arises, should be carefully considered on its merits, and the fact not too easily admitted, but only in those passages where the proof is clear. It may also happen that the sense of a passage remains ambiguous, and in this case good hermeneutical methods will greatly assist in clearing up the obscurity. But it is *absolutely wrong and forbidden, either to narrow inspiration to certain parts only of Holy Scripture, or to admit that the sacred writer has erred.* For the system of those who, in order to rid themselves of these difficulties, do not hesitate to concede that divine inspiration regards the things of faith and morals, and nothing beyond, because (as they wrongly think) in a question of the truth

or falsehood of a passage, we should consider not so much what God has said as the reason and purpose which He had in mind in saying it—this system cannot be tolerated. For all the books which the Church receives as sacred and canonical are written wholly and entirely, with all their parts, at the dictation of the Holy Spirit. And so far is it from being possible that any error can co-exist with inspiration, that inspiration not only is essentially incompatible with error, but excludes and rejects it as absolutely and necessarily as it is impossible that God Himself, the supreme Truth, can utter that which is not true. This is the ancient and unchanging faith of the Church, solemnly defined in the Councils of Florence and of Trent, and finally confirmed and more expressly formulated by the Council of the Vatican.[33]

Since God is the principal author of Scripture, historical errors in the Bible would still be attributed to God, even if they do not seem to concern matters of faith and morals directly. And God, the Truth Itself, cannot be directly responsible for what is contrary to truth any more than He can be directly responsible for sin. Some have objected to this reasoning by seeking to distinguish the divine and human authors. There could be errors in Scripture, they would hold, not because God is directly teaching the error, but because He simply allows the human author to remain in a certain ignorance of non-essential matters and to make erroneous assertions in their regard. Leo XIII responds to this kind of objection:

Hence, because the Holy Spirit employed men as His instruments, we cannot therefore say that it was these inspired instruments who, perchance, have fallen into error, and not the primary author. For, by supernatural power, He so moved and impelled them to write—He was so present to them— that the things which He ordered, and those only, they, first, rightly understood, then willed faithfully to write down, and

---

[33] *SD*, 55 (my italics).

finally expressed in apt words and with infallible truth. Otherwise, it could not be said that God was the author of the entire Scripture.[34]

In other words, the inspiration of Scripture applies to all of Scripture; all of Scripture is inspired and is the Word of God. It cannot be said that only the parts of Scripture dealing directly with religious truths are inspired by God and free from error, whereas other parts are the product only of the human author who could have fallen into error (in minor or historical matters). For, if some parts of Scripture are the product of the human author alone, left to his own unaided natural powers, then it could not be said that God is truly the author of the whole of Scripture.

It is true that the purpose of Scripture is the salvation of man, but it is inspired in its entirety, and hence it must also be true and free in its entirety from what is incompatible with divine authorship. Nor can it be said that possible errors are not to be attributed to the divine Author, but only to the human one, who is certainly fallible insofar as he works in his own power. The reason for this is that God interiorly moved the sacred writer to write all that God wished, so that we cannot ever separate the two authors. Everything that is affirmed by the sacred author we must believe to be also affirmed by God, for, in the words of St. Augustine cited by Leo XIII, "they wrote the things which He showed and uttered to them."

The error that Leo XIII condemns here (attributing error only to the human author) would imply a kind of biblical Nestorianism, as if we could separate the work of the human and divine authors and attribute some parts of Scripture to the human author alone.

Despite the forceful condemnation by this Pope, the error of limiting inerrancy to matters of faith and morals has continued to be affirmed by theologians, with considerable damage to the faith of Catholics. His teaching was confirmed by Popes St. Pius X, Benedict XV, and Pius XII.

---

[34] *Providentissimus Deus* §20 (*SD*, 55–56).

THE TRUTH OF SCRIPTURE

On Conflicts of Science and the Bible

Leo XIII also treats alleged conflicts between modern science and the Bible to show that they are not real conflicts, but capable of a resolution in which the truth of the Bible is not impaired. The key principle is that Scripture speaks about the physical world according to its appearances and according to the language of the culture in which it was written and does not seek to give a scientific explanation as would be expected of an empirical scientist:

> We must remember, first, that the sacred writers, or to speak more accurately, the Holy Spirit "who spoke by them, did not intend to teach men these things (that is to say, the essential nature of the things of the visible universe), things in no way profitable unto salvation."[35] Hence they did not seek to penetrate the secrets of nature, but rather described and dealt with things in more or less figurative language, or in terms which were commonly used at the time, and which in many instances are in daily use at this day, even by the most eminent men of science. Ordinary speech primarily and properly describes what comes under the senses; and somewhat in the same way the sacred writers—as the Angelic Doctor also reminds us— "went by what sensibly appeared," or put down what God, speaking to men, signified, in the way men could understand and were accustomed to.[36]

Thus it is not contrary to the truth of Scripture that it speaks of the "firmament of the heavens" (Gen 1) or of the sun moving in the sky,[37] for that is indeed how it appears to us, and we continue to speak in that way in ordinary language despite the fact that we know it is the earth that is moving around the sun. This principle resolves many supposed conflicts between science and Scripture. Similarly, Genesis speaks of the work of creation as occurring in stages using the con-

---

[35] St. Augustine, *De Genesi ad litteram imperfectus liber* 9.30.

[36] Leo XIII, *Providentissimus Deus* §18.

[37] See, for example, Josh 10:13.

crete and familiar term "day," rather than a more abstract term proper to modern Western culture but foreign to ancient Israel.

Benedict XV

Benedict XV further developed Leo XIII's teaching on inerrancy in *Spiritus Paraclitus*, commemorating the fifteenth centenary of St. Jerome, the patron of biblical studies. He commends the use of critical methods (§18) to explain the difficulties in Scripture. He laments, however, that some theologians continue to restrict inerrancy to only the religious dimension of Scripture, even though they claim to accept the teaching that all of Scripture is inspired:

> For while conceding that inspiration extends to every phrase—and, indeed, to every single word of Scripture—yet, by endeavoring to distinguish between what they style the primary or religious and the secondary or profane element in the Bible, they claim that the effects of inspiration—namely, absolute truth and immunity from error—are to be restricted to that primary or religious element. Their notion is that only what concerns religion is intended and taught by God in Scripture, and that all the rest—things concerning "profane knowledge," the garments in which Divine truth is presented—God merely permits, and even leaves to the individual author's greater or less [sic] knowledge.[38]

Benedict XV also reproves the position held by some that historical narratives in Scripture might be said to be true insofar as they are in accordance with common opinion at the time, even if they are not in accord with historical fact.[39] This opinion attempted to base itself on the statement in *Providentissimus Deus* in which Leo XIII says that

---

[38] *Spiritus Paraclitus* §20 (*SD*, 88).

[39] This position was held by Franz von Hummelauer, S.J.; see James T. Burtchaell, *Catholic Theories of Biblical Inspiration Since 1810: A Review and Critique* (London: Cambridge University Press, 1969), 228, 187.

it is not contrary to the truth of Scripture that it speak according to the appearances of things, rather than physical truth.[40] But this principle cannot be applied in the same way to history, as if biblical narratives could be assumed to be spoken merely according to opinion rather than to truth. There are two principal reasons for this. First, when we speak about the truth of a historical narration, we do not mean that it corresponds to popular opinion (which might be false), but to what actually occurred in reality. For example, it would not be true to say that the Shoah did not occur just because that statement is in accordance with the opinion of a large number of people in a given society (Holocaust-deniers)! Second, God reveals Himself precisely through salvation history, and the historical dimension of revealed truth is intrinsic to it. Benedict XV explains:

> Those, too, who hold that the historical portions of Scripture do not rest on the absolute truth of the facts but merely upon what they are pleased to term their relative truth, namely, what people then commonly thought, are—no less than are the aforementioned critics—out of harmony with the Church's teaching, which is endorsed by the testimony of Jerome and other Fathers. Yet they are not afraid to deduce such views from the words of Leo XIII on the ground that he allowed that the principles he had laid down touching the things of nature could be applied to historical things as well. Hence they maintain that precisely as the sacred writers spoke of physical things according to appearance, so, too, while ignorant of the facts, they narrated them in accordance with general opinion or even on baseless evidence; neither do they tell us the sources whence they derived their knowledge, nor do they make other peoples' narrative their own. Such views are clearly false, and constitute a calumny on our predecessor. After all, what analogy is there between physics and history? For whereas physics is concerned with "sensible appearances" and must consequently square with phenomena,

---

[40] See *Providentissimus Deus* §18, cited above.

history on the contrary, must square with the facts, since history is the written account of events as they actually occurred. If we were to accept such views, how could we maintain the truth insisted on throughout Leo XIII's Encyclical—viz. that the sacred narrative is absolutely free from error?[41]

Pius XII and the Importance of Rightly Identifying Literary Forms

Pius XII reaffirms the doctrine of Leo XIII on inerrancy in his great encyclical on the Bible, *Divino afflante Spiritu*, in which he quotes *Providentissimus Deus* §20 and makes it his own:

Finally it is absolutely wrong and forbidden "either to narrow inspiration to certain passages of Holy Scripture, or to admit that the sacred writer has erred," since divine inspiration "not only is essentially incompatible with error but excludes and rejects it as absolutely and necessarily as it is impossible that God Himself, the supreme Truth, can utter that which is not true. This is the ancient and constant faith of the Church." This teaching, which Our Predecessor Leo XIII set forth with such solemnity, We also proclaim with Our authority and We urge all to adhere to it religiously.[42]

Pius XII returned briefly to the subject of inerrancy in his 1950 encyclical, *Humani generis* §22:

To return, however, to the new opinions mentioned above, a number of things are proposed or suggested by some even against the divine authorship of Sacred Scripture. For some go so far as to pervert the sense of the Vatican Council's definition that God is the author of Holy Scripture, and they put forward again the *opinion, already often condemned, that as-*

---

[41] *Spiritus Paraclitus* §22 (SD, 89).

[42] *Divino afflante Spiritu* §3–4 (SD, 117).

serts that immunity from error extends only to those parts of the Bible that treat of God or of moral and religious matters. They even wrongly speak of a human sense of the Scriptures, beneath which a divine sense, which they say is the only infallible meaning, lies hidden.[43]

He does not limit himself to condemning any restriction of biblical inerrancy to matters directly of faith and morals. As Leo XIII had done with regard to conflicts with science, Pius XII provides a principle to resolve difficulties in Scripture with regard to objections of historical error. This principle is the necessity of rightly analyzing the literary genre and conventions used by the sacred author so as to rightly judge what is actually being affirmed by him, for it can easily happen that an inexperienced reader mistakes what the sacred author means to affirm through a lack of understanding of literary conventions.[44] Pius XII states that the first task of the exegete is to determine the literal sense of Scripture, which is what the author intends to convey by his *words*.[45] This sense could also be called the *literary* sense,[46] for it presupposes that the literary techniques are rightly understood. The literal sense is metaphorical when the words are meant to be understood in a metaphorical or symbolic way. In this case, the literal sense is what the words are intended to convey through the metaphor, allegory (which is a kind of extended metaphor), symbol, or other literary form. For example, when Scripture speaks about the "outstretched arm of God" by which He brought the Chosen People out of the house of bondage, we are not to understand the literal sense

---

[43] DS, 3887; SD, 141 (my italics).

[44] This principle of literary genres had been affirmed as the proper way to defend the truth of the Bible with regard to objections of historical error by, among others, Marie-Joseph Lagrange in "L'inspiration et les exigences de la critique; Réponse à la lettre précédente," *Revue Biblique* 5 (1896): 496–518, and in his *Historical Criticism and the Old Testament*, trans. Edward Myers (London: Catholic Truth Society, 1906), 103.

[45] See CCC §116: "The literal sense is the meaning conveyed by the words of Scripture and discovered by exegesis, following the rules of sound interpretation: 'All other senses of Sacred Scripture are based on the literal'" (quoting ST 1, q. 1, a. 10, ad 1). For the priority of the literal sense, see *Divino afflante Spiritu* §23.

[46] See Scott Hahn, ed., *Catholic Bible Dictionary* (New York: Doubleday, 2009), 392.

of these texts as implying that God—in the divine nature—has arms or hands! The literal sense is what the metaphor intends to represent: the power of God to accomplish His will.[47] Similarly, Christ is said to be seated at the right hand of God in the sense that His sacred humanity in heaven is associated with all the power of God, so that He is King of heaven and earth. St. Thomas explains these two forms of the literal sense:

> There are two ways in which something can be signified by the literal sense: either according to the usual construction, as when I say, "the man smiles"; or according to a likeness or metaphor, as when I say, "the meadow smiles." Both of these are used in Sacred Scripture; as when we say, according to the first, that Jesus ascended, and when we say according to the second, that He sits at the right hand of God. Therefore, under the literal sense is included the parabolic or metaphorical.[48]

Presupposing the proper meaning of the "literal sense," Pius XII writes:

> What is the "literal" sense of a passage is not always as obvious in the speeches and writings of the ancient authors of the East as it is in the works of our own time. For what they wished to express is not to be determined by the rules of grammar and philology alone nor solely by the context; the interpreter must, as it were, go back wholly in spirit to those remote centuries of the East and with the aid of history, archaeology, ethnology, and other sciences, accurately determine what modes of writing, so to speak, the authors of that ancient pe-

---

[47] Some of the Fathers and ecclesiastical writers of the early Church, such as Origen, sometimes use the term "literal sense" to refer to the literalistic sense, as can be seen from the context. Normally, however, scholastic theologians use the term "literal sense" to refer not to the literalistic, but to the literary sense.

[48] St. Thomas, *Super Epistolam B. Pauli ad Galatas lectura: Commentary on Saint Paul's Epistle to the Galatians*, ch. 4, lec. 7 (on Gal 4:24, Marietti no. 254), trans. F.R. Larcher, O.P. (Lander: Aquinas Institute for the Study of Sacred Doctrine, 2012), 112.

riod would be likely to use, and in fact did use. For the ancient peoples of the East, in order to express their ideas, did not always employ those forms or kinds of speech which we use today, but rather those used by the men of their times and countries. What those exactly were the commentator cannot determine as it were in advance, but only after a careful examination of the ancient literature of the East.[49]

Although we must believe that what the sacred author affirms is affirmed by the Holy Spirit, it is not always easy to be certain about what the sacred author actually meant to affirm![50] For example, no error is present when an author expresses himself in what we might regard as exaggerated language using the literary conventions of Semitic hyperbole,[51] or when an author expresses a profound truth through a narration in which symbolic events are put in a historical setting that is not purely factual and is not meant to be taken at the letter.

Pius XII, therefore, calls on Catholic exegetes to make prudent use of "genre criticism"—the identification of literary genres and conventions—to defend Scripture from charges of error:

The Catholic commentator, in order to comply with the present needs of biblical studies in explaining the Sacred Scripture and in demonstrating and proving its immunity from

---

[49] *Divino afflante Spiritu* §§35–36 (*SD*, 128–129).

[50] See Lagrange, *Historical Criticism and the Old Testament*, 103: "Certain as the principles may be, their application remains extremely difficult. What the sacred writers teach, God teaches, and it is therefore true. But what do the sacred writers teach? They teach, we are told, what they categorically affirm! Now it has long since been pointed out that the Bible is not a mere collection of theses or categorical affirmations. There are certain forms of literary composition in which no absolute statement is made as to the reality of the facts related: they are used merely as the groundwork of a moral lesson."

[51] See *Divino afflante Spiritu* §37: "Nevertheless, no one who has a correct idea of biblical inspiration will be surprised to find, even in the sacred writers, as in other ancient authors, certain fixed ways of expounding and narrating, certain definite idioms, especially of a kind peculiar to the Semitic tongues, so-called 'approximations' and certain hyperbolical, even at times paradoxical, modes of expression, which help to impress the ideas more deeply on the mind. For of the modes of expression which, among ancient peoples and especially those of the East, human language used to express its thought, none is excluded from the sacred Books, provided the way of speaking adopted in no wise contradicts the holiness and truth of God" (*SD*, 129).

all error, should also make a prudent use of this means, determining, that is, to what extent the manner of expression or the literary mode adopted by the sacred writer may lead to a correct and genuine interpretation. And let him be convinced that this part of his office cannot be neglected without serious detriment to Catholic exegesis. Not infrequently—to mention only one instance—when some persons reproachfully charge the sacred writers with some historical error or inaccuracy in the recording of facts, on closer examination it turns out to be nothing else than those customary modes of expression and narration peculiar to the ancients, which used to be employed in the mutual dealings of social life and which in fact were sanctioned by common usage.[52]

This emphasis on rightly understanding literary genres is taken up in *Dei Verbum* §12, as will be seen in the following chapter. The 1993 document of the Pontifical Biblical Commission, *The Interpretation of the Bible in the Church*, warns of the danger of not taking into account the use of metaphor and other literary forms in understanding Scripture. It explains that the literal sense is "not to be confused with the 'literalist' sense to which fundamentalists are attached. It is not sufficient to translate a text word for word in order to obtain its literal sense. One must understand the text according to the literary conventions of the time."[53]

This needs to be kept in mind when we affirm the inerrant truth of Scripture. The Bible is true in that it has God for its author, but we must correctly understand the literary conventions used in the text. For example, it would be a mistake to assume that the literal meaning of the first chapter of Genesis necessarily implies that the creation of

---

[52] Ibid. §38 (*SD*, 129–130).

[53] PBC, *The Interpretation of the Bible in the Church* (1993), II.B.1 (*SD*, 280). The text continues: "The literal sense of Scripture is that which has been expressed directly by the inspired human authors. Since it is the fruit of inspiration, this sense is also intended by God, as principal author. One arrives at this sense by means of a careful analysis of the text, within its literary and historical context."

the world was accomplished in six twenty-four-hour periods.[54] The Church (in a document by the PBC in1909) tells us that a "day" (*yom*, in Hebrew) of creation may be taken metaphorically to mean an undetermined period of time.[55] Indeed, how can we speak of a twenty-four-hour day when the sun was not created until the fourth day? The six "days" of creation thus intend to speak of six ascending "stages" of creation portrayed as an unfolding temporal process. This is still the *literal* sense, rightly understood.[56]

Another example where the literal sense involves the use of metaphor is Genesis 6:6, which speaks of God's *repentance* and *inner sorrow of heart* for having created man. The literal meaning is not that God has actually "repented" and changed His mind, for the counsels of God are eternal and immutable, as is the divine nature. "Repentance" here is used as a kind of metaphor. God, according to His eternal plan, punished the sin of the men of that time, as we, in our temporal condition, destroy things that we "repent having made." That is, the metaphor of human regret is used to help us understand God's sorrow over the proliferation of sin and the motivation for God's act of permitting the Deluge. Scripture must be read with intelligence. For this reason, it is not an easily accessible and straightforward book, nor has the Church ever claimed that it was! This is why the faithful are always counseled to read the Bible with the aid of good commentaries that explain the figures and metaphors and the correct interpretation of the text.

---

[54] See Mark P. Shea, *Making Senses out of Scripture: Reading the Bible As the First Christians Did* (San Diego: Basilica Press, 1999), 168: "What the modern reader often hears, however, is 'The universe was made in six twenty-four-hour days.' This is as wrong-headed as taking me to mean I actually stood in line a million years or that my cardiac tissue has been torn in half or that Christ had delusions of being a grape plant. It is necessary therefore to distinguish between the literal meaning of an author and the various literary devices he may employ to communicate that meaning."

[55] See the June 30, 1909 Response by the PBC (DS, 3519).

[56] See the PBC, *The Inspiration and Truth of Sacred Scripture*, §74: "The distribution of the various works of creation over six days does not intend to affirm as a truth to be believed that the world really took form in six days, while God rested on the seventh; it intends to communicate, rather, that there exists an order and a purpose in creation. Humans can and must participate in this order."

The parable is another example of a literary form. It is a kind of allegory or extended metaphor whose literal sense is the point made by the parable. Thus the parables of Christ in Matthew 13 have a literal metaphorical sense concerning the growth of the Church, represented through the analogy of a mustard seed, the sowing of a field, the fermentation of dough, the precious pearl, etc.

Allegory as a literary form does not affirm the literal historical truth of the story it tells. For example, after King David sinned by committing adultery and murder, the prophet Nathan told him an allegory of a rich man who, not wishing to use his own flocks, took the sole lamb of a poor man to make a feast (2 Sam 12:1–7). Obviously the rich man represented David, and the poor man Uriah, whose wife David took in adultery and whom he had killed. This allegory belongs to the literal sense, for its meaning is the one that the prophet Nathan meant to signify by his words.

Within the broad genre of history, there can be very different types, some of which may be told in a more allegorical or metaphorical way than others. Books such as Tobit, Judith, Job, and Jonah can have varying degrees of literary artifice and symbolism in their historical setting that need to be understood according to the literary intentions of their authors.

One of the texts that poses the greatest difficulties in rightly understanding its literary conventions is Genesis 1–11.[57] Pius XII states in *Humani generis* that the literal sense of the first eleven chapters of Genesis belongs to the genre of history in a broad sense, although of a unique kind expressed in archaic language and metaphor. These texts are not to be considered simply as myth or legend, but as a primordial history written in a unique way, in which the origins of man are narrated in primeval and symbolic terms proper to the ancient Near East. He writes:

> In a particular way must be deplored a certain too free interpretation of the historical books of the Old Testament. Those

---

[57] On the category of primitive history found in Genesis 1–11, see Lagrange, *Historical Criticism and the Old Testament*, 180–213.

who favor this system, in order to defend their cause, wrongly refer to the Letter which was sent not long ago to the Archbishop of Paris by the Pontifical Commission on Biblical Studies.[58] This letter, in fact, clearly points out that the first eleven chapters of Genesis, although properly speaking not conforming to the historical method used by the best Greek and Latin writers or by competent authors of our time, do nevertheless *pertain to history in a true sense,* which however must be further studied and determined by exegetes; the same chapters (the Letter points out), in simple and metaphorical language adapted to the mentality of a people but little cultured, both state the principal truths which are fundamental for our salvation, and also give a popular description of the origin of the human race and the chosen people. If, however, the ancient sacred writers have taken anything from popular narrations (and this may be conceded), it must never be forgotten that they did so with the help of divine inspiration, through which they were rendered immune from any error in selecting and evaluating those documents.

Therefore, whatever of the popular narrations have been inserted into the Sacred Scriptures must in no way be considered on a par with myths or other such things, which are more the product of an extravagant imagination than of that striving for truth and simplicity which in the Sacred Books, also of the Old Testament, is so apparent that our ancient sacred writers must be admitted to be clearly superior to the ancient profane writers.[59]

---

[58] January 16, 1948 (*AAS*, 40:45–48).

[59] Encyclical Letter Concerning Some False Opinions Threatening to Undermine the Foundations of Catholic Doctrine *Humani generis* (1950), §38–39 (*SD*, 143, my italics).

Vatican II: *Dei Verbum* §11

Dei Verbum §11 treats the subject of the truth of Scripture in a much-discussed passage:[60]

> In composing the sacred books, God chose men and while employed by Him they made use of their powers and abilities, so that with Him acting in them and through them, they, as true authors, consigned to writing everything and only those things which He wanted.
>
> Therefore, since everything asserted by the inspired authors or sacred writers must be held to be asserted by the Holy Spirit, it follows that the books of Scripture must be acknowledged as teaching solidly, faithfully and without error that truth which God wanted put into sacred writings for the sake of salvation.[61]

The foundation of biblical inerrancy is the principle that God so guided the sacred authors in their work that they put in writing everything He wanted and only what He wanted. It is for this reason that "everything asserted by the inspired authors or sacred writers must be held to be asserted by the Holy Spirit."[62]

There has been much discussion about the meaning of the clause that modifies the word "truth": *quam Deus nostrae salutis causa Litteris Sacris consignari voluit* ("which God wanted put into sacred writings

---

[60] See the collection of essays on the interpretation of *DV* §11 in *Letter & Spirit* 6 (2010).

[61] The Official Latin text is: "Cum ergo omne id, quod auctores inspirati seu hagiographi asserunt, retineri debeat assertum a Spiritu Sancto, inde Scripturae libri veritatem, quam Deus nostrae salutis causa Litteris Sacris consignari voluit, firmiter, fideliter et sine errore docere profitendi sunt." Perhaps a more accurate translation of the Latin would be the following: "... it follows that the books of Scripture must be acknowledged as teaching solidly, faithfully, and without error the truth that God wanted to make known through the sacred writings for the sake of salvation." The Latin original of this text is from the *Acta Synodalia Sacrosancti Concilii Oecumenici Vaticani II* [Synodal Acts of the Ecumenical Council Vatican II], 32 vols. (Rome: Typis Polyglottis Vaticanis, 1970–), vol. 4, pt. 5, 708.

[62] This formulation is based on a Response of the PBC of June 18, 1915, Question 2: "... Catholic dogma regarding the inspiration and inerrancy of the Scriptures, whereby all that the sacred writer asserts, enunciates, and suggests must be held to be asserted, enunciated, and suggested by the Holy Spirit" (DS, 3629). *DV* §11 simplifies by eliminating "enunciates and suggests."

for the sake of salvation"). The discussion focuses on whether this clause should be understood as limiting the doctrine of inerrancy to only those texts in Scripture that have a direct bearing on human salvation (restrictive inerrancy), or should be understood as giving the final cause for the whole of Scripture, all of which would be inerrant in the service of human salvation (plenary inerrancy).[63] There are three weighty reasons for decisively rejecting the restrictive interpretation.

First of all, as we have seen, earlier magisterial documents, as well as the teaching of the Fathers and Doctors, explicitly and repeatedly reject the restrictive interpretation, and the fundamental rule for reading magisterial documents is the "hermeneutic of continuity."[64] Furthermore, the footnote in this part of *Dei Verbum* §11 refers to *Providentissimus Deus* and *Divino afflante Spiritu*, indicating that it is to be read in accordance with them.[65]

Secondly, the first rule of interpretation of any text is to look at its context. *Dei Verbum* §11 has two paragraphs, the first of which defines the plenary *inspiration* of Scripture, in all its parts and assertions. The second paragraph argues from inspiration to the *truth* (inerrancy) of Scripture, which thus must also be a property of the whole of Scripture. Since all is inspired and everything asserted by the sacred authors must be held to be asserted by the Holy Spirit without restriction because they wrote *only* what the Holy Spirit wanted, it follows that all of their assertions, rightly understood, have the property of truth. Hence, *all* of their assertions are to be received by the faithful as the Word of God, and not just *some* assertions bearing more closely on salvific or theological matters (according to each reader's private judgment?).

---

[63] In grammatical terms, the question is whether the clause beginning with the words, "which God wanted . . . ," should be interpreted as a limiting clause regarding the truth of Scripture, or as a final clause that indicates the purpose of God regarding His promulgation of Scripture. In other words, because God desires our salvation, He made His Revelation known through Scripture.

[64] See Benedict XVI, Address to the Roman Curia, Dec. 22, 2005, at http://www.vatican.va/holy_father/benedict_xvi/speeches/2005/december/documents/hf_ben_xvi_spe_20051222_roman-curia_en.html.

[65] The footnote to *DV* §11 refers to Leo XIII, *Providentissimus Deus* §§18 and 20–21, and Pius XII, *Divino afflante Spiritu* §3.

Thirdly, the history of the debate at the Council on the successive drafts of *Dei Verbum* §11 (recorded in the Acts of the Council) clearly shows that a restrictive interpretation was not intended. A good summary is given by Pablo Gadenz:

> As for the proper interpretation of the phrase "for the sake of our salvation," it is helpful to recall that the penultimate schema or draft of *Dei Verbum* 11 instead spoke of "saving truth" *(veritatem salutarem)*, in order to make reference also to the events of salvation history. Many Council fathers expressed concerns about this terminology, as it appeared to restrict inerrancy to matters of faith and morals, an idea that, as we have seen, was condemned by Leo XIII. The doctrinal commission overseeing the drafting process was of the opinion that this terminology did not introduce any "material limitation" to the truth of Scripture, but rather indicated its "formal specification."[66] The matter was brought to the attention of Pope Paul VI, who, sharing the concern of the Council fathers, asked the doctrinal commission to consider omitting the expression, in part because it could be open to wrong interpretation. After Cardinal Augustin Bea, a trusted adviser of the Pope, explained the matter to the commission, it voted to drop the adjective "saving" and replace it with the clause "for the sake of our salvation." This clause went on to become part of the definitive text.[67]

---

[66] This clarification of the doctrinal commission is translated by Brian W. Harrison in his excellent article, "Restricted Inerrancy and the 'Hermeneutic of Discontinuity,'" *Letter & Spirit* 6 (2010): 234: "By the term 'salvific' *(salutarem)* it is by no means suggested that sacred Scripture is not in its integrity the inspired Word of God.... This expression does *not* imply any *material limitation* of the truth of Scripture; rather, it indicates Scripture's *formal specification*, the nature of which must be kept in mind in deciding in what sense all things *affirmed* in the Bible are true—not only matters of faith and morals and facts bound up with the history of salvation. For this reason the [doctrinal commission overseeing the drafting process] has decided that the expression should be retained."

[67] Pablo T. Gadenz, "Magisterial Teaching on the Inspiration and Truth of Scripture: Precedents and Prospects," *Letter & Spirit* 6 (2010): 80–81.

Augustin Cardinal Bea gives an authoritative commentary on this part of *Dei Verbum* §11. He was in a uniquely privileged position to interpret this text because of his involvement in the Council and his position as Rector of the Biblical Institute in Rome and expert on this subject. He defends the position that it affirms an unlimited inerrancy as follows:

> In fact, we declare in general that there is no limit set to this inerrancy, and that it applies to all that the inspired writer, and therefore all that the Holy Spirit by his means, affirms.
>
> Our reasons are these. First of all, the Constitution itself says that in holy Scripture the truth and holiness of God must always remain inviolable [*DV* §13]. This thought . . . is here clearly understood in a sense which excludes the possibility of the Scriptures containing any statement contrary to the reality of the facts.
>
> In particular, these documents of the magisterium require us to recognize that Scripture gives a true account of events, naturally not in the sense that it always offers a complete and scientifically studied account, but in the sense that what is asserted in Scripture—even if it does not offer a complete picture—never contradicts the reality of the fact.
>
> If therefore the Council had wished to introduce here a new conception, different from that presented in these documents of the supreme teaching authority, which reflects the beliefs of the early Fathers, it would have had to state this clearly and explicitly.
>
> Let us now ask whether there may be any indications to suggest such a restricted interpretation of inerrancy. The answer is decidedly negative. There is not the slightest sign of any such indication. On the contrary everything points against a restrictive interpretation. . . .
>
> Does the text of *DV* we have before us now imply a restrictive interpretation of inerrancy? Here also the answer is firmly negative. The first proof of this is seen in the fact that

all those (and in the first place the Pope himself) who had been anxious to prevent the possible misunderstandings that might have arisen from the expression "the saving truth" have instead accepted the present form. This means that they consider that this does not present the same danger of mis-understanding. In fact, the phrasing we now have does not admit of any such interpretation because the idea of salvation is no longer directly linked with the noun "truth," but with the verbal expression "wanted put into the sacred writings." In other words, the phrase in which the text speaks of salva-tion explains God's purpose in causing the Scriptures to be written, and not the nature of the truth enshrined therein.[68]

Cardinal Bea is thus saying that the phrase "for the sake of our salvation" is not to be understood as a limitation of what is inerrant in Scripture, but rather as an indication of the final cause or purpose of Scripture: the salvation of man. It is not a limiting clause, but a final clause.

The 2014 document by the Pontifical Biblical Commission, *The Inspiration and Truth of Sacred Scripture*, also holds that the phrase "for the sake of our salvation" should not be interpreted as a limiting clause, but rather as expressing the finality for the sake of which God has revealed His truth:

> This must not, however, be taken to mean that the truth of Sa-cred Scripture concerns only those parts of the Sacred Book that are necessary for faith and morality, to the exclusion of other parts (the expression *veritas salutaris* of the fourth sche-ma had not been accepted precisely to avoid such an interpre-tation). The meaning of the expression "the truth which God wanted put into sacred writings for the sake of our salvation" is rather that the books of Scripture, with all their parts, in-sofar as they are inspired by the Holy Spirit and have God as

---

[68] Augustin Cardinal Bea, "Vatican II and the Truth of Sacred Scripture," *Letter & Spirit* 6 (2010): 381–382.

their author, intend to communicate the truth insofar as it relates to our salvation, which is, in fact, the purpose for which God reveals himself.[69]

It is interesting to note that the CDF, in the Doctrinal Commentary on the *Professio fidei*, spoke of the inerrancy of Scripture as a truth revealed by God, infallibly proposed by the Church in her universal and ordinary Magisterium, and taught by *Dei Verbum* §11.[70]

Study Questions

1. What is the teaching of the Church on the inerrancy of Scripture? Explain the relationship between plenary inspiration and inerrancy. What are the relevant magisterial texts?
2. How does Leo XIII resolve conflicts between science and the Bible?
3. What is the importance of rightly recognizing literary genres for resolving conflicts between our knowledge of history and the Bible?
4. What is meant by the "literal sense" of Scripture? How is it determined?
5. Explain the teaching of *Dei Verbum* §11 on the inerrancy of Scripture. Does it support restrictive or plenary inerrancy? Justify your answer.

Suggestions for Further Reading

Pope Leo XIII. Encyclical Letter on the Study of Holy Scripture *Providentissimus Deus*. September 30, 1893.

Pope Benedict XV. Encyclical Letter Commemorating the Fifteenth Centenary of the Death of St. Jerome *Spiritus Paraclitus*. September, 1920.

---

[69] PBC, *The Inspiration and Truth of Sacred Scripture*, 71.

[70] CDF, Commentary on the *Professio fidei* §11. This commentary accompanied John Paul II's *Ad tuendam Fidem*.

Pope Pius XII. Encyclical Letter Promoting Biblical Studies *Divino afflante Spiritu*. November 18, 1943.

Pontifical Biblical Commission, *The Inspiration and Truth of Sacred Scripture: The Word that Comes from God and Speaks of God for the Salvation of the World*. Collegeville: Liturgical Press, 2014.

Letter & Spirit 6 (2010). Volume title: *"For the Sake of Our Salvation: The Truth and Humility of God's Word."*

Ramage, Matthew J. "Violence Is Incompatible with the Nature of God: Benedict, Aquinas, and Method C Exegesis of the 'Dark' Passages of the Bible." *Nova et Vetera* (English) 13, no. 1 (2015): 273–295.

CHAPTER TWELVE

Principles and Methods of Biblical Interpretation

Two Principles of Biblical Interpretation Based on Human and Divine Authorship

Two Principles of Biblical Interpretation According to Dei Verbum §12

Like the Incarnation, biblical inspiration is a mystery of the divine condescension in which God speaks "through men in human fashion" such that whatever is "asserted by the inspired authors or sacred writers must be held to be asserted by the Holy Spirit" (*DV* §11). This twofold origin of the Bible—divine and human—gives rise to two fundamental principles of biblical interpretation. (1) Since every book of Scripture has a human writer, every text must be interpreted in light of its historical context and original language, with attention to everything that can help us understand the mentality, cultural and historical context, original language, and literary forms or genres used by the sacred author. Exegesis therefore must make use of the human sciences of philology, history, and archeology, and thus employ a historical-critical methodology.[1] (2) But no less importantly, since God is the Author of Scripture, every text must be understood also in light of the unity of the entire Bible, the faith of the Church, and her Tra-

---

[1] See, for example, Pius XII, Encyclical Letter Promoting Biblical Studies *Divino afflante Spiritu* (1943), §§16–17.

dition as it bears on a given text. Thus the Old Testament should be read in the light of the New[2] and in the light of Christ.[3] In general, every part of the Bible should be read in the light of every other. All of it, finally, should be read in light of the Church's Creed, life, Tradition, and worship, and in the context of the whole of salvation history.[4] *Dei Verbum* §12 explains these two fundamental principles of biblical interpretation:

> However, since God speaks in Sacred Scripture through men in human fashion, the interpreter of Sacred Scripture, in order to see clearly what God wanted to communicate to us, should carefully investigate what meaning the sacred writers really intended, and what God wanted to manifest by means of their words.
>
> To search out the intention of the sacred writers, attention should be given, among other things, to "literary forms." For truth is set forth and expressed differently in texts which are variously historical, prophetic, poetic, or of other forms of discourse. The interpreter must investigate what meaning the sacred writer intended to express and actually expressed in particular circumstances by using contemporary literary forms in accordance with the situation of his own time and culture. For the correct understanding of what the sacred author wanted to assert, due attention must be paid to the customary and characteristic styles of feeling, speaking, and narrating which prevailed at the time of the sacred writer and to the patterns men normally employed at that period in their everyday dealings with one another.

---

[2] See *DV* §16: "God, the inspirer and author of both Testaments, wisely arranged that the New Testament be hidden in the Old and the Old be made manifest in the New." This text is based on St. Augustine, *Quaestiones in heptateuchum* 2.73 (PL, 34:623).

[3] See Hugh of St. Victor, *De arca Noe morali* 2.8: "All of Sacred Scripture is one single book, and that one book is Christ" (PL, 176:642); cited in Ignace de la Potterie, S.J., "Interpretation of Holy Scripture in the Spirit in Which It Was Written (*Dei Verbum* 12c)," in *Vatican II Assessment and Perspectives: Twenty-five Years After (1962–1987)*, vol. 1 (New York: Paulist, 1988), 252.

[4] See De la Potterie, "Interpretation of Holy Scripture," 254.

But, since Holy Scripture must be read and interpreted in the same Spirit in which it was written,[5] no less serious attention must be given to the content and unity of the whole of Scripture if the meaning of the sacred texts is to be correctly worked out. The living tradition of the whole Church must be taken into account along with the harmony which exists between elements of the faith.[6]

First, the fact that Scripture has a human author means that exegesis must consider the natural order on which inspiration builds, and which theology uses as a handmaid. God condescends to speak to man using human means of expression, and so the Church must carefully study those human forms of expression to grasp the meaning of what God wished to reveal.

Second, the fact that God is the principal author of Scripture means that the exegete must use the supernatural method proper to theology as the science of faith, keeping in mind that it is God who speaks through different human means of expression throughout Scripture. Biblical interpretation can fulfill its great task in the Church only when these two dimensions—human and divine—are understood and kept in balance. As we have seen, *Dei Verbum* §13 beautifully compares this union of divine and human sources with the union of the divine and human natures in Christ. As we must acknowledge and reverence both natures in Christ, so we must reverence both dimensions of the Word of God and investigate its meaning accordingly.

Dei Verbum §12 mentions three criteria that must be used by the exegete in order to grasp the theological meaning of Scripture: the unity of Scripture, the living Tradition of the Church, and the "analogy of faith." The analogy of faith refers to the relation that a biblical

---

[5] I have slightly modified the translation to accord more exactly with the official Latin text, which capitalizes *Spiritu* so that it clearly refers to the Holy Spirit: "Sed, cum Sacra Scriptura *eodem Spiritu* quo scripta est etiam legenda et interpretanda sit." For an excellent commentary on this text, see De la Potterie, "Interpretation of Holy Scripture," 220–266. The Latin original of this text is from the *Acta Synodalia Sacrosancti Concilii Oecumenici Vaticani II* [Synodal Acts of the Ecumenical Council Vatican II], 32 vols. (Rome: Typis Polyglottis Vaticanis, 1970–).

[6] DS, 4217–4219.

text has with the truths of the faith.[7] In other words, the analogy of faith as a criterion of interpretation means that any scriptural text needs to be understood not in isolation, but in harmony with all the truths of faith in their progressive unfolding.[8]

Joseph Ratzinger gives a good explanation of the intimate inter-relationship of these three criteria in his well-known lecture, "Biblical Interpretation in Conflict":

> The fundamental presupposition on which the theological understanding of the Bible is based, it said, is the unity of Scripture; the method to follow, corresponding to that pre-supposition, is the *analogia fidei*—that is, the understanding of individual texts on the basis of the whole. Then there are two further indications as to method. Scripture is one, on the basis of its continuing historical vehicle, the one people of God. Reading it as a unity therefore means reading it on the basis of the Church as its locus in life and regarding the faith of the Church as the true hermeneutic key. That means, in the first place, that tradition does not obstruct access to Scripture; rather, it opens it up; and secondly, that it is for the Church, through her official organs, to pronounce the decisive word in the interpretation of Scripture.[9]

Two Principles of Interpretation According to Pius XII and Benedict XVI

This great text (*DV* §12) was prepared for by *Divino afflante Spiritu* §§23–24, in which Pope Pius XII states that the first task of the biblical exegete is to set forth the literal sense of Scripture, which is what

---

[7] The term "analogy of faith" is explained in CCC §114: "By 'analogy of faith' we mean the coherence of the truths of faith among themselves and within the whole plan of Revelation."

[8] See First Vatican Council, Dogmatic Constitution on the Catholic Faith *Dei Filius*, ch. 4 (DS, 3016), which teaches that theology seeks an understanding of the mysteries by considering "the analogy with the objects of its natural knowledge and from the connection of these mysteries with one another and with man's ultimate end."

[9] Ratzinger, *God's Word: Scripture—Tradition—Office*, trans. Henry Taylor, (San Francisco: Ignatius Press, 2008), 96–97.

the sacred author intended to communicate through his words. In order to do this properly, the exegete must be attentive to the meaning of the words in their context, as one would do with non-biblical texts. But at the same time, they should "no less diligently" investigate their theological meaning using a properly theological method:

> Aided by the context and by comparison with similar passages, let them therefore by means of their knowledge of languages search out with all diligence the literal meaning of the words; all these helps indeed are wont to be pressed into service in the explanation also of profane writers, so that the mind of the author may be made abundantly clear.
>
> The commentators of the Sacred Letters, mindful of the fact that here there is question of a divinely inspired text, the care and interpretation of which have been confided to the Church by God Himself, should no less diligently take into account the explanations and declarations of the teaching authority of the Church, as likewise the interpretation given by the Holy Fathers, and even "the analogy of faith" as Leo XIII most wisely observed in the Encyclical Letter *Providentissimus Deus*.[10]

Pius XII gives three things that the interpreter of Scripture must be especially attentive to in order to grasp its theological meaning: magisterial teachings that bear on the text, interpretations of the Fa-

---

[10] The reference is to Leo XIII, Encyclical Letter on the Study of Holy Scripture *Providentissimus Deus* §14: "Wherefore the first and dearest object of the Catholic commentator should be to interpret those passages which have received an authentic interpretation either from the sacred writers themselves, under the inspiration of the Holy Ghost (as in many places of the New Testament), or from the Church, under the assistance of the same Holy Spirit, whether by her solemn judgment or her ordinary and universal *magisterium*—to interpret these passages in that identical sense, and to prove, by all the resources of science, that sound hermeneutical laws admit of no other interpretation. In the other passages, the analogy of faith should be followed, and Catholic doctrine, as authoritatively proposed by the Church, should be held as the supreme law; for, seeing that the same God is the author both of the Sacred Books and of the doctrine committed to the Church, it is clearly impossible that any teaching can by legitimate means be extracted from the former which shall in any respect be at variance with the latter. Hence it follows that all interpretation is foolish and false which either makes the sacred writers disagree one with another, or is opposed to the doctrine of the Church."

thers, and the "analogy of faith." It is interesting to compare the three theological criteria given by Pius XII with *Dei Verbum* §12. The later text improves on *Divino afflante Spiritu* by adding the unity of the Bible as the primary theological criterion. Then, instead of mentioning only the Fathers, it speaks of the "living Tradition of the whole Church" as a criterion of interpretation. This includes the Fathers and Doctors, the Magisterium, and the liturgy.

Pius XII laments that certain modern commentaries focus only the first of these tasks—the natural principles of interpretation—but neglect the supernatural and theological dimension. The exegete, on the contrary, is to interpret the Bible in a way that brings out above all its aspect of divine Revelation so as to build up the faith and spiritual life of the faithful:

> With special zeal should they apply themselves, not only to expounding exclusively these matters which belong to the historical, archaeological, philological and other auxiliary sciences—as, to Our regret, is done in certain commentaries—but, having duly referred to these, in so far as they may aid the exegesis, they should set forth in particular the theological doctrine in faith and morals of the individual books or texts so that their exposition may not only aid the professors of theology in their explanations and proofs of the dogmas of faith, but may also be of assistance to priests in their presentation of Christian doctrine to the people, and in fine may help all the faithful to lead a life that is holy and worthy of a Christian.[11]

In large areas of academic biblical studies in the last century, the historical-critical method has been used in a rather exclusive sense, without being sufficiently balanced by a complementary theological method of interpretation.[12] With regard to *Dei Verbum*'s insistence

---

[11] *Divino afflante Spiritu* §24.

[12] See De la Potterie, S.J., "Interpretation of Holy Scripture," 255–257, and Joseph Atkinson, "The Interpenetration of Inspiration and Inerrancy as a Hermeneutic for Catholic Exegesis," *Letter & Spirit* 6 (2010): 191–198. See especially 192n6 in Atkinson, in which he cites the following

that Scripture be "interpreted in the sacred Spirit in which it was written," Ignacio de la Potterie remarks that "strangely enough, after the Council, this remained a dead letter."[13]

Pope Benedict XVI also alluded to this danger of the neglect of the second of the two principles given in *Dei Verbum* §12 in his Apostolic Exhortation, *Verbum Domini* §§34–35:

> While today's academic exegesis, including that of Catholic scholars, is highly competent in the field of historical-critical methodology and its latest developments, it must be said that comparable attention needs to be paid to the theological dimension of the biblical texts....
>
> In this regard we should mention the serious risk nowadays of a dualistic approach to sacred Scripture. To distinguish two levels of approach to the Bible does not in any way mean to separate or oppose them, nor simply to juxtapose them. They exist only in reciprocity. Unfortunately, a sterile separation sometimes creates a barrier between exegesis and theology, and this "occurs even at the highest academic levels." Here I would mention the most troubling consequences, which are to be avoided.
>
> a) First and foremost, if the work of exegesis is restricted to the first level alone, Scripture ends up being *a text belonging only to the past*: "One can draw moral consequences from it, one can learn history, but the Book as such speaks only of the past, and exegesis is no longer truly theological, but becomes

---

works that criticize a unilateral use of the historical-critical method: Claus Westermann, *Genesis 1–11: A Commentary*, trans. John J. Scullion (Minneapolis: Augsburg, 1984), 567–606; Gordon Wenham, *Genesis 1–15*, Word Biblical Commentary 1 (Waco: Word, 1987), xxv–xlv; Yehezkel Kaufmann, *The Religion of Israel: From Its Beginnings to the Babylonian Exile*, trans. Moshe Greenberg (Chicago: University of Chicago Press, 1960); Issac M. Kikawadia and Arthur Quinn, *Before Abraham Was* (Nashville: Abingdon, 1986); and Umberto Cassuto, *A Commentary on the Book of Genesis*, trans. Israel Abrahams (Jerusalem: Magnes, 1961).

[13] De la Potterie, "Biblical Exegesis: A Science of Faith," in *Opening Up the Scriptures: Joseph Ratzinger and the Foundations of Biblical Interpretation*, eds. José Granados, Carlos Granados, and Luis Sanchez-Navarro (Grand Rapids: Eerdmans, 2008), 36; see also 42: "Vatican II opened up new horizons, but they were not taken advantage of or even seen."

pure historiography, history of literature."[14] Clearly, such a reductive approach can never make it possible to comprehend the event of God's revelation through his word, which is handed down to us in the living Tradition and in Scripture.

b) The lack of a hermeneutic of faith with regard to Scripture entails more than a simple absence; in its place there inevitably enters another hermeneutic, a positivistic and secularized hermeneutic ultimately based on the conviction that the Divine does not intervene in human history. According to this hermeneutic, whenever a divine element seems present, it has to be explained in some other way, reducing everything to the human element. This leads to interpretations that deny the historicity of the divine elements.

c) Such a position can only prove harmful to the life of the Church, casting doubt over fundamental mysteries of Christianity and their historicity—as, for example, the institution of the Eucharist and the resurrection of Christ. A philosophical hermeneutic is thus imposed, one which denies the possibility that the Divine can enter and be present within history. The adoption of this hermeneutic within theological studies inevitably introduces a sharp dichotomy between an exegesis limited solely to the first level and a theology tending towards a spiritualization of the meaning of the Scriptures, one which would fail to respect the historical character of revelation. All this is also bound to have a negative impact on the spiritual life and on pastoral activity.

The divine inspiration of Scripture is the basis for the theological principles that must be the principal tools and foundation of biblical interpretation. The human means are presupposed and are necessary, but they must not be allowed to dominate. Otherwise the interpretation will be purely natural, arid, and lacking in piety. If they are not only allowed to dominate, but to conflict with theological principles,

---

[14] Benedict XVI, Intervention at the Fourteenth General Congregation of the Synod, October 14, 2008; see *Insegnamenti di Benedetto XVI*, vol. 4.2 (Rome: Libreria Editrice Vaticana, 2009), 493.

the interpretation will be not only arid but erroneous and reductive.

An exegete must be first and foremost a theologian, even when he makes expert use of history, archeology, and the study of ancient languages. Biblical exegesis is a part of *theology*.[15] The Pontifical Biblical Commission's *The Interpretation of the Bible in the Church* (1993) rightly stresses this point, saying: "Catholic exegesis does not have the right to become lost, like a stream of water, in the sands of a hypercritical analysis."[16] Today not a few exegetes consider exegesis to be a "pre-theological" discipline, which would be basically historical and philological, scientifically neutral and free from presuppositions of faith. This is not the view of the Church!

Historical-Critical Methods of Exegesis

Analytic and Synthetic Methods

In order to interpret Scripture according to *Dei Verbum* §12, various complementary exegetical methods need to be used. Some of these methods are suited to investigate the meaning of the text in accordance with the first principle given there, and these are generally referred to as "historical-critical" methods. Others, such as canonical criticism and attention to Patristic exegesis, are consequences of the second principle.

Methods of biblical criticism, like all rational thought and discourse, involve two distinct procedures: analysis and synthesis. The analytic approach takes apart the biblical text to distinguish different

---

[15] See De la Potterie, S.J., "Interpretation of Holy Scripture," 257: "Exegesis, like theology, seeks to *interpret* the Christian message, but it does so according to its own methods, seeking the meaning of the inspired words, which were written by believers and for believers. Exegesis too is therefore a *fides quaerens intellectum* and must be carried out in faith. And this is maybe the precise point on which one of the greatest ambiguities or misunderstandings exists today."

[16] PBC, *The Interpretation of the Bible in the Church* (1993), in *SD*, 315. See also 314–315: "Through fidelity to the great tradition, of which the Bible itself is a witness, Catholic exegesis should . . . maintain its identity as a *theological discipline*, the principal aim of which is the deepening of faith. This does not mean a lesser involvement in scholarly research of the most rigorous kind, nor should it provide an excuse for abuse of methodology out of apologetic concern. Each sector of research (textual criticism, linguistic study, literary analysis, etc.) has its own proper rules, which it ought follow with full autonomy."

sources and historical stages of development. The synthetic approach seeks to understand the manifold unity of Revelation underlying the differences that have been analyzed. As we shall see, source criticism and form criticism are analytic methods, whereas narrative criticism and especially the canonical approach focus on the synthetic aspect. The narrative approach seeks the unity of purpose in a given literary unit. Canonical criticism looks at the unity of the Bible as a whole as a criterion for interpretation.

The aspects of analysis and synthesis are frequently referred to under another set of terms: diachronic and synchronic. Diachronic refers to an analysis that distinguishes different historical moments of time. Synchronic refers to an approach that bridges or synthesizes what stems from distinct moments of time. Its tendency is synthetic and holistic. Biblical exegesis must always involve the use of both kinds of procedures, analytic (diachronic) and synthetic (synchronic).[17] The Pontifical Biblical Commission gives a good introduction to the various methods used in biblical exegesis in *The Interpretation of the Bible in the Church*.[18] Here we give a brief overview of the most important methods with a few applications.

Textual Criticism

Historical-critical exegesis begins with textual criticism, which has the task of seeking to determine the best reading of the biblical text

---

[17] See the conclusion of *The Interpretation of the Bible* (*SD*, 314) and Paul VI's Address to the Members of the Pontifical Biblical Commission on the Ecclesial Role of Biblical Studies, March 14, 1974 (*SD*, 151).

[18] For a study of this document of the PBC, see Peter Williamson, *Catholic Principles for Interpreting Scripture: A Study of the Pontifical Biblical Commission's The Interpretation of the Bible in the Church* (Rome: Pontifical Biblical Institute, 2001). Paul VI altered the status of the PBC after the Second Vatican Council so that its documents no longer would pertain to ordinary papal Magisterium; rather the Commission now has consultative status as a commission of respected biblical scholars, parallel to the International Theological Commission. See Cardinal Ratzinger's preface to the 1993 document: "The Pontifical Biblical Commission, in its new form after the Second Vatican Council, is not an organ of the Teaching Office, but rather a commission of scholars who, in their scientific and ecclesial responsibility as believing exegetes, take positions on important problems of scriptural interpretation and know that for this task they enjoy the confidence of the Teaching Office" (*SD*, 245).

from among the variants found in different manuscripts that have come down to us from antiquity.[19]

> Textual criticism, as practiced for a very long time, begins the series of scholarly operations. Basing itself on the testimony of the oldest and best manuscripts, as well as of papyri, certain ancient versions, and Patristic texts, textual criticism seeks to establish, according to fixed rules, a biblical text as close as possible to the original.[20]

Literary Criticism in Exegesis

After textual criticism, the historical-critical method analyzes the biblical text from a literary point of view to distinguish distinct literary units and forms. The PBC describes this process:

> It is the role of literary criticism to determine the beginning and end of textual units, large and small, and to establish the internal coherence of the text. The existence of doublets, of irreconcilable differences and of other indicators is a clue to the composite character of certain texts. These can then be divided into small units, the next step being to see whether these in turn can be assigned to different sources.[21]

It is interesting to compare the historical-critical method of literary criticism with the work of "division of the text" in medieval exegesis. In his biblical commentaries, St. Thomas Aquinas begins with a division of the text into different parts and subparts and determines the particular finality of the larger and smaller units.[22] Historical-

---

[19] Key sources for textual criticism include the *Biblia Hebraica Stuttgartensia*, ed. Albrecht Alt et al. (Stuttgart, Germany: Deutsche Bibelstiftung, 1984), and the *Novum Testamentum Graece*, eds. Barbara Aland, Kurt Aland, Eberhard Nestle, and Erwin Nestle, 28th ed. (Stuttgart, Germany: Deutsche Bibelges, 2014).

[20] PBC, *The Interpretation of the Bible* (SD, 252). See Pius XII, *Divino afflante Spiritu* §§17–19.

[21] PBC, *The Interpretation of the Bible* (SD, 252).

[22] See, for example, *Super Evangelium S. Matthaei: Lectura*, Marietti no. 11 (on Matt 1:1), ed. R.

critical exegesis uses literary criticism in large part to establish hypotheses about sources and the historical development of the text. St. Thomas and other scholastics use this method to analyze the text as it currently exists to grasp its inner logic and argumentative and rhetorical structure. In other words, medieval and scholastic analysis used a synchronic approach, whereas historical-critical literary criticism in its classical form works in a primarily diachronic manner.

Genre Criticism

As seen above, *Dei Verbum* §12 and Pius XII, in *Divino afflante Spiritu*, have emphasized the importance of rightly identifying the literary genre of a biblical text, and understanding the literary conventions used in that genre. The PBC explains: "Genre criticism seeks to identify literary genres, the social milieu that gave rise to them, their particular features and the history of their development."[23]

Source Criticism

Source criticism seeks to analyze and identify as far as possible the various sources (oral or written) that can be shown to lie behind or under the canonical text.[24] A problem with this sort of criticism is that results that are quite hypothetical in nature may be presented as if they were more or less certain.[25]

Cai (Turin: Marietti, 1951), 3–4; and *Commentary on the Epistle to the Hebrews*, no. 6, trans. Chrysostom Baer (South Bend: St. Augustine's Press, 2006), 8–9.

[23] PBC, *The Interpretation of the Bible* (SD, 252).

[24] See the definition of source criticism by D. R. Catchpole, "Source, Form and Redaction Criticism of the New Testament," in *Handbook to Exegesis of the New Testament* (Leiden: Brill, 1997), 168: "Source criticism is the process of bringing to light the earlier resources available to an author. Although used conventionally of documents, written resources, and tending to be concerned with literary relationships, there is, it must be said, no reason in principle why it should not include the study of unwritten or oral resources."

[25] See the critique of an unbalanced use of source and form criticism by Joseph Ratzinger in "Biblical Interpretation in Conflict," in *God's Word: Scripture—Tradition—Office*, 92–93: "Thus in opposition to the history depicted, another, 'real' history must be constructed; behind the surviving sources—the books of the Bible—more original sources must be found, which then become the criteria for interpretation. No one can be surprised that in the course of this, hypotheses increasingly branch out and subdivide and finally turn into a jungle full of contradictions. In the

Old Testament Application of Source Criticism

Source criticism with regard to the Old Testament has focused on identifying various sources that are thought to underlie our canonical text. With regard to the Pentateuch, these sources are generally correlated with the use of the divine names—Elohim and YHWH. It is assumed that the different sources of the Pentateuch are distinguished, among other things, by a preference for one or the other of the principal divine names. Other criteria to distinguish different sources are repetition, contrasting viewpoints, and variations in language and style. The hypothetical sources are indicated by letters: J (Jahwist), E (Elohist), P (Priestly), and D (Deuteronomist). This theory of sources of the Pentateuch is often called the "Documentary Hypothesis."[26]

The Jewish biblical scholar Umberto Cassuto, who makes an interesting critique of this theory, gives a good description:

> Until recently, the doctrine known as the Theory of Documents was counted among the strongest edifices of science. Although it was still designated a 'theory' as at the time of its formulation, it seemed as if this, its original character, had been entirely forgotten, and that a kindly fate had saved it from being mortal like other scientific hypotheses. There was not a scholar who doubted that the Torah was compiled in the period of the Second Temple from various documents or sources: one source was J [Jahwist], which used the name YHWH from the beginning of the story of Creation; another source was E [Elohist], according to which the Tetragramma-

---

end, we find out, no longer what the text says, but what it ought to say and to what components it can be traced back."

[26] See PBC, *The Interpretation of the Bible*: "According to this hypothesis, four documents, to some extent parallel with each other, had been woven together: that of the Yahwist (J), that of the Elohist (E), that of the Deuteronomist (D) and that of the priestly author (P); the final editor made use of this latter (priestly) document to provide a structure for the whole" (*SD*, 250). For a classic presentation of this hypothesis, see Martin Noth, *A History of Pentateuchal Traditions*, trans. Bernhard Anderson (Englewood Cliffs: Prentice-Hall, 1972). For a brief summary of its development, see Antony F. Campbell and Mark A. O'Brien, *Sources of the Pentateuch: Texts, Introductions, Annotations* (Minneapolis: Fortress Press, 1993), 1–9.

ton was first revealed to Moses, and hence it employed the designation אֱלֹהִים *'Elohim* in all the narratives preceding the revelation of God to Moses on Mount Horeb; a third was P [Priestly Code], which emanated from priestly circles and also refrained from mentioning the name YHWH before the generation of Moses; there was still a fourth source D, which comprises the main part of the Book of Deuteronomy. It is true that differences of opinion with regard to details were not lacking: one exegete declared this source the earlier and another exegete that source; some attributed a given section or verse to one document and some to another; certain scholars divided a section or verse among the sources in one way and others in another way; there were those who broke down the documents themselves into different strata and others who added new sources to those already mentioned, and so forth. Nevertheless, even though no two scholars held completely identical views, and though these divergences of opinion betrayed a certain inner weakness in the theory as a whole, yet in regard to the basic principles of the hypothesis almost all the expositors were agreed.[27]

Today the classic source theory of the Old Testament has lost much of its former dogmatic acceptance.[28] Part of the reason is that the classical source theory dividing the Pentateuch into various sources has had the effect of fragmenting many biblical narratives, which, according to the theory, would become a kind of collage composed of the interweaving of the hypothetical sources.[29] For example,

---

[27] Umberto Cassuto, *The Documentary Hypothesis and the Composition of the Pentateuch: Eight Lectures*, trans. Israel Abrahams (Jerusalem: Magnes Press, 1961), 6.

[28] See Antony F. Campbell and Mark A. O'Brien, *Rethinking the Pentateuch: Prolegomena to the Theology of Ancient Israel* (Louisville: Westminster John Knox Press, 2005), 5: "The classical documentary hypothesis may be 'broke'; whether it is beyond repair is a question we do not try to answer."

[29] See Campbell and O'Brien, *Sources of the Pentateuch*, 7: "In 1922, Otto Eissfeldt published a synopsis of the sources. . . . The process of compilation as presented by Eissfeldt could only be imagined as that of an author-compiler with four or five scrolls spread out, selecting now a passage from this one, now a passage from another, without any attempt to maintain the character and

in the narrative of the Flood, a division of the sources according to the divine names used would imply an interweaving of the P and J sources, as if an editor took two separate accounts, cut them into pieces and wove them together.[30] If that were the case, how could one explain the marvelous narrative unity and drama of the whole? Furthermore, one of the classic criteria for distinguishing the different sources was repetition in the text. It was held that repetition was an indication that two parallel texts were juxtaposed, creating a reduplication of certain narratives. Repetition, however, is a fundamental feature of the Semitic style of narrative, used to introduce greater solemnity. The repetitions thus are better viewed as elements of style rather than indications of a collage of sources![31] Thus modern synchronic methods focusing on narrative have tended to undermine some of the previous certainty that existed with regard to the sources of the Pentateuch.[32]

A better explanation of the different use of divine names in the Pentateuch, to my mind, is the hypothesis of Umberto Cassuto. He proposes that the two principal divine names—'Elohim and YHWH—have different connotations and serve to reveal and emphasize different divine attributes. The use of different divine names, therefore, does not reveal a difference of documentary sources but rather a difference of connotation and context. The title 'Elohim, like our word "God," is a generic and abstract term for God (or gods), related to the names for God used by other nations surrounding Israel, such as Egypt. The name YHWH (also referred to as the Tetragrammaton), on the other hand, is the name proper to the God who revealed Himself to Moses in the burning bush (see Exod 3:13–15), and then to Israel through Moses. Cassuto writes:

---

integrity of any of the scrolls. As one critic remarked at the time, the publication of such a synopsis would undoubtedly sound the death knell of all source criticism; it revealed in full clarity the absurdity of the process."

[30] See ibid., 25–26 (P source) and 95–97 (J source).

[31] A good example of this is the repetition of the entrance of Noah's family and the animals into the ark, recounted in Gen 6:19–20; 7:1–3; 7:7–9; and 7:13–16. Familiarity with Hebrew style shows this and other similar examples to be quite deliberate and not the accidental result of a process of cutting and pasting.

[32] See ibid., x–xi, 10–19.

The language of the Torah is always scrupulously exact in its minutest details, and it is inconceivable that just in this respect, the most important and exalted, it failed to act with meticulous care and exactitude. We must conclude, therefore, that there is, without doubt, some significance in the changing of the Names. What is it? . . . The designation *'Elohim* was originally a common noun, an appellative, that was applied both to the One God of Israel and to the heathen gods (so, too, was the name *'El*). On the other hand, the name YHWH is a proper noun, the specific name of Israel's God, the God whom the Israelites acknowledged as the Sovereign of the universe and as the Divinity who chose them as His people.[33]

Cassuto holds that the name *'Elohim*, because of its international and abstract character, is used preferentially to speak of God's omnipotence and creative power. The Tetragrammaton, on the other hand, because it is associated with God's concrete intervention in history to save the Israelites from bondage in Egypt, it is the name used preferentially to refer to the divine mercy and God's interventions in salvation history. Cassuto summarizes:

It selected the name YHWH when the text reflects the Israelite conception of God, which is embodied in the portrayal of YHWH and finds expression in the attributes traditionally ascribed to Him by Israel, particularly in His ethical character; it preferred the name *'Elohim* when the passage implies the abstract idea of the Deity prevalent in the international circles of 'wise men'—God conceived as the Creator of the physical universe, as the Ruler of nature, as the Source of life. . . . The name YHWH is employed when God is presented to us in His personal character and in direct relationship to people or nature; and *'Elohim*, when the Deity is alluded to as a Transcendental Being who exists completely outside and above the physical universe.[34]

---

[33] Cassuto, *The Documentary Hypothesis*, 18.

[34] Ibid., 31.

It is interesting to relate Cassuto's analysis of the divine names in the Old Testament to the names given to Jesus and the Father in the New Testament, which Cassuto does not do. We see in the New Testament that the divine title preferentially used to refer to the Son of God is the title *Kyrios* (Κύριος) or "Lord" which is intimately associated with the Tetragrammaton, whereas the Person of the Father is frequently associated with the name *Theos* (θεός).

The Jews, out of reverence for the Tetragrammaton, would substitute the name *Adonai* (Lord), which was read instead of YHWH. When the Pentateuch was translated into the Greek of the Septuagint, the title *Kyrios* was regularly put where the Hebrew had YHWH, whereas Elohim was translated with *Theos*. Thus the fact that *Kyrios*, rather than *Theos*, is associated with Jesus seems to be not insignificant, for the Incarnation of the Son of God is the maximum work of God's mercy, condescension, and salvation.

New Testament Application of Source Criticism: The Synoptic Problem

Source criticism as applied to the New Testament has focused above all on the Synoptic Gospels (Matthew, Mark, and Luke), seeking to establish their literary relationship in what is known as the "Synoptic Problem." The most prominent position over the past century has been the so-called "Two-Source Theory," which holds that the Gospel of Mark is the earliest of the three and that Matthew and Luke were composed on the basis of the Gospel of Mark and another common source of the sayings of Jesus that is supposed to have existed and is referred to in the theological literature by the name of "Q," which stands for *Quelle*, meaning "source" in German.

The PBC document, *Interpretation of the Bible in the Church*, observes that this theory, together with the documentary hypothesis, "retains prominence in scientific exegesis today—though they are also under challenge."[35] The major problem with this theory is

---

[35] PBC, *The Interpretation of the Bible* (SD, 250). For some interesting works on the Synoptic problem that challenge the conventional view of Markan priority and give more weight to the Patristic testimony and the role of the apostolic oral Tradition in the formation of the Gospels,

that it has little foundation in the early testimony of the Fathers of the Church on the writings of the Gospels.

In the context of the condemnation of Modernist errors during the pontificate of St. Pius X, the Pontifical Biblical Commission pronounced on this topic in responses from 1911 and 1912. It stated that, on account of the unanimous weight of the testimony of the Fathers, "the testimony of tradition sufficiently supports the opinion that Matthew wrote before the other Evangelists and that he composed this first Gospel in the native dialect then in use by the Jews of Palestine, for whom this work was intended."[36] It is not necessary, however, to hold that the canonical Greek translation of Matthew was made before the writing of Mark and Luke. Its Greek therefore may show influences from Mark and Luke.[37]

The PBC also stated that, while respecting the traditional Patristic testimony about the order of the Gospels, "it is permissible for exegetes to explain the similarities and dissimilarities between them by disputing freely about the varying and opposing opinions of authors and by appealing to hypotheses of a tradition, written or oral, that proceeded from a single or multiple sources." One should not, however, "easily embrace . . . the 'Two-Source Theory,' which seeks to explain the composition of the Greek Gospel of Matthew and the Gospel of Luke mainly by their common dependence on the Gospel of Mark and on a so-called collection of the sayings of the Lord."[38] The reason

---

see William R. Farmer, *The Gospel of Jesus: The Pastoral Relevance of the Synoptic Problem* (Louisville: Westminster/John Knox Press, 1994); John Rist, *On the Independence of Matthew and Mark* (Cambridge, UK: Cambridge University Press, 1978); and B. C. Butler, *The Originality of St. Matthew: A Critique of the Two-Document Hypothesis* (Cambridge, UK: Cambridge University Press, 1951).

[36] Decree on the Authorship, Date of Composition, and Historicity of the Gospel of Matthew (1911), Second Question (*SD*, 197).

[37] PBC, Response on the Authorship, Date of Composition, and Historicity of the Gospels of Mark and Luke of June 26, 1912, Fifth Question: "Whether, with regard to the chronological order of the Gospels, it is permissible to abandon the claim, supported as it is by the most ancient and perduring testimony of tradition, that, after Matthew, who first of all wrote his Gospel in his own native dialect, Mark wrote second and Luke third; and whether we must regard this traditional claim as opposed to the opinion which asserts that the second and third Gospels were composed before the Greek version of the first Gospel. Response: Negative to both parts" (*SD*, 200).

[38] Ibid., Second Question (*SD*, 202).

that is given is that it does not have sufficient support in tradition or ancient historical sources.

Pope St. Pius X, in a *motu proprio* on the Decisions of the Biblical Commission *Praestantia Scripturae Sacrae* clarified the magisterial character of these responses:

> All are bound in conscience to submit to the decisions of the Biblical Commission, which have been given in the past and shall be given in the future, in the same way as to the Decrees pertaining to doctrine, issued by the Sacred Congregations and approved by the Sovereign Pontiff.[39]

These responses should be regarded therefore as non-definitive ordinary Magisterium of the Church requiring the third grade of assent, which is "religious submission of mind and will." In 1955, the secretary of the PBC, Athanasius Miller, made an important clarification concerning their binding nature:

> The decrees of the Pontifical Biblical Commission have great significance. However, as long as these decrees propose views that are neither immediately or mediately connected with truths of faith and morals, it goes without saying that the interpreter of Sacred Scripture may pursue his scientific research with complete freedom and may utilize the results of these investigations, provided always that he respects the teaching authority of the Church.[40]

---

[39] *SD*, 79.

[40] Ibid., 327. Cardinal Ratzinger also spoke about the provisional nature of some of the material in these responses of the PBC, in reference to the CDF's *Donum veritatis*: "It states—perhaps for the first time with such candor—that there are magisterial decisions which cannot be the final word on a given matter as such but, despite the permanent value of their principles, are chiefly also a signal for pastoral prudence, a sort of provisional policy. Their kernel remains valid, but the particulars determined by circumstances can stand in need of correction. In this connection, one will probably call to mind both the pontifical statements of the last century regarding freedom of religion and the anti-Modernist decisions of the beginning of this century, especially the decisions of the then Biblical Commission"; see *The Nature and Mission of Theology* (San Francisco: Ignatius Press, 1995), 106.

In other words, when it is a matter of a literary or historical question that does not touch either directly or indirectly on truths of the faith, scholars would be free to follow the results of their research and would not be bound by these decrees. It seems, however, that many of these responses concerning the Gospels are at least indirectly concerned with truths of faith. Indeed, the apostolic origin of the Gospels and their true historical character are intimately connected with truths of faith and thus pertain to Catholic doctrine. To the extent that the Synoptic problem is merely a question of literary relationship, then it would seem to be neither directly nor indirectly connected with truths of faith and scholars could freely follow their research. However, different opinions on the Synoptic problem can often have important implications for their apostolic origin and historicity, which do pertain to Catholic doctrine. William Farmer has written:

> We argue that our understanding of Christian faith is vitally affected by the research paradigm we use when we interpret the Gospel texts. Specifically, we argue that the Two-Source Hypothesis, especially in the hands of the Thomas Q school of exegesis, gives us a different Jesus than the Jesus that has been transmitted by the church since the time of the apostles.[41]

Form Criticism

The method of form criticism (*Formgeschichte*) was developed above all by Hermann Gunkel (1862–1932), with regard to the Old Testament, and by Martin Dibelius (1883–1947)[42] and Rudolf Bultmann (1884–1976),[43] with regard to the New Testament, especially the Gospels. The form critics presupposed the work of source criticism

---

[41] Farmer, *The Gospel of Jesus*, 5.

[42] See Martin Dibelius, *From Tradition to Gospel*, trans. Bertram Lee Woolf (New York: Scribner, 1965).

[43] See, above all, his *The History of the Synoptic Tradition*, trans. John Marsh, 2nd edition (New York: Harper & Row, 1968, originally published 1921).

and sought to carry further the work of analysis to show not only the sources of a particular text, but also the modifications the text underwent in the process of its oral development through the influence of the particular needs of the Christian community that transmitted it.[44] Form criticism had the merit of highlighting the oral tradition, principally in the form of preaching, out of which the Gospels were formed. It made the assumption that this oral tradition involved distinct units (*pericopae*) that underwent modification through time according to certain laws of development that form criticism seeks to delineate.[45]

Bultmann defines form criticism at the beginning of his book, *The History of the Synoptic Tradition*. Form criticism, as applied to the Synoptic Gospels, involves

> discovering what the original units of the Synoptics were, both sayings and stories, to try to establish what their historical setting was, whether they belonged to a primary or secondary tradition or whether they were the product of editorial activity.... The following investigation therefore sets out to give an account of the history of the *individual units of the tradition*, and how the tradition passed from a fluid state to the fixed form in which it meets us in the Synoptics.... Form-criticism ... does not consist of identifying the individual units of the tradition according to their aesthetic or other characteristics and placing them in their various categories. It is much rather "to rediscover the origin and the history of the particular units and thereby to throw some light on the history of the tradition before it took literary form." The proper understanding of form-criticism rests upon the judgment that

---

[44] See the description by Catchpole, "Source, Form and Redaction Criticism of the New Testament," 168: "Form criticism recognizes that source material may have been in written form, but that it was not necessarily so. It aims therefore to separate out the distinct units of material that the compilers of the sources selected, to establish the earliest forms of those units, to classify them on the basis of 'family likeness,' and, by the exercise of informed imagination, to posit for each a setting and a purpose in the life of a community."

[45] See Eric Eve, *Behind the Gospels: Understanding the Oral Tradition* (Minneapolis: Fortress Press, 2014), 15–32.

the literature in which the life of a given community, even the primitive Christian community, has taken shape, springs out of quite definite conditions and wants of life from which grows up a quite definite style and quite specific forms and categories.[46]

Bultmann's goal was to trace the history of the development of the Gospel materials as they grew under the influence of the needs of the primitive Christian community in the time intervening between the death of Jesus and the definitive redaction of the Gospels. The method involves seeking to identify the precise context in the life of the primitive Christian community in which a given Gospel text originated (*Sitz im Leben*). Texts are analyzed by their literary type or form, and compared with one another so as to trace out a hypothetical reconstruction of the path of development from the historical Jesus to the Gospel text.[47] Form critics seek to discover "laws" by which oral material about Jesus was progressively transformed and "divinized," with the multiplication of miracles, in the course of the decades from the historical Jesus to the final form of the Gospels.

The comparison of similar literary forms, however, need not be tied to rationalistic presuppositions (such as those used by Bultmann) and can be illuminating in clarifying the intention of the evangelist or sacred writer. The 1964 instruction from the Pontifical Biblical Commission summarizes:

---

[46] *The History of the Synoptic Tradition*, 2–4. Bultmann has quoted Dibelius, from *Theologische Rundschau* 1 (1929): 187.

[47] See the summary of form criticism in an article by Craig A. Evans, "The Life of Jesus," in *Handbook to Exegesis of the New Testament*, ed. Stanley E. Porter, New Testament Tools and Studies 25 (Leiden: Brill, 1997), 433–434: "Form criticism attempts to identify specific literary or sub-literary forms and infer from these forms their function or setting in the life of the early Christian community (i.e. *Sitz im Leben*). It is assumed that the tradition of the life of Jesus was 'minted by the faith of the primitive Christian community in its various stages.' Of the three traditional criticisms, form criticism is the most problematic. It is problematic because, by its very nature, a great deal of subjectivity comes into play. We really do not know what the practices were of first-century Christians who told and retold the sayings of and stories about Jesus. Therefore, we can never be sure of precisely what setting a piece of tradition may reflect."

In appropriate cases the interpreter is free to seek out what sound elements there are in the "method of form-criticism," and these he can duly make use of to gain a fuller understanding of the Gospels. He must be circumspect in doing so, however, because the method in question is often found alloyed with principles of a philosophical or theological nature, which are quite inadmissible, and which not infrequently vitiate both the method itself and the conclusions arrived at regarding literary questions. For certain exponents of this method, led astray by rationalistic prejudices, refuse to admit that there exists a supernatural order, or that a personal God intervenes in the world by revelation properly so called, or that miracles and prophecies are possible and have actually occurred. There are others who have as their starting-point a wrong notion of faith, taking it that faith is indifferent to historical truth and is indeed incompatible with it. Others practically deny *a priori* the historical value and character of the documents of revelation. Others, finally, there are who on the one hand underestimate the authority that the apostles had as witnesses of Christ and the office and influence that they wielded in the primitive community, while on the other hand they overestimate the creative capacity of the community itself. All these aberrations are not only opposed to Catholic doctrine but are also devoid of any scientific foundation and foreign to the genuine principles of the historical method.[48]

A more complete critique of Bultmann's method and presuppositions will be made in the following chapter.

Redaction Criticism

Redaction criticism can be understood as a complementary procedure to source criticism. It puts the emphasis not on the hypothetical

---

[48] Instruction on the Historical Truth of the Gospels *Sancta Mater Ecclesia* (1964), §5 (*SD*, 228–229).

original sources but on the contribution of the final redactor and his theological intentions in molding his sources and composing the biblical text as we have canonically received it.[49] With regard to the Gospels, redaction criticism focuses on the contribution of the four evangelists in shaping the material received through the oral tradition or eyewitnesses. It thus focuses on each Gospel as a whole and seeks to discern the principal theological concerns and themes of the evangelist and his community. Redaction criticism applied to the Synoptic Gospels must presuppose a certain theory of the relationship of the Synoptic Gospels (the Synoptic problem). For example, if one holds that the Gospel of Matthew is based on Mark and Q, then redaction criticism seeks to ascertain how the evangelist modified his sources in Mark and Q. However, since the solution of source criticism to the Synoptic problem is uncertain, redaction criticism rests on an uncertain foundation in that regard.[50]

Newer Synchronic Methods: Rhetorical and Narrative Criticism

The PBC accords great value to the historical-critical method, while recognizing its limitations:

> To be sure, the classic use of the historical-critical method reveals its limitations. It restricts itself to a search for the meaning of the biblical text within the historical circumstances that gave rise to it and is not concerned with other possibilities of meaning which have been revealed at later stages of the biblical revelation and history of the church.[51]

---

[49] See PBC, *The Interpretation of the Bible*: "Eventually, form criticism was supplemented by *redaktionsgeschichte* (redaction criticism), the 'critical study of the process of editing.' This sought to shed light upon the personal contribution of each evangelist and to uncover the theological tendencies which shaped his editorial work" (*SD*, 251).

[50] See Craig Evans, "The Life of Jesus," 441: "Redaction criticism's single greatest vulnerability lies, of course, in whether or not source critics have found the solution to the Synoptic Problem. I have argued above that Markan priority, which is held by most New Testament scholars today, is the most probable solution. If I am wrong, then my redaction-critical judgments are inaccurate and misleading. However, it is redaction criticism itself that lends support to Markan priority."

[51] *The Interpretation of the Bible* (*SD*, 253).

To offset some of these limitations, other complementary methods of exegesis have been developed in recent decades. These methods tend to be more synthetic and synchronic, rather than analytic and diachronic. In the last half-century, many exegetes have given greater attention to the literary aspects of the biblical text, applying methods of literary analysis used also for non-biblical literature.[52]

Rhetorical criticism analyzes the use of classical and Semitic rhetorical literary devices. Rhetoric is the art of making a discourse effective for the purposes of persuasion, and rhetorical criticism seeks to be attentive to the rhetorical elements of biblical texts so as to better understand the intentions of the authors.[53] Many Fathers of the Church, such as Origen, St. John Chrysostom, and St. Jerome, had already been quite attentive to the rhetorical aspect of the biblical text.

Synthetic and Theological Methods of Interpretation

Canonical Criticism

Canonical criticism is an approach to the interpretation of biblical texts that takes very seriously the fact that each is part of an inspired and normative whole that is ultimately one book with one divine Author working through many human authors of diverse times and cultures. This means that each text has meanings that come to it from the unity of the Bible and that would not be evident if it were considered as an isolated text. This approach stems from the second hermeneutical principle given in *Dei Verbum* §12:

> But, since Holy Scripture must be read and interpreted in the sacred spirit in which it was written, no less serious attention must be given to the content and unity of the whole of Scripture if the meaning of the sacred texts is to be correctly worked out. The living tradition of the whole Church must

---

[52] See Hans Frei, *The Eclipse of Biblical Narrative: A Study in Eighteenth and Nineteenth Century Hermeneutics* (New Haven: Yale University Press, 1974), and Mark Allan Powell, *What is Narrative Criticism?* (Minneapolis: Fortress, 1990).

[53] See PBC, *The Interpretation of the Bible* (SD, 254–256).

be taken into account along with the harmony which exists between elements of the faith.

Canonical criticism is a very different exegetical approach from form criticism, source criticism, or redaction criticism.[54] Whereas those methods generally approach the biblical text by way of analysis, division, and the multiplication of hypotheses, canonical criticism begins with the canon of the Bible as a theological unity and seeks to understand how an individual text is illuminated by being understood as a part of the Bible as a whole.[55] Thus its nature is principally synthetic. All biblical typology, to be examined below, presupposes the principle of canonical interpretation.

The Pontifical Biblical Commission speaks of the importance of canonical criticism:

The Dogmatic Constitution *Dei Verbum* (n. 12) and the Post-Synodal Exhortation *Verbum Domini* (nn. 40–41) indicate how only an approach which takes account of the entire canon of Scripture is adequate to unveil its full theological and spiritual sense. Every biblical tradition, in fact, must be interpreted in the canonical context in which it was articulated, which permits one to explain the diachronic and synchronic connections with the entire canon. The canonical approach thus points out the relationships between the traditions of the Old Testament and those of the New Testament.[56]

---

[54] See Bartholomew, Craig, Scott Hahn, Robin Parry, Christopher Seitz, and Al Wolters, eds., *Canon and Biblical Interpretation* (Grand Rapids: Zondervan, 2006). A seminal work in the development of the canonical approach is Brevard Childs, *Biblical Theology in Crisis* (Philadelphia: Westminster, 1970).

[55] See Ignace De la Potterie, "Biblical Exegesis: A Science of Faith," 36: "If it is true that in order to interpret the Bible, we must pay attention to profane literature, we absolutely cannot forget this fundamental principle: even when the sacred writer makes use of modes of expression that prevailed at his time, he uses them according to a new perspective. His thought can never be reduced to that of the profane authors from whom he often drew inspiration. . . . His text takes on a *new sense* in the *new context* of Sacred Scripture."

[56] PBC, in *The Inspiration and Truth of Sacred Scripture: The Word that Comes from God and Speaks of God for the Salvation of the World* (Collegeville: Liturgical Press, 2014), 119–120.

An interesting example of canonical criticism is the comparison of Genesis 3:15 with Revelation 12:1, Galatians 4:4, John 2:4, and John 19:26. All of these texts use the word "woman" in a very significant way to refer to Mary, the Mother of God. Revelation 12:1 puts the woman also in contrast with a dragon (serpent), and with her offspring. This confrontation of these five texts from different epochs and authors, but united in the biblical canon, mutually enriches the meaning of each one. The reference to Mary as "the woman" brings out Mary's identity as the New Eve, in parallel with her son as the New Adam, and alludes to the universal import of her maternal mission. It also shows how God's plan of salvation history is continuous and harmonious from the beginning to the end of salvation history.

Another contribution of a canonical reading of Scripture with respect to Mary is the uncovering of the variety of ways in which Mary is prefigured in the Old Testament, as in the great mothers who are naturally barren but fruitful according to the promise (Sarah and Hannah), the women of valor such as Judith and Esther, the personification of Israel as the "daughter of Zion" or the "virgin Israel," and finally the figure of Wisdom.[57]

Connection of the Old and New Testaments

Canonical interpretation is most significant in bringing out the connection between the Old and New Testaments and how they mutually enrich each other when the Bible is read as a unity.[58] Benedict XVI speaks about this in *Verbum Domini* §41:

---

[57] See the excellent studies on Mary prefigured in the Old Testament by Joseph Ratzinger, *Daughter Zion*, trans. John M. McDermott (San Francisco: Ignatius Press, 1983), and Ignace De la Potterie, *Mary in the Mystery of the Covenant*, trans. Bertrand Buby (New York: Alba House, 1992). See also Feingold, *The Mystery of Israel and the Church*, vol. 1, *Figure and Fulfillment* (St. Louis: The Miriam Press, 2010), 191–200.

[58] See Scott Hahn, *Covenant and Communion: The Biblical Theology of Pope Benedict XVI* (Grand Rapids: Brazos Press, 2009), 100–106.

"The New Testament is hidden in the Old and the Old is made manifest in the New,"[59] as Saint Augustine perceptively noted. It is important, therefore, that in both pastoral and academic settings the close relationship between the two Testaments be clearly brought out, in keeping with the dictum of Saint Gregory the Great that "what the Old Testament promised, the New Testament made visible; what the former announces in a hidden way, the latter openly proclaims as present. Therefore the Old Testament is a prophecy of the New Testament; and the best commentary on the Old Testament is the New Testament."

An interesting example of the canonical approach to Scripture is found in Joseph Ratzinger's *Jesus of Nazareth: The Infancy Narratives*, in which he speaks of certain Old Testament texts as "words in waiting"[60] for the future context that will unlock their meaning. With regard to the prophecy of the virgin birth and the Emmanuel in Isaiah 7:14, he reviews the attempts made by recent scholarship to identify explanations of the text that would have been intelligible at the time of King Ahaz in which the prophecy was given and concludes that these efforts have failed:

So what are we to say? The passage about the virgin who gives birth to Emmanuel, like the great Suffering Servant song in Is 53, is a word in waiting. There is nothing in its own historical context to correspond to it. So it remains an open question: it is addressed not merely to Ahaz. Nor is it addressed merely to Israel. It is addressed to humanity. The sign that God himself announces is given not for a specific political situation, but it concerns the whole history of humanity.

Should Christians not hear this word as their own? On

---

[59] St. Augustine, *Quaestiones in heptateuchum* 2.73 (PL, 34:623).

[60] See also Ratzinger, *Feast of Faith: Approaches to a Theology of the Liturgy*, trans. Graham Harrison (San Francisco: Ignatius Press, 1986), 67, in which the Jewish Passover is spoken of in this way as "waiting" for an enlargement of its meaning given by Jesus at the Last Supper.

listening to this verse, should they not come to the conviction that the message which always seemed so strange, waiting to be deciphered, has now come true? Should they not be convinced that God has now given us this sign in the birth of Jesus from the Virgin Mary? Emmanuel has come. . . . I believe that in our own day, after all the efforts of critical exegesis, we can share anew this sense of astonishment at the fact that a saying from the year 733 B.C., incomprehensible for so long, came true at the moment of the conception of Jesus Christ.[61]

Use of Patristic Exegesis

The second theological principle given by *Dei Verbum* §12 directs us not only to recognize the unity of Scripture, with God as its primary author, but also to read the text in the light of the Tradition of the Church. In particular, the Fathers of the Church are an irreplaceable source. Biblical exegesis always needs to be nourished by the wisdom of Fathers.[62] The Council of Trent taught that the teaching of the consensus of the Fathers of the Church on the interpretation of Scripture is binding for theology[63] because such a consensus demonstrates apostolic Tradition and the ordinary and universal Magisterium. Even when there is not properly a consensus, the Fathers are a uniquely important source for biblical interpretation, as Leo XIII emphasizes in *Providentissimus Deus* §14:

The Holy Fathers "to whom, after the Apostles, the Church owes its growth—who have planted, watered, built, gov-

---

[61] *Jesus of Nazareth: The Infancy Narratives*, trans. Philip J. Whitmore (New York: Image, 2012), 50–51.

[62] For Patristic exegesis, see Manlio Simonetti, *Biblical Interpretation in the Early Church: An Historical Introduction to Patristic Exegesis*, trans. John A. Hughes (Edinburgh: T&T Clark, 1994), and Bertrand de Margerie, *An Introduction to the History of Exegesis*, 3 volumes (Petersham, MA: Saint Bede's, 1991–1995).

[63] Council of Trent, Session 4 (April 8, 1546): "No one may dare to interpret the Scripture in a way contrary to the unanimous consensus of the Fathers" (DS, 1507)

erned, and cherished it,"[64] the Holy Fathers, We say, are of supreme authority, whenever they all interpret in one and the same manner any text of the Bible, as pertaining to the doctrine of faith or morals; for their unanimity clearly evinces that such interpretation has come down from the Apostles as a matter of Catholic faith. The opinion of the Fathers is also of very great weight when they treat of these matters in their capacity of doctors, unofficially; not only because they excel in their knowledge of revealed doctrine and in their acquaintance with many things which are useful in understanding the apostolic Books, but because they are men of eminent sanctity and of ardent zeal for the truth, on whom God has bestowed a more ample measure of His light. Wherefore the expositor should make it his duty to follow their footsteps with all reverence, and to use their labors with intelligent appreciation.

Pius XII is no less eloquent in calling for exegetes to be steeped in the biblical interpretation of the Fathers:

In the accomplishment of this task the Catholic exegete will find invaluable help in an assiduous study of those works in which the Holy Fathers, the Doctors of the Church and the renowned interpreters of past ages have explained the Sacred Books. For, although sometimes less instructed in profane learning and in the knowledge of languages than the scripture scholars of our time, nevertheless by reason of the office assigned to them by God in the Church, they are distinguished by a certain subtle insight into heavenly things and by a marvelous keenness of intellect, which enables them to penetrate to the very innermost meaning of the divine word and bring to light all that can help to elucidate the teaching of Christ and to promote holiness of life. It is indeed regrettable

---

[64] St. Augustine, *Against Julian* 2.10.37.

that such precious treasures of Christian antiquity are almost unknown to many writers of the present day.[65]

He expresses the hope that contemporary biblical scholarship will be able to forge a fruitful synthesis capable of bringing together Patristic insights with the greater erudition in historical and literary matters made possible by modern historical-critical studies:

> Would that many, by seeking out the authors of the Catholic interpretation of Scripture and diligently studying their works and drawing thence the almost inexhaustible riches therein stored up, might contribute largely to this end, so that it might be daily more apparent to what extent those authors understood and made known the divine teaching of the Sacred Books, and that the interpreters of today might thence take example and seek suitable arguments. For thus at long last will be brought about the happy and fruitful union between the doctrine and spiritual sweetness of expression of the ancient authors and the great erudition and more refined knowledge of the moderns.[66]

Dei Verbum §23 also mentions the need for exegetes to draw from the wealth of the Fathers of East and West and also of the liturgy. Liturgical texts, like the writings of the Fathers, are witnesses of the Tradition and make much use of Sacred Scripture, revealing its inner depths.

Benedict XVI also refers to the importance of the Fathers in exegesis in *Verbum Domini* §37:

> A significant contribution to the recovery of an adequate scriptural hermeneutic, as the synodal assembly stated, can also come from renewed attention to the Fathers of the Church and their exegetical approach. The Church Fathers present a

---

[65] *Divino afflante Spiritu* §28–29.

[66] Ibid. §29.

theology that still has great value today because at its heart is the study of sacred Scripture as a whole. Indeed, the Fathers are primarily and essentially "commentators on sacred Scripture."[67] Their example can "teach modern exegetes a truly religious approach to sacred Scripture, and likewise an interpretation that is constantly attuned to the criterion of communion with the experience of the Church, which journeys through history under the guidance of the Holy Spirit."

Exegetical Methods Are to Be Used to Deepen Theological Insight

In accordance with *Dei Verbum* §12, the various methods that make up historical-critical exegesis should never be used in isolation from theological principles and should deepen theological reflection. In *Sancta Mater Ecclesia*, the PBC gives the following recommendation to those who teach Scripture in the seminary:

> Professors should make theological doctrine the main subject-matter of their exposition, so that the Sacred Scriptures "may become for future priests of the Church a pure and never-failing source of spiritual life for themselves and of nourishment and vigor for the office of sacred preaching which they are to undertake." Professors, when they make use of critical methods, especially of what is called literary criticism, should not do so for the mere sake of criticism but with a view to gaining by means of it a *deeper insight into the sense intended by God speaking through the sacred writer.* They should not stop halfway, therefore, resting on the discoveries they have made from the literary point of view, but should go on to show how such findings make a real contribution towards the better understanding of revealed doctrine or, if occasion arises, towards the refutation of misleading views. By following these

---

[67] Cf. St. Augustine, *De libero arbitrio* 3.21.59 (PL, 32:1300), and *De Trinitate* 2.1.2 (PL, 42:845).

guiding principles, teachers will ensure that their pupils find in Sacred Scripture themes of a nature "to raise their minds to God, nourish their souls and foster their interior life."[68]

Study Questions

1. Explain the two principles of biblical interpretation given in *Dei Verbum* §12.
2. Explain the relationship between these two principles and the Incarnation.
3. Explain how overly unilateral attention to one or the other of these principles of interpretation is detrimental to a right understanding of Revelation (and how this would be analogous with Christological heresies).
4. Why is textual criticism important?
5. Give a description of the various historical-critical methods and explain their complementarity and potential shortcomings.
6. What is canonical criticism and how is it related to the principles of interpretation given in *Dei Verbum* §12?
7. Why must biblical interpretation make use of Patristic interpretation?

Suggestions for Further Reading

Dei Verbum §12.
Pope Pius XII. Encyclical Letter Promoting Biblical Studies *Divino afflante Spiritu*. September 30, 1943.

---

[68] *Sancta Mater Ecclesia* §12 (SD, 232–233). See also Pius XII, *Divino afflante Spiritu* §54, on the biblical courses that should be given in seminaries: "Hence their exegetical explanation should aim especially at the theological doctrine, avoiding useless disputations and omitting all that is calculated rather to gratify curiosity than to promote true learning and solid piety. The literal sense and especially the theological let them propose with such definiteness, explain with such skill and inculcate with such ardor that in their students may be in a sense verified what happened to the disciples on the way to Emmaus, when, having heard the words of the Master, they exclaimed: 'Was not our heart burning within us, whilst He opened to us the Scriptures?'"

Pope Benedict XVI. Post-synodal Apostolic Exhortation On the Word of God in the Life and Mission of the Church *Verbum Domini*. September 30, 2010.

Ratzinger, Joseph. "Biblical Interpretation in Conflict." In *God's Word: Scripture—Tradition—Office*, 91–126. Edited by Peter Hünermann and Tomas Söding. Translated by Henry Taylor. San Francisco: Ignatius Press, 2008.

De la Potterie, Ignace, S.J. "Biblical Exegesis: A Science of Faith," in *Opening Up the Scriptures: Joseph Ratzinger and the Foundations of Biblical Interpretation*, 30–64. Edited by José Granados, Carlos Granados, and Luis Sanchez-Navarro. Grand Rapids: Eerdmans, 2008.

———. "Interpretation of Holy Scripture in the Spirit in Which It Was Written (*Dei Verbum* 12c)." In *Vatican II Assessment and Perspectives: Twenty-five Years After (1962–1987)*, 1:220–266. New York: Paulist, 1988.

Pontifical Biblical Commission. *The Interpretation of the Bible in the Church*. Vatican City: Libreria Editrice Vaticana, 1993.

Simonetti, Manlio. *Biblical Interpretation in the Early Church: An Historical Introduction to Patristic Exegesis*. Translated by John A. Hughes. Edinburgh: T&T Clark, 1994.

PART 5

Historicity of the Gospels

CHAPTER THIRTEEN

Was Christ's Claim a Myth? Challenge to the Historicity of the Gospels

A particular application of the debate about the truth of Scripture is the question of the historical truth of the Gospels. This has crucial importance for Fundamental Theology, for Christ is the center and culmination of divine Revelation. The entire Christian faith rests upon the four Gospels and their historical witness of the life of Christ. For the Gospels contain Christ's claim to be God (made in a great variety of ways), the witness of His Passion and Resurrection, His teaching and the miracles that confirm them, His founding His Kingdom on the Apostles, and the institution of the sacraments.[1]

We will examine this question in three parts: (a) the challenge to the historicity of the Gospels on the part of many biblical scholars, exemplified by Rudolf Bultmann and the Catholic Modernists such as Alfred Loisy, (b) the apostolic origin of the Gospels, and (c) the Magisterium's defense of the historicity of the Gospels and arguments of reason to support the Magisterium's claims.

---

[1] See Leo XIII, Encyclical Letter on the Study of Holy Scripture *Providentissimus Deus* §17: "But since the divine and infallible *magisterium* of the Church rests also on the authority of Holy Scripture, the first thing to be done [by exegetes] is to vindicate the trustworthiness of the sacred records at least as human documents, from which can be clearly proved, as from primitive and authentic testimony, the Divinity and the mission of Christ our Lord, the institution of a hierarchical Church and the primacy of Peter and his successors."

The importance of the question is evident. When the historicity of the Gospels is put into doubt, the entire edifice of Christian faith and prayer is undermined. Concerning the multitude of attempts to give us a picture of the historical Jesus significantly different from that in the Gospels, Pope Benedict XVI highlights the drama of our current situation:

> All these attempts have produced a common result: the impression that we have very little certain knowledge of Jesus and that only at a later stage did faith in his divinity shape the image we have of him. This impression has by now penetrated deeply into the minds of the Christian people at large. This is a dramatic situation for faith, because its point of reference is being placed in doubt: Intimate friendship with Jesus, on which everything depends, is in danger of clutching at thin air.[2]

The Trilemma Concerning Christ's Identity

We have seen that many thinkers in the Enlightenment rejected the possibility of miracles and prophecy, excluding God's direct action in the world and the supernatural order. Since a great number of miracles are recounted in the Gospels, as well as the most supernatural actions of all—the Incarnation of the Son and His Resurrection from the dead—it is not surprising that the historical character of the Gospels has been the subject of intense attack over the past 250 years.

Another way to look at the attack on the historicity of the Gospels is to see it as a way of trying to escape or blunt the power of Christ's claim to divinity. This claim is simply "the most shocking thing that has ever been uttered by human lips."[3] As the crowds in Jerusalem said: "No man ever spoke like this man" (John 7:46).

---

[2] Joseph Ratzinger, *Jesus of Nazareth: From the Baptism in the Jordan to the Transfiguration*, trans. Adrian J. Walker (New York: Doubleday, 2007), xii.

[3] C. S. Lewis, *Mere Christianity* (San Francisco: Harper, 2001), 51.

The Divine Claim

The Gospels show us that Christ made a claim to divine identity in a great many different ways. The most common form is through Jesus's miracles, which involve an implicit divine claim not from the mere fact of the miracles themselves, but from the fact that they are not attributed to the power of another. From the beginning of His public ministry, Jesus works miracles in His own name, unlike the prophets of the Old Testament and unlike the Apostles. This can be seen in the cleansing of the leper related in Mark 1:40–41 (Matt 8:2–3). The leper says to Him: "If you will, you can make me clean." Jesus "stretched out his hand and touched him, and said to him, 'I will; be clean.'" Jesus thus attributes the miracle to His own power and His own will.

In the Sermon on the Mount, Jesus presents himself as Legislator of the moral law when He uses the following formula five times to proclaim a moral truth: "You have heard that it was said ... but I say to you."[4] Cardinal Ratzinger observed that "the Sermon on the Mount is in many respects the clearest expression of his claim to divinity,"[5] for He does not merely place Himself on a level with Moses, but with the divine Legislator Himself. Moses never said, "*I* say unto you," but rather he told the people "the words which the Lord had commanded him" (Exod 19:7).[6] No prophet of Israel could speak as Jesus spoke in the Sermon on the Mount. The prophets always prefaced their inspired teaching by calling attention to the fact that it was not their word, but God's: "The word of the Lord came to me";[7] "Thus says the Lord";[8] "The Lord says";[9] "The Lord said to me";[10] or "Hear the word of the Lord."[11] Jesus never uses those formulas, but says rather, "*I* say to you."

---

[4] Matt 5:22; 5:32; 5:34; 5:39; and 5:44.

[5] Ratzinger, *God and the World: A Conversation with Peter Seewald* (San Francisco: Ignatius Press, 2002), 282.

[6] See Exod 35:1; 24:3; Deut 5:5; etc.

[7] See, for example, Ezek 30:1; 33:1; 34:1; Jer 6:22; 16:1; 32:6; Hos 1:1; and Joel 1:1.

[8] See, for example, Ezek 34:11; Jer 15:19; 19:1; 25:32; 31:15, 16, 23, 35, and 37; and Amos 1:6.

[9] See, for example, Isa 1:24 and Ezek 30:10.

[10] See, for example, Jer 14:11.

[11] Ezek 34:7.

Just as John the Baptist proclaimed Jesus as the "Lamb of God who takes away the sins of the world," so too Jesus proclaims that He has the power to forgive sins. This first appears with the miracle of the paralytic narrated in Mark 2:3–12, Matthew 9:2–8, and Luke 5:18–26. Who can forgive sins but God Himself, as the rightly scandalized Pharisees observe? For only the offended party has the right to forgive an offense.[12] And yet, who could doubt the historicity of the unforgettable account of the synoptic Gospels about the cure of the paralytic lowered on a stretcher through the roof? Jesus backed up his claim to forgive sins with the miracle of the man's cure before a huge crowd. In the same way, He proclaimed that the sins of the woman in the house of Simon the Pharisee were forgiven (Luke 7:47–49), scandalizing those present, who say, "Who is this, who even forgives sins?"

Furthermore, Jesus demands faith in His person parallel to faith in God. When the crowds asked Him how they could do the works of God, Jesus replies, "This is the work of God, that you believe in him whom he has sent" (John 6:29). Again, at the Last Supper, He says (John 14:1), "Believe in God, believe also in me." No prophet had ever spoken like this, demanding belief in himself on a par with God. In fact, the phrase "to believe *in*,"[13] properly speaking, can only be directed to God Himself, for it implies not only a belief in his word, but a motion of hope towards the one believed in.[14] Indeed, Jesus promises eternal life to those who believe *in Him*, repeating this six times in the Gospel of John.[15]

In various ways, Christ claims a love and allegiance from man that is proper to God alone. For example, He says: "He who loves father or mother more than me is not worthy of me" (Matt 10:37). Only God can claim this from us.[16]

---

[12] Lewis develops this point very eloquently in *Mere Christianity* (51–52).

[13] It seems that this expression, which occurs frequently in the Gospel of John, was not common earlier in classical Greek or in the Septuagint.

[14] See St. Thomas Aquinas, *ST* II-II, q. 2, a. 2.

[15] John 3:15 and 36; 5:24; 6:47; 7:38; and 11:25–26.

[16] See also Luke 12:8–9: "And I tell you, every one who acknowledges me before men, the Son of man also will acknowledge before the angels of God; but he who denies me before men will be denied before the angels of God." See also Matt 10:32–33. On this point, see John McDermott,

At various times, Jesus upbraids His contemporaries for failing to recognize Him by comparing Himself with past prophets and sages, saying that something greater is here present. For example, in Matthew 12:41–42, He says: "The men of Nineveh will arise at the judgment with this generation and condemn it; for they repented at the preaching of Jonah, and behold, something greater than Jonah is here. The queen of the South will arise at the judgment with this generation and condemn it; for she came from the ends of the earth to hear the wisdom of Solomon, and behold, something greater than Solomon is here."

He also says that "something greater than the Temple is here" (Matt 12:6), and that "the Son of man is lord of the Sabbath" (Matt 12:8). Could Moses or Solomon have said that they were "lord of the Sabbath" or "greater than the Temple"? It is unthinkable. That is only proper to God, in Whose honor the Sabbath is celebrated and the Temple consecrated. Just as Christ is superior to Jonah and Solomon, so He is superior to the angels and to all the elect, for the angels minister to Him, and He speaks of them as "His angels," "His elect": "He [the Son of man] will send out *his angels* with a loud trumpet call, and they will gather *his elect* from the four winds."[17] Only one who is God can speak of the angels and the elect in this way.

Christ also presents Himself as the future judge of mankind. The power to judge all men and nations presupposes a fullness of authority over all nations. Who can claim the power to judge all of mankind and all of history, but God alone?[18] By presenting Himself as the judge, Christ is presenting Himself as God. This is apparent

---

S.J., "Didn't Jesus Know He Was God? Mark 10:17–22," *Irish Theological Quarterly* 73 (2008): 322.

[17] Matt 24:31. See also Matt 13:41. That Christ is the Lord of the angels is also implied in John 1:51, in which He says to Nathanael: "Truly, truly, I say to you, you will see heaven opened, and the angels of God ascending and descending upon the Son of man."

[18] See, for example, Pss 50:4 and 96:13. See the PBC, *Inspiration and Truth of Sacred Scripture: The Word that Comes from God and Speaks of God for the Salvation of the World*, (Collegeville: Liturgical Press, 2014)29: "According to the Synoptic Gospels, the strict relationship of Jesus with God is manifested not only in the fact that the life of Jesus is the fulfillment of the history of God with Israel, but also in the fact that the whole of history is brought to its fulfillment through Jesus's return in glory."

also in His response to Caiaphas at His trial before the Sanhedrin.

When Christ proclaims that He, the Son of man, will be the judge of all peoples and nations, he also proclaims that every act of charity done to any human person is reckoned as an act of charity to Himself that will be eternally rewarded; and, on the contrary, every act against charity to any human person is an offense to Christ Himself and will be punished accordingly.[19] No one else in history has ever made any claim remotely like this. Hence, this criterion that Christ gives for the Last Judgment is itself a proclamation of His divinity.

Although Jesus's preferred way of speaking of Himself is as the "Son of man," He sometimes simply refers to Himself as "the Son" of the Father,[20] and accepts the title, "Son of God," in Peter's confession,[21] in His trial before Caiaphas,[22] and before the Sanhedrin.[23] It could be objected that this title is not unique to Jesus and thus does not directly indicate His divinity, for we too are said to be "sons of God," and "gods." However, it is clear that Christ claims to be the Son of God in a different way than we are. We are sons in the plural and without a definite article, whereas He is *the Son*."[24] In other words, each of us is *a* son of God by participation in His unique Sonship. Catholic theology expresses this by saying that Christ is the *natural* Son of the Father, whereas we are *adopted* sons through Christ. He is the "only-begotten son who is in the bosom of the Father" (John 1:18), whereas we are *sons in the Son*. Furthermore, in Matthew 11:27–29, Jesus not only refers to Himself as "the Son," but puts himself on the level of reciprocal intimacy of knowledge with the Father. By saying that no one knows the Son except the Father, and vice versa, He implicitly says that He is consubstantial with the Father. For, like the Father, He transcends all creaturely knowledge.[25]

---

[19] In Matt 25:31–46.

[20] Matt 11:27 and Luke 10:22. Jesus also implicitly signifies that He is the Son of the Father in the parable of the wicked husbandmen in Matt 21:37.

[21] Matt 16:16.

[22] Matt 26:63–64 and Mark 14:61–62.

[23] Luke 22:70.

[24] See Mark 13:32.

[25] See St. Thomas Aquinas, *Super Evangelium S. Matthaei*, lec. 11.27 (Rome: Marietti, 1951), no.

After the Last Supper, the Apostle Thomas tells Jesus that they do not know where Jesus is going, nor do they know the way. Jesus responds: "I am the way, and the truth, and the life; no one comes to the Father, but by me" (John 14:6). By saying that He is the truth and the life, Jesus is clearly professing His divinity. Creatures participate in truth and life. We say that we "have" life and that we possess some truths. Only God *is* the truth and the life, such that He sums up in Himself all truth and life and is its infinite source and exemplar. Jesus is the "way" because He is the truth and the life. He leads to the Father because He is the same infinite life and truth as the Father. Hence He can say, "no one comes to the Father but by me." In the same way, Jesus can say that He is "the resurrection and the life" (John 11:25). He *is* the resurrection only because He is the infinite life of God that gives life to all creatures.

Another clear claim to divinity can be seen in Jesus's not infrequent use of the phrase, "I am," which is emphasized in the Gospel of John.[26] This is clearly an allusion to the solemn title of God revealed to Moses in the burning bush: "I am who am" (Exod 3:14).[27] In John 8:24, Jesus says, "I told you that you would die in your sins, for you will die in your sins unless you believe that *I am he*."[28] A few verses later, He says, "when you have lifted up the Son of man, then you will know that *I am he*, and that I do nothing on my own authority but

---

965. See also Reginald Garrigou-Lagrange, *Our Savior and His Love for Us* (Rockford: TAN Books, 1998), 20–21.

[26] See the discussion of this theme in Ratzinger, *Jesus of Nazareth: Baptism in the Jordan to the Transfiguration*, 345–352.

[27] God also uses the "I am" with great solemnity in Deut 32:39: "See now that I, even *I, am he*, and there is no god beside me." The preceding verses offer no antecedent for the masculine third-person pronoun. The Hebrew phrase here is "*ani hu*" (literally, "I he"—the "am" is understood). It seems reasonable to think that, when Jesus used the "I am" formula, He was using the Aramaic version of "*ani hu*." The same form appears in Isa 43:10 (again, with no antecedent): "'You are my witnesses,' says the Lord, 'and my servant whom I have chosen, that you may know and believe me and understand that *I am He*. Before me no god was formed, nor shall there be any after me.'" See also Isa 43:13: "I am God, and also henceforth *I am He*; there is none who can deliver from my hand"; and 51:12: "I, *I am he* that comforts you."

[28] The Greek text is ἐγώ εἰμι, which could be translated simply: "I am." Jesus seems to be making reference to Isa 43:25, where God says: "I, *I am He* who blots out your transgressions for my own sake, and I will not remember your sins."

speak thus as the Father taught me. And he who sent me is with me" (John 8:28–29). Here Jesus is saying that the people will recognize His divine identity only after He has been lifted up on the Cross. Another example occurs as the Apostles see Jesus walking on the water in John 6:20. He says to them: "It is I [*ego eimi*]; do not be afraid." This expression also occurs in John 18:6, when the Temple guards came to Gethsemane to capture Jesus: "When he said to them, 'I am he,' they drew back and fell to the ground."[29] In both cases, the solemn "I am" is coupled with a prodigious miracle. Perhaps the strongest use of the phrase, "I am," occurs in John 8:58, when He says, "Before Abraham was, I am." Thus He claims to have always existed in the eternal present proper to God. No other historical figure has ever made such a statement.

Finally, Jesus claimed that to see Him was to see the invisible Father. The most explicit statement He made in this regard was after the Last Supper, in response to Philip's request: "Lord, show us the Father, and we shall be satisfied." Jesus replied, "Have I been with you so long, and yet you do not know me, Philip? He who has seen me has seen the Father; how can you say, 'Show us the Father'? Do you not believe that I am in the Father and the Father in me?" (John 14:8–10). Jesus's humanity reveals the Father because it is the humanity of the Son, who is in the Father, and in whom is the Father. No other man has ever claimed anything remotely similar. Earlier, in John 10:30, He had proclaimed, "I and the Father are one." Christ and the Father are one in divinity, and thus Christ's humanity reveals the Father. Not surprisingly, the crowd tried to stone Him. Although Jesus's oneness with the Father is most explicitly proclaimed in these texts from John, it nevertheless is implicit throughout Christ's public ministry in all the Gospels, as seen above.

In all of these very different ways Jesus makes a divine claim, not by directly saying that He is God, but in more subtle, striking, natural, and unforgettable ways He reveals His oneness with the Father.

---

[29] Other emphatic examples of this phrase occur in John 4:26; 6:20; 8:24, 28, and 58; 13:19; and 18:5, 8; and in Mark 6:50 and 14:62.

It is not something He said once or twice. In order to eliminate Jesus's divine claim, one would have to tear out most of the pages of the Gospels.

Trilemma

This divine claim leads every person who thinks about it to a dilemma—or better, a trilemma (that is, a choice between three difficult alternatives). Either Christ was what He said He was, or he was mad, or He was something worse than a liar. C. S. Lewis formulates this crucial point with brilliance in his great work of apologetics, *Mere Christianity*. He says:

> I am trying here to prevent anyone saying the really foolish thing that people often say about Him: 'I'm ready to accept Jesus as a great moral teacher, but I don't accept His claim to be God.' That is the one thing we must not say. A man who was merely a man and said the sort of things Jesus said would not be a great moral teacher. He would either be a lunatic— on a level with the man who says he is a poached egg—or else he would be the Devil of Hell. You must make your choice. Either this man was, and is, the Son of God, or else a madman or something worse. You can shut Him up for a fool, you can spit at Him and kill Him as a demon; or you can fall at His feet and call Him Lord and God. But let us not come with any patronizing nonsense about His being a great human teacher. He has not left that open to us. He did not intend to.[30]

The Gospels clearly do not leave us the option of Christ's being a lunatic, although this charge was sometimes made.[31] The true alternatives are between Christ being God as He claimed to be, or being the greatest offense to God in human history precisely because

---

[30] Lewis, *Mere Christianity*, 52.

[31] See John 10:20: "Many of them said, 'He has a demon, and he is mad; why listen to him?'"

He claimed to be God. This was the way the situation was framed at Christ's trial in which He was condemned for His claim.[32]

View of Modernism and Rudolf Bultmann: Christ's Claim Is a Myth

There is a fourth alternative to C. S. Lewis's trilemma that has gained the favor of many of our contemporaries and thus needs to be dealt with in a special way in our times. The trilemma is dismissed by holding that the historical Jesus never made an explicit claim to divinity and that the texts that impose this triple alternative on us have legendary elements that are the product of a kind of transfiguration of the figure of Jesus.[33] Thus the Jesus of history, who never claimed to be God, is separated from the Christ of faith, who is the invention of the early Christian community. This would convert the trilemma into a *quadrilemma* (choice between four difficult alternatives). Either (a) Christ's divine claim is true, or (b) he is a madman, or (c) a liar, or (d) he never made a divine claim and the texts which transmit this claim are the fruit of a legendary transfiguring development.[34]

The last option is the position of many biblical scholars of the rationalist school of the nineteenth and twentieth centuries, such as David Friedrich Strauss, the Modernist movement in the Catholic Church condemned by St. Pius X as the "synthesis of all heresies,"[35] Rudolf Bultmann, and the Jesus Seminar.[36] Why do they hold this position?

---

[32] This was also the position of pagan opponents of Christianity, such as Celsus, who wrote a book against Christianity in about AD 180, *The True Doctrine*, which was massively refuted in the mid-third century by Origen, in his *Against Celsus*. For Celsus, Jesus possessed magical powers that he learned in Egypt, and on the strength of these, "gave himself out to be a god" (*Contra Celsum* 1.28); in *Against Celsus*, trans. Henry Chadwick (Cambridge: University Press, 1965), 28.

[33] See Pope St. Pius X's analysis of the Modernist understanding of the presentation of Jesus in the Gospels, in his Encyclical Letter on the Doctrines of the Modernists *Pascendi dominici gregis* (1907), §§9 and 30.

[34] See Craig L. Blomberg, *The Historical Reliability of the Gospels* (Downer's Grove: IVP Academic, 2007), 22.

[35] *Pascendi dominici gregis* §39. See also Holy Office, Decree Condemning Certain Errors of the Modernists *Lamentabili sane* (1907).

[36] See Robert W. Funk, Roy W. Hoover, and the Jesus Seminar, *The Five Gospels: The Search for the*

The answer seems clear: in order to escape the force of the trilemma. Indeed, the Modernist understanding of Christ has basically been an attack on the logic of these three alternatives. Previous opponents of Christ's claim did not deny that He made the claim, but held that the claim was false and He was a blasphemer. The novelty of Modernism is that it is an attack on the very fact of Christ's divine claim, made from within the Church by those who accept the New Testament as the Word of God. These theologians deny that He was a blasphemer and defend His goodness, while rejecting the idea that He made any claim to divinity at all! Oddly enough, many theologians who hold that Jesus never made a divine claim do not reject the divine claim itself and have no difficulty with the Nicene Creed. What they reject is the belief that Christ made the divine claim that the Gospels attribute to Him. Why?

Starting in the Enlightenment, many intellectuals began to reject all notion of supernatural intervention of God in history. God Himself was not rejected at first; He was turned into a clockmaker God who created the world but, once the laws of nature were established, is left with His hands bound, unable or unwilling to intervene in the order He has created. Such a view of God is known as Deism, which stems from a rationalist philosophy. It is obvious that, in such a context, where God cannot intervene in the world, the Incarnation of Christ becomes impossible and incomprehensible. However, because of the force of established piety, rather than simply rejecting Christianity, many thinkers in the eighteenth, nineteenth, and twentieth centuries sought to accommodate Christianity to a "religion within the bounds of pure reason." In order to fit the mold, Christ had to be stripped of all His supernatural actions, attributes, and mysteries and be retained simply as a sublime teacher of morality, neighborly love, and revolutionary idealism. Out had to go all the claims to divinity, the divine prerogatives, and all the miracles, including the Virgin Birth and the bodily Resurrection. However, what was to be done with the Gospels, which give us our historical knowledge of Christ wrapped in such supernatural events and claims? They had to be turned into legends and

Authentic Words of Jesus: New Translation and Commentary (New York: MacMillan, 1993).

myths. They simply could not be historical, for they contradict the theory that God does not intervene in history in miraculous ways.

A new history of Jesus had to be forged in which all "unbelievable" claims were eliminated and censored. How could such a re-writing of history be justified? It was alleged that the New Testament did not give us true history, but a mythological or legendary account in which the actual historical memories were submerged in a mythologizing process of embellishment. The religious sense of the primitive Christians, according to this theory, led them to make their own pious additions to what they knew of the historical Jesus, and thus the historical data was gradually transformed in a mythical or "supernatural" direction. Thus it was considered necessary to strip away these added elements—which have collectively been called the "Christ of faith"— to get at the underlying historical facts—the "Jesus of history."

In the course of the nineteenth century, various "biographies" of Jesus were written, attempting to reconstruct his life according to Deism—the idea that God does not intervene in history. One of the first of these was by David Friedrich Strauss, the father of biblical rationalism. In 1835, he published his *Life of Jesus Critically Examined*, in which, using the Hegelian categories of thesis, antithesis, and synthesis, he interpreted the Gospels as *myth* rather than history. The Gospels present us with the "Christ of faith," which he held to be very different from the real events and from the actual "Jesus of history." In order to arrive at the Jesus of history, we have to strip away all the supernatural and mythical elements. Nevertheless, the mythological elements are not without interest for Strauss, for he thinks that they contain philosophical or theological ideas expressed in a symbolic mode of thought (often called a *theologoumenon*).

This work of "de-mythologizing" was begun by the liberal Protestants, especially in Germany. However, it soon entered the Catholic camp at the end of the nineteenth century, especially through Alfred Loisy and his associates, whose views have come to be known as "Modernism," which was explained and condemned in 1907 by Pope St. Pius X in his great encyclical *Pascendi dominici gregis*. One of the key elements of the Modernist method was the radical distinction, forged earlier by liberal Protestants, between the Jesus of history and the Christ of faith. In order to unearth the true Jesus of history, one has to strip away mythological elements that have been imported into the image of Christ given to us in the Gospels ("Christ of faith"). Among these Christological elements are Christ's divine claim and His miracles.[37]

At about the same time (1906), Albert Schweitzer, philanthropist and German biblical scholar, wrote an account of the results of over a century of historical research into the life of Jesus. The result, he claimed, was that after so many learned tomes, we knew practically nothing at all about the life of Jesus. The search for the historical life of Jesus was a complete failure.[38] He said: "We thought we really had him at last, and now he has passed by our age and gone back to being himself."[39]

The culmination of this tendency was reached in the second quarter of the twentieth century by the German Lutheran scholar, Rudolf

---

[37] See Pius X, *Pascendi dominici gregis* §30, in which the modernist method of Gospel criticism is summarized: "In things where a double element, the divine and the human, mingles, in Christ, for example, or the Church, or the sacraments, or the many other objects of the same kind, a division must be made and the human element assigned to history while the divine will go to faith. Hence we have that distinction, so current among the Modernists, between the Christ of history and the Christ of faith, between the sacraments of history and the sacraments of faith, and so on. Next we find that the human element itself, which the historian has to work on, as it appears in the documents, has been by faith transfigured, that is to say raised above its historical conditions. It becomes necessary, therefore, to eliminate also the accretions which faith has added, to assign them to faith itself and to the history of faith: thus, when treating of Christ, the historian must set aside all that surpasses man in his natural condition, either according to the psychological conception of him, or according to the place and period of his existence. Finally, by virtue of the third principle, even those things which are not outside the sphere of history they pass through the crucible, excluding from history and relegating to faith everything which, in their judgment, is not in harmony with what they call the *logic* of facts and in character with the persons of whom they are predicated. Thus, they will not allow that Christ ever uttered those things which do not seem to be within the capacity of the multitudes that listened to Him. Hence they delete from His *real* history and transfer to faith all the allegories found in His discourses."

[38] *The Quest of the Historical Jesus: A Critical Study of Its Progress from Reimarus to Wrede* (New York: Macmillan, 1942), 398: "There is nothing more negative than the result of the critical study of the Life of Jesus."

[39] Ratzinger, *God and the World*, 203, paraphrasing Schweitzer, *Quest of the Historical Jesus*, 399. Schweitzer goes on to say: "The mistake was to suppose that Jesus could come to mean more to our time by entering into it as a man like ourselves. That is not possible. First, because such a Jesus never existed."

Bultmann, who carried the task of "demythologization" through in a radical way, stripping from the Jesus of history everything supernatural. He saw the New Testament as clothed in a "mythical world picture" that, in principle, could be separated from its salvific nucleus.[40] Demythologization thus is presented as an exigency for evangelization of the modern world. Speaking of the Gospel presentation of the central elements of the Christian kerygma (such as the Atonement, Resurrection, Ascension, and the Second Coming), he wrote:

All of this is mythological talk, and the individual motifs may be easily traced to the contemporary mythology of Jewish apocalypticism and of the Gnostic myth of redemption. Insofar as it is mythological talk it is incredible to men and women today because for them the mythical world picture is a thing of the past. Therefore, contemporary Christian proclamation is faced with the question whether, when it demands faith from men and women, it expects them to acknowledge this mythical world picture of the past. If this is impossible, it then has to face the question whether the New Testament proclamation has a truth that is independent of the mythical world picture, in which case it would be the task of theology to demythologize the Christian proclamation. . . .

We cannot use electric lights and radios and, in the event of illness, avail ourselves of modern medical and clinical means and at the same time believe in the spirit and wonder world of the New Testament. And if we suppose that we can do so ourselves, we must be clear that we can represent this as

---

[40] Rudolf Bultmann, "New Testament and Mythology: The Problem of Demythologizing the New Testament Proclamation," in *New Testament and Mythology and Other Basic Writings*, trans. Schubert M. Ogden (Philadelphia: Fortress, 1984), 1: "The world picture of the New Testament is a mythical world picture. The world is a three-story structure, with earth in the middle, heaven above it, and hell below it. Heaven is the dwelling place of God and of heavenly figures, the angels; the world below is hell, the place of torment. But even the earth is not simply the scene of natural day-to-day occurrences, of foresight and work that reckon with order and regularity; rather, it, too, is a theater for the working of supernatural powers, God and his angels, Satan and his demons. These supernatural powers intervene in natural occurrences and in the thinking, willing, and acting of human beings; wonders are nothing unusual."

the attitude of Christian faith only by making the Christian proclamation unintelligible and impossible for our contemporaries.[41]

However, (as Schweitzer saw) if one strips away everything supernatural from the Gospels, what is left? Not much. Bultmann, in effect, claimed that the only thing that we know about the historical Jesus is that he was a Palestinian Jew who died on the cross.[42] This is all that is left when we thoroughly "de-mythologize" the Gospels to eliminate all claims to divinity and all supernatural action done to confirm that claim. This absolute failure of the quest for the "historical Jesus" (who could not have claimed to be God) is surely instructive, for it shows how integral Christ's claim to divinity is to the Gospel narratives. Nothing at all is left if we strip it away.

Nevertheless, Bultmann counted this failure of the quest for the historical Jesus a paradoxical blessing. He held that it gives us the "freedom" to fashion the Christ of faith according to our own needs (inevitably leaving the Gospels behind, despite the erudition devoted to them). He proceeded to fashion an existentialist Christ (a prophet of "authentic existence") based on the philosophy of his colleague, Martin Heidegger.[43] Liberation theology in the second half of the twentieth century is another form of this type of de-mythologizing

---

[41] Ibid., 2–5.

[42] See Bultmann's work (originally of 1921), *The History of the Synoptic Tradition*, trans. John Marsh, 2nd edition (New York: Harper & Row, 1968), and his 1941 essay on "The New Testament and Mythology," in *Kerygma and Myth: A Theological Debate*, vol. 1, trans. R.H. Fuller (London, 1953). See also his *Jesus and the Word*, trans. Louise Pettibone Smith and Erminie Huntress Lantero (New York: Scribner, 1958), 8: "I do indeed think that we can now know almost nothing concerning the life and personality of Jesus, since the early Christian sources show no interest in either, and are moreover fragmentary and often legendary; and other sources about Jesus do not exist."

[43] See, for example, Bultmann, *New Testament and Mythology*, 23: "Above all, Martin Heidegger's existentialist analysis of human existence seems to be only a profane philosophical presentation of the New Testament view of who we are: beings existing historically in care for ourselves on the basis of anxiety, ever in the moment of decision between the past and the future, whether we will lose ourselves in the world of what is available and of the 'one,' or whether we will attain our authenticity by surrendering all securities and being unreservedly free for the future. Is this not how we are also understood in the New Testament?"

and reconstruction of a new Christ who fits our "needs." In this case Christ was re-fashioned as a Marxist revolutionary instead of a Heideggerian philosopher.[44]

Problems with Bultmann's Project

Bultmann and Form Criticism: Presuppositions

In his well-known essay, "Biblical Interpretation in Conflict," Joseph Ratzinger analyzed three major presuppositions of Bultmann's exegetical method: the priority of proclamation over event, the principle of discontinuity, and a concept of evolution from the simple to the complex.[45]

The priority of proclamation over event refers to Bultmann's presupposition that the New Testament only gives us the proclamation of the early Church, without enabling us to attain to the actual events —the life of Jesus—on which that proclamation is founded and about which it speaks. The only certainties that we can obtain from the New Testament are about the proclamation of the early Church, not about the events themselves that the proclamation proclaims.

This fundamental presupposition is a kind of Kantian epistemology applied to the New Testament. According to Kant, we can only know what has been projected by the human mind itself. The actual reality that lies beneath, although it is supposed to exist, must be acknowledged as unknowable to human reason.[46] In a similar way, Bultmann holds that the actual reality of Jesus in His deeds and words is unattainable from the New Testament. All we can come to know is the proclamation of the early Church about Jesus. Or to put it another way, all that we can know is what the early Church *projected* onto the figure of Jesus. This projection then, in good Kantian fashion,

---

[44] See the CDF, Instruction on Certain Aspects of the "Theology of Liberation" (1984).

[45] See Ratzinger, "Biblical Interpretation in Conflict: The Question of the Basic Principles and Path of Exegesis Today," in *God's Word: Scripture—Tradition—Office*, 104–107 (this essay is the text of a talk given in New York in 1988 as the Erasmus Lecture).

[46] This is, however, a contradiction, for to know that reality is unknowable is to know something about it and about our intellectual power.

becomes the object of a very complex and subtle investigation. This investigation, however, will never enable us to get to the reality itself that lies under the projection. All that it can do is shed light on the process of projection. However, the impression is made—although in contradiction to Bultmann's principles—that if one could only strip away all that has been projected, one would get closer to the actual Jesus. Thus, instead of revealing Jesus, the proclamation of the early Church actually hides Him, and so must be stripped back, layer by layer. This becomes one of the major goals of the exegetical method known as *form criticism*.

The second presupposition, the principle of discontinuity, separates the proclamation of the early Church, which is seen as Hellenized, from the previous unknowable preaching of Jesus Himself, assumed to be not Hellenized. Both are set off against the Old Testament by another discontinuity. The only way to get back to Jesus Himself is to strip away the Hellenizing overlay in dialectical fashion. Not only must one strip away the apostolic proclamation, but one must look for something in dialectical opposition to it! However, the proclamation lies in such complete discontinuity with Jesus Himself that there is no way to get back to Him in His historical reality. Here we can see the heritage of the Hegelian dialectical understanding of history.

The third presupposition involves applying a notion of biological evolution to the New Testament. The evolution must go from simple to complex. An obvious problem with this principle is that it leaves undefined the notion of what is "simple." What is seen as simple to one may appear complex to another. However, the problem does not lie principally in the vagueness of the principle. Still more serious is the naturalism that it presupposes. The priority of the simple presupposes that all change is from the less to the more, the lower to the higher. This shuts off, in advance, any notion of inspiration from above and any divine initiative. Ratzinger gives a good critique of this presupposition:

We have to dispute the fundamental notion that is based on a simple transfer of the evolutionary model from natural science to the history of the mind. Mental processes do not follow the law of animal genealogies. In this case, it is frequently the opposite way around: a great breakthrough is followed by generations of imitators, who bring down the bold new beginning to the banality of school theories and bury and obscure it. . . . Examples could be produced through the whole of history. All judgments based on the theory of the discontinuity of tradition and on the evolutionist assertion of the priority of the "simple" over the "complex" must therefore from the outset be challenged as having no real foundation.[47]

Archeology of the Gospel Texts

In addition to his naturalism that excludes the supernatural, Bultmann's method is based on two other closely related presuppositions that seem to lack foundation. First, he assumes that the Gospels are like archeological sites that one could excavate and divide into different layers or strata. Secondly, in order to distinguish these layers, Bultmann presupposes that there are objective laws that govern the development of the oral tradition and create the different archeological layers. Without such laws, there would be no way to identify any given text as lying in a certain stage of development of the tradition.

Bultmann describes the method of form criticism as an attempt to distinguish these different layers of tradition in the Gospel accounts and other works of the New Testament:

> Critical investigation shows that the whole tradition about Jesus which appears in the three synoptic gospels is composed of a series of layers which can on the whole be clearly distinguished, although the separation at some points is difficult and doubtful. (The Gospel of John cannot be taken into account at all as a source for the teaching of Jesus.)[48]

---

[47] Ratzinger, "Biblical Interpretation in Conflict: The Question of the Basic Principles and Path of Exegesis Today," in *God's Word: Scripture—Tradition—Office*, 106.

[48] Bultmann, *Jesus and the Word*, 12.

In other words, the intent of form criticism is to serve as a kind of archeology performed on the biblical text so as to separate out different strata of tradition.[49]

There is an obvious difficulty with such an archeology of the biblical text. In normal archeology, the archeologist encounters physical layers that are physically superimposed on one another. Thus, dating can be established, in part, by the fact that one layer is physically above another, and this fact can be empirically verified. In the archeology of the biblical text, on the other hand, there is no empirically verifiable control such as archeology possesses in finding one artifact above or below another. The biblical text does not come with any means of empirically verifying higher or lower texts. Thus the layers that form criticism seeks to compare are purely hypothetical constructions of some prior oral tradition for which we have no direct records.

This means that such an archeology, by the nature of the enterprise, will rest on some hypothetical reconstructions being used as if they were equivalent to the physical strata encountered by the archeologist. In practice, this implies some pre-conceived notion of religious development, as well as the supposition that this development follows objective laws that can be formulated like the law of gravity.

This presupposition has been criticized by many. Martin Hengel writes: "An errant judgment that misled form-critical research from the beginning was the claim that there are unequivocal 'laws' for the oral (and written) folklore tradition, which must have also determined the 'history of the synoptic tradition.'"[50]

---

[49] Such investigation continues in radical form in, e.g., Funk, Hoover, and the Jesus Seminar, *The Five Gospels*.

[50] See Martin Hengel, "Eye-Witness Memory and the Writing of the Gospels," in *The Written Gospel*, eds. Markus Bockmuehl and Donald A. Hagner (Cambridge, UK: Cambridge University Press, 2005), 84–85. Hengel quotes E. P. Sanders, *The Tendencies of the Synoptic Tradition*, SNTSMS 9 (Cambridge, UK: Cambridge University Press, 1969), 272: "There are no hard and fast laws of the development of the Synoptic tradition. On all counts, the tradition developed in opposite directions. It became both longer and shorter, both more and less detailed, and both more and less Semitic. . . . For this reason, dogmatic statements that a certain characteristic proves a certain passage to be earlier than another are never justified. . . . For this reason, we must always give room for human differences and be alert to editorial tendencies of each particular writer." See also Eric Eve, *Behind the Gospels: Understanding the Oral Tradition* (Minneapolis: Fortress Press, 2014), 27: "Bultmann's entire analysis of the synoptic tradition is in danger of reifying oral tradi-

Methodological Problem of the Vicious Circle

Rudolf Bultmann acknowledged that the method of form criticism practiced by himself and Martin Dibelius involved a certain amount of circular reasoning, which he thought was unavoidable in similar historical questions. He writes:

> It is essential to realize that form-criticism is fundamentally indistinguishable from all historical work in this, that it has to move in a circle. The forms of the literary tradition must be used to establish the influences operating in the life of the community, and the life of the community must be used to render the forms themselves intelligible.[51]

To this it must be said that there are grades of moving in a vicious circle. All historical scholarship seeks to reduce to a minimum the degree to which it engages in the fallacy of arguing in a vicious circle by presupposing, in a hidden way, what one is attempting to demonstrate. This procedure is also known in logic as the fallacy of *petitio principii*. In other words, Bultmann's conclusions are not based on the method of form criticism *per se*, but on his presuppositions concerning the primitive Christian community, especially with regard to its Hellenistic character that supposedly imposes itself on the primitive Jesus-tradition.[52]

The methodological problem of the vicious circle is not peculiar to Bultmann. Rather, in greater or lesser degree, it has plagued the "higher criticism" of the nineteenth century and the work of scholars

---

tion into a series of archaeological layers that can be excavated, when in reality oral tradition is nothing of the sort."

[51] Bultmann, *History of the Synoptic Tradition*, 5.

[52] Even Dibelius, Bultmann's colleague in the foundation of form criticism, criticized the objectivity of Bultmann's conclusions that minimized the historicity of the Gospels: "It must be said quite emphatically that Bultmann's skepticism in all questions of historicity is not necessarily connected with form-critical criteria but with his conception of the nature of the primitive Christian community as well as his emphasis upon the difference between Palestinian and Hellenistic Christianity"; see *Deutsche Literaturzeitung* 53, no. 24 (1932):1105–1111 (quoted in Hengel, "Eye-Witness Memory," 81–82). See also his review of Bultmann's *Die Geschichte der synoptischen Tradition* in *Deutsche Literaturzeitung* 43, no. 7/8 (1922): 128–134.

after Bultmann. The fallacy of the vicious circle is present whenever a particular theory of the development of theological ideas—whether Hegelian or Heideggerian—rather than external evidence is used as the *principal* criterion to provide dates for scriptural texts. Then the dates given to the texts on the basis of this theory are used, even if unintentionally, to corroborate the theory that established them and to prevent these texts from offering any substantial contrary evidence. The theory of development that is the real guiding principle of the historical reconstruction remains without substantial scientific control or verification.

Or to put it another way, there is a vicious circle whenever one's preconceived idea of what the historical Jesus must have been like is used to determine which sources about the historical Jesus are primary and which are secondary. The result is that one's preconceived picture of Jesus seems to emerge from the research, whereas in reality it preceded and guided it.[53] The great danger is that this method easily allows Jesus to appear as we think He should have been, rather than how the apostolic Tradition and the New Testament presents Him. Ratzinger pointed to this kind of methodological circle on numerous occasions. He writes:

> I think all these attempts are reconstructions in which we can always see the face of the architect. Whether you take Adolf Harnack's Christ—who reflects the typical liberal—or whether you take Bultmann's Christ, who portrays his kind of existential philosophy. All these constructions have been undertaken with one guiding idea: There can be no such thing as God made man. Those events that presuppose his existence cannot therefore have happened.[54]

---

[53] See Eve, *Behind the Gospels*, 27: "He [Bultmann] seemed to know in advance that the historical Jesus was an eschatological prophet who issued a radical call to repentance, so that material that reflected such a radical immanent eschatology was most likely to be authentic: his method thus delivered the historical Jesus he expected to find."

[54] *God and the World*, 203.

In the foreword to the first volume of his *Jesus of Nazareth*, Ratzinger writes: "If you read a number of these reconstructions one after the other, you see at once that far from uncovering an icon that has become obscured over time, they are much more like photographs of their authors and the ideals they hold."[55]

In terms of scientific method, the theory of development that lies at the heart of Bultmann's use of the critical method remains without any effective means of falsification. For, if a particular text, dated according to external sources, seems to be contrary to the theory of development, then the date indicated by external sources is disregarded and replaced by one in accordance with the theory of development. For example, Bultmann writes: "The aim of form-criticism is to determine the original form of a piece of narrative, a dominical saying or a parable. In the process we learn to distinguish secondary additions and forms, and these in turn lead to important results for the history of the tradition."[56] But how is the original form of a piece of narrative determined? The theory of development is the measure that determines what is secondary and what is primary. Without a theory of development, form criticism would be unable to assign one part of the tradition as secondary with respect to another. But the theory of development itself, which is moving the entire critical machine, never gets tested.

Bultmann presents his theory of development as if it consists in general laws that govern the development of tradition. Thus biblical criticism is treated on the analogy of physical sciences that formulate general laws and then use those laws to make predictions. However, the laws of development that Bultmann is using are not deduced from empirical observation in the same way that physical laws are. Bultmann himself admits as much:

> For the most part the history of the tradition is obscure, though there is one small part which we can observe in our sources, how Marcan material is treated as it is adapted by

---

[55] *Jesus of Nazareth: Baptism in the Jordan to the Transfiguration*, xii.

[56] Bultmann, *History of the Synoptic Tradition*, 6.

Matthew and Luke. . . . In the case of Q admittedly, we are dependent upon a reconstruction from Matthew and Luke; but even here it is possible on occasion, by comparing Matthew and Luke to recognize what laws governed the development of material from Q to Matthew and Luke. If we are able to detect any such laws, we may assume that they were operative on the traditional material even before it was given its form in Mark and Q, and in this way we can infer back to an earlier stage of the tradition than appears in our sources.[57]

In other words, the laws of development have to be inferred by induction from cases in which we know by other means that one text is prior to another and observe the differences between the primary and the secondary text. From such a comparison, one infers laws that can then be applied to other material to determine what is primary and what is secondary. But even in this most obvious case, one is still assuming a particular theory of development in order to establish Marcan priority, which is then used as a basis to infer the general laws of development. But if the foundation is uncertain, the entire edifice will be far more uncertain.

Furthermore, this kind of argumentation is entirely based on induction of "general laws" from a very small number of examples. It is well known that an argument of induction never yields certainty. Just because something has occurred in a particular way 1,000 times does not mean that it will necessarily happen in the same way on time 1,001. For there may be other variables at play that we do not know anything about, especially since we are dealing with divine inspiration. But, as Bultmann admits, we are not speaking here about regularities that have been observed as many as 1,000 times. The "laws" are inferred by generalizing on the basis of just a handful of examples, which are themselves all uncertain.[58] For Marcan pri-

---

[57] Ibid.

[58] See the critique of Bultmann's method in Hengel's "Eye-Witness Memory," 84; E. P. Sanders, *The Tendencies of the Synoptic Tradition*, SNTSMS 9 (Cambridge, UK: Cambridge University Press, 1969), 272 (quoted above, in note 50, p. 393).

ority and reconstructions of Q cannot be held to be certain.

In order to avoid this kind of vicious circle, the historical data must be given due weight by preferring external criteria to internal ones and giving them greater methodological importance precisely because the external criteria are independent of one's theory of development and can either falsify or corroborate it.

Barth's Criticism of Bultmann

One of the most penetrating critiques of Bultmann's theological method that I am aware of is an essay by Karl Barth entitled "Rudolf Bultmann—An Attempt to Understand Him."[59] In this brilliant essay, Barth charges Bultmann with using a particular philosophical theory as the privileged lens through which the New Testament is seen and interpreted. This, in Barth's eyes, is like the ancient Gnostic heresy. It also could be seen to be a form of idolatry, in which a construction of one's own making is used as the matrix into which the New Testament has to be made to fit. Barth writes:

> How can we decide even before we have read the text what it actually says, and what is only temporary imagery? And what happens if we use this alien criterion as an infallible instrument rather than as a provisional clue? Is not Bultmann's very concept of myth, the infallible criterion which dominates his hermeneutics, quite alien to the New Testament? Whether or not it is the contemporary fashion, as Bultmann claims it is, the question is how can it be used to decide what belongs to the substance of the New Testament and what is merely outward imagery?[60]

Barth rightly points out that Bultmann is raising his philosoph-

---

[59] Karl Barth, "Rudolf Bultmann—An Attempt to Understand Him," in *Kerygma and Myth: A Theological Debate*, ed. Hans-Werner Bartsch, trans. Reginald H. Fuller (London: S.P.C.K, 1962), 2:83–132.

[60] Ibid., 2:108.

ical presuppositions to the level of an infallible interpretative key by which he decides what is to be retained in the New Testament and what re-interpreted. This is a classic instance of rationalism: elevating some philosophical system into a means of judging Revelation. This puts philosophy above Revelation and faith. Barth continues:

> We have no right to try and barricade ourselves behind the limits of our understanding in order to protect ourselves from the Word of God. Of course, everyone approaches the New Testament with some kind of preconceptions. . . . But have we any right to elevate all this into a methodological principle? . . . What business has the modern world view here, however tenaciously we cling to it and imagine we are morally obliged to uphold it? And what business has existentialism and anthropological interpretation here, however much we ourselves may be convinced by them and accept them as binding for ourselves? What is the relevance here of idealism or positivism, to which our fathers were so attached? Or—as may occur and has in fact occurred to some—Marxism or some kind of nationalism? Do these elements of the world make us competent to quibble with the Spirit and the Word of God? How can we listen to the New Testament if we are always thrusting some *conditio sine qua non* between ourselves and the text? . . . Surely it would be better to cultivate as flexible and open-minded an approach as we can, instead of donning the existentialist straitjacket?[61]

The Most "Primitive" Is Not Necessarily the Most Faithful

Even if one grants the assumptions of a radical use of the historical-critical method and accepts that one could separate out a first portrait of Christ that lies behind the Gospel image, this would not be any real help in getting to the historical Jesus. For, why should one think

---

[61] Ibid., 2:124.

that the first portrait of Jesus is the complete and faithful portrait? The axiom—everything that is received is received according to the mode of the receiver—implies that the full realization of who Jesus is required an enlarging of the recipients. Jesus Himself explains that there are many things that the Apostles could not yet bear (John 16:12), and precisely for this reason the Holy Spirit had to come. The more faithful portrait is the one that is more deeply meditated on. Thus, *the portrait that we seek is not the first draft, but the portrait born in the Church through the development of apostolic Tradition.*

Two complementary arguments can be offered against Bultmann in this regard. First, as we have seen, it is impossible to separate out a first portrait of Christ without a methodological circle, since the unproven presuppositions will predetermine the conclusion. Second, there is no need to separate out a first portrait of Christ because, even if one succeeded, it would have little value compared with the more fully developed portraits. A first portrait could not be trusted to have more historical accuracy of what is essential in Christ and His divine claim. The portrait that can be trusted is that of the apostolic Church as a whole. And the portrait of the apostolic Church is the four Gospels in their entirety.

St. Irenaeus, in his defense of the four Gospels, made this point against the Gnostics: the increased understanding acquired at Pentecost is the guarantee of the historical accuracy of the apostolic witness. Far from being a hindrance to objectivity, that fuller faith is a *sine qua non* of the apostolic mission of giving accurate witness:

> We are not permitted to say that they preached before they had received "perfect knowledge," as some dare to state, boasting that they are the correctors of the apostles. For, after our Lord had risen from the dead, and they "were clothed with power from on high when the Holy Spirit came upon them," they had full assurance concerning all things, and had "perfect knowledge." Only then did "they go forth to the ends of the earth, bringing" us "the good news," . . . inasmuch as

they collectively, and each of them individually, equally possessed the Gospel of God.[62]

James Dunn has had the merit of recalling this capital truth that the Easter faith of the Apostles was not a hindrance to their mission of giving accurate witness. Indeed, the Gospel witness cannot be discussed or understood without the context of faith.[63] Dunn argues that it is a mistake to make a radical discontinuity between the understanding of the disciples before Easter and their response of faith after Easter. From the beginning, the response of the disciples was faith in Jesus's implicit divine claims as expressed by His miracles and teachings. Easter did not introduce a response of faith that would cloud the Jesus of history. Rather, Easter deepened their faith by including in it His death and Resurrection and making it luminous through the gift of the Spirit.[64]

And as the disciples always had to give a response of faith to Christ's claim, so too all readers of the Gospels are called to the same response of faith. The Gospel, or the encounter with Jesus, cannot be had without the perspective of faith that He calls forth and demands.

Furthermore, a passionate interest in the subject of a history should not be regarded as something that would create a distorting bias concerning that history. Personal neutrality and lack of subjective involvement do not guarantee memory. Rather, lack of interest or involvement would beget oblivion, error, or instrumentalization.

---

[62] *Adversus haereses* 3.1.1, in *St. Irenaeus of Lyons: Against the Heresies Book 3*, trans. Dominic J. Unger, Ancient Christian Writers 64 (New York: The Newman Press, 2012), 30. St. Irenaeus is here countering a Gnostic argument that the apostolic witness in the four canonical Gospels is untrustworthy because they were written by Apostles who were imperfect in understanding the secret mysteries, of which the Gnostics prided themselves on having an exclusive knowledge.

[63] See his *A New Perspective on Jesus: What the Quest for the Historical Jesus Missed* (Grand Rapids: Baker Academic, 2005) and his *Christianity in the Making*, vol. 1, *Jesus Remembered* (Grand Rapids: Eerdmans, 2003).

[64] See James Dunn, *New Perspective on Jesus*, 28 (speaking of the so-called Q tradition): "It was formulated as an expression of faith, indeed, but of the faith of the disciples that drew them into following him. As such, it takes us back not merely to the 70s or 80s when the Gospels were written, and not merely to the 40s, 50s, or 60s when the Jesus tradition was being circulated round the first churches, but to the late 20s or early 30s, to the time and mission of Jesus himself. As such, it enables us to hear, much more clearly than has regularly been assumed by Jesus researchers, Jesus himself as these first disciples heard him."

Profound interest in an event is precisely what equips an eyewitness or historian to remember the event and transmit it faithfully for its own sake. As Samuel Byrskog has stressed, the classical historians such as Thucydides, Xenophon, Polybius, and Josephus saw active involvement in the events that they narrate as the best qualification for the fidelity of their history.[65]

If the personal high-level involvement of Josephus in the Jewish War made him an ideal historian of that war, how much more the Apostles were qualified by their interest in Jesus to faithfully transmit their memories of the words and deeds of one whom they believed was the "Author of life."[66] In Acts 3:15, Peter tells the crowds in Jerusalem that they have "killed the Author of life, whom God raised from the dead. To this we are witnesses." The words of one regarded as the "Author of life" are less likely to be forgotten or treated cavalierly as instruments for any kind of propaganda than are any other words.

Bultmann's Account Is Incompatible with the Portrait of the Apostolic Generation in Acts

One of the greatest problems with Bultmannian form criticism is that it presupposes a picture of the primitive Christian community

---

[65] See Samuel Byrskog, *Story as History—History as Story: The Gospel Tradition in the Context of Ancient Oral History* (Tübingen: Mohr Siebeck, 2000), 149–176, esp. 154–156: "The historians preferred the participating eyewitness to the passive observer. Involvement was not an obstacle to what they perceived as historical truth. It was rather the essential means to a correct understanding of what had really happened. We actually detect a development among the Greek historians, with an increasing emphasis on direct participation. Thucydides is the first one. . . . Xenophon confirms this ideal. . . . In the second century BCE, Polybius draws the development of autopsy from observation to direct participation and personal experience to its extreme. . . . When he chose an informant, he was interested in finding out to what extent that person had an active part in the matters of interest. . . . For Josephus . . . autopsy in the sense of direct participation in the events was more or less taken for granted as an essential criterion of the suitability of a person intending to write about the recent past."

[66] See ibid., 165–167: "The oral history approach takes very seriously the fact that accurate memory depends on social interest and need. *A person involved remembers better than a disinterested observer.* . . . Why would the involvement, the keen and enthusiastic attachment to the person and teaching of Jesus, be an obstacle to the truth of history for them? Was not historical truth, as they thought, instead embedded precisely within this matrix of involvement and dedication?" (italics original).

very different from that which is given, for example, in the Acts of the Apostles or the prologue of Luke. Acts shows us the early Church as unified by the tremendous prestige of the apostolic teaching. Bultmann's methodology totally neglects the authority that would have been exercised by the apostolic college and their oral witness to the words and deeds of Jesus. He conceives the primitive tradition as anonymous and creative, instead of centering on the concrete witness of the Apostles.[67] Furthermore, he completely discounts the apostolic origin of the Gospels.

Bultmann Used the Categories of "Oral Poetry" Rather than "Sacred Oral History"

Bultmann and other form critics have used a model of the development of oral folk traditions as the paradigm for studying the Synoptic tradition. One of the crucial problems of this method is precisely that it confuses these two very different types of oral tradition. In a tradition of oral poetry, inventive addition would naturally occur over time as a kind of improvisation on a traditional theme. Form critics make use of this observation in order to maintain, for example, that the names of minor figures in the Gospels are added as a kind of free composition to "flesh out" the narrative and satisfy the curiosity of hearers.[68]

---

[67] See Ben F. Meyer, "Some Consequences of Birger Gerhardsson's Account of the Origins of the Gospel Tradition," in *Jesus and the Oral Gospel Tradition*, ed. Henry Wansbrough (Sheffield, UK: JSOT Press, 1991), 424: "Classical NT form criticism supposed a primitive Christian state of affairs that was open to any imaginable account of the origins of primitive Christianity. Or, rather, it was open to many imaginable accounts, but not to that suggested by the endings of the Gospels, by the Lukan prologue, and by the first chapters of the Acts of the Apostles. If such texts were taken at anything like face value, the controlling suppositions of classical New Testament form criticism would have to be adjudged radically defective." See also ibid., 432: "The Church that the Bultmannian account of tradition has conjured up is a phenomenon of which we have never otherwise heard and which we would never otherwise have imagined. It is unrecognizable. Gerhardsson, on the contrary, has offered an account of tradition that indirectly brings into our field of vision a Church that we have heard of from the letters of Paul and from the Acts of the Apostles; it is familiar; we recognize it."

[68] See Bultmann, *History of the Synoptic Tradition*, 269, 282–283, and 309–312.

However, oral history actually presents the opposite tendency. The evangelists did not understand themselves as operating within a context of oral poetry for the purpose of entertainment! The names of witnesses are given especially in the earlier accounts when the eye-witnesses were still available for verification of the testimony. They may then tend to drop out in later accounts when they no longer serve a purpose of corroboration. For example, Mark gives the names of the two sons of Simon the Cyrene. This has been understood to indicate that these two men would have been known in the Roman community in which Mark's Gospel was written.

Hengel calls attention to this confusion between the models of oral poetry and oral history:

> This means that instead of "oral poetry," which dominates the form-critical perspective, the related phenomenon of "oral history," which is closer to the situation of Jesus' disciples as well as to the missionary churches of later decades, should be drawn upon more strongly for the understanding of the Jesus tradition. In the Gospels, and especially the Synoptics, it is not primarily a matter of literary fiction; instead, they claim to describe a real event of the past, i.e., "history" narrated in the form of "stories" about Jesus' words and deeds, which are ultimately founded upon eye-witnesses and their memory, even if, time and again, they were newly shaped and changed by the tradition-bearers and authors for the purpose of effective missionary proclamation and teaching in worship. In John, this occurred in a radical way, and yet the claim to eye-witness testimony is strikingly emphasized. Also, the sentence in Luke 1:2 . . . is to be taken seriously. Because the *autoptai* are a reality for him, he does not need to invent any witnesses.[69]

I would add that, not only does Luke not need to invent any witnesses, but he would have seen such a procedure as blasphemous. For the Gospel, even in its oral form, was conceived by the apostolic

---

[69] Hengel, "Eye-Witness Memory and the Writing of the Gospels," 87–88.

generation as transmission of the witness of God. What St. Paul says about himself in 1 Corinthians 15:15 would apply to all the Evangelists: "We are even found to be misrepresenting God, because we testified of God that he raised Christ, whom he did not raise if it is true that the dead are not raised."

Bultmann's Christ Is without a Face

Perhaps the most important and catastrophic consequence of Bultmann's method, from the perspective of the evangelizing mission of the Church, is Bultmann's conclusion that we cannot know anything about the personality of Jesus Christ. His method debars any attempt to encounter Him as He appears on the pages of the Gospels. This is not a problem of which Bultmann was unaware. Quite the contrary, he embraced this consequence as something positive. He writes:

> *Interest in the personality of Jesus* is excluded—and not merely because, in the absence of information, I am making a virtue of necessity. I do indeed think that we can now know almost nothing concerning the life and personality of Jesus, since the early Christian sources show no interest in either, are moreover fragmentary and often legendary; and other sources about Jesus do not exist.[70]

This conclusion of Bultmann is amazing. Of all the figures in history, countless numbers of people—and not only Christians—have found Jesus as portrayed in the New Testament to be the Person who is *most vivid*, most individual, most puzzling and inscrutable in His intensity, *the one whose Personality most powerfully encounters us*. I think that it is fair to say that there is no figure delineated with a greater ring of authenticity than the Jesus we meet in the pages of the four Gospels.[71]

---

[70] *Jesus and the Word*, 8 (italics original).

[71] It is should be observed that this mark of authenticity is utterly absent from Gnostic "gospels" like that of Thomas. On this question, see the masterful essay by C. S. Lewis, "Modern Theolo-

However, despite the plethora of ways in which the Gospels convey a divine claim to us, Bultmann holds that one cannot know with certainty whether Jesus even knew that He was the Messiah (let alone God), and in fact Bultmann says his "personal opinion"[72] is not only that Jesus did not know that He was the Messiah, but that in fact He (Jesus) thought He was not. And if one cannot know even this, what could one know about Jesus's inner life?

> Considering that it was really no trifle to believe oneself Messiah, that, further, whoever so believed must have regulated his whole life in accordance with this belief, we must admit that if this point is obscure we can, strictly speaking, know nothing of the personality of Jesus. I am personally of the opinion that Jesus did not believe himself to be the Messiah, but I do not imagine that this opinion gives me a clearer picture of his personality.[73]

Let it be noted that this conclusion of Bultmann's is possible only if one accepts his method of dismissing the historicity of almost every chapter of the Gospels. For, almost every page communicates not only a messianic, but an implicit divine claim, as shown above. When the historicity of the Gospels is put into doubt, the face of Jesus is lost.

To encounter the face of Jesus in prayer, we have to know Him as He is portrayed so vividly in the pages of the Gospels, believing in the historical truth of those accounts. Pope John Paul II, in his Apostolic Letter on the Jubilee *Novo millennio ineunte*, speaks repeatedly of the Church's contemplation of the face of Jesus Christ. He says that the principal fruit of the Jubilee consists in this "contemplation of the face of Christ"[74] as He is presented in the Gospels. This is possible because the Gospels "faithfully hand on what Jesus Christ, while liv-

---

gy and Biblical Criticism," in *The Seeing Eye and Other Selected Essays from Christian Reflections* (New York: Ballantine Books, 1992), 208–210.

[72] Bultmann, *Jesus and the Word*, 9.

[73] Ibid.

[74] *Novo millennio ineunte* (2001), §15.

ing among men, really did and taught for their eternal salvation" (*DV* §19). He writes:

> The Gospels do not claim to be a complete biography of Jesus in accordance with the canons of modern historical science. From them, nevertheless, *the face of the Nazarene emerges with a solid historical foundation*. The Evangelists took pains to represent him on the basis of trustworthy testimonies which they gathered (cf. Luke 1:3) and working with documents which were subjected to careful ecclesial scrutiny.[75]

Study Questions

1. What are some of the ways in which Jesus made a divine claim in the Gospels?
2. What is the trilemma (or quadrilemma) used by C.S. Lewis to show Christ's divinity?
3. Why is it impossible to hold that Christ's claim to divinity was a myth or legend that formed in the early Christian community?
4. What is meant by the distinction between the Jesus of history and the Christ of faith? What philosophical ideas motivated the search for the historical Jesus in the nineteenth and early twentieth century?
5. How is the danger of a vicious circle present in the method used by Bultmann?
6. Is it possible or reasonable to seek to reconstruct a more "primitive" portrait of Jesus than that given in the Gospels?
7. What would be the consequences for Christian prayer and contemplation if one accepted Bultmann's radical skepticism regarding the historical Jesus?

---

[75] Ibid. §18.

Suggestions for Further Reading

Ratzinger, Joseph Cardinal. *Jesus of Nazareth: From the Baptism in the Jordan to the Transfiguration*, especially xi–xxiv. Translated by Adrian J. Walker. New York: Doubleday, 2007.

———. "Biblical Interpretation in Conflict." In *God's Word: Scripture—Tradition—Office*, 91–126. Edited by Peter Hünermann and Tomas Söding. Translated by Henry Taylor. San Francisco: Ignatius Press, 2008.

Pope St. John Paul II, Apostolic Letter at the Close of the Great Jubilee of the Year 2000 *Novo millennio ineunte*. January 6, 2001.

Pope St. Pius X. Encyclical on the Doctrine of the Modernists *Pascendi dominici gregis*. September 8, 1907.

Bultmann, Rudolf. "New Testament and Mythology: The Problem of Demythologizing the New Testament Proclamation." In *New Testament and Mythology and Other Basic Writings*, 1–43. Translated by Schubert M. Ogden. Philadelphia: Fortress, 1984.

Schweitzer, Albert. *The Quest of the Historical Jesus: A Critical Study of Its Progress from Reimarus to Wrede*. New York: Macmillan, 1942.

Barth, Karl. "Rudolf Bultmann—An Attempt to Understand Him." In *Kerygma and Myth: A Theological Debate*, 2:83–132. Edited by Hans-Werner Bartsch. Translated by Reginald H. Fuller. London: S.P.C.K, 1962.

Lewis, C. S. "Modern Theology and Biblical Criticism." In *The Seeing Eye and Other Selected Essays from Christian Reflections*, 208–210. New York: Ballantine Books, 1992.

CHAPTER FOURTEEN

Apostolic Origin of the Four Gospels

In responding to the skepticism of Bultmann and others about the historical truth of the portrait of Christ in the Gospels, *Dei Verbum* makes two fundamental claims: (a) the four Gospels have an apostolic origin, and (b) they have a truly "historical character" and "faithfully hand on what Jesus Christ, while living among men, really did and taught"[1] until He ascended into heaven, notwithstanding the lapse of time between the life of Jesus and the final redaction of the Gospels. In this chapter we shall examine the first claim and the Patristic evidence supporting it.

Apostolic Origin of the Gospels according to *Dei Verbum* §18

Today, many put in doubt the direct apostolic origin of the four Gospels.[2] The question is crucial, for the credibility of the historical veracity of the Gospels depends on the fact that they substantially transmit

---

[1] *DV* §19.

[2] See Denis Farkasfalvy, *Inspiration & Interpretation: A Theological Introduction to Sacred Scripture* (Washington, DC: Catholic University of America Press, 2010), 195: "In spite of *Dei Verbum*'s statement to the contrary, the majority of leading Catholic biblical scholars in the post-conciliar period began to call the canonical gospels anonymous works. It became customary, in fact, to regard the so-called 'superscriptions' in the ancient manuscripts ('Gospel according to N.') as later additions without historical foundation."

the preaching and witness of the Apostles—the most intimate and authoritative eyewitnesses—being written either by Apostles (Matthew and John) or by intimate disciples of the Apostles (Mark and Luke), who substantially transcribe their oral teaching, within the living historical memory of the events. This topic was addressed by the Second Vatican Council in *Dei Verbum* §18, which observes that the apostolic origin of the four Gospels has *always and everywhere been held in the Church*:

> The Church has always and everywhere held and continues to hold that the four Gospels are of apostolic origin. For what the Apostles preached in fulfillment of the commission of Christ, afterwards they themselves and apostolic men, under the inspiration of the divine Spirit, handed on to us in writing: the foundation of faith, namely, the fourfold Gospel, according to Matthew, Mark, Luke and John.[3]

The text makes the distinction between Apostles and "apostolic men" because the Church's Tradition is that the Gospels according to Matthew and John were written by Apostles, whereas those of Mark and Luke were written not by Apostles but by the intimate collaborators of the Apostles Peter and Paul. Mark was the spiritual son of Peter, accompanying him in Rome,[4] while Luke was the spiritual son and

---

[3] See St. Irenaeus, *Adversus haereses* 3.11.8 (*ANF* 1:428). St. Irenaeus, writing about AD 180, says: "It is not possible that the Gospels can be either more or fewer in number than they are. For, since there are four zones of the world in which we live, and four principal winds ... it is fitting that she (the Church) should have four pillars, breathing out immortality on every side, and vivifying men afresh. From which fact, it is evident that the Word ... has given us the Gospel under four aspects, but bound together by one Spirit." The four Gospels that St. Irenaeus is referring to, of course, are our four canonical Gospels, which he goes on to name.

[4] Martin Hengel gives a very good argument for the traditional claim that the authority of Peter stands behind Mark in "Eye-Witness Memory and the Writing of the Gospels," in *The Written Gospel*, eds. Markus Bockmuehl and Donald A. Hagner (Cambridge, UK: Cambridge University Press, 2005), 91–92: "He certainly still had contact with eyewitnesses. This is true above all for Simon Peter, upon whose tradition he primarily drew according to multiple early ancient church accounts, and who suffered martyrdom in Rome only five or six years before the origin of the work. This is already shown by the unique, predominant role of Peter, who is highlighted by Mark in a striking way through a consciously formed *inclusio*. The Peter tradition in the back-

collaborator of Paul, as we can see in the "we" sections of the Acts of the Apostles, in which St. Luke accompanied St. Paul.

Because of the foundational importance of this question, *Dei Verbum* formulates this truth as something that the Church has "always and everywhere held and continues to hold." This language indicates that this teaching is a definitive teaching of the universal and ordinary Magisterium of the Church.[5] Such teachings are infallible, as stated in *Lumen gentium* §25.[6]

The Catholic Church understands the apostolic Tradition about Christ as the rock on which the Church is founded. It is in this sense that St. Paul, for example, speaks of the Church as "built on the foundation of the Apostles and the prophets, Christ Jesus himself being the cornerstone" (Eph 2:20). The apostolic Tradition is first and foremost the witness of the Apostles about the person, life, and teaching of Jesus Christ. The Church has always held that this apostolic witness is contained in a preeminent way in the four Gospels.

---

ground gives this Gospel (which from a superficial perspective was relatively quickly outdated by Luke and Matthew) lasting authority. The claim that the author was an unknown Gentile Christian, i.e., an anonymous Mr. Nobody without any authority, is absolutely absurd. Also, there is no evidence that it originated in Syria.... The numerous Aramaisms together with the Jewish milieu necessitate a close connection with Palestine; the striking Latinisms as well as church tradition suggest Rome. Behind such a 'revolutionary work' *an authority must stand.*"

[5] See Farkasfalvy, *Inspiration & Interpretation*, 195: "This leaves little doubt that the Council meant to affirm the apostolic origin of the gospels as a tenet of faith taught by the consensus of all Church Fathers and the Magisterium."

[6] *LG* §25: "Although the individual bishops do not enjoy the prerogative of infallibility, they nevertheless proclaim Christ's doctrine infallibly whenever, even though dispersed through the world, but still maintaining the bond of communion among themselves and with the successor of Peter, and authentically teaching matters of faith and morals, they are in agreement on one position as definitively to be held." This teaching would require the second grade of assent indicated in the *Professio fidei*: "I also firmly accept and hold each and every thing definitively proposed by the Church regarding teaching on faith and morals" (see ch. 9, "Three Grades of Assent," above). See CDF, Instruction on the Ecclesial Vocation of the Theologian *Donum veritatis* (1990) §16: "By its nature, the task of religiously guarding and loyally expounding the deposit of divine Revelation (in all its integrity and purity), implies that the Magisterium can make a pronouncement 'in a definitive way' on propositions which, even if not contained among the truths of faith, are nonetheless intimately connected with them, in such a way, that the definitive character of such affirmations derives in the final analysis from revelation itself."

Responses of the Pontifical Biblical Commission

The Church previously addressed the question of the apostolic origin of the Gospels in various Responses of the Pontifical Biblical Commission between 1907 and 1912.[7] These responses are short but precisely formulated documents with a nuanced question and an affirmative or negative answer. They were given in the context of the Church's condemnation of Modernism. *Dei Verbum* §18 is in complete harmony with these responses of the PBC on the apostolic origin of the Gospels, but without addressing the subsidiary questions about the order in which the Gospels were written and their dates.

Matthew

With regard to St. Matthew, the question is raised whether it is certain that the Apostle himself is the author of the Gospel. The reasons for authorship by him rest on the solid testimony of the Fathers of the Church, the titles of the earliest codices, translations, and catalogues of the books of Scripture, and the universal usage of the liturgy.[8] There

---

[7] For the dogmatic character of these decrees and the assent required by them from the faithful, see St. Pius X, *Motu proprio* on the Decisions of the Biblical Commission *Praestantia Scripturae Sacrae* (1907) §79: "All are bound in conscience to submit to the decisions of the Biblical Commission, which have been given in the past and shall be given in the future, in the same way as to the Decrees pertaining to doctrine, issued by the Sacred Congregations and approved by the Sovereign Pontiff. And no one can escape the stigma of disobedience and temerity nor be free of serious guilt whenever they impugn these decisions orally or in writing" (SD, 79). See the clarification of the binding nature of these decrees by Athanasius Miller in 1955: "The decrees of the Pontifical Biblical Commission have great significance. However, as long as these decrees propose views that are neither immediately or mediately connected with truths of faith and morals, it goes without saying that the interpreter of Sacred Scripture may pursue his scientific research with complete freedom and may utilize the results of these investigations, provided always that he respects the teaching authority of the Church" (SD, 327). However, it seems incorrect to assume that most of these responses concerning the Gospels are not at least indirectly concerned with truths of faith, especially when they are referring to the apostolic origin of the Gospels and their true historical character. See also L. C. Fillion, "Décisions de la Commission biblique," *Revue Apologétique* 33 (1921/22): 484–498 and 672–686.

[8] PBC, Response of June 19, 1911, First Question: "Whether, in view of the universal and constant tradition of the Church dating form the first centuries, which is found clearly recorded in the expressed testimony of the Fathers, in the inscriptions of the codices of the Gospel, in the oldest translations of the sacred Books, as well as in the catalogues transmitted to us by the holy Fathers, the ecclesiastical writers, the supreme Pontiffs, and the Councils, and, finally, in the liturgical

are no dissenting voices from antiquity. All our sources agree that the author of the first Gospel is the eyewitness, St. Matthew, also named Levi, the tax collector. It is absurd to think that such a solid tradition could be unfounded.[9]

The Pontifical Biblical Commission also responded affirmatively to the question of whether "the testimony of tradition sufficiently supports the opinion that Matthew wrote before the other Evangelists and that he composed this first Gospel in the native dialect then in use by the Jews of Palestine, for whom this work was intended."[10] With regard to the time of writing, it states that the more probable position is a date before the coming of St. Paul to Rome about the year AD 60.[11]

The Commission also touched on the order of the Gospels in two decrees of June 26, 1912. They affirmed that one should hold, with the ancient tradition, that Matthew is the first Gospel, but it is not necessary to hold that the canonical Greek translation of Matthew was made before the writing of Mark and Luke.[12] It is

---

usages of the Eastern and Western Church, it may and must be affirmed with certainty that Matthew, an apostle of Christ, is truly the author of the Gospel published under his name. Response: Affirmative" (SD, 197).

[9] For modern commentaries that maintain this basic position, see R. Gundry, *Matthew: A Commentary on His Literary and Theological Art* (Grand Rapids: Eerdmans, 1982), 599–622, and R. T. France, *The Gospel of Matthew* (Grand Rapids: Eerdmans, 2007), 15 and 19. See also L. Morris, *The Gospel According to Matthew* (Grand Rapids: Eerdmans, 1992), 12–15.

[10] PBC, Response of June 19, 1911, Second Question (SD, 197).

[11] Ibid., Third Question: "Whether the publication of the original text of this work may be deferred beyond the time of the destruction of Jerusalem so that the prophecies of this event herein recorded must have been written after it; and whether the frequently quoted testimony of Irenaeus (*Adversus haereses* 3.1.2), the uncertain meaning of which is disputed, is yet to be considered of such weight as to require us to reject the opinion of those who consider it more in conformity with tradition that the publication of the Gospel was completed before Paul's arrival in Rome. Response: Negative to both parts" (SD, 197–198).

[12] PBC, Response on the Authorship, Date of Composition, and Historicity of the Gospels of Mark and Luke of June 26, 1912, Fifth Question: "Whether, with regard to the chronological order of the Gospels, it is permissible to abandon the claim, supported as it is by the most ancient and perduring testimony of tradition, that, after Matthew, who first of all wrote his Gospel in his own native dialect, Mark wrote second and Luke third; and whether we must regard this traditional claim as opposed to the opinion which asserts that the second and third Gospels were composed before the Greek version of the first Gospel. Response: Negative to both parts" (SD, 200).

also stated that one should not "easily embrace" the "Two-Source Theory."[13]

Mark and Luke

The PBC addressed similar questions about the Gospels of Mark and Luke in a decree of June 26, 1912. First it affirms the identity of Mark, the disciple of St. Peter, and Luke, the disciple of St. Paul, as the authors of the second and third Gospels.[14] It also affirms that one should hold that their written accounts are in accordance with the preaching of Peter and Paul and "other trustworthy sources."[15]

With regard to the date, the question is posed whether one can hold that these Gospels were written after the destruction of Jerusalem in AD 70, on account of their containing prophecies of that destruction. The answer is negative.[16] Luke's Gospel, furthermore, should be dated to the time of Paul's imprisonment in Rome (ca. AD

---

[13] PBC, Response on the Synoptic Question or the Mutual Relations Among the First Three Gospels of June 26, 1912, Second Question (SD, 202).

[14] PBC, Response on the Authorship, Date of Composition, and Historicity of the Gospels of Mark and Luke of June 26, 1912, First Question: "Whether the clear witness of the tradition, which is remarkably harmonious from the very beginning of the Church and well supported by numerous arguments—namely, by the testimony of the holy Fathers and other ecclesiastical writers expressed in the citations and allusions occurring in their writings, by the usage of ancient heretics, by the versions of the books of the New Testament, by the most ancient and almost universal manuscript codices, and also by the intrinsic evidence from the text of these sacred books—compels us to affirm with certainty that Mark, the disciple and interpreter of Peter, and Luke the physician, the assistant and companion of Paul, were truly the authors of the Gospels respectively attributed to them. Response: Affirmative" (SD, 199).

[15] PBC, Response on the Synoptic Question or the Mutual Relations Among the First Three Gospels of June 26, 1912, Eighth Question: "Whether, considering both the testimony of tradition and the intrinsic arguments with regard to sources used by both Evangelists in the writing of their Gospels, we can fairly call into question the claim that, while Mark wrote according to preaching of Peter and Luke wrote according to Paul, these Evangelists also had at their disposal other trustworthy sources, either oral or written. Response: Negative" (SD, 201).

[16] PBC, Response on the Authorship, Date of Composition, and Historicity of the Gospels of Mark and Luke of June 26, 1912, Sixth Question: "Whether it is permissible to set the time for the composition of the Gospels of Mark and Luke as late as the destruction of the city of Jerusalem; or whether, in view of the fact that Luke's version of the Lord's prophecy of this event appears to be more definite, it may at least be held that his Gospel was written after the siege had begun. Response: Negative to both parts" (SD, 200).

62). The reason given for this is that Luke's Gospel was written before the Acts of the Apostles and the latter can be dated to the close of St. Paul's imprisonment in Rome, for the account of the Acts ends with that and it seems unreasonable to suppose that Luke would have omitted the glorious martyrdom of his two major protagonists, St. Peter and St. Paul, if he were writing after that occurred (ca. AD 64–67).[17] Interestingly, this verdict coincides with the view of the liberal Protestant critic, Adolf von Harnack, who wrote:

> The concluding verses of the acts of the Apostles, taken in conjunction with the absence of any reference in the book to the result of the trial of St Paul and to his martyrdom, make it in the highest degree probable that the work was written at a time when St Paul's trial in Rome had not come to an end.[18]

Gospel of John

The apostolic authorship of the Gospel of John was addressed in a decree of the PBC from May 2, 1907. The first question concerns the authorship of the Gospel by the Apostle John. Here it is affirmed that the "Apostle John and no other must be acknowledged as the author of the fourth Gospel,"[19] not on account of a theological theory or hy-

---

[17] PBC, Response of June 26, 1912, Seventh Question: "Whether it is to be affirmed that the Gospel of Luke was written before the book of the Acts of the Apostles (Acts 1:1–2), and, since the latter book, also written by Luke, was completed at the end of the apostle's Roman imprisonment (Acts 28:30–31), whether his Gospel was composed not after this date. Answer: In the affirmative" (SD, 200). See also the Response of June 12, 1913, Fourth Question: "Whether from the fact that the book itself abruptly concludes after barely mentioning the first two-year captivity of Paul in Rome it may be inferred that the author wrote another volume, now lost, or intended to write one, and that the time of the composition of the Book of Acts can, therefore, be deferred to a time long after this captivity; or whether, instead, it is right and proper to hold that Luke completed this book at the end of the first Roman captivity of the Apostle Paul. Response: Negative to the first part; Affirmative to the second part" (SD, 203).

[18] Adolf von Harnack, Date of Acts and the Synoptic Gospels, trans. J.R. Wilkinson (London: Williams & Norgate; New York: G.P. Putnam's Sons, 1911), 99 (italics original).

[19] PBC, Response On the Authorship and Historicity of the Fourth Gospel of May 29, 1907, First Question (SD, 190).

pothesis, but on the basis of the "constant, universal, and solemn Tradition of the Church." This Tradition is manifested in four kinds of sources:

> (a) from the testimonies and allusions of the holy Fathers, ecclesiastical writers, and even heretics, which, having been certainly derived from the disciples or first successors of the apostles, are linked by a necessary connection to the very origin of the book; (b) from the fact that the name of the author of the Fourth Gospel was received always and everywhere in the canon-lists of the sacred books; (c) from the most ancient manuscripts, codices, and early translations of the same books; and (d) from the public use in liturgy obtaining throughout the whole world from the very beginnings of the Church.[20]

The Value of the Church's Tradition with Regard to the Authorship, Apostolicity, and Historicity of the Gospels

In studying a historical question such as the authorship and dating of the four Gospels, what method ought to be principally employed? Should one put principal importance on the testimony of our earliest historical sources that speak about this question or on the internal evidence of the four Gospels themselves? These two are referred to as external and internal criteria, respectively.

Obviously, both factors must be employed. However, the relative weight that is placed on each will often give rise to very different conclusions. This is manifestly the case with regard to the question of the origins of the Gospels. The Christian tradition until the late eighteenth century put the principal emphasis on external witnesses. This was challenged in Protestant exegesis in the nineteenth century, which increasingly came to prefer internal criteria.[21] Catholic ex-

---

[20] Ibid.

[21] See E. Gutwenger, "The Gospels and Non-Catholic Higher Criticism," in *A Catholic Commentary*

egesis remained anchored to the primacy of the external witness of Christian antiquity until about the middle of the twentieth century. After that time, many Catholic biblical scholars have tended to follow the trend of minimizing the importance of the Patristic tradition in this regard.

The preference for internal evidence is understandable in the Protestant world, which tends to go under the banner of Scripture alone, rejecting Tradition as a secure channel of the transmission of Revelation. Nevertheless, it still goes against sound historical method and devalues the witness of the early Church. For, in historical questions in general, external evidence, because of its objective nature, is almost always to be preferred to merely internal evidence.[22] The devaluation of the Patristic evidence is far less understandable, however, in the world of Catholic theology,[23] in which the consensus of the Fathers of the Church is recognized as a sure witness of apostolic Tradition.

Pope Leo XIII wrote about this question in his encyclical on Scripture, *Providentissimus Deus* §17:

There has arisen, to the great detriment of religion, an inept method, dignified by the name of the "higher criticism,"

---

on Holy Scripture, ed. Bernard Orchard (New York: Thomas Nelson and Sons, 1953), 753: "The important point to be noticed is the easy way in which the savants of the age [the Enlightenment] separated themselves from the historical evidence provided by the documents of early Christian literature. On the whole it must be said that both in its origins and in its later development higher criticism has signally failed in respect for external historical evidence about the composition of the gospels. Right from the beginning it put its trust in its power of literary analysis rather than in the broader approach which includes analysis and historical tradition alike."

[22] See ibid., 756: "The question which of the gospels is the oldest is a historical question. The choice between the two possibilities should be guided by historical evidence which is amply provided in early Christian literature. But historical evidence is in favor of the priority of Matthew."

[23] See James R. Edwards, *The Hebrew Gospel and the Development of the Synoptic Tradition* (Grand Rapids: William B. Eerdmans, 2009), 1: "In defining and investigating the Synoptic Problem, modern scholarship has by and large favored literary evidence and hypotheses over historical testimony from the church fathers. Since Schleiermacher, approaches to the problem have limited themselves almost exclusively to internal evidence among Matthew, Mark, and Luke. Little reference has typically been devoted to the evidence of the church fathers relating to the formation of the gospel tradition. Several reasons contribute to this neglect of the early tradition, among which are the elevation of Scripture over tradition in Protestantism, a bias against Roman Catholic scholarship and dogma that has characterized some streams of Protestant scholarship, and a predisposition in favor of Greek over Hebrew origins of the Christian tradition."

which pretends to judge of the origin, integrity and authority of each Book from internal indications alone. It is clear, on the other hand, that in historical questions, such as the origin and the handing down of writings, the witness of history is of primary importance, and that historical investigation should be made with the utmost care, and that in this matter internal evidence is seldom of great value, except as confirmation. To look upon it in any other light will be to open the door to many evil consequences. It will make the enemies of religion much more bold and confident in attacking and mangling the Sacred Books; and this vaunted "higher criticism" will resolve itself into the reflection of the bias and the prejudice of the critics. It will not throw on the Scripture the light which is sought, or prove of any advantage to doctrine; it will only give rise to disagreement and dissension, those sure notes of error, which the critics in question so plentifully exhibit in their own persons; and seeing that most of them are tainted with false philosophy and rationalism, it must lead to the elimination from the sacred writings of all prophecy and miracle, and of everything else that is outside the natural order.

His remark that the use of internal criteria alone will give rise to disagreement and dissension has been amply borne out in the past 120 years since *Providentissimus Deus*. Not a few scholars in recent decades, Protestants and Catholics, have called for greater caution in the use of internal indications and for giving greater importance to external testimony.[24]

---

[24] See John A. T. Robinson, *Redating the New Testament* (Philadelphia: Westminster Press, 1976); and E. Earle Ellis, *History and Interpretation in New Testament Perspective* (Leiden: Brill, 2001), 50–51: "The literary criticism of New Testament literature accepted by most scholars today, and the New Testament chronology based upon it, has underpinnings that are tenuous and that in some cases can be shown to be historically false. If this is so, the dating of the documents must perforce rely less upon internal literary characteristics and more upon the book's attributions of authorship, upon early Patristic tradition and upon historical correlations such as those that J. A. T. Robinson pointed to." See also, among others, Jean Carmignac, *The Birth of the Synoptic Gospels*, trans. Michael J. Wrenn (Chicago: Franciscan Herald Press, 1987); Craig L. Blomberg, *The Historical Reliability of the Gospels*, 2nd ed. (Downer's Grove: IV Academic, 2007); Blomberg,

Patristic Witness on the Apostolic Origin of the Gospels

St. Papias

The earliest witness on the authorship of the Gospels is St. Papias, Bishop of Hierapolis in Phrygia (now Turkey) and a contemporary of St. Ignatius of Antioch. His testimony is very important, for, according to St. Irenaeus, he was a disciple of St. John the Evangelist,[25] whom Papias refers to as John the Elder [presbyter].[26] Papias wrote a five-volume treatise called *An Exposition of the Oracles* [Scriptures] *of the Lord*,[27] which has been lost, but some fragments of it have been preserved by Eusebius. In one of these fragments, Papias speaks of the composition of the Gospel of Mark, attributing the information to the "presbyter" John:

> This also the Presbyter [John] used to say: "When Mark became Peter's interpreter, he wrote down accurately, although not in order, all that he remembered of what was said or done by the Lord. For he had not heard the Lord nor followed Him, but later, as I have said, he did Peter, who made his teaching fit

---

The Historical Reliability of John's Gospel: Issues & Commentary (Downer's Grove: InterVarsity Press, 2001); and Richard Bauckham, *Jesus and the Eyewitnesses: The Gospels as Eyewitness Testimony* (Grand Rapids: Eerdmans, 2006).

[25] St. Irenaeus says that Papias was "a hearer of John, and companion of Polycarp" (*Adversus haereses* 5.33.4; in *ANF* 1:563). St. Irenaeus himself was a disciple of Polycarp in his youth, so that his information about Papias ought to have been reliable.

[26] As will be seen below, Eusebius thought that "John the Elder" was a disciple distinct from John the Apostle, but it seems that Eusebius was mistaken. In either case, however, this John is said to be a direct disciple of the Lord, which means someone who followed Jesus during His public ministry. We know that John the Apostle lived to a very advanced age, and he would fittingly be referred to as "the Elder" *par excellence* on account of his age and apostolic dignity. In 2 and 3 John, the author refers to himself as "the presbyter" (or "elder"). See John Chapman, *John the Presbyter and the Fourth Gospel* (Oxford, UK: Clarendon, 1911), 35–40.

[27] Λογίων Κυριακῶν Ἐξήγησις. See John Chapman, "Papias," in the *Catholic Encyclopedia*, vol. 11 (New York: Appleton, 1911), 11:458: "*Logia kyriaka* in Papias, in Irenaeus, in Photius, means 'the divine oracles' of the Old or New Testament or both." Scholars assign different dates for the work; probably the work was written between the years 100 and 140. Recent scholars incline for the earlier date; see William R. Schoedel, "Papias," in *The Anchor Bible Dictionary*, ed. David Noel Freedman, vol. 5 (New York: Doubleday, 1992), 140.

his needs without, as it were, making any arrangement of the Lord's oracles,[28] so that Mark made no mistake in thus writing some things down as he remembered them. For to one thing he gave careful attention, to omit nothing of what he heard and to falsify nothing in this.[29]

Papias tells us, on the authority of John, that the Gospel of Mark records for us the direct testimony of St. Peter about Christ in His public ministry, Passion, and Resurrection. This affirmation is of great importance, for St. Peter was certainly a rather crucial eyewitness! The Gospel of Mark is in harmony with this identification, for it is full of particular and incidental details such as an eyewitness would give. Furthermore, the Gospel of Mark has the peculiarity that the merits and dignity of St. Peter are kept out of view, whereas his faults are sincerely confessed. For example, it contains Jesus's strong reproof of St. Peter after his confession of faith ("Get thee behind me, Satan"), but it is does not give the Lord's words of praise and the promise of primacy, uttered on the same occasion (according to St. Matthew): "On this rock I will build my Church." The most probable reason for this is St. Peter's humility. It would not be proper for St. Peter to preach words of praise or honor with regard to himself.[30] In the same way, through humility the Blessed Virgin could not tell St. Joseph that she had been chosen to be the Mother of God.

It can also be inferred from this account of Papias that the Gospel of Mark had perhaps been criticized by some as lacking an ordered narration of the teaching of the Lord, such as that which is found in Matthew and Luke. In fact, the Gospel of Mark is much less frequently cited by the early Fathers than the other three Gospels.[31] Papias

---

[28] The Greek term here is λογια. It seems to refer to the whole Gospel, not just to the sayings or discourses of the Lord. The same word appears in the title of Papias's book and in his description of the Gospel of Matthew.

[29] *Historia ecclesiastica* 3.39, in Eusibius, *Ecclesiastical History*, vol. 1 (Fathers of the Church 19), trans. R. J. Deferrari (Washington, DC: The Catholic University of America Press, 1953), 206.

[30] Eusebius makes this argument in *The Proof of the Gospel: Being the Demonstratio Evangelica of Eusebius of Caesarea*, trans. W. J. Ferrar (New York: Macmillan, 1920), 139.

[31] See Édouard Massaux, *The Influence of the Gospel of Saint Matthew on Christian Literature Before*

defends the Gospel of Mark by stating that Mark did not have the intention of making an ordered account, but rather to be faithful to the oral preaching of St. Peter as he had heard it. It is significant that Papias attributes this defense of the Gospel of Mark to the authority of John.

With regard to Matthew, Papias has made the following brief statement: "Now Matthew collected the oracles [*logia*] in the Hebrew language, and each one interpreted [translated] them as he was able."[32] There has been a great deal of discussion about the meaning of the word *logia* here. In general Papias seems to use the word to indicate the Gospel in general and its contents, which are the "Lord's sayings and doings." There is no reason to limit it to "sayings" as opposed to narrative material.[33] This question has been thoroughly studied by R. Gryson, who comes to the conclusion that the word *logia* in the writings of the Apostolic Fathers[34] almost always refers to the Scriptures in general, and not specifically to "sayings" or "discourses."[35]

It makes perfect sense that the first Gospel would have been written in Hebrew or Aramaic, for the Church's first effort of evangelization—in her first quarter century of existence—was directed primarily to the Jews in Israel.[36] The Gospel of Matthew would thus be a

---

Saint Irenaeus, trans. Norman J. Belval and Suzanne Hecht, ed. Arthur J. Bellinzoni, 3 vols. (Macon: Mercer University, 1993), especially 3:188: "The literary influence of the Gospel of Mk. is practically nil on these writings. This characteristic of the early tradition constitutes a strange phenomenon. How can we explain this silence of tradition if, as is generally believed, Mk. was the first of the canonical gospels? How can we explain that the first Christians hardly resorted to it, so that it appeared almost nonexistent?"

[32] In Eusebius, *Historia ecclesiastica* 3.39 (Deferrari, 206).

[33] See R. Gryson, R. "A propos du témoignage de Papias sur Matthieu: le sens de logion chez les Pères du second siècle," *Ephemerides Theologicae Lovanienses* 41 (1965): 530–547; Carmignac, *The Birth of the Synoptic Gospels*, 53–54; and Edwards, *Hebrew Gospel and the Development of the Synoptic Tradition*, 3–6.

[34] For examples, see Clement I, *Letter to the Corinthians* 19.1, 53.1, and 62.3; in Michael Holmes, *The Apostolic Fathers: Greek Texts and English Translations*, 3rd ed. (Grand Rapids: Baker Books, 2007), 72 (19.1), 114 (53.1), and 128 (62.3); Polycarp to Philippians 7.1 (ibid., 288); 2 Clement 13.3 (ibid., 154); St. Irenaeus, *Adversus haereses* 1.8.1 (*ANF*, 1:326).

[35] Gryson, "A propos du témoignage de Papias sur Matthieu."

[36] See George Howard, *The Gospel of Matthew according to a Primitive Hebrew Text* (Macon: Mercer University Press, 1987).

record of the first apostolic preaching in Palestine. Papias also seems to infer that at first there was no official translation of Matthew into Greek, but that one already existed in Papias's time. Our canonical Greek Gospel of Matthew would thus be a translation that was officially adopted by the Church in the latter part of the first century, as Greek became her predominant language.

Since the fragments of Papias's work are our earliest direct source on the origins of the Gospels, it is important to consider the quality of his sources. In another fragment quoted by Eusebius, Papias speaks about the great importance he put on collecting the oral tradition that he heard directly from the disciples of the Apostles and from John himself, as well as from a disciple of the Lord named Aristion:[37]

> I will not hesitate to set down for you, along with my interpretations, everything I carefully learned then from the elders and carefully remembered, guaranteeing their truth. For unlike most people I did not enjoy those who have a great deal to say, but those who teach the truth. Nor did I enjoy those who recall someone else's commandments, but those who remember the commandments given by the Lord to the faith and proceeding from the truth itself. And if by chance someone who had been a follower of the elders should come my way, I inquired about the words of the elders—what Andrew or Peter said, or Philip, or Thomas, or James, or John, or Matthew, or any other of the Lord's disciples, and whatever Aristion and the elder John, the Lord's disciples, were saying.[38] For I did not think that information from books would profit me as much as information from a living and abiding voice.[39]

---

[37] Aristion is listed in the *Roman Martyrology* as one of the seventy-two disciples, and his martyrdom is commemorated on Feb. 22, together with St. Papias; see *The Roman Martyrology*, ed. J. B. O'Connell (Westminster: The Newman Press, 1962), 38.

[38] The Greek verb here is in the present tense.

[39] Quoted in Eusebius, *Historia ecclesiastica* 3.39.3–4 (Holmes, *Apostolic Fathers*, 735). For a commentary on this text of Papias, see Bauckham, *Jesus and the Eyewitnesses*, 12–38, and Chapman, *John the Presbyter*, 35–40.

There are two important points to be noticed. First, Papias considered the oral testimony of the eyewitnesses of Christ and the Apostles to be of greater importance than written texts. Secondly, some of these eyewitnesses (the "elder John,"[40] a disciple named Aristion, and the disciples of the other Apostles) were still active in the Church towards the end of the first century. Papias was still in the time of living memory of the Apostles and at the end of the time of living memory of Jesus.

It should be noticed that Papias speaks about his interest in what the disciples of the Lord *had said* and were *still saying*.[41] Of the disciples of the Lord, only Aristion and the venerable John were still alive and active during this period so as to give contemporary testimony. The most obvious interpretation of this text, which I believe is correct, is that Papias is distinguishing past and present witness. For, he inquired into what the elders/direct disciples had said, and also what those among them who were still alive were saying. Those of the direct disciples who were still alive when Papias was writing this are said to be Aristion and John. That John the Apostle and Evangelist was still alive in the reign of Trajan is confirmed by many other sources.[42]

This text has generated much controversy, especially on account of Eusebius' commentary on it. Eusebius, who is anxious to discredit the apostolicity and canonicity of the book of Revelation because of the millenarianism that Papias, Irenaeus, and others drew from it,[43] distinguishes between two Johns: the apostle and the elder. This

---

[40] Although some have disputed this, Papias seems to use the term "elder" to refer to the Apostles. Papias also speaks of the "disciples of the Lord," which refers to *direct* disciples of Jesus during His public ministry, including the Apostles and other disciples, such as the seventy-two. It appears that Aristion should be counted among the seventy-two, for he is said to be a disciple, although he is not given the title of Elder. This way of speaking of an Apostle with the title "elder" is in harmony with the 1 and 3 John, in which the author refers to himself as "the elder." Similarly, it corresponds to 1 Pet 5:1, in which the author refers to himself as "a fellow elder and a witness of the sufferings of Christ."

[41] See William R. Schoedel, *Polycarp, Martyrdom of Polycarp, Fragments of Papias* (Camden: Thomas Nelson, 1967), 97–100.

[42] See Eusebius, *Historia ecclesiastica* 3.23, who cites St. Irenaeus and Clement of Alexandria in support of this.

[43] See Gundry, *Matthew*, 612: "To be sure, Eusebius distinguishes between the Apostle John and the Elder John (HE 3.39.6). But the distinction is tendentious. Eusebius does not like the Book

distinction suits his purpose because he can thus attribute the fourth Gospel to the Apostle and the book of Revelation to another John, the elder, who lacks apostolic status. Eusebius writes:

> His mentioning the name of John twice is worth noting here. The first of these he reckons along with Peter and James and Matthew and the other Apostles, meaning clearly the Evangelist, but the other John, after expanding his statement, he places outside the number of the Apostles, placing Aristion before him, and he distinctly calls him a presbyter. Thus, by these words is proved the truth of the story of those who have said that two persons in Asia bore the same name, and that there were two tombs in Ephesus and each of these even today is said to be John's. We must give attention to this, for it is probable that the second (unless you would prefer the first) saw the Revelation which passes under the name of John.[44]

With all due respect, I think that Eusebius is mistaken, for it is much more reasonable to think that Papias is concerned to distinguish two different periods of testimony—past and present—rather than two different persons. Papias wants to point out that he bases himself on eyewitness testimony, and especially on the testimony of eyewitnesses who were still alive. Of the eyewitnesses, most had passed away before his time, except for Aristion and John, who are both said to be "disciples of the Lord." For this reason, John is mentioned twice, first together with the other Apostles whose past testimony was transmitted to him by others, and then with Aristion alone as one remaining alive and whose word was still reaching him directly in person.[45]

---

of Revelation—the millenarianism that Papias, Irenaeus, and others have drawn from it seems crassly materialistic to him (HE 3.339.12–13)—so he wants to belittle the book by making it unapostolic, i.e., written by an elder named John as opposed to the apostle named John."

[44] Eusebius, *Historia ecclesiastica* 3.39.5–6 (Deferrari, 203–204).

[45] See Gundry, *Matthew*, 613: "Thus it appears that Papias repeats John's name because John is the last surviving elder and therefore is one whose current statements Papias has been hearing by first-hand report."

In other words, the double mention of John seems pointless to Eusebius and those who follow his line of interpretation unless the two-fold mention corresponded to two distinct persons. However, Papias has a perfectly good reason to mention John twice. On the one hand he belongs to the group of Apostles whose witness has maximum authority, even if it comes second-hand. Secondly, he is mentioned again because only he and Aristion are personal disciples or eyewitnesses of the Lord still alive and speaking close to the time of Papias's writing.

This mention of Aristion and John as still speaking at the time of the writing of Papias's work also provides crucial evidence for determining its date. It should be dated to the end of the lifetime of St. John and Aristion, direct disciples of the Lord, or not long after. Thus it may have been written some eighty years after the death of Jesus, which again puts it during the reign of the Emperor Trajan, which is the time-period in which Eusebius discusses Papias.

St. Justin Martyr (ca. AD 100–165)

St. Justin Martyr mentions the Gospels in his description of the Sunday liturgy in his *First Apology*, written in the middle of the second century:

> For the Apostles in the memoirs composed by them, which are called Gospels, thus handed down what was commanded them: that Jesus took bread and having given thanks, said: "Do this for my memorial, this is my body"; and likewise He took the chalice and having given thanks said: "This is my blood;" and gave it to them alone. . . . And on the day called Sunday all who live in cities or in the country gather together in one place, and the memoirs of the Apostles or the writings of the prophets are read, as long as time permits. Then when the reader has finished, the Ruler in a discourse instructs and exhorts to the imitation of these good things.[46]

---

[46] Justin Martyr, *First Apology* 66–67, in *St. Justin Martyr: The First and Second Apologies*, trans. Leslie William Barnard (New York: Paulist Press, 1997), 70–71.

It is significant that, in the middle of the second century, the Gospels are read in the liturgy together with the writings of the prophets (which probably means the Old Testament in general), and that Justin refers to them with the description "memoirs of the Apostles." This manifests the conviction of St. Justin's time as to their apostolic origin.

St. Irenaeus (ca. AD 120–203)

A native Greek from Smyrna (Asia Minor), St. Irenaeus was, in his youth, a disciple of St. Polycarp, who in his turn was a disciple of St. John the Apostle. St. Irenaeus came to prominence after migrating to the Latin west. In the year 177, he was appointed bishop of Lyons, France, where he soon published his five-volume work, *Against Heresies* (*Refutation and Overthrow of What Is Wrongly Called "Knowledge"*). In book 3 of this work, he argues against the Gnostics on the basis of Scripture and Tradition. He begins, therefore, by speaking about the authority of the four Gospels and the apostolic Tradition.

He stresses, against the Gnostics, that the Gospels come from the "perfect understanding" that the Apostles acquired on Pentecost. He distinguishes an initial phase of oral apostolic preaching that preceded the writing of the Gospels. He then classifies the Gospels into three groups, marked by three different geographical locations and times:

> In point of fact, we received the knowledge of the economy of our salvation through no others than those through whom the Gospel has come down to us. This Gospel they first preached orally, but later by God's will they handed it on [*tradiderunt*] to us in the Scriptures, so that it would be "the foundation and pillar of our faith." ... Matthew, accordingly, produced a writing of the Gospel among the Hebrews in their own language, whereas Peter and Paul evangelized at Rome and founded the Church [there]. But after their departure, Mark, Peter's disciple and translator, handed down to us in

writing what was preached by Peter. Luke too, Paul's follower, set down in a book the Gospel that was preached by Paul. Later, John likewise, the Lord's disciple who had also rested on His breast, issued the Gospel while living at Ephesus of Asia.[47]

This testimony is extremely important, for it comes from a disciple of a disciple of St. John and a bishop familiar with the traditions both of the Eastern and Western churches, for he was a native of Asia Minor and a bishop of France. According to St. Irenaeus, the first and the last Gospels were written by Apostles—Matthew and John—whereas the second and the third Gospels were written by disciples of Peter and Paul, the princes of the Apostles, whose oral preaching they record. Therefore, all four Gospels have apostolic authority and are based on eyewitnesses designated by Jesus Christ as Apostles, the most authentic witnesses of all that He did and taught. Indeed, St. Irenaeus's principal concern in this text is to tie the four Gospels to the authoritative witness and prior oral preaching of four principal Apostles: Matthew and John directly, and Peter and Paul indirectly through the instrumentality of Mark and Luke.[48]

St. Irenaeus also stresses that there are but four canonical Gospels that stand at the foundation of the Church's faith on account of the apostolic witness that they give of Jesus Christ. The number four is compared to the four directions and the four faces of the cherubim

---

[47] *Adversus haereses* 3.1.1, in *St. Irenaeus of Lyons: Against the Heresies; Book 3*, trans. Dominic J. Unger, Ancient Christian Writers 64 (New York: The Newman Press, 2012), 30. On Luke, see also *Adversus haereses* 3.14.1: "Luke, who always preached with Paul and was called 'beloved,' and together with him proclaimed the good news and was entrusted with recording the Gospel for us" (Unger, 73).

[48] For a good analysis of St. Irenaeus's intention in this text, see John T. Curran, "St. Irenaeus on the Dates of the Gospels," *Catholic Biblical Quarterly* 5 (1943): 34–46 (article part 1), 160–178 (part 2), 301–310 (part 3), and 445–457 (part 4). See also M. C. Steenberg's introduction to *St. Irenaeus of Lyons: Against the Heresies; Book 3*: "For Irenaeus, the oral origins of the Gospel are part and parcel of the common voice of the Church's true witness—for the four gospel accounts do not emerge out of the independent textual or historical traditions, but out of the same, common oral preaching that was the product of the apostolic experience of Christ.... In the same way, Irenaeus is keen to identify and stress the apostolic origins of each account of what he does not call 'the four Gospels' (as we are wont to do today), but, rather, the 'fourfold Gospel which is held together by the one Spirit' (3.11.8)—stressing its common and divinely united proclamation" (Unger, 8).

in the visions of Ezekiel 1:10 and Revelation 4:7. Although, at this time, the New Testament canon was not fully determined, for some churches had doubts with regard to a few books (such as Revelation, Hebrews, 2 Peter, and 2 and 3 John), the canon was closed and certain with regard to the four Gospels. He writes:

> It is not possible that there be more Gospels in number than these, or fewer. By way of illustration, since there are four zones in the world in which we live, and four cardinal winds, and since the Church is spread over the whole earth, and since "the pillar and bulwark" of the Church is the Gospel and the Spirit of life, consequently she has four pillars, blowing imperishability from all sides and giving life to men. From these things it is manifest that the Word, who is Artificer of all things and "is enthroned upon the Cherubim and holds together all things," and who was manifested to men, gave us the four-fold Gospel, which is held together by the one Spirit.[49]

St. Irenaeus also mentions that even the heretics have to recognize the great authority of the Gospels, for they have no choice but to try to base their claims on at least one of them: "Now, the authority of these Gospels is so great that the heretics themselves bear witness to them, and each one of them tries to establish his doctrine with the Gospels as a starting point."[50]

St. Irenaeus sees the four Gospels as a unitary witness to Christ, the "fourfold Gospel," which he contrasts to the very different depictions of Christ found in the Gnostic gospels, such as in Valentinus's

---

[49] *Adversus haereses* 3.11.8 (Unger, 56).

[50] Ibid. 3.11.7 (Unger, 55). The text continues: "The Ebionites use only the Gospel of Matthew. But by this same Gospel they are convicted of not teaching the right things about the Lord. Marcion, on the other hand, mutilated the Gospel according to Luke; but by the passages he retains he is shown to be a blasphemer against the only God who exists. Those, however, who prefer the Gospel of Mark and divide Jesus from Christ, and assert that Christ remained impassible but that Jesus suffered, can be corrected if they read this Gospel with a love for the truth. Finally, the followers of Valentinus, who make very ample use of the Gospel according to John ... are by this very Gospel exposed to be entirely false.... Since, therefore, those who contradict us bear witness to and use these [Gospels], our proof drawn from them is solid and true" (Unger, 55–56).

so-called "Gospel of Truth." St. Irenaeus mocks Valentinus for daring to fabricate a work on Christ and give it such a title:

> On the other hand, the followers of Valentinus, living without any fear whatever, put forth their own writings and boast of having more Gospels than there really are. Indeed, they have carried their boldness so far that they give the title *Gospel of Truth* to a book which they have but recently composed, and which agrees in no wise with the Gospels of the apostles. . . . That these alone, however, are the true and authentic Gospels, and that there cannot be more than we have predicated, nor fewer, I have proved by many and strong arguments. For since God arranged and harmonized all things well, it is necessary that also the form of the Gospel be arranged and fitted together well.[51]

Today scholars tend to make much about the discrepancies between the four Gospels, whereas for St. Irenaeus, the only significant discrepancy was between the four Gospels, on the one hand, and the Gnostic gospels, on the other.

Pantaenus

We have an interesting testimony regarding the Gospel of Matthew from Pantaenus, who died around AD 200. He was the founder of the catechetical school in Alexandria and the teacher of Clement of Alexandria. In his *Ecclesiastical History*, Eusebius recounts Pantaenus's journey to India, where he found the Gospel of Matthew in Hebrew, and the tradition that the Gospel had been brought there by St. Bartholomew.[52] St. Jerome confirms this testimony in his *Lives of Illustrious Men*:

---

[51] *Adversus haereses* 3.11.9 (Unger, 58).

[52] Eusebius, *Historia ecclesiastica* 5.10: "Pantaenus . . . is said to have gone among the Indians, where a report is that he discovered the Gospel according to Matthew among some there who knew Christ, which had anticipated his arrival; Bartholomew, one of the Apostles, had preached to them and had left them the writing of Matthew in Hebrew letters, which writing they preserved until the aforesaid time" (Deferrari, 303).

Pantaenus, a philosopher of the stoic school . . . was of so great prudence and erudition both in scripture and secular literature that, on the request of the legates of that nation, he was sent to India by Demetrius bishop of Alexandria, where he found that Bartholomew, one of the twelve apostles, had preached the advent of the Lord Jesus according to the gospel of Matthew, and on his return to Alexandria he brought this with him written in Hebrew characters.[53]

Tertullian

Tertullian speaks of the apostolic authority of the four Gospels in his polemical work *Adversus Marcionem* (*Against Marcion*), completed in 208 (although a first edition dates from perhaps 198).[54] Marcion was a gnostic whose doctrine was radically anti-Jewish. He considered the God of the Old Testament to be different from the God proclaimed by Christ. Consequently, he did not recognize the Old Testament and radically mutilated the canon of the New Testament, keeping only an adulterated version of Luke and some of the Letters of St. Paul, which he stripped of their references to the Old Testament. In book four of *Against Marcion*, Tertullian emphasizes that the apostolic authority of the four Gospels is the foundation for theological controversy. This authority rests on the fact that (as proclaimed by *Dei Verbum* §18) two of the four Gospels have Apostles as their authors—Matthew and John—and the remaining two were written by "apostolic men," Mark and Luke, who were close disciples of the principal apostles, Peter and Paul:

I lay it down to begin with that the documents of the gospel have the apostles for their authors, and that this task of pro-

---

[53] St. Jerome, *Lives of Illustrious Men* 36 (trans. Ernest Cushing Richardson in *NPNF2*, 3:370). Carmignac comments: "This story of a Hebrew Gospel of Matthew discovered in the Indies is so improbable that it just might be true" (*Birth of the Synoptic Gospels*, 56).

[54] See Ernest Evans's introduction to Tertullian, *Adversus Marcionem*, trans. E. Evans (Oxford: Clarendon Press, 1972), 1:xviii.

mulgating the gospel was imposed upon them by our Lord himself. If they also have for their authors apostolic men, yet these stand not alone, but as companions of apostles or followers of apostles: because the preaching of disciples might be made suspect of the desire of vainglory, unless there stood by it the authority of their teachers, or rather the authority of Christ, which made the apostles teachers. In short, from among the apostles the faith is introduced to us by John and by Matthew, while from among apostolic men Luke and Mark give it renewal, [all of them] beginning with the same rules [of belief], as far as relates to the one only God, the Creator, and to his Christ, born of a virgin, the fulfilment of the law and the prophets. It matters not that the arrangement of their narratives varies, so long as there is agreement on the essentials of the faith—and on these they show no agreement with Marcion.[55]

With regard to the Gospel of Luke, the one Gospel recognized by Marcion, Tertullian insists that it has its authority through its acceptance by the Apostles and its essential agreement with them.[56] Tertullian then goes on to reproach Marcion for discarding the other three Gospels (Matthew, Mark, and John), which have no less authority

---

[55] *Adversus Marcionem* 4.2 (Evans, 261–263).

[56] Ibid. (Evans, 263–265): "Now Luke was not an apostle but an apostolic man, not a master but a disciple, in any case less than his master, and assuredly even more of lesser account as being the follower of a later apostle, Paul, to be sure: so that even if Marcion had introduced his gospel under the name of Paul in person, that one single document would not be adequate for our faith, if destitute of the support of his predecessors. For we should demand the production of that gospel also which Paul found [in existence], that to which he gave his assent, that with which shortly afterwards he was anxious that his own should agree: for his intention in going up to Jerusalem to know and to consult the apostles, was lest perchance he had run in vain—that is, lest perchance he had not believed as they did, or was not preaching the gospel in their manner. At length, when he had conferred with the original [apostles], and there was agreement concerning the rule of the faith, they joined the right hands [of fellowship], and from thenceforth divided their spheres of preaching, so that the others should go to the Jews, but Paul to Jews and gentiles. If he therefore who gave the light to Luke chose to have his predecessors' authority for his faith as well as his preaching, much more must I require for Luke's gospel the authority which was necessary for the gospel of his master."

than that of Luke, an authority derived from the apostolic Church. In doing so, he gives a summary account of what was believed concerning the origin of the four Gospels:

> That same authority of the apostolic churches will stand as witness also for the other gospels, which no less [than Luke's] we possess by their agency and according to their text—I mean John's and Matthew's, though that which Mark produced is stated to be Peter's, whose interpreter Mark was. Luke's narrative also they usually attribute to Paul. It is permissible for the works which disciples published to be regarded as belonging to their masters. And so concerning these also Marcion must be called to account, how it is that he has passed them over, and preferred to take his stand upon Luke's, as though these too, no less than Luke's, have not been in the churches since the beginning—indeed it is to be supposed that they have even greater claim to have been since the beginning, since they were earlier, as written by apostles, and established along with the churches. Otherwise, if the apostles published nothing, how can it have come about that their disciples published things instead, when they could not even have existed as disciples apart from some instruction by their masters?[57]

Here Tertullian supposes that the Gospel according to Matthew and John (at least in oral form)—and the preaching of Peter on which Mark was based—were earlier than that of Luke. The reasoning is that the Gospel of the Apostles must have been substantially present from the beginning of the establishment of the apostolic churches.[58]

---

[57] Ibid. 4.5 (Evans, 271–273).

[58] See also the continuation of the text (ibid.): "These are the sort of summary arguments I use when skirmishing light-armed against heretics on behalf of the faith of the gospel, arguments which claim the support of that succession of times which pleads the previous question against the late emergence of falsifiers, as well as that authority of the churches which gives expert witness to the tradition of the apostles: because the truth must of necessity precede the false, and proceed from those from whom its tradition began" (Evans, 273). See also *On the Prescriptions of Heretics* chs. 19–21 and 37, in which Tertullian holds the priority of Tradition over Scripture.

This, however, does not mean that the written Gospels of Matthew and John in their current form predate the Gospel of Luke. Rather, it implies that their oral teaching, together with those of the other Apostles, pre-existed as the foundation of the churches, as well as of the written Gospels.[59] Indeed, Luke tells us in his prologue that he assiduously consulted the eyewitness sources, which could have been in oral or written form.

Clement of Alexandria

After St. Irenaeus and Papias, the most important witness is that of Clement of Alexandria at the beginning of the third century. Eusebius quotes from Clement's lost *Hypotyposes*, in which the latter spoke about the Gospels of Mark and John:

> Clement gives the tradition of the earliest presbyters, as to the order of the Gospels, in the following manner: The Gospels containing the genealogies, he says, were written first. The Gospel according to Mark had this occasion. As Peter had preached the Word publicly at Rome, and declared the Gospel by the Spirit, many who were present requested that Mark, who had followed him for a long time and remembered his sayings, should write them out. And having composed the Gospel, he gave it to those who had requested it. When Peter learned of this, he neither directly forbade nor encouraged it. But, last of all, John, perceiving that the external facts had been made plain in the Gospel, being urged by his friends, and inspired by the Spirit, composed a spiritual Gospel.[60]

There is much discussion about the meaning of the phrase, "the Gospels containing the genealogies were *written first*," because it

---

[59] See John Rist, *On the Independence of Matthew and Mark* (Cambridge, UK: Cambridge University Press, 1978), 102: "It is clear from Paul's letters and above all from Acts that the words and the authority of the eyewitnesses provided the basic evidence on which the Churches were founded."

[60] Eusebius, *Historia ecclesiastica* 6.14.5–7 (NPNF2, 1:251).

seems to conflict with all other Patristic evidence.[61] Otherwise, the tradition about Mark coincides generally with that of Papias.

Stephen C. Carlson has given a new interpretation of Clement's text that makes good sense. He argues that the word προγεγράφθαι should not be translated "written first," but rather "published open-ly,"[62] or "officially sanctioned," or publicly proclaimed.[63] Thus it would read: "The Gospels containing the genealogies, he says, were pub-lished officially (or publicly)." This would presumably mean officially sanctioned by the leading Apostles. Perhaps it would refer to being sanctioned by the Apostles for liturgical reading. Then Clement goes on to say that Mark's Gospel was not officially sanctioned in that way by Peter, but was tolerated by him when requested by the faithful.

When Clement speaks of a "spiritual gospel," he means a work that records the most profound and lofty teaching of Christ. For this reason, John the Evangelist was symbolized as an eagle soaring far above the plain. However, the fact that it is a "spiritual gospel" does not in itself make it less historical. John, in the selection of his mate-rial, chose to record those more profound discourses and dialogues that were not recorded by the other Evangelists who came before him.

Origen

Origen (ca. 184–254), a disciple of Clement of Alexandria and the greatest Scripture scholar of his time, gives an important witness of the Church's tradition concerning the four Gospels in the first half of

---

[61] See C. S. Carlson, "Clement of Alexandria on the 'Order' of the Gospels," in *New Testament Studies* 47 (2001): 118–125, and D. Farkasfalvy, "The Presbyter's Witness on the Order of the Gospels as Reported by Clement of Alexandria," *Catholic Biblical Quarterly* 54 (1992): 260–270.

[62] See Carlson, "Clement of Alexandria," 123: "If προγεγράφθαι is taken in the sense of writing publicly, Clement's statement would mean: 'He said that those gospels having the genealogies were published openly,' with an implication that their publication was official. In contrast with the standard chronological interpretation, this sense provides a better fit with its literary context and poses no difficulty for Origen's ordering of the gospels. Finally, Clement's statement under this proposal suits its context in Eusebius."

[63] In Gal 3:1, this verb has the sense of "publicly" or "authoritatively proclaimed": "O foolish Galatians! Who has bewitched you, before whose eyes Jesus Christ was *publicly portrayed* as cruci-fied?" Other texts Carlson brings in for comparison are Josephus, *Antiquities* 12.33 and Clement, cited by Eusebius shortly before the passage under consideration in *Historia ecclesiastica* 6.14.2.

the third century. Eusebius preserves a fragment from the beginning of Origen's commentary on the Gospel of Matthew:

> For I learned by tradition concerning the four Gospels, which alone are indisputable in the Church of God under heaven, that first there was written that according to the one-time tax-collector and later Apostle of Jesus Christ, Matthew, who published it for those who from Judaism came to have the faith, being composed in the Hebrew language; secondly, that according to Mark, which he wrote as Peter guided him, whom also Peter acknowledged as son in his Catholic Epistle [1 Pet 5:13], speaking with these words: "The church that is in Babylon, elected together with you, salutes you: and so does my son Mark"; and thirdly, that according to Luke, who composed this Gospel, which was praised by Paul,[64] for Gentile converts; and in addition to them all, that according to John.[65]

It is significant that Origen attributes his knowledge of the authorship and circumstances of the four Gospels to *Tradition*, and not simply to personal research, a particular authority such as Papias, or a theory of a particular theological school.

Furthermore, according to Origen, the chronological order in which the Gospels were written corresponds to their order in our Bibles: Matthew, Mark, Luke, and John. Origen, like Papias and St. Irenaeus, confirms that Matthew was written by the Apostle who had been a publican and was written first in Hebrew. Like St. Irenaeus, he is concerned to show the apostolic origin of all four Gospels, linking Mark and Luke to Peter and Paul, respectively.

---

[64] This is a reference to 2 Cor 8:18: "We have sent with him the brother whose praise is in the gospel through all the churches." Origen understands this text as referring to Luke. See also Origen, Homily 1 on Luke 1:1–4: "Hence the Apostle praises him deservedly when he says, 'He is praised for his Gospel throughout all the churches.' Scripture says this about no one else; it uses the expression only for Luke"; see *Origen: Homilies on Luke: Fragments on Luke*, trans. Joseph T. Lienhard, S.J., The Fathers of the Church 94 (Washington, DC: The Catholic University of America Press, 1996), 6.

[65] Eusebius, *Historia ecclesiastica* 6.25 (Deferrari, 48–49).

In his Homilies on Luke, Origen again stresses that there are only four canonical Gospels, although heretical sects have circulated many others:

> The Church has four Gospels. Heretics have very many. One of them is entitled *According to the Egyptians*, another *According to the Twelve Apostles*. Basilides, too, dared to write a gospel and give it his own name. . . . I know of one gospel called *According to Thomas*, and another *According to Matthias*. . . . But in all these questions we approve of nothing but what the Church approves of, namely only four canonical Gospels.[66]

In his first homily on Luke, Origen also mentions that John collected and approved the three synoptic Gospels during the reign of Nero, before writing his own to complement theirs. He bases this on a traditional source.[67]

Eusebius

Eusebius's *Ecclesiastical History* is the most valuable source of information about the authorship of the four Gospels, for he collects the most important testimonies of the Fathers before his time. He gives his own view of the four Gospels in book 3.24, where he begins by saying that, of the eyewitnesses of the Lord among the twelve Apostles and seventy-two disciples, only Matthew and John wrote Gospels, after having preached orally. He also mentions that Matthew wrote first in his "native tongue" and that John wrote last.

Eusebius indicates here that he is basing himself on a record or document of tradition, although he does not give his source. It has

---

[66] Origen, Homily 1 on Luke 1:1–4 (Lienhard, 5–6).

[67] Translation by Charles E. Hill in "What Papias Said about John (and Luke): A 'New' Papian Fragment," *Journal of Theological Studies* 49 (1998): 605: "A report noted down in writing that John collected the written Gospels in his own lifetime in the reign of Nero, and approved of and recognized those of which the deceit of the devil had not taken possession." For a dating of this fragment, see H. Crouzel, F. Fourier, and P. Périchon, *Homilies sur S. Luc Texte latin et fragments grecs: introduction et notes* Sources Chrétiennes 87 (Paris: Editions du Cerf, 1962), 81, who place it in Caesarea in 233–234.

been argued persuasively that the source is the book of Papias that he discusses and quotes from shortly thereafter:[68]

> Nevertheless, of all the disciples of the Lord, only Matthew and John have left us written memorials, and they, tradition says, were led to write only under the pressure of necessity. For Matthew, who had at first preached to the Hebrews, when he was about to go to other peoples, committed his Gospel to writing in his native tongue, and thus compensated those whom he was obliged to leave for the loss of his presence.
>
> And when Mark and Luke had already published their Gospels, they say that John, who had employed all his time in proclaiming the Gospel orally, finally proceeded to write for the following reason. The three Gospels already mentioned having come into the hands of all and into his own too, they say that he accepted them and bore witness to their truthfulness; but that there was lacking in them an account of the deeds done by Christ at the beginning of his ministry.
>
> And this [account] indeed is true. For it is evident that the three evangelists recorded only the deeds done by the Saviour for one year after the imprisonment of John the Baptist, and indicated this in the beginning of their account.[69]

In this very important text, Eusebius compares the chronology of the Synoptic Gospels and John, showing their compatibility and noting John's more complete picture of Jesus's public ministry. Like Origen, he mentions that John received and approved the three Synoptic Gospels and finally wrote his to complement their account, compelled by the urging of others.

Interestingly, Eusebius implies that the Gospels of Matthew, Mark, and John came not from the spontaneous desire of each Evan-

---

[68] See Hill, "What Papias Said about John (and Luke)," 582–629.

[69] Eusebius, *Historia ecclesiastica* 3.24.5–8 (trans. Arthur C. McGiffer in *NPNF2*, 1:152–153). See also the translation in Hill, "What Papias Said about John (and Luke)," 582–629.

gelist, which could be regarded as presumptuous (like the presumption of the Gnostic gospels), but from the urging of the Church, as well as the inspiration of the Spirit. And all have the seal of the apostolic witness and approval.

With regard to the dating of John's Gospel, Eusebius also states:

> At that time the apostle and evangelist John, the one whom Jesus loved, was still living in Asia, and governing the churches of that region, having returned after the death of Domitian from his exile on the island. And that he was still alive at that time may be established by the testimony of two witnesses. They should be trustworthy who have maintained the orthodoxy of the Church; and such indeed were Irenaeus and Clement of Alexandria. The former in the second book of his work *Against Heresies*, writes as follows: "And all the elders that associated with John the disciple of the Lord in Asia bear witness that John delivered it to them. For he remained among them until the time of Trajan." And in the third book of the same work he attests the same thing in the following words: "But the church in Ephesus also, which was founded by Paul, and where John remained until the time of Trajan, is a faithful witness of the apostolic tradition."[70]

Eusebius also speaks about the authorship of the four Gospels in his work, *The Proof of the Gospel (Demonstratio evangelica)*. Here he points out a general rule that the Evangelists, when speaking of themselves, omit what is to their glory and point out what is to their dishonor.[71] This rule is the opposite of what one normally expects in secular writings, but is what one should expect from disciples of the Lord who emptied Himself to take on the form of a slave. Thus, one can see some confirmation of the testimony of tradition with regard to Matthew's authorship of the first Gospel, or Peter's testimony standing behind the Gospel of Mark, when one sees that what is dis-

---

[70] Ibid., 3.23.1–4 (*NPNF2*, 1:150).

[71] *Demonstratio evangelica* 3.5 (Ferrar, 137–140).

honorable and humiliating for the author is emphasized and what is glorious is omitted.

With regard to Matthew, Eusebius writes:

> The Apostle Matthew, if you consider his former life, did not leave a holy occupation, but came from those occupied in tax-gathering and over-reaching one another. None of the evangelists has made this clear, neither his fellow apostle John, nor Luke nor Mark, but Matthew himself, who brands his own life, and becomes his own accuser. . . . And again further on, when he gives a list of the disciples, he adds the name "Publican" to his own. . . . Thus Matthew, in excess of modesty, reveals the nature of his own old life, and calls himself a publican, he does not conceal his former mode of life, and in addition to this he places himself second after his yoke-fellow. . . . For he is paired with Thomas, . . . and he puts Thomas before himself . . . while the other evangelists have done the reverse. If you listen to Luke, you will not hear him calling Matthew a publican, nor subordinating him to Thomas. . . . Mark has done the same.[72]

Eusebius makes the same point with regard to Peter, whose preaching has been preserved by Mark.[73] With regard to John, Eusebius here observes:

> And you would find John like Matthew. For in his epistles he never mentions his own name, or call himself the Elder, or Apostle, or Evangelist; and in the Gospel, though he declares himself as the one whom Jesus loved, he does not reveal himself by name.

---

[72] Ibid. (Ferrar, 137–138).

[73] Ibid. (Ferrar, 138–140).

St. Epiphanius (ca. 310–403)

Various references to the Gospels are found in St. Epiphanius' massive work, *Panarion*. He was born in Palestine and formed by St. Hilarion in the monastic life. Later he was made bishop of Salamis in Cyprus and became a friend of St. Jerome. The *Panarion*, which means "Medicine Chest," is a description of eighty heresies and was written between 374 and 378.[74] One of the heresies that he describes is that of the Nazarenes [Nazoraeans], who are "Hebrew Catholics" descended from those of the apostolic generation who fled Jerusalem before its destruction in AD 70. The only fault that he finds with this sect is their continued observance of the ceremonial Law of Moses. They continue to read the Old Testament Scriptures in Hebrew, as do the Jews.[75] They also have "the Gospel according to Matthew in its entirety in Hebrew. For it is clear that they still preserve this, in the Hebrew alphabet, as it was originally written."[76]

Epiphanius also asserts that the Gospel of Matthew was the first to be written:

> For Matthew was the first to become an evangelist. He was directed to issue the Gospel first, . . . and this was absolutely right. Because he had repented of many sins, and had risen from the receipt of custom and followed Him who came for man's salvation and said, "I have not come to call the righteous, but sinners to repentance," it was Matthew's duty to present the message of salvation first, as an example for us, who would be saved like this man who was restored in the tax office and turned from his iniquity. . . . Matthew himself wrote and issued the Gospel in the Hebrew alphabet, and did

---

[74] See *The Panarion of Epiphanius of Salamis: Book I (Sects 1–46)*, trans. Frank Williams, Nag Hammadi and Manichaean Studies 35 (Leiden: Brill, 1987), xvi.

[75] See *Panarion* 29.9.7: "They are trained to a nicety in Hebrew. For among them the entire Law, the prophets, and the so-called Writings . . . are read in Hebrew, as they surely are by Jews. They are different from Jews, and different from Christians, only in the following. They disagree with Jews because they have come to faith in Christ; but since they are still fettered by the Law—circumcision, the Sabbath, and the rest—they are not in accord with Christians" (Williams, *Book 1*, 118–119).

[76] Ibid. 29.9.9 (Williams, *Book I*, 119).

not begin at the beginning, but traced Christ's pedigree from Abraham.[77]

The Hebrew Gospel according to Matthew was also conserved by a heretical sect known as the Ebionites. This Gospel, however, was corrupted by them, being stripped of the genealogy and the infancy narrative, and perhaps receiving various additions.[78] The Ebionites referred to this Gospel as the Gospel according to the Hebrews.[79]

With regard to the Gospel of Mark, he writes: "Mark, who came directly after Matthew, was ordered to issue the Gospel by St. Peter at Rome, and after writing it was sent by St. Peter to Egypt."

Epiphanius also addresses the question of the divergences between the four Gospels. He lays down the principle that the Evangelists did not always intend to repeat what had already been written, but to supplement the account of the prior Gospels with different and complementary accounts. For example, with regard to the infancy narratives, he writes:

> Because Matthew did not report the events which Luke related [in the infancy narrative], can St. Matthew be at odds with the truth? Or is St. Luke not telling the truth, because he has said nothing about the first things Matthew dealt with? Didn't God give each evangelist his own assignment, so that each of the four evangelists whose duty was to proclaim the Gospel could find what he was to do and proclaim some things in agreement and alike to show that they were from the same source, but otherwise describe what another had omitted, as each received his proportionate share from the Spirit?[80]

---

[77] Ibid. 51.4–5, in *The Panarion of Epiphanius of Salamis: Books II and III*, trans. Frank Williams (Leiden: Brill, 1994), 29.

[78] Ibid. 30.13.2: "Now in what they call a Gospel according to Matthew, though it is not entirely complete, but is corrupt and mutilated" (Williams, *Book I*, 129).

[79] Ibid. 30.3.7–8: "They too accept the Gospel according to Matthew. Like the Cerinthians and Merinthians, they too use it alone. They call it, 'According to the Hebrews'" (Williams, *Book I*, 122).

[80] Ibid. 51.6.1–2 (Williams, *Books II and III*, 30).

With regard to Mark's omission of the infancy narrative, he writes:

Is Mark lying, then? Of course not! There was no reason for him to repeat information which had already been given. Similarly, the things St. John discussed, and confirmed in the Holy Spirit, were not just meant to repeat what had already been proclaimed, but to speak of the teachings the others had had to leave to John.[81]

St. Jerome

St. Jerome, the great translator of the Vulgate and the Patristic Church's greatest expert on Scripture, discusses the authorship of the Gospels in the preface to his commentary on the Gospel of Matthew, from about 398, and in his *Lives of Illustrious Men*, written about 392–393.

Of St. Matthew, St. Jerome writes:

Matthew, surnamed Levi, first publican, then apostle, composed a gospel of Christ at first published in Judea in Hebrew for the sake of those of the circumcision who believed, but this was afterwards translated into Greek, though by what author is uncertain. Moreover, the Hebrew itself has been preserved until the present day in the library at Caesarea which Pamphilus the martyr so diligently gathered. I have also had the opportunity of having the volume described to me by the Nazarenes of Beroea, a city of Syria, who use it.[82]

---

[81] Ibid. 51.6.5 (Williams, *Books II and III*, 30–31).

[82] *On Illustrious Men* 3, trans. Thomas Halton (Washington DC: Catholic University of America Press, 1999), 10. He gives the same testimony in his commentary on Matthew: "The first of all is Matthew, the tax collector, who is also named Levi [Luke 5:27], who published a Gospel in Judea in the Hebrew language, chiefly for the sake of those from the Jews who had believed in Jesus"; see *Commentary on Matthew*, trans. Thomas P. Scheck, The Fathers of the Church 117 (Washington, DC: The Catholic University of America Press, 2008), 53. He also mentions that he himself translated it into Greek and Latin around 390. See *On Illustrious Men* 2.11 (Halton, 8).

On Mark, St. Jerome writes:

Mark, the disciple and interpreter of Peter, wrote a short gospel at the request of the brethren at Rome, embodying what
he had heard Peter tell. When Peter had heard it, he approved
it and issued it to the churches to be read by his authority, as
Clement, in the sixth book of his *Hypotyposes*, and Papias, the
bishop of Hierapolis, record. Peter also mentions this Mark
in his First Epistle [5:13], figuratively indicating Rome under
the name of Babylon: "She who is in Babylon, chosen together
with you, salutes you; and so does my son Mark." ... He died
in the eighth year of Nero [emperor 54–68] and was buried in
Alexandria, leaving Annianus as his successor.[83]

In his commentary on Matthew he writes concerning Mark:

Mark is the second, the interpreter of the apostle Peter and the
first bishop of the Alexandrian church, who indeed did not
himself see the Lord and Savior, but he narrated the things
which he had heard his master preaching in accordance with
the reliability of the events rather than their sequence.[84]

On Luke, he records:

Luke, a physician of Antioch, as his writings indicate, was not
unskilled in the Greek language. An adherent of the apostle
Paul and companion of all his journeying, he wrote a *Gospel*,
concerning whom the same Paul says, "We send with him a
brother whose praise in the gospel is among all the churches
[2 Cor 8:18]," and to the Colossians [4:14], "Luke, the dearly
beloved physician, salutes you," and to Timothy [2 Tim. 4:11],
"Luke only is with me."

---

[83] *On Illustrious Men* 8 (Halton, 15–16). See also St. Jerome's Epistle *Ad Hebidiam*, Epistula 120, 11
(ca. 406/407): "He (St. Paul), thus, had Titus as an interpreter, just as the blessed Peter also had
Mark, whose gospel was composed with Peter narrating and him writing" (*PL*, 22:1002).

[84] *Commentary on Matthew*, preface (Scheck, 53).

He also wrote another excellent volume to which he pre-fixed the title *Acts of the Apostles*, a history which extends to the second year of Paul's sojourn at Rome, that is, to the fourth year of Nero, from which we learn that the book was composed in that same city.

... Some suppose that whenever Paul in his epistle says, "according to my gospel," he means the book of Luke and that Luke not only had learned the gospel from the apostle Paul, who had not been with the Lord in the flesh, but also from the other apostles. He declares this also at the beginning of his work. ... So he wrote the *Gospel* as he had heard it, but composed the *Acts of the Apostles* as he himself had seen.[85]

In his commentary on Matthew, he adds that Luke composed his Gospel "in the regions of Achaia and Boeotia, tracing out certain matters more deeply, and as he himself admits in the preface, describing things that had been heard rather than seen."[86]

On John, St. Jerome writes:

John, the Apostle whom Jesus loved most, the son of Zebedee, and brother of the apostle James, whom Herod, after our Lord's passion, beheaded, most recently of all, at the request of the bishops of Asia, wrote a Gospel against Cerinthus and other heretics, and especially against the then-arising doctrine of the Ebionites, who assert that Christ did not exist prior to Mary. On this account he was compelled to maintain His divine birth.

But there is said to be yet another reason for this work, in that, when he had read the volumes of Matthew, Mark, and Luke, he approved, indeed, the substance of the history and declared that the things they said were true, but that they had given the history of only one year, the one, that is, which follows the imprisonment of John and in which he was put to death.

---

[85] *On Illustrious Men* 7 (Halton, 15–16).

[86] *Commentary on Matthew*, preface (Scheck, 53).

So, skipping this year, the events of which had been set forth by these, he related the events of the earlier period before John was shut up in prison, so that it might be manifest to those who should diligently read the volumes of the four Evangelists. This also takes away the *diafonia*, the discrepancy, which seems to exist between John and the others.[87]

In his Commentary on Matthew, he writes of John:

When he was in Asia, even then the seeds of the heretics were already sprouting, of Cerinthus, of Ebion, and of the others who deny that Christ came in the flesh. John himself in his epistle calls them antichrists, and the apostle Paul frequently smites them. At that time John was compelled by nearly all the bishops of Asia and delegations from many churches to write more deeply concerning the divinity of the Savior and to break through, so to speak, unto the very Word of God, through a boldness that was not so much audacious as blessed. This is the source of the church's historical tradition that when he was compelled by the brothers to write, he answered that he would do so if a universal fast were proclaimed and everyone would pray to the Lord. When this had been carried out and he had been abundantly filled with revelation, he poured forth that heaven-sent prologue: "In the beginning was the Word."[88]

St. Augustine

St. Augustine repeats the testimony of his predecessors:

Now, those four evangelists whose names have gained the most remarkable circulation over the whole world, and whose number has been fixed as four ... are believed to have written in the order which follows: first Matthew, then Mark, thirdly

---

[87] *On Illustrious Men* 9 (Halton,19).

[88] *Commentary on Matthew*, preface (Scheck, 53).

Luke, lastly John. Hence, too, [it would appear that] these had one order determined among them with regard to the matters of their personal knowledge and their preaching [of the gospel], but a different order in reference to the task of giving the written narrative. As far, indeed, as concerns the acquisition of their own knowledge and the charge of preaching, those unquestionably came first in order who were actually followers of the Lord when He was present in the flesh, and who heard Him speak and saw Him act. . . . But as respects the task of composing that record of the gospel which is to be accepted as ordained by divine authority, there were (only) two, belonging to the number of those whom the Lord chose before the passover, that obtained places,—namely, the first place and the last. For the first place in order was held by Matthew, and the last by John. And thus the remaining two, who did not belong to the number referred to, but who at the same time had become followers of the Christ who spoke in these others, were supported on either side by the same, like sons who were to be embraced, and who in this way were set in the midst between these twain.[89]

In other words, Matthew and John have priority over Mark and Luke in the source of their knowledge, for they were Apostles and eye-witnesses, but Mark and Luke have the chronological priority over John in *writing* their Gospels, for John wrote his down last towards the end of his very long life.

St. Augustine also repeats the testimony that Matthew alone wrote in Hebrew, whereas the other Gospels were written down first in Greek. He also briefly alludes to the literary inter-relationship between the Gospels:

Of these four, it is true, only Matthew is reckoned to have written in the Hebrew language; the others in Greek. And however they may appear to have kept each of them a certain

---

[89] Augustine, *De consensu evangelistarum* (ca. 400) 1.2.3 (trans. S. D. F. Salmond in *NPNF1*, 6:78).

order of narration proper to himself, this certainly is not to be taken as if each individual writer chose to write in ignorance of what his predecessor had done, or left out as matters about which there was no information things which another nevertheless is discovered to have recorded. But the fact is, that just as they received each of them the gift of inspiration, they abstained from adding to their several labors any superfluous conjoint compositions. For Matthew is understood to have taken it in hand to construct the record of the incarnation of the Lord according to the royal lineage, and to give an account of most part of His deeds and words as they stood in relation to this present life of men. Mark follows him closely, and looks like his attendant and epitomizer.[90]

With regard to the so-called Synoptic problem (the literary relationship between Matthew, Mark, and Luke), St. Augustine makes three principal points. First, the order of the Gospels is the same as what appears in our canonical Bibles: Matthew, Mark, Luke, and John. Second, the later Gospels are not written entirely independently, but with knowledge of the earlier Gospels (and of the pre-existing oral traditions). Thus Mark was written with knowledge of Matthew, and Luke with knowledge of Mark and Matthew. John, obviously, wrote with knowledge of all three Synoptics. Third, St. Augustine emphasizes that where a Gospel omits what is presented in another Gospel, this should not be attributed to *ignorance* of what is omitted. Rather, it should be attributed either to the fact that it was already narrated by another (and thus can be presupposed as already known by the faithful), or to the fact that it does not find room in the particular narrative scheme of the Evangelist. In other words, the later Evangelists often wish to complement the account in the earlier Gospels by adding new material of one kind or another, according to their narrative purpose.[91]

---

[90] Ibid. 1.3.4 (*NPNF1*, 6:78).

[91] For some interesting works on the Synoptic problem challenging the conventional view of Markan priority and giving more weight to the Patristic testimony and the role of the apostolic oral Tradition in the formation of the Gospels, see Rist, *Independence of Matthew and Mark*; William

St. John Chrysostom

St. John Chrysostom speaks about the four Gospels, their authors, and the discrepancies between them in the first homily in his commentary on the Gospel of Matthew. He argues that the very discrepancies in the narration are a manifestation of the independent witness of the Evangelists' sources. This independence in details, together with harmony in the substance of the Gospel, adds an important motive of credibility to the fourfold Gospel witness.

> And why can it have been, that when there were so many disciples, two write only from among the apostles, and two from among their followers? (For one that was a disciple of Paul, and another of Peter, together with Matthew and John, wrote the Gospels.) It was because they did nothing for vainglory, but all things for use.
>
> "What then? Was not one evangelist sufficient to tell all?" One indeed was sufficient; but if there be four that write, not at the same times, nor in the same places, neither after having met together and conversed one with another, and then they speak all things as it were out of one mouth, this becomes a very great demonstration of the truth.
>
> "But the contrary," it may be said, "hath come to pass, for in many places they are convicted of discordance." Nay, this very thing is a very great evidence of their truth. For if they had agreed in all things exactly even to time, and place, and to the very words, none of our enemies would have believed but that they had met together, and had written what they wrote by some human compact, because such entire agreement as this cometh not of simplicity. But now even that discordance which seems to exist in little matters delivers them from all suspicion, and speaks clearly in behalf of the character of the writers.

R. Farmer, *The Gospel of Jesus: The Pastoral Relevance of the Synoptic Problem* (Louisville: Westminster/John Knox Press, 1994); and B. C. Butler, *The Originality of St. Matthew: A Critique of the Two-document Hypothesis* (Cambridge, UK: Cambridge University Press, 1951).

... Of Matthew again it is said, that when those who from amongst the Jews had believed came to him, and besought him to leave to them in writing those same things, which he had spoken to them by word, he also composed his Gospel in the language of the Hebrews. And Mark too, in Egypt, is said to have done this self-same thing at the entreaty of the disciples.[92]

Conclusion

The Patristic witness unanimously bears out the affirmation of *Dei Verbum* §18 as to the apostolic origin of the four Gospels.[93] All four Gospels were written within living memory[94] of the events narrated. The first and the last Gospels were written by most authoritative eye-witnesses—two Apostles—whereas the second and third Gospels were written by intimate disciples of Sts. Peter and Paul. The fourth Gospel perhaps stands at the limit of living memory, but was itself the work of the most important eyewitness, spoken of as "the beloved disciple," who put his head on the heart of Christ at the Last Supper and was present at the foot of the Cross during the Passion, to whose guardianship Mary was entrusted as Mother.

---

[92] *The Homilies of St. John Chrysostom on the Gospel according to St. Matthew*, Homily 1.5–7 (trans. George Prevost in *NPNF*1, 10:2–3).

[93] See the summary of the early historical evidence by E. Gutwenger, "The Gospels and Non-Catholic Higher Criticism," 754: "Not only did the Apostolic Fathers allude to our canonical gospels, but Papias, *c* 120, reports the words of the Elder who almost certainly is identical with John the Apostle. We are told that Matthew wrote in Hebrew (= Aramaic) and that Mark, the interpreter of Peter, wrote down what Peter had preached in Rome about Jesus. For accurate information about Papias I must refer the reader to Dom Chapman's *John the Presbyter and the Fourth Gospel*, 1911. But our chief witness is St Irenaeus. For he knew the tradition of Asia Minor, where he came from, of Rome and Gaul. Besides, he was conversant with the writings of Papias, and as a youth had heard St Polycarp the disciple of the Apostle John. He again *c* 185 testifies to the authenticity of the gospels and to the order in which they were written. It is the traditional order. In all this he is supported by the tradition of Italy, Africa and Alexandria as represented by St Justin († *c* 165), the old Latin prologues, the Muratorian fragment (*c* 180), Tertullian († 220), Clement of Alexandria († *c* 215) and Origen († 253)."

[94] Living memory marks a period of time in which witnesses of a past event or person are still alive and can confirm or deny what people say about those events or persons.

Study Questions

1. What does *Dei Verbum* §18 affirm about the origins of the Gospels?

2. What do the Responses of the PBC affirm about the authors of the Gospels?

3. What does Papias say about the Gospels and why is it important?

4. What does St. Irenaeus say about the Gospels?

5. Summarize the Patristic testimony about the authorship of the Gospels.

Suggestions for Further Reading

Dei Verbum §18.

Eusebius. *Ecclesiastical History.* Translated by Roy J. Deferrari. 2 Volumes (The Fathers of the Church 19 and 29). Washington, DC: Catholic University of America Press, 1953–1955.

Pontifical Biblical Commission. Responses. In *The Scripture Documents: An Anthology of Official Catholic Teachings*, 190–191 and 197–202. Edited by Dean P. Béchard, S.J. Collegeville: Liturgical Press, 2002.

CHAPTER FIFTEEN

Historical Character of the Four Gospels

Magisterial Teaching on the Historical Character of the Four Gospels

Historical Character of the Four Gospels according to Dei Verbum §19

After asserting the apostolic origin of the Gospels, *Dei Verbum* §19 goes on to affirm, with still greater emphasis and solemnity, the historical character of the four Gospels that transmit the apostolic testimony about Jesus:

> Holy Mother Church has firmly and with absolute constancy held, and continues to hold, that the four Gospels just named, whose historical character the Church unhesitatingly asserts, faithfully hand on what Jesus Christ, while living among men, really did and taught for their eternal salvation until the day He was taken up into heaven (see Acts 1:1).

The solemn affirmation of the "historical character" of the Gospels means that they "faithfully hand on what Jesus . . . really did and taught." This is affirmed on the basis of the constant Tradition of the Church.

The dogmatic and definitive character of this affirmation is manifested first in the fact that this passage is introduced by the words, "Holy Mother Church." Secondly, it is manifested in the words "firmly and with absolute constancy held, and continues to hold." This shows that this teaching pertains to the deposit of faith and requires the second grade of assent. Third, it does not simply affirm, but "unhesitatingly affirms," the historicity of the four Gospels. This shows the definitive nature of this teaching. Augustin Cardinal Bea, who was intimately involved in the crafting of this text, stresses the solemnity of the passage in his commentary on *Dei Verbum*:

> With regard to the initial affirmation we must point out the unusual emphasis—unique of its kind in the whole document—with which the Constitution affirms the historical nature of the gospels. It begins with the solemn assertion: "Holy Mother Church," adding emphatically "firmly and with absolute constancy." As if this were not enough, it speaks of the gospels "whose historical character the Church unhesitatingly asserts." This emphasis is not surprising when we are aware of the grave damage done by form criticism, and especially by the movement for the so-called "demythologization" of the gospels. It is the expression of the Council's grave concern when confronted by the all too real dangers which come from this direction to undermine the faith of so many Christians, Catholic and non-Catholic alike.[1]

Like the affirmation of the apostolic origin, we should regard this affirmation of the historical character of the Gospels as a truth pertaining to the deposit of faith that requires an irrevocable assent by the faithful.

---

[1] Augustin Cardinal Bea, *The Word of God and Mankind*, trans. Dorothy White (Chicago: Franciscan Herald Press, 1967), 254–255.

Responses of the Pontifical Biblical Commission

As with the question of apostolic origin, *Dei Verbum's* affirmation of the historical character of the Gospels is in complete harmony with the Responses of the Pontifical Biblical Commission on the Gospels from 1907 to 1912. Although a denial of the substantial historicity of many of the Gospel accounts became widespread in liberal Protestantism of the nineteenth century, it first began to be asserted by Catholic theologians—such as Alfred Loisy and other Modernists—at the turn of the twentieth century. The first magisterial defense of the historicity of the Gospels thus occurred in the context of the condemnation of various Modernist errors.

These Responses take the form of detailed and precise questions giving the objections against and/or the evidence for the very brief negative or affirmative response. The question of the historicity of Matthew is posed by asking whether Matthew's apologetic aim to convince and confirm his audience in the faith that Jesus is the Messiah foretold by the prophets, and the fact that the narration "does not always follow the chronological order," imply that the Gospel can be assumed to deviate from historical truth. In other words, should one think that

> the narratives of the deeds and words of Christ found in the Gospel have undergone certain alterations and adaptations under the influence both of the Old Testament prophecies and of the more developed perspective of the Church, and that, in consequence, this Gospel narrative is not in conformity with historical truth?[2]

The Modernist answer to these questions was affirmative, as would be that of Rudolf Bultmann and his school. The PBC, however, responds in the negative.

The affirmation of historicity is stressed in a particular way with regard to some key texts of Matthew, such as the infancy narrative,

---

[2] PBC, Response on the Authorship, Date of Composition, and Historicity of the Gospel of Matthew of June 19, 1911, Sixth Question (DS, 3566; *SD*, 198).

"the primacy of Peter (16:17–19), the form of baptism given to the apostles together with the universal mission of preaching (28:19–20), [and] the apostles' profession of faith in the divinity of Christ (14:33)."[3]

With regard to Mark and Luke, the PBC affirms their historical character through posing the question:

> Whether it is right to continue the Church's practice of crediting historical veracity to the sayings and deeds that are accurately and, as it were, graphically narrated by Mark, according to the preaching of Peter, and that are most faithfully set forth by Luke, who "investigated everything accurately anew" (Luke 1:3) from eminently trustworthy sources, indeed from those "who were eyewitnesses from the beginning and ministers of the word" (Luke 1:2); or whether, on the contrary, we must regard these same sayings and deeds as devoid of historical truth, at least in part, because the writers were not eyewitnesses, or because often in both evangelists there is found a lack of order and a discrepancy in the arrangement of events, or because these evangelists, writing later, must necessarily have related not only conceptions foreign to the mind of Christ and the apostles but also facts more or less contaminated by popular imagination, or, finally, because each, in the pursuit of his own purposes, was guided by preconceived dogmatic claims. Response: Affirmative to the first part; Negative to the second part.[4]

As can be seen from the formulation of the question, the key concern is how to guarantee the fidelity of the transmission between the death of Christ and the writing of the Gospels. The objection contained in the question is that, since decades elapsed from the life of Christ to the writing of the Gospels, how were the Gospel accounts

---

[3] Ibid., Seventh Question (DS, 3567; SD, 198–199).

[4] PBC, Response on the Authorship, Date of Composition, and Historicity of the Gospels of Mark and Luke of June 26, 1912, Ninth Question (DS, 3576; SD, 201).

not subject to distortions coming from the popular imagination and preconceived dogmatic ideas?

This accusation of historical distortion for theological purposes was most keenly proclaimed by the Modernists with regard to the Gospel of John, whose historical character was defended in a response of the PBC in 1907. The question is posed whether the facts and discourses in John's Gospel are, as the Modernists such as Loisy hold, "wholly or in part, invented in order to serve as allegories or instructional symbols, and that the discourses are not properly and truly the discourses of the Lord himself but the theological compositions of the writer."[5] The answer is negative, and the principal reason for this—the Church's constant awareness of their historical character—is given in the first part of the question, citing

> the practice, continuously maintained throughout the universal Church from the very beginning, of arguing from the Fourth Gospel as from a truly historical document, yet considering the peculiar character of this Gospel and the author's manifest intention of illustrating and vindicating the divinity of Christ from the very deeds and words of the Lord.[6]

In other words, the Church has constantly held that the Gospel of John gives us true historical information about Jesus, even though the Gospel is very carefully crafted to convey the deeper theological significance of Jesus's words and deeds.[7] This constant understanding of the Church is foundational for all her theology.

---

[5] PBC, Response on the Authorship and Historicity of the Fourth Gospel of May 29, 1907, Third Question (DS, 3400; SD, 191).

[6] Ibid., (SD, 190–191).

[7] See also Holy Office, Decree Condemning Certain Errors of the Modernists *Lamentabili sane* (1907), Condemned Proposition 16: "The narrations of John are not properly history but a mystical contemplation of the gospel. The discourses contained in his Gospel are theological meditations on the mystery of salvation that lack historical truth" (DS, 3416).

Sancta Mater Ecclesia

Fifty years after its Responses during the Modernist crisis, the Pontifical Biblical Commission returned to the problem of the historicity of the Gospels in a 1964 Instruction entitled *Sancta Mater Ecclesia*. The intention of this important document is to respond to the radical questioning of the historicity of the Gospels by scholars like Rudolf Bultmann and his school using a more positive approach than during the Modernist crisis. The document was also intended to aid the Fathers of the Second Vatican Council in their work on *Dei Verbum*, which was promulgated in the following year.

Sancta Mater Ecclesia mentions three erroneous presuppositions that lead some biblical scholars to deny the historical character of the Gospels. First, if one denies the possibility of miracles, prophecy, or any knowledge of His divine identity on the part of Jesus, then clearly the Gospel accounts that contain miracles, fulfill prophecy, or contain a divine claim will be assumed to be historically impossible. Closely related to this would be the second erroneous presupposition, the view that the realm of faith (in which one could affirm Christ's divine claims) and that of history (from which the supernatural would be excluded) are two distinct realms that do not intersect.

The third erroneous presupposition is to minimize the role of the authoritative witness of the Apostles in the transmission of the faith in the period from the death of Christ to the writing of the Gospels, stressing, on the contrary, the creativity of the anonymous Christian community as a whole, as if the Apostles had disappeared with the Ascension of the Lord.[8] All the talk about anonymous creative Chris-

---

[8] PBC, Instruction on the Historical Truth of the Gospels *Sancta Mater Ecclesia* (1964): "Certain exponents of this method, led astray by rationalistic prejudices, refuse to admit that there exists a supernatural order, or that a personal God intervenes in the world by revelation properly so called, or that miracles and prophecies are possible and have actually occurred. There are others who have as their starting-point a wrong notion of faith, taking it that faith is indifferent to historical truth and is indeed incompatible with it. Others practically deny *a priori* the historical value and character of the documents of revelation. Others, finally, there are who on the one hand underestimate the authority that the apostles had as witnesses of Christ and the office and influence that they wielded in the primitive community, while on the other hand they overestimate the creative capacity of the community itself. All these aberrations are not only opposed to Catholic doctrine but are also devoid of any scientific foundation and foreign to the genuine principles of the historical method" (*SD*, 229).

tian communities as the soil in which the Gospel traditions grew over-looks the picture of the Church that our sources give us—a Church in which the Apostles enjoy a tremendous authority, as we see in Acts 2:42–43; 4:33; 5:12–15.

Process of Redaction of the Gospels: Three Stages

Sancta Mater Ecclesia then goes on to illuminate the historical character of the Gospels by distinguishing three stages in the genesis and transmission of the Gospel material: first there is the public ministry of Jesus, then the preaching of the Apostles, and finally the redaction of the four Gospels on the basis of the preceding oral traditions. The document examines each of these phases to bring out elements that manifest the fidelity of the transmission of the life and teaching of Jesus.

As we have seen, the key objection raised against the historicity of the Gospels is the supposition that, in the decades that intervened between the earthly life of Jesus and the writing of the Gospels, the memory of Jesus was altered over time so as to create a radical and perhaps unbridgeable gap between the real Jesus of history and the Christ of faith that emerges in the four Gospels. This was the view of the Modernists, and it was further developed by Rudolf Bultmann and his disciples. Faced with this objection, it is not enough merely to affirm the historicity of the Gospels; we must also ask what guarantees the fidelity of the transmission of the life and words of the Jesus of history to the pages of the Gospels. The answer of the Church, as given in *Sancta Mater Ecclesia* and *Dei Verbum* §19, is the apostolic preaching, which predates the Gospels and is their foundation and the foundation of the Church's faith. This apostolic preaching was then put authoritatively in writing by two Apostles and two intimate disciples of the leading Apostles, so that the Gospels truly transmit to us the substance of the apostolic preaching, which in turn presented the substance of Jesus's words and deeds.

Preaching of Jesus

Christ chose certain close disciples—the twelve Apostles—to be authoritative witnesses of His life and teaching. This special election reveals that Jesus was concerned not merely to teach the crowds and disciples and work miracles, but also, and more importantly, to have His deeds (especially the Passion and Resurrection) and words, in their authentic meaning, faithfully transmitted by the witness of the Apostles. Furthermore, we see that Jesus varied His message according to the capacities of His hearers, setting the example for His Apostles to do likewise. Finally, as will be seen below, the Gospels show us that Jesus used techniques of the oral style to facilitate the memorization and transmission of His words.

Preaching of the Apostles

After Jesus's Ascension, the Apostles preached and, "bearing testimony to Jesus, proclaimed first and foremost the death and Resurrection of the Lord, faithfully recounting his life and words (cf. Acts 10:36–41) and, as regards the manner of their preaching, taking into account the circumstances of their hearers."[9] During this period, the apostolic witness was not falsified, but strengthened by the deeper faith in His divinity that the Apostles received after His Resurrection, Ascension, and the gift of the Spirit at Pentecost.

The objection is often made that the Gospels cannot give us a reliable picture of what Jesus actually did and taught during His earthly ministry because the memory of the early Church was necessarily colored by the fuller faith that they acquired after Christ's Resurrection and after Pentecost. Thus, it is commonly supposed that much of the Gospels reflects more the situation after Easter than before. This supposition is in fact one of the foundational principles of form criticism and is a serious challenge to the historicity of the Gospels.

The reasoning can be schematized as follows: (a) The Apostles and disciples had a very incomplete and often erroneous idea of Jesus's identity and mission before Pentecost; but (b) the Gospels were

---

[9] Ibid. (SD, 229).

written long after Pentecost, at which time the Apostles had a completely different understanding of the Lord; and therefore (c), the Gospels cannot give an accurate portrayal of what Jesus actually did and said during the public ministry, but rather they manifest the situation (*Sitz im Leben*) of the early Church.

In response to this objection, it should be pointed out that a greatly improved understanding of Jesus's mission and identity through an increase of faith does not hinder a historically accurate portrayal, but rather greatly enhances it. *Sancta Mater Ecclesia* explains:

> The faith of the disciples, far from blotting out the remembrance of the events that had happened, rather consolidated it, since their faith was based on what Jesus had done and taught (cf. Acts 2:22; 10:37–39). Nor was Jesus transformed into a "mythical" personage and his teachings distorted by reason of the worship which the disciples now paid him, revering him as Lord and Son of God. Yet it need not be denied that the apostles, when handing on to their hearers the things which in actual fact the Lord had said and done, did so in the light of that fuller understanding which they enjoyed as a result of being schooled by the glorious things accomplished in Christ and of being illumined by the Spirit of Truth.[10]

As Jesus had interpreted to them the meaning of the Old Testament Scriptures, so too the Apostles now interpreted the meaning of the events of Jesus's life, death, and Resurrection.

Cardinal Bea makes a similar point in his commentary on *Dei Verbum* §19:

> It is also true that the account of the deeds and words of Jesus were given, as our document points out, by the Apostles with that clearer understanding which they enjoyed after they had been instructed by the events of Christ's risen life and taught by the Spirit of truth, which descended on them at Pentecost.

---

[10] *SD*, 230.

Their faith had ripened and they could now understand many things which they had not understood during the earthly life of Jesus, but this is a question of a more thorough understanding and explanation of events which had actually been spoken by Jesus, not a case of invention or of "creative activity." To understand and explain more thoroughly does not mean to alter the truth, but rather to be *more faithful to it*, for by so doing the reliability of the historical facts recounted, far from being impaired, is strengthened! That the apostles took care not only to expound the truth but also to preserve it intact is shown by what we have already said about the primitive Christian community and the discipline it exercised in order to preserve doctrine in all its purity.[11]

Redaction of the Gospels

The final stage of the genesis of the Gospels was their written redaction by Matthew, Mark, Luke, and John on the basis of the prior apostolic preaching. Each Evangelist selected and synthesized the Gospel material in a distinct and personal way, according to the needs of the churches that were their intended audience and according to their apostolic aims. *Sancta Mater Ecclesia* explains:

The sacred authors, for the benefit of the churches, took this earliest body of instruction, which had been handed on orally at first and then in writing—for many soon set their hands to "drawing up a narrative" (Luke 1:1) of matters concerning the Lord Jesus—and set it down in the four Gospels. In doing this each of them followed a method suitable to the special purpose that he had in view. They selected certain things out of the many that had been handed on; some they synthesized, some they explained with an eye to the situation of the churches, painstakingly using every means of bringing home to the readers the *solid truth* of the things in which they

---

[11] Bea, *Word of God and Mankind*, 259–260 (my italics).

had been instructed. For, out of the material that they had received, the sacred authors selected especially those items that were adapted to the varied circumstances of the faithful as well as to the end that they themselves wished to attain; these they recounted in a manner consonant with those circumstances and with that end. And since the meaning of a statement depends, among other things, on the place which it has in a given sequence, the Evangelists, in handing on the words or the deeds of our Savior, explained them for the advantage of their readers by respectively setting them, one Evangelist in one context, another in another.[12]

Dei Verbum §19 borrows heavily from this paragraph of *Sancta Mater Ecclesia* in describing the activity of the Evangelists and our reasons for trusting their historical veracity, which it emphasizes still more strongly:

The sacred authors wrote the four Gospels, selecting some things from the many which had been handed on by word of mouth or in writing, reducing some of them to a synthesis, explaining some things in view of the situation of their churches and preserving the form of proclamation, but always in such fashion that they told us the honest truth about Jesus.[13] For their intention in writing was that either from their own memory and recollections, or from the witness of those who "themselves from the beginning were eyewitnesses and ministers of the Word" we might know "the truth" concerning those matters about which we have been instructed (see Luke 1:2–4).

This text reminds us that the Gospel accounts are very succinct, compressing three years of public ministry into a short account, which inevitably implies the selection of some elements at the expense of

---

[12] *Sancta Mater Ecclesia* 9 (*SD*, 230–231; my italics).

[13] Here the conciliar text cites *Sancta Mater Ecclesia* §9 (*AAS* 56 (1964): 715; *SD*, 230).

others, so that we have many omissions and summarized accounts. However, an omission is not an error, nor does it compromise the infinite truth and wisdom of God, the primary author of Scripture. As St. John says at the end of his Gospel, "But there are also many other things which Jesus did; were every one of them to be written, I suppose that the world itself could not contain the books that would be written" (John 21:25).

After describing the activity of the Evangelists, *Sancta Mater Ecclesia* touches on the question of the truth of the Gospels, clarifying that the differences in the order of events and in the selection of events and discourses in the four Gospels do not pose an obstacle to their truth. The text cites St. Augustine's work, *On the Harmony of the Gospels*, in which this question is treated at length:

> For the truth of the narrative is not affected in the slightest by the fact that the Evangelists report the sayings or the doings of our Lord in a different order, and that they use different words to express what he said, not keeping to the very letter, but nevertheless preserving the sense. For, as St. Augustine says: "Where it is a question only of those matters whose order in the narrative may be indifferently this or that without in any way taking from the truth and authority of the Gospel, it is probable enough that each Evangelist believed he should narrate them in that same order in which God was pleased to suggest them to his recollection. 'The Holy Spirit distributes his gifts to each one according as he wills' [1 Cor 12:11]; therefore, too, for the sake of those books, which were to be set so high at the very summit of authority, he undoubtedly guided and controlled the minds of the holy writers in their recollection of what they were to write; but as to why, in doing so, he should have permitted them, one to follow this order in his narrative, another to follow that—that is a question whose answer may possibly be found with God's help, if one seeks it out with reverent care."[14]

---

[14] *SD*, 231, quoting St. Augustine, *On Agreement among the Evangelists* 2.21.51–52 (PL, 34:1102).

It is not an error to report an event in its substance, leaving out circumstantial elements, synthesizing it with other events, and departing from chronological order according to one's plan and intention. Every historian must select, synthesize, and arrange. The Evangelists did this also, guided by divine inspiration. An error would be present, on the other hand, when something is affirmed as historical which did not truly occur at all. For example, in the Gospel of St. Matthew, in Caesarea Philippi, Christ makes a momentous promise/prophecy to St. Peter: "And I tell you, you are Peter, and on this rock I will build my church, and the powers of death shall not prevail against it" (Matt 16:18). Now, if the substance of this dialogue did not actually take place, if it is a fictional construction, or if something substantially different was said, then the Gospel would be leading us to believe that something of tremendous importance occurred in human history that did not actually occur. Thus God, the principal Author of the Gospel (as of all the Scriptures), would be leading us astray.

The same could be said of the other texts of the Gospel: if Christ did not truly affirm that He was the Son of God before Caiaphas and the Sanhedrin, or if He did not physically rise from the dead and appear to the Apostles as recounted in the Gospels, then God, the primary Author of Scripture, would be deceiving us in matters of the greatest importance. If these and the other events narrated did not truly occur, then the Gospels are not telling us "the plain truth about Jesus," as Vatican II affirms and all the Christian centuries have believed.

Likewise, if Jesus did not really speak, in their substance, the discourses put in His mouth in the Gospel of John, then God would have led the Church astray for twenty centuries by leading all Christians to believe that the substance of these discourses came from the mouth of Christ.

This does not mean that we have the *exact words* of our Lord in chronological order, but rather the *true substance of what He did and said*, although paraphrased and summarized. After all, our Gospel accounts are translations and summaries. But nevertheless, they give us the *honest truth about Jesus*. In fact, the very divergences of the

Gospels on many accidental matters, showing that they are distinct witnesses, is precisely what makes their substantial agreement historically credible.

Furthermore, the affirmation of *Dei Verbum* §19 on the historicity of the Gospels also explicitly includes the events from Easter to the Ascension, for it speaks of all that he "really did and taught . . . until the day He was taken up into heaven." Cardinal Bea comments:

> In fact, this period of the forty days after the resurrection may also properly be considered as the life of Jesus among men. This ample scope of the gospel accounts shows that even the fact of Christ's resurrection and his appearances after he has risen again, although they belong, strictly speaking, to another order of events (a supernatural order) are nevertheless also facts which have their place in human history, and are guaranteed by the historical veracity of the gospels.[15]

Historicity of the Gospels in the Post-Conciliar Magisterium

The teaching of *Dei Verbum* §§18–19 was reiterated by Pope John Paul II several times. In his *Redemptoris missio*, he implies that the separation of the Jesus of history from the Christ of faith is a kind of Nestorianism:

> To introduce any sort of separation between the Word and Jesus Christ is contrary to the Christian faith. St. John clearly states that the Word, who "was in the beginning with God," is the very one who "became flesh" (John 1:2, 14). Jesus is the Incarnate Word—a single and indivisible person. One cannot separate Jesus from the Christ or speak of a "Jesus of history" who would differ from the "Christ of faith." The Church acknowledges and confesses Jesus as "the Christ, the Son of the living God" (Matt 16:16): Christ is none oth-

---

[15] Bea, *The Word of God and Mankind*, 255.

er than Jesus of Nazareth: he is the Word of God made man for the salvation of all. In Christ "the whole fullness of deity dwells bodily" (Col 2:9) and "from his fullness have we all received" (John 1:16). The "only Son, who is in the bosom of the Father" (John 1:18) is "the beloved Son, in whom we have redemption. . . . For in him all the fullness of God was pleased to dwell, and through him to reconcile to himself all things, whether on earth or in heaven, making peace by the blood of his Cross" (Col 1:13–14, 19–20). It is precisely this uniqueness of Christ which gives him an absolute and universal significance, whereby, while belonging to history, he remains history's center and goal.[16]

Another text that develops the teaching of *Dei Verbum* 18–19 is John Paul II's *Novo millennio ineunte*. In order for the Church to be able to give witness to Christ in the third millennium as in the past, the disciples of Christ need to be able to contemplate the face of Christ as He lived among us during His earthly ministry. To do this, we must have faith in the truth of the Gospel witness:

Remaining firmly anchored in Scripture, we open ourselves to the action of the Spirit from whom the sacred texts derive their origin, as well as to the *witness of the Apostles* (cf. John 15:27), who had a first-hand experience of Christ, the Word of life: they saw him with their eyes, heard him with their ears, touched him with their hands (cf. 1 John 1:1). What we receive from them is a vision of faith based on precise historical testimony: a true testimony which the Gospels, despite their complex redaction and primarily catechetical purpose, pass on to us in an entirely trustworthy way.

The Gospels do not claim to be a complete biography of Jesus in accordance with the canons of modern historical science. From them, nevertheless, *the face of the Nazarene emerg-*

---

[16] John Paul II, Encyclical Letter on the Permanent Value of the Church's Missionary Mandate *Redemptoris missio* (1990), §6.

es with a solid historical foundation. The Evangelists took pains to represent him on the basis of trustworthy testimonies which they gathered (cf. Luke 1:3) and working with documents which were subjected to careful ecclesial scrutiny.[17]

John Paul II here also addresses the historicity of the Gospel accounts which speak of Jesus's self-awareness of being the Son of God:

This divine-human identity emerges forcefully from the Gospels, which offer us a range of elements that make it possible for us to enter that "frontier zone" of the mystery, represented by Christ's self-awareness. The Church has no doubt that the Evangelists in their accounts, and inspired from on high, have correctly understood in the words which Jesus spoke the truth about his person and his awareness of it. Is this not what Luke wishes to tell us when he recounts Jesus's first recorded words, spoken in the Temple in Jerusalem when he was barely twelve years old? Already at that time he shows that he is aware of a unique relationship with God, a relationship which properly belongs to a "son." . . . It is no wonder therefore that later as a grown man his language authoritatively expresses the depth of his own mystery, as is abundantly clear both in the Synoptic Gospels (cf. Matt 11:27; Luke 10:22) and above all in the Gospel of John. In his self-awareness, Jesus has no doubts: "The Father is in me and I am in the Father" (John 10:38).[18]

---

[17] John Paul II, Apostolic Letter *Novo millennio ineunte* (2000), §§17–18.

[18] Ibid., §24. The text continues: "However valid it may be to maintain that, because of the human condition which made him grow 'in wisdom and in stature, and in favor with God and man' (Luke 2:52), his human awareness of his own mystery would also have progressed to its fullest expression in his glorified humanity, there is no doubt that already in his historical existence Jesus was aware of his identity as the Son of God. John emphasizes this to the point of affirming that it was ultimately because of this awareness that Jesus was rejected and condemned: they sought to kill him 'because he not only broke the sabbath but also called God his Father, making himself equal with God' (John 5:18). In Gethsemane and on Golgotha Jesus's human awareness will be put to the supreme test. But not even the drama of his Passion and Death will be able to shake his serene certainty of being the Son of the heavenly Father."

The rejection of the historicity of the Gospel accounts of Jesus has been especially directed against the discourses presented in the Gospel of John, which are all too often regarded as purely theological constructs (*theologoumena*, or "Jesus poems") put into the mouth of Jesus, never pronounced in reality. Such a view is clearly incompatible with the text of *Dei Verbum* §19, as well as with the constant Tradition of the Church. Joseph Ratzinger discusses this in *Jesus of Nazareth*:

> If "historical" is understood to mean that the discourses of Jesus transmitted to us have to be something like a recorded transcript in order to be acknowledged as "historically" authentic, then the discourses of John's gospel are not "historical." But the fact that they make no claim to literal accuracy of this sort by no means implies that they are merely "Jesus poems" that the members of the Johannine school gradually put together, claiming to be acting under the guidance of the Paraclete. What the Gospel is really claiming is that it has correctly rendered the *substance of the discourses*, of Jesus's self-attestation in the great Jerusalem disputes, so that the readers really do encounter the decisive content of this message and, therein the authentic figure of Jesus.[19]

The *Catechism of the Catholic Church* provides a good example of how the teaching of *Dei Verbum* §19 should be put into practice. As Ratzinger observes:

> The *Catechism* trusts the biblical word. It holds the Christ of the Gospels to be the real Jesus. It is also convinced that all the Gospels tell us about this same Jesus and that all of them together help us, each in its own way, to know the true Jesus of history, who is no other than the Christ of faith.

---

[19] Joseph Ratzinger, *Jesus of Nazareth: From the Baptism in the Jordan to the Transfiguration*, trans. Adrian J. Walker (New York: Doubleday, 2007), 229 (my italics).

This basic position has earned the *Catechism* vehement attacks. The *Catechism*, it is alleged, has slept through an entire century of exegesis, is utterly ignorant of literary genres, form and redactional history, and the like, and has not progressed beyond a "fundamentalistic" exegesis. . . . However, the many-layered, plastic portrayal of Jesus that modern research has uncovered in the Gospels in no way forces us to go behind the texts and to construct another, allegedly purely historical Jesus from a combination of conjectured sources, while stigmatizing the Gospel portrait of Jesus as a product of the community's faith. As to the further contention that different communities or representatives of the tradition believed in different, incompatible Christs, it is hard to see how such minimal historical reality, such a contradictory mass of fabrications by the communities, could still produce in such a short time that common faith in Christ that transformed the world.[20]

Pope Benedict has said that the *Catechism* is one of the principal fruits of the Second Vatican Council.[21] It can be argued that the *Catechism*'s trust that the Christ of the Gospels is the real Christ is a good example of the implementation of Vatican II, and in particular of *Dei Verbum* §§18–19. Attacks on the *Catechism*'s use of the Gospels reveals, on the other hand, a lack of implementation or understanding of §19.

---

[20] Joseph Ratzinger, *Gospel, Catechesis, Catechism: Sidelights on the Catechism of the Catholic Church* (San Francisco: Ignatius Press, 1997), 64–66.

[21] Benedict XVI, Apostolic Letter (issued *motu proprio*) For the Indiction of the Year of Faith *Porta fidei* (2011), §11: "In order to arrive at a systematic knowledge of the content of the faith, all can find in the *Catechism of the Catholic Church* a precious and indispensable tool. It is one of the most important fruits of the Second Vatican Council."

Apostolic Witness, Oral Tradition, and Living Memory: Arguments of Reason in Support of the Historical Character of the Gospels

Link Between the Apostolic Witness and the Gospel Accounts

The key question with regard to the historicity of the Gospel narratives, as we have seen, is what guarantees, even to the eyes of reason alone, the fidelity of the transmission from the words and deeds of Jesus to the written Gospels as we have them. On what grounds can we trust that the Gospels accurately transmit the substance of what Jesus truly did and said? Or why should we think that the apostolic witness was not substantially altered, by addition or omission, in the course of this transmission?

There are several fundamental reasons for this confidence, even aside from the inspiration and inerrancy of Scripture and the infallibility of the Church. These arguments of reason serve as motives of credibility for faith. First, Jesus formed an inner group of disciples—the Apostles—precisely for this purpose of forming them as eyewitnesses to retain what He had taught, understand it more and more intimately, and pass it on with authority. As seen above, their testimony was first oral but then redacted into the Gospels by Apostles (Matthew and John) and by intimate disciples of Peter and Paul (Mark and Luke). Second, the Apostles had good reason to retain Christ's words, which they believed with increasing clarity were the "words of eternal life" (John 6:68). Third, the apostolic preaching and the redaction of the Gospels occurred during the time of living memory, in which many other eyewitnesses were still around to confirm the apostolic and Gospel accounts. For example, we are told that some of those resurrected by Christ in the Gospels (such as the daughter of Jairus, the son of the widow of Naim, and Lazarus) were alive until about the end of the first century.[22] Now, if the Gospel accounts said something dif-

---

[22] See the *Testimony of Quadratus*, an apologetic work addressed to Hadrian that is cited in Eusebius, *Historia ecclesiastica* 4.3: "But the works of our Saviour were always at hand, for they were true, those who were cured, those who rose from the dead, who were seen not only when being

ferent from what eyewitnesses such as these knew to be the case, they would have protested, as Holocaust survivors protest when someone denies the historicity of the events of which they are a living witness. But we have no trace of any such protests, except later with regard to the Gnostic "gospels."[23] Similarly, St. Paul wrote to the Corinthians (1 Cor 15:6) that the Risen Christ appeared to over five hundred witnesses, most of whom were still alive and could be questioned over twenty years after the event. St. Paul's account of the Resurrection is thus greatly strengthened by the fact that it could be corroborated by many other eyewitnesses. Fourth, Christ and the Apostles preached in an oral culture conditioned for over a millennium to reverence the Word of God, memorize it, and faithfully transmit it.[24]

In summary, the Gospels were written either by the most authoritative eyewitnesses themselves (Matthew and John) or by the intimate disciples (Mark and Luke) of the leading Apostles, Peter and Paul, in the time of living memory of the life of Jesus, in a culture accustomed to oral teaching, memorization, and faithful oral transmission. To this must be added the conviction that they were transmitting the most important words and deeds of human history, for which they had a maximum religious reverence.

The Gospels Claim to Give Eyewitness Testimony

The New Testament itself makes the claim in various places that it is transmitting eyewitness accounts. Cardinal Bea points out that the New Testament speaks of the notion of "witness" and "testimony," in its various forms, over 150 times.[25]

---

cured and when rising, but also, being always at hand, not only when the Savior was on earth, but even after he had departed, survived for a considerable time, so that some of them have even come down to our own time"; see *Ecclesiastical History*, vol. 1 (Fathers of the Church 19), trans. R. J. Deferrari (Washington, DC: The Catholic University of America Press, 1953), 210.

23 See St. Irenaeus, *Adversus haereses* 3.11.9.

24 The Jewish reverence for the Word of God at the time of Christ is nicely described by Flavius Josephus in *Against Apion* I.8, in *Josephus: Complete Works*, trans. William Whiston (Grand Rapids: Kregel, 1978), 609.

25 Augustin Cardinal Bea, *The Study of the Synoptic Gospels; New Approaches and Outlooks*, trans. Joseph A. Fitzmyer (New York: Harper & Row, 1965), 23: "For a witness is a person who is in a

Luke's Prologue

At the very beginning of Luke's Gospel (1:1–4), he makes sure to indicate the eyewitness sources on which his account is based:

> Inasmuch as many have undertaken to compile a narrative of the things which have been accomplished among us, just as they were delivered to us by those who from the beginning were eyewitnesses and ministers of the word, it seemed good to me also, having followed all things closely for some time past, to write an orderly account for you, most excellent Theophilus, that you may know the truth concerning the things of which you have been informed.

This text indicates Luke's intent, which was to transmit an orderly account of the "things accomplished among us" in the life of Christ, "just as they were delivered to us by those who from the beginning were eyewitnesses and ministers of the word" (Luke 1:2). We see here that Luke's principal concern is to base himself on eyewitnesses, particularly those entrusted by Christ and the Church to transmit this testimony as "ministers of the word," which was the role of the Apostles, as we see in Acts 6:4.[26] The word "delivered" (παρέδοσαν) is a term that indicates the authoritative transmission of tradition. St. Paul uses the same verb in his account of the words of the institution of the Eucharist in 1 Corinthians 11:23: "For I received (παρέλαβον) from the Lord what I also delivered (παρέδωκα) to you, that the Lord Jesus on the night when he was betrayed took bread . . ." The Greek word παραδίδωμι is translated in Latin as *tradere*, from which our English word *tradition* derives.

---

position to affirm something officially, as it were, on the basis of his own immediate experience. The apostles refer to themselves repeatedly as witnesses of the events of the life of Jesus (Acts 1:22; 2:32; 3:15; 5:32; 10:39; 13:31; 23:14; 26:16; 1 Peter 5:1)." See also Bea, *Word of God and Mankind*, 257–259.

[26] See Bea, *Study of the Synoptic Gospels*, 23: "Neither Luke's predecessors nor the evangelist himself made it a rule to cull everything that was recounted in the community about Jesus, but only that which the authorized eyewitnesses had passed on who had become in time the ministers of the word."

We also see from this prologue that several other accounts already existed. These may have included the Gospels of Matthew and Mark. Nevertheless, Luke does not say that he is basing himself on pre-existing written accounts, but rather on the authoritative *tradition* received from the Apostles and other direct disciples and eyewitnesses of Jesus's life.

John Rist gives a good summary:

Luke [in his prologue] certainly gives the impression—some might say disingenuously—of a stage when the tradition is still the dominant authority, and where the written versions are to be checked out against the tradition. This account seems eminently reasonable in view of the attitude of the early believers . . . and the obvious authority during their lifetimes of the primary witnesses.[27]

Furthermore, Luke explicitly states that the authoritative eyewitnesses on which he relies were present "from the beginning." In other words, his entire account is an orderly record of what has been transmitted to him by those who were there. Samuel Byrskog comments:

What the prologue does imply, however, is the author's conviction that the material from the eyewitnesses and ministers of the word was not limited only to small portions of the past events, but pertained way back to their beginning. *The tradition available to the author was, according to the Lukan perspective, rooted in its entirety in the oral history of persons present at the events themselves.*[28]

---

[27] John M. Rist, *On the Independence of Matthew and Mark* (Cambridge, UK: Cambridge University Press, 1978), 100.

[28] Samuel Byrskog, *Story as History—History as Story: The Gospel Tradition in the Context of Ancient Oral History* (Tübingen: Mohr Siebeck, 2000), 232 (italics original).

John

The Gospel of John makes the claim several times that it is the testimony of the "beloved disciple" who was an eyewitness of the key events that he relates. For example, in John 19:35, after the account of the crucifixion, the Evangelist says: "He who saw it has borne witness—his testimony is true, and he knows that he tells the truth—that you also may believe."[29]

The account of the doubting Thomas is a powerful assertion of eyewitness evidence and its importance. St. Thomas insists on seeing the wounds of the Risen Christ and touching them before giving his assent of faith to the report of the other Apostles. Christ obliges him, for the sake of the faith of the Church, which he shall then build up with his account of touching the wounds of the Risen One:

> Now Thomas, one of the twelve, called the Twin, was not with them when Jesus came. So the other disciples told him, "We have seen the Lord." But he said to them, "Unless I see in his hands the print of the nails, and place my finger in the mark of the nails, and place my hand in his side, I will not believe." Eight days later, his disciples were again in the house, and Thomas was with them. The doors were shut, but Jesus came and stood among them, and said, "Peace be with you." Then he said to Thomas, "Put your finger here, and see my hands; and put out your hand, and place it in my side; do not be faithless, but believing." Thomas answered him, "My Lord and my God!" Jesus said to him, "Have you believed because you have seen me? Blessed are those who have not seen and yet believe."[30]

---

[29] The Modernists denied the truth of John's claims to be an eyewitness, and this denial was condemned by the Holy Office in *Lamentabili sane* (1907), Condemned Proposition 18: "John claims for himself the quality of witness concerning Christ. In reality, however, he is only a distinguished witness of the Christian life, or of the life of Christ in the Church at the close of the first century" (DS, 3418).

[30] John 20:24–29.

This text continues (John 20:30–31): "Now Jesus did many other signs in the presence of the disciples, which are not written in this book; but these are written that you may believe that Jesus is the Christ, the Son of God, and that believing you may have life in his name."

John's Gospel ends with an affirmation of its eyewitness nature and consequent veracity. Peter asks Jesus what will become of the "disciple whom Jesus loved, who had lain close to His breast at the Supper and had said, 'Lord, who is it that is going to betray you?'" After Jesus refuses to answer, saying "What is that to you?" John states: "This is the disciple who is bearing witness to these things, and who has written these things; and we know that his testimony is true" (John 21:24).

His final words, however, stress that the oral tradition is much larger than what got written down in his Gospel: "But there are also many other things which Jesus did; were every one of them to be written, I suppose that the world itself could not contain the books that would be written" (John 21:25).

1 John 1:1–4

Perhaps the most expressive affirmation of eyewitness testimony in all of literature is given by the opening of the First Letter of John, which begins:

> That which was from the beginning, which *we have heard*, which we have *seen with our eyes*, which we have *looked upon and touched with our hands*, concerning the word of life—the life was made manifest, and *we saw it, and testify to it*, and proclaim to you the eternal life which was with the Father and was made manifest to us—*that which we have seen and heard* we proclaim also to you, so that you may have fellowship with us; and our fellowship is with the Father and with his Son Jesus Christ. And we are writing this that our joy may be complete.

John, in good Semitic fashion, uses the literary device of repetition to give maximum solemnity to an idea. In case we might otherwise pass over it too lightly, he repeats the notion of the apostolic eyewitness by giving three senses: seeing with his eyes, hearing, and touching with his hands. And then he repeats these over and over, so that *seeing* the Word of life is mentioned four times, framed by *hearing*.

It seems that John uses the plural "we," instead of "I," to underscore the public nature of the witness of the apostolic college. The "we" of the Apostles serves as the foundation for the incorporation of all others into the apostolic faith by which we come to share in the life of God.[31]

To get a good idea of the reverence with which the Apostles and the early Christian community transmitted the events of the life of Christ, one must meditate on these verses. The Apostles were conscious that they had been in intimate contact with—seeing, listening to, and touching—a man whom they believed to be "the word of life" and "the eternal life with the Father." St. Peter refers to Christ in a similar way, as "the author of life" (Acts 3:15), after he cures the paralytic shortly after Pentecost.

In a society that cultivated the fear of the Lord as the beginning of wisdom, the Jews who were chosen as Apostles would have had a maximum fear of the Lord, in the sense of the most extreme reverence for "the word of life." People in the Old Testament who were granted a vision of an angel from God generally feared that they would die as a result, for it was a proverb that "no one can see God and live."[32] We see that mentality at work in Peter after the miraculous catch of fish in Luke 5:8, when he says to Jesus: "Depart from me, for I am a sinful man, O Lord." All the reverence built up over the centuries in Israel would have given to the Apostles a supreme zeal to preserve the truth of that encounter with the "word of life" and "author of life."

---

[31] See Byrskog, *Story as History—History as Story*, 241–242.

[32] See, for example, Gen 32:30; Exod 20:19 and 33:20; and Judg 6:23–24 and 13:22.

2 Peter 1:16–18

The Second Letter of Peter asserts that the Gospel of Christ was not a "cleverly devised myth," for the author of the Letter, speaking of the Transfiguration, says that "we were eyewitnesses of his majesty. . . . We heard this voice borne from heaven, for we were with him on the holy mountain."

1 Corinthians 11 and 15

Although not directly referring to written Gospels, St. Paul speaks twice in the First Letter to the Corinthians of a tradition that he has received and transmitted.[33]

Acts 1:21–22

The replacement of Judas in the Apostolic College by St. Matthias sheds light on the value placed by the Apostles on eyewitness testimony. In order to replace Judas and fill up the number of the Twelve, Peter asks the brethren to put forth candidates who can serve as eyewitnesses of the public ministry and Resurrection of Christ: "So one of the men who have accompanied us *during all the time that the Lord Jesus went in and out among us, beginning from the baptism of John until the day when he was taken up from us*—one of these men must become with us a *witness to his resurrection*" (Acts 1:21–22). We see here that the apostolic office was essentially conceived as an authorized eyewitness of the historicity of all the events that were proclaimed in the Gospel accounts, starting from the beginning of Jesus's public ministry.[34]

Another interesting text in this regard is Acts 4:20. After the Apostles were forbidden to teach in the name of Jesus, they replied that they had to obey God rather than men, "for we cannot but speak

---

[33] 1 Cor 11:23 and 15:3. For a discussion of the implications of these two texts, see Birger Gerhardsson, *The Reliability of the Gospel Tradition* (Peabody: Hendrickson Publishers, 2001), 21–22.

[34] See Byrskog, *Story as History—History as Story*, 233.

of what we have *seen* and *heard*." Their eyewitness testimony cried out to be shared as the foundation of the Church's faith.

The Gospels Were Composed in an Oral Culture

We live in a culture inundated by written matter, in which it is hardly necessary for us to memorize anything. Our natural tendency, there-fore, is to suppose that the cultural context of the first century AD was similar to our own. Many biblical scholars of the last two centuries have tended to treat the four Gospels as if they were texts[35] originat-ing in a culture like ours that lives on the printed rather than spoken word, and in which oral memory is largely atrophied, deprived of the very significant social or cultural role that the spoken word and oral tradition formerly enjoyed.[36] This type of supposition has shaped the way people frame the Synoptic problem—the investigation of liter-ary influences between the three synoptic Gospels—and has con-

---

[35] See Gerhardsson, *Reliability of the Gospel Tradition*, xxiii–xxiv: "Many scholars confine them-selves today to studying the New Testament documents as *texts*—their nature, structure, con-tent, and way of functioning, as well as their readers' reading and reception of them—and to ex-pressing an opinion about their reliability as historical sources without discussing the question how the material may have been preserved during the decades between the Master's ministry in Israel and the evangelists' writings. They fail to give any attention to two centuries of assiduous attempts to elucidate how the sayings of Jesus and the memories of his ministry were preserved during the first decades of the church. To me it seems clear that the question whether the New Testament documents give us a historically reliable picture of Jesus of Nazareth cannot be an-swered without a thorough study of the early Christian tradition problem." See also James Dunn, *A New Perspective on Jesus: What the Quest for the Historical Jesus Missed* (Grand Rapids: Baker Academic, 2005), 42: "This, I suggest to you, is the second major flaw in the quest of the histor-ical Jesus: an ability to envisage the transmission of the Jesus tradition tightly constricted by the literary paradigm inbred in us; an unwillingness to take seriously the question whether oral tradition would have functioned like literary tradition; a negative evaluation of oral tradition as to its reliability as testimony to Jesus; and consequently a negative judgment as to the questers' ability to say anything with much confidence about Jesus."

[36] See, for example, Gerhardsson, *Reliability of the Gospel Tradition*, 2: "My chief objection to the form-critical scholars—whom I agree with in part, but in part decidedly differ from—is that their work is not sufficiently historical. They do not show sufficient energy in anchoring the ques-tion of the origin of the gospel tradition within the framework of the question concerning how holy, authoritative tradition was transmitted in the Jewish milieu of Palestine and elsewhere at the time of the NT. This must surely be the starting point if one wants to understand the origins of the early Christian tradition historically."

ditioned modern presuppositions about the composition of the New Testament.

Instead, one ought to take the paradigm of oral culture and memorization, as well as reverence for what is passed on, as the norm for understanding the origin of the Gospels. We tend to think that oral transmission would cause constant errors and changes in the texts. It can be shown, however, that oral cultures are tremendously conservative, in great contrast to our dynamic modern Western culture. Certain men were trained to memorize extremely long texts, composed in a style appropriate for such memorization, full of repetition, set phrases, and parallelism (as are the Gospels). It stands to reason also that oral memory is enhanced where written texts are very limited.

It is well known that the Jewish culture of the time of Our Lord was an oral culture in which it was customary for very large texts to be transmitted in an exclusively oral fashion. This can be seen in the transmission of the oral Jewish Law, which was finally written down centuries later in the Mishnah and the Talmud. Before the writing of the Talmud, this tremendous mass of material (far greater than our four Gospels) was memorized by the rabbis and passed from master to disciple as their most precious inheritance.[37]

St. Jerome witnesses to the capacity of memorization of Jews that he met in the Holy Land:

> Just as we who are Latins easily commit to memory Latin names and things that originate in our language, so from earliest infancy they have imbibed in their deepest thoughts terms that are indigenous to their speech (and from the beginning with Adam until the end in Zerubbabel, they run through the generations of everyone so swiftly and accurately that you would think they are referring to their own name).[38]

---

[37] See Jacob Neusner, *The Oral Torah: The Sacred Books of Judaism: An Introduction* (San Francisco: Harper & Row, 1986).

[38] St. Jerome, *Commentary on Titus* 3:9, in *St. Jerome's Commentaries on Galatians, Titus, and Philemon*, trans. Thomas P. Scheck (Notre Dame: University of Notre Dame Press, 2010), 342–343.

The exhortation of Deuteronomy 6:6–7 shaped the life of Israel: "And these words which I command you this day shall be upon your heart; and you shall teach them diligently to your children, and shall talk of them when you sit in your house, and when you walk by the way, and when you lie down, and when you rise." This exhortation to memorize and transmit would have been applied by the Apostles to the words of Jesus with no less reverence than in the case of the words of Moses, but rather more.

Oral transmission of religious texts has a threefold value. On the one hand, oral transmission allows a text to continue to live through the generations and is not dependent on libraries, books, or literacy in a culture in which those are rare. Secondly, oral transmission, because it involves memorization—learning by heart—allows the teaching to be carried with one in one's heart when traveling, working, or resting, as in Deuteronomy 6:7.[39] What comes in through the ears is better retained than what comes in through the eyes. St. Paul alludes to the importance of hearing the Word in Romans 10:14–17: "How are they to believe in him of whom they have never heard? And how are they to hear without a preacher? . . . So faith comes from what is *heard*, and what is heard comes by the preaching of Christ." Third, oral transmission has an essential social dimension, for it involves public recitation. When religious texts are involved, this public recitation is liturgical.

The value of oral transmission can be seen above all in the example of Christ Himself, who chose not to write anything and devoted Himself entirely to oral preaching and the formation of disciples who would not only carry on His words, but their spirit, substance, and authoritative meaning. Indeed, He did not order His disciples to *write*, but rather to *preach* the Gospel to every creature (Mark 16:15 and Matt 28:20).

Several twentieth-century scholars have had the significant merit of calling attention to the oral culture of Israel at the time of Christ

---

[39] See Robert Oswald Patrick Taylor, *The Groundwork of the Gospels: With Some Collected Papers* (Oxford, UK: Blackwell, 1946), 61, cited in Bernard Orchard, *Matthew, Luke, and Mark* (Manchester, UK: Koinonia Press, 1976), 32: "To the men of Jesus's day oral transmission was natural and normal. . . . whereas we regard any system of oral transmission as a mere makeshift for the written word, they had an actual and decided preference for records inscribed in men's brains."

and its implications for our understanding the origins of the Gospels. Of particular importance in this regard are Marcel Jousse (1886–1961) and Birger Gerhardsson.[40] Others who have carried on this line of thought are Samuel Byrskog and Werner Kelber. Jousse, a French Jesuit, anthropologist, and philologist, dedicated much of his life to the study of oral cultures from a psychological and anthropological perspective and applied this material to the problem of the origins of the Gospels.[41] He speaks of the "oral style" in which a culture transmits its religious and historical patrimony primarily through memorization and oral recitation.[42] Obviously, all illiterate cultures have an oral style, but literate cultures can also prefer to transmit their most important teachings orally. In the course of oral transmission, it can happen that what is orally transmitted also gets written down without interrupting the oral nature of what was transmitted and the emphasis on oral transmission.

The early Church conserved the oral style that she inherited from the synagogue, even after the written redaction of the Gospels. The importance of the homily in the Christian liturgy is an echo and

---

[40] See Birger Gerhardsson, *Memory and Manuscript with Tradition and Transmission in Early Christianity*, trans. Eric Sharpe, foreword by Jacob Neusner (Grand Rapids: Eerdmans, 1998). *Memory and Manuscript* was originally published in 1961, and *Tradition and Transmission* in 1964. On the importance of Gerhardsson's work, see Ben F. Meyer, "Some Consequences of Birger Gerhardsson's Account of the Origins of the Gospel Tradition," in *Jesus and the Oral Gospel Tradition*, ed. Henry Wansbrough (Sheffield, UK: JSOT Press, 1991), 425: "If Gerhardsson's account of the origins of the Synoptic tradition is true, much of the discussion of historical criteriology over the past two generations has been misplaced or defective. For example, Ernst Käsemann's famous principle, that we have 'somewhat firm ground under our feet' only when a tradition for whatever reason is unattributable either to Judaism or to Christianity, will have ceased to be meaningful. Why? Because its numerous presuppositions on the nature of tradition, for example, a rather free formation of tradition designed almost exclusively to serve immediately practical communitarian concerns, no longer obtain."

[41] See Marcel Jousse, *The Oral Style*, trans. Edgard Sienaert and Richard Whitaker (New York: Garland, 1990). This seminal work was originally published in French in 1924. See also the three works published posthumously: *L'anthropologie du geste* (Paris: Editions Resma, 1969); *L'anthropologie du geste*, vol. 2, *La Manducation de la parole* (Paris: Éditions Gallimard, 1975); and *L'anthropologie du geste*, vol. 3, *Le Parlant, la Parole et le Souffle* (Paris: Éditions Gallimard, 1978).

[42] Other important works on the oral style include Albert Bates Lord, *The Singer of Tales* (Cambridge: Harvard University Press, 1960), Walter J. Ong, *Orality and Literacy: The Technologizing of the Word* (London: Routledge, 1982), Jan Vansina, *Oral Tradition as History* (Madison: University of Wisconsin Press, 1985), and Henry Wansbrough, ed., *Jesus and the Oral Gospel Tradition* (Sheffield, UK: JSOT Press, 1991).

preservation of the oral style. More generally, it forms the heart of the Catholic understanding of the role of Tradition and its oral transmission.

Oral Style in the Gospels

As analyzed by Jousse and others, the oral style is marked above all by elements that facilitate memorization, retention, and faithful transmission. The hallmarks of this style are extensive parallelism, antithetical opposition, repetition of key words and phrases, rhythm, the use of stereotyped formulae, parables, and pithy summarizing phrases. Written cultures, on the contrary, tend to avoid parallelism and repetition, whether of words, metaphors or rhythms.

These techniques of the oral style are evident throughout the Old Testament, especially in the prophets, psalms and other canticles, and proverbs or wisdom literature. They are likewise present in the sayings of the rabbis that were passed on orally in Israel and which were eventually written down and gathered into the Mishnah and Talmud. And it is easy to see that they are also present in the Gospels, especially in the discourses of Jesus.

To a culture that is unfamiliar with the oral style and unpracticed in memorization through repeated oral recitation, it may seem difficult to believe that Jesus's discourses could have been remembered accurately and faithfully preserved orally for some twenty to fifty years before they were written down. Would not such a gap of time result in the change of the preaching of Jesus into something quite different, colored by the mentality of the milieu in which it was written down? Form criticism and the various quests for the historical Jesus have answered in the affirmative. The early Church, however, did not see anything incredible about the faithful oral transmission of the preaching of Jesus for a generation before its rendition in writing because they lived in an oral culture not yet too dissimilar from that of Jesus and the Apostles.

If, on the other hand, the Gospels failed to show us the clear hallmarks of the oral style as it was used in Israel, then the objection might have real force. If the Gospels showed us teaching that was clearly thought in written terms (like modern academic works or like the medieval *Summas*) that did not lend itself to easy memorization and oral recitation and required writing to be preserved, only then would the lack of writing for a generation be a major problem for the credibility of the Gospel tradition. But that is not the case, for Jesus deliberately spoke and acted in a way that would make His words and deeds supremely memorable for the Apostles.

Cardinal Bea draws attention to this in his *Study of the Synoptic Gospels*:

> Considering the matter *from the point of view of Christ* himself, we must say that he certainly must have repeated many times over the same truth with the same incisive formulae. His purpose was to inculcate his doctrine when speaking in public or else to fix it in the minds of the apostles. This was actually the traditional method among the Rabbis, the only one available at a time when the use of books or scrolls was rare and difficult. The rhythmic formulas and mnemonic sentences still found in the Gospels testify to the use of this method.[43]

The Scandinavian school of New Testament scholarship has much credit for developing the thesis that Jesus would have taught in such a way that His essential words would be remembered. In an essay from 1959, Harald Riesenfeld argued that the origin of the Gospel tradition is to be attributed not to later sources such as Mark or Q, but to Jesus Himself during His public ministry. Granted that Jesus was aware of His messianic mission, it is perfectly reasonable that Jesus would be quite concerned about the transmission of His teaching to the entire world.[44] It was for this reason that He chose the Twelve and gave them a unique formation, instructing them in public and in private for three years.

---

[43] *The Study of the Synoptic Gospels*, 67.

[44] See *"The Gospel Tradition and Its Beginnings,"* in *The Gospel Tradition: Essays*, trans. Margaret Rowley and Robert Kraft (Philadelphia: Fortress, 1970), 20.

This claim that the Gospel materials go back to the discourses of Jesus, rather than merely to the redactors, is strongly supported by the fact that the discourses of Jesus are magnificent examples of the oral style proper to oral preachers. Gerhardsson writes:

> The sayings of Jesus in the Synoptic Gospels . . . consist of brief, laconic, well-rounded texts, of pointed statements with a clear profile, rich in content and artistic in form. The artistic devices show through clearly even in the tradition's Greek form: picturesque content, strophic construction, *parallelismus membrorum*, verbatim repetitions, and so on. These features can be seen all the more clearly if one translates back into Aramaic. Then one sees in the sayings of Jesus such characteristics as rhythm, assonance, and alliteration as well. It is obvious that we are dealing here with carefully thought out and deliberately formulated statements.[45]

Joachim Jeremias has also analyzed the characteristic oral style present in the discourses of Jesus in the Synoptic Gospels. He observes that the use of certain forms of rhythm is carefully chosen to make certain formulations more memorable and emphatic:

> Because of its brevity, the two-beat line necessitates terse and abrupt formulations, whose sparseness and monotony lends them the utmost urgency. A further look at the themes of the examples given above will immediately show that Jesus used the two-beat line . . . to impress upon his hearers *central ideas* of his message.[46]

Parallelism

The Old Testament makes very abundant use of parallelism. It is regarded as the chief characteristic of Hebrew poetry and of the oral

---

[45] *Reliability of the Gospel Tradition*, 42.

[46] *New Testament Theology: The Proclamation of Jesus* (New York: Charles Scribner's Sons, 1971), 22.

style. Parallelism aids memory by the repetition of the same idea in parallel phrases. David Biven explains:

> Hebrew poetry is not like English poetry. It is not rhyming the ends of verses of the poem. It is not a repetition of the same sound, but a repetition or echoing of the same thought. One says the same thing twice, but each time in a different way, in different though equivalent words. This feature of Hebrew poetry is called parallelism. Parallelism, the placing of two synonymous phrases or sentences side by side, is the essence of Hebrew poetry.[47]

The poetic structure of the teaching of Jesus is somewhat hidden by the fact that this teaching is almost always printed as if it were simply prose. However, it is easy to see that Jesus's discourses are a kind of orally proclaimed verse, and are masterpieces of the oral style. Rainer Riesner notes that the great majority of Jesus's sayings are structured in this way:

> As hypothetical as this must remain, only if we try to retrovert the sayings of Jesus into Aramaic or sometimes also into Hebrew can we evaluate fully their often poetical structure. According to my estimate, about 80 percent of the separate saying units are formulated in some kind of *parallelismus membrorum*. To this one has to add other poetical techniques such as alliteration, assonance, rhythm, and rhyme.[48]

Sermon on the Mount

The Sermon on the Mount in St. Matthew's Gospel has a large amount of parallelism to facilitate memorization. The most evident is the structure of the beatitudes. Another good example is the house built on rock or on sand. Matthew 7:7–11 is also rich in parallelism:

---

[47] David Bivin and Roy Blizzard Jr., *Understanding the Difficult Words of Jesus: New Insights from a Hebrew Perspective* (Kindle Locations 704–707). Kindle Edition.

[48] "Jesus as Preacher and Teacher," in Wansbrough, *Jesus and the Oral Gospel Tradition*, 202.

[7] **Ask**, and it will be *given* you;
seek, and you will *find*;
knock, and it will be *opened* to you.
[8] For every one who **asks** *receives*,
and he who **seeks** *finds*,
and to him who **knocks** it will be *opened*.
[9] Or what man of you, if his son **asks** him for bread, will *give* him
a stone?
[10] Or if he **asks** for a fish, will *give* him a serpent?
[11] If you then, who are *evil*, know how to *give* **good** gifts to your
children, how much more will your Father who is in heaven *give*
good things to those who **ask** him!

Sending of the Apostles:

Parallelism can be seen again in the sending of the Apostles in Matthew 10:32–33:

[32] So every one who **acknowledges me**   before men,
I also will **acknowledge**   before my Father
who is in heaven;
[33] but whoever *denies me*   before men,
I also will *deny*   before my Father
who is in heaven.

Matthew 16:13–23

One of the texts in the Gospel of Matthew that has greatest theological significance is surely Matthew 16:13–23, in which Christ asks the Apostles who they say He is, and in which He declares that He will build His Church on the rock of Peter. This text is also one in which we can most closely see the parallelism and antithesis typical of Hebrew prophetic literature and poetry. This was recognized also by liberal theologians such as Adolf von Harnack, who wrote that "there are not many longer sections in the Gospels from which the Aramaic basis shines through in form and content so surely as from this tightly compact pericope."[49]

Oral Tradition in the Early Church Was Ecclesial, Apostolic, and Liturgical

Oral tradition in oral societies involves three aspects that were especially important in the early Church. First, it is profoundly communal, for it preserves the lifeblood and foundational history of the community.[50] Second, because of its communal importance, oral tradition is preserved above all by those entrusted with safeguarding and transmitting the foundational history of the society.[51] Third, it is predominantly liturgical in character, for it concerns the celebration of the *magnalia Dei*, the great works of God that lie at the foundation of a society (see Acts 2:11).

All three of these aspects can be clearly seen in Israel. Oral tradition was intensely communal, giving and preserving Israelite identity. It was transmitted by authoritative witnesses, beginning with Moses and Aaron, and passing through the lines of priests and prophets. Finally, oral tradition was liturgical. The tradition was passed on above all in the liturgical recitation of God's Word. Even when the Word of God was written down, it was still known only in its oral form by the great majority of the people, and even those who preserved the written Torah learnt it by heart.

---

[49] Quoted in Joseph Ratzinger, *Called to Communion: Understanding the Church Today*, trans. Adrian Walker (San Francisco: Ignatius Press, 1996), 60.

[50] See Dunn, *A New Perspective on Jesus*, 43: "Oral tradition was group tradition; it existed in and for the churches; that is why it took the forms it did take." See also ibid., 48: "Oral tradition continues in existence because there are communities for whom the tradition is important. The tradition is performed with greater or less regularity (depending on its importance) in the gatherings of the community, kept alive for the community by the elders, teachers, or those acknowledged as proficient performers of the tradition."

[51] See ibid., 49: "In the oral community there would be one or more who were recognized as having *primary responsibility for maintaining and performing the community's tradition*— the singer of tales, the bard, the elders, the teachers, the rabbis.... In NT terms this certainly accords with the role of the apostle in providing what can properly be called foundation tradition for the churches he founded, as clearly attested in the Pauline letters."

Applying this to the early Church, it can be seen that the oral tradition about the words and works of Jesus—the oral Gospel—was ecclesial, apostolic, and liturgical. The transmission of the oral Gospel is the very foundation of the Christian community. Every church would receive the patrimony of the "Gospel" from the Apostles, who founded the churches, and this foundational patrimony would be received and renewed above all in the celebration of the liturgy.

It follows that the guarantee that we encounter the real Jesus in the Gospels, as affirmed by *Dei Verbum* §19, rests on the fact that apostolic Tradition has transmitted the portrait of Jesus to us through the fourfold witness of the Gospels, and that the Church has always seen in them the faithful record of "what Jesus Christ, while living among men, really did and taught for their eternal salvation."

In *Lumen fidei* §38, Pope Francis poses the question concerning the reliability of the Gospels:

> It is through an unbroken chain of witnesses that we come to see the face of Jesus. But how is this possible? How can we be certain, after all these centuries, that we have encountered the "real Jesus"? Were we merely isolated individuals, were our starting point simply our own individual ego seeking in itself the basis of absolutely sure knowledge, a certainty of this sort would be impossible. I cannot possibly verify for myself something which happened so long ago. But this is not the only way we attain knowledge. Persons always live in relationship. We come from others, we belong to others, and our lives are enlarged by our encounter with others. Even our own knowledge and self-awareness are relational; they are linked to others who have gone before us: in the first place, our parents, who gave us our life and our name. Language itself, the words by which we make sense of our lives and the world around us, comes to us from others, preserved in the living memory of others. Self-knowledge is only possible when we share in a greater memory. The same thing holds true for faith, which brings human understanding to its fullness.

Faith's past, that act of Jesus's love which brought new life to the world, comes down to us through the memory of others—witnesses—and is kept alive in that one remembering subject which is the Church. The Church is a Mother who teaches us to speak the language of faith. Saint John brings this out in his Gospel by closely uniting faith and memory and associating both with the working of the Holy Spirit, who, as Jesus says, "will remind you of all that I have said to you" (John 14:26). The love which is the Holy Spirit and which dwells in the Church unites every age and makes us contemporaries of Jesus, thus guiding us along our pilgrimage of faith.

Christian faith rests on the witness of the Gospels to Jesus Christ. But why should we trust the Gospels? The veracity of the witness of the Gospels rests, in turn, on the assurance of the Tradition of the Church, who is our Mother. For this reason, St. Augustine famously wrote: "For my part, I should not believe the gospel except as moved by the authority of the Catholic Church."[52]

Faith Is the Proper Response to the Gospel Witness about Christ

The proclamation of the witness about Christ calls forth an act of faith on the part of the recipient. This act of faith is dual: (1) belief in the testimony of the Apostles who transmit in manifold ways Christ's unique claim that shines through His life, death, and Resurrection, and (2) belief in the divinity of Christ, whose divine claim is transmitted by that apostolic witness. In the genesis of the act of faith through an encounter with the New Testament, one first comes to believe in the apostolic witness through human faith, which makes possible divine faith in Christ as being who He said He is. This faith then leads one to the Church and the inspiration of her Scriptures. Thus, one then comes to have divine faith also in the words of the Apostles.

Reception of the apostolic witness in faith enables the recipient to

---

[52] St. Augustine, *Against the Epistle of Manichaeus Called 'Fundamental'* 5.6 (*NPNF1*, 4:131).

enter into a dual communion: with the Apostles and with Christ (and indeed the whole Trinity) who is proclaimed. John states in 1 John 1:3: "That which we have seen and heard we proclaim also to you, so that you may have fellowship with us; and our fellowship is with the Father and with his Son Jesus Christ."

The implication is that if I do not believe the apostolic testimony about Christ, I cannot enter into that communion. I cannot believe in Christ without believing the Apostles. Any attempt to reconstruct a Jesus of history distinct in any substantial way from the Jesus proclaimed in the Gospels, is equivalent to challenging the apostolic witness and refusing to enter into the communion of the Church. To be a disciple of Christ means to believe the apostolic witness about Christ contained preeminently in the Gospels, as well as the rest of Scripture and Tradition.

Conclusion

The defense of the historicity of the Gospels is of the greatest importance for the Christian faith. An attitude of general distrust or suspicion with regard to their substantial historicity would destroy the foundation of the Christian faith in a way similar to the heresy of the Gnostics in the second and third century AD, who held that Christ did not assume a real human nature, notwithstanding the testimony of the Gospels. Of them, St. Thomas Aquinas writes:

> This position wipes out the authority of Scripture. Since the likeness of flesh is not flesh . . . Scripture lies in saying: "The Word was made flesh" (John 1:14)—if it was but phantasy flesh. It also lies when it says that Jesus Christ walked, ate, died, and was buried—if these things took place only in an apparent phantasy. But, *if even in a moderate way the authority of Scripture be decried, there will no longer be anything fixed in our faith which depends on sacred Scripture*, as in John's words (20:31): "These are written, that you may believe."[53]

---

[53] *SCG*, bk. 4, ch. 29, no. 2 (my italics).

Study Questions

1. What does the Magisterium of the Church teach about the historical character of the Gospels?
2. What are the three steps in the genesis of the Gospels spoken of in *Dei Verbum* §19 and *Sancta Mater Ecclesia*?
3. What are some of the ways in which the notion of eyewitness is emphasized in the New Testament?
4. Describe some of the elements of "oral style" that are evident in the discourses of Jesus. How do they facilitate memorization?
5. What do Papias and St. Irenaeus say about the importance of oral tradition in the early Church?

Suggestions for Further Reading

Dei Verbum §19.

Pontifical Biblical Commission. Instruction on the Historical Truth of the Gospels *Sancta Mater Ecclesia*. April 21, 1964.

Bauckham, Richard. *Jesus and the Eyewitnesses: The Gospels as Eyewitness Testimony*. Grand Rapids: Eerdmans, 2006.

Blomberg, Craig L. *The Historical Reliability of the Gospels*. Downer's Grove: IVP Academic, 2007.

Byrskog, Samuel. *Story as History—History as Story: The Gospel Tradition in the Context of Ancient Oral History*. Tübingen: Mohr Siebeck, 2000.

Dunn, James. *A New Perspective on Jesus: What the Quest for the Historical Jesus Missed*. Grand Rapids: Baker Academic, 2005.

Eve, Eric. *Behind the Gospels: Understanding the Oral Tradition*. Minneapolis: Fortress, 2014.

Gerhardsson, Birger. *The Reliability of the Gospel Tradition*. Peabody: Hendrickson, 2001.

Jousse, Marcel, S.J. *The Oral Style*. Translated by Edgard Sienaert and Richard Whitaker. New York: Garland, 1990.

PART 6

Biblical Typology

CHAPTER SIXTEEN

The Four Senses of Scripture

Words and Deeds

A theological study of Revelation and its transmission would be incomplete without studying biblical typology, by which God reveals Himself through the events of salvation history narrated by the words of Scripture.

As we have seen in the first chapter, God reveals Himself to mankind not just through words, but also through deeds or events. This is eloquently stated in *Dei Verbum* §2:

> This plan of revelation is realized by deeds and words having an inner unity: the deeds wrought by God in the history of salvation manifest and confirm the teaching and realities signified by the words, while the words proclaim the deeds and clarify the mystery contained in them.

The central deed of Revelation is the Incarnation of the Word and His Passion and Resurrection (the Paschal mystery). However, many other events of salvation history in various ways prepare for or point to supernatural mysteries and are also revelatory. Biblical typology is concerned with the revelatory aspect of *deeds* in sacred history, and constitutes what is known as the *spiritual* sense of Scripture. The literal sense of Scripture is the proper meaning conveyed through its *words*.

Because God is the principal author of the Bible, it has a richness of meaning that other books cannot rival. Most non-fictional human writings have only one meaning in each text, which is called the literal sense. This is the meaning that the words are intended to convey. Works of literary fiction, on the other hand, often have passages with more than one sense, when an author uses literary techniques to make one event symbolize or foreshadow another. If writers of literature and poetry can give more than one meaning to a text, then certainly God can put a still greater richness of meaning into the Word He inspires.

What the poet does with the events that he invents, God can do with the events of sacred history that He guides through His providence. This distinguishes the historical texts of the Bible from purely human historical works. The historical events, institutions, and persons recounted in the Bible can signify future or supernatural events and realities because biblical history has for its principal author the Author of history. *This meaning by which a biblical event signifies a reality or future event in salvation history is called the typological or spiritual meaning.*[1]

Distinction between the Literal and the Spiritual Senses of Scripture

St. Thomas Aquinas distinguishes the literal and the typological/spiritual senses of Scripture with this simple distinction between words and deeds. The literal sense is the meaning conveyed directly by the words of Scripture. The spiritual (typological) senses are meanings conveyed directly by the events or deeds that the words express. Thus the spiritual senses are conveyed indirectly by the words of Scripture,

---

[1] See the definition of typology by Devin Roza, *Fulfilled in Christ: The Sacraments: A Guide to Symbols and Types in the Bible and Tradition* (Steubenville: Emmaus Academic, 2015), 23: "Typology is the discernment of realities, events, deeds, words, symbols, or signs in the Bible that foreshadow the fulfillment of God's plan in Jesus Christ."

but directly by the events or realities. The events of sacred history are intended by God to have a meaning that goes beyond their own intrinsic significance to function as signs or pointers of future mysteries. However, St. Thomas also holds that "nothing necessary to faith is contained under the spiritual sense which is not elsewhere put forward by Scripture in its literal sense."[2]

In the last article of the first question in part I of the *Summa theologiae*, St. Thomas explains the difference between the literal and the spiritual senses of Scripture:

> Therefore that first signification whereby words signify things belongs to the first sense, the historical or literal. That signification whereby things signified by words have themselves also a signification is called the spiritual sense, which is based on the literal, and presupposes it.[3]

The same distinction is further explained in a parallel text in *Quodlibet*:

> Holy Scripture is divinely ordained to manifest to us the truth necessary for salvation. The manifestation or expression of a truth can be made in two ways—through events[4] or words—in that words signify events, and one event can be the figure of another. The author of Sacred Scripture, the Holy Spirit, is not only the author of the words, but also the author of the events, so that He is able not only to use words to signify something, but also can dispose the events to be figures of something else. And thus truth is manifested in a twofold fashion in Holy Scripture. In one way, insofar as events are signified by words, and this is the literal sense. In another way, insofar as events are figures of other things, and the spiritual

---

2   *ST* I, q. 1, a. 10, ad 1. See also *Quodlibet* 7, q. 6, a. 1 ad 1; in *Opera Omnia*, vol. 25/1 (Rome: Commissio Leonina, 1996), 28.

3   *ST* I, q. 1, a. 10.

4   The Latin word is "res," which can be translated as "event," "thing," or "reality."

sense consists in this. And thus it belongs to Sacred Scripture to have more than one sense.[5]

This Thomistic understanding of the difference between the literal and the spiritual senses of Scripture has been taken up in the *Catechism of the Catholic Church* §117: "Thanks to the unity of God's plan, not only the text of Scripture but also the realities and events about which it speaks can be signs." The text of Scripture gives rise to the literal sense, whereas the deeds narrated by the text can themselves be signs of other realities, which is the spiritual or typological sense.

Type and Antitype

Typology comes from the Greek word "*typos*," from whence comes the English word "type," which broadly means "figure" or "model" and is the root of many English words containing the word "type" (such as "prototype," "typecast," "archetype," and the adjective, "typical").[6] The English word "type" is taken here in the sense in which it means "that by which something is symbolized or figured; anything having a symbolical signification; a symbol, emblem."[7] A type is that which serves as a model for other things.

"Typology" literally means "the study or science of types." In biblical interpretation, typology is the systematic study of the various types in Scripture. As St. Justin Martyr stated, "The Holy Spirit sometimes caused something that was to be a type of the future to be done openly."[8] Typology studies the architecture of God's progressive Revelation through the interconnected deeds of salvation history.

---

[5]   St. Thomas, *Quodlibet* 7, q. 6, a. 1 (*Opera Omnia*, vol. 25/1:28).

[6]   See John J. O'Keefe and R. R. Reno, *Sanctified Vision: An Introduction to Early Christian Interpretation of the Bible* (Baltimore: John Hopkins University Press, 2005), 70.

[7]   *Oxford English Dictionary*, 2nd ed. (Oxford, UK: Clarendon Press, 1989), 18:786. See also K. J. Woollcombe, "The Biblical Origins and Patristic Development of Typology," in *Essays on Typology*, eds. G. W. H. Lampe and K. J. Woollcombe, (London: SCM Press, 1957), 60–65.

[8]   St. Justin, *Dialogue with Trypho* 104.1; in *The First Apology, The Second Apology, Dialogue with Trypho, Exhortation to the Greeks, Discourse to the Greeks, The Monarchy or The Rule of God*, trans. T. B. Falls, The Fathers of the Church 6 (Washington, DC: The Catholic University of America Press, 1948), 323.

In Romans 5:14, St. Paul uses the word *typos* to show the connection between Adam and Christ: "Adam, who was a *type* of the one who was to come." When "type" is used of events or persons, two events or persons can be related as type and "antitype," the type being the model or figure of the antitype. This language is used in 1 Peter 3:21, in which the flood is presented as the type and Baptism as the antitype prefigured by the earlier event.[9] Typology is essentially Christocentric because Christ (and our incorporation into Him) is the principal antitype of all the types in Scripture.[10]

Three Typological Senses

We have seen that the first division of senses of Scripture is twofold: the literal or historical sense, on the one hand, and the typological or spiritual sense, on the other. The typological sense can be further divided into three categories, generally referred to as the allegorical, moral (tropological), and anagogical senses. All three of these typological senses refer to the Christian mystery, but in three different ways. Typology is said to be "allegorical" when the type prefigures Christ, His Church, and her sacraments. Typology is said to be "moral" when the type prefigures the Christian life in its spiritual and moral dimension. It is said to be anagogical, finally, when the type prefigures the Church triumphant and the Last Things. St. Thomas explains:

---

[9] The word "antitype" (ἀντίτυπος) is also used in Heb 9:24: "For Christ has entered, not into a sanctuary made with hands, a copy ["antitypical"] of the true one, but into heaven itself, now to appear in our behalf." This text uses "antitypical" to refer to the type of the Old Testament rather than to its fulfillment in the New. This shows that the terminology with regard to typology was still fluid in the period of the New Testament. Modern authors generally use "antitype" in the sense of 1 Pet 3:21, rather than Heb 9:24.

[10] See St. Ambrose, *De excessu fratris sui Satyri* 2.109: "But all is Christ's, and all is in Christ, whom now we cannot see according to the reality, but we see him, as it were, in a kind of likeness of future things. Of which we have seen the shadow in the Law" (PL, 16:1347). This is also quoted in Bertrand de Margerie, S.J., *An Introduction to the History of Exegesis*, vol. 2, *The Latin Fathers*, trans. Pierre de Fontnouvelle (Petersham: Saint Bede's, 1995), 92. See also Paul M. Quay, *The Mystery Hidden for Ages in God* (New York: Peter Lang, 1997), 154–158.

Now this spiritual sense has a threefold division. Therefore, so far as the things of the Old Law signify the things of the New Law, there is the allegorical sense; so far as the things done in Christ, or so far as the things which signify Christ, are types of what we ought to do, there is the moral sense. But so far as they [things of the Old and New Testament] signify what relates to eternal glory, there is the anagogical sense.[11]

The *Catechism of the Catholic Church* §§115–117 follows the Thomistic understanding of the senses of Scripture. §115 summarizes the traditional teaching of the Church on the literal and spiritual senses of Scripture:

According to an ancient tradition, one can distinguish between two *senses* of Scripture: the literal and the spiritual, the latter being subdivided into the allegorical, moral, and anagogical senses. The profound concordance of the four senses guarantees all its richness to the living reading of Scripture in the Church.

It follows that, if the spiritual senses are neglected in theology or preaching, our understanding of the Word of God would lose the guarantee of "all its richness."

The three categories of the spiritual sense are explained in §117. From the allegorical sense, "we can acquire a more profound understanding of events by recognizing their significance in Christ; thus

---

[11] *ST* I, q. 1, a. 10. A fuller parallel description of the three spiritual senses is given in St. Thomas's *Commentary on Galatians*, ch. 4, lec. 7 (on Gal 4:24; Marietti no. 254): "However, the mystical or spiritual sense is divided into three types. First, as when the Apostle says that the Old Law is the figure of the New Law. Hence, insofar as the things of the Old Law signify things of the New Law, it is the *allegorical* sense. Then, according to Dionysius in the book *On The Heavenly Hierarchy*, the New Law is a figure of future glory; accordingly, insofar as things in the New Law and in Christ signify things which are in heaven, it is the *anagogical* sense. Furthermore, in the New Law the things performed by the Head are examples of things we ought to do—because "whatever things were written, were written for our learning" (Rom 15:3)—accordingly insofar as the things which in the New Law were done in Christ and done in things that signify Christ are signs of things we ought to do, it is the *moral* sense" (*Super Epistolam B. Pauli ad Galatas lectura*, trans. Fabian Larcher [Lander: Aquinas Institute for the Study of Sacred Doctrine, 2012], 112–113).

the crossing of the Red Sea is a sign or type of Christ's victory and also of Christian Baptism." With regard to the *moral* sense: "The events reported in Scripture ought to lead us to act justly. As St. Paul says, they are written 'for our instruction.'" This instruction may also be through an example that we are *not* to follow, as when Esau sold his birthright for a plate of lentils, which is a type of all mortal sin, or when the Israelites desired to return to the fleshpots of Egypt. With regard to the *anagogical* or *eschatological* sense, "we can view realities and events in terms of their eternal significance, leading us toward our true homeland: thus the Church on earth is a sign of the heavenly Jerusalem." The entering into the Promised Land after crossing the Red Sea represents not only the entrance into the Church through Baptism, but also the entrance into the kingdom of heaven.

Thus there are four biblical senses: literal, allegorical, moral, and anagogical. Every text of Scripture has a literal sense, and in addition, it may have one, two, or (rarely) all three of these spiritual senses. The four senses of Scripture were popularized by a Latin poem written by a disciple of St. Thomas:

The Letter speaks of deeds; Allegory to faith;
The Moral how to act; Anagogy our destiny.[12]

To give an example of the four senses, St. Thomas chooses the words of Genesis 1:3: "Let there be light." In the literal sense this refers to the creation of physical light. However, St. Thomas sees three spiritual senses in which the creation of light is seen to prefigure Christ as the true light.

For when I say, "Let there be light," referring literally to corporeal light, it is the literal sense. But if it be taken to mean "Let Christ be born in the Church," it pertains to the allegorical sense. But if one says, "Let there be light," i.e., "Let

---

[12] Augustine of Dacia, *Rotulus pugillaris* 1: "Lettera gesta docet, quid credas allegoria, moralis quid agas, quo tendas anagogia"; ed. A. Walz in *Angelicum* 6 (1929): 256. See Henri de Lubac, *Medieval Exegesis*, vol. 1, *The Four Senses of Scripture*, trans. Mark Sebanc (Grand Rapids: Eerdmans, 1998), 1–4.

us be conducted to glory through Christ," it pertains to the anagogical sense. Finally, if it is said "Let there be light," i.e., "Let us be illumined in mind and inflamed in heart through Christ," it pertains to the moral sense.[13]

St. Thomas's procedure here is not arbitrary, but is based on the literal sense of other texts of Scripture that speak of light in a spiritual sense. His reading of the first line of the Bible is enriched by John 1:4–9, 8:12, and 9:5 and 2 Corinthians 4:6, in which Christ is presented according to the literal sense as the light of the world and of the Christian life.[14] It seems that St. John's presentation of Christ as the light of the world in the prologue of his Gospel is intended precisely to evoke this connection with Genesis 1:3. Thus, it is not unreasonable to understand the creation of physical light in Genesis 1:3 as a divinely intended prefiguration of the Incarnation, by which God would introduce the maximum supernatural, spiritual light into the world. This example pertains to the allegorical sense, showing a parallel between the work of creation and that of redemption.

The moral sense in which the creation of light is seen to prefigure the Christian life by which Christ's members are "illumined in mind" is also supported by the literal sense of Matthew 5:14: "You are the light of the world." Finally, the anagogical sense is based on the fact that the beatific vision will be the maximum imparting of light—the light of glory by which we shall see God as He is. Revelation 21:23–25 speaks of the light of glory as illuminating the heavenly Jerusalem: "And the city has no need of sun or moon to shine upon it, for the glory of God is its light, and its lamp is the Lamb. By its light shall the nations walk . . . and there shall be no night there."

---

[13] St. Thomas, *Commentary on Galatians*, ch. 4, lec. 7 (Marietti no. 254; Larcher, 113).

[14] 2 Cor 4:6 directly connects Gen 1:3 with the light of Christ: "For it is the God who said, 'Let light shine out of darkness,' who has shone in our hearts to give the light of the knowledge of the glory of God in the face of Christ."

The Meaning of "Spiritual" Sense

We have said that the typological meanings of Scripture are also referred to as *spiritual senses*. A word of caution: the word "spiritual" here is not being used in the ordinary sense of the word, but in a technical sense by which it is distinguished from the literal sense and synonymous with the typological. The fact that it is called *spiritual* should not lead us to think that the literal sense is not also "spiritual" in the ordinary sense of the word (dealing with lofty spiritual realities), especially when it teaches us directly about God, life in Christ, and our moral obligations. For example, the teaching of the Sermon on the Mount about the Christian life belongs to the literal rather than to the spiritual sense, for this teaching is made known directly by the *words* of Jesus in Matthew 5–7.[15]

The term "spiritual sense" has its roots in several texts of St. Paul that contrast the spirit and the letter (2 Cor 3:6 and Rom 2:29 and 7:6). This distinction is related to, but does not exactly correspond with, the distinction between spiritual senses and the literal sense as explained above, and as used, for example, by St. Thomas. St. Paul contrasts the spirit and the letter to express the difference between two kinds of worship. Spiritual worship has supernatural efficacy by being offered in Christ and the Spirit under the influence of faith, hope, and charity, and through the sacraments of the New Covenant that efficaciously give what they represent. Worship merely according to the letter would be worship according to the forms of the Mosaic Law, but not animated by faith, hope, and charity, failing to see Christ in it.

In 2 Corinthians 3:6, St. Paul says that God "has made us competent to be ministers of a new covenant, not in a written code [letter; *gramma*] but in the Spirit; for the written code kills, but the Spirit gives life." The same distinction is present in Romans 2:29: "He is a Jew who is one inwardly, and real circumcision is a matter of the heart, spiritual and not literal." Likewise, Romans 7:6 states: "We serve not under the old written code [letter; *gramma*] but in the new life of the

---

[15] For this reason, I think that it is less confusing for modern readers to refer to this non-literal sense as "typological," rather than "spiritual."

Spirit." In these texts, spiritual worship is one moved by the theological virtues, whereas a literal worship is the use of a corporal sign of the Old Covenant, such as circumcision, without being animated by right faith, hope, and charity.[16]

While this distinction between the letter and the spirit is applied by St. Paul above all to contrast two forms of worship, it can also be applied analogically to the interpretation of Scripture. Reading according to the letter would be reading the Old Testament without seeing Christ in it, whereas interpretation in the Spirit would be grasping the Christocentric content by which we receive supernatural life in Christ. Thus, reading the Old Testament "in the spirit" would be to understand the typology in Old Testament events that prefigure Christ. Bertrand de Margerie explains:

> For Paul, on whom the Fathers of the Church drew, the letter designates the Scripture interpreted ... not in the light of Christ, while the spirit of Scripture, likewise for Paul, is the meaning which the revelation of the mystery of Christ has given to it, the interpretation of the texts of the Old Testament in the light of Christ: the letter kills, the spirit gives life (2 Cor 3:6; cf. Rom 2:29; 7:6). Hence we have the expression spiritual sense and, by way of opposition, that of the *literal* or *corporal* or *historical* sense.[17]

After St. Paul, it is above all through the influence of Origen that the typological sense is referred to as spiritual. Origen makes an analogy between three aspects of the human person—body, soul, and

---

[16] St. Paul received this distinction from the prophetic texts, Ezek 36:26–27 and Jer 31:33. The latter proclaims that there will be a new covenant in which God promises that "I will put my law within them, and I will write it upon their hearts." The former makes a similar promise: "A new heart I will give you, and a new spirit I will put within you; and I will take out of your flesh the heart of stone and give you a heart of flesh. And I will put my spirit within you, and cause you to walk in my statutes and be careful to observe my ordinances."

[17] De Margerie, *Introduction to the History of Exegesis*, vol. 1, *The Greek Fathers*, trans. Leonard Maluf (Petersham: Saint Bede's, 1993), 9–10.

spirit—and three levels of meaning in Scripture.[18] The literal sense is associated with the body; the moral sense is associated with the soul; and the prefigurement of supernatural mysteries is associated with the spirit. Pope Benedict XVI gives a good summary of Origen's division of three senses of Scripture:

> Also in his *Homilies,* Origen took every opportunity to recall the different dimensions of the sense of Sacred Scripture that encourage or express a process of growth in the faith: there is the "literal" sense, but this conceals depths that are not immediately apparent. The second dimension is the "moral" sense: what we must do in living the word; and finally, the "spiritual" sense, the unity of Scripture which throughout its development speaks of Christ. It is the Holy Spirit who enables us to understand the Christological content, hence, the unity in diversity of Scripture.[19]

The spiritual sense is named above all from the Holy Spirit, both because the Spirit inspired the Scriptures, giving it a spiritual sense, and because He assists the interpreter to understand the spiritual meaning of biblical events.

Other Synonyms for Typological: Allegorical and Mystical

Two other terms that can serve as synonyms for the typological sense in general are the "mystical" and "allegorical" sense. Both expressions are used by St. Paul.

---

[18] See *On First Principles* 4.2.4: "Thus, just as a human being is said to be made up of body, soul, and spirit, so also is sacred Scripture, which has been granted by God's gracious dispensation for man's salvation"; in *Origen: An Exhortation to Martyrdom; Prayer; First Principles: Book IV; Prologue to the Commentary on the Song of Songs; Homily XXVII on numbers,* trans. Rowan Greer (New York: Paulist Press, 1979), 182. Origen's tripartite anthropological division comes from St. Paul, 1 Thess 5:23. See Arthur Calkins, "The Tripartite Biblical Vision of Man: A Key to the Christian Life," last modified January 24, 2014, at http://www.christendom-awake.org/pages/calkins/biblanth.htm.

[19] Benedict XVI, "Origen of Alexandria: Life and Work," General Audience of April 25, 2007; in *Church Fathers from Clement of Rome to Augustine* (San Francisco: Ignatius Press, 2008), 35–36.

The term "mystical sense" comes from the Greek word *mysterion*, used by St. Paul in Ephesians 5:32, in which he quotes Genesis 2:24 and says that "this mystery is a profound one, and I am saying that it refers to Christ and the Church." The typological sense is said to be mystical because Christ, who is Himself the great Mystery, is hidden in this way in the Old Testament.[20]

The term "allegorical sense" has its basis in Galatians 4:24: "Now this is an allegory: these women are two covenants." Unfortunately, there is considerable ambiguity with the term "allegorical" with regard to the Bible, for the term can be taken in three different senses. Sometimes the literal sense is intended to be allegorical. This occurs whenever the human author intends his words to be understood as an allegory, which is a particular literary genre in which certain events or persons are meant by the author to signify other realities in an extended metaphor. Good examples of literary allegories are Judges 9:8–15 (in which different kinds of trees are related to the consequences of kingship), Ezekiel 16, Psalm 80:8–16, and 2 Samuel 12:1–4 (Nathan's parable illustrating David's sin).

Sometimes the term "allegory" is used to refer to typology in general and not just to a particular kind of typology. I shall avoid this usage for the sake of clarity. However, it is good to be aware that the Fathers not infrequently speak of allegory in this general sense. St. Ambrose, for example, says: "There is allegory when one thing is being accomplished, another is being prefigured."[21] This is a good definition of typology in general.[22]

In common usage today, however, which began with the Scholastics, the allegorical sense refers to a particular kind of typological

---

[20] See de Lubac, *Medieval Exegesis*, vol. 2: *The Four Senses of Scripture* (Grand Rapids: Eerdmans, 1998), 20: "The mystical sense is the sense related to the mystery, which is a reality, at first hidden in God, and then revealed to human beings at the same time as realized in Jesus Christ. It will therefore be the sense which contains the plenitude of the doctrine."

[21] St. Ambrose, *De Abraham* 1.4.28 (PL, 14:432C; quoted also in de Lubac, *Medieval Exegesis*, 2:7). See also St. Augustine, *De Trinitate* 15.9.15: "When the Apostle spoke of an allegory, he does not find it in the words, but in the fact" (*NPNF*1, 3:207).

[22] See also Honorius, *Elucidarium* 2.27: "Holy Scripture is understood in two ways, historically and allegorically" (PL, 172:1154B; quoted also in de Lubac, *Medieval Exegesis*, 2:25). "Allegorically" here clearly refers to typology in general, and not just to one form of typology.

sense in which an earlier event (usually from the Old Testament, but sometimes from the New) is a type of Christ, the Church, or the sacraments. This is the normal sense in which I shall use the term, following the *Catechism of the Catholic Church* §115.

Why this plethora of synonymous terms (typology, spiritual sense, mystical sense, and allegory) to express one idea?[23] Although the plurality of terms can certainly lead to confusion, it is also an indirect indication of the importance of this topic. A plurality of names generally shows the significance and richness of a theme that has merited the attention of various ages in history. Each term emphasizes a different aspect of the reality of typology.

Typology and the Stages of Salvation History

Biblical typology and the distinction of three spiritual senses is based on the fact that salvation is marked in progressive stages that center on the Incarnation of the Word in the fullness of time. We can identify the following stages: the creation of man in original justice in Eden; man after the Fall but before the Old Covenant; the Old Covenant; the Incarnation, the New Covenant, and the time of the Church; and the Last Things. The fact that salvation history is fashioned by God with these progressive stages makes it possible for God to prepare for each succeeding stage in two ways: by words of prophecy and by events that foreshadow future realities. The event becomes a type that prefigures a reality of a future stage.

The various stages of salvation history also determine the kind of typological sense. Insofar as earlier events prefigure the mysteries of Christ and the Church, we have the allegorical sense. Insofar as they refer to the Christian life, we have the moral sense. Insofar as they refer to the last things, we have the anagogical sense.

Since the type must precede the antitype, the allegorical sense is principally found in the Old Testament. Nevertheless, there are three

---

[23] See de Lubac, *Medieval Exegesis*, 2:21: "Spirit, mystery, allegory: these then are the three major, practically synonymous vocabulary items. They and their derivatives are frequently intermingled in diverse combinations."

exceptions to this general rule. First, the earlier events in the life of Christ can prefigure later ones. Thus, the loss of the child Jesus in the Temple prefigures the three days in the tomb and would be an example of the allegorical sense. Second, the mysteries in the life of Christ are types of His Mystical Body who is formed in His image. A third type is when what "is said of the early Church [is] interpreted of a future state of the present Church."[24] Thus the picture of the Church painted in the second chapter of Acts is the type or model of what the Church is called to be throughout her history.

The moral sense can be found both in the events of the Old Testament and the New, for Christian life follows on both. Similarly, the anagogical sense can be found in the events of both Testaments, for it is the final end for which everything is a preparation. In heaven, there are no more types, for all veils will be taken away, and all the types of history will be perfectly manifested. St. Thomas explains the possible typological senses in the New Testament as follows:

> What is said literally about Christ our Head can be interpreted allegorically, with respect to the Mystical Body; and morally, referring to our acts which are to be reformed in His image; and anagogically, in that our path to glory has been made manifest in Christ. But when something is said about the Church in the literal sense, it cannot be interpreted allegorically, unless that which is said of the early Church be interpreted of a future state of the present Church. They can, however, be interpreted morally and anagogically. Those things that according to the literal sense have a moral meaning, can only be interpreted anagogically.[25] Those things finally that according to the literal sense pertain to the state of glory, cannot be interpreted in any other sense, because that

---

[24] St. Thomas, *Quodlibet* 7, q. 6, a. 2, ad 5 (*Opera Omnia*, vol. 25/1:31).

[25] An example of this would be the Sermon on the Mount. The literal sense transmits a moral teaching about the Christian life. There is no further allegorical or moral sense. It can have an anagogical sense, however, for the Christian life outlined in the Sermon on the Mount according to the literal sense, is itself the type of the life of the blessed in heaven.

state is not a figure of any other state, but is prefigured by all others.[26]

The Literal Sense Is the Foundation of the Spiritual Senses

Since the events narrated in Scripture are described through words, it is not hard to see that the spiritual senses depend on the literal sense, but not the reverse. Before considering the typological meaning of events narrated in Scripture, one must first rightly understand the meaning of the words of the narration. The spiritual sense, therefore, never supplants the literal sense, but always presupposes it. These two senses are never in conflict, but always stand in an analogous relationship. Their relationship is like those between nature and grace and between reason and faith. As "grace does not destroy nature but perfects it," [27] so the spiritual sense of Scripture does not threaten the literal sense, but rather is built on it and could not exist without it. *The Catechism of the Catholic Church* §116, quoting St. Thomas, stipulates that "'all other senses of Sacred Scripture are based on the literal.'"[28] Deeds or events can serve as signs only if they have first been communicated through the literal sense.

Since the literal sense is the foundation of the spiritual senses, it is the first task of the exegete to understand the literal sense. In *Divino afflante Spiritu* §23, Pope Pius XII states that, in the work of expounding the true meaning of Scripture:

> Let the interpreters bear in mind that their foremost and greatest endeavor should be to discern and define clearly that sense of the biblical words which is called literal. Aided by the context and by comparison with similar passages, let them

---

[26] *Quodlibet* 7, q. 6, a. 2, ad 5 (*Opera Omnia*, vol. 25/1:31–32).

[27] *ST* I, q. 1, a. 8, ad 2.

[28] Ibid., a. 10, ad 1. This was also the teaching of St. Jerome; see Benedict XV, *Spiritus Paraclitus* (1920), §51.

therefore by means of their knowledge of languages search out with all diligence the literal meaning of the words.

The spiritual senses build on and enrich, but never replace, the literal meaning of the text.

One objection to the spiritual senses of Scripture is that they would introduce confusing multiplicity and ambiguity into the biblical text. St. Thomas answers that this would occur if the literal and spiritual senses were unrelated. A multiplicity of unrelated meanings would not be helpful! The spiritual sense must always be related to the literal sense as to its foundation:

> Thus in Holy Writ no confusion results, for all the senses are founded on one—the literal—from which alone can any argument be drawn, and not from those intended in allegory, as Augustine says (Epistle 48). Nevertheless, nothing of Holy Scripture perishes on account of this, since nothing necessary to faith is contained under the spiritual sense which is not elsewhere put forward by the Scripture in its literal sense.[29]

The purpose of the typological sense of Scripture is not principally to provide the basis for theologians to define doctrine, but rather to provide material to be contemplated by the faithful as well as by the theologian. The typological sense enriches our knowledge of the faith, helping us to see the mystery and beauty of God's Providence throughout history.

Not All of Scripture Has a Typological Sense

Although all of Scripture has a literal sense, not all has a typological sense. The relationship between the typological and the literal sense is roughly analogous to that between nature and grace. When one thing builds on another, the foundation can exist without what is built

---

[29] *ST* I, q. 1, a. 10, ad 1. See also *Quodlibet* 7, q. 6 a. 1 ad 1 (*Opera Omnia*, 25/1:28).

upon it, but not the reverse. Grace presupposes and builds on human nature. Every human being has human nature, but not everyone has sanctifying grace. Similarly, every text of Scripture has a literal sense, but that literal sense does not always represent another reality, and so have a typological meaning.

Although Origen has great merit with regard to biblical typology, one of his excesses was to think that every detail of Scripture has a spiritual sense. Such an exaggeration is dangerous because it can lead to the opposite extreme and the denial of typology altogether. St. Isidore of Pelusium gives a good critique of an excessive typology:

> Those who wish to apply the Old Testament in its entirety to Christ are far from correct. In doing so, they provide arguments to the pagans and heretics who reject this principle. They do violence to the texts in attempting to extract from them a Christological sense they do not have, and in so doing they end up throwing into discredit the texts that speak quite clearly of Christ. There is a truth that seems evident to me: if the Old Testament does not always speak of Christ, it does at least sometimes, refer to him.[30]

De Margerie comments:

> The principle according to which every passage of Scripture has a symbolic sense is foreign to the primitive Christian conception. It is the principle of universal allegory. Origen is so penetrated with this principle that he does not hesitate to write: "Everything in Scripture is mystery" [*Tenth Sermon on Genesis* 9.1]. Two negative consequences follow from this. On the one hand, the typological interpretation of Scripture is frequently reduced in Origen to hardly convincing subtleties (especially in the case of Leviticus); on the other hand, his

---

[30] St. Isidore of Pelusium, Epistle 195, (PG, 78:642; also in de Margerie, *History of Exegesis*, 1:110).

perception of a historical development in the Old Testament is sometimes imperiled. The general tendency of allegorism is toward the negation of history.[31]

A similar warning is given by St. Hilary:

We have often warned you that it is necessary to bring to the reading of Holy Writ a zeal capable of ascertaining, through careful study and well-reasoned judgment, when one should understand the account of historical events in its simplicity or in the typical sense, lest by using one and the other indiscriminately both of them become useless to the listeners, if the knowledge of simple events were impaired by an unjustified claim to find prefigurations therein, or if on the contrary the cogency of any prefigurations were ignored under the pretext of a belief that one is dealing with simple events.[32]

The Pontifical Biblical Commission under Pius XII declared that it was a serious excess to discover "a symbolic sense everywhere, even to the detriment of the literal and historical sense."[33] This is also implied in his *Divino afflante Spiritu* §26, which exhorts exegetes to expound the spiritual sense, "provided it is clearly intended by God."[34]

The Existence of Typology Is Taught by the Magisterium

In addition to the *Catechism of the Catholic Church*, other important magisterial documents on Scripture affirm the existence and importance of typology. Pope Leo XIII speaks of the typological sense in *Providentissimus Deus*:

---

[31] De Margerie, *History of Exegesis*, 1:110

[32] St. Hilary, *Traité des Mystères* 2.11, ed. Brisson, in *Sources Chrétiennes*, vol. 19 (Paris: Editions du Cerf, 1967), 73–75 (de Margerie, *History of Exegesis*, 2:56).

[33] PBC, Letter to the Archbishops and Bishops of Italy, August 20, 1941, (*SD*, 214).

[34] See also *Divino afflante Spiritu* (1943), §27.

Neither should those passages be neglected which the Fathers have understood in an allegorical or figurative sense, more especially when such interpretation is justified by the literal, and when it rests on the authority of many. For this method of interpretation has been received by the Church from the Apostles, and has been approved by her own practice, as the holy Liturgy attests.[35]

A document from 1941 by the Pontifical Biblical Commission asserts that the existence of a spiritual sense is a doctrine of faith. It also gives the general criteria for discerning its existence in any given case:

Although it is a dogma of faith and a fundamental principle of interpretation, as the practice of our Lord and the Apostles proves, that there is in Holy Scripture, over and above the literal sense, a meaning that is spiritual or typical, nevertheless, not every sentence or narrative has a typical meaning. This was the grave exaggeration of the Alexandrian school, that they wished to find a symbolic meaning everywhere, even to the detriment of the literal and historical meaning of the text. The spiritual or typical sense, besides being based on the literal sense, must conform to the practice of our Lord, of the Apostles, and of inspired writers, as well as to the traditional usage of the holy Fathers of the Church, especially as they express themselves in the voice of the Sacred Liturgy, for "the rule of prayer is the rule of faith." A freer application of the sacred text is permissible in sermons and ascetical works for the expression of an edifying idea, but the resulting thought, no matter how beautiful it may be, if it has not been established as above explained, cannot be proposed truly and strictly as the sense of the Bible, nor as inspired by God in the sacred text.[36]

---

[35] Encyclical Letter on the Study of Holy Scripture *Providentissimus Deus* (1893), §15.

[36] PBC, Letter to the Archbishops and Bishops of Italy, August 20, 1941 (*SD*, 214).

Pius XII likewise affirms the existence of this spiritual sense as follows:

> For what was said and done in the Old Testament was ordained and disposed by God with such consummate wisdom, that things past prefigured in a spiritual way those that were to come under the new dispensation of grace. Wherefore the exegete, just as he must search out and expound the literal meaning of the words intended and expressed by the sacred writer, so also must he do likewise for the spiritual sense, provided it is clearly intended by God. For God alone could have known this spiritual meaning and have revealed it to us. Now Our Divine Savior Himself points out to us and teaches us this same sense in the Holy Gospel; the Apostles also, following the example of the Master, profess it in their spoken and written words; the unchanging tradition of the Church approves it; and finally the most ancient usage of the liturgy proclaims it, wherever may be rightly applied the well-known principle: "The rule of prayer is the rule of faith." Let Catholic exegetes then disclose and expound this spiritual significance intended and ordained by God with that care which the dignity of the divine word demands; but let them scrupulously refrain from proposing as the genuine meaning of Sacred Scripture other figurative senses.[37]

Identifying the typological or spiritual sense is not left to the caprice of exegetes or theologians. It must be shown, with reasonable certainty, to be divinely intended through its presence in the New Testament itself, in the Tradition of the Church, or in the liturgy. These are the three principal sources for ascertaining the validity of a possible typological meaning of Scripture.

Dei Verbum §§15–16 refers to the importance of typology in its teaching on the significance of the Old Testament:

---

[37] *Divino afflante Spiritu* §26 (DS, 3828). The existence of the typological sense is also affirmed by the authoritative Response of the Pontifical Biblical Commission of June 30, 1909 (DS, 3517).

The principal purpose to which the plan of the old covenant was directed was to prepare for the coming of Christ, the redeemer of all and of the messianic kingdom, to announce this coming by prophecy (see Luke 24:44; John 5:39; 1 Pet 1:10), and to indicate its meaning through various types (see 1 Cor 10:12).

... God, the inspirer and author of both Testaments, wisely arranged that the New Testament be hidden in the Old and the Old be made manifest in the New.[38] For, though Christ established the new covenant in His blood (see Luke 22:20; 1 Cor 11:25), still the books of the Old Testament with all their parts, caught up into the proclamation of the Gospel, acquire and show forth their full meaning in the New Testament (see Matt 5:17; Luke 24:27; Rom 16:25–26; 2 Cor 3:14–16) and in turn shed light on it and explain it.

The Pontifical Biblical Commission also briefly discusses typology and the spiritual sense of Scripture,[39] defining "spiritual sense" in a very broad way:

As a general rule we can define the spiritual sense, as understood by Christian faith, as the meaning expressed by the biblical texts when read under the influence of the Holy Spirit, in the context of the paschal mystery of Christ and of the new life which flows from it.[40]

This definition is much broader than that given in the *Catechism of the Catholic Church* §117 and makes impossible a clear distinction between the literal and the typological/spiritual sense. As the Commission's document points out, the literal sense of Scripture is very

---

[38] St. Augustine, *Quaestiones in heptateuchum* 2.73 (PL, 34:623).

[39] It should be noted that the documents of the Pontifical Biblical Commission after 1965 are no longer intended to have magisterial force, but reflect the theological expertise of the members of the Commission.

[40] PBC, *On the Interpretation of the Bible in the Church* (1993), 2.B.2 (*SD*, 281–282).

frequently "spiritual," according to this broad sense of the word "spiritual."[41] To avoid confusion, I will not use the term "spiritual sense" in this broad way, but only as synonymous with "typological sense," in harmony with the terminology of the Fathers and Scholastic doctors such as St. Thomas Aquinas.

The Commission also briefly mentions typology as one aspect of the spiritual sense:

> One of the possible aspects of the spiritual sense is the typological. This is usually said to belong not to Scripture itself but to the realities expressed by Scripture: Adam as the figure of Christ (cf. Rom 5:14), the flood as the figure of baptism (1 Pet 3:20–21), etc. Actually, the connection involved in typology is ordinarily based on the way in which Scripture describes the ancient reality (cf. the voice of Abel: Gen 4:10; Heb 11:4; 12:24) and not simply on the reality itself. Consequently, in such a case one can speak of a meaning that is truly Scriptural.[42]

Even though the typological sense refers to the meaning of the events narrated, rather than the words of Scripture, the words themselves (by which the type is described) generally contribute to manifesting the typological sense.

Study Questions

1. How does St. Thomas distinguish the literal sense from the spiritual senses?

---

[41] See ibid.: "Contrary to a current view, there is not necessarily a distinction between the two senses. When a biblical text relates directly to the paschal mystery of Christ or to the new life which results from it, its literal sense is already a spiritual sense. Such is regularly the case in the New Testament. It follows that it is most often in dealing with the Old Testament that Christian exegesis speaks of the spiritual sense. But already in the Old Testament there are many instances where texts have a religious or spiritual sense as their literal sense. Christian faith recognizes in such cases an anticipatory relationship to the new life brought by Christ" (SD, 282).

[42] Ibid. (SD, 283).

2. How are the spiritual senses divided into three categories? Give examples. How are the three spiritual senses related and unified?
3. Does all of Scripture have all four senses? Can a text have a spiritual/typological meaning, but not a literal meaning? Explain.
4. What is the relationship between typology and the progressive nature of salvation history?

Suggestions for Further Reading

Catechism of the Catholic Church §§114–117.

De Lubac, Henri. *Medieval Exegesis.* Vols. 1–2: *The Four Senses of Scripture.* Translated by Mark Sebanc. Grand Rapids: Eerdmans, 1998–2000.

O'Keefe, John J. and Russel R. Reno. *Sanctified Vision: An Introduction to Early Christian Interpretation of the Bible.* Baltimore: The Johns Hopkins University Press, 2005.

CHAPTER SEVENTEEN

Scriptural References to Typology

Typological Interpretation of the Exodus in the Old Testament Prophets

Although the typological interpretation of events of the Old Testament is principally gained from the New Testament, the major prophets of Israel give a typological reading of the Exodus by seeing it as the pattern of a new and greater Exodus to come in the messianic age. This second Exodus will involve a new ingathering of scattered Israel, a new miraculous passing through the waters, a new indwelling of God with His people as in the column of cloud and fire, a new law written this time on the heart, a new and more universal gift of the Holy Spirit, and a new Covenant. The new Exodus will transcend the former one through its spiritual gifts.[1]

---

[1] See Jean Cardinal Daniélou, S.J., *From Shadows to Reality: Studies in the Biblical Typology of the Fathers*, trans. Dom Wulstan Hibberd (Westminster: The Newman Press, 1960), 153–154: "The Exodus, more than anything, brings home that typology is rooted in the Old Testament. Two aspects are involved here. The Historical Books, especially the Pentateuch, recall the mighty works which God has done for Israel; while the Prophetical Books foretell equally great works which God will perform for his people in time to come. The Old Testament is both a memory and a prophecy. We can go further, and say that it is the prophecy which makes it a memory: the mighty works of the past are recalled only as the foundation of future hope. For it is very noticeable that the Prophets foretell events to come as the recovery of what has passed. When we turn to the theme in hand we find that Isaiah and Jeremiah hold up to the Jews of the Captivity the future which God has in store for them as a new Exodus, of which the earlier one was the type. A. G. Hebert can rightly say that we have here 'the beginning of mystical interpretation of the

The typology of the new Exodus is especially presented in Isaiah, Jeremiah, and Ezekiel. Isaiah 43:16–20 speaks of a future time in which the events of the Exodus will be fulfilled in a higher way:

> Thus says the Lord, who makes a way in the sea, a path in the mighty waters, who brings forth chariot and horse, army and warrior; they lie down, they cannot rise, they are extinguished, quenched like a wick: "Remember not the former things, nor consider the things of old. Behold, I am doing a new thing; now it springs forth, do you not perceive it? I will make a way in the wilderness and rivers in the desert. The wild beasts will honor me, the jackals and the ostriches; for I give water in the wilderness, rivers in the desert, to give drink to my chosen people."

Isaiah 52:11–12 also makes reference to a new going forth, as a new Exodus. However, its character will be different, for it will not be "in haste" nor "in flight." Like the first Exodus, it will be accompanied by the presence of the Lord going before and behind as in the pillar of cloud and fire:

> Depart, depart, go out thence, touch no unclean thing; go out from the midst of her, purify yourselves, you who bear the vessels of the Lord. For you shall not go out in haste, and you shall not go in flight, for the Lord will go before you, and the God of Israel will be your rear guard.

Jeremiah also prophesies the new Exodus. In Jeremiah 23:7–8 he says:

> Therefore, behold, the days are coming, says the Lord, when men shall no longer say, "As the Lord lives who brought up the people of Israel out of the land of Egypt," but, "As the

---

story of the Exodus.'" The last quotation is from Arthur Gabriel Hebert, *The Authority of the Old Testament* (London: Faber and Faber, 1947), 146.

Lord lives who brought up and led the descendants of the house of Israel out of the north country and out of all the countries where he had driven them." Then they shall dwell in their own land.[2]

Jeremiah 31:31–33 interprets the Old Covenant in general as a type of a New Covenant to be established:

> Behold, the days are coming, says the Lord, when I will make a new covenant with the house of Israel. . . . I will put my law within them, and I will write it upon their hearts . . . for I will forgive their iniquity, and I will remember their sin no more.

The covenant sealed at the foot of Mt. Sinai was the spiritual center of the Exodus. Jeremiah is saying that a new and higher Exodus will result in a New Covenant entailing the forgiveness of sin and the infusion of grace by which the Law is written on the heart.

Ezekiel speaks of a new messianic ingathering into the Promised Land in the great prophecy of 36:24–27:

> For I will take you from the nations, and gather you from all the countries, and bring you into your own land. I will sprinkle clean water upon you, and you shall be clean from all your uncleannesses, and from all your idols I will cleanse you. A new heart I will give you, and a new spirit I will put within you; and I will take out of your flesh the heart of stone and give you a heart of flesh. And I will put my spirit within you, and cause you to walk in my statutes and be careful to observe my ordinances.

---

[2] See also Jer 16:14–15: "Therefore, behold, the days are coming, says the Lord, when it shall no longer be said, 'As the Lord lives who brought up the people of Israel out of the land of Egypt,' but 'As the Lord lives who brought up the people of Israel out of the north country and out of all the countries where he had driven them.' For I will bring them back to their own land which I gave to their fathers."

Here the new Exodus of ingathering does not involve a passage through the Red Sea, but a sprinkling of "clean water," which clearly prefigures Baptism. The Church is gathered together by passing through the waters of Baptism. Not surprisingly, this text is read in the baptismal liturgy of the Easter vigil.[3]

The writers of the New Testament and the Fathers of the Church had these prophetic texts in mind, and they underlined their fulfillment in Jesus and the Church. Jean Cardinal Daniélou writes:

> We can now put together the various features which the different texts afford us, and shall find the various themes which make up the picture of the future Exodus: crossing of the sea, the desert march, living water pouring from rocks, the cloud and the new covenant. And it is these features that we find again in the New Testament, and the Fathers who will use the Exodus from the point of view of the first typology which the Prophets have given. The Prophets, in the very heart of the Old Testament, are the first who have dwelt on the significance of the Exodus, and their work is of primary importance, for it makes clear that the principles of typology were to be found already among these Prophets. We have only to add that they think of this New Exodus as something superior to the old (Isa 43:16) and of a more spiritual character (Jer 31:33).
>
> ... When the New Testament shows that the life of Christ is the truth and fulfillment of all that was outlined and typified in the Exodus, it is only taking up and continuing the typology outlined by the Prophets. The basic difference does not lie in the typology, but in the fact that what is presented by the Prophets as something yet to come is shown by the New Testament writers as fulfilled in Jesus Christ. . . . Prophecy, which thus becomes the first degree in the evolution of typology, is seen as establishing a relationship between the

---

[3] A good summary of the elements of the new Exodus prophesied by Isaiah, Jeremiah, and Ezekiel is given by Hebert in *Authority of the Old Testament*, 145.

New Testament and the Exodus. The organic relation between typology and prophecy, *typos* and *logos*,[4] is quite clear, for so far from being distinct categories, prophecy is the typological interpretation of history.[5]

Prophecies of the Messiah in the Old Testament generally make some use of typology to speak of the messianic events that they are announcing. In other words, not only do prophecies of the Messiah use words to reveal future messianic events, but those words also point to events in the history of Israel that are signs or types of future salvific events and provide the best way to understand them. The literal sense of the messianic prophecies thus includes an element of typology that is a key clue to the full sense of the prophecy. For example, the New Covenant spoken of in Jeremiah 31:31 cannot be understood without typological reflection on the Mosaic Covenant and how it can be the sign of a more perfect covenant between God and His People. The same is true of prophecies of Christ as the new Moses and as the new Davidic king. Daniélou therefore rightly stresses the harmony between prophecy and the typological interpretation of history.

A good example of the interpenetration of prophecy and typology is Moses' prophecy of a "new Moses" in Deuteronomy 18:15–19:

> The Lord your God will raise up for you a prophet like me from among you, from your brethren—him you shall heed. . . . And the Lord said to me, "I will raise up for them a prophet like you from among their brethren; and I will put my words in his mouth, and he shall speak to them all that I command him. And whoever will not give heed to my words which he shall speak in my name, I myself will require it of him."

This prophecy alludes to the fact that, at the foot of Mt. Sinai, the people of Israel were afraid that they would not be able to bear it if

---

4 "*Logos*" means "word" in Greek. Daniélou is using the pair "*typos*" and "*logos*" to contrast "deed" and "word," or "type" and "prophecy."

5 Daniélou, *From Shadows to Reality*, 156–157.

God spoke to them directly, and so they begged God to speak to them through the mediation of Moses.[6] Here Moses is saying that God will do something similar for Israel in the future. He will raise up a new prophet like Moses to act as a mediator between God and men, a prophet whom the people will have to believe and obey in the same way.

The literal sense of this particular text points to a typological sense of much of the book of Deuteronomy, as well as of Exodus, Leviticus, and Numbers. The future prophet foretold here who will mediate between the people and God cannot be understood without typological reflection on the entire figure of Moses, his unique contemplation of God, and his role as lawgiver, judge, mediator, and liberator.

Another example of the blending of prophecy and typology is found in Psalm 110:4. This messianic psalm speaks of the Messiah as "a priest for ever after the order of Melchizedek." The literal sense of this text assigns a mysterious priestly role to the protagonist of the psalm that is to be understood not in the sense of the Aaronic priesthood, but rather through the type of Melchizedek. This typology is greatly developed in Hebrews 7.

Christ Uncovers the Typological Sense of the Old Testament

The Christian way of reading the Bible was obviously deeply shaped by Israel's way of interpreting her Scriptures. Above all, the Church inherited Israel's faith in the inspiration and inerrancy of the Old Testament, the conviction that God's great works in salvation history provide the decisive light for understanding the present and future of the People of God, and the expectation of a messianic new Exodus.

However, the Church differs from the synagogue in two decisive ways. First of all, it recognizes the books of the New Testament as equally inspired by the same Spirit of Truth. Secondly, the Church reads the Old Testament Scriptures in the light of explicit faith in Jesus Christ as the Messiah. This faith in Christ is the key to the deepest

---

[6] See Exod 20:18–19.

understanding of the history of Israel, in which it is possible to see a prefiguring of the Christ, the Paschal mystery, and the Church prepared by God from the beginning.

Jesus revealed Himself as the key to understanding the Old Testament while accompanying two disciples on the road to Emmaus. These disciples were walking sadly on Easter Sunday from Jerusalem to the village of Emmaus and discussing the events of the Passion. They were approached by Jesus Himself, who kept Himself from being recognized by them, appearing as a stranger:

> And he said to them, "What is this conversation which you are holding with each other as you walk?" And they stood still, looking sad. Then one of them, named Cleopas, answered him, "Are you the only visitor to Jerusalem who does not know the things that have happened there in these days?" And he said to them, "What things?" And they said to him, "Concerning Jesus of Nazareth, who was a prophet mighty in deed and word before God and all the people, and how our chief priests and rulers delivered him up to be condemned to death, and crucified him. But we had hoped that he was the one to redeem Israel. . . . And he said to them, "O foolish men, and slow of heart to believe all that the prophets have spoken! Was it not necessary that the Christ should suffer these things and enter into his glory?" And *beginning with Moses and all the prophets, he interpreted to them in all the scriptures the things concerning himself.*[7]

These two disciples had lost their faith in Jesus as the Messiah because He had died a miserable death on the Cross and thus failed to "redeem Israel" in the earthly sense they were expecting. Jesus explains to them that Scripture foretells that the Messiah had to "suffer these things" and die to redeem mankind, and so enter into His glory. Part of His explanation must have consisted in an interpretation of the messianic prophecies, as in Isaiah. However, Luke says that Jesus

---

[7] Luke 24:17–27.

began with Moses and interpreted to them things concerning Himself in "all the Scriptures." This makes it extremely likely that Jesus explained not only prophetic *words*, but also how the central *events* of the Old Testament prefigured His Paschal mystery. The second aspect is biblical typology. The importance of the revelation of the typological meaning of the Scriptures is brought out by the comment of the disciples on their return to Jerusalem: "Did not our hearts burn within us while he talked to us on the road, while he *opened to us the scriptures?*" (Luke 24:32).

The same lesson on the inner hidden meaning of the Old Testament was given some hours later when the disciples had returned from Emmaus to Jerusalem and gathered with the eleven Apostles in the upper room. At that moment Jesus walked through the locked doors and said, "*Shalom aleichem.*" After showing them the wounds in His hands and feet, and eating in front of them, He said:

> "These are my words which I spoke to you, while I was still with you, that everything written about me in the law of Moses and the prophets and the psalms must be fulfilled." Then he opened their minds to understand the scriptures, and said to them, "Thus it is written, that the Christ should suffer and on the third day rise from the dead, and that repentance and forgiveness of sins should be preached in his name to all nations, beginning from Jerusalem. You are witnesses of these things."[8]

Part of this explanation, as on the road to Emmaus, must have concerned the messianic prophecies. However, the text tells us not only that Jesus spoke of how the prophets spoke of His Passion, but also that He began with the books of Moses, showing how they also spoke of His sufferings, death, and glory. The books of Moses contain very little direct prophecy about Christ's Passion, but they contain a great deal of symbolic prefiguring of it: in the sacrifice of Isaac, in the story of Joseph and his brothers, in the Exodus, and in various events

---

[8] Luke 24:44–48.

during the wandering in the desert. Jesus must have explained not only the messianic prophecies, but also the spiritual sense of the Old Testament in general regarding all that concerned His Passion, death, and Resurrection.[9]

How we wish we had been there with the disciples on the way to Emmaus or in the upper room to hear Jesus open the Scriptures and show how it all speaks of Him! However, even though these particular discourses have not been recorded, they have certainly passed into the Tradition of the Church, molding the way that the Apostles and their successors—the early Fathers of the Church—read the Old Testament. The Christian interpretation of the Old Testament has its origin in this teaching of the Risen Christ to His disciples and Apostles.

The Sign of Jonah

On several occasions, Jesus explicitly explains that both persons and events in the Old Testament were types of Him. He uses this kind of typology to reveal His identity and to announce that He is greater than the types of old. One of the clearest examples is Jonah.

Some of the Pharisees were saying that He was casting out demons in the name of Beelzebul and asked for a sign from Him to prove His divine origin. Of course, He had given very many signs already, as recorded in the Gospel. Thus He reproved them for asking for some sign above what had already been given, but promised that they would indeed be given the "sign of Jonah" (Matt 12:40–42), consisting in His death and Resurrection and the conversion of the Gentiles:

> For as Jonah was three days and three nights in the belly of the whale, so shall the Son of man be three days and three nights in the heart of the earth. The men of Nineveh will arise at the judgment with this generation and condemn it; because they repented at the preaching of Jonah, and behold, something greater than Jonah is here. The queen of the South will arise at the judgment with this generation and condemn

---

[9] See Paul Quay, *The Mystery Hidden for Ages in God* (New York: Peter Lang, 1997), 193–194.

it; for she came from the ends of the earth to hear the wisdom of Solomon, and behold, something greater than Solomon is here.[10]

The story of Jonah is indeed very rich in the spiritual or typological sense. The prophet Jonah represents both Jesus and Israel as a whole with regard to their role in the salvation of the Gentiles. The prophet is told by God to preach repentance to the people of Nineveh, who were enemies and persecutors of the Jews, and to warn them of their impending destruction if they remain obstinate. However, Jonah flees from God, taking a boat to Tarshish, in the opposite direction from Nineveh. A great storm arises, he confesses his guilt, and at his own request he is thrown overboard. He is swallowed by a whale, from the belly of which he prays to the Lord, who hears him and allows him to be spit up on the shore.

Christ tells us that the three days Jonah spent in the belly of the whale represent the three days the Body of Christ spent in the tomb before rising in glory. Jonah's being spit out of the whale on the third day represents the Resurrection of Christ. However, the parallel does not end there. For Jonah goes on to preach repentance to the people of Nineveh, who were not Jews, but gentiles and fierce enemies. Surprisingly, they convert and repent, and the city is not destroyed, which is also part of the figure. The Apostles, as an antitype of Jonah, preach Christ to the Gentiles, represented by the people of Nineveh, and very surprisingly, like the Ninevites, the Gentiles are converted and do penance.

Jonah is also a figure of Israel. As Jonah converted the Ninevites, so Israel has played a great part in the conversion of the Gentiles to Christianity. Indeed, Christ tells us that "salvation is from the Jews" (John 4:22). The Messiah was from the seed of Abraham, Isaac, Jacob, and David, and "born under the Law" (Gal 4:4). The Old Testament was given to the Jewish people and preserved, passed on, and revered

---

[10] See also the parallel passage in Luke 11:30, in which the aspect of the conversion of the Gentiles is especially emphasized: "For as Jonah became a sign to the men of Nineveh, so will the Son of man be to this generation."

by them. The Apostles, finally, were all faithful Jews commissioned to preach the Jewish Messiah to the ends of the earth.

However, there is one final aspect to the figure. Jonah is distressed by the conversion of the Ninevites because they were enemies of the Jewish people. (In fact, the Ninevites took the ten northern tribes into a captivity from which they never returned.) It is not unreasonable to see this negative attitude of Jonah as also a figure of the attitude of a large part of Israel to the conversion of the Gentiles to Christianity. And like the Ninevites, Christians have been the instrument of suffering and persecution for the Jewish people.

In short, Christ used the story of Jonah to make a prophecy about His own death, entombment, and Resurrection, as well as the subsequent conversion of the nations and the rancor between Jews and Christians that would occur afterwards. What happens in the story of Jonah is recapitulated in a higher way in the death and Resurrection of Christ and the formation of His Church from all peoples. The story of Jonah is fascinating even without seeing this spiritual sense, but it becomes far more marvelous when read in the light of Christ's explanation.

King Solomon

In the same passage in which Christ relates the story of Jonah, He also alludes to Solomon as a figure of Christ and to the Queen of Sheba as a figure of the conversion of the Gentiles (Matt 12:39–42). Solomon is a figure of Christ through his wisdom, the building of the Temple, the territorial extent of his reign, which was the largest in the history of Israel, and the peace that it enjoyed. The fact that the Queen of Sheba came from "the ends of the earth" to hear the wisdom of Solomon prefigures how the Gentile nations will gradually flock to the true Temple—Christ and His Church—to hear the divine wisdom of salvation.

The Bronze Serpent

Another example of an Old Testament narrative referred to by Jesus as a figure of Himself is Numbers 21:4–9. This text recounts an episode during the wandering of the Chosen People in the desert in which they murmured against God and Moses, complaining about the lack of the fleshpots of Egypt and expressing their loathing for the manna sent them by God. Because of their complaining God sent fiery serpents in punishment, and the people cried out to Moses in repentance:

> From Mount Hor they set out by the way to the Red Sea, to go around the land of Edom; and the people became impatient on the way. And the people spoke against God and against Moses, "Why have you brought us up out of Egypt to die in the wilderness? For there is no food and no water, and we loathe this worthless food." Then the Lord sent fiery serpents among the people, and they bit the people, so that many people of Israel died. And the people came to Moses, and said, "We have sinned, for we have spoken against the Lord and against you; pray to the Lord, that he take away the serpents from us." So Moses prayed for the people. And the Lord said to Moses, "Make a fiery serpent, and set it on a pole; and every one who is bitten, when he sees it, shall live." So Moses made a bronze serpent, and set it on a pole; and if a serpent bit any man, he would look at the bronze serpent and live.

It is a mysterious text. All those guilty of this ingratitude and afflicted by serpent bites could be healed by looking at a bronze serpent set on a pole and erected as a kind of standard. What was the significance of the bronze serpent on a pole? Read simply in the context of the five books of Moses, the detail of the bronze serpent makes little sense.

Jesus explained this detail in His nocturnal discussion with Nicodemus, a wealthy member of the Sanhedrin, as recorded in John 3:14–15. He said: "And as Moses lifted up the serpent in the wilderness, so must the Son of man be lifted up, that whoever believes in him may have eternal life."

The bronze serpent raised up as a sign to the penitent and capable of giving life to him is a figure of Christ who would be raised up on the Cross. Like the serpent, Christ on the Cross appears as a sign of suffering due to sin, but when seen through the eyes of faith, becomes the means of salvation. The difference is that the bronze serpent was a lifeless statue, working a physical cure in one instance and one place alone, whereas Christ on the Cross works the spiritual salvation of all men of all times and places, if we but cooperate with His grace through faith, hope, and charity.

In addition, the serpent is a symbol of sin, and of the tempter who drew Adam and Eve to perform the first sin. Thus the serpent bound to a pole is also a symbol of victory over sin through Christ, who bore all human sin and hung on a Cross in order to redeem men from its slavery. As St. Paul says in 2 Corinthians 5:21, God "made him to be sin who knew no sin, so that in him we might become the righteousness of God."

The Bread of Life

In the Bread of Life discourse in John 6, Jesus presents Himself as the true bread from heaven. His listeners give Him a suitable occasion for this teaching by asking Him whether He would give them a sign similar to the manna in the desert.

> Jesus then said to them, "Truly, truly, I say to you, it was not Moses who gave you the bread from heaven; my Father gives you the true bread from heaven. For the bread of God is that which comes down from heaven, and gives life to the world." They said to him, "Lord, give us this bread always." Jesus said to them, "I am the bread of life; he who comes to me shall not hunger, and he who believes in me shall never thirst."[11]

---

[11] John 6:32–35.

Jesus thus indicates that the manna that fed the Israelites in the wilderness for forty years was a figure of the spiritual nourishment He would give the world through the Sacrament of His Body and Blood. Furthermore, He clearly states that the type falls immeasurably short of the Antitype, which is the Eucharist. Only the Eucharist is the "*true* bread from heaven." The type was a great sign, for it was literally bread that came physically down from heaven like dew to nourish the Israelites physically in their pilgrimage in the desert. Christ's Body and Blood is a spiritual bread—being Christ, true God and true man—that nourishes the faithful not physically, but in sanctifying grace and charity, by which we gain access to eternal life. Furthermore, Christ's Body comes from heaven not physically, but through the supreme mystery of the hypostatic union by which the Word of God, pre-existing from eternity, "became flesh and dwelt among us" (John 1:14). "No man has ascended into heaven, but he that descended from heaven" (John 3:15). This Body continues to come to us "from heaven" through transubstantiation, by which He who sits now in heaven at the right hand of the Father is truly and substantially present in the Eucharist under the appearances of bread and wine.

Typology in the Letters of St. Paul and the Catholic Epistles

The Spiritual Sense of the Old Testament According to St. Paul

St. Paul refers to the spiritual sense of the Old Testament in an interesting text from 1 Corinthians 10:1–11, in which he speaks about the moral sense of the wandering of the Chosen People in the desert for forty years:

> For I would not have you ignorant, brethren, that our fathers were all under the cloud, and all passed through the sea. And all in Moses were baptized, in the cloud, and in the sea. And all ate the same spiritual food, and drank the same spiritual drink (for they drank from the spiritual rock which followed

them, and the rock was Christ). Yet with most of them God was not well pleased, for "they were laid low in the desert." Now these things *came to pass as examples to us,* that we should not lust after evil things even as they lusted. And do not become idolaters, even as some of them were. . . . Neither let us tempt Christ, as some of them tempted, and perished by the serpents. Neither murmur, as some of them murmured, and perished at the hands of the destroyer. Now *all these things happened to them as a type, and they are written for our correction,* upon whom the final age of the world has come.[12]

St. Paul affirms that the Israelites in the Exodus in some sense mysteriously received a prefiguration of the mysteries of Christ revealed and sacramentally given in the New Testament. The figures of the crossing of the Red Sea, the pillar of cloud, the manna, and the water from the rock "embodied a hidden presence of the future mystery, they implied a mysterious participation in its reality."[13]

St. Paul also explains the typological moral sense of the repeated rebellions of the Chosen People during their forty-year sojourn in the desert. Because of the infidelity of the Israelites, God punished them by prolonging their stay in the desert for two generations, so that all but two of the original Israelites who left Egypt died without entering the Promised Land. St. Paul says this happened to them to serve as a lesson to Christians of the necessity of vigilance and of resistance to temptation. The Israelites were allowed to fall into a series of archetypical sins of rebellion, followed by exemplary punishments, to provide a graphic example of spiritual sins. Just as the first generation of Israelites perished in the desert for lack of docility to God, so it may happen that Christians fail to reach the spiritual Promised Land through the same cause.

The last sentence of this text of St. Paul—*"all these things happened to them as a type, and they are written for our correction"*—is the most

---

[12] Confraternity of Christian Doctrine translation (New York: Benziger Bros., 1958).

[13] Bertrand de Margerie, S.J., *An Introduction to the History of Exegesis,* vol. 1, *The Greek Fathers* (Petersham: Saint Bede's, 1993), 8.

explicit biblical statement affirming the principle of typological interpretation. We could state it as follows: The events of Israel narrated in
Scripture happened to them (in many cases) as a type of the Church
and her members, for our instruction. Both Patristic exegesis and the
liturgical usage of the Old Testament are founded on this principle.[14]
Its significance extends far beyond the particular use that St. Paul
made of it in the preceding verses, for it is the general or universal
principle behind the typological interpretation of the Old Testament.

Typology of the Passover According to 1 Corinthians 5:6–8

In 1 Corinthians 5:6–8, St. Paul interprets the unleavened bread in
the Jewish Passover as a type of the Christian life:

> Do you not know that a little leaven leavens the whole lump?
> Cleanse out the old leaven that you may be a new lump, as
> you really are unleavened. For Christ, our paschal lamb, has
> been sacrificed. Let us, therefore, celebrate the festival, not
> with the old leaven, the leaven of malice and evil, but with the
> unleavened bread of sincerity and truth.

Joseph Ratzinger comments:

> Here the two essential elements of the Old Testament Pasch
> appear: the sacrificial lamb and the unleavened bread; thus
> appears the Christological basis and the anthropological, be-
> havioral implications of the sacrifice of Christ. If the lamb an-
> ticipates Christ, so the bread becomes the symbol of Chris-
> tian existence. The unleavened bread becomes the sign of a
> new beginning: to be a Christian is described as a permanent
> feast whose source is this new life. One could speak of an in-

---

[14] Ibid., 7: "Such a principle, set forth so broadly and without limitation, constitutes the inspired
basis of patristic exegesis, even if the latter occasionally abused it." See also Pierre Grelot, *Sens
chrétien de l'Ancien Testament: esquisse d'un traité dogmatique* (Tournai, BE: Desclée, 1962), 25–
26.

terpretation of the Old Testament Pasch that is at the same time Christological and existential.[15]

The Allegory of the Two Covenants in Galatians 4

According to St. Paul in the Letter to the Galatians, the Law of Moses is essentially a kind of pedagogy leading towards faith in Christ. The newly evangelized Gentile Christians of Galatia had been persuaded by certain Jewish Christians that they needed to observe the ceremonial rites of the Law of Moses in addition to the precepts of Christ in order to be saved. St. Paul explained that these ceremonial rites were not obligatory for them, since they are but a figure of the realities they had received through faith in Christ, in whom the Old Testament was completely fulfilled. To observe the ceremonial law of the Old Testament after the coming of the Messiah would be to continue to use the figures when the reality represented by the figures—Christ and His Redemption of mankind—had been revealed and accomplished, giving rise to a new and everlasting covenant.

In Galatians 3:23–25, he states, "Now before faith came, we were confined under the law, kept under restraint until faith should be revealed. So that the law was our tutor until Christ came, that we might be justified by faith. But now that faith has come, we are no longer under a tutor." Later, in Galatians 4:21–31, he applies biblical typology in service of his argument that they were not to observe the ceremonial law of Moses:

> Tell me, you who desire to be under law, do you not hear the law? For it is written that Abraham had two sons, one by a slave and one by a free woman. But the son of the slave was born according to the flesh, the son of the free woman through promise. Now this is an allegory: these women are two covenants. One is from Mount Sinai, bearing children for slavery; she is Hagar. Now Hagar is Mount Sinai in Arabia; she corresponds to the present Jerusalem, for she is in slavery with

---

[15] "Eucharist and Mission," *Irish Theological Quarterly* 65 (2000): 250–251.

her children. But the Jerusalem above is free, and she is our mother. For it is written, "Rejoice, O barren one who does not bear; break forth and shout, you who are not in travail; for the children of the desolate one are many more than the children of her that is married." Now we, brethren, like Isaac, are children of promise. But as at that time he who was born according to the flesh persecuted him who was born according to the Spirit, so it is now. But what does the scripture say? "Cast out the slave and her son; for the son of the slave shall not inherit with the son of the free woman." So, brethren, we are not children of the slave but of the free woman.

St. Paul teaches that Isaac, physically the forefather of the Jewish people, nevertheless allegorically represents the Church, the heavenly Jerusalem; whereas Ishmael, physically the forefather of Arab nations, allegorically represents the synagogue, the physical Jerusalem that is here below. The Church is said to be free in that she possesses the spiritual realities—the channels of grace to attain to heaven—that were only prefigured in the Old Covenant.

This is not to denigrate the dignity of the Chosen People. Their dignity consists in being specially prepared to receive the Messiah and Redeemer, and for this reason they were under the tutorship of the Law, which was an *immense privilege*. Nevertheless, the Old Covenant was never meant to be an end in itself, but was always conceived by God as a preparation for the Church that was to issue from it.

St. Paul speaks of the Old Covenant as a servant, the child of a bondwoman, in the sense that, although it prepared for the Church and symbolically represented it, it did not yet attain to "the glorious freedom of the sons of God." It did not have the seven glorious sacraments of the New Law, which not only represent grace, but actually confer grace to all those who pose no obstacle to its action. The Old Covenant is allegorically a "bondwoman" because it attained only to the figure, and not to the reality signified by the figure, which is the sacramental bestowal of sanctifying grace, the treasure of the Church.

Adam as a Figure of Christ

Another crucial Pauline text that serves as a foundation for typology is the understanding in Romans 5:14 of Christ as the "new Adam": "Yet death reigned from Adam to Moses, even over those whose sins were not like the transgression of Adam, who was a *type* of the one who was to come." Here St. Paul shows that Adam is the type of Christ in two contrary ways. Adam's headship over humanity as the first man is a figure of Christ's headship over redeemed humanity. But whereas Adam's headship brought death to all men, Christ's headship brings eternal life to all who are incorporated into Him.

This Pauline typology of Christ as the new Adam will become the exemplar of the early Christian typology of Mary as the New Eve. The Marian typology follows the same pattern of being like Eve in being a universal mother, but opposite to her regarding the fruit of that maternity.

Another Pauline text, Ephesians 5:31–32, refers to the marriage of Adam and Eve as a figure of the union of Christ and His Church: "'For this reason a man shall leave his father and mother and be joined to his wife, and the two shall become one flesh.' This mystery is a profound one, and I am saying that it refers to Christ and the church."

The Incarnation as the Archetype of the Christian Life According to St. Paul

St. Paul not only views events of the Old Testament as types of Christ and the Christian life, but he also sees the Incarnation and the mysteries of Christ's life as types—or better, archetypes—of the entire Christian life. Christ is the archetype of the Christian life in a different sense than that in which Old Testament events are types of Christ. The Old Testament events fall short of the reality they prefigure. The deeds of Christ, of course, infinitely exceed all of the Christian life that they prefigure as their infinite archetype and model. In philosophical language, the life of Christ is the "exemplar cause" of the Christian life.

In the famous Christological hymn in Philippians 2:2–9, St. Paul presents the event of the Incarnation, with Christ's self-emptying unto the Cross, as the archetype of all Christian humility. Thus the Christian moral life is fundamentally Christological and consists in participating in the great Exemplar:

> Complete my joy by being of the same mind, having the same love, being in full accord and of one mind. Do nothing from selfishness or conceit, but in humility count others better than yourselves. Let each of you look not only to his own interests, but also to the interests of others. Have this mind among yourselves, which was in Christ Jesus, who, though he was in the form of God, did not count equality with God a thing to be grasped, but emptied himself, taking the form of a servant, being born in the likeness of men. And being found in human form he humbled himself and became obedient unto death, even death on a cross. Therefore God has highly exalted him and bestowed on him the name which is above every name.

In a similar way, when St. Paul wishes to exhort the Corinthians to generosity in aiding the Christians in Judea, he grounds his exhortation in the exemplar of the Incarnation: "For you know the grace of our Lord Jesus Christ, that though he was rich, yet for your sake he became poor, so that by his poverty you might become rich" (2 Cor 8:9).

Christ Recapitulates All Things: Summary of Typology in Ephesians 1:9–12

In Ephesians 1:9–12, St. Paul gives not merely an example of typology, as in the texts above, but rather summarizes the theory behind all typology, when he speaks of Christ as *recapitulating* all things:

> For he has made known to us in all wisdom and insight the mystery of his will, according to his purpose which he set

forth in Christ as a plan for the fullness of time, to *unite all things in him*, things in heaven and things on earth. In him, according to the purpose of him who accomplishes all things according to the counsel of his will, we who first hoped in Christ have been destined and appointed to live for the praise of his glory.

The Greek word in Ephesians 1:10 that the RSV translates as "unite" is literally "recapitulate," which means "to bring things back to their head." Christ recapitulates all things in Himself by being the culmination and goal of salvation history. Everything before the Incarnation was a preparation for and prefigurement of Christ, and everything after Him is to be conformed to His image in the Church, which shall finally be brought into the splendor of His glory. Christ is the Antitype both of what came before (allegorical sense) and what comes afterward (moral and anagogical senses). Christ can be the recapitulation of everything because, in His Person, He unites two natures: human and divine. Through His humanity He recapitulates human history, especially the history of Israel. Through His divine nature He recapitulates and is the Exemplar of the glory of which He makes us partakers, both in the Church and in heaven.

St. Irenaeus put great emphasis on this notion of "recapitulation" in *Against the Heresies*, and it becomes perhaps the key element of his theological synthesis. He stresses that Christ recapitulates salvation history, for it was all modeled on Him as the Exemplar:

When He became incarnate and was made man, He recapitulated in Himself the long unfolding of humankind, granting salvation by way of compendium, that in Christ Jesus we might receive what we had lost in Adam, namely, to be according to the image and likeness of God.[16]

---

[16] *Adversus haereses* 3.18.1, in *St. Irenaeus of Lyons: Against the Heresies Book 3*, trans. Dominic J. Unger, Ancient Christian Writers, no. 64 (New York/Mahwah: The Newman Press, 2012), 87–88.

And again he writes:

> There is, therefore, one God the Father and one Christ Jesus
> our Lord, who comes through every economy and recapitu-
> lates in Himself all things. Now, man too, God's handiwork,
> is contained in this "all." So He also recapitulated in Him-
> self humanity; the invisible becoming visible; the incompre-
> hensible, comprehensible; the impassible, passible; the Word,
> man. Thus He recapitulated in Himself all things, so that, just
> as the Word of God is the sovereign Ruler over superceles-
> tial, spiritual, and invisible beings, so too He might possess
> sovereign rule over visible and corporeal things; and thus, by
> taking to Himself the primacy, and constituting Himself the
> Head of the Church, He might draw all things to Himself at
> the proper time.[17]

Christ's Passion and Resurrection Is the Type of Christian Baptism

In Romans 6:3–11, St. Paul presents Christ's Paschal mystery as
the type or exemplar of Christian Baptism, which is a participation
in Christ's death and Resurrection. Through Baptism the Christian
dies, crucified with Christ, to the old man, and rises to a supernatural
life animated by sanctifying grace, on the pattern of Christ's Resurrection:

> Do you not know that all of us who have been baptized into
> Christ Jesus were baptized into his death? We were buried
> therefore with him by baptism into death, so that as Christ
> was raised from the dead by the glory of the Father, we too
> might walk in newness of life. For if we have been united with
> him in a death like his, we shall certainly be united with him
> in a resurrection like his. We know that our old self was cruci-
> fied with him so that the sinful body might be destroyed, and

---

[17] Ibid., 3.16.16–17 (Unger, 82).

we might no longer be enslaved to sin. For he who has died is freed from sin. But if we have died with Christ, we believe that we shall also live with him. For we know that Christ, being raised from the dead, will never die again; death no longer has dominion over him. The death he died he died to sin, once for all, but the life he lives he lives to God. So you also must consider yourselves dead to sin and alive to God in Christ Jesus.

The implication is that the entire sacramental life of the Christian is typological. The mysteries of Christ's life are the source and archetype of the spiritual life of the Christian, in which source the Christian mystically or spiritually shares. Christ accomplished these mysteries for us so that we could be incorporated into them.

Christ's Resurrection Is the Type of Our Future Resurrection (Anagogical Sense)

In a similar way, Christ's Resurrection is the archetype of our future resurrection. In 1 Corinthians 15, St. Paul develops this anagogic typology at length and with great power. His concern here is to correct a heretical view present among some of the faithful in Corinth—influenced by a Platonic conception—that the promised resurrection is a purely spiritual affair. They apparently did not dare directly question the physical Resurrection of Christ. Nevertheless, St. Paul saw that a doubt about the future physical general resurrection of the faithful implied a corresponding, unexpressed doubt about the historical physical Resurrection of Christ, who is the "first fruit of the dead," the victor over sin and death. To counter this doubt, St. Paul develops the intrinsic connection between the Resurrection of Christ and the general resurrection of the dead:

Now if Christ is preached as raised from the dead, how can some of you say that there is no resurrection of the dead? But if there is no resurrection of the dead, then Christ has not been raised; if Christ has not been raised, then our preaching is in vain and your faith is in vain. We are even found to be misrepresenting God, because we testified of God that he raised Christ, whom he did not raise if it is true that the dead are not raised. For if the dead are not raised, then Christ has not been raised.... But in fact Christ has been raised from the dead, the first fruits of those who have fallen asleep. For as by a man came death, by a man has come also the resurrection of the dead. For as in Adam all die, so also in Christ shall all be made alive. But each in his own order: Christ the first fruits, then at his coming those who belong to Christ.[18]

Christ's Resurrection and the general resurrection of the just are so intimately connected that denial of one implies a denial of the other. For, everything worked by Christ is for the sake of His Mystical Body, the Church. Christ's Resurrection makes no sense if His Church is not to share in His bodily glory. Christ's Resurrection is the exemplar, figure, and cause of our future resurrection. Precisely for this reason Christ's Resurrection had to precede the general resurrection. His Resurrection is the first fruit, harbinger, pledge, and seed of the future general resurrection. It is the foundation on which the entire faith and hope of the Church is built.

Typology in Hebrews 8–10

Hebrews 8–10 develops a typology of the worship of Israel, of the Church, and of the heavenly liturgy in which Christ is seated at the right hand of the Father. The religious rites of Israel (including its priesthood, sacrifices, Temple, and the Holy of Holies) are described as a kind of replica or copy of Christ's true sacrifice (8:5; 9:23–24; 10:1), of which the Church possesses the "true form" (10:1). The Greek word translated by the RSV as "true form" is *eikōn*, which literally means icon, likeness, image, or form.

---

[18] 1 Cor 15:12–23.

The worship of Israel is designated as a kind of *shadow*, "a shadow of the good things to come" (10:1). The worship of the present Church is said to be an *icon* or image, whereas the heavenly liturgy is the *reality* to which both shadow and icon refer, but in two different ways: remote and proximate. Thus, salvation history is a progression from shadow to icon to reality. The shadow—the events and worship of the Old Covenant—is a type both of the icon and of the reality, whereas the icons—the Incarnation and the sacraments of the Church—are types of the realities of the Church triumphant and of the heavenly liturgy. Hebrews 8:5 states: "They [the priests of the Old Covenant] serve a copy and shadow of the heavenly sanctuary; for when Moses was about to erect the tent, he was instructed by God, saying, 'See that you make everything according to the pattern which was shown you on the mountain.'" The Letter to the Hebrews interprets this "pattern" to be not just a visual image or blueprint shown to Moses (which would be the literal sense), but Christ's Paschal mystery itself. The Paschal mystery is the true model and exemplar of Israel's religious rites, and thus those rites prefigure it.

The Church's worship is a higher kind of representation of the Paschal mystery, so that it qualifies as a "true form" or "likeness," rather than a "shadow." It is a "likeness" and not a mere shadow because it truly contains what it represents. St. Ambrose gives a marvelous exegesis of this:

> The carnal Jews had the shadow, the likeness is ours, the reality theirs who shall rise again. For we know that according to the Law there are these three, the shadow, the image or likeness, and the reality; the shadow in the Law, the image in the Gospel, the truth in the judgment. But all is Christ's, and all is in Christ, whom now we cannot see according to the reality, but we see him, as it were, in a kind of likeness of future things. Of which we have seen the shadow in the Law.[19]

---

[19] St. Ambrose, *On Belief in the Resurrection* 2.109 (trans. H. de Romestin in *NPNF2*, 10:192–193).

Origen (who is probably Ambrose's source) gives a similar reading:

Paul distinguishes three levels in the law: the shadow, the image, and the truth. . . . The law contains the shadow of future good things, but not the very image of the realities, and this clearly shows that the image of the realities is different from what is designated as the shadow of the law. If anyone can describe the ceremonies of the Jewish worship, let him view the temple as not having had the image of realities, but only their shadow. Let him see the altar as a mere shadow, and the rams and the calves brought to sacrifice also as a shadow, according to the Scripture: "our days on earth are like a shadow" (1 Chr 29:15).

If someone wishes to go beyond this shadow, let him come to the image of the realities and let him behold the coming of Christ made flesh: let him contemplate him in his role as High Priest offering victims to the Father henceforth and in the future; let him understand that all this is an image of spiritual realities and that heavenly functions are denoted by corporal functions. We employ the term image to refer to that which is intelligible at present and which human nature can observe.

If you can penetrate the heavens with your understanding and your mind and follow Jesus who has penetrated the heavens and who stands as our intercessor before the face of God, you will find there those good things whose shadow the law contained and whose image Christ revealed through his Incarnation, those good things that have been prepared for the blessed, which neither eye has seen nor ear heard, and which man has never even imagined or thought of.[20]

---

[20] Origen, *Homily in Psalm* 38.2.2 (PG, 12:402A), in de Margerie, *History of Exegesis*, 1:102–103.

Study Questions

1. How do the prophets anticipate biblical typology?
2. How did Jesus use biblical typology?
3. Explain typology in the Pauline Epistles.
4. Explain the notion of recapitulation as used by St. Paul in Ephesians 1:9–10, and as explained by St. Irenaeus. How is this notion important for understanding typology?
5. Explain typology as developed in Hebrews 8:5 and 10:1. What is the distinction between "shadow," "image" (translated in the RSV as "true form"), and "reality"?
6. Explain the typology of Baptism developed in Romans 6:3–11.
7. Explain the typology in 1 Corinthians 15 connecting the general resurrection with the Resurrection of Christ.

Suggestions for Further Reading

Daniélou, Jean Cardinal, S.J. *The Bible and the Liturgy*. Notre Dame: University of Notre Dame Press, 1956.

———. *From Shadows to Reality: Studies in the Biblical Typology of the Fathers*. Translated by Dom Wulstan Hibberd. Westminster: The Newman Press, 1960.

CHAPTER EIGHTEEN

Fittingness of Biblical Typology

Why is it fitting that God reveal Himself to man not just through words, but also through prophetic deeds or events? Why did God give Scripture spiritual senses in addition to the literal sense? We have said above that salvation history is fashioned by God in progressive stages, culminating in the Incarnation of Christ in the fullness of time. Earlier stages of Revelation present God's plan in a way that prepares for His full Revelation in Christ.

Order of Human Knowing: From the Sensible to the Spiritual

The fittingness of biblical typology rests on human nature. God speaks to man in a way that corresponds with the human nature He created. As rational animals, all of our knowledge begins with sense knowledge and we come to know spiritual truths by abstraction from that sense knowledge. Even after we grasp spiritual truths, however, we still have to accompany all our knowledge with images of the imagination by which the spiritual truths are given concrete imaginative form.

For this reason, God does not simply reveal abstract propositions to man. On the contrary, He teaches man in the manner of a perfect teacher, using sensible objects to illustrate and embody the abstract truths. In the words of St. Thomas, "the Lord wills that we be led by the hand from sensible things unto intelligible and spiritual things."[1] Thus, it is out of respect for our nature that God reveals spiritual truths through sensible images and historical narratives. Typology realizes this divine pedagogy in a marvelous way, for the types are sensible and concrete events that make a strong impression on their own level (as, for example, the Flood or the Exodus), but they also have the power to lead the mind to spiritual and transcendent things, of which they are signs. St. Thomas explains:

> As Dionysius says (*Celestial Hierarchy* 1), the things of God cannot be manifested to men except by means of sensible similitudes. Now these similitudes move the soul more when they are not only expressed in words, but also offered to the senses. Wherefore the things of God are set forth in the Scriptures not only by similitudes expressed in words, as in the case of metaphorical expressions; but also by similitudes of things set before the eyes.[2]

Typology is similar to the sacraments in this regard. In both, sensible things or events are put forward as the signs of invisible spiritual realities. The *Catechism of the Council of Trent* develops this idea with regard to the fittingness of the sacraments:

> We are so constituted by nature that we can understand nothing intellectually unless it is first perceived through the senses. Out of his goodness, the Creator of all things wisely decreed that the mysterious effect of his infinite power should be made intelligible to us by means of certain signs evident to our senses. If man were not clothed, as it were, in a material body, St. John Chrysostom tells us, goodness would have

---

[1] *Commentary on the Epistle to the Hebrews*, ch. 8, lec. 1 (Marietti no. 389), trans. Chrysostom Baer (South Bend: St. Augustine's Press, 2006), 166.

[2] *ST* I-II, q. 99, a. 3, ad 3. In this article, St. Thomas is considering the typological meaning of the ceremonial precepts of the Mosaic Law.

been presented to him in a manner likewise unclothed; but since his soul is in fact embodied, it is absolutely necessary that certain sensory signs be used if he is to have any understanding of what goodness is.[3]

With regard to the sacraments, St. Thomas explains that it is fitting for human nature that we come to partake in spiritual goods through sensible signs and ends by comparing that to the method of Scripture:

Divine wisdom provides for each thing according to its mode; hence it is written (Wisd 8:1) that "she . . . orders all things sweetly." For this reason we are also told (Matt 25:15) that she "gave to everyone according to his proper ability." Now it is part of man's nature to acquire knowledge of the intelligible from the sensible. But a sign is that by means of which one attains to the knowledge of something else. Consequently, since the sacred things which are signified by the sacraments are the spiritual and intelligible goods by means of which man is sanctified, it follows that the sacramental signs consist in sensible things, just as in the divine Scriptures spiritual things are set before us under the guise of things sensible.[4]

Both the sacraments and biblical typology are based on the principle that the natural human order of learning is to learn about spiritual realities through sensible images. Thus it is fitting that we be brought to spiritual truths and gifts through sensible signs.

---

[3] *The Roman Catechism*, part 2, intro., section 14, trans. Robert I. Bradley and Eugene Kevane (Boston: St. Paul, 1985), 151.

[4] *ST* III, q. 60, a. 4. See also *ST* III, q. 61, a. 1: "Sacraments are necessary unto man's salvation for three reasons. The first is taken from the condition of human nature which is such that it has to be led by things corporeal and sensible to things spiritual and intelligible. Now it belongs to Divine providence to provide for each one according as its condition requires. Divine wisdom, therefore, fittingly provides man with means of salvation, in the shape of corporeal and sensible signs that are called sacraments."

Typology Shows Divine Preparation and Is a Motive of Credibility

Typology can serve as an important motive of credibility in the Christian faith, because it reveals mysteries worthy of the divine Wisdom hidden under the letter of the events of the Old Testament. This hidden meaning reveals God's providential plan in the course of human history leading to Christ and the Church.

When, on Easter Sunday, Jesus "opened the Scriptures" to the Apostles and disciples who had fallen into despair, this revelation of scriptural typology revived their faith. Typology enabled them to see the plan of God hidden under the apparently contradictory "accidents" of history and how everything prepared for Christ's Paschal mystery. For this reason their hearts burned within them.

A very different example of the power of typology to reinforce faith is given in the life of St. Augustine. In his *Confessions*, he reveals that the discovery of biblical typology in the sermons of St. Ambrose was one of the crucial steps in his coming back to faith. The Manicheans had drawn him away from the Catholic faith, in part, because they ridiculed many of the events of the Old Testament as unedifying according to the literal sense. In the sixth book of the *Confessions*, he writes:

> Thus, since we are too weak by unaided reason to find out truth, and since, because of this, we need the authority of the Holy Writings, I had now begun to believe that thou wouldst not, under any circumstances, have given such eminent authority to those Scriptures throughout all lands if it had not been that through them thy will may be believed in and that thou mightest be sought. For, as to those passages in the Scripture which had heretofore appeared incongruous and offensive to me, now that I had heard several of them expounded reasonably, I could see that they were to be resolved by the mysteries of spiritual interpretation. The authority of Scripture seemed to me all the more revered and worthy of devout belief because, although it was visible for all to read, it

reserved the full majesty of its secret wisdom within its spiritual profundity. While it stooped to all in the great plainness of its language and simplicity of style, it yet required the closest attention of the most serious-minded—so that it might receive all into its common bosom.[5]

Coming to understand the typological or spiritual sense of Scripture enabled St. Augustine to have the proper reverence for the Word of God as containing immeasurable depths of meaning, although it speaks to all on the level of the literal sense.

Richness of Biblical Senses

As stated above, an objection to biblical typology is that a multiplicity of levels of meaning in a text causes ambiguity and obscurity.[6] Indeed, there is no doubt that many texts of Scripture have a difficulty that comes not from poverty of expression and ideas, but from overabundance. The richness of different levels of meaning in the Bible is what makes it the most difficult book to understand fully. However, the very difficulty and richness add greatly to the fascination of the biblical text and make it capable of speaking on many levels at the same time.

St. Augustine speaks, in his *De doctrina christiana*, on the fittingness of the richness of meaning in the Bible:

Some of the expressions are so obscure as to shroud the meaning in the thickest darkness. And I do not doubt that all this was divinely arranged for the purpose of subduing pride by toil, and of preventing a feeling of satiety in the intellect, which generally holds in small esteem what is discovered without difficulty.

. . . But why I view them with greater delight under that aspect than if no such figure were drawn from the sacred books,

---

[5] *Confessions* 6.5.8, trans. Albert Outler, Library of Christian Classics 7 (Philadelphia: Westminster Press, 1955), 85.

[6] See *ST* I, q. 1, a. 10, obj. 1 and ad 1.

though the fact would remain the same and the knowledge the same, is another question, and one very difficult to answer. Nobody, however, has any doubt about the facts, both that it is pleasanter in some cases to have knowledge communicated through figures, and that what is attended with difficulty in the seeking gives greater pleasure in the finding. For those who seek but do not find suffer from hunger. Those, again, who do not seek at all because they have what they require just beside them often grow languid from satiety. Now weakness from either of these causes is to be avoided. Accordingly the Holy Spirit has, with admirable wisdom and care for our welfare, so arranged the Holy Scriptures as by the plainer passages to satisfy our hunger, and by the more obscure to stimulate our appetite. For almost nothing is dug out of those obscure passages which may not be found set forth in the plainest language elsewhere.[7]

Creation Has a Typological Aspect

Clement of Alexandria saw in creation itself a kind of typology. In creating the universe, God made physical realities symbols of spiritual realities. This aspect of the thought of Clement captivated Cardinal Newman while still an Anglican. He writes:

> The broad philosophy of Clement and Origen carried me away. . . . Some portions of their teaching, magnificent in themselves, came like music to my inward ear, as if the response to ideas, which, with little external to encourage them, I had cherished so long. These were based on the mystical or sacramental principle, and spoke of the various Economies or Dispensations of the Eternal. I understood them to mean that the exterior world, physical and historical, was but the outward manifestation of realities greater than itself. Nature was a parable: Scripture was an allegory: pagan literature,

---

[7] *De doctrina christiana* 2.6.7–8 (NPNF1, 2:537).

philosophy, and mythology, properly understood, were but a preparation for the Gospel.[8]

The typology of creation is frequently mentioned in Scripture. Psalm 19:1–2 summarizes: "The heavens are telling the glory of God; and the firmament proclaims his handiwork. Day to day pours forth speech, and night to night declares knowledge." God is manifested at times in the tempest and storm, in the clouds, the mountains, the sea, the dove, or in the gentle breeze. Nature also provides images of moral evil, as in the serpent or swarms of locusts. St. Ephrem gives a magnificent expression of the Christocentric nature of the typology of creation:

> In every place, if you look, His symbol is there,
> and when you read, you will find His types.
> For by Him were created all creatures,
> And He engraved His symbols upon His possessions.[9]

Biblical typology continues the kind of divine artistry manifested in creation, transferring it to the realm of history.

Typology: A Divine Bridge between the Old and New Testaments

Biblical typology provides a divine bridge between the Old and New Testaments. God Himself prepared the events and religious ceremonies of the Old Testament so as to make them figures, signs, or symbols of the New. We may ask why God wished to make this bridge between the Testaments, creating a subtle symbolism that most readers would never understand unless they were expressly taught. Why did God create these figures?

---

[8] John Henry Newman, *Apologia pro vita sua* (New York: Modern Library, 1950), 55.

[9] St. Ephrem, *Hymn on Virginity* 20.12, in *Ephrem the Syrian: Hymns*, trans. Kathleen McVey (Mahwah: Paulist Press, 1989), 348.

In reality, our question here is deeper. Why did God create two covenants and frame two divine laws, the Law of Moses and the law of the New Testament? Why did the New Testament and the New Covenant sealed with the Blood of Christ need to be preceded by an Old Testament and an Old Covenant sealed with the blood of animals at Mt. Sinai?

The Chosen People was elected to receive the prophecies concerning the Messiah and His Church and to prepare for His coming *also through the symbolism of their ceremonies and their history.* The Fathers of the Church, following the teaching of Jesus and of St. Paul, see the entire framework of the Old Testament—its history and ceremonial laws—as essentially a sensible figure of future spiritual realities that would be brought by Christ. The sensible figures prepared mankind to receive and understand the spiritual blessings that were represented under them.

Biblical typology therefore plays a crucial role in grasping the veiled continuity of God's salvific plan. It reveals that the liturgy of ancient Israel, which continually commemorated the Exodus, mystically foreshadows the Paschal mystery of Christ. The typological sense of Scripture binds the contents of the Old and New Testaments intimately together.[10] It also helps us to understand the teaching of the Gospel, for knowledge of the types and figures allows the doctrines to take flesh, to live within us, to appeal to our imagination, to be more memorable, to show us the unity of God's providence in history, and to show us graphically that Christ and His Passion are the center of history around which everything else revolves and to which all is oriented in the plan of God. Typology is admirably suited to show God's power, while adapted to our sensible and corporeal nature. The Fathers and Doctors of the Church drew heavily on this way of understanding Scripture.

---

[10] Lev 23:14 proclaims observance of the Passover to be "a statute forever in all your dwellings throughout your generations"; Lev 23:31 proclaims Yom Kippur to be "a statute forever throughout your generations"; and Lev 23:41 proclaims that Sukkot shall be "a statute forever throughout your generations." This perpetual celebration is realized (in a typological sense) insofar as these feasts are figures that are eternally fulfilled in the Sacrifice of Christ, perpetuated throughout the ages in the Holy Mass.

It is a great shame that present-day Christians have very little familiarity with biblical typology. Scholars pride themselves on their knowledge of history and languages, but most of them do not concern themselves with the typological sense of the Bible, where the deepest and most important meaning of the texts is found. The generally illiterate populace of the Middle Ages was better versed in understanding biblical typology, for it fills the Gothic cathedrals, their stained glass windows, and the glorious art of the Renaissance, and above all, it completely permeates the liturgy of the Church. The typological sense of Scripture is beautiful and sublime precisely because it demonstrates the reality and power of God's providence over history. It shows us the presence of the finger of God in events of this world. It is a divine work of art written within history itself. However, it can only be grasped by those who have the key to the Scriptures, which is Christ and the Church, since this is the principal content of the typological sense.

Connection between the Two Testaments

The study of typology is based on faith in the profound relationship between the Old and the New Covenants. In the first two centuries of the Church, this typological relationship between the two Testaments was under attack from Gnostic heresies that sought to sever the relationship of Christ and the Church with the Old Testament. Many Gnostics went so far as to deny the identification of the God of the Old Testament with that of the New. In such an interpretative framework, typology can have no place. The logical result is the irrelevance of the Old Testament for Gnostic Christianity. One form of Gnosticism, that of Marcion, took this position to its logical conclusion, as we have seen, and excised the Old Testament from the canon of Scripture!

The fact that the Old Testament was read typologically in the Church saved it from receiving the fate given it by Marcion. Pope Benedict XVI commented on the importance of typology in this regard in an audience on Origen:

It was especially on this route that Origen succeeded in effectively promoting the "Christian interpretation" of the Old Testament, brilliantly countering the challenge of the heretics, especially the Gnostics and Marcionites, who made the two Testaments disagree to the extent that they rejected the Old Testament.[11]

Given that typology has increasingly fallen out of the consciousness of modern Catholics, it is not surprising that the Old Testament has become an object of profound ignorance and neglect to many.[12] An understanding and appreciation of typology is crucial for the revival of the interest of the Catholic faithful in the Old Testament!

Typology Is Christocentric

Typology manifests the fact that the divine plan centers on Christ. Typology connects events occurring before and after Christ with the Incarnation and the Paschal mystery. Salvation history before Christ is essentially a preparation for Christ, and so prefigures Him. The Christian life after Christ is even more closely connected with the Incarnation, for the Church lives the life of Christ through the gift of the Spirit and the sacraments through which the Spirit is given. History culminates in heaven, in which Christ will be "all in all." Typology, therefore, is always pointing to Christ. This pointing is of three kinds:

---

[11] "Origen of Alexandria: Life and Work," General Audience of April 25, 2007, in *Church Fathers from Clement of Rome to Augustine* (San Francisco: Ignatius Press, 2008), 36.

[12] See G. W. H. Lampe and K. J. Woollcombe, *Essays on Typology* (London: SCM Press, 1957), 17: "It is true, perhaps, that so far as the ordinary reader is concerned the consequence of this great change has been to present him once more with the dilemma which confronted the Church of the second century: either the typological and allegorical method of dealing with the Old Testament, so as to make it readable as a Christian book, or the more drastic solution advocated by Marcion. Either follow such rules of exegesis as will allow the Gospel to be read out of the Hebrew Scriptures, or throw away the Old Testament as irrelevant to those who live under the New Covenant. Since at the same time the modern reader was convinced by the historical method that the Old Testament could not be read as a directly Christian book, there can be little doubt that one of the most far-reaching effects of the growth of the critical attitude has been the impression gained by the general reader and the ordinary Christian that the Old Testament is of no great significance to him and is of little real interest except to the student of religions."

pointing to the Incarnation (allegorical sense), pointing to the participation of the Church militant in Christ's life (moral sense), and pointing to the more perfect participation of the Church triumphant in that same life (anagogical sense).[13]

Typology thus enables the whole of Scripture to be Christocentric, even when the literal sense is not referring to Christ. In controversy with the Manicheans who ridiculed the Old Testament, St. Augustine writes:

> All those passages speak of Christ. The head now ascended into heaven along with the body still suffering on earth is the full development of the whole purpose of the authors of Scripture, which is well called Sacred Scripture.[14]

Rejections of the centrality of typology, therefore, imply a loss of Christocentric perspective. This cannot fail to be a most serious symptom of a crisis of faith.

Typology in the Fathers of the Church

As seen above, the Fathers have a special importance in the interpretation of Scripture because of their proximity to the Apostles. Their importance thus does not depend entirely on the scientific precision of their methods, but on their special insight into the apostolic Tradition, as Pope Leo XIII emphasizes in *Providentissimus Deus*.[15] *Dei*

---

[13] See Bertand de Margerie, *History of Exegesis*, vol. 1, *The Greek Fathers* (Petersham: Saint Bede's, 1991), 9: "But it appears, in the light of the Letter to the Hebrews, that the figures of the Old Covenant point toward a single reality in three stages: Christ and his already passed history, Christ in his present Church (image), Christ in his future manifestation or reality. Christ thus appears as both the eternal and prior *archetype*, and the final *teleotype* illuminating our present and historical experience in the Church."

[14] St. Augustine, *Contra Faustum* 22.94 (trans. R. Stothert in *NPNF*1, 4:310).

[15] Encylical Letter on the Study of Holy Scripture *Providentissimus Deus* (1893), §14: "The Holy Fathers, We say, are of supreme authority, whenever they all interpret in one and the same manner any text of the Bible, as pertaining to the doctrine of faith or morals; for their unanimity clearly evinces that such interpretation has come down from the Apostles as a matter of Catholic faith. The opinion of the Fathers is also of very great weight when they treat of these matters in their

Verbum §23 also emphasizes the importance of the Fathers, both Eastern and Western, and the sacred liturgies for "a more profound understanding of the sacred Scriptures."

In interpreting the Bible, all the Fathers, like the ancient liturgies, make very liberal use of typology.[16] This is a sign that this mode of interpretation comes from the teaching of the Apostles. It has been rightly said that "without typology it is difficult to imagine Patristic theology and the concept of Christian orthodoxy it defined and supported as existing at all."[17]

The Fathers see Jesus Christ as the key to understanding the mysteries hidden in the Old Testament. They investigate the typological meaning of texts in the light of what Christ has revealed. This method, used by Our Lord Himself and by St. Paul and the other Apostles, is metaphorically signified in Revelation 5:4–5:

> I wept much that no one was found worthy to open the scroll or to look into it. Then one of the elders said to me, "Weep not; lo, the Lion of the tribe of Judah, the Root of David, has conquered, so that he can open the scroll and its seven seals."

Christ alone, the Lion of the tribe of Judah, the culmination of Jewish yearning and the great Antitype of all the figures of the Old

---

capacity of doctors, unofficially; not only because they excel in their knowledge of revealed doctrine and in their acquaintance with many things which are useful in understanding the apostolic Books, but because they are men of eminent sanctity and of ardent zeal for the truth, on whom God has bestowed a more ample measure of His light. Wherefore the expositor should make it his duty to follow their footsteps with all reverence, and to use their labors with intelligent appreciation." See also Pius XII, Encyclical Letter on Promoting Biblical Studies *Divino afflante Spiritu* (1943) §§28–30, and the Congregation for Catholic Education, *Instruction on The Study of the Fathers of the Church in Priestly Formation* (1989).

[16] Jean Cardinal Daniélou, S.J., and Henri de Lubac have a great merit in studying the importance of biblical typology in the theology of the Fathers of the Church. See de Lubac, *Medieval Exegesis*, vols. 1 and 2: *The Four Senses of Scripture*, trans. Mark Sebanc (Grand Rapids: Eerdmans, 1998–2000), and Daniélou, *The Bible and the Liturgy* (Notre Dame: University of Notre Dame Press, 1956) and *From Shadows to Reality: Studies in the Biblical Typology of the Fathers*, trans. Dom Wulstan Hibberd (Westminster: The Newman Press, 1960).

[17] John J. O'Keefe and R. R. Reno, *Sanctified Vision: An Introduction to Early Christian Interpretation of the Bible* (Baltimore: John Hopkins University Press, 2005), 69.

Testament, can open the scroll of the Scriptures by revealing the fullness of meaning hidden in it. St. Gregory the Great says of this text: "Our Redeemer alone opened the scroll, and having become man, dying, rising, ascending, He laid open all the mysteries that had been locked up in Scripture."[18] St. Irenaeus proclaims the same conviction, saying that every part of Scripture, when read in the light of Christ, is "a treasure, hid indeed in a field, but brought to light by the cross of Christ."[19]

Typology was also crucial in the combat of the Fathers against the first heresies that concerned the relationship between the two Testaments. For example, typology is the best refutation of the anti-Jewish heretics such as Gnostics like Marcion who rejected the Old Testament Revelation and the divine origin of the Law of Moses. At the same time, typology protects against the Judaizing error in which the newness of the Christian sacramental economy would be overlooked and the Mosaic ceremonial law would be regarded as on the same level as Christian sacraments.

Biblical typology shows the subordinate place of the mysteries of the Old Testament compared to those of the New—for the former prefigure the latter—without thereby eliminating their value and beauty. Rather, typological understanding enhances their beauty by revealing their intrinsic ordination to Christ and the Church, thus showing their transcendence and the beauty of God's plan, which exceeds what any human mind could have conceived.

Biblical typology, as developed by the Fathers, thus shows the proper relationship between the Old and the New Testaments to be one of preparation and fulfillment. It shows that God's intention was not simply to replace the Old with the New, as in some supersessionist models of understanding, but to *fulfill* the Old through the New. Thus it is perfectly in harmony with Jesus's claim that He came not to

---

[18] Pope St. Gregory the Great, *Dialogue* 4.42 (PL, 77:401A): "Quam solus Redemptor noster aperuit, qui homo factus, moriendo, resurgendo, ascendendo, cuncta mysteria quae in eo fuerant clausa patefecit."

[19] *Adversus haereses* 4.26.1 (*ANF*, 1:496). See also earlier in 4.26.1: "For Christ is the treasure which was hid in the field, that is, in this world (for 'the field is the world'); but the treasure hid in the Scriptures is Christ, since He was pointed out by means of types and parables" (*ANF*, 1:496).

abolish the Law and the prophets, but to fulfill them.[20] Typology is thus crucial for understanding the right relationship between Israel and the Church.

Typology in the Liturgy

The Lectionary and Divine Office

The Second Vatican Council stresses the importance of looking to the liturgy for a right understanding of Scripture, for it is "above all in the sacred Liturgy that the Church continuously takes the bread of life from the table of the word of God and offers it to the faithful."[21] The bringing together of readings from the Old and the New Testaments is based on a typological understanding of their relationship.

Scott Hahn gives an entertaining account of his discovery of typology in the Catholic liturgy. As a Protestant, he saw the connection between Isaiah 22:19–23[22] and Matthew 16:13–20 as something he had come upon through his own research. After becoming Catholic, he found that the Church put these texts together in the liturgy (twenty-first Sunday of ordinary time), not by chance, but to show us the typology. He writes:

> Sunday after Sunday, the Church gives us a pattern of biblical interpretation, showing us how the promises of the Old Testament are fulfilled in the New Testament. It's no wonder the Church does it this way. The Church learned this from the New Testament writers, who learned it from Jesus.[23]

---

[20] See Matt 5:17.

[21] *DV* §21; see also *DV* §23.

[22] Isa 22:19–23: "Thus says the Lord to Shebna, master of the palace: 'I will thrust you from your office and pull you down from your station. On that day I will summon my servant Eliakim, son of Hilkiah; I will clothe him with your robe, and gird him with your sash, and give over to him your authority. He shall be a father to the inhabitants of Jerusalem, and to the house of Judah. I will place the key of the House of David on Eliakim's shoulder; when he opens, no one shall shut; when he shuts, no one shall open. I will fix him like a peg in a sure spot, to be a place of honor for his family.'"

[23] Scott Hahn, *Spirit & Life: Essays on Interpreting the Bible in Ordinary Time* (Steubenville: Emmaus Road, 2009), 114.

Biblical typology is thus crucial for understanding the structure of the Church's liturgy. Catholic liturgy springs organically from the prayer of ancient Israel, but is yet entirely centered on the Messiah, who is the key of all of salvation history. In Him the prayer and yearning of Israel comes to fruition.

Typology in the Sacraments

Typology not only regards the lectionary, but underlies the very structure of the sacramental action. Through the use of typology, the sacraments mysteriously bring together fundamental levels of time: the past of salvation history, the Paschal mystery in which that history culminates, the present of the Church in which we celebrate the liturgy and live our Christian lives, and a mysterious anticipation of future glory. The *Catechism of the Council of Trent* explains the threefold temporal dimension of the sacraments:

> These mysterious, divinely instituted signs called sacraments properly signify, by the same divine ordinance, more than just one reality. Besides the reality already mentioned, viz., the divine grace and our sanctification, there are in each of the sacraments two other realities, both of which are most intimately connected with that grace and sanctification. These other realities are, first, the Passion of our Lord, and secondly, the life of the blessed in heaven. They are related to our sanctification as its source and as its culmination, respectively. Thus each sacrament of its very nature, as the Doctors of the Church have taught us, has a threefold signification: it recalls something from the past, it indicates something in the present, and it anticipates something in the future.
>
> This teaching is more than a mere opinion, for it is solidly based on the authority of the Sacred Scriptures. When St. Paul says, "All of us who have been baptized into Christ Jesus were baptized into his death" (Rom 6:3), he shows that Baptism is a sign in that it reminds us of the Passion and Death of

our Lord. When he goes on to say, "We were buried therefore with him by baptism into death, so that as Christ was raised from the dead by the glory of the Father, we too might walk in newness of life" (Rom 6:4), he also shows that Baptism signifies the infusion of divine grace into the soul, by which we are enabled to renew our lives and fulfill what is expected of us. Finally, when he says, "If we have been united with him in a death like his, we shall certainly be united with him in a resurrection like his" (Rom 6:5), he shows that Baptism also signifies the eternal life itself—the life which through Baptism we shall one day attain.[24]

St. Thomas Aquinas explains these three temporal dimensions of the sacraments in the *Summa* (III, q. 60, a. 3):

A sacrament properly speaking is that which is ordained to signify our sanctification. In which three things may be considered: the very cause of our sanctification, which is Christ's passion; the form of our sanctification, which is grace and the virtues; and the ultimate end of our sanctification, which is eternal life. And all these are signified by the sacraments. Consequently a sacrament is a sign that is both a reminder of the past, i.e. the passion of Christ; and an indication of that which is effected in us by Christ's passion, i.e. grace; and a prognostic, that is, a foretelling of future glory.

Sacraments have this marvelous capacity to bring together the past, present, and future in a way greater than any other human action because they are efficacious types of grace and future glory, as well as antitypes with respect to the history of the Old Covenant and its sacramental rites. The typological sense of the Old Testament mirrors the typological richness of the sacramental action and prepares for it. This is one of the reasons why, in the wisdom of the Church, the liturgy of the Word precedes the Eucharistic liturgy.

---

[24] *The Roman Catechism*, part 2, intro., section 12, trans. Robert I. Bradley and Eugene Kevane (Boston: St. Paul, 1985), 150–51.

The Eucharistic Prayer itself is rich in typology. Consider the words of consecration: "For this is the cup of my blood, the blood of the new and eternal covenant, which will be poured out for you and for many for the forgiveness of sins." The new and eternal covenant and the sacramental pouring out of Christ's blood in sacrifice by which the new covenant is sealed are antitypes of the Old Covenant itself and of its many sacrifices.

The Roman Canon then goes on to mention three great typological figures of the offering of the Eucharist: the sacrifices of Abel, Abraham, and Melchizedek:

> Be pleased to look upon these offerings with a serene and kindly countenance, and to accept them, as you were pleased to accept the gifts of your servant Abel the just, the sacrifice of Abraham, our father in faith, and the offering of your high priest Melchizedek, a holy sacrifice, a spotless victim.

Typology is found in a spectacular way in the Easter vigil, the most solemn liturgy of the liturgical year, with its long series of Old Testament readings that marvelously prefigure Baptism.

A magnificent exposition of typology is contained in the solemn hymn of the *Exsultet*:

> These, then, are the feasts of Passover, in which is slain the Lamb, the one true Lamb, whose Blood anoints the doorposts of believers. This is the night, when once you led our forebears, Israel's children, from slavery in Egypt and made them pass dry-shod through the Red Sea. This is the night that with a pillar of fire banished the darkness of sin. This is the night that even now, throughout the world, sets Christian believers apart from worldly vices and from the gloom of sin, leading them to grace and joining them to his holy ones. This is the night, when Christ broke the prison-bars of death and rose victorious from the underworld. . . . O truly necessary sin of Adam, destroyed completely by the Death

of Christ! O happy fault that earned so great, so glorious a Redeemer![25]

Relationship between the Structure of the Sacraments and Typology

Another parallel between the sacraments and biblical typology is that both exhibit a threefold structure. In the Scholastic tradition the sacraments are distinguished into three parts: *sacramentum tantum* (sacramental sign alone), *res et sacramentum* (both sign and reality), and *res tantum* (reality alone). The *sacramentum tantum* is the outward sign. The *res et sacramentum* is an invisible reality signified by the outward sacramental sign (such as the invisible character conferred by Baptism, Confirmation, and Holy Orders), and itself also signifying an invisible grace. Finally, the *res tantum* (reality alone) is the grace alone.

These three levels can be seen most clearly in the Eucharist. The sacramental sign is the bread and wine and the words of the consecration; the intermediate level is the invisible reality of the Body and Blood of Christ; and the third level is the communication of an increase of sanctifying grace and charity.[26] There is also a causal relation between the three levels. The realization of the sacramental sign causes the presence of the Body and Blood, and worthy reception of the Body causes spiritual nourishment in grace and charity.

The Word of God displays a similar structure. The Bible is composed of words that are signs that signify events or realities. These events or realities may, in turn, signify other higher and more invisible events and realities. Thus we have the threefold progression: first there is the literal level of the words that describe an event; there is the event itself, which has its own historical reality; and the event may signify salvific realities in Christ and the Church.

---

[25] *Roman Missal*, 3rd edition.

[26] In Baptism, the sacramental sign is the pouring of water and the words of the Baptismal formula, the *res et sacramentum* is the imprinting of the indelible Baptismal character, and the *res tantum* is the infusion of sanctifying grace and the theological virtues.

Thus the words of Scripture are analogous to the sacramental sign (*sacramentum tantum*), for the words are sacred signs of holy things. The words signify events and realities in salvation history, which is their literal sense. These literal events or realities often signify other sacred realities. The events are like the *res et sacramentum* (or the Body and Blood of Christ). They are realities signified by the words, as well as mysterious signs or figures of other salvific realities, such as Christ, the Church and her sacraments, the Christian life, and the Last Things. Mysteries represented by the events are like the *res tantum* (the communication of grace). These mysteries of Christ and the Church are signified both by words and by events, but they do not represent anything further beyond Christ and the Church (militant and triumphant).[27]

Importance of Typology for Preaching and Contemplation

In his *Life of Moses*, St. Gregory of Nyssa uses the life of Moses as a model of spiritual growth and perfection. His treatment is divided into two parts: the first focuses on the literal or historical sense, and the second focuses on the spiritual or typological sense. St. Gregory refers to the latter sense with the term *theoria*, which means contemplation. The spiritual sense is particularly suited for contemplation on the mysteries of salvation history.

Christian contemplation involves a prolonged consideration of the mysteries of the faith under the guidance of the Holy Spirit. The mind reflects on how a particular mystery relates to one's own life as a member of Christ's Mystical Body and to our final destiny. Contemplation thus naturally considers salvation history in a typological sense in which the sensible dimension points to the spiritual, and in which all the events are brought together in Christ, the Church, one's own personal life in Christ, and the fullness of that life in heaven to which we direct our hope.

---

[27] See M. D. Mailhiot, O.P., "La pensée de S. Thomas sur la sens spirituelle," *Revue Thomiste* (1959): 630–633 ; and de Margerie, *An Introduction to the History of Exegesis*, vol. 3, *Saint Augustine*, trans. Pierre de Fontnouvelle (Petersham: Saint Bede's, 1991), 17.

Just as typology is central to the liturgy because of its Christo-centrism, so it is profoundly important for preaching and contempla-tion. As we have seen, the readings in the sacred liturgy are frequent-ly placed together to bring out typology. Homilies ought to explain this typological connection. Typology enables the events of the Old Testament, without diminishing their own reality, to point to what is most important for the spiritual life of the faithful: Christ, the Church, the sacraments, the Christian life, judgment, and heaven.[28] A purely historical-critical exposition of Scripture would fail to edify the faithful. Pope Benedict XVI has pointed to this danger in *Verbum Domini* §35: "If the work of exegesis is restricted to the first level alone [historical-critical analysis], Scripture ends up being *a text belonging only to the past.*" Typology enables the preacher to show—and the per-son doing *lectio divina* to see and taste—how texts belonging to the past in their literal and historical sense speak to the present in Christ and the Church and to the future in the heavenly Jerusalem that is the object of our hope. Typology thus is God's own device for bursting open any reading that seeks to imprison the text in the past and for centering it on the mystery of Christ and the Church in her present pilgrimage and in eternal glory.

Study Questions

1. Explain the fittingness of biblical typology.
2. What makes it possible for Scripture to have typological senses in addition to the literal sense? In other words, what are the foundations of typology?
3. Explain the typological relationship between the rewards and punishments promised in the Old and the New Testaments.

---

[28] See also de Margerie, *History of Exegesis*, 1:15: "It is clear that many of the works produced by contemporary exegetes lead to a kind of atomization in the reading of Scripture. . . . We have today at our disposal more accurate and more numerous scientific tools for discovering the spir-itual sense of the Scriptures, but many of our present works of exegesis are scarcely oriented, as were those of the Fathers, toward the disclosure of the anagogical sense, toward man's return to God, through the practice of the virtues and through the sacraments, through the reading of Scriptures. Whence the crisis in pastoral homiletics, and more radically, the crisis of faith, not of the Church, but within the Church."

4. Explain how the liturgy has an essential typological dimension.
5. What is the importance of typology for Christian contemplation and *lectio divina*?
6. Explain the importance of typology for preaching.

Suggestions for Further Reading

Hahn, Scott. *Letter and Spirit: From Written Text to Living Word in the Liturgy.* New York: Doubleday, 2005.

BIBLIOGRAPHY

Allison, Dale C., Jr. *The Historical Christ and the Theological Jesus.* Grand Rapids: Eerdmans, 2009.

Alonso-Schökel, Luis. *The Inspired Word: Scripture in the Light of Language and Literature.* Translated by Francis Martin. New York: Herder, 1965.

The Apostolic Fathers: Greek Texts and English Translations. Edited by Michael W. Holmes. 3rd edition. Grand Rapids: Baker Academic, 2007.

Aquinas, Thomas. *The Aquinas Catechism: A Simple Explanation of the Catholic Faith by the Church's Greatest Theologian.* Edited by Ralph McInerny. Manchester: Sophia Institute Press, 2000.

———. *Catena aurea.* Translated by John Henry Newman. 4 vols. Oxford, UK: John Henry Parker, 1841–1845. Reprinted with an introduction by Aidan Nichols. London: Saint Austin Press, 1997.

———. *Commentary on the Gospel of St. John.* Translated by Fabian R. Larcher and James A. Weisheipl. Washington, DC: Catholic University of America Press, 2010.

———. *Commentary on St. Paul's Epistle to the Ephesians.* Translated with introduction by Matthew L. Lamb. Albany: Magi Books, 1966.

———. *Commentary on the Epistle to the Hebrews.* Translated by Chrysostom Baer. South Bend: St. Augustine's Press, 2006.

———. *Commentary on the Letter of Saint Paul to the Romans.* Translated by Fabian R. Larcher. Lander: Aquinas Institute for the Study of Sacred Doctrine, 2012.

———. *Commentaries on St. Paul's Epistles to Timothy, Titus, and Philemon.* Translated by Chrysostom Baer. South Bend: St. Augustine's Press, 2007.

———. *Commentary on Saint Paul's First Letter to the Thessalonians and the Letter to the Philippians.* Translated by Fabian R. Larcher and Michael Duffy. Albany: Magi Books, 1966.

———. *Commentary on Saint Paul's Epistle to the Galatians.* Translated by Fabian R. Larcher. Albany: Magi Books, 1966.

———. *Introduction to St. Thomas Aquinas.* Edited by Anton C. Pegis. New York: Modern Library, 1948.

———. *Summa contra gentiles.* Translated by Anton Pegis, James Anderson, Vernon Bourke, and Charles O'Neil. 4 vols. Notre Dame: University of Notre Dame Press, 1975.

———. *Summa theologiae of St. Thomas Aquinas.* 2nd edition. Translated by Dominican Fathers of the English Province. London: Burns, Oates, & Washbourne, 1920–1932.

———. *Super epistolas S. Pauli lectura.* Edited by Raphael Cai. 2 vols. Turin: Marietti, 1953.

Aristotle. *Basic Works of Aristotle.* Edited by Richard McKeon. New York: Random House, 1970.

Atkinson, Joseph C. "The Interpenetration of Inspiration and Inerrancy as a Hermeneutic for Catholic Exegesis." *Letter & Spirit* 6 (2010): 191–224.

Aubert, Roger. *Le problème de l'acte de foi; données traditionnelles et resultats des controverses recentes.* Louvain, BE: Nauwelaerts, 1969.

Augustine. *The City of God.* NPNF1, 2:1–511.

———. *Confessions.* NPNF1, 1:45–207.

———. *Contra Faustum Manichaeum.* Translated by Richard Stothert. NPNF1, 4:155–345.

———. *Harmony of the Gospels.* NPNF1, 6:65–236.

———. *Letters (1–82).* Translated by Wilfrid Parsons. Washington, DC: The Catholic University of America Press, 1951.

Barry, John D., ed. *Lexham Bible Dictionary.* Bellingham: Lexham Press, 2012.

Bartholomew, Craig G., Stephen Evans, Mary Healy, and Murray Rae, eds. *"Behind" the Text: History and Biblical Interpretation.* Grand Rapids: Zondervan, 2003.

————, Scott Hahn, Robin Parry, Christopher Seitz, Al Wolters, eds. *Canon and Biblical Interpretation*. Grand Rapids: Zondervan, 2006.

Bauckham, Richard, ed. *The Book of Acts in Its Palestinian Setting*. Grand Rapids, MI: William B. Eerdmans, 1995.

————. *A Cloud of Witnesses: The Theology of Hebrews in Its Ancient Contexts*. London: T & T Clark, 2008.

————. *Jesus and the Eyewitnesses: The Gospels as Eyewitness Testimony*. Grand Rapids: William B. Eerdmans, 2006.

————. *The Testimony of the Beloved Disciple: Narrative, History, and Theology in the Gospel of John*. Grand Rapids: Baker Academic, 2007.

Bea, Cardinal Augustin. *De inspiratione et inerrantia Sacrae Scripturae: notae historicae et dogmaticae quas in usum privatum auditorum composuit*. Rome: Pontifical Biblical Institute, 1954.

————. *The Study of the Synoptic Gospels; New Approaches and Outlooks*. Edited by Joseph A. Fitzmeyer. New York: Harper & Row, 1965.

————. "Vatican II and the Truth of Sacred Scripture." *Letter & Spirit* 6 (2010): 377–382. Originally published in *The Word of God and Mankind*.

————. *The Word of God and Mankind*. Translated by Dorothy White. Chicago: Franciscan Herald Press, 1967.

Bell, David N. *A Cloud of Witnesses: An Introductory History of the Development of Christian Doctrine to 500 AD*. 2nd revised edition. Cistercian Studies series. Kalamazoo: Cistercian Publications, 2007.

Bellamah, Timothy, O.P. "In the Name of Jesus Christ: A Few Historical Perspectives on the Functioning of Authority in Biblical Interpretation." *Nova et Vetera* (English) 13, no.1 (2015): 57–86.

Benedict XV, Pope. Encyclical Letter Commemorating the Fifteenth Centenary of the Death of St. Jerome *Spiritus Paraclitus*. September 15, 1920.

Benedict XVI, Pope. Regensburg Lecture: "Faith, Reason and the University." September 12, 2006.

———. Christmas Discourse to the Roman Curia of December 22, 2005. In *Origins* 35, no. 32 (January 26, 2006): 534–539.

———. Address of February 14, 2013. In *Origins* 42, no. 38 (February 28, 2013): 601–608.

———. Apostolic Letter issued *motu proprio* for the Indiction of the Year of Faith *Porta fidei*. October 11, 2011.

———. Encyclical Letter on Christian Hope *Spe salvi*. November 30, 2007.

———. Post-synodal Apostolic Exhortation on the Word of God in the Life and Mission of the Church *Verbum Domini*. September 30, 2010.

———. *The Essential Pope Benedict XVI: His Central Writings and Speeches*. Edited by John F. Thornton and Susan B. Varenne. New York: HarperCollins, 2007.

Benoit, André. "Ecriture et Tradition chez St. Irenée." *Revue d'Histoire et Philosophie Religieuses* 40 (1960): 32–43.

Benoit, Pierre. *Aspects of Biblical Inspiration*. Translated by Jerome Murphy-O'Connor and Keverne Ashe. Chicago: Priory Press, 1965.

Biemer, Günter. *Newman on Tradition*. Translated by Kevin Smyth. New York: Herder and Herder, 1967.

Billot, Ludovicus. *De inspiratione Sacrae Scripturae*. Rome: Pontifical Gregorian University, 1929.

Black, Edith. "Historicity of the Bible." *Homiletic and Pastoral Review* (December 1980): 12–23; (January 1981): 24–32.

Blomberg, Craig L. *The Historical Reliability of the Gospels*. Downer's Grove: IVP Academic, 2007.

———. *The Historical Reliability of John's Gospel: Issues & Commentary*. Downer's Grove: InterVarsity Press, 2001.

———. *Jesus and the Gospels: An Introduction and Survey*. 2nd edition. Nashville: B & H Academic, 2009.

Blondel, Maurice. *The Letter on Apologetics and History and Dogma*. Translated by Alexander Dru and Illtyd Trethowan. New York: Holt, Rinehart and Winston, 1965.

Bockmuehl, Markus, and Donald A. Hagner, eds. *The Written Gospel*. Cambridge: Cambridge University Press, 2005.

Bouillard, Henri, S.J. "Human Experience as the Starting Point of Fundamental Theology." In *The Church and the World: Fundamental Theology*, 79–91. Concilium 6. New York: Paulist Press, 1965.

Bouyer, Louis. "Liturgie et exégèse spirituelle." *Maison-Dieu* 7 (1946): 27–50.

Boyle, John P. *Church Teaching Authority: Historical and Theological Studies.* Notre Dame: University of Notre Dame Press, 1995.

Breck, John. *Scripture in Tradition: The Bible and Its Interpretation in the Orthodox Church.* Crestwood: St. Vladimir's Seminary, 2001.

Breen, A. E. *A General Introduction to Holy Scripture.* 2nd edition. Reprint: Fort Collins: Roman Catholic Books, 2000.

Brown, Colin. *Miracles and the Critical Mind.* Grand Rapids: Eerdmans, 1984.

Brown, Raymond Edward. *The Critical Meaning of the Bible.* New York: Paulist Press, 1981.

———, Joseph Fitzmyer, and Roland Murphy, eds. *The New Jerome Biblical Commentary.* Englewood Cliffs: Prentice-Hall, 1990.

Bruce, F. F. *The New Testament Documents: Are They Reliable?* Grand Rapids: Eerdmans, 1960; reprinted 2003.

Bultmann, Rudolf. *Existence and Faith: Shorter Writings of Rudolf Bultmann.* Selected and translated with introduction by Schubert M. Ogden. New York: Meridan Books, 1960.

———. *Faith and Understanding.* Edited with introduction by Robert W. Funk. Translated by Louise Pettibone Smith. New York: Harper & Row, 1969.

———. *The Gospel of John: a Commentary.* Translated by G. R. Beasley-Murray. Edited by R. W. N. Hoare and J. K. Riches. Oxford: Blackwell, 1971.

———. *The History of the Synoptic Tradition.* Translated by John Marsh. 2nd edition. New York: Harper & Row, 1968.

———. *The Johannine Epistles: a Commentary on the Johannine Epistles.* Translated by R. Philip O'Hara, Lane C. McGaughy, and Robert Funk. Edited by Robert W. Funk. Philadelphia: Fortress Press, 1973.

———. *New Testament and Mythology and Other Basic Writings*. Edited and translated by Schubert M. Ogden. Philadelphia: Fortress Press, 1984.

Burtchaell, James T. *Catholic Theories of Biblical Inspiration since 1810: A Review and Critique*. London: Cambridge University Press, 1969.

Burney, Charles F. *The Poetry of Our Lord: An Examination of the Formal Elements of Hebrew Poetry in the Discourses of Jesus Christ*. Oxford: Clarendon Press, 1925.

Butler, Basil C. *The Originality of St. Matthew: A Critique of the Two-document Hypothesis*. Cambridge: Cambridge University Press, 1951.

Byrskog, Samuel. *Jesus the Only Teacher: Didactic Authority and Transmission in Ancient Israel, Ancient Judaism and the Matthean Community*. Stockholm, SE: Almqvist & Wiksell International, 1994.

———. *Story as History—History as Story: The Gospel Tradition in the Context of Ancient Oral History*. Tübingen: Mohr Siebeck, 2000.

Cahill, John, O.P. *The Development of the Theological Censures after the Council of Trent (1563-1709)*. Fribourg: The University Press, 1955.

Campbell, Antony F. and Mark A. O'Brien. *Rethinking the Pentateuch: Prolegomena to the Theology of Ancient Israel*. Louisville: Westminster John Knox Press, 2005.

———. *Sources of the Pentateuch: Texts, Introductions, Annotations*. Minneapolis: Fortress Press, 1993.

Carl, Scott, ed. *Verbum Domini and the Complementarity of Exegesis and Theology*. Grand Rapids: Eerdmans, 2015.

Carmignac, Jean. *The Birth of the Synoptic Gospels*. Translated by Michael J. Wrenn. Chicago: Franciscan Herald Press, 1987.

Castellani, Leonardo. *El Evangelio de Jesucristo*. Buenos Aires: Vortice, 1997.

Cassuto, Umberto. *A Commentary on the Book of Genesis*. Translated by Israel Abrahams. Jerusalem: Magnes, 1961.

———. *The Documentary Hypothesis and the Composition of the Pentateuch*. Translated by Israel Abrahams. Jerusalem: Magnes Press, 1961.

Catchpole, David R. "Source, Form and Redaction Criticism of the New Testament." In *Handbook to Exegesis of the New Testament*, 167–188. Leiden: Brill, 1997.

Catechism of the Catholic Church. 2nd edition. Washington, DC: United States Catholic Conference, 2000.

A Catholic Commentary on Holy Scripture. Edited by Bernard Orchard. New York: Thomas Nelson and Sons, 1953.

Cessario, Romanus, O.P. *Christian Faith and the Theological Life*. Washington, DC: Catholic University of America Press, 1996.

Chapman, John. *John the Presbyter and the Fourth Gospel*. Oxford: Clarendon, 1911.

———. "Papias." In *Catholic Encyclopedia*, 11:457–459. New York: Robert Appleton Co., 1911.

Chesterton, Gilbert K. *The Everlasting Man*. New York: Image Books, 1955. Originally published 1925.

———. *Orthodoxy*. Garden City, NY: Image Books, 1956. Originally published 1908.

Congar, Yves M. J. *The Meaning of Tradition*. Translated by A. N. Woodrow. San Francisco: Ignatius Press, 2004.

———. *Tradition and Traditions: An Historical and a Theological Essay*. New York: The Macmillan Company, 1967.

Congregation for Catholic Education. Instruction on the Study of the Fathers of the Church in the Formation of Priests. November 10, 1989. In *Origins* 19, no. 34 (January 25, 1990).

Congregation for the Doctrine of the Faith. Declaration in Defense of the Catholic Doctrine on the Church Against Certain Errors of the Present Day *Mysterium ecclesiae*. June 24, 1973.

———. Instruction on the Ecclesial Vocation of the Theologian, *Donum veritatis*. May 24, 1990.

———. Letter on Some Aspects of the Church Understood as Communion *Communionis notio*. May 28, 1992.

———. Doctrinal Commentary on the Concluding Formula of the *Professio fidei*. In *Origins* 28, no. 8 (July 16, 1998): 116–119.

———. Declaration on the Unicity and Salvific Universality of Jesus Christ and the Church *Dominus Iesus*. August 6, 2000.

———. Notification on the Book *Jesus, Symbol of God* by Father Roger Haight S.J. December 13, 2004.

———. Notification on the Works of Father Jon Sobrino, S.J.: *Jesucristo liberador: Lectura histórico-teológica de Jesús de Nazaret* (Madrid, 1991) and *La fe en Jesucristo: Ensayo desde las víctimas* (San Salvador, 1999). November 26, 2006.

———. *The Primacy of the Successor of Peter in the Mystery of the Church*. October, 1998.

———. "*Responses to Some Questions Regarding Certain Aspects of the Doctrine on the Church.*" June 29, 2007.

Costello, Charles J. *St. Augustine's Doctrine on the Inspiration and Canonicity of Scripture*. Washington, DC: Catholic University of America Press, 1930.

Craig, William L. *Reasonable Faith: Christian Truth and Apologetics*. Wheaton: Crossway Books, 1994.

Dalley, Stephanie. *Myths from Mesopotamia: Creation, the Flood, Gilgamesh and Others*. Oxford: Oxford University Press, 1989.

Daniélou, Cardinal Jean, S.J. *The Bible and the Liturgy*. Notre Dame: University of Notre Dame Press, 1956.

———. *From Shadows to Reality: Studies in the Biblical Typology of the Fathers*. Translated by Dom Wulstan Hibberd. Westminster: The Newman Press, 1960.

Dauphinais, Michael, and Matthew Levering, eds. *Wisdom and Holiness, Science and Scholarship: Essays in Honor of Matthew L. Lamb*. Naples: Sapientia Press, 2007.

De la Potterie, Ignace, S.J. "Biblical Exegesis: A Science of Faith." In *Opening Up the Scriptures: Joseph Ratzinger and the Foundations of Biblical Interpretation*, 30–64. Edited by José Granados, Carlos Granados, Luis Sanchez-Navarro. Grand Rapids: Eerdmans, 2008.

———. "Interpretation of Holy Scripture in the Spirit in Which It Was Written (*Dei Verbum* 12c)." In *Vatican II Assessment and Per-*

spectives: Twenty-five Years After (1962–1987). Vol. 1, 220–266. New York: Paulist, 1988.

———. *Mary in the Mystery of the Covenant*. Translated by Bertrand Buby. New York: Alba House, 1992.

De la Soujeole, Benoît-Dominique, O.P. *Introduction to the Mystery of the Church*. Translated by Michael J. Miller. Washington, DC: Catholic University of America Press, 2014.

De Lubac, Henri. *Catholicism: Christ and the Common Destiny of Man*. Translated by Lancelot Sheppard and Elizabeth Englund. San Francisco: Ignatius Press, 1988.

———. *The Discovery Of God*. Translated by Alexander Dru. Chicago: Henry Regnery Company, 1967.

———. *Medieval Exegesis*. Vols. 1–2, *The Four Senses of Scripture*. Translated by Mark Sebanc. Grand Rapids: Eerdmans, 1998–2000.

———. *The Motherhood of the Church*. Translated by Sergia Englund. San Francisco: Ignatius Press, 1982.

———. *Scripture in the Tradition*. Translated by Luke O'Neill. New York: Herder and Herder, 2000.

———. "Sens spiritual." *Recherches de Science Religieuse* 36 (1949): 542–576.

———. *The Splendor of the Church*. Translated by Michael Mason. San Francisco: Ignatius Press, 1986.

De Margerie, Bertrand, S.J. *An Introduction to the History of Exegesis*. 3 vols. Petersham: Saint Bede's Publications, 1991–1995.

Denzinger, Heinrich. *Enchiridion Symbolorum: Compendium of Creeds, Definitions, and Declarations on Matters of Faith and Morals*. 43rd edition. Edited by Peter Hünermann. English edition edited by Robert Fastiggi and Anne Englund Nash. San Francisco: Ignatius Press, 2012.

Dewan, Lawrence, O.P. *Wisdom, Law, and Virtue: Essays in Thomistic Ethics*. New York: Fordham University Press, 2007.

Dubay, Thomas, S.M. *The Evidential Power of Beauty: Science and Theology Meet*. San Francisco: Ignatius Press, 1999.

———. *Faith and Certitude*. San Francisco: Ignatius Press, 1985.

Dulles, Avery, S. J. *The Assurance of Things Hoped For: A Theology of Christian Faith*. New York: Oxford University Press, 1994.

———. *The Craft of Theology: From Symbol to System*. New York: Crossroad, 1992.

———. *A History of Apologetics*. San Francisco: Ignatius Press, 2005. Originally published 1971.

———. *Magisterium: Teacher and Guardian of the Faith*. Naples: Sapientia Press, 2007.

———. *Models of Revelation*. 2nd edition. Maryknoll: Orbis Books, 1992.

———. *The Survival of Dogma*. Garden City: Image Books, 1973.

———. "Wisdom as the Source of Unity for Theology." In *Wisdom and Holiness, Science and Scholarship: Essays in Honor of Matthew L. Lamb*, 59–71. Edited by Michael Dauphinais and Matthew Levering. Naples: Sapientia Press, 2007.

Dunn, James. *Jesus Remembered*. Vol. 1, *Christianity in the Making*. Grand Rapids: Eerdmans, 2003.

———. *A New Perspective on Jesus: What the Quest for the Historical Jesus Missed*. Grand Rapids: Baker Academic, 2005.

———. *The Oral Gospel Tradition*. Grand Rapids: Eerdmans, 2013.

——— and Scot McKnight, editors. *The Historical Jesus in Recent Research*. Winona Lake: Eisenbrauns, 2005.

Dupuis, J., and Jacob Neuner. *The Christian Faith in the Doctrinal Documents of the Catholic Church*. 7th edition. New York: Alba House, 2001.

Ecumenical Study Group of Protestant and Catholic Theologians in Germany. *Binding Testimony: Holy Scripture and Tradition*. Edited by Theodor Schneider and Wolfhart Pannenberg. Translated by Martha Matesich. Frankfurt am Main: Peter Lang, 2014.

Ellis, E. Earle. "Dating the New Testament." *New Testament Studies* 26 (1980): 487–502.

———. *History and Interpretation in New Testament Perspective*. Leiden: Brill, 2001.

———. *The Making of the New Testament Documents*. Leiden: Brill, 1999.

———. *Prophecy and Hermeneutic in Early Christianity*. Grand Rapids: Eerdmans, 1978.

Eusebius, *Ecclesiastical History*. Translated by Roy J. Deferrari. 2 vols. The Fathers of the Church 19 and 29. Washington, DC: Catholic University of America Press, 1953–1955.

Evans, Craig A. "The Life of Jesus." In *Handbook to Exegesis of the New Testament*, 427–476. Leiden: Brill, 1997.

Eve, Eric. *Behind the Gospels: Understanding the Oral Tradition*. Minneapolis: Fortress Press, 2014.

———. *The Jewish Context of Jesus' Miracles*. New York: Sheffield Academic Press, 2002.

Farkasfalvy, Denis. "The Apostolic Gospels in the Early Church." In *Canon and Biblical Interpretation*, 112–122. Edited by Craig Bartholomew et al. Grand Rapids, MI: Zondervan, 2006.

———. "Inspiration and Incarnation." In *Verbum Domini and the Complementarity of Exegesis and Theology*, 3–11. Edited by Scott Carl. Grand Rapids: Eerdmans, 2015.

———. *Inspiration & Interpretation: A Theological Introduction to Sacred Scripture*. Washington, DC: Catholic University of America Press, 2010.

Farmer, William R. *Jesus and the Gospel: Tradition, Scripture, and Canon*. Philadelphia: Fortress Press, 1982.

———. *The Gospel of Jesus: The Pastoral Relevance of the Synoptic Problem*. Louisville: Westminster John Knox Press, 1994.

———. *The Synoptic Problem: A Critical Analysis*. New York: Macmillan, 1964.

———, ed. *New Synoptic Studies: The Cambridge Gospel Conference and Beyond*. Macon: Mercer University Press, 1983.

——— and Denis M. Farkasfalvy. *The Formation of the New Testament Canon: an Ecumenical Approach*. Edited by Harold W. Attridge with introduction by Albert C. Outler. New York: Paulist Press, 1983.

Farnell, F. David. "The Synoptic Gospels in the Ancient Church: The Testimony to the Priority of Matthew's Gospel." *The Master's Seminary Journal* 10, no. 1 (Spring, 1999): 53–86.

Fastiggi, Robert L. "Communal or Social Inspiration: A Catholic Critique." *Letter & Spirit* 6 (2010): 247–263.

Feingold, Lawrence. *The Mystery of Israel and the Church.* Vol. 1, *Figure and Fulfillment.* St. Louis: The Miriam Press, 2010.

———. *The Mystery of Israel and the Church.* Vol. 2, *Things New and Old.* St. Louis: The Miriam Press, 2010.

———. *The Mystery of Israel and the Church.* Vol. 3, *The Messianic Kingdom of Israel.* St. Louis: The Miriam Press, 2010.

———. *The Natural Desire to See God According to St. Thomas Aquinas and His Interpreters.* Ave Maria: Sapientia Press, 2010.

Finan, Thomas, and Vincent Twomey. *Scriptural Interpretation in the Fathers: Letter and Spirit.* Dublin: Four Courts Press, 1995.

Foster, R. J. "The Formation and History of the Canon." In *A Catholic Commentary on Holy Scripture,* 13–18. Edited by Bernard Orchard. New York: Thomas Nelson and Sons, 1953.

Francis, Pope. Encyclical Letter on Faith *Lumen fidei.* June 29, 2013.

Francis de Sales. *The Catholic Controversy: St. Francis de Sales' Defense of the Faith.* Translated by Henry B. Mackey. Rockford: TAN Books, 1992.

Gadenz, Pablo T. "Magisterial Teaching on the Inspiration and Truth of Scripture: Precedents and Prospects." *Letter & Spirit* 6 (2010): 67–91.

Gaillardetz, Richard R. *By What Authority?: A Primer on Scripture, the Magisterium, and the Sense of the Faithful.* Collegeville: Liturgical Press, 2003.

———. *Teaching with Authority: A Theology of the Magisterium in the Church.* Collegeville: The Liturgical Press, 1997.

Galbiati, Enrico. "I generi letterari secondo il P. Lagrange e la *Divino afflante Spiritu.*" *La Scuola Cattolica,* 75 (1947): 117–86 and 282–92.

Gallagher, Edmon. "The Old Testament 'Apocrypha' in Jerome's Canonical Theory." *Journal of Early Christian Studies* 20.2 (Summer 2012): 213–233.

Garrigou-Lagrange, Réginald. *The Principles of Catholic Apologetics.* Translated by Thomas J. Walsh. Eugene, OR: Wipf & Stock, 2009. Originally published 1926.

Gerhardsson, Birger. *The Gospel Tradition.* Malmö, SE: CWK Gleerup, 1986.

———. *Memory and Manuscript with Tradition and Transmission in Early Christianity.* Translated by Eric Sharpe with foreword by Jacob Neusner. Grand Rapids: Eerdmans, 1998.

———. *The Origins of the Gospel Traditions.* Philadelphia: Fortress Press, 1979.

———. *The Reliability of the Gospel Tradition.* Peabody: Hendrickson, 2001.

Giambrone, Anthony. "The Quest for the *Vera et Sincera de Jesu*: *Dei Verbum* §19 and the Historicity of the Gospels." *Nova et Vetera* (English) 13. no 1 (2015): 87–123.

Giussani, Luigi. *At the Origin of the Christian Claim.* Translated by Vivianne Hewitt. Montreal: McGill-Queen's University Press, 1998.

———. *The Religious Sense.* Translated by John Zucchi. Montreal: McGill-Queen's University Press, 1997.

———. *Why the Church?* Translated by Vivianne Hewitt. Montreal: McGill-Queen's University Press, 2001.

Gondreau, Paul. "Set Free by First Truth: *Ex corde Ecclesiae* and the Realist Vision of Academic Freedom for the Catholic Theologian." In *Wisdom and Holiness, Science and Scholarship: Essays in Honor of Matthew L. Lamb*, 73–107. Edited by Michael Dauphinais and Matthew Levering. Naples: Sapientia Press, 2007.

Granados, José, Carlos Granados, and Luis Sanchez-Navarro, eds. *Opening Up the Scriptures: Joseph Ratzinger and the Foundations of Biblical Interpretation.* Grand Rapids: Eerdmans, 2008.

Grant, Robert M. *Eusebius as Church Historian.* Oxford: Clarendon Press, 1980.

Grelot, Pierre. "Tradition as Source and Environment of Scripture." In *Scripture: The Dynamism of Biblical Tradition*, 7–28. Edited by Pierre Benoit. Concilium 20. New York: Paulist Press, 1967.

Grisez, Germain. "The Inspiration and Inerrancy of Scripture." *Letter & Spirit* 6 (2010): 181–190.

Green-Armytage, Adrian H. N. *John Who Saw: A Layman's Essay on the Authorship of the Fourth Gospel.* London: Faber and Faber, 1952.

Guardini, Romano. "Holy Scripture and the Science of Faith." *Letter & Spirit* 6 (2010): 401–432.

Güttgemanns, Erhardt. *Candid Questions Concerning Gospel Form Criticism: a Methodological Sketch of the Fundamental Problematics of Form and Redaction Criticism.* Pittsburgh: Pickwick Press, 1979.

Gutwenger, Engelbert. "The Gospels and Non-Catholic Higher Criticism," in *A Catholic Commentary on Holy Scripture.* Edited by Bernard Orchard. New York: Thomas Nelson and Sons, 1953, pp. 752–759.

Habermas, Gary R. *The Historical Jesus: Ancient Evidence for the Life of Christ.* Joplin: College Press, 1996.

Hahn, Scott. "Canon, Cult and Covenant." In *Canon and Biblical Interpretation*, 207–235. Edited by Craig Bartholomew et al. Grand Rapids: Zondervan, 2006.

———. *Consuming the Word: The New Testament and The Eucharist in the Early Church.* New York: Image, 2013.

———. *Covenant and Communion: The Biblical Theology of Pope Benedict XVI.* Grand Rapids: Brazos Press, 2009.

———. "For the Sake of Our Salvation: The Truth and Humility of God's Word." *Letter & Spirit* 6 (2010): 21–46.

———. *Kinship by Covenant: A Canonical Approach to the Fulfillment of God's Saving Promises.* New Haven: Yale University Press, 2009.

———. *Letter and Spirit: From Written Text to Living Word in the Liturgy.* New York: Doubleday, 2005.

———. *Reasons to Believe: How to Understand, Explain, and Defend the Catholic Faith.* New York: Doubleday, 2007.

———, general ed. *Catholic Bible Dictionary.* New York: Doubleday, 2009.

────── and Benjamin Wiker. *Answering the New Atheism: Dismantling Dawkins' Case Against God*. Steubenville: Emmaus Road, 2008.

──────. *Politicizing the Bible: The Roots of Historical Criticism and the Secularization of Scripture: 1300–1700*. New York: Crossroad Publishing, 2013.

Harnack, Adolf von. *Date of Acts and the Synoptic Gospels*. Translated by J. R. Wilkinson. New York: G .P. Putnam's Sons, 1911.

──────. *What Is Christianity?: Sixteen Lectures Delivered in the University of Berlin During the Winter-Term 1899–1900*. Translated by Thomas Bailey Saunders. New York: G. P. Putnam's Sons, 1901.

Harrison, Brian W. "Restricted Inerrancy and the 'Hermeneutic of Discontinuity.'" *Letter & Spirit* 6 (2010): 225–246.

Harvey, A. E. *Jesus and the Constraints of History*. London: Duckworth, 1982.

Healy, Mary. "Biblical Interpretation as a Prophetic Charism in the Church." *Nova et Vetera* (English) 13, no. 1 (2015): 219–240.

Heidel, Alexander. *The Gilgamesh Epic and Old Testament Parallels*. Chicago: University of Chicago Press, 1946.

Hengel, Martin. *The Four Gospels and the One Gospel of Jesus Christ: An Investigation of the Collection and Origin of the Canonical Gospels*. Harrisburg: Trinity Press International, 2000.

──────. "Eye-Witness Memory and the Writing of the Gospels." In *The Written Gospel*. Edited by Markus Bockmuehl and Donald A. Hagner. Cambridge: Cambridge University Press, 2005.

──────. *Studies in the Gospel of Mark*. London: SCM Press, 1985.

──────. *The Septuagint as Christian Scripture: Its Prehistory and the Problem of Its Canon*. Translated by Mark E. Biddle. Edinburgh: T&T Clark, 2002.

Hill, Charles E. *The Johannine Corpus in the Early Church*. Oxford: Oxford University Press, 2004.

──────. *Who Chose the Gospels? Probing the Great Gospel Conspiracy*. Oxford: Oxford University Press, 2010.

Hochschild, Paige. "John Henry Newman: Mariology and the Scope of Reason in the Modern Age." *Nova et Vetera* (English) 11, no. 4 (2013): 993–1016.

Holmes, Jeremy. "Tradition and the Individual Exegete." *Nova et Vetera* (English) 13, no. 11 (2015): 241–251.

Hütter, Reinhard. *Dust Bound for Heaven: Explorations in the Theology of Thomas Aquinas.* Grand Rapids: Eerdmans, 2012.

———. "What Is Faith? The Theocentric, Unitive, and Eschatologically Inchoative Character of Divine Faith." *Nova et Vetera* (English) 11, no. 2 (2013): 317–340.

——— and Matthew Levering, eds. *Ressourcement Thomism: Sacred Doctrine, the Sacraments, and the Moral Life.* Washington, DC: Catholic University of America Press, 2010.

International Theological Commission. *Theology Today: Perspectives, Principles and Criteria. Origins* 41, no. 40 (March 15, 2012).

Irenaeus. *Against Heresies.* In *ANF,* 1:315–567. Peabody: Hendrickson, 1994.

Jerome. *Commentary on Matthew.* Translated by T. P. Scheck. The Fathers of the Church 117. Washington, DC: Catholic University of America Press, 2008.

———. *On Illustrious Men.* Translated by Thomas Halton. The Fathers of the Church 100. Washington, DC: Catholic University of America Press, 1999.

John Paul II, Pope. Apostolic Letter (issued *motu proprio*) *Praestantia Scripturae Sacrae.* May 18,1998.

———. Apostolic Letter on Keeping the Lord's Day Holy *Dies Domini.* May 31, 1998.

———. Encyclical Letter on the Holy Spirit in the Life of the Church and the World *Dominum et vivificantem.* May 18, 1986.

———. Encyclical Letter on the Relationship between Faith and Reason *Fides et ratio.* September 14, 1998.

———. *Man and Woman He Created Them: A Theology of the Body.* Translated with introduction by Michael Waldstein. Boston: Pauline Books & Media, 2006.

————. *Mary: God's Yes to Man: John Paul's Encyclical* Redemptoris mater. Introduction by Joseph Ratzinger. San Francisco: Ignatius Press, 1988.

————. Apostolic Letter at the Close of the Great Jubilee of the Year 2000 *Novo millennio ineunte.* January 6, 2001.

————. Encyclical Letter at the Beginning of His Papal Ministry *Redemptor hominis.* March 4, 1979.

Journet, Charles. "The Mysterious Destinies of Israel." In *The Bridge: A Yearbook of Judaeo-Christian Studies,* 2:35–90. Edited by John Oesterreicher. New York: Pantheon Books, 1956.

————. *Theology of the Church.* Translated by Victor Szczurek. San Francisco: Ignatius Press, 2004. (French original 1958)

————. *What Is Dogma?* Translated by Mark Pontifex, with an Introduction by Roger W. Nutt. San Francisco: Ignatius Press, 2011 Originally published 1963 in French.

Jousse, Marcel, S.J. *L'anthropologie du geste.* Paris: Editions Resma, 1969.

————. *The Oral Style.* Translated by Edgard Sienaert and Richard Whitaker. New York: Garland, 1990.

St. Justin Martyr. *The First Apology, The Second Apology, Dialogue with Trypho, Exhortation to the Greeks, Discourse to the Greeks, The Monarchy or The Rule of God.* Translated by T. B. Falls. The Fathers of the Church 6. Washington, DC: Catholic University of America Press, 1948.

Käsemann, Ernst. *Essays on New Testament Themes.* Translated by W. J. Montague. Naperville: Allenson, 1964.

Kaufmann, Yehezkel. *The Religion of Israel: From Its Beginnings to the Babylonian Exile.* Translated by Moshe Greenberg. Chicago: University of Chicago Press, 1960.

Kelber, Werner H. *The Oral and the Written Gospel: The Hermeneutics of Speaking and Writing in the Synoptic Tradition, Mark, Paul, and Q.* Philadelphia: Fortress Press, 1983.

————. "The Oral-Scribal-Memorial Arts of Communication in Early Christianity." In *Jesus, the Voice, and the Text: Beyond the Oral and Written Gospel,* 235–62. Edited by Tom Thatcher. Waco: Baylor University Press, 2008.

—————— and Samuel Byrskog, eds. *Jesus in Memory: Traditions in Oral and Scribal Perspectives.* Waco: Baylor University Press, 2009.

Kevane, Eugene. *The Lord of History: Christocentrism and the Philosophy of History.* Boston: St. Paul Editions, 1980.

Kreeft, Peter. *A Summa of the Summa.* San Francisco: Ignatius Press, 1990.

—————— and Ronald K. Tacelli. *Handbook of Christian Apologetics.* Downers Grove: InterVarsity Press, 1994.

Lagrange, Marie-Joseph. *The Gospel of Jesus Christ.* Translated by members of the English Dominican Province. Westminster: Newman Bookshop, 1938.

——————. *Évangile selon Saint Jean.* 3rd edition. Paris: J. Gabalda, 1927.

——————. *Évangile selon saint Luc.* 2nd edition. Paris: J. Gabalda, 1921.

——————. *Évangile selon saint Marc.* Paris: J. Gabalda, 1947.

——————. *Évangile selon saint Matthieu.* 2nd edition. Paris: J. Gabalda, 1923.

——————. *Histoire ancienne du canon du Nouveau Testament.* Paris: J. Gabalda, 1933.

——————. *Historical Criticism and the Old Testament.* Translated by Edward Myers. London: Catholic Truth Society, 1906.

——————. "L'inspiration et les exigences de la critique; Réponse à la lettre précedente." *Revue Biblique* 5 (1896): 496–518.

——————. *Introduction a l'étude du Nouveau Testament: Critique Historique I: Les Mystères, L'Orphisme.* Paris: J. Gabalda, 1937.

——————. *Introduction à l'étude du Nouveau Testament; deuxième partie, Critique textuelle; II: La critique rationelle.* Paris: J. Gabalda, 1935.

——————. *Le Judaisme avant Jésus Christ.* Paris: J. Gabalda, 1931.

——————. *Saint Paul Épitre aux Romains.* Paris: Libraire Lecoffre, 1950.

——————. "Une pensée de Saint Thomas sur l'inspiration scripturaire." *Revue Biblique* 4 (1896): 563–571.

Lapide, Pinchas. *The Resurrection of Jesus: a Jewish Perspective.* Minneapolis: Augsburg, 1983.

Latourelle, Rene, S.J. "A New Image of Fundamental Theology." Translated by Matthew J. O'Connell. In *Problems and Perspectives of Fundamental Theology.* Edited by Rene Latourelle and Gerald O'Collins. New York: Paulist Press, 1982.

————. *Theology of Revelation*. Staten Island: Alba House, 1966.

————. *Christ and the Church: Signs of Salvation*. Translated by Sr. Dominic Parker. Staten Island: Alba House, 1972.

Leo XIII, Pope. Encyclical Letter on the Study of Scripture *Providentissimus Deus*. November 18, 1893.

————. Encylical Letter on the Unity of the Church *Satis cognitum*. June 29, 1896.

Léon-Dufour, Xavier. *The Gospels and the Jesus of History*. Translated by John McHugh. London: Collins, 1968.

Levering, Matthew. *Christ's Fulfillment of Torah and Temple: Salvation According to Thomas Aquinas*. Notre Dame: University of Notre Dame Press, 2002.

————. "Ecclesial Exegesis and Ecclesial Authority: Childs, Fowl, and Aquinas." *The Thomist* 69 (2005): 407–467.

————. *Engaging the Doctrine of Revelation: Mediation of the Gospel Through Church and Scripture*. Grand Rapids: Baker Academic, 2014.

————. "The Inspiration of Scripture: A *Status Quaestionis*." *Letter & Spirit* 6 (2010): 281–314.

————. "Israel and the Shape of Thomas Aquinas's Soteriology." *The Thomist* 63 (1999): 65–82.

————. *Sacrifice and Community: Jewish Offering and Christian Eucharist*. Malden: Blackwell, 2005.

————. *Scripture and Metaphysics: Aquinas and the Renewal of Trinitarian Theology*. Malden: Blackwell, 2004.

Lewis, Clive Staples. *Mere Christianity*. San Francisco: HarperCollins, 2001. Originally published 1952.

————. *Miracles*. San Francisco: HarperCollins, 2001. Originally published 1947.

————. "Modern Theology and Biblical Criticism." In *The Seeing Eye and Other Selected Essays from Christian Reflections*, 203–223. New York: Ballantine Books, 1986.

Lienhard, Joseph T., S.J. *The Bible, the Church, and Authority: The Canon of the Christian Bible in History and Theology*. Collegeville: Liturgical Press, 1995.

Linnemann, Eta. *Biblical Criticism on Trial: How Scientific Is "Scientific Theology"?* Translated by Robert Yarbrough. Grand Rapids: Kregel, 2001.

―――. *Historical Criticism of the Bible: Methodology or Ideology? Reflections of a Bultmannian Turned Evangelical.* Translated by Robert Yarbrough. Grand Rapids: Kregel, 1990.

―――. *Is There a Synoptic Problem? Rethinking the Literary Dependence of the First Three Gospels.* Translated by Robert W. Yarbrough. Grand Rapids: Baker Book House, 1992.

Lonergan, Bernard. *Method in Theology.* 2nd edition. Toronto: University of Toronto Press, 2012.

Mailhiot, M. D., O.P., "La pensée de S. Thomas sur la sens spirituelle." *Revue Thomiste* (1959): 613–663.

Marchetto, Agostino. *The Second Vatican Ecumenical Council: A Counterpoint for the History of the Council.* Translated by Kenneth D. Whitehead. Scranton: University of Scranton Press, 2010.

Marin-Sola, Francisco. *La evolución homogénea del dogma católico.* Madrid: Biblioteca de Autores Cristianos, 1952.

Marshall, Bruce D. "*Quod Scit Una Uetula*: Aquinas on the Nature of Theology." In *The Theology of Thomas Aquinas*, 1–35. Edited by Rik Van Nieuwenhove and Joseph Wawrykow. Notre Dame: University of Notre Dame Press, 2005.

Marshall, I. Howard, ed. *New Testament Interpretation: Essays on Principles and Methods.* Milton Keynes, UK: Paternoster, 1997.

Martin, Francis. *Sacred Scripture: The Disclosure of the Word.* Naples: Sapientia Press, 2006.

―――. "Revelation and Understanding Scripture: Reflections on the Teaching of Joseph Ratzinger, Pope Benedict XVI." *Nova et Vetera* (English) 13, no. 1 (2015): 253–272.

McCarthy, Dennis J., S.J., "God as Prisoner of Our Own Choosing: Critical-Historical Study of the Bible, Why and Whither." In *Proceedings of the Fellowship of Catholic Scholars, 1979 Convention: Historicism and Faith*, 17–47. Edited by Paul L. Williams. Scranton: Northeast Books, 1980.

McGovern, Thomas. "The Gospels as History." *Letter & Spirit* 6 (2010): 333–343.

Melina, Livio. "The Role of the Ordinary Universal Magisterium: On Francis Sullivan's Creative Fidelity." *The Thomist* 61 (1997): 605–615.

Metzger, Bruce M. *The Canon of the New Testament: Its Origin, Development, and Significance.* Oxford: Clarendon, 1987.

Morerod, Charles, O.P. *The Church and the Human Quest for Truth.* Ave Maria: Sapientia Press, 2008.

Most, William G. *Free from All Error.* Libertyville: Franciscan Marytown Press, 1985.

Muller, Julius. *The Theory of Myths in Its Application to the Gospel History Examined and Confuted.* London: Chapman, 1844.

Nash, Ronald H. *The Gospel and the Greeks: Did the New Testament Borrow from Pagan Thought?* 2nd edition. Phillipsburg: P & R Publishing, 2003.

Neuner, Josef, S.J. and Jacques Dupuis, S.J., eds. *The Christian Faith: Doctrinal Documents of the Catholic Church.* 6th edition. New York: Alba House, 1996.

Neusner, Jacob. *The Oral Torah: The Sacred Books of Judaism, an Introduction.* San Francisco: Harper & Row, 1986.

———. *A Rabbi Talks with Jesus.* Revised edition. Montreal: McGill-Queen's University Press, 2000.

——— and Bruce Chilton. *Jewish-Christian Debates: God, Kingdom, Messiah.* Minneapolis: Fortress Press, 1998.

Newman, Blessed John Henry Cardinal. *Apologia pro vita sua.* London: J. M. Dent, 1993.

———. *Discourses Addressed to Mixed Congregations.* Boston: Patrick Donahoe, 1853.

———. *Discussions and Arguments on Various Subjects.* New York: Longmans, Green, and Co., 1897.

———. *An Essay in Aid of a Grammar of Assent.* New York: Catholic Publication Society, 1870.

———. *An Essay on the Development of Christian Doctrine.* 6th edition. Notre Dame: University of Notre Dame Press, 1989.

————. "Private Judgment." In *Essays, Critical and Historical*, 2:336–374. London: Basil Montagu Pickering, 1871.

————. *Sermons, Chiefly on the Theory of Religious Belief, Preached Before the University of Oxford*. London: Francis & John Rivington, 1844.

Nichols, Aidan, O.P. *Chalice of God: A Systematic Theology in Outline*. Collegeville: Liturgical Press, 2012.

————. *A Grammar of Consent*. Notre Dame: University of Notre Dame Press, 1991.

————. *A Key to Balthasar: Hans Urs von Balthasar on Beauty, Goodness, and Truth*. Grand Rapids: Baker Academic, 2011.

————. *Redeeming Beauty: Soundings in Sacral Aesthetics*. Burlington: Ashgate, 2007.

————. *The Shape of Catholic Theology*. Collegeville: The Liturgical Press, 1991.

Nicolau, Michaele, S.J. and Ioachim Salaverri, S.J. *Theologia Fundamentalis*. Vol. 1 of *Sacrae Theologiae Summa*. Madrid: Biblioteca de Autores Cristianos, 1958.

Noth, Martin. *A History of Pentateuchal Traditions*. Englewood Cliffs: Prentice-Hall, 1972.

O'Callaghan, José. "Papiros neotestamentarios en la cueva 7 de Qumran?" *Biblica* 53 (1972): 91–100.

Ocáriz, Fernando and Arturo Blanco. *Fundamental Theology*. Woodridge: Midwest Theological Forum, 2009.

Ocáriz, Fernando, Lucas F. Matteo Seco, and José A. Riestra. *The Mystery of Jesus Christ*. Portland: Four Courts Press, 1994.

O'Collins, Gerald. *Rethinking Fundamental Theology: Toward a New Fundamental Theology*. New York: Oxford University Press, 2011.

O'Keefe, John J. and Russel R. Reno. *Sanctified Vision: An Introduction to Early Christian Interpretation of the Bible*. Baltimore: Johns Hopkins University Press, 2005

Orchard, Bernard. *Matthew, Luke & Mark*. Manchester, UK: Koinonia Press, 1976.

———— and Harold Riley. *The Order of the Synoptics: Why Three Synoptic Gospels?* Macon: Mercer University Press, 1987.

Origen. *Origen: An Exhortation to Martyrdom; Prayer; First Princi-ples: Book IV; Prologue to the Commentary on the Song of Songs; Homily XXVII on Numbers.* Translated by Rowan Greer. New York: Paulist Press, 1979.

Ott, Ludwig. *Fundamentals of Catholic Dogma.* Rockford: TAN Books, 1974.

Pascal, Blaise. *Pensées.* Translated by A. J. Krailsheimer. New York: Penguin Classics, 1966.

Patai, Raphael. *The Messiah Texts.* Detroit, MI: Wayne State University Press, 1979.

Persson, Per Erik. *Sacra Doctrina: Reason and Revelation in Aquinas.* Philadelphia: Fortress Press, 1970.

Pius IX, Pope. Letter to the Archbishop of Munich-Freising *Tuas libenter* of December, 21, 1863. *Acta Sanctae Sedis* 8 (1874): 436–442. English translation in *The Church*, 171–174. Translated by E. O'Gorman. Papal Teaching. Boston: Daughters of St. Paul, 1962.

Pius XII, Pope. Encyclical Letter on Promoting Biblical Studies *Divino afflante Spiritu.* September 30, 1943.

———. Encyclical Letter Concerning Some False Opinions Threatening to Undermine the Foundations of Catholic Doctrine *Humani generis.* August 12, 1950.

———. Apostolic Constitution Defending the Dogma of the Assumption *Munificentissimus Deus.* November 1, 1950.

Pontifical Biblical Commission. Instruction on the Historical Truth of the Gospels *Sancta Mater Ecclesia.* April 21, 1964.

———. *The Inspiration and Truth of Sacred Scripture: The Word That Comes from God and Speaks of God for the Salvation of the World.* Translated by Thomas Esposito and Stephen Gregg. Collegeville: Liturgical Press, 2014.

———. *The Interpretation of the Bible in the Church.* Vatican City: Libreria Editrice Vaticana, 1993.

———. *The Jewish People and Their Sacred Scriptures in the Christian Bible.* Vatican City: Libreria Editrice Vaticana, 2002.

Porter, Stanley E., ed. *Handbook to Exegesis of the New Testament.* Leiden: Brill, 1997.

Quay, Paul M., S.J. *The Mystery Hidden for Ages in God.* New York: Peter Lang, 1997.

Rahner, Karl. *Inspiration in the Bible.* Translated by C. H. Henkey. New York: Herder, 1961.

Ramage, Matthew J. *Dark Passages of the Bible: Engaging Scripture with Benedict XVI & Thomas Aquinas.* Washington, DC: Catholic University of America Press, 2013.

———. "Violence Is Incompatible with the Nature of God: Benedict, Aquinas, and Method C Exegesis of the 'Dark' Passages of the Bible." *Nova et Vetera* (English) 13, no. 1 (2015): 273–295.

Ratzinger, Cardinal Joseph. *Daughter Zion.* Translated by John M. McDermott. San Francisco: Ignatius Press, 1983.

———. *Feast of Faith: Approaches to a Theology of the Liturgy.* Translated by Graham Harrison. San Francisco: Ignatius Press, 1986.

———. *God's Word: Scripture—Tradition—Office.* Edited by Peter Hünermann and Tomas Söding. Translated by Henry Taylor. San Francisco: Ignatius Press, 2008.

———. *Gospel, Catechesis, Catechism: Sidelights on the Catechism of the Catholic Church.* San Francisco: Ignatius Press, 1997.

———. *In the Beginning: A Catholic Understanding of Creation and the Fall.* Grand Rapids: Eerdmanns, 1995.

———. *Introduction to Christianity.* San Francisco: Ignatius Press, 1990. Originally published 1968 in German.

———. *Jesus, the Apostles, and the Early Church.* San Francisco: Ignatius Press, 2007

———. *Jesus of Nazareth: From the Baptism in the Jordan to the Transfiguration.* Translated by Adrian J. Walker. New York: Doubleday, 2007.

———. *Jesus of Nazareth: Holy Week: from the Entrance into Jerusalem to the Resurrection.* Translated by Philip J. Whitmore. San Francisco: Ignatius Press, 2011.

———. *Jesus of Nazareth: The Infancy Narratives.* Translated by Philip J. Whitmore. New York: Image, 2012.

———. *Many Religions—One Covenant: Israel, the Church, and the World.* Translated by Graham Harrison. San Francisco: Ignatius Press, 1999.

———. *The Nature and Mission of Theology*. San Francisco: Ignatius Press, 1995.

———. *Principles of Catholic Theology: Building Stones for a Fundamental Theology*. Translated by Sr. Mary Frances McCarthy, S.N.D. San Francisco: Ignatius Press, 1987. Originally published 1982 in German.

———. *Truth and Tolerance: Christian Belief and World Religions*. Translated by Henry Taylor. San Francisco: Ignatius Press, 2004.

Rist, John M. *On the Independence of Matthew and Mark*. Cambridge: Cambridge University Press, 1978.

Robinson, John A. T. *Redating the New Testament*. Philadelphia: Westminster Press, 1976.

Rondet, Henri, S.J. *Do Dogmas Change?* London: Burns & Oates, 1961.

Roza, Devin. *Fulfilled in Christ: The Sacraments: A Guide to Symbols and Types in the Bible and Tradition*. Steubenville: Emmaus Academic, 2015.

Sanders, E. P. *The Tendencies of the Synoptic Tradition*. SNTSMS 9. Cambridge, UK: Cambridge University Press, 1969.

Sayers, Dorothy. *Christian Letters to a Post-Christian World*. Grand Rapids: Eerdmans, 1969. Reissued as *The Whimsical Christian: 18 Essays* by MacMillan (New York), 1978.

———. *The Mind of the Maker*. San Francisco: Harper & Row, 1987.

Schall, James V., S.J. *The Regensburg Lecture*. South Bend: St. Augustine's Press, 2007.

Scheeben, Matthias Joseph. *The Mysteries of Christianity*. Translated by Cyril Vollert, S.J. St. Louis: Herder, 1946.

Schoedel, William R. "Papias." In *Anchor Bible Dictionary* 5:140–142.

———. *Polycarp, Martyrdom of Polycarp, Fragments of Papias*. Camden; London; Toronto: Thomas Nelson, 1967.

Schroeder, Francis J. *Père Lagrange and Biblical Inspiration*. Washington, DC: Catholic University of America Press, 1954.

———. "Père Lagrange: Record and Teaching on Inspiration." *Catholic Biblical Quarterly* 20 (1958): 206–217.

Schulz, Hans-Joachim. *Die apostolische Herkunft der Evangelien.* Freiburg: Herder, 1993.

The Scripture Documents: An Anthology of Official Catholic Teachings. Edited by Dean P. Béchard. Collegeville: The Liturgical Press, 2002.

Schweitzer, Albert. *The Quest of the Historical Jesus: A Critical Study of Its Progress from Reimarus to Wrede.* New York: Macmillan, 1942.

Shea, Mark P. *By What Authority? An Evangelical Discovers Catholic Tradition.* Huntington: Our Sunday Visitor, 1996.

———. *Making Senses out of Scripture: Reading the Bible As the First Christians Did.* San Diego: Basilica Press, 1999.

Sheed, Frank J. *Theology For Beginners.* Ann Arbor: Servant Books, 1981. Originally published 1958.

———. *Theology and Sanity.* San Francisco: Ignatius Press, 1993 (Original 1947).

Simonetti, Manlio. *Biblical Interpretation in the Early Church: An Historical Introduction to Patristic Exegesis.* Translated by John A. Hughes. Edinburgh: T&T Clark, 1994.

Sokolowski, Robert. *Eucharistic Presence: A Study in the Theology of Disclosure.* Washington, DC: Catholic University of America Press, 1994.

———. *The God of Faith and Reason: Foundations of Christian Theology.* Washington, DC: Catholic University of America Press, 1995.

Suárez, Francisco. *Opera omnia.* Vol. 1. Paris: Vivès, 1856.

Sullivan, Francis A. *Creative Fidelity: Weighing and Interpreting Documents of the Magisterium.* New York: Paulist Press, 1996.

———. *From Apostles to Bishops: the Development of the Episcopacy in the Early Church.* New York: Newman Press, 2001.

———. *Magisterium: Teaching Authority in the Catholic Church.* New York: Paulist Press, 1983.

———. *Salvation Outside the Church?: Tracing the History of the Catholic Response.* New York: Paulist Press, 1992.

Sundberg, Albert. "The 'Old Testament': A Christian Canon." *Catholic Biblical Quarterly* 30 (1968): 143–155.

Synave, Paul, and Pierre Benoit. *Prophecy and Inspiration; A Commentary on the* Summa theologica *II-II, questions 171–178*. Translated by Avery R. Dulles, S.J., and Thomas L. Sheridan. New York: Desclee, 1961.

Tábet, Miguel Ángel. *Introducción general a la Biblia*. 3rd edition. Madrid: Ediciones Palabra, 2009.

Taguchi, Cardinal Paul. "Sacred Scripture and the Errors of the 'New' Exegesis." *Letter & Spirit* 6 (2010): 383–400.

Taylor, Robert Oswald P. *The Groundwork of the Gospels, with Some Collected Papers*. Oxford: Blackwell, 1946.

Taylor, Vincent. *The Formation of the Gospel Tradition*. London: Macmillan, 1960. 1st edition 1933.

Thiede, Carsten P. *The Dead Sea Scrolls and the Jewish Origins of Christianity*. New York: Palgrave, 2001.

———— and Matthew D'Ancona. *The Jesus Papyrus*. New York: Doubleday, 1996.

Thomas, Robert L., ed. *Three Views on the Origins of the Synoptic Gospels*. Grand Rapids: Kregel, 2002.

Thomas, Robert L., and F. David Farnell, eds. *The Jesus Crisis: The Inroads of Historical Criticism into Evangelical Scholarship*. Grand Rapids, MI: Kregel, 1998.

Turner, Denys. *Eros and Allegory: Medieval Exegesis of the Song of Songs*. Kalamazoo: Cisterician, 1995.

Vall, Gregory. "Word and Event: A Reappraisal." *Nova et Vetera* (English) 13, no. 1 (2015): 181–218.

Vatican Council II. *The Sixteen Documents of Vatican II*. Edited by Marianne Lorraine Trouvé with introduction by Douglas Bushman. Boston: Pauline Books and Media, 1999.

Waldstein, Michael. "Analogia Verbi: The Truth of Scripture in Rudolf Bultmann and Raymond Brown." *Letter & Spirit* 6 (2010): 93–140.

Welch, Lawrence J. *The Presence of Christ in the Church*. Ave Maria: Sapientia Press, 2012.

Wenham, John. *Redating Matthew, Mark and Luke: A Fresh Assault on the Synoptic Problem*. Downer's Grove: InterVarsity Press, 1992.

White, Thomas Joseph. *Wisdom in the Face of Modernity: A Study in Thomistic Natural Theology.* Ave Maria: Sapientia Press, 2009.

Wicks, Jared, S.J. *Doing Theology.* Mahweh: Paulist Press, 2009.

Williamson, Peter. *Catholic Principles for Interpreting Scripture: A Study of the Pontifical Biblical Commission's* The Interpretation of the Bible in the Church. Rome: Pontifical Biblical Institute, 2001.

Woods, Thomas E. *How the Catholic Church Built Western Civilization.* Washington, DC: Regnery, 2005.

Wright, William M., IV. "Inspired Scripture as a Sacramental Vehicle of Divine Presence in the Gospel of John and *Dei Verbum.*" *Nova et Vetera* (English) 13, no. 1 (2015): 155–180.

INDEX

revealed Himself to Moses, 57

revealing both natural and supernatural truths, 100–101

revealing Himself, 4, 5, 13, 94, 98–102, 322, 493

revealing mysteries, 109–110

seeing face to face, 20, 79

seeing Him as He is, 25

seeing through Jesus, 23

selecting sacred writers, 291

self-communication of, 306

as the Source of love, 75

sources of knowledge about, 102

speaking through different human means of expression, 341

speaking through the mediation of Moses, 522

speaking to a society, 10

speaking to mankind socially, 55

as subject of theology, 117–118

as sufficient witness, 30

teaching man using sensible objects, 545

those ready to believe in, 50

union of man with, 8

unveiling His mystery first, 20

using "I am," 381n27

using weak things to confound the proud, 219

God of the Old Testament, 430

Godel's theorem, 96n5

God's Word. *See* Word of God

"golden rule," 114n4

Good Samaritan, allegorical interpretation of, 14

"goods of salvation," transmission of, 215

Gospel

commandment to preach, 194

as four-fold, 428

meaning of the word, 7–8

oral origins of, 427n48, 477–487

principal content of, 7–9

Gospel accounts, as very succinct, 461–462

Gospel material

going back to the discourses of Jesus, 483

stages in the genesis (origin) and transmission of, 457

tracing the history of the development of, 360

Gospel of John

apostolic authorship of, 415–416

dating of according to Eusebius, 438

discourses presented in, 467

ending with an affirmation of its eyewitness nature, 474

historical character defended in a response of the PBC, 455

testimony of the "beloved disciple," 473

Gospel of Luke

authority through its acceptance by the Apostles, 431

authorship of, 414n14

dated to the close of St. Paul's imprisonment in Rome, 415

dated to the time of Paul's imprisonment in Rome, 414–415

dependence on the Gospel of Mark, 356

prologue indicating eyewitness sources, 471–472

written before the book of the Acts, 415n17

Gospel of Mark, 414

authorship of, 414n14

composition of, 419–420

as earliest of Synoptic Gospels, 355

lacking an ordered narration, 420

literary influence of, 421n31

much less frequently cited by the early Fathers, 420

Peter's testimony recorded in, 410, 410n4, 414, 419–421, 426–427, 432–435, 439, 441, 443

on St. Peter, 410n4, 420

Gospel of Matthew

author of, 412–414

Christ making a promise/prophecy to St. Peter, 463

dependence on the Gospel of Mark, 356

Ebionites using only, 428n50

as the first Gospel, 413, 421, 426, 435, 440, 445

Hebrew or Aramaic, written in, 413, 421, 426, 429–430, 435, 437, 440, 442

Jesus. *See also* God; Holy Spirit; Son of
God
as Antitype for all of salvation history,
537
apostles' profession of faith in the
divinity of, 454
appearing to the Apostles, 524
as archetype of the Christian life, 535
"author of faith," 23
aware of his identity as the Son of God,
466n18
aware of relationship with God at age
of twelve, 466
beatific vision possessed by, 23
being God as He claimed to be, 383
being truly born of a virgin, 312
belief in the divinity of, 488
"biographies" reconstructing his life,
386
as Bridegroom, 9
called Twelve Apostles, 196
center of the divine plan, 7–9, 17–21,
375, 554
choosing not to write anything, 479
as "the Christ, the Son of the living
God," 464
claiming divine identity, 375–385
claiming He came not to abolish the
Law and the prophets, but to fulfill
them, 557–558
claiming love and allegiance from
man, 378
concerned about transmission of His
teaching to the entire world, 482
connection with Adam, 497
deliberately spoke and acted to make
His words and deeds memorable,
482
demanding faith in His person parallel
to faith in God, 378
died on the cross, 312
on disposition for faith, 53
division of the vestments of, 64
as eschatological shepherd, 197
existence of, 387n39
explicit faith in, 522–523
as future judge of mankind, 379
as God and man, 161
having a vision of God in His human
soul, 263n50

hidden in the Old Testament, 504
holiness of the Revelation in the
Person of, 72–74
humanity continuing in time and
space through the sacraments, 224
humanity of, 55
as Incarnate Word, 464
interpreted parables and Old
Testament texts, 201
as invisible head of the Church, 222
as Jesus of Nazareth, 464–465
as key to understanding mysteries
hidden in the Old Testament, 556
as the key to understanding the Old
Testament, 523
knowing He was the Messiah, 406
life and personality of, 405
limiting his mission to Israel alone,
197
as Lord of the angels, 379n17
loss of, as a child in the Temple
prefiguring three days in the tomb,
506
making frequent use of parables and
metaphors, 136
as the Mediator between God and
man, 220
miracles of, 63
missionary mandate given by, 194
moral and religious teaching of, 71
mystery of the Trinity revealed in, 20
as natural Son of the Father, 380
as the "new Adam," 535
not transformed into a "mythical"
personage, 459
one in divinity with the Father, 382
parables of, 329
personality of, 405
preaching of, 458
as principal antitype, 497
as the principal motive of credibility,
68
proclaiming He has the power to
forgive sins, 378
promise to St. Peter, 242, 463
promising eternal life to those who
believe in Him, 378
public Revelation culminating in, 18
reality of unattainable from the New
Testament, 390

Mary
Church called to imitate, 181, 209
entrusted as Mother to guardianship
of John, 449
humility of, 420
the mother of God, 365
mystery of the divine maternity, 110,
312, 365
as the New Eve, 535
prefigured in the Old Testament,
365–367
as the "woman," 365
Mary's Assumption, definition of,
248n14
Mass
perpetuating the Sacrifice of Christ,
552n10
sacrifice of, 7
Thomas Aquinas absorbed by, 145
mass conversions, as remarkable, 79
"mass media," theologians avoiding, 274
"material heresy," 47
material limitation, of the truth of
Scripture, 333n66
material object, 123
materialism, main principle of, 86, 96
Matthew (saint and apostle), 476
St Augustine on, 446–447
as author of the Gospel, 412, 413n8
branding his own life, 439
composed his Gospel in the language
of the Hebrews, 421, 426, 435, 449,
449n93
constructing the record of the
incarnation of the Lord, 447
the tax collector, named Levi, 442,
442n82
Matthias (saint), 228
mediation
of angels, 21n32
of Apostles, 220, 487–489
of the Church, 10, 179–184, 219–220,
488
of the humanity of Christ, 23, 220
minimizing human, 220
of Moses, 10, 57–58, 211, 521–522
principle of, 10, 220, 221
of Revelation, 10, 23, 55, 152, 220
social function of, 10, 120, 486

mediators
Apostles and their successors, 219–
227
between God and mankind, 10, 55,
220, 223
the Church as, 10, 179–184, 219–220
God revealing Himself through, 193
God speaking through, 55
Jesus as supreme mediator, 23, 220
prophets as, 10
in two dimensions, 223
Melchizedek, 522, 561
"memoirs of the Apostles," Gospels as,
426
"Memorial" (Pascal), 106
Mere Christianity (Lewis), 383
Messiah, as "priest for ever after the order
of Melchizedek," 522
messianic prophecies
interpretation of, 523
literal sense of, 521
as a motive of credibility, 60–62
on transmission of apostolic Tradition,
195–196
metaphor, literal sense of, 325
metaphysical certainty, 42
metaphysics
defined, 105
described, 138
distinguished from sacred theology,
104
knowing God only as First Cause and
Final End, 139–140
as science, 114
Metaphysics (Aristotle), 134
Metzger, Bruce, 300
Middle Ages, populace better versed in
biblical typology, 553
Miller, Athanasius, 357, 412n7
mind
natural desire to understand a given
truth, 156
"seeing" first principles of reason, 27
something seen by, 28
"ministers of the word," transmitting
testimony as, 471
miracles
accepting the evidence for, 85
a priori argument against any, 84

SCRIPTURE INDEX